MW00441060

UNDERSTANDING, ASSESSING, AND RESPONDING TO TERRORISM

The Wiley Bicentennial–Knowledge for Generations

Each generation has its unique needs and aspirations. When Charles Wiley first opened his small printing shop in lower Manhattan in 1807, it was a generation of boundless potential searching for an identity. And we were there, helping to define a new American literary tradition. Over half a century later, in the midst of the Second Industrial Revolution, it was a generation focused on building the future. Once again, we were there, supplying the critical scientific, technical, and engineering knowledge that helped frame the world. Throughout the 20th Century, and into the new millennium, nations began to reach out beyond their own borders and a new international community was born. Wiley was there, expanding its operations around the world to enable a global exchange of ideas, opinions, and know-how.

For 200 years, Wiley has been an integral part of each generation's journey, enabling the flow of information and understanding necessary to meet their needs and fulfill their aspirations. Today, bold new technologies are changing the way we live and learn. Wiley will be there, providing you the must-have knowledge you need to imagine new worlds, new possibilities, and new opportunities.

Generations come and go, but you can always count on Wiley to provide you the knowledge you need, when and where you need it!

William J. Pesce
President and Chief Executive Officer

Peter Booth Wiley
Chairman of the Board

UNDERSTANDING, ASSESSING, AND RESPONDING TO TERRORISM

PROTECTING CRITICAL INFRASTRUCTURE AND PERSONNEL

Brian T. Bennett

WILEY-INTERSCIENCE
A JOHN WILEY & SONS, INC., PUBLICATION

Published by John Wiley & Sons, Inc., Hoboken, New Jersey
Published simultaneously in Canada

For general information on our other products and services or for technical support, please contact our Customer Care Department within the United States at 877-762-2974, outside the United States at 317-572-3993 or fax 317-572-4002.

Wiley also publishes its books in a variety of electronic formats. Some content that appears in print may not be available in electronic formats. For more information about Wiley products, visit our web site at www.wiley.com.

Wiley Bicentennial Logo: Richard J. Pacifico

Library of Congress Cataloging-in-Publication Data:

Bennett, Brian T.
Understanding, assessing, and responding to terrorism : protecting critical infrastructure and personnel / Brian T. Bennett.
p. cm.
Includes index.
978-0-471-77152-4 (Cloth)
1. Civil defense—United States. 2. Terrorism—United States—Prevention. I. Title.
UA927.B38 2007
363.325′170973—dc22 2006030755

Printed in the United States of America

10 9 8 7 6 5 4 3 2 1

To my wife, Sharon, and my son, Tim, for their endless love, support, and patience through this and many other professional endeavors.

To my parents, Barbara and Jerry, who laid the foundation for my achievements.

My successes belong to the family.

CONTENTS

PREFACE

This book could serve as an introductory text for the student new to homeland security, as well as a valuable reference for the experienced security professional.

September 11, 2001 was a watershed moment in our nation's history. The attacks that occurred that day were our first taste of a significant international terrorist attack occurring in our homeland. Much like previous generations who can instantly recall where they were and what they were doing when Pearl Harbor was attacked or President John F. Kennedy was assassinated, many Americans have the same vivid recollections with regard to the September 11th attacks. The images of the World Trade Center Towers first being struck and then collapsing, the Pentagon in flames, and the crater in the Pennsylvania countryside resulting from the crash of United Flight 93 were forever seared in our memories thanks to real time media reporting. Our way of life was forever changed on that fall morning. From that day forward, security issues will reign paramount in our daily activities. As an example, the most involved reorganization of our government, which led to the creation of the Department of Homeland Security, was a direct result of the September 11th attacks and an indication of the newfound importance of homeland security. Although international terrorism may be a new concept to some in America, terrorism has been around for thousands of years as illustrated in the many examples through this book.

This book was written to assist organizations, both private or public, in identifying what is critical to them and protecting them from hazards. All organizations must take the appropriate actions to reduce risk and protect their assets. Although each organization will deem what is important to them, it should be remembered that when they are grouped together with other assets in a municipality or region, they may not maintain that same level of criticality or importance.

Chapter 2 provides suggestions on how to identify critical infrastructure and key assets. The principles and examples in this book apply equally regardless of jurisdiction. Each organization has a responsibility to identify their key assets, assess the threat posed against them, and evaluate the risk that those assets may be degraded or destroyed. In keeping with the all hazards theme of this book, Chapter 3 introduces the reader to the three types of destruction events and how an asset may be adversely affected. However, emphasis is placed on the intentional destructive event that could be perpetrated by an adversary, including their tactics, whether they are an insider, outsider, or one working in collusion with an insider. The target selection process, including basic screening methodologies that can be used to determine your asset's attractiveness as a target, are also provided.

The premise of this book is that our assets should be protected from all hazards and all risks, not just terrorism. The principles covered are designed for all threats from minor criminal activity through the use of a weapon of mass destruction by a terrorist. Many of the basic principles that are applied to assessing and protecting an asset from being bombed by a terrorist can also be applied to reduce the likelihood of theft. The principles covered in a comprehensive emergency preparedness and response plan that address how to mitigate and recover from a terrorist attack can likewise be used to recover from the damage caused by a hurricane. There are various scenarios and case studies presented to assist in the implementation of an assessment and countermeasures process.

The most horrific attack a terrorist could initiate would involve a weapon of mass destruction. These weapons, which would involve the use of a biological, chemical, or radiological agent, or an incendiary or explosive device, would be truly devastating if executed properly. Therefore, an entire chapter is devoted to describing these weapons, and how a terrorist may go about turning an apparently innocuous or commonly available material into a weapon. Having this understanding will greatly assist in performing the vulnerability and risk assessment processes as well as developing appropriate countermeasures.

Chapter 5 addresses the various preattack preparations an adversary may undertake before executing an attack. Included are eight potential indicators of terrorism; these indicators are the core of a training program for personnel to help them recognize that a plot may be afoot. The next logical step after conducting a vulnerability analysis will be to evaluate the risk of adverse consequences, and implement the appropriate level of security countermeasures. Chapter 6 presents several examples of worksheets that can be used to assess asset criticality, asset value, threat analysis, and consequences of a successful attack. Risk and threat assessment and analysis techniques are also discussed, including examples of both qualitative and quantitative risk analysis. Chapter 7 presents a key asset screening methodology and the process of conducting a security vulnerability assessment for all types of potential loss. Several examples and sample worksheets are provided.

Just as all organizations and jurisdictions have an obligation to assess their vulnerabilities and risk, they have an obligation to implement effective countermeasures. These countermeasures can take many forms, and will certainly vary from organization to organization and jurisdiction to jurisdiction based on the threat and risk assessment. Chapter 8 details the principles of protective security and introduces the concept of rings of protection. Rings of protection involve the use of several overlapping and complementary security measures that can be implemented to reduce vulnerabilities and hence risk. Chapter 9 provides some basic guidance and templates for various countermeasures that can be customized to fit specific applications.

Chapter 10 provides some basic principles of emergency response, including an introduction to the National Incident Management System (NIMS). These basic principles are valid for any type of emergency situation. Chapter 11 provides some basic guidance on how to respond to an incident involving the use of a weapon of mass destruction.

There were many who have supported and encouraged me in this endeavor. To these behind the scene friends whose names do not appear in print, I extend my sincere appreciation and gratitude for your support.

To the practitioners in the field of homeland security, this work is submitted in the hope it will be a useful tool in strengthening our critical infrastructure and in helping to prevent casualties and loss in the future.

BRIAN BENNETT

Woodbridge, NJ

CHAPTER 1

The Terrorist Threat

1.1 WHAT IS TERRORISM?

Terrorism is derived from the Latin word *terrere*, which means to tremble. Terrorism is defined by the U.S. Department of State in the *United States Code*, Title 22, Section 2656f (d), as "premeditated, politically motivated violence perpetrated against non-combatant targets by subnational groups or clandestine agents, usually intended to influence an audience." Terrorism is often random: attacks intentionally and indiscriminately impact noncombatants. Terrorism is premeditated, criminal in nature, politically motivated, potentially including religious, philosophical, ideological, or culturally symbolic motivations, violent, and perpetrated against a noncombatant target. Terrorism primarily seeks to assist an organization in the furtherance of its ideological ideals. Thus there are four key distinguishing elements of terrorism:

1. It is premeditated—planned in advanced and not conducted as an impulsive act of rage.
2. It is political—designed to change the existing political order.
3. It is aimed at civilians—not military personnel or facilities.
4. It is carried out by subnational groups—not a country's army.

In the world of terrorism, physical assets including people, products, services, information, and property are viewed as targets. What sets terrorism apart from mass murder is not only that it's an attack carried out against civilians (noncombatants), but it also has psychological effects that must be dealt with across the general population. From the terrorists' point of view, they need to conduct just one significant attack every year or two to maintain the public's fear and anxiety. Terrorist attacks are often spectacular, designed to disturb and influence a wide audience beyond the victims of the attack itself. There are both direct and indirect victims of terrorism. The direct victims include those who were the target of an attack and became a casualty. Indirect victims of a terrorist attack are those who were

Understanding, Assessing, and Responding to Terrorism: Protecting Critical Infrastructure and Personnel By Brian T. Bennett

remote from the attack, yet suffered some harm anyway. An example of a direct victim of terrorism would be a person who was killed in a suicide bomb attack at a hotel. An indirect victim from this attack would be the hotel itself, which lost business because of the attack on its property. Terrorism is more than just brutal violence; there is a strategy behind all terrorist actions. That strategy is the deliberate use of violence against civilians to achieve political, social, or religious goals. Terrorism will disrupt foreign policy, disrupt peace initiatives, and sow discomfort and domestic unrest in a geopolitical region. The true target of the terrorist is society as a whole.

1.2 TERRORISM STATISTICS

The U.S. count of major world terrorist attacks more than tripled in 2004. The number of "significant" international terrorist attacks rose to about 650 in 2004, from about 208 in 2003. A total of 625 persons were killed, including 35 U.S. citizens, and 3646 persons were wounded in attacks that occurred in 2003. The increase of attacks in 2004 from previous years reflects the numerous indiscriminate attacks on "soft targets," such as places of worship, hotels, and commercial districts, intended to produce mass casualties. Most of the attacks that have occurred during Operation Iraqi Freedom and Operation Enduring Freedom do not meet the longstanding U.S. definition of international terrorism because they were directed at combatants, that is, U.S. and coalition forces on duty. Attacks against noncombatants, that is, civilians and military personnel who at the time of the incident were unarmed and/or not on duty, are judged to be terrorist attacks [1].

1.3 PURPOSE OF TERRORISM

The purpose of terrorism, as the name implies, is to terrify and spread fear and destruction. The randomness of an attack to inflict casualties on innocent victims is the very essence of terror—it can strike at any place and at any time and can adversely impact someone who had the misfortune to be at the wrong place at the wrong time. Terrorism strikes at our core values—the right to life, peace, and security. Terrorism is a tactic used by an adversary to accomplish one of five things:

1. Instill a sense of fear in a population.
2. Influence the policy of a government.
3. Effect the conduct of a government.
4. Get the affected population to change their daily routine.
5. Coerce or intimidate a population in furtherance of social, religious, or political objectives.

1.4 GOALS OF TERRORISM

Terrorists can operate individually or in large groups and can perpetrate their attacks in different ways for different goals. Terrorist goals include the following:

1. Causing casualties (injuries and fatalities).
2. Damaging or destroying critical infrastructure.
3. Disrupting the economy.
4. Harassing, weakening, or embarrassing the government.
5. Discouraging tourism or investments due to perceived insecurity.

Terrorist organizations remain intent on obtaining and using devastating weapons against the United States to cause casualties and economic damage. The development of more sophisticated weapons in the twentieth century has allowed terrorists to kill more people from a greater distance. Many terrorist organizations are not concerned about killing large numbers of innocent victims indiscriminantly, so precise targeting is not necessary. Suicide terrorism has reemerged, not because of lack of technology, but because suicide terrorism generates fear among the general population, and it allows for accurate, large-scale attacks without the use of sophisticated weapons and tactics. Suicide terrorists are not crazy but rather are extremely committed to their mission and see themselves as martyrs. Suicide bombers are often viewed as heroes; they believe that they will receive rewards in death. Their surviving family receives both financial and psychological rewards for their sacrifice. Martyrdom is the perfect manifestation of jihad.

Terrorists worldwide have favored the old reliable, low-tech high-impact weapons, such as vehicle bombs, suicide bombs, and automatic weapons, and will probably continue to do so. However, some terrorist organizations will increasingly exploit advances in science and technology as these technologies become more widespread and accessible to maximize their destructive impact. The more readily available and accessible these technological developments become, the more likely the terrorists will adapt them for nefarious purposes. Terrorist groups have embraced technology and are using the Internet to formulate plans, recruit members, communicate between individual members and cells, raise funds, and spread propaganda. The enemy adapts. As we step up security, the terrorists shift tactics in response. As examples, the Tamil Tigers have used rudimentary stealth technology to mask their suicide speedboats, and Colombia's FARC has deployed remotely controlled automobiles to deliver car bombs. The current generation of terrorists can learn their trade without traveling to a distant training camp in another country. They can train at home using materials broadcast over the Internet.

The disturbing fact is that the terrorist will change and adapt as precautions against attacks are implemented. Recent intelligence suggests that some of al Qaeda's leaders may favor smaller scale operations that employ simple technology, take less preparation, and require fewer operatives. The terrorists may be executing attacks that focus more on the psychological and economic effects resulting from smaller attacks than the mass casualties and damage caused by a large-scale event.

Terrorism has become a strategic weapon. It is capable of disrupting foreign policy and peace initiatives and has become a force multiplier in certain regions of the world, causing discomfort and domestic unrest.

1.5 CASE STUDY: ECONOMIC EFFECTS OF A TERRORIST ATTACK

As an example, consider the economic effects the September 11, 2001 terrorist attack in the United States had on domestic and international markets. The U.S. monetary loss as a result of the September 11 attack is estimated at $500 billion, besides the loss of a huge number of jobs. The economy of lower Manhattan, which by itself is the third largest business district in the United States, was devastated in the immediate aftermath of the attack. Approximately 30% (34.5 million square feet) of lower Manhattan office space was either damaged or destroyed. The attack resulted in $50–70 billion in insured losses. The New York Stock Exchange and NASDAQ did not open on September 11 and remained closed until September 17, 2001 due to damage to the communications facilities near the World Trade Center Complex. This closure of the markets was the longest since the Great Depression of 1929. When the markets finally reopened on September 17, 2001, the Dow Jones Industrial Average stock market index fell 684 points, or 7.1%. This decline was the biggest ever one-day point decline. By Friday, September 21, 2001, the Dow Jones had dropped 1369.7 points, or 14.3%, its largest one-week point drop in history. United States stocks lost $1.2 trillion in value for the week [2]. There has been even greater cascading economic effects caused the September 11 attack. Washington, DC's Reagan National Airport was closed for 23 days due to its proximity to many potential targets in the Nation's capital. The air space over North America was closed after the attack until September 13. When flights resumed, air travel decreased by approximately 20% due to several factors, including people's unwillingness to wait in long lines due to increased security measures and fear of additional attacks involving airplanes.

1.6 OBJECTIVES OF TERRORISM

Terrorist groups exist for the purpose of planning and executing attacks to accomplish their mission. Included among the objectives of terrorism are:

- Demonstrate the group's power over the population and government.
- Show the existing government's lack of power to interfere or stop terrorist operations.
- Exact revenge for perceived persecution and satisfy the group's vengeance.
- Gain worldwide, national, or local publicity for the group's cause by attracting media coverage.

Terrorists need money, membership, and media to accomplish their goals. Therefore terrorists depend on the media to publicize their attacks, and hence their cause, which will lead to more volunteers and financial support. Terrorist groups have become expert at leveraging the media to assist in their objectives. The worldwide media, perhaps unwillingly in some cases, contributes to terrorism. Terrorism depends on the masses listening, reading, and watching terrorist attacks unfold in real time. The terrorists need their attack to garner worldwide attention to have the desired impact; 24/7 media coverage helps achieve that goal. The end result is the media attention helps the terrorists' recruiting and financing goals.

1.7 THE TERRORISM CHALLENGE

Advanced warning of terrorist attacks remains difficult due to the terrorists' operational security practices and their ability to take full advantage of the West's open and free society. Terrorists are fully aware that attacks lead to political fallout. That, combined with the likelihood that Western countries are prone to "cut and run" when sustaining casualties, ensures Islamic terrorists will factor political considerations into future attacks. Individual terrorist cells are now starting to finance their operations locally by criminal activity, primarily narcotics trafficking. Al Qaeda has mutated into a global insurgency, with no central leadership and many local branches, fighting the West with or without allegiance to Osama bin Laden. Osama bin Laden doesn't necessarily authorize attacks; he merely inspires them. It is now a network of global relationships. In order to stop al Qaeda, the cycle of terrorist recruitment must be broken and the appeal of radicalism diminished. Efforts must be undertaken to ensure the jihad does not become self-sustaining.

History has shown the best way to defeat and demoralize an enemy is to bring the fight to their homes. An attack from covert al Qaeda operatives inside the homeland is the biggest threat posed to the United States.

1.8 WHAT IS HOMELAND SECURITY?

Homeland security is a concerted national effort to prevent terrorist attacks within the United States, reduce America's vulnerability to terrorism, and minimize the damage and recover from attacks that do occur. The mission of homeland security is a very complex task that requires a long-term coordinated and focused effort from the federal government, state government, local government, the private sector, and the American people. Homeland security must be a cooperative public and private effort.

The strategic objectives of homeland security [3] in order of priority are the following:

- Prevent terrorist attacks within the United States.
- Reduce America's vulnerability to terrorism.
- Minimize the damage and recover from attacks that do occur.

In order to prepare for the many challenges associated with homeland security, the most extensive reorganization of the federal government in the past fifty years has been completed. The newly created Office of Homeland Security has been tasked with the overall responsibility for coordinating the various national homeland security missions. In July 2002, the Office of Homeland Security issued the *National Strategy for Homeland Security*. The purpose of this document was to mobilize and organize the nation to secure the U.S. homeland from terrorist attacks. This exceedingly complex mission requires coordinated and focused effort from our entire society—the federal government, state and local governments, the private sector, and the American people. The *National Strategy for Homeland Security* provides direction for the federal government departments and agencies that have a role in homeland security. It suggests steps that state and local governments, private companies and organizations, and individual Americans can take to improve our security and offers them incentives for doing so. The *National Strategy for Homeland Security* establishes a foundation on which to organize our efforts and provides initial guidance to prioritize the work ahead.

Critical Mission Areas

The *National Strategy for Homeland Security* [3] aligns and focuses the homeland security functions into six critical mission areas, which are discussed next.

Intelligence and Warning. For terrorism to be effective in causing damage or casualties, the attack must be a surprise. Most Americans were taken by surprise by the events of September 11, 2001. However, upon further review, it was found there were a number of indicators that were known before the attack that might have provided a clue as to al Qaeda's plans had they been routed to a central organization for processing and review. It is critical that systems are in place to collect, analyze, evaluate, and respond to intelligence information that may provide advance warning of an impending attack. Once the intelligence has been thoroughly analyzed, it must be shared with the appropriate agencies, critical infrastructure sectors, and in some cases the general public, so the proper immediate safeguards can be implemented to prevent the attack, or at least minimize its consequences. Intelligence agencies must also look beyond the near-term information that has been collected. To be in a position to thwart future attacks by terrorists, a thorough understanding of the terrorist organizations must be developed. Knowing the identities, financial and political sources of support, motivation, goals, current and future capabilities, and vulnerabilities of these organizations will assist us in preventing future attacks and in taking long-term actions that can weaken support for organizations that seek to damage our interests. The *National Strategy for Homeland Security* identifies five major initiatives in this area:

- *Enhance the Analytical Capabilities of the FBI.* The FBI's top priority is preventing terrorist attacks. They are creating an analytical capability within the FBI that can combine lawfully obtained domestic information with information lawfully derived from investigations, thus facilitating prompt investigation of possible terrorist activity within the United States.

- *Building New Capabilities Through the Information Analysis and Infrastructure Protection Division of the Office of Homeland Security.* The Office of Homeland Security will coordinate and oversee the effort of conducting comprehensive vulnerability assessments of critical infrastructure and key assets. These assessments will reveal gaps in security, evaluate the potential effects of a given attack, and identify protective measures that can be implemented.
- *Implement the Homeland Security Advisory System.* The Homeland Security Advisory System disseminates information regarding the risk of terrorism to federal, state, and local authorities, the private sector, and the American people. Each threat condition has corresponding suggested measures to be taken in response to the terrorist threat.
- *Utilize Dual-Use Analysis to Prevent Attacks.* "Dual-use" items are equipment and materials that have both a legitimate commercial use as well as potential terrorist applications that can be purchased on the open market. Examples of dual-use items include fermentors, crop dusters, and disease-causing agents.
- *Employ "Red Team" Techniques.* By applying homeland security intelligence and information, personnel view the United States from the perspective of the terrorists, seeking to discern and predict the methods, means, and targets of the terrorists.

Border and Transportation Security. America has historically relied on two vast oceans and two friendly neighbors for border security. Transportation security was provided by the individual carriers. All people and goods legally entering the United States must be processed through an air, land, or sea port of entry. America must now redevelop its systems for border and transportation security. With global travel readily accessible and relatively inexpensive, systems must be enhanced to tighten control of who can enter the country. American communities are tied into the global transportation network, with virtually every community connected by airports, seaports, highways, railroads, waterways, and pipelines that move people, goods, and services across our borders and into our neighborhoods. Transportation security must be enhanced to ensure terrorists do not use our transportation infrastructure to convey weapons of mass destruction but yet not impede the flow of people and goods.

The *National Strategy for Homeland Security* identified six major initiatives in this area:

- *Ensure Accountability in Border and Transportation Security.* The principal border and transportation security agencies are now part of the Office of Homeland Security. The Office of Homeland Security also controls the issuance of visas to foreigners and coordinates the border control activities.
- *Create "Smart Borders."* Today's borders will be a continuum framed by land, sea, and air dimensions, where a layered management system enables greater

visibility of vehicles, people, and goods coming into and departing from the country. The United States will screen and verify the security of goods and identities of people before they can harm the international transportation system and well before they reach our shores or land borders.

- *Increase the Security of International Shipping Containers.* Approximately 90% of the world's cargo moves by container. Each year, nearly 50% of the value of all U.S. imports arrives via 16 million containers. The core elements of this initiative are to establish security criteria to identify high-risk containers; prescreen containers before they arrive at U.S. ports; use technology to inspect high-risk containers; and develop and use smart and secure containers.
- *Implement the Aviation and Transportation Security Act of 2001.* The act establishes a series of challenging but important milestones toward achieving a secure air travel system. The act fundamentally changed the way transportation security is performed and managed in the United States. Protection of critical transportation assets such as ports, pipelines, rail and highway bridges, and more than 10,000 Federal Aviation Administration facilities is another key requirement established by the act.
- *Recapitalize the U.S. Coast Guard.* This initiative will support the recapitalization of the U.S. Coast Guard's aging fleet, as well as targeted improvements in the areas of maritime domain awareness, command and control systems, and shore-side facilities.
- *Reform Immigration Services.* This reform aims to ensure full enforcement of the laws that regulate the admission of aliens to the United States and to improve greatly the administration of immigration benefits to more than 7 million annual applicants.

Domestic Counterterrorism. The mission of preventing and interdicting terrorism on U.S. soil has been assigned to law enforcement agencies. These agencies will use all legal means—both traditional and nontraditional—to identify, halt, and, where appropriate, prosecute terrorists in the United States. Not only will the individuals directly responsible in the terrorist activity be pursued, but also their supporting cast: the people and organizations that knowingly provide the terrorists with logistical and financial assistance. The federal government has instituted initiatives that have increased information sharing and the coordination of operations throughout the law enforcement communities.

The *National Strategy for Homeland Security* identifies six major initiatives in this area:

- *Improve Intergovernmental Law Enforcement Coordination.* An effective counterterrorism effort requires the participation of law enforcement personnel at all levels of government, as well as the coordination of all relevant agencies and officials.

- *Facilitate Apprehension of Potential Terrorists.* Law enforcement officers must have access to information on suspected terrorists in order to apprehend them before they have an opportunity to execute their plans. Various crime information databases and watch lists are being updated and expanded to make this critical information available to all state and local law enforcement officers.
- *Continue Ongoing Investigations and Prosecutions.* Counterterrorism efforts include the investigation and prosecution of foreign and domestic terrorists, as well as the pursuit of individuals who provide logistical support to terrorists. The September 11 attack has resulted in the largest and most extensive criminal investigation in history, involving numerous federal, state, and local law enforcement agencies, and the intelligence and law enforcement agencies of foreign countries.
- *Complete FBI Restructuring to Emphasize Prevention and Terrorist Attacks.* Our nation's highest law enforcement objective is the prevention of terrorist acts. The FBI has made several structural changes to reflect the primacy of the counterterrorism mission. New positions have been established for strengthening information sharing and coordination with state and local authorities. The FBI's counterterrorism investigative capabilities and flexibility have been increased by shifting hundreds of field agents from criminal investigations to counterterrorism investigations and activities. These changes will ensure the FBI has a concentrated, national, centralized, and deployable expertise on terrorism issues.
- *Target and Disrupt Terrorist Financing.* Terrorists cannot operate without financial resources. The U.S. Treasury Department has spearheaded the terrorist finance interdiction effort. The department works to freeze the accounts of, and seize the assets of, individuals and organizations that finance terrorist groups.
- *Track Foreign Terrorists and Bring Them to Justice.* The federal government has two key missions in regard to tracking foreign terrorists: barring terrorists or terrorist supporting aliens from the United States and tracking down and deporting any who have illegally entered our country.

Protecting Critical Infrastructure and Key Assets. Our modern society and day to day activities are dependent on networks of critical infrastructure—both physical networks such as energy and transportation systems and virtual networks such as the Internet. If terrorists attack a piece of critical infrastructure, they will disrupt our standard of living and cause significant physical, psychological, and financial damage to our nation. Particular attention must be given to protecting our critical infrastructure and key assets, not only from terrorist attacks but from other, more common illegal activities such as theft, industrial espionage, and computer hackers.

The *National Strategy for Homeland Security* identifies eight major initiatives in this area:

- *Unify America's Infrastructure Protection Efforts in the Office of Homeland Security.* The Office of Homeland Security has been charged with the responsibility of integrating and coordinating federal infrastructure protection.
- *Build and Maintain a Complete and Accurate Assessment of America's Critical Infrastructure and Key assets.* Threat information must be translated into appropriate action in the shortest possible time, a critical factor in preventing or mitigating attacks, particularly those involving weapons of mass destruction. The Office of Homeland Security maintains a complete, current, and accurate assessment of the vulnerabilities and preparedness of key assets across the critical infrastructure sectors. The office has the ability to continuously evaluate threat information against our current vulnerabilities, inform the president, issue warnings, and effect action accordingly.
- *Enable Effective Partnership with State and Local Governments and the Private Sector.* Government at the federal, state, and local levels must actively collaborate and partner with the private sector to protect our nation's critical infrastructure. In many cases, the private sector, not the government, possesses the technical expertise and means to protect the infrastructure it controls. Government at all levels must enable, not inhibit, the private sector's ability to protect the infrastructure it controls.
- *Develop a National Infrastructure Protection Plan.* The Office of Homeland Security developed and coordinates the implementation of a comprehensive national plan to protect America's critical infrastructure from terrorist attack. The national plan provides a methodology for identifying and prioritizing critical assets, systems, and functions, and for sharing protection responsibility with state and local governments and the private sector.
- *Secure Cyberspace.* Our potential enemies have the intent, the tools of destruction are broadly available, and the vulnerabilities of our systems are myriad and well known. In cyberspace, a single act can inflict damage in multiple locations simultaneously without the attacker ever having physically entered the United States.
- *Harness the Best Analytic and Modeling Tools to Develop Effective Protective Solutions.* High-end modeling and simulation tools can greatly enhance our ability to quickly make decisions based on the best possible understanding of their consequences. State-of-the-art modeling and simulation provides another important tool for determining what assets, systems, and functions are critical, a process that involves many factors that interact with one another in complex ways.
- *Guard America's Critical Infrastructure and Key Assets Against "Inside" Threats.* The "insider threat" and personnel reliability are increasingly serious concerns for protecting critical infrastructure. Personnel with privileged

access to critical infrastructure, particularly control systems, may serve as terrorist surrogates by providing information on vulnerabilities, operating characteristics, and protective measures.

- *Partner with the International Community to Protect our Transnational Infrastructure.* We share and interconnect much of our critical infrastructure with our neighbors in Canada and Mexico, and increasingly with countries around the world. Thus terrorists need not gain access to our country to attack our infrastructure.

Defending Against Catastrophic Threats. The expertise, knowledge, and materials necessary to build the most deadly weapons of mass destruction—chemical, biological, radiological/nuclear, and explosive—are readily available. Several terrorist organizations have stated they are actively trying to acquire such weapons. If a weapon of mass destruction were obtained, it is likely to be used against us. The results of an effectively deployed weapon of mass destruction would be catastrophic, and the consequences of such an attack would be far more devastating than those we suffered on September 11, 2001. Much work is required to enhance our ability to detect and respond to an attack using chemical, biological, radiological/nuclear, or explosive materials.

The *National Strategy for Homeland Security* identifies six major initiatives in this area:

- *Prevent Terrorist Use of Nuclear Weapons Through Better Sensors and Procedures.* New inspection procedures and detection systems protect against the entry of nuclear materials at all ports of entry in the United States and at major overseas cargo loading facilities. Additional inspection procedures and detection systems are being added throughout our national transportation structure to detect the movement of nuclear materials within the United States.
- *Detect Chemical and Biological Materials and Attacks.* New sensitive and highly selective systems that detect the release of chemical or biological agents have been developed. The Environmental Protection Agency has upgraded air monitoring stations to allow for the detection of certain chemical, biological, or radiological substances.
- *Improve Chemical Sensors and Decontamination Techniques.* The Office of Homeland Security is funding and coordinating a national research program to develop, test, and field detection devices and networks that provide immediate and accurate warnings. The office is also supporting research into decontamination technologies and procedures.
- *Develop Broad Spectrum Vaccines, Antimicrobials, and Antidotes.* In many cases, our medical countermeasures cannot address all possible biological agents or may not be suitable for use by the general population. Therefore new defenses will be pursued that will increase efficacy while reducing side effects.

Short- and long-term efforts will expand the inventory of diagnostics, vaccines, and other therapies such as antimicrobials and antidotes that can mitigate the consequences of a chemical, biological, radiological, or nuclear attack.

- *Harness the Scientific Knowledge and Tools to Counter Terrorism.* Substantial research into relevant medical sciences is necessary to better detect, diagnose, and treat the consequences of chemical, biological, radiological, or nuclear attacks. The Office of Homeland Security is leveraging the expertise of America's cutting edge medical and biotechnology infrastructure to advance the state of knowledge in infectious disease prevention and treatment, forensic epidemiology, and microbial forensics.
- *Implement the Select Agent Program.* The Office of Homeland Security oversees the Select Agent Program to regulate the shipment of certain hazardous biological organisms and toxins. Through the laboratory registration process, the Select Agent Program has significantly increased oversight and security of pathogens that could be used for bioterrorism.

Emergency Preparedness and Response. It is critical that we are prepared to respond to any future terrorist attack. Although our primary effort is geared toward the prevention of such an attack, it is prudent to have the proper capability to have an effective response to properly mitigate a major terrorist attack. Therefore a comprehensive national system to coordinate and deploy the appropriate response assets quickly and effectively is needed. Emergency response organizations must plan, equip, train, and exercise together and with the private sector so they can mobilize without warning for any emergency, be it a terrorist attack or natural disaster.

Many pieces of this national emergency response system are in place and have been so for many years. America's first line of defense in the aftermath of a terrorist attack is its local first responders—firefighters, police officers, emergency medical services, and emergency management officials. Nearly three million first responders at the state and local levels regularly put their lives on the line to save lives, protect property, and make our country safer.

The *National Strategy for Homeland Security* identifies twelve major initiatives in this area:

- *Integrate All Separate Federal Response Plans into a Single, All-Discipline Incident Management Plan.* All existing federal government emergency response plans have been consolidated into one genuinely all-discipline all-hazard plan—the National Emergency Response Plan. This plan covers all incidents of national significance, including acts of terrorism.
- *Create a National Incident Management System.* The Office of Homeland Security, working with federal, state, local, and nongovernmental public safety organizations has created the comprehensive National Incident Management System (NIMS) to respond to terrorist incidents and other disasters. The NIMS ensures that there is now a national system of common terminology, provides a uniform command structure, and is scalable to address incidents of all sizes.

- *Improve Tactical Counterterrorist Capabilities.* With advance warning, we have various federal, state, and local response assets that can intercede and prevent terrorists from carrying out attacks. In the most dangerous of incidents, particularly when terrorists have chemical, biological, radiological, or nuclear weapons in their possession, it is crucial that the individuals who preempt the terrorists do so flawlessly. It is also crucial that these individuals be prepared and are able to work effectively with each other and with other specialized response personnel.
- *Enable Seamless Communication Among All Responders.* In the aftermath of any major terrorist attack, emergency response efforts would likely involve hundreds of officials from across the government and the country. It is crucial for response personnel to have and use equipment, systems, and procedures that allow them to communicate with one another.
- *Prepare Health Care Providers for Catastrophic Terrorism.* The Office of Homeland Security will support training and equipping of state and local health care personnel to deal with the growing threat of chemical, biological, radiological, and nuclear terrorism. The hospital preparedness grant program is used to help prepare hospital and poison control centers to deal specifically with biological and chemical attacks and to expand their surge capacity to care for a large number of patients in a mass casualty incident.
- *Augment America's Pharmaceutical and Vaccine Stockpiles.* The National Pharmaceutical Stockpile ensures America's ability to respond rapidly to a bioterrorist attack. This program maintains twelve strategically placed "push packs" containing 600 tons of antibiotics, antidotes, vaccines, bandages, and other medical supplies. The federal government can transport these packs to an incident site in less than 12 hours for rapid distribution by state and local authorities.
- *Prepare for Chemical, Biological, and Radiological/Nuclear Decontamination.* The Office of Homeland Security will provide grant money to emergency responders for planning, equipping, training, and exercising first responders for chemical, biological, radiological, and nuclear attacks. It has launched a national research and development effort to create new technologies for the detection and cleanup of such attacks.
- *Plan for Military Support to Civil Authorities.* The importance of military support to civil authorities as the latter respond to threats or acts of terrorism is recognized in presidential decision directives and legislation. Military support to civil authorities pursuant to a terrorist threat or attack may take the form of providing technical support and assistance to law enforcement; assisting in the restoration of law and order; loaning specialized equipment; and assisting in consequence management.
- *Build the Citizen Corps.* Under the president's proposal, the Office of Homeland Security is expanding the Citizen Corps, a national program to prepare

volunteers for terrorism-related response support. These citizen volunteers would supplement the formal governmental emergency response with personnel who have been trained to perform certain tasks (such as traffic control), thus releasing the more highly trained emergency responders for life-saving missions.

- *Implement the First Responder Initiative of the Fiscal Year 2003 Budget.* The purpose of this initiative is to improve dramatically first responder preparedness for terrorist incidents and disasters. The Office of Homeland Security consolidates all grant programs that distribute federal funds to state and local first responders.
- *Build a National Training and Evaluation System.* The Office of Homeland Security launched a consolidated and expanded training and evaluation system. The system is predicated on a four-phase approach: requirements, plans, training (and exercises), and assessments (comprising evaluations and corrective action plans). The office serves as the central coordinating body responsible for overseeing curriculum standards and for training the instructors who will train the first responders.
- *Enhance the Victim Support System.* The United States must be prepared to assist the victims of terrorist attacks and their families, as well as other individuals affected indirectly by the attacks. The Office of Homeland Security will lead federal agencies and provide guidance to state, local, and volunteer organizations in offering victims and their families various forms of assistance, including crisis counseling, cash grants, low-interest loans, unemployment benefits, free legal counseling, and tax refunds.

The Foundations of Homeland Security

The *National Strategy for Homeland Security* also describes four foundations—unique American strengths that cut across all of the mission areas, all levels of government, and all sectors of our society.

Law. Laws have been used throughout our nation's history to promote and safeguard our security and our liberty. The law will provide mechanisms for the government to act and will define the appropriate limits of action. The *National Strategy for Homeland Security* identifies twelve initiatives in this area.

Federal Level

- *Enable Critical Infrastructure Information Sharing.* Homeland security officials need quick and complete access to information relevant to the protection of critical infrastructure. We must meet this need by narrowly limiting public disclosure of such information in order to facilitate its voluntary submission without compromising the principles of openness that ensure government accountability. Legislative reform or guidance regarding statutes governing public disclosure is needed.

- *Streamline Information Sharing Among Intelligence and Law Enforcement Agencies.* Homeland security requires improved information sharing between the intelligence community, law enforcement agencies, and government decision makers. Laws controlling intelligence operations need to be modified.
- *Expand Existing Extradition Authorities.* The war on terrorism is and must be a global effort. Our country must continue to work cooperatively with nations around the world. To that end, current extradition laws should be amended. First, new legislation must be adopted that would authorize extradition for certain crimes where the United States already has an extradition treaty, but where the treaty applies only to a limited set of crimes. Second, Congress should grant authority to extradite individuals from the United States for serious crimes in the absence of an extradition treaty, on a case by case basis.
- *Review the Authority for Military Assistance in Domestic Security.* United States federal law prohibits military personnel from enforcing law within the United States except as expressly authorized by the Constitution or an Act of Congress. The threat of catastrophic terrorism requires a thorough review of the laws permitting the military to act within the United States in order to determine whether domestic preparedness and response efforts would benefit from greater involvement of military personnel, and if so, how.
- *Revive the President's Reorganization Authority.* Only Congress can create a new department of government. Congress should revive the president's ability to reorganize and restructure the federal government to eliminate redundancies within executive agencies and address homeland security more efficiently and economically.
- *Provide Substantial Management Flexibility for the Office of Homeland Security.* The Office of Homeland Security must have the advantage of twenty-first century approaches to personnel and procurement policies. With these and other flexible practices, the secretary would have the managerial freedom necessary to accomplish not only the office's primary mission of homeland security but also the important agency functions that are not directly related to homeland security.

State Level

- *Coordinate Suggested Minimum Standards for State Driver's Licenses.* There is no national standard for content, format, or license acquisition procedures. Terrorist organizations, including al Qaeda operatives involved in the September 11 attack, have exploited these differences. The federal government should support state led efforts to develop minimum standards for driver's licenses.
- *Enhance Market Capacity for Terrorism Insurance.* The need for insurance coverage for terrorist events has increased dramatically. State regulation will play an integral role in ensuring the adequate provision of terrorism insurance. To establish a regulatory approach that enables American businesses to spread

and pool risk efficiently, states should work together and with the federal government to find a mutually acceptable approach to enhance market capacity to cover terrorist risk.

- *Train for Prevention of Cyber Attacks.* State and local officials have requested federal training regarding the identification, investigation, and enforcement of cyber-related crimes and terrorism. The FBI should take the lead in assisting state and local law enforcement in obtaining training in this area.
- *Suppress Money Laundering.* Terrorists use unregulated financial services, among other means, to fund their operations. The Money Laundering Suppression Act (Public Law 103-325) urges states to enact uniform laws to license and regulate certain financial services. The USA PATRIOT Act also relies on state law to establish the regulatory structure necessary to combat money laundering.
- *Ensure Continuity of the Judiciary.* In the aftermath of a terrorist attack, our judicial system must continue to operate effectively. State and federal authorities should develop a system to expediently appoint judges, to ensure interaction and coordination among federal and state judiciaries, and to deal with other matters necessary to the continued functioning of the judiciary in times of crisis.
- *Review Quarantine Authorities.* State quarantine laws fail to address the dangers presented by modern biological warfare and terrorism. States should update quarantine laws to improve intrastate response while working with federal regulators to assure compliance with minimum public health standards.

Science and Technology. New technologies for analysis, information sharing, detection of attacks, and countering chemical, biological, and radiological/nuclear weapons of mass destruction will help prevent and minimize the damage from future terrorist attacks.

The *National Strategy for Homeland Security* identified eleven major initiatives in this area:

- *Develop Chemical, Biological, and Radiological/Nuclear Countermeasures.* Key initiatives include research and development to prevent terrorist use of nuclear weapons, to detect chemical and biological materials and attacks, to develop high-efficacy vaccines and antivirals against biological agents, and to track laboratory use of biological agents.
- *Develop Systems for Detecting Hostile Intent.* Terrorists may behave in a manner that reveals their criminal intent. The Office of Homeland Security is developing systems that highlight such behavior and can trigger further investigation and analysis of suspected individuals. This would allow security officials at points of interest such as airports and borders to examine more closely individuals who exhibit such characteristics and also have other indications of potentially hostile intent in their background.

- *Apply Biometric Technology to Identification Devices.* A terrorist may sneak past security personnel at an airport or border crossing thanks to false documents and a simple disguise. These challenges require new technologies and systems to identify and find individual terrorists. The Office of Homeland Security is supporting research and development efforts in biometric technology. The office is focusing on improving accuracy, consistency, and efficiency in biometric systems.
- *Improve the Technical Capabilities of First Responders.* If our first responders are not protected from the dangerous effects of chemical, biological, radiological, and nuclear attacks, we may lose the very people we depend on to minimize the damage of any such attacks. The Office of Homeland Security has launched a long-term effort to provide first responders with technical capabilities for dealing with the effects of catastrophic threats—capabilities that would aid both first responders and the victims of the attack. These capabilities include protective gear and masks, prophylactic treatments, detection equipment, and decontamination equipment.
- *Coordinate Research and Development of the Homeland Security Apparatus.* The Office of Homeland Security has set the overall direction for our nation's homeland security research and development. It has based these efforts on a continuous evaluation of the nation's vulnerabilities, on continual testing of security systems, and on updated evaluations of the threat.
- *Establish a National Laboratory for Homeland Security.* The Office of Homeland Security is establishing a network of laboratories that provide a multidisciplinary environment for developing and demonstrating new technologies for homeland security.
- *Solicit Independent and Private Analysis for Science and Technology Research.* The Office of Homeland Security will fund independent analytic support for our homeland security science and technical endeavors. These efforts will support planning activities, including net assessment, preparing agency guidance, and reviewing agency programs and budgets; systems analyses; requirements analyses; assessments of competing technical and operational approaches; and the Office's use of "red team" techniques.
- *Establish a Mechanism for Rapidly Producing Prototypes.* The Office of Homeland Security will work with other federal agencies to provide a means for rapid prototyping of innovative homeland security concepts based on existing technologies. It will collect unsolicited ideas, evaluate them, and maintain a capability for funding the most promising ideas.
- *Conduct Demonstrations and Pilot Deployments.* The Office of Homeland Security would systematically engage in pilot deployments and demonstrations to provide a conduit between the state and local users of technology and the federal developers of that technology. The pilot deployments and demonstrations serve as a focal point for the development of regional solutions and testing how well new technologies work under local conditions.

- *Set Standards for Homeland Security Technology.* The Office of Homeland Security will work with state and local governments and the private sector to build a mechanism for analyzing, validating, and setting standards for homeland security equipment. The office will develop comprehensive protocols for certification of compliance with these standards.
- *Establish a System for High-Risk, High-Payoff Homeland Security Research.* The Office of Homeland Security will establish a program with a high level of programmatic and budgetary flexibility to solicit private industry for innovative concepts.

Information Sharing and Systems. Although America's information technology system is the most advanced in the world, it has not been used adequately to support the homeland security mission. Databases maintained by different agencies need to be connected in ways that allow information gaps or redundancies to be identified. Communications systems are not compatible to allow most state and local first responders to communicate directly with each other.

The *National Strategy for Homeland Security* identifies five major initiatives in this area:

- *Integrate Information Sharing Across the Federal Government.* The Office of Homeland Security coordinates the sharing of essential homeland security information through the Critical Infrastructure Assurance Office. Enhancements include better information sharing methods; transportation security; emergency response; chemical, biological, radiological, and nuclear countermeasures; and infrastructure protection.
- *Integrate Information Sharing Across State and Local Governments, Private Industry, and Citizens.* Several efforts are under way to enhance the timely dissemination of information from the federal government to state and local homeland security officials by building and sharing law enforcement databases, secure computer networks, secure video teleconferencing, and more accessible websites.
- *Adopt Common "Metadata" Standards for Electronic Information Relevant to Homeland Security.* The administration has begun several initiatives to integrate terrorist-related information from databases of all government agencies responsible for homeland security. This complements the effort to analyze the information with advanced "data mining" techniques to reveal patterns of criminal behavior and detain suspected terrorists before they act.
- *Improve Public Safety Emergency Communications.* The Office of Homeland Security is working to develop comprehensive emergency communications systems. These systems would disseminate information about vulnerabilities and protective measures, as well as allow first responders to better manage incidents and minimize damage.

- *Ensure Reliable Public Health Information.* The Office of Homeland Security is working to ensure reliable public health communications. Prompt detection, accurate diagnosis, and timely reporting and investigation of disease epidemics require reliable communications between medical, veterinary, and public health organizations. Once an attack is confirmed, it is crucial to have real-time communication with other hospitals, public health officials, health professionals, law enforcement, emergency management officials, and the media. Providing the public with timely and accurate risk communication during a public health emergency will inform as well as reassure concerned Americans.

International Cooperation. The terrorist threat pays no respect to traditional borders; therefore our strategy for homeland security cannot stop at our borders. America must pursue a sustained, steadfast, and systematic international agenda to counter the global terrorist threat and improve our homeland security. It is critical that we work diligently and cooperatively with our friends and allies to overcome the terrorist threat.

The *National Strategy for Homeland Security* identifies nine major initiatives in this area:

- *Create "Smart Borders."* The United States is working closely with its neighbors to improve efforts to stop terrorists and their instruments of terror from entering the United States. The United States has entered into "smart border" agreements with Mexico and Canada to meet this objective.
- *Combat Fraudulent Travel Documents.* More than 500 million people cross our borders every year. Verifying that each has a legitimate reason to enter the United States requires international support. The United States is working with its international partners to set improved security standards for travel documents such as passports and visas.
- *Increase the Security of International Shipping Containers.* Sixteen million containers enter our nation every year. The United States is working with its trading partners and international organizations to identify and screen high-risk containers and develop and use smart and secure containers.
- *Intensify International Law Enforcement Cooperation.* The U.S. government is working with individual countries and through multilateral international organizations to improve cooperation on law enforcement action against terrorists. These efforts have focused on freezing the assets of terrorists and affiliated persons and organizations. Efforts have also been taken to prevent terrorist recruitment, transit, and safe haven, as well as cooperating with other countries to bring terrorists to justice.
- *Help Foreign Nations Fight Terrorism.* The U.S. government provides other countries with specialized training and assistance to help build their capabilities to combat terrorism. Some of these programs are military in nature, but many focus on improving the efforts of civilian authorities.

- *Expand Protection of Transitional Critical Infrastructure.* The United States will continue to work with both Canada and Mexico to improve physical and cyber security of critical infrastructure that overlaps with both countries.
- *Amplify International Cooperation on Homeland Security Science and Technology.* The U.S. government encourages and supports complementary international scientific initiatives. The Office of Homeland Security is also working with several close allies to improve techniques and develop new technologies for detecting hostile intent.
- *Improve Cooperation in Response to Attacks.* The United States will continue to work with other nations to ensure smooth provision of international aid in the aftermath of terrorist attacks. It will initiate bilateral and multilateral programs to plan for efficient burden sharing between friendly nations in the case of attack.
- *Review Obligations to International Treaties and Law.* The United States is party to all twelve counterterrorism instruments adopted by the United Nations in recent years. The United States is actively encouraging all United Nations members to join and fully implement all twelve conventions.

1.9 THE MOTIVATION FOR TERRORISM

What would give a person or group the motivation to resort to a terrorist act? Why would someone perpetrate terrorism to achieve his/her goals? How can the murder of innocent people be justified? There are many motivations for terrorism, including:

- *Religion.* Religion is an external influence that may affect the actions of a terrorist if they believe there is no other recourse. Religion often generates very strong feelings on many sensitive issues.
- *Accomplish a Goal.* The primary reason a person or group would perpetrate an act of terrorism would be to accomplish a goal, which, in the case of terrorism, is to achieve social, religious, or political change.
- *Revenge.* A terrorist may desire to avenge a previous perceived wrong.
- *Publicity.* Terrorists may perpetrate an attack to draw attention to their cause and influence people to provide support for their efforts.

1.10 COMMON TERMS IN TERRORISM

Fatwa

A fatwa is an Islamic legal pronouncement, issued by a religious law specialist, concerning a specific issue. A fatwa is usually issued to address a question posed by an individual or judge. The scholar who issues the fatwa is known as a Mufti. Islam has no centralized priestly hierarchy; thus there is no uniform method to determine who can issue a valid fatwa and who cannot. According to the Islamic science called "Usul al-fiqh" (Principles of Jurisprudence), a fatwa is binding when the following four conditions are met:

1. It is in line with the relevant legal proofs, deducted from Koranic verses and hadiths (traditions relating to the sayings and doings of the prophet Muhammad).
2. It is issued by a person (or a board) having due knowledge and sincerity of heart.
3. It is free from individual opportunism and does not depend on political servitude.
4. It is adequate with the needs of the contemporary world.

A fatwa is not binding on all Muslims, only on the Mufti who issued it and his followers. Perhaps the best known fatwa was issued in 1989 by Iran's Ayatollah Ruhollah Khomeini, calling for the death of Salman Rushdie, author of the novel *The Satanic Verses*. The argument posed by the fatwa was that Rushdie had included a blasphemous statement concerning the prophet Muhammad.

The Islamic Commission of Spain, which represents about 70% of the mosques in Spain, proclaimed a fatwa against Osama bin Laden in March 2005 as a result of the Madrid train bombings. The fatwa was issued on the one-year anniversary of the Madrid train bombings. The commission's secretary general reported that the group had consulted in other countries including Morocco, Algeria, and Libya and had their support. The fatwa stated [4]: "the terrorist acts of Osama bin Laden and his organization al Qaeda ... are totally banned and must be roundly condemned as part of Islam .... In as much as Osama bin Laden and his organization defend terrorism as legal and try to base it on the Qur'an ... they are committing the crime of 'istihlal' (meaning making up one's own laws) and thus become apostates that should not be considered Muslims or treated as such."

Osama bin Laden's Fatwas

Osama bin Laden has issued several fatwa's to justify his "holy war" or "jihad" against America and its allies. The first major fatwa, "Declaration of War Against the Americans Occupying the Land of the Two Holy Places," was issued by Osama bin Laden in August 1996. In this fatwa, bin Laden points out that the people of Islam have suffered from aggression, iniquity, and injustice imposed by the Zionist crusaders (the U.S.) alliance and their allies. Bin Laden fears the presence of the U.S. and allied military forces on the land, air, and sea of the Islamic Gulf states as the greatest danger threatening the largest oil reserves in the world. He is concerned that the United States would rather burn the oil than see it fall into the hands of its legitimate owners and would like to cause economic damage to its competitors in Europe or the Far East. Bin Laden warns that "the money you pay to buy American goods will be transformed into bullets and used against our brothers in Palestine and tomorrow against our sons in the land of the two holy places. By buying these goods we are strengthening their economy while our dispossession and poverty increases." Bin Laden therefore calls for the boycotting of American goods, along with the military operations of the Mujahideen, to defeat the United States. Finally, bin Laden declares "it is a duty now on every tribe in the Arab Peninsula to fight, Jihad, in the cause of Allah and to cleanse the land from those occupiers. Allah knows that their blood is permitted to be spilled, and their wealth is a booty; their wealth is a booty to those who kill them."

The second major fatwa, "Kill Americans Everywhere," states the killing of Americans and their allies, civilian and military, is an individual duty on every Muslim who can do so in any country in which it is possible to do it, in order that American and allied armies move out of all the land of Islam defeated and unable to threaten any Muslim in compliance with the words of Almighty God. Justifying the call to kill U.S. civilians and military personnel, the statement declares that "U.S. aggression is affecting Muslim civilians, not just the military." This fatwa, proclaimed on February 23, 1998 in the name of the World Islamic Front for Jihad Against Jews and Crusaders, was issued by Osama bin Laden, jointly with Ayman al-Zawahiri, leader of the Jihad group in Eqypt; Abu-Yasir Rifa'I Ahmad Taha, a leader of the Egyptian Islamic group; Sheik Mir Hamzah, secretary of the Jamiat ul-Ulema Pakistan; and Fazlul Rahman, leader of the Jihad Movement in Bangladesh. The fatwa declared that in compliance with God's order "the ruling to kill the Americans and their allies—civilians and military—is an individual duty for every Muslim who can do it in any country in which it is possible to do it, in order to liberate the al Aqsa Mosque [in Jerusalem] and the holy Mosque [in Mecca] from their grip, and in order for their armies to move out of all the lands of Islam, defeated and unable to threaten any Muslim. This is in accordance with the words of Almighty God, and fight the pagans all together as they fight you all together, and fight them until there is no more tumult or oppression, and there prevail justice and faith in God." The justification for this fatwa was based on three grievances:

- "First, for over seven years, the United States has been occupying the lands of Islam in the holiest of places, the Arabian Peninsula, plundering its riches, dictating to its rulers, humiliating its people, terrorizing its neighbors, and turning its bases in the peninsula into a spearhead through which to fight the neighboring Muslin peoples."
- "Second, despite the great devastation inflicted on the Iraqi people by the crusader–Zionist alliance, and despite the huge number of those killed, in excess of 1 million . . . despite all this, the Americans are once again trying to repeat the horrific massacres, as though they are not content with the protracted blockade imposed after the ferocious war or the fragmentation and devastation."
- "Third, if the Americans' aims behind these wars are religious and economic, the aim is also to serve the Jews' petty state and divert attention from its occupation of Jerusalem and murder of Muslims there."

The fatwa also "calls on every Muslim who believes in God and wishes to be rewarded to comply with God's order to kill the Americans and plunder their money wherever and whenever they find it. We also call on Muslim, Ulema

(Muslim scholars of Islamic studies), leaders, youths, and soldiers to launch the raid on Satan's U.S. troops and the devil's supporters allying with them, and to displace those who are behind them so that they may learn a lesson" [5].

Jihad

Jihad is an Islamic word meaning "to exert utmost effort, to strive, struggle," which can mean a number of things: anything from an inward spiritual struggle to attain perfect faith to a political or military struggle to further the Islamic cause. In as much as jihad is a struggle, it is a struggle against all that is perceived as evil in the Muslim world. The term jihadist is sometimes used to describe militant Islamic groups. Returnees from Afghanistan in the 1980s were the global jihad's first generation of terrorists.

Muslims generally classify jihad in two forms. Jihad al-Akbar, the greater jihad, is said to be inward seeking, the struggle against one's soul, while Jihad al-Asgar, the lesser jihad, is external rebellion and is in reference to physical effort (i.e., fighting). Islam exalts jihad as the greatest deed in its canonical literature. Jihad is widely used to mean "holy war." Traditional Islamic doctrine divided the world into two parts: the Dar al-Islam (land of Islam) and the Dar al-Harb (land of war). The former were the Muslim territories, governed by Islam as a political movement, while the latter were the non-Muslim territories of the world. The concept of warfare in Islam is of two distinct types: defensive jihad, which is the defense of the Dar al-Islam, and the offensive jihad, which is the military conquests of the Dar al-Harb by Islam as a political movement. In addition to this doctrine of international relations, Islamic law also lays down the basic rules of war in Islam. There are specific legal issues concerning the basic laws of jihad, such as treatment of prisoners of war, questions about who can be killed in the course of warfare, and questions about what kinds of military tactics are permissible [6].

Mujahid

A person who engages in any form of jihad is called a mujahid, which means "striver or struggler," though it most often means a person who engages in fighting.

1.11 TYPES OF TERRORISTS

There are seven basic types of terrorists.

1. *Nationalist Terrorists.* These terrorists seek to form a separate state for themselves. They have been successful at gaining sympathy from others and concessions from governments by fighting for their "national liberation." The two most widely known national terrorist groups are the Irish Republican Army and the Palestine Liberation Organization.

2. *Religious Terrorists.* These terrorists use violence to further their own interpretation of divine will and perception of world order. They feel free to

target anyone who is not a member of their religion or cult. The four most widely known religious terrorist groups are al Qaeda, Hamas, Hezbollah, and Aum Shinrikyo.

3. *State Sponsored Terrorists.* These terrorists are used by their radical government as violent foreign policy tools. Since these groups are supported by their government, they have significantly more resources and can operate freely within their territory without fear of prosecution. Perhaps the best known state sponsored terrorist organization was the Iranian militants who were used to seize the American embassy in Tehran in 1979. Other examples of state sponsored terrorist groups include Hezbollah (backed by Iran), Abu Nidal (which has been backed by Syria, Libya, and Iraq), and al Qaeda (backed by the former Taliban government in Afghanistan). The U.S. State Department has accused Iran, Cuba, Iraq, Libya, North Korea, Sudan, and Syria of sponsoring terrorism.

4. *Left Wing Terrorists.* Left wing terrorists generally profess a revolutionary socialist doctrine and view themselves as protectors of the people against "dehumanizing effects" of capitalism and imperialism and therefore are out to destroy capitalism and replace it with a communist or social regime. Leftist groups are on the liberal end of the political spectrum. Leftists often see themselves as defending the equality, freedom, and well-being of the common citizens. In the late nineteenth century, immigrants from eastern Europe sympathetic to the international anarchist movement launched the first domestic terrorist attacks in the United States. Anarchist Alexander Berkman attempted to murder steel tycoon Henry Clay Frick in 1892 due to his ruthless anti-union policy, and anarchists bombed Chicago's Haymarket in 1886 because of perceived differences between the business class and working class. Left wing terrorists often use tactics that focus on hampering capitalism, such as adversely impacting businesses, and destroying government facilities. They aim to bring about change in the United States through revolution rather than through the established political process. Terrorist groups seeking to secure full Puerto Rican independence from the United States through violent means represent one of the remaining active vestiges of left wing terrorism. During the 1970s and 1980s, numerous leftist groups, including extremist Puerto Rican separatist groups such as the Armed Forces for Puerto Rican National Liberation (FALN), carried out bombings on the U.S. mainland, primarily in and around New York City. The threat posed by Puerto Rican extremist groups to mainland U.S. communities decreased during the past decade. Acts of terrorism continue to be perpetrated, however, by violent separatists in Puerto Rico. Three acts of terrorism have taken place in various Puerto Rican locales in recent years, including the March 1998 bombing of a super-aqueduct project in Arecibo, the bombings of bank offices in Rio Piedras and Santa Isabel in June 1998, and the bombing of a highway in Hata Rey. The extremist Puerto Rican separatist group Los Macheteros is suspected in each of these attacks [7]. Other examples of left wing groups include the Japanese Red Army and the Italian Red Brigades. Radical factions of otherwise reputable causes, including environmental groups such as the Earth Liberation Front, are also considered left wing terrorist groups.

5. *Right Wing Terrorists.* Right wing terrorists are the most loosely organized terrorists and often adhere to the principles of racial supremacy and embrace antigovernment, antiregulatory beliefs. Right wing terrorism can be motivated by opposition to federal taxation and regulation. These groups seek to eliminate liberal democratic governments and install fascist states in their place. Right wing terrorists are also racist and anti-Semitic. Generally, right wing extremists engage in activities that are protected by the constitutional guarantees of free speech and assembly. In 1999, the FBI interrupted plans by members of the Southeastern States Alliance—an umbrella organization of militias in Florida, Georgia, South Carolina, Alabama, and other southern states—to steal weapons from National Guard armories in central Florida, attack power lines in several states, and ambush federal law enforcement officers. The goal of this group was to create social and political chaos, thereby forcing the U.S. government to declare martial law, an act the group believed would lead to a violent overthrow of the government by the American people [7]. The most infamous right wing terrorist organizations include the skinheads, Ku Klux Klan, Aryan Nation, and the National Alliance.

6. *Anarchist Terrorists.* In the late nineteenth and early twentieth centuries, anarchist terrorism was a significant global phenomenon. Anarchists and other extremist socialist groups seek to overthrow the existing government using violence. President William McKinley was assassinated on September 6, 1901 at the Pan American Exposition in Buffalo, New York by Hungarian refugee and anarchist sympathizer Leon Czolgosz. Anarchists, operating individually and in small groups, caused a significant amount of damage during the 1999 World Trade Organization meetings in Seattle, Washington. The Workers World Party, Reclaim the Streets, and Carnival Against Capitalism are all anarchist groups.

7. *Special Interest Terrorists.* Special interest terrorism differs from traditional right wing and left wing terrorism in that extremist special interest groups focus on single issues and seek to resolve these specific issues rather than effect more widespread political change. Special interest extremists conduct acts of politically motivated violence to force segments of society, including the general public, to change attitudes about issues considered important to their causes.

Not all special interest groups, and their members, can be considered terrorists. These extremists are violent subgroups of otherwise well meaning legitimate organizations that have noble causes, such as right to life, protection of the environment, and animal rights. However, these extremist subgroups have chosen to resort to violence and other criminal activities to further their cause and hence have been designated as terrorist groups by federal law enforcement organizations.

In recent years, elements of the Animal Liberation Front (ALF) have become some of the most active extremists in the United States. Despite the violence and damage caused by ALF's operations, its operational philosophy discourages acts that harm "any animal, human and non-human." Factions of the Earth Liberation Front (ELF) are also very active in using criminal activities to promote their cause. They claimed responsibility for the arson fires set at a Vail, Colorado ski resort in October 1998 that destroyed eight separate structures and caused $12 million in damages. Special interest groups include ALF, ELF, and Stop Huntington Animal Cruelty.

1.12 HISTORICAL TERRORIST ATTACKS

For many Americans, September 11, 2001 represented our first exposure to the devastating effects of international terrorism, and the day the war on terrorism began. Others believe America's first exposure to terrorism began with the seizing of the U.S. embassy in Tehran, Iran. In reality, terrorism has existed for centuries. Terrorism is not something new.

One of the first links to terrorism involves the Greek superhero Hercules, who appears to have used the world's first biological weapon referenced in Western literature. After Hercules killed Hydra, the many headed serpent, Hercules dipped his arrowheads in Hydra's venom to increase their lethality. In 200 BC, Hannibal's sailors catapulted pots containing venomous snakes onto the decks of enemy ships. In the first century, Jewish zealots would publicly slit the throats of Romans and their collaborators. In AD 199, the Romans threw pots filled with poisonous scorpions over the walls of the city of Hatra. In seventh century India, the Thuggee cult would strangle passersby as sacrifices to the Hindu deity Kali. In the mid-fourteenth century in the Tartar attack on Caffa, plague-infected corpses were catapulted into the ranks of the enemy to spread disease. British soldiers sent Native American Indians smallpox-infected blankets during the French and Indian Wars. During the U.S. Civil War in the 1860s, Confederate troops dropped dead animals into drinking water wells. In 1914, Austrian Archduke Franz Ferdinand was assassinated by a Serb extremist, helping to trigger World War I. During World War II, Germany experimented with biological agents on prisoners of war. British scientists were conducting experiments with anthrax on the Scottish Isle of Gruinard. Results of the testing and the remaining contamination left the island uninhabitable for years. The Popular Front for the Liberation of Palestine executed the first terrorist hijacking of a commercial airliner on July 22, 1968.

The earliest documented use of chemical weapons occurred in the fourth century BC during the Peloponnesian War between Athens and Sparta. Using a crude but effective system, the Spartans used a chemical irritant (sulfur-laden smoke) against the fort at Delium, forcing the soldiers to flee. The use of chemical weapons continued in the following centuries, with mixtures of pitch, sulfur, lime, and other chemicals being placed into clay pots and thrown or catapulted against an enemy. The resulting odors when the clay pots broke and released their contents were suffocating to those exposed. Modern chemical weapons were born with the French and German military developing tear gas. On April 22, 1915, the German's unleashed the full fury of modern chemical warfare, with the use of 150 tons of chlorine against French and British troops. By the end of 1915, both sides were utilizing chlorine and phosgene as weapons. By 1917, the Germans began using mustard blister agents against Allied troops. In the Viet Nam War, the United States made extensive use of tear gas to clear tunnels of guerillas. The United States also developed and deployed numerous defoliant agents in the jungles of Viet Nam, most notably Agent Orange. Chemical weapons have reportedly also been used by Egypt, by the Soviet armies in their war with Afghanistan, and by Iraq in their war with Iran as well as against their own Kurdish population.

1.13 INTERNATIONAL TERRORISM

International terrorism transcends national boundaries in terms of attacks, the persons they are intended to coerce or intimidate, or the locale in which the adversaries operate. International terrorism involves violent acts that are a violation of the criminal laws of the United States or any state. Although terrorist groups are based all across the globe, today's greatest threats stem from terrorist organizations that originated in or have ties to the Middle East.

In general terms, the international terrorist threat can be divided into three categories: loosely affiliated extremists operating under the radical international jihad movement, formal terrorist organizations, and state sponsors of terrorism.

- *Loosely Affiliated Extremists.* These terrorists are motivated by political or religious beliefs. Within this category are the Sunni Islamic extremists, such as groups affiliated with the al Qaeda organization, which have demonstrated a willingness and capability to carry out attacks resulting in large-scale casualties and destruction against U.S. citizens, facilities, and interests. However, the threat from al Qaeda is only part of the overall threat from the international jihad movement. The movement is comprised of individuals from many different nationalities and ethnic groups, who work together to achieve the extremist Sunni goals. The primary Sunni goal is the removal of U.S. military forces from the Persian Gulf, particularly Saudi Arabia. The single common element among all of these groups is the call for the use of violence against the "enemies of Islam" to overthrow all governments that are not ruled by Sharia (conservative Islamic law).
- *Formal Terrorist Organizations.* These are typically autonomous transnational organizations that have their own infrastructure, personnel, financial resources, and training facilities. These groups are capable of planning, financing, and executing attacks on a worldwide basis. A number of these organizations maintain operations and support cells throughout the world. For example, Hamas and Hezbollah have operations in both the western and eastern hemispheres, engaged in fund raising, recruiting, and intelligence gathering.
- *State Sponsors of Terrorism.* These are countries that view terrorism as a tool of foreign policy. Presently, the U.S. Department of State lists seven countries as state sponsors of terrorism: Iran, Iraq, Sudan, Libya, Syria, Cuba, and North Korea. Of these, Iran represents the greatest terrorist threat to the United States. Despite a moderation in its public anti-United States rhetoric since the election of Mohammed Khatemi as president, the government of Iran remains controlled by conservative clerics opposed to reform and normalization of relations with Western countries. The government of Iran continues to target dissidents living outside the country and supports financially and logistically anti-Western acts of terrorism by others [7].

Terrorist organizations are always seeking financial resources needed to conduct their activities. There are many different sources of financial support, some of which may be legal and some illegal. *Narcoterrorism* refers to terrorist acts carried out by groups that are directly or indirectly involved in cultivating, manufacturing, transporting, or distributing illegal drugs. These terrorists use the drug trade to fund their operations. Narcoterrorist groups include the Revolutionary Armed Forces of Colombia (FARC), National Liberation Army, and the Liberation Tigers of Tamil Eelam.

Sleeper cells are terrorists who are already in place within the Unites States but are not currently active. America is an open society, with people free to come and go as they please. There are hundreds of mosques, where radicals can preach propaganda to assist in recruiting new members and solicit funds. Sleeper cells are groups of terrorists who are loyal to a cause but are living quietly in society. The group lies dormant until such time as the members receive an assignment to act. Sleeper cells may be empowered to act on their own if a target of opportunity presents itself. The general modus operandi of a sleeper cell is that members move into a community, assimilate into society as well as they can, and wait for the opportunity or order to attack.

Table 1.1 is a compilation of foreign terrorist organizations designated by the U.S. Department of State as of March 2006. The Office of Counterterrorism in the Department of State continually monitors the activities of terrorist groups active

TABLE 1.1. United States Department of State, Foreign Terrorist Organizations, March 2006

Abu Nidal Organization	Kach
Abu Sayyaf Group	Kurdistan Workers Party
Al-Aqsa Martyrs Brigade	Lashkar-e-Jhangvi
Al-Gama'a al-Islamiyya	Lashkar-e-Taiba
Armed Islamic Group	Liberation Tigers of Tamil Eelam
Al Qaeda	Libyan Islamic Fighting Group
Al Qaeda Organization in the Land of Two Rivers	Moroccan Islamic Combatant Group
Ansar al-Sunnah Army	Mujahedeen-e-Khaig
Armed Islamic Group	National Liberation Army
Asbat al-Ansar	New People's Army
Aum Shinrikyo	Palestine Liberation Front
Basque Fatherland and Freedom	Palestinian Islamic Jihad
Continuity Irish Republican Army	Popular Front for the Liberation of Palestine
DHKP-C	Popular Front for the Liberation of Palestine—General Command
Egyptian Islamic Jihad	Real Irish Republican Army
Hamas	Revolutionary Armed Forces of Colombia
Harakat ul-Mujahideen	Revolutionary Nuclei
Hezbollah	Revolutionary Organization 17 November
Islamic Jihad Group	Salafist Group for Call and Combat
Islamic Movement of Uzbekistan	Shining Path
Jaish-e-Mohammed	United Self-Defense Forces of Colombia
Jemaah Islamiya	

TABLE 1.2. United States Department of State, Terrorist Exclusion List, March 2006

Aden Abyan Islamic Army (AAIA)
Afghan Support Committee
Al-Hamati Sweets Bakery
Al-Ittihaad al-Islami (AIAI)
Al-Ma'unah
Al-Manar
Al-Nur Honey Center
Al-Rashid Trust
Al-Shifa Honey Press for Industry and Commerce
Al-Wafa al-Igatha al-Islamia
Alex Boncayao Brigade (ABB)
Allied Democratic Forces (ADF)
Anarchist Faction
Army for the Liberation of Rwanda (ALIR)
Babbar Khalsa International (BKI)
Bank Al Taqwa Ltd.
Black Star
Communist Party of Nepal-Maoist (CPN-M)
Continuity Irish Republican Army (CIRA)
Darkazanli Company
Dhamat Houmet Daawa Salafia
Eastern Turkistan Islamic Movement (ETIM)
First of October Antifascist Resistance Group (GRAPO)
Harakat ul-Jihad-i-Islami (HUJI)
International Sikh Youth Federation
Islamic International Peacekeeping Brigade (IIPB)
Jaish-e-Mohammad (JeM)
Jamiat al-Ta'awum al-Islamiyya
Jamiat ul-Mujahideen (JuM)
Japanese Red Army (JRA)
Jayshullah
Jerusalem Warriors
Lashkar-e-Taiba (LeT)
Libyan Islamic Fighting Group (LIFG)
Lord's Resistance Army (LRA)
Loyalist Volunteer Force (LVF)
Makhtab al-Khidmat
Moroccan Islamic Combatant Group
Nada Management Organization
New People's Army (NPA)
New Red Brigades/Communist Combatant Party
Orange Volunteers (OV)
Overthrown Anarchist Faction
People Against Gangsterism and Drugs (PAGAD)

(*Continued*)

TABLE 1.2. (*Continued*)

Rajah Solaiman Movement
Red Hand Defenders (RHD)
Revival of Islamic Heritage Society
Revolutionary Proletarian Nucleus
Revolutionary United Front (RUF)
Riyad us-Saliheyn Martyrs Brigade
Salafist Group for Call and Combat (GSPC)
Special Purpose Islamic Regiment (SPIR)
The Pentagon Gang
Tunisian Combatant Group (TCG)
Turkish Hezbollah
Ulster Defence Association/Ulster Freedom Fighters
Ummah Tameer E-Nau
Youssef M Nada & Co. Gesellschaft M.B.H.

around the world to identify potential organizations for designation. When reviewing potential targets, the Office of Counterterrorism looks not only at the actual terrorist attacks that a group has carried out, but also at whether the group has engaged in planning and preparations for possible future acts of terrorism or retains the capability and intent to carry out such attacks. The legal ramifications of being designated as a foreign terrorist organization include the following:

1. It is unlawful for a person in the United States or subject to the jurisdiction of the United States to knowingly provide "material support or resources" to a designated foreign terrorist organization.
2. Representatives and members of a designated foreign terrorist organization, if they are aliens, are inadmissible to and, in certain circumstances, removable from the United States.
3. Any U.S. financial institution that becomes aware that it has possession of or control over funds in which a designated foreign terrorist organization or its agent has an interest must retain possession of or control over the funds and report the funds to the Office of Foreign Assets Control of the U.S. Department of the Treasury [8].

Table 1.2 is the U.S. State Department's Terrorist Exclusion List (TEL). The USA PATRIOT Act of 2001 authorized the Secretary of State, with the assistance of the U.S. Attorney General, to designate terrorist organizations for immigration purposes. A TEL designation increases homeland security efforts by facilitating the ability to exclude aliens associated with entities on the TEL from entering the United States.

Table 1.3 is the U.S. State Department's List of Other Selected Terrorist Organizations, which includes other selected terrorist groups deemed of relevance in the global war on terrorism.

TABLE 1.3. United States Department of State, List of Other Selected Terrorist Organizations, March 2006

Aden Abyan Islamic Army (AAIA)
Al-Badr
Al-Ittihaad al-Islami (AIAI)
Alex Boncayao Brigade (ABB)
Anti-Imperialist Territorial Nuclei for the Construction of the Fighting Communist Party
Army for the Liberation of Rwanda (ALIR)
Cambodian Freedom Fighters (CFF)
Communist Party of India-Maoist
Communist Party of Nepal-Maoist (CPN-M)
Democratic Front for the Liberation of Rwanda (FDLR)
Easter Turkistan Islamic Movement (ETIM)
First of October Antifascist Resistance Group (GRAPO)
Harakat ul-Jihad-i-Islami
Harakat ul-Jihad-i-Islami/Bangladesh
Hizb-I Islami Gulbuddin
Hizbul Mujahideen
Irish National Liberation Army
Irish Republican Army
Islamic Great Eastern Raiders Front
Islamic International Peacekeeping Brigade
Jamatul Mujahedin Bangladesh
Jamiat ul-Mujahedin (JuM)
Japanese Red Army (JRA)
Kumpulah Mujahidin Malaysia
Lord's Resistance Army (LRA)
Loyalist Volunteer Force (LVF)
New Red Bridgades/Communist Combatant Party
People Against Gangsterism and Drugs (PAGAD)
Rajah Solaiman Movement
Red Hand Defenders (RHD)
Revolutionary Proletarian Nucleus
Revolutionary Struggle
Riyad us-Saliheym Martyrs Brigade
Special Purpose Islamic Regiment (SPIR)
Tunisian Combatant Group (TCG)
Tupac Amaru Revolutionary Movement
Turkish Hezbollah
Ulster Defense Association/Ulster Freedom Fighters
Ulster Volunteer Force
United Liberation Front of Assam

1.14 EXAMPLES OF INTERNATIONAL TERRORIST GROUPS

Al Qaeda

The primary terrorist threat facing the United States today is al Qaeda and its affiliates. Osama bin Laden's plan is to attack the United States until it is bankrupt.

Osama bin Laden and his associate, Mohammed Atef, became involved in the Mujadeen rebellion to fight the Soviets after the Soviet Union invaded Afghanistan in December 1979. Bin Laden apparently received training from the Central Intelligence Agency, which was backing the Afghan holy warriors (the mujahideen) in their fight against Soviet forces. Bin Laden used his family's money and his own business experience to recruit young Muslim men from around the world to join the mujahideen. He also used his money to buy equipment for the Afghan resistance. In 1984, Osama bin Laden moved to Pakistan and cofounded Maktub al-Khidamat (MAK) to organize approximately 20,000 anti-Soviet mujahideen rebels and to channel overseas weapons and funds to the group. In 1986, bin Laden established his own training camp in Afghanistan for Persian Gulf Arabs called al Masadah (the Lion's Den). In 1988, as the Soviet occupation in Afghanistan was failing, al Qaeda (the base) was organized from Osama bin Laden's former mujahideen members. Al Qaeda seeks to rid the Muslim regions of the world of what it believes is the profane influence of the West and to replace their governments with fundamentalist Islamic regimes. In 1989, the Soviet Union withdrew from Afghanistan, and bin Laden returned to Saudi Arabia to join his family's construction company.

In the 1980s, al Qaeda's primary focus was to depose the Saudi monarchy (and that goal remains very important today). The 1990s was the period of al Qaeda recruitment and training. After the Iraqi invasion of Kuwait in August 1991, Saudi Arabia rejected Osama bin Laden's offer to assist in fighting Iraq and allowed U.S. forces to use its military bases, fueling bin Laden's hatred of both the United States and Saudi Arabia. He moved the al Qaeda headquarters to Sudan in 1991. In 1992, Osama bin Laden established legal businesses (farms, a tannery, and a construction firm) in Sudan to increase his available funds for al Qaeda. In 1994, bin Laden's citizenship was revoked by Saudi Arabia, and his family and friends publicly disowned him due to his crimes. Bin Laden was forced to leave Sudan for Afghanistan in 1996 following intense pressure from the U.S. government after he issued the fatwa "Declaration of War Against the Americans Occupying the Land of the Two Holy Places." In 1998, Osama bin Laden released a fatwa entitled "Kill Americans Everywhere," declaring that "to kill Americans and their allies, civilians, and military is an individual duty for every Muslim who can do it, in any country in which it is possible to do it." By the late 1990s, bin Laden had taken up residence in Afghanistan and had become a mentor, guest, and inspiration to the Taliban government. Bin Laden and his followers helped the Taliban fight against the Northern Alliance. In March 2003, Osama bin Laden's plan to create a "nuclear hell storm" by constructing and detonating a radiological weapon on U.S. soil was uncovered when Kalid Sheik Mohammed, al Qaeda's military operations chief, was arrested in Pakistan. Currently, Osama bin Laden and other top al Qaeda leaders are reportedly hiding in Iran, Afghanistan, and Pakistan as the United States and the coalition prosecute the war on terrorism. To date approximately 75% of al Qaeda's leadership have been killed or captured.

Despite the valiant and somewhat effective efforts of the United States to capture or kill the al Qaeda terrorists, and disperse and degrade their leadership, al Qaeda has not gone out of business. Regional al Qaeda extremist cells have a newfound importance in the new order of al Qaeda and pose an increasing threat. There are literally thousands of al Qaeda trainees spread out across the globe. Additional operatives are being trained daily in Iraq. Can al Qaeda remain effective with Osama bin Laden and other top leaders removed from the day to day operations of the organization? Unfortunately, the answer is yes. There is no need for bin Laden or other top leaders to be involved. Under bin Laden's leadership, the jihadist movement has been boosted to new heights. Despite thousands of worldwide arrests, al Qaeda is still capable of planning and launching attacks. Bin Laden has created the phenomenon, and now his followers are taking up the cause and running local terrorist cells. It is also quite possible that some attacks have been in the planning stages for years, and that al Qaeda has regrouped to some extent, and the new leaders are simply giving the orders to carry out attacks. Some individual cells may be operating on their own, planning and executing local attacks without coordination with the overall al Qaeda organization. These local cells have demonstrated a propensity for planning and executing their attacks in only a few months using locally available resources. Al Qaeda is more an ideology than an organization. The 2005 London subway bombings prove the movement continues to be viable. The bombings demonstrate a willingness and ability to strike against the very heart of the West.

In his statement to the American public on October 29, 2004, Osama bin Laden stated that his hatred toward the United States started when America permitted the Israelis to invade Lebanon and the U.S. Navy's Sixth Fleet assisted. Bin Laden stated that as he looked at the demolished towers in Lebanon, it gave birth to a strong resolve to punish the oppressors (America). This is when the idea to attack the World Trade Center first came to him. He decided that America should be punished in kind, and al Qaeda should destroy towers in America in order to taste some of what the Lebanese tasted, and so America would be deterred from killing women and children. Osama bin Laden believes that the reasons justifying the September 11 attack still exist today, thus enabling al Qaeda to execute another attack on a similar scale.

According to most Islamist religious doctrine, the jihadist is obligated to forewarn the prospective targets and provide them the opportunity to repent and rectify their actions. Osama bin Laden has been criticized several times for not providing sufficient prewarnings of attacks.

The hallmark of an al Qaeda attack is multiple, near simultaneous mass casualty attacks against separate targets.

Al Qaeda's strategic plan includes:

- Murder of infidels (all non-Muslims and Muslims who do not follow al Qaeda).
- Removal of Westerners from Muslim countries.
- Abandonment by the West of its Arab allies.
- Removal of the Western presence from the Muslim world.
- Replacement of secular leaders in the Muslim world.
- Infusion of Sharia as law of the Muslim world.

It is essential to differentiate between the threat posed by the "corporate" al Qaeda and its "franchise" groups. The al Qaeda corporate group still remains interested in executing a large-scale, mass casualty, economically damaging, and symbolic attack against the United States. With the war on terror having some success in disrupting al Qaeda's ability to plan, communicate, and most likely execute a large-scale attack, and with key leaders being removed from the organization, the corporate group is shrinking while the number of franchise groups is rapidly growing. These franchise groups are small groups and individuals who view themselves as part of the global jihad but do not have hard links to the al Qaeda organization. These smaller cells are most likely operating independently from the corporate organization without receiving funding, operational direction, or approval for their attack plans. The franchise groups are more likely to conduct smaller, less sophisticated attacks that do not require extensive planning, funding, or logistics to execute. They have carried out several smaller scale, unsophisticated, but successful attacks (e.g., the Madrid and London train bombings) that were put together fairly quickly and did not take a lot of resources to execute. The war in Iraq has provided support for the franchise concept, much like Afghanistan spawned many of today's terrorists during the battle against the Soviets in the 1980s. Eager individuals or small groups travel to Iraq to join the jihad. They are able to receive hands-on training on the planning of attacks, they get to build and deploy improvised explosive devices, and they execute attacks against real targets. After gaining the relevant experience, they return home and wait for the opportune time to mount domestic terror campaigns.

On April 14, 2004, Osama bin Laden issued an audio tape statement proposing a "reconciliation initiative" with Europe. The truce was a "commitment to stop operations against any state which vows to stop attacking Muslims or interfere in their affairs." The truce was effective for three months. In Osama bin Laden's April 14, 2004 statement he said: "I offer a peace initiative, whose essence is our commitment to stopping operations against every country that commits itself to not attacking Muslims or interfering in their affairs. The peace will start with the departure of its last soldier from our country. For those who reject peace and want war, we are ready."

Al Qaeda has used terrorist attacks to influence elections. There have been a number of attacks that immediately preceded elections, including Spain in March 2004, the Philippines in July 2004, Chechnya in August 2004, Afghanistan in October 2004, Australia in October 2004, and Iraq in January 2005.

Al-Aqsa Martyrs Brigades

The brigades, formed in 2000 as an offshoot of Yasir Arafat's Palestinian nationalist movement, Fatah, are a group of West Bank militias and have been one of the driving forces behind the Palestinian uprising. The organization's goals are to create a Palestinian state and eliminate the presence of Israeli soldiers and settlers in the Palestinian occupied territories. Al-Aqsa does not claim to be intent on destroying the state of Israel.

Initially, al-Aqsa militants exclusively attacked the Israeli Defense Force and Israeli settlers, but in 2002 they began targeting civilians in Israel. Al-Aqsa does not directly target U.S. interests. The group uses mostly knifings, shootings, kidnapping, and suicide bombings in their terror attacks. In January 2002 the group introduced the use of female suicide bombers.

Aum Shinrikyo

Aum Shinrikyo, established in 1987, is a Japanese religious cult obsessed with the apocalypse. Aum aimed to control Japan and the world, and subsequently create a global utopian society after the apocalypse. The cult's leader, Asahara, preached that his followers, a race of superhumans, would rule the world after the apocalyptic war and herald a new order from chaos. Aum has sought to develop nuclear, chemical, and biological weapons. The group has successfully deployed Sarin nerve agent in Japan on two occasions. On June 27, 1994 Aum released Sarin in central Japan, killing seven people and injuring hundreds. In their most infamous attack, on March 20, 1995, ten Aum followers punctured bags of diluted Sarin in five subway stations located under government offices and the National Police Agency's headquarters. Twelve people were killed and over 5000 wounded. They have also tried unsuccessfully to aerosolize the biological agents anthrax and botulism. Aum has not targeted Americans or U.S. interests.

Hamas

Hamas was spawned in 1987 by the Muslim Brotherhood, the leading Islamic-Jihadist movement in the Muslim world. Hamas is the Palestinian's largest and most influential Muslim fundamentalist movement. Hamas is a determined foe of Israeli–Palestinian peace and is determined to destroy Israel. Hamas initially sought to expel Jews and the state of Israel from Palestine, and to establish an Islamic Palestinian state based on Islamic law. Hamas operates primarily inside Israel, in Gaza, and the West Bank. Hamas has used suicide bombers (their first suicide bombing took place in April 1993), mortars, short-range rockets, and small arms fire. Hamas provides the family of a suicide bomber a bounty between $3000 and $5000 and assures them their son died a martyr in the holy jihad. Hamas also provides funding for extensive social, welfare, cultural, and educational services such as schools, orphanages, mosques, healthcare clinics, soup kitchens, summer camps, and sports leagues. The group has not targeted U.S. interests.

Hezbollah

Hezbollah was founded in 1982 by Lebanese Shiite clerics in response to Israel's invasion of Lebanon. The group is a Lebanese umbrella organization of radical Islamic Shiite groups and organizations. It opposes the West, seeks to create a Muslim fundamentalist state modeled on Iran, and is a bitter enemy of Israel. According to their manifestos, Hezbollah is dedicated to the liberation of Jerusalem, the destruction of

Israel, and the ultimate establishment of an Islamic state in Lebanon. Hezbollah is a significant force in Lebanon's politics and a major provider of social services, operating schools, hospitals, and agricultural services for thousands of Lebanese Shiites. The group reportedly shares members with the Palestinian Islamic Jihad and is an ally of Hamas. The group also reportedly has ties to al Qaeda, cooperating on logistics and training. Hezbollah has engaged in kidnappings, bombings, and hijackings, as well as rocket strikes against Israeli settlements and the firing of surface-to-air missiles at Israeli aircraft. The group was the principal supporter of anti-Western and anti-American terrorism in the 1980s. Their most significant attack against Americans was the 1983 Beirut embassy bombing and the 1983 U.S. Marine barracks bombing. Until September 11, 2001, Hezbollah was responsible for more American deaths than all other terrorist groups combined.

Liberation Tigers of Tamil Eelam (LTTE)

The Liberation Tigers of Tamil Eelam, also known as the Tamil Tigers, are a separatist terrorist group founded in 1976 that seeks an independent state in areas of Sri Lanka inhabited by ethnic Tamils. The Tamils are an ethnic group who live in southern India and on Sri Lanka. The LTTE have been involved in a twenty year bloody civil war. The LTTE is notorious for suicide bombings and has perfected the jacket style apparatus worn by individual suicide bombers, which has been copied and used by al Qaeda, Hezbollah, Hamas, and the al-Aqsa Martyrs Brigades. The LTTE is also noted for the first and most active use of female suicide bombers, who have carried out 30–40% of the suicide attacks of LTTE. Their first suicide attack was on July 5, 1987, when a rebel drove a truckload of explosives into the Nelliyady army camp in northern Sri Lanka, killing 40 soldiers. The LTTE has also used conventional bombs against political and civilian targets and has assassinated both Sri Lankan officials and civilians, most notably former Indian Prime Minister Rajiv Gandhi in 1991 and Sri Lankan Prime Minister Ranasinghe Premadasa in 1993. LTTE terrorists wear cyanide capsules around their necks so they can commit suicide if they are captured. The LTTE is the only non-Muslim group that has practiced suicide bombings on a large scale. The LTTE has not targeted or attacked U.S. interests.

1.15 TERRORIST GROUPS THAT CLAIMED RESPONSIBILITY FOR TERRORIST ATTACKS IN 2004

In 2002 [9], the following groups perpetrated 651 attacks, leaving 1907 people dead and 6704 wound.

Abu Musab al-Zarqawi
Revolutionary Armed Forces of Colombia (FARC)
Informal Anarchic Federation
United Jihad Council
Al-Aqsa Martyrs Brigade

Hamas
Hizbul-Mujahedin
Al-Mansurian
National Front for the Liberation of Corscia (FLNC)
Ansar al-Sunna
Save Kashmir Movement
Karachayev Djamaat
Indomitable Marxists
Taliban
Jamiat ul-Mujahedin
Popular Front for the Liberation of Palestine (PFLP)
Jama'at al-Tawid wa'al Jihad
Jaish-e-Mohammed
Al Qaeida
Ansar al-Islam
Brigades of Martyr Ahmed Yassim
Palestine Islamic Jihad
Communist Party of Nepal (Maoist)/United People's Front
Ansar al-Din
The Mujahideen Brigades (Saraya al-Mujahedin)
Abu Sayyaf Group
The Green Battalion
Lashkar-e-Tayyiba
Islamic Rage Brigade
Comando Jaramillista 23 de Mayo
Waqas Islamic Brigade
Sudanese Liberation Army
Jihad Squadrons
Islamic Anger Brigades
Al-Nasreen
All Tripura Tiger Force
The National Liberation Front of Tripura
The Izz al-Din al-Qassam Brigades
MLKP-FESK
Khaled ibn al-Walid Brigade
Iraqi Legitimate Resistance
Abu al-Rish Brigades
Black Banners Division of the Islamic Secret Army
Islamic Army in Iraq, the 1920 Revolution Brigades

Usd Allah (Lions of God)
Mujahideen Corps in Iraq
Islamic Jihad Group of Uzbekistan
Mujahideen of Iraq, the Group of Death
United Liberation Front of Assam
National Democratic Front of Bodoland
Freedom Falcons of Kurdistan
Abu Hafs al-Masri Brigade
Kongra-Gel
Abu al-Abbas
Mahdi Army
Ukranian People's Party (PUP)
Basque Fatherland and Liberty (ETA)
Islambouli Brigades
Riyad us-Saliheyn Martyrs Brigade
Islamic Resistance Movement, Nu'man Brigades
Fallujah Mujahideen
Jemaah Islamiya (JI)
Brigades of Al Tawhid Lions
United Self-Defense Forces of Colombia (AUC)
Salafist Brigades
Abu Bakr al-Siddiq
Jaish-e-Muslimeen
Battalions of the Martyr Abdullah Azzam
Tanzim Qa'idat al-Jihad fi Bilad al-Rafidayn (QJBR)
Al Khandaq
Fatah Hawks
Lord's Resistance Army (LRA)

1.16 RECENT INTERNATIONAL TERRORIST ATTACKS

Terrorism is not exclusive to the Middle East, but rather has been used across the globe. A sampling of worldwide terrorist activity over the past thirty-five years includes the following:

February 10, 1970. Three terrorists attack El Al passengers in a bus at the Munich Airport with guns and grenades. One passenger is killed, and 11 are injured. The Action Organization for the Liberation of Palestine and the Popular Democratic Front for the Liberation of Palestine claim responsibility.

May 1972. The Irish Republican Army plots to blow up the British cruise ship *Queen Elizabeth II*.

July 21, 1972. Irish Republican Army bomb attacks in Belfast, Northern Ireland kill 11 and injure 130.

March 2, 1973. The U.S. Ambassador to Sudan and other diplomats are assassinated at the Saudi Arabian Embassy by members of the Black September organization.

January 27, 1975. Puerto Rican nationalists bomb a New York City bar, killing four and injuring 60.

March 16, 1978. Italian Prime Minister Aldo Moro is kidnapped by the Red Brigade and assassinated 55 days later.

August 27, 1979. The Irish Republican Army explodes the British yacht *Shadow V*, killing Britain's Lord Mountbatten.

November 4, 1979. The U.S. Embassy in Tehran, Iran is seized by fundamentalist Islamic students; 52 American diplomats are taken hostage and held for 444 days.

August 31, 1981. The Red Army explodes a bomb at the U.S. Air Force base in Ramstein, Germany.

October 6, 1981. Egyptian President Anwar Sadat is assassinated by members of the Takfir Wal-Hajira Muslim extremists.

April 18, 1983. Sixty-three people, including 17 Americans, are killed and 120 injured when a suicide pickup truck loaded with explosives is detonated at the U.S. Embassy in Beirut. The Islamic Jihad claims responsibility.

October 23, 1983. A suicide truck bomb is detonated at a U.S. military barracks in West Beirut, Lebanon, killing 242 U.S. Marines. The Islamic Jihad claims responsibility.

November 8, 1983. All 130 passengers and crew are killed when an Angolan Airlines Boeing 737 is hit by a surface-to-air missile in Angola.

December 12, 1983. The U.S. Embassy in Kuwait is bombed, resulting in five deaths and 80 injuries.

March 16, 1984. The U.S. Central Intelligence Agency Station Chief, William Buckley, is kidnapped, tortured, and executed in Beirut, Lebanon by members of the Islamic Jihad.

September 20, 1984. A suicide bomb explodes at the U.S. Embassy in Beirut, Lebanon, killing 23.

April 12, 1985. A bomb explodes in a restaurant near a U.S. Air Force base in Madrid, Spain, killing 18 and wounding 82.

June 14, 1985. TWA Flight 847 is hijacked enroute from Athens to Rome and forced to land in Beirut, where the hijackers hold the plane for 17 days. A U.S. Navy diver is shot and killed when the hijackers' demands are not met.

June 23, 1985. A bomb destroys an Air India 747 over the Atlantic Ocean, killing all 329 aboard. Both Sikh and Kashmiri terrorists are blamed.

August 8, 1985. A car bomb is detonated in a parking lot at the U.S. Air Force base in Frankfurt, Germany, killing two and injuring 20.

October 7, 1985. Palestinian Liberation Front terrorists hijack the Italian passenger liner *Achille Lauro*, killing one American.

March 30, 1986. A Palestinian splinter group detonates a bomb as TWA Flight 840 approaches the Athens airport, killing four U.S. citizens.

April 5, 1986. LaBelle discotheque in West Berlin, Germany, a spot frequented by U.S. servicepeople, is bombed by a Libyan group, killing two soldiers and injuring 79.

February 17, 1988. United States Marine Corps Lieutenant Colonel William Higgins is kidnapped and murdered by the Iranian backed Hezbollah group.

July 1988. Terrorists open fire with automatic weapons and throw hand grenades at passengers on the Greek day excursion ship *City of Poros*, killing nine and wounding 100.

December 21, 1988. Pan Am Flight 103 from London to New York explodes over the town of Lockerbie, Scotland. All 259 people on board are killed, along with 11 people on the ground.

September 19, 1989. A bomb destroys UTA Flight 772 over the Sahara Desert in southern Niger. All 170 persons aboard are killed. Six Libyans are later found guilty in absentia.

November 30, 1989. The Red Army Faction assassinates Deutsche Bank Chairman Alfred Herrhausen in Frankfurt.

May 13, 1990. The New People's Army murders two U.S. Air Force personnel in the Philippines.

May 21, 1991. A female member of the Liberation Tigers of Tamil Eelam kills herself, former Indian Prime Minister Rajiv Gandi, and 16 others by detonating an explosive vest.

March 17, 1992. Hezbollah claims responsibility for a bombing that leveled the Israeli Embassy in Buenos Aires, killing 29 and injuring 242.

February 26, 1993. A truck bomb is detonated by Islamic terrorists in the underground parking garage at the World Trade Center, killing six and causing over 1500 injuries.

December 11, 1994. Ramzi Ahmed Yousef, mastermind of the 1993 World Trade Center bombing, detonates a bomb on PAL flight 434 enroute to Japan, killing one passenger.

December 24, 1994. An Air France jumbo jet laden with fuel is hijacked in a failed attempt to fly the plane to Paris to destroy the Eiffel Tower. Four Armed Islamic Group terrorists with ties to Osama bin Laden carried out the hijackings.

March 20, 1995. Japan's Aum Shinrikyo cult organization releases the nerve agent Sarin in the Tokyo subway system, killing 12 people and injuring 5700.

November 19, 1995. Islamic Jihad explodes a suicide truck bomb at the Eqyptian Embassy in Islamabad, Pakistan, killing 16 people and injuring 60.

January 31, 1996. Members of the Liberation Tigers of Tamil Eelam ram an explosives laden truck into the Central Bank of Colombo, Sri Lanka, killing 90 and injuring more than 1400.

June 25, 1996. A truck bomb is detonated at the U.S. Air Force Khobar Towers barracks in Dhahran, Saudi Arabia, killing 19 U.S. servicepeople and wounding an additional 515.

September 4, 1997. Three suicide bombers from Hamas detonate bombs in a shopping mall in Jerusalem, killing five and wounding nearly 200.

August 7, 1998. Nearly simultaneous suicide car bombings hit the U.S. embassies in Dar es Salaam, Tanzania and Nairobi, Kenya, killing 291 people, including 12 Americans, and wounding 5000. Osama bin Laden is held responsible for the attack.

October 10, 1998. All 41 passengers and crew are killed when a Congo Airlines Boeing 727 is hit by a surface-to-air missile.

February 25, 1999. FARC kidnaps three U.S. citizens working for the Hawaii based Pacific Cultural Conservatory International. On March 4, their bodies are found in Venezuela.

August 12, 2000. The Islamic Movement of Uzbekistan takes four U.S. citizens hostage in Kyrgyzstan. They later escape.

October 12, 2000. Suicide attackers ram an explosives laden boat into the U.S. destroyer *Cole* off the Yemen coast, killing 17 American sailors.

December 30, 2000. Explosions in Manila strike a train, a bus, the airport, a park near the U.S. embassy, and a gas station, killing 22 people. The attack is attributed to Jemaah Islamiyah, a Southeast Asian militant group tried to al Qaeda.

September 11, 2001. Hijackers fly two jetliners into the World Trade Center in New York City, one jetliner into the Pentagon in Washington, DC, and one jetliner into the ground in Pennsylvania, killing almost 3000 people.

April 11, 2002. A truck loaded with propane gas is blown up near El Ghriba synagogue in Djerba, Tunisia, killing 16 people.

June 14, 2002. A suicide bomber blows up a truck at the U.S. Consulate in Karachi, Pakistan, killing 11 Pakistanis. Harkat ul-Mujahideen, linked to al Qaeda, is blamed.

October 2, 2002. Suspected Abu Sayyaf guerillas, who are linked to al Qaeda, detonate a nail laden bomb in a market in Zamboanga, Philippines. An American Green Beret and three others are killed. The group detonates several more bombs during the month, killing an additional 16 people.

October 10, 2002. A small suicide boat crashes into the French oil tanker *Limburg* as it enters the port of Ash Shir, off the southeast Yemen coast, and explodes, killing one crew member, injuring 12, and releasing 90,000 barrels of oil into the Arabian Sea. Al Qaeda is suspected.

October 12, 2002. A pair of bombings in the nightclub district of Bali, Indonesia kill 202 people, including two Americans, and wound over 300. Jemaah Islamiyah is suspected.

November 28, 2002. Suicide bombers kill 15 people and wound 15 by driving a vehicle packed with bombs into the lobby of an Israeli owned hotel in Kenya; two shoulder launched surface-to-air missiles narrowly miss an airliner taking off with Israeli tourists. Al Qaeda is one of the groups suspected of executing the attack.

February 22, 2003. Al Qaeda operatives open fire at a World Cup cricket match in Karachi, Pakistan, killing nine.

May 11, 2003. A bomb explodes in a crowded market in the Philippines, killing nine people. The blast is blamed on the Muslim separatist Moro Islamic Liberation Front.

May 12, 2003. Four explosions rock Riyadh, Saudi Arabia in American housing compounds. Eight Americans are among the 34 people killed. The suspected bombers are linked to al Qaeda.

May 16, 2003. A team of 12 suicide bombers attack five targets in Casablanca, Morocco, killing 43 people and injuring over 100. The targets include a Spanish restaurant, a Jewish community, a Jewish cemetery, a hotel, and the Belgian consulate. Local militant groups linked to al Qaeda are blamed.

February 6, 2004. Terrorists detonate explosives in a train car in a Moscow subway during the morning rush hour, killing at least 40 people and injuring at least 110.

March 11, 2004. A group of al Qaeda connected Moroccan Islamic extremists set off ten bombs on four commuter trains in Madrid, Spain, killing 201 people and injuring more than 1800. Three other bombs did not detonate.

July 7, 2005. Suicide bombers detonate bombs on three subway trains and one bus, killing 56 people in London.

April 26, 2006. Suicide bomber detonates a bomb inside military headquarters in Sri Lanka, killing ten people and wounding 30.

Case Study: Hezbollah

On October 23, 1983, Hezbollah attacked the buildings housing the U.S. Marine's peacekeeping force with a truck containing explosives being driven by a suicide bomber; 242 soldiers were killed and 81 injured. Most of the dead were asleep at the time of the 6:20 am attack. The terrorists hijacked a water delivery truck on its way to the Beirut International Airport Marine barracks and sent the explosives laden truck in its place. The driver, an Iranian, drove the 19 ton truck over a barbed wire fence and past two guardhouses and then detonated the explosives. A separate and simultaneous suicide bombing killed 58 French paratroopers in an attack at their barracks.

A U.S. federal court order issued in 2003 in a case brought by the relatives of the victims summarized the effects of the explosion [10]:

- "The resulting explosion was the largest non-nuclear explosion that had ever been detonated on the face of the earth. It was equal in force to between 15,000 and 21,000 pounds of TNT."

- "The force of its impact ripped locked doors from their doorjambs at the nearest building, which was 256 feet away. Trees located 370 feet away were shredded and completely exfoliated."
- "All the windows at the airport control tower, half a mile away, shattered. A crater eight feet deep was carved into the earth, and 15 feet of rubble was all that remained of the four story Marine barracks."
- "The force of the explosion ripped the building from its foundation. The building then imploded upon itself."

Previously, in April 1983, Hezbollah attacked the U.S. Embassy in Beirut with a 400 pound suicide truck bomb that killed 63 people, including 17 Americans.

The attacks were motivated by the American involvement in the Lebanese civil war.

Case Study: Tamil Tigers

Sri Lanka's Tamil Tigers claimed responsibility for a suicide bomb attack against a top military official on April 26, 2006. The bomber disguised herself as a pregnant woman and detonated her explosives near the motorcade carrying Sri Lanka's highest ranking general, Lieutenant General Sarath Fonseca. Ten people were killed and 30 wounded, including Fonseca. According to the Associated Press, the bombing occurred inside the military headquarters' complex, which is protected by fences and troops guarding all entrances. The attacker entered the grounds using fake identification and claiming to have a prenatal appointment at the army's hospital.

Case Study: Madrid Train Bombing, March 11, 2004

A cell of al Qaeda connected to the Moroccan Islamic Combatant Group extremists, who had recently immigrated to Spain, perpetrated the March 11, 2004 bombings of commuter trains in Madrid, Spain that killed 200 and injured hundreds more. The terrorists boarded commuter trains outside Madrid during the morning rush hour and placed 13 improvised explosive devices (IEDs) in passenger cars on four trains bound for Madrid. The IEDs were concealed in backpacks and sport bags. After placing the IEDs, the terrorists disembarked the trains. The bombs were set to detonate when the trains were in the station. The backpacks contained approximately 10 kilograms of a gelatin dynamite, more than $\frac{1}{2}$ kilogram of nails to produce additional shrapnel, a cellular phone timing device that initiated the explosion via its alarm feature, and a detonator. Ten of the 13 devices were successfully detonated. Three of the IEDs failed to detonate. Authorities detonated two of them near the scene of the attack. One device was inadvertently brought to a police station along with the victims' personal belongings. The attack was inspired by seasoned radicals who had attended al Qaeda's Afghan training camps before September 11, 2001. Intelligence indicates that the cell was, like most in the new order, self-driven and operated independently, despite links to al Qaeda. Several suspects, including a Tunisian believed to be the ringleader of the bombings, and several Moroccans committed suicide by detonating explosives in their apartment on April 3, 2004 when law enforcement personnel raided the apartment in a Madrid suburb. The primary goal of the terrorists who perpetrated this attack was certainly to inflict mass casualties on the commuters. However, the very timing of the attack may be indicative of a more sinister goal: to influence the March 14th national election that was to occur in an important coalition ally nation in the war against terror. In fact, the bombing contributed to the incumbent government being removed from office, in favor of a new government that was committed to withdrawing its troops from Iraq. Osama bin Laden had threatened Spain for several months for their involvement in the war on terrorism. Jihadist propaganda websites had also posted threats against Spain. These attacks demonstrated the relative ease and speed with which local terrorist networks can develop and execute highly lethal attacks that do not require significant operational expertise. These attacks demonstrate a trend of increased operational activity by local terrorist cells, apparently without coordination or approval from the "corporate" al Qaeda organization. A Spaniard with ties to the mining community helped the terrorists obtain the explosives and the detonators used in the attack. The explosives were stolen from northern Spain over several months. The attack apparently was financed locally via criminal activity, primarily narcotics trafficking.

1.17 DOMESTIC TERRORISM

Domestic terrorism has existed in the United States for more than a century. It is the unlawful use, or threatened use, of violence by a group or individual based and operating entirely within the United States (or its territories) without foreign direction and which is committed against persons or property with the intent of intimidating or coercing a government or its population in furtherance of political or social objectives. The USA PATRIOT Act adds acts that are "dangerous to human life" to the definition. Americans were responsible for about three-quarters of the 335 domestic incidents between 1980 and 2000 that the FBI has classified as suspected or confirmed terrorism. However, not all politically motivated violence can be considered domestic terrorism. Domestic terrorist groups represent interests that span the full spectrum of political, social, and economic viewpoints. During the past decade, right wing extremism overtook left wing terrorism as the most dangerous domestic terrorist threat to the United States. As an example of the problem associated with domestic terrorism, right to life extremists have killed seven doctors, and there have also been approximately 16 attempted murders, 99 acid attacks, 153 arson incidents, and 39 bombings in the past two decades [11].

White supremacy is a racist ideology in which it is believed that the white race is superior to other races and therefore should dominate society. White supremacists most often view Europeans (those of white skin) as the superior race. Although white supremacists most often attack Blacks and Jews, they have also targeted Native Americans, Asians, Roman Catholics, Communists, and homosexuals among others. The group maintains a strong opposition to racial mixing, especially interracial relationships and marriage. White supremacist groups include the American Front, Aryan Nation, Ku Klux Klan, National Alliance, and the Posse Comitatus.

The FBI defines *ecoterrorism* as the use or threatened use of violence of a criminal nature against innocent victims or property by an environmentally oriented, subnational group for environmental–political reasons, or aimed at an audience beyond the target, often of a symbolic nature. Ecoterrorist groups include Green Peace and Sea Shepherd Conservation Society. Hometown ecoterrorists and animal rights extremists have claimed credit for more than 1200 terrorist crimes and $110 million in damage since 1990, including arson, assault, vandalism, and other crimes against scores of individuals and American companies [12]. Most animal rights and ecoextremists so far have refrained from violence against humans. Domestic terrorist groups have been used in direct action campaigns to cause economic damage or disrupt or destroy the operations of university research labs, restaurants, sports utility vehicle dealerships, new home construction developments, fur farms, the pharmaceutical and cosmetics industry, and logging operations. Over the past few years, these groups have used explosive and incendiary devices more and more. No deaths have been blamed on attacks by these groups so far, but the attacks have increased in frequency and size. ELF activists have been known to leave banners or graffiti near the attack. ELF activists have also been known to conduct burglaries in the general vicinity of the target prior to an attack. There is a growing network of support for eco and animal rights extremists. Environmental and animal rights activists who use arson and explosives are the U.S. top domestic terrorism threat. Groups such as the Animal Liberation Front (ALF), the Earth Liberation Front (ELF), and Stop Huntington Animal Cruelty (SHAC) are the leaders in terms of damage and number of violent crimes.

American militant extremists are right wing domestic terrorists opposed to federal taxation, federal regulation, the U.S. government itself, and the United Nations and have a hatred of racial and religious minorities.

Cyber terrorism refers to unlawful attacks and threats of attack by spies, thieves, and saboteurs against computers (hardware infrastructure), networks (using computer networks to take over the control systems for other critical infrastructure, such as power plants), and the information (disrupting the information systems) they contain for the same reasons as other forms of terrorism. Cyber terrorism also involves the use of computers to steal, alter, or destroy information. To qualify as cyber terrorism, an attack should result in violence against persons or property, or at least generate fear. Terrorist organizations can use cyberspace as a medium for reaching a global audience. Terrorist cells can use encryption to conceal their communications via the Web to share surveillance, planning, and operational information preparatory to an attack. The Web can also be used to broadcast a terrorist group's message and spread propaganda to the general public in multiple countries simultaneously. With American society increasingly interconnected and ever more dependent on information technology, cyber terrorist attacks could cause as much devastation as more traditional forms of terrorism. Cyber terrorism allows terrorists to leverage limited resources to instill fear. Cyber terrorism can be accomplished with limited funds, small teams, and from remote locations. Cyber terrorism attacks could include diverse methods of exploiting vulnerabilities in network security: computer viruses, stolen passwords, insider collusion, software with secret "back doors" that could be penetrated undetected, and waves of electronic traffic that overwhelms computer systems. There could be attacks on the physical components of the information technology system itself, such as an explosive device or electromagnetic discharge that physically destroys the electronic components or the physical assets and systems.

Third positionists espouse a political ideology that emphasizes the commonalities between the extreme left and the extreme right. Third positionists advocate a redistribution of wealth, a ban on animal testing, and respect for the environment.

Agroterrorism is the intentional contamination of human food sources.

Lone wolf terrorism involves individual extremists who usually operate alone or on the fringes of established extremist groups, inflicting serious harm or causing significant damage. Lone wolves generally have no direct links to terrorist groups. Their activities can encourage others to act and often result in copycat crimes. Antiabortionist Eric Rudolf is an example of a lone wolf extremist.

Example of Cyber Terrorism

According to an April 26, 2003, MSNBC report, Gazprom, one of Russia's gas monopolies, was attacked by a hacker. The report said the hackers worked with a Gazprom insider to elude the company's security and break into the system controlling gas flow in pipelines. This put the central control panel of gas flows under the control of the external hackers.

1.18 EXAMPLES OF DOMESTIC TERRORIST GROUPS

American Coalition of Life Activists (ACLA)

The ACLA is nationwide radical antiabortion group that intimidates abortion clinic owners, doctors, nurses, and patients. The group feels that abortion providers are committing a crime against humanity and should be punished. The group started a project in 1997 called the Nuremburg Files. The creator of the project eventually put the information onto the World Wide Web. The website features a "wanted poster" alleging crimes against humanity that targets abortion doctors. The site distributes personal information about over 200 abortion providers, including names, family members, business and home addresses, and photographs. Although the website does not threaten violence to any one person, it does provide information to radical antiabortionists looking for a target. Several providers were advised by law enforcement to wear bulletproof vests and take other precautionary measures, and some were offered protection by federal marshals. This type of activity serves to intimidate and instill fear in abortion providers. The fear is certainly well placed, as several doctors performing abortions have been killed since 1977. There have also been approximately 16 attempted murders, 99 acid attacks, 153 arson incidents, and 39 bombings in the last two decades [11].

Animal Liberation Front (ALF)

The Animal Liberation Front was established in Great Britain in the mid-1970s. It is a nationwide violent animal rights activist group that began operations in the United States in the late 1970s, committed to ending the abuse and exploitation of animals. The ALF has become one of the most active extremist elements in the United States. Despite the destructive aspects of ALF's operations, its operational philosophy discourages acts that harm "any animal, human and nonhuman." ALF says on its website that it's a small, autonomous group of people who take direct action against animal abuse by rescuing animals and causing financial loss to animal exploiters, usually by destroying property.

Aryan Nation (AN)

Aryan Nation is a nationwide highly militant antigovernment, white supremist group with smaller regional groups. This group espouses the overthrow of the U.S. government using bank robberies, armed resistance, and the murder of nonwhites.

Earth First

Formed in 1980 by disaffected environmentalists, this radical group engaged in a series of protests and civil disobedience events. In 1984, Earth First introduced "tree spiking," which is the insertion of metal or ceramic spikes into trees to damage the saws of lumberjacks as a tactic to thwart logging.

Earth Liberation Front (ELF)

ELF was founded in 1992 in Brighton, England by Earth First members who refused to abandon criminal acts as a tactic. In the United States, the group consists of nationwide, violent, high-tech ecological activists protesting the destruction of forests, the development of open spaces, and the use of genetically altered seeds and crops. The ELF advocates acts of sabotage and property destruction against industries and other entities perceived to be damaging the natural environment. ELF is an underground movement with no public leadership, membership, or spokesperson. The group has claimed responsibility for the destruction of U.S. Forest Service facilities and equipment (attacked because the group believed the U.S. Forest Service is not doing its job of protecting the nation's forests) and have committed arson at several lumberyards, bioaltered seed facilities, and building developments across the nation. The most destructive practice of ELF is arson. ELF members consistently use improvised incendiary devices equipped with crude but effective timing mechanisms. These devices are constructed based on instructions found on the ELF website.

Ku Klux Klan (KKK)

The Ku Klux Klan is a nationwide, long-lived Protestant Christian white supremacy group organized before the Civil War. The group is violently opposed to black freedoms and has used assault, murder, bombings, and arson against blacks and black supporters.

Michigan Militia

This Michigan based, antigovernment, weapons resistance militia group is the largest antigovernment group in the United States. The Michigan Militia advocates the purchase of weapons, ammunition, and explosives.

National Alliance (NA)

This regional white suppremist group takes violent action against blacks and Jews and has a very active Internet site. The group advocates the halting of nonwhite immigration and the deportation of nonwhite populations. The group also espouses the withdrawal of economic and technical aid to the undeveloped areas of the nonwhite world.

The Order

The group, based in the Midwest, is an extremely violent right wing neo-Nazi, white suppremist, anti-Semitic group. The group has been linked to several murders and has planned various attacks including bank robbery, assault, murder, bombings, and poisoning a reservoir.

Stop Huntington Animal Cruelty (SHAC)

The SHAC is a British based worldwide campaign (since 1999) to rescue animals tortured in research labs and shut down the businesses that rely on their use.

Texas Militia

This is a Texas based antigovernment, weapons rights group that advocates the manufacturing and stockpiling of automatic weapons and explosives.

1.19 RECENT DOMESTIC TERRORIST ATTACKS

September 1984. The followers of Indian born guru Bhagwan Shree Rajneesh try to gain political control by disrupting a local election in Oregon by spraying water contaminated with salmonella bacteria on salad bar fruits, vegetables, and coffee creamers in ten restaurants; 751 people became ill and 45 were hospitalized.

April 19, 1995. Timothy McVeigh, a U.S. citizen, uses a massive truck bomb to blow up the Alfred Murrah Federal Building in Oklahoma City, Oklahoma, killing 168 people.

November 10, 1995. An abortion doctor is shot and injured in his home in Ohio.

July 27, 1996. A bomb is detonated at Centennial Park during the Atlanta Olympics, killing one and injuring more than 100. The attack was perpetrated by right wing extremist Eric Robert Rudolph. The justification for the attack was political. According to Rudolph, the purpose of the attack was to confound, anger, and embarrass the Washington government in the eyes of the world for its abominable sanctioning of abortion on demand. The plan was to force the cancellation of the games, or at least create a state of insecurity to empty the streets around the venues and thereby eat into the vast amounts of money invested.

October 28, 1997. An abortion doctor is shot and injured in his home in Rochester, New York.

November 11, 1997. An abortion doctor is shot and injured in his home in Manitoba, Canada.

November 29, 1997. The Animal Liberation Front (ALF) and Earth Liberation Front (ELF) burned down a Bureau of Land Management horse corral complex in Burns, Oregon, resulting in $500,000 in damages.

January 29, 1998. Police Officer Robert Sanderson is killed during an abortion clinic bombing in Birmingham, Alabama. Nurse Emily Lyons is severely injured.

June 28, 1998. The ALF and ELF claim responsibility for an arson fire that destroyed a U.S. Department of Agriculture building near Olympia, Washington, causing $2 million in damage.

October 19, 1998. ELF claims responsibility for the arson of the Two Elk Lodge, a Vail, Colorado ski facility, destroying seven structures and resulting in over $12 million in damages.

October 23, 1998. Abortion doctor, Dr. Barnett Slepian, is shot and killed in his home in Amherst, New York.

March 27, 1999. The ALF firebombs circus trailers in Franklin, New Jersey.

July 2, 1999. An arsonist sets fire to the Country Club Medical Center Building in Sacramento, California, which houses an abortion clinic.

Summer 1999. Shooting sprees by lone gunmen in the Chicago and Los Angeles areas kill three people.

September 18 and October 9, 2001. Letters containing anthrax are mailed from a post office in New Jersey, ultimately killing five people in the eastern United States.

August 25, 2003. Animal Liberation Front activists release over 10,000 mink from a mink farm in Sultan, Washington.

May 26, 2004. Seven members of Stop Huntington Animal Cruelty are charged with burning New Jersey animal testing lab employees' cars, vandalizing the homes of company shareholders, and threatening employees' families.

June 14, 2004. Two terrorists from the Earth Liberation Front are convicted of an arson attack on a West Jordan, Utah lumber company that caused $1.5 million in damage.

REFERENCES

1. U.S. Department of State, *Patterns of Global Terrorism 2003.*
2. www.answers.com/topic/september-11-attacks.
3. *National Strategy for Homeland Security*, Office of Homeland Security, July 16, 2002.
4. www.cbc.ca/storyview/MSN/world/national/2005/03/11/fatwa-050311.html.
5. www.ict.org.il/articles/fatwah.htm.
6. www.en.wikipedia.org.
7. Testimony of Louis J. Freeh, FBI Director, before the United States Senate, Committees on Appropriations, Armed Services, and Select Committee on Intelligence, May 10, 2001.
8. *Foreign Terrorist Organizations Fact Sheet*, U.S. Department of State, March 23, 2005.
9. National Counterterrorism Center, *Chronology of Significant International Terrorism for 2004.*
10. www.cbsnews.com/stories/2003/10/23/world/main579638.shtml.
11. Elaine Lafferty, "Ruling Against Anti-Abortion Websites Raises Storm in US Over Rights." *The Irish Times*, February 4, 1999.
12. *Homeland Defense Journal*, June 2005, page 5.

CHAPTER 2

Critical Infrastructure

2.1 INTRODUCTION

Terrorists will continue to have an interest in attacking hard targets but are showing an increased interest in soft targets that are ill protected. Based on the success of the September 11, 2001 attack, there will also be a strong emphasis on attacking targets that will result in economic damage. These attacks will be perpetrated against both hard and soft targets of critical infrastructure, key assets, and key resources. Government agencies and the private sector must cooperatively work together to identify and prioritize the infrastructure most essential to the United States' economic and social well-being so that scarce resources can be allocated to the most critical in a planned and logical manner.

The *American Heritage Dictionary, Fourth Edition*, defines infrastructure as the basic facilities, services, and installations needed for the functioning of a community or society, such as transportation and communications systems, water and power lines, and public institutions including schools, post offices, and prisons. Critical infrastructures are the major physical components of our modern industrialized society.

2.2 EVOLUTION OF THE DEFINITION OF CRITICAL INFRASTRUCTURE

One of the first attempts by the government to identify the nation's infrastructure was in the 1983 Congressional Budget Office report entitled *Public Works Infrastructure: Policy Considerations for the 1980s*. This report defined infrastructure as "facilities with the common characteristics of capital intensiveness and high public investment at all levels of government. They are, moreover, directly critical to activity in the nation's economy" [1]. The Congressional Budget Office issued a second report in September 1988 entitled *New Directions for the Nation's Public Works*. This report started to identify critical infrastructure and therefore eliminated

Understanding, Assessing, and Responding to Terrorism: Protecting Critical Infrastructure and Personnel By Brian T. Bennett

such "facilities often thought of as infrastructure—such as public housing, government buildings, private rail service, and schools—some environmental facilities such as hazardous or toxic waste sites where the initial onus of responsibility is on private individuals" [2].

In 1984, Congress enacted a bill that established the National Council on Public Works Improvement (Public Law 98-501), which required the states to report on public works infrastructure systems. Infrastructure systems were defined as "any physical asset that is capable of being used to produce services or other benefits for a number of years, including but not limited to roadways or bridges; airports or airway facilities; mass transportation systems; wastewater treatment or related facilities; water resources projects; hospitals; resource recovery facilities; public buildings; space or communication facilities; railroads; and federally assisted housing" [3]. The council established by P.L. 98-501 developed its own definition of infrastructure: "facilities with high fixed costs, long economic lives, strong links to economic development, and a tradition of public sector involvement." The services that they provide "form the underpinnings of the nation's defense, a strong economy, and our health and safety" [4].

In the 1990s, the focus shifted from infrastructure adequacy to infrastructure protection due to the increasing threat of international terrorism. On July 15, 1996, President William Clinton signed Executive Order 13010, entitled "Critical Infrastructure Protection," which established the President's Commission on Critical Infrastructure Protection. The Executive Order established eight critical infrastructure sectors, including, for the first time, two owned predominantly by the private sector. Threats against critical infrastructure were broken down into two categories: physical threats to tangible property (physical threats) and threats of electronic, radio frequency, or computer based attacks on the information or communications components that control critical infrastructures (cyber threats). Executive Order 13010 further stated that "certain national infrastructures are so vital that their incapacity or destruction would have a debilitating impact on the defense or economic security of the United States" and called for the government and the private sector to work together to develop a strategy for protecting them and assuring their continued operation [5]. Appendix 2.1 is a copy of Executive Order 13010.

In response to the President's Commission on Critical Infrastructure Protection final report, President Clinton issued Presidential Decision Directive 63 (PDD 63) on May 22, 1998. The goal of the PDD was to establish a national capability within five years to protect critical infrastructure from intentional disruption. PDD 63 defined critical infrastructures as "those physical and cyber based systems essential to the minimum operations of the economy and government" and included assets in both public and private sectors. This definition included cyber security within the realm of critical infrastructure for the first time. The first version of a National Plan for Critical Infrastructure, called for in PDD 63, defined critical infrastructures as "those systems and assets—both physical and cyber—so vital to the Nation that their incapacity or destruction would have a debilitating impact on national security, national economic security, and/or national public health and safety" [6]. Appendix 2.2 is a copy of PDD 63.

Following the terrorist attacks on the United States on September 11, 2001, President George Bush issued Executive Order 13228 on October 8, 2001. This Executive Order established the new Office of Homeland Security and the Homeland Security Council. The order assigned the Office of Homeland Security the responsibility to protect the nation's nine critical infrastructure sectors. For the first time, nuclear sites, special events, and agriculture were included in the critical infrastructure sectors. Appendix 2.3 is a copy of Executive Order 13228. A separate Executive Order 13231, which was signed on October 16, 2001, established the President's Critical Infrastructure Protection Board. The Executive Order referred primarily to information systems, including "telecommunications, energy, financial services, manufacturing, water, transportation, health care, and emergency services." Appendix 2.4 is a copy of Executive Order 13231.

2.3 CURRENT DEFINITION OF CRITICAL INFRASTRUCTURE

In response to the terrorist attacks of September 11, 2001, Congress passed the USA PATRIOT Act of 2001 (Public Law 107-56). The USA PATRIOT Act was intended to "deter and punish terrorist acts in the United States and around the world, to enhance law enforcement, investigatory tools, and for other purposes." The Act goes on to define *critical infrastructure* in Section 1016(e) and includes the personnel, physical assets, cyber, and communications systems that must be intact and operational to ensure survivability, continuity of operations, and mission success. Critical infrastructures are so vital that the incapacitation or destruction of such systems and assets would have a debilitating effect on security, national economic security, national public health, safety, or psychology or any combination of those matters.

The President's National Strategy for Homeland Security, issued in July 2002, restates the definition of critical infrastructure from the USA PATRIOT Act. The National Strategy summarizes the classification of critical infrastructure sectors. "Our critical infrastructures are particularly important because of the functions or services they provide to our country. Our critical infrastructures are also particularly important because they are complex systems: the effects of a terrorist attack can spread far beyond the direct target, and reverberate long after the immediate damage. America's critical infrastructure encompasses a large number of sectors. Our agriculture, food, and water sectors, along with the public health and emergency services sectors, provide the essential goods and services Americans need to survive. Our institutions of government guarantee our national security and freedom, and administer key public functions. Our defense industrial base provides essential capabilities to help safeguard our population from external threats. Our information and telecommunication sector enables economic productivity and growth, and is particularly important because it connects and helps control many other infrastructure sectors. Our energy, transportation, banking and finance, chemical industry, and postal and shipping sectors help sustain our economy and touch the lives of Americans everyday" [7, p. 30].

2.4 DEFINITION OF KEY RESOURCES

Key resources are defined in Section 2(9) of the Homeland Security Act of 2002 as the publicly or privately controlled individual resources essential to the minimal operation of the economy and government. Destruction of a key resource would not endanger vital systems but could cause large-scale injury, death, or destruction of property and/or profound damage to our national prestige and confidence.

2.5 DEFINITION OF KEY ASSETS

Definition of an Asset. An asset is any real or personal property, tangible or intangible, that a company or individual owns that can be given or assigned a monetary value. Intangible property includes things such as good will, proprietary information, and elated property.

Key assets, a subset of nationally important key resources, is defined in *The National Strategy for Homeland Security* as "individual targets whose destruction would not endanger a vital system, but could create local disaster or profoundly damage our Nation's morale or confidence. Key assets include symbols or historical attractions, such as prominent national, state, or local monuments or icons. In some cases, these include quasi-public symbols that are identified strongly with the United States as a nation. Key assets also include individual or localized facilities that deserve special protection because of their destructive potential or their value to the local community" [7, p. 31].

The Bush administration's *National Strategy for the Physical Protection of Critical Infrastructures and Key Assets*, which was released in February 2003, defines three categories of key assets. "One category of key assets comprises the diverse array of national monuments, symbols, and icons that represent our Nation's heritage, traditions, and values, and political power. They include a wide variety of sites and structures, such as prominent historical attractions, monuments, cultural icons, and centers of government and commerce. Another category of key assets includes facilities and structures that represent our national economic power and technological advancement. Many of them house significant amounts of hazardous materials, fuels, and chemical catalysts that enable important production and processing functions. A third category of key assets includes such structures as prominent commercial centers, office buildings, and sports stadiums, where large numbers of people regularly congregate to conduct business or personal transactions, shop, or enjoy a recreational pastime" [7, p. 71].

2.6 DISCUSSION OF CRITICAL INFRASTRUCTURE

What Is Critical Infrastructure?

Not all infrastructures are critical. A critical infrastructure is a collection of indispensable assets. An asset, a subset of a critical infrastructure, is something of high importance or high value and can include people, property, or information systems. Critical infrastructures are best selected by each individual jurisdiction, as they know their specific circumstances best. However, it must be realized that what may be deemed critical infrastructure by a jurisdiction may not meet the definition when compared to other national or regional assets. An individual jurisdiction may decide they will expand their own resources to protect what they have deemed critical.

Critical infrastructures are very complex systems that provide the products and services we rely on every day. Quite simply, critical infrastructures are those important assets that we need and want. Our increasing dependence on these systems has caused them to become larger and even more complex. Critical infrastructures drive all of the necessary functions on which our society depends and help keep our country functioning. America's critical infrastructures provide the foundation for our national security, governance, economic vitality, and way of life. Continued reliability, robustness, and resiliency of our critical infrastructures create a sense of confidence and form an important part of our national identity and purpose. Historically, we have just assumed that these critical infrastructures would always be there, getting the job done. We have grown accustomed to their output and have ignored the need to protect their ability to provide the products and services they do, because it has never been necessary to do so. Over time these critical infrastructures have evolved in complexity and have been threatened by natural disasters, accidental damage, and now intentional acts. Little consideration was given to protect them from adversaries intent upon their destruction. Assets that were lightly designed or did not have robust security countermeasures in place were considered "soft." Therefore these ill protected critical infrastructures are vulnerable to attack and very brittle, unable to resist or sustain the type of damage that might result from a terrorist attack.

Critical infrastructure and key assets can be static or mobile. Static assets are those that are fixed in place, such as a hospital. Mobile assets are those that move around from place to place, such as a subway car. The attacks against critical infrastructure and key assets can be either a physical attack or a cyber attack. Physical attacks are those that are conducted at the location of the asset and employ physical weapons such as an explosive device. A cyber attack can be executed great distances from the target, using the World Wide Web to perpetrate an attack against a computer target, such as an asset's website. Some targets carry value for both the damage inflicted based on their disruption and their potential for causing mass casualties. A power generation plant may be targeted because a successful attack can disrupt its ability to generate and distribute electricity to its customers. This disruption of service will have a downstream effect on people and other critical infrastructure, perhaps causing additional casualties and economic damage. Some critical infrastructure or key assets typically have large amounts of people present in a relatively small, confined area such as a sports stadium. This type of asset may be targeted with a weapon such as a chemical device because it would cause many injuries and fatalities among the attendees. Much of our critical infrastructure and key assets are dangerously exposed to simple attacks, which require little or no planning or resources. The July 2005 suicide bomb attacks against the London subway system illustrate just how difficult it can be to protect critical infrastructure in an open society, especially one that must be readily accessible to the general public.

Critical Infrastructure Sectors

Critical infrastructure can have like resources grouped together into sectors. The U.S. Department of Homeland Security has grouped critical infrastructure into the sectors shown in Table 2.1.

For comparative purposes, the Canadian Critical Infrastructure Sectors described by the Office of Critical Infrastructure Protection and Emergency Preparedness are:

- Energy and utilities
- Communications
- Services (such as financial services, food distribution, and health care)
- Transportation
- Safety (such as nuclear safety, search and rescue, and emergency services)
- Government

Federal key resources in the United States are:

- Commercial assets.
- Dams.
- Government facilities.
- Nuclear power plants.

Where Are Critical Infrastructures Located?

Critical infrastructure, key resources, and key assets are located everywhere and anywhere. They are present in all aspects of our daily routine. It is easy to define them as a collection of assets present within a jurisdiction. A jurisdiction is a responsible party that has authority and control over the activities within a specific

TABLE 2.1. Critical Infrastructure Sectors as Defined by the Office of Homeland Security

Agriculture	Government
Banking and finance	Information and telecommunications
Chemical industry	Postal and shipping
Defense industrial base	Public health
Emergency services	Transportation
Energy	Water
Food	

geographical area. A jurisdiction can be private sector or public sector. A private sector jurisdiction is privately owned and operated by an individual or a legal entity such as a corporation and has control of the asset. A public sector jurisdiction is one in which the assets are owned by the citizens and controlled and operated by a government agency, entity, or employee.

In the United States, 85% of the critical infrastructure is owned by the private sector.

It is possible that an asset can be classified as critical infrastructure to both the private sector and the public sector. An example would be a privately owned medical clinic that is operated by a private concern and intended to earn a profit, but it supplies a critical service on which the public depends.

What Makes an Infrastructure Critical?

A product or service is critical when either it provides an essential contribution in maintaining a defined minimum level of national or international law and order, pubic safety, economic life, public health, and environmental protection, or if the disruption of its ability to provide product or services hurts citizens or government administration and may endanger security. Some are critical only when others are damaged (e.g., emergency services).

The following qualifications impact the criticality of infrastructure:

- The more dependencies, the more critical. The more things that depend on a particular asset, the more important it is and the more damaging its loss.
- The more vulnerable, the more critical. If an asset has many vulnerabilities, it becomes more critical because its loss is more likely.
- Lack of alternatives increases its criticality. If a substitute does not exist to replace a degraded asset, it becomes more critical as its loss would be more significant.

Why Protect Critical Infrastructure?

Critical infrastructures enable Americans to enjoy one of the highest overall standards of living in the world. Without our critical infrastructure, our economy would fail to operate. Critical infrastructure and key assets are both physical and cyber based and span all sectors of our economy. Critical infrastructure and key assets provide the essential services on which American society depends. The nation possesses numerous key assets, whose exploitation or destruction by terrorists could cause catastrophic health effects or mass casualties, or could profoundly affect our national prestige and morale. In addition, there are critical infrastructure and key assets so vital that their incapacitation, exploitation, or destruction through a terrorist attack could have a debilitating effect on security and economic well-being [8].

The physical critical infrastructure or key asset may not be physically damaged in an attack, but it may be debilitated. An asset is considered debilitated when it is rendered ineffective or unable to fulfill its mission of providing essential products or services. To address this issue, a critical infrastructure or key asset is considered "mission critical" if its damage or destruction would have a debilitating effect on its ability to perform its essential function or provide its essential service.

Terrorists seek to destroy, incapacitate, or exploit critical infrastructure and key assets across the United States in order to:

- *Threaten National Security.* A successful attack against some critical infrastructure or key asset, such as our defense industrial base, may have an adverse effect on national security.
- *Cause Mass Causalities.* A weapon of mass destruction (WMD) attack targeting a large concentration of people in a small area may result in hundreds or even thousands of injuries or fatalities.
- *Weaken our Economy.* A successful attack against a critical infrastructure or key resource could result in significant direct and indirect economic loss based on the asset's inability to provide its product or service.
- *Damage Public Morale and Confidence in the Government.* A successful attack may instill a sense of fear in the population. The fear could translate into the perception that the government cannot provide the security necessary to protect people from harm.
- *Cause Inconvenience and Changes in our Daily Activities.* A successful attack against a critical infrastructure or key resource will certainly cause people to adapt their day to day activities due to the loss of the essential product or service, and will most likely result in some type of inconvenience for the average citizen.

Creation of Homeland HSPD 7

To help prevent terrorists from using our critical infrastructure as a weapon against us, President George W. Bush issued Homeland Security Presidential Directive (HSPD) 7, entitled *Critical Infrastructure Identification, Prioritization, and Protection*, on December 17, 2003. The directive requires that the Department of Homeland Security and other federal agencies collaborate with appropriate private sector entities in sharing information and protecting critical infrastructure. HSPD 7 supersedes Presidential Decision Directive 63 (PDD 63). HSPD 7 adopts, by reference, the definitions of critical infrastructure and key resources in Section 6 of the Homeland Security Act. It also adopts the critical infrastructure and key asset categories from the *National Strategy for the Physical Protection of Critical Infrastructure and Key Assets*. Appendix 2.5 is a copy of HSPD 7.

Public Versus Private Critical Infrastructure

Terrorists will plan attacks where the possibility of success is greatest. Since most publicly owned critical infrastructure and key resources have been hardened to some degree, they will likely look to attack softer targets within the private sector. The concentration on high profile targets has diminished steadily in response to increased efforts to protect them against well established threats. Historically, al Qaeda's attacks have been directed at large, high value targets. Although al Qaeda has not given up aspirations to attack major, highly visible targets in the U.S. homeland, soft targets are the kind of targets al Qaeda has traditionally hit successfully in terms of planning, surveillance, and execution. Recent intelligence suggests that Osama bin Laden has instructed his cells to focus on a campaign of simple attacks against these lightly defended soft targets.

Example of Critical Infrastructure: Agriculture Sector

Consider the possibility that an adversary may attack our food supply, animals, or crops, which is known as agroterrorism. Agroterrorism is the malicious use or threatened use of biological, chemical, or radiological agents against some component of the agriculture sector (livestock, food supply, crops, or workers) in such a way as to adversely impact a component of the agriculture industry, the economy, or the consuming public. As such, an agroterrorist attack would primarily be an attack on our economy. CIA official Peter Probst was quoted in the October 4, 2001 *New York Times*, stating "agriculture is the soft underbelly of the American economy. It's an absolutely vital sector, but it's terribly difficult to protect." Tommy Thompson, the U.S. Department of Health and Human Services secretary, was quoted in December 2004: "For the life of me, I cannot understand why the terrorists have not attacked our food supply because it is so easy to do." Figure 2.1 illustrates the location and relative density of farms in the United States.

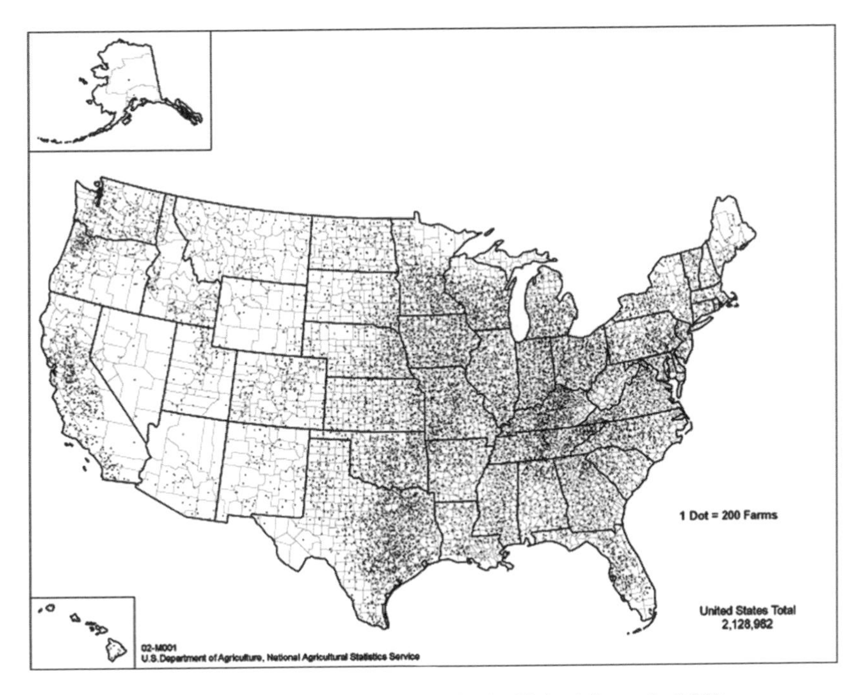

FIGURE 2.1. Number of farms in the United States in 2002.

Why is the agriculture sector such an attractive target? The U.S. agricultural sector generates over $1 trillion per year in economic activity, which accounts for over 12% of the U.S. gross domestic product, and over $55 billion in annual exports. Twenty-two percent of American workers are employed in the agriculture sector. The production of food in the United States is so extensive (most of it comes from 500,000 farms on over one billion acres of land and is handled by 57,000 food processors and 6000 meat, poultry, and egg product processors) that if even a small number of contaminants were intentionally introduced into some part of the food chain, such an incident could seriously damage public confidence in the safety of the nation's food supply and could result in staggering economic losses for the agriculture industry [9]. There are a large number of easily accessible targets within a relatively small area. Although spread out over several states, 70% of U.S. beef cattle are raised in an area with a 200 mile radius [10]. There are also a large number of biological and chemical agents that can be introduced into the agricultural sector very easily. A successfully executed attack on the food supply could provide many benefits to the terrorist organization including the following:

- Destruction of consumer confidence in the agriculture sector (the sector cannot provide a safe product to the public).
- Effect on vulnerable segments of society (especially children and the elderly).
- Instillation of fear in people and creation of chaos (people are afraid to eat certain foods due to adulteration).
- Economic damage (people won't buy certain foods).
- Farm crisis (no markets for commodities due to fear of contaminated food).
- Mass disruption (people change purchasing patterns and diet).
- Weakening of the agriculture sector (potential for significant short-term job loss due to decreased sales of services and product).
- Destabilization of the government (sense that the government cannot provide security to and inspection of the agriculture sector).

The agriculture sector is so critical to the Unites States, that President Bush issued Homeland Security Presidential Directive (HSPD) 9 in 2002, which outlined the need to defend the agriculture and food systems. We trust that our food is safe, and with good reason—the United States has the world's safest food supply. However, our food supplies are vulnerable to assorted types of biological attack.

Scenario: Attack on the Agriculture Sector

One scenario would be to infect cattle with foot and mouth disease. Foot and mouth disease is not indigenous to North America, but it could be brought into the United States by an adversary. Cattle in the United States are not vaccinated against this disease. This disease is not a direct threat to humans but decimates cloven hoofed animals such as cattle and swine. The disease causes fever and large blisters on the mouth and hooves, making it difficult for the animal to eat, drink, and walk. Foot and mouth disease is a major threat because infecting just one animal with the contagious virus would lead to the infection of hundreds of thousand of cattle within days. Aerosols from animals that contain the virus can spread for miles through the air. Cattle that are infected with the disease would develop symptoms approximately two weeks later. Once the disease was discovered and identified, the infected herd plus all other susceptible animals within a 2 mile radius must be killed, burned, and buried. There would also be a ban on U.S. meat exports, causing economic losses in the billions of dollars and a loss in public confidence in the food supply. There would also be quarantined farms, road closures, and stoppage of animal transport. Food prices would skyrocket, and there would likely be short-term food shortages. In 2001, there was an actual foot and mouth disease outbreak in the United Kingdom, which led to the slaughter and burning of more than five million animals. A Price Waterhouse Coopers estimate put the economic loss at between $3.6 and $11.6 billion. An attack against our food supply, which is considered a soft target, could lead to food shortages, mass panic, and significant economic losses.

Neil Speer, an associate professor of animal science at Western Kentucky University's agriculture department, who has studied the economic effects of a foot and mouth disease attack, says halts on shipments and quarantines in the Kansas–Texas region, in which 40% of the nation's slaughtering capability is located, would result in lost cattle sales of $207 million a day [11].

The following news report outlines what could happen in case of a virus attack on U.S. herds. "In 2001, more than 4 million farm animals, out of herds of approximately 60 million, have been eliminated in Great Britain due to foot and mouth disease. That is a large number of animals, but it is only a fraction of the damage that would be caused if a foot and mouth disease outbreak of the same scale occurred in the United States, where the herds total an estimated 160 million head. One report estimated that if foot and mouth disease became established in the United States, it would cost livestock producers an estimated $12 billion just to deal with the direct consequences of the crisis, such as the cost of drugs and veterinary services, lost production, and lower prices. In addition, the public would bear the multibillion dollar cost of depopulating herds, and other industries linked to the dairy and livestock industries would suffer losses and unemployment. Finally, U.S. exports of meat and dairy products would halt abruptly and would not resume for at least six months, but probably much longer" [12].

Categorizing Critical Infrastructure and Key Resources

When comparing critical infrastructure and key resources from several different jurisdictions, it may be necessary to categorize or rank assets. This categorization may be necessary to ensure that proper resources, especially funding, are directed at the proper asset so that it can be protected. For this purpose, critical infrastructure and key resources are categorized based on national level of importance, state or regional level of importance, and local community level of importance.

2.7 SOFT TARGETS

Soft targets are those infrastructures or key resources that usually lack proper security or are difficult to protect and defend because they are open to the general public by their very design, such as a shopping center. An adversary would generally have largely unimpeded access to large concentrations of people. They are not designed to limit or restrict free and easy access by the general public. Enhanced security or access restriction would likely cause disruption of people's normal activities and would cause the perception of adverse or inconvenient effect on the general public. Soft targets are relatively unguarded or difficult to secure effectively. They are typically undefended civilian assets easy to attack or obtain an advantage from because they are not very secure due to their perceived low risk of exploitation. Most jurisdictions have many more soft targets than hard targets. Examples of soft targets include shopping centers, hotels, places of worship, buses, trains, nightclubs, and restaurants.

The list of soft targets will vary depending on the makeup and size of the city or town. The intent of attacks on soft targets will not only be to kill or injure, but to generate terror, create chaos, and intimidate the population. Imagine a terrorist attack at a local elementary school, with coordinated and simultaneous attacks against the local police, fire, and emergency medical services along with the hospital. There would be immediate chaos within the city, which would rapidly spread to neighboring communities and eventually the entire country.

The basic nature of our free and open society greatly facilitates the tactics and operations espoused by terrorists and make soft targets attractive. Critical infrastructure and key assets must be readily accessible to those who need or desire access, yet be protected sufficiently to avoid damage or destruction. This need for public access hinders our ability to predict, prevent, or mitigate the effects of a terrorist attack.

The protection of critical infrastructure, key resources, and key assets takes precedence over protection of soft targets as they serve the masses and are needed to maintain our standard of living.

2.8 HARD TARGETS

A *hard target* is an asset that has sufficient security countermeasures in place to provide a high degree of protection against an attack. Hard targets typically have restricted access that would prevent free and easy access by the general public. A significant amount of both physical hardening as well as administrative countermeasures would be in place to deter an attack by an adversary. Although hard targets are highly protected, an adversary may decide to attack anyway, as the results of a successful attack would most likely be spectacular. A successful attack against a hard target should validate the adversary as a meaningful force. Hard targets include government facilities, airports, and nuclear power plants.

2.9 CASCADING EFFECTS FROM INTERDEPENDENCIES OF CRITICAL INFRASTRUCTURES

It is likely that a successful attack on a particular critical infrastructure sector will have an adverse cascading effect on other sectors. For example, the chemical sector depends on the transportation sector to move manufactured products to market. If various key assets of the transportation sector are eliminated or services degraded through a terrorist attack, the chemical sector will suffer losses as well.

Critical infrastructures are not mutually exclusive and are often dependent on one another. There are many interdependencies and interconnectivities between the various critical infrastructure sectors. In the event of an attack, these cross sector interdependencies will cause adverse consequences and hinder the ability of another sector to function properly. A catastrophic event in one could cause a series of disruptions, degradation, or interruptions in essential services. These cascading effects can lead to an adversary realizing indirect or exploitative results. Indirect effects are the hidden results that are achieved and may not be as obvious as the direct effects. The loss of life and destruction of the World Trade Center towers were the direct effects of the September 11 terrorist attacks in New York City. The indirect effect was the massive economic damage that followed. Exploitation is when a vulnerability to damage is taken advantage of to cause even more damage. Again referring to the September 11 attack, the hijackers exploited weak airport security to smuggle weapons aboard aircraft that were then used as missiles.

The Gulf Coast hurricanes of September 2005 illustrated not only the cascading effect, but also the interdependencies among critical infrastructures. As a result of the hurricanes striking land, a significant amount of critical infrastructure was damaged or destroyed, and this had a dramatic effect, showing just how intimately some critical infrastructures are tied together. The remaining critical infrastructures were severely taxed to provide their services or products. A tremendous amount of help was provided from nearby unaffected critical infrastructure to help fill the shortfall. A successful terrorist attack against an already compromised critical infrastructure, or against a critical infrastructure in a neighboring community that was providing assistance, could have been disastrous.

Example: Cascading Effect on Interdependent Critical Infrastructures

As a result of hurricane damage to the Gulf Coast of the United States in 2005, there was a loss of the electrical generating capability. This in turn led to the loss of the domestic water supply, as there was no power to operate the supply pumps. Petroleum refineries were also shut down due to the lack of electricity. Communications systems were adversely impacted due to electrical outages. Each of the critical infrastructures that were degraded had an effect on the emergency services infrastructure and its ability to provide services. Firefighters were at a disadvantage because there was no water for the fire hydrants. The lack of fuel led to fire trucks, ambulances, and police cars sitting unused. The emergency services were unable to communicate via radio or cellular phones. This example illustrates how the emergency services sector, even though not directly attacked, lost its ability to provide critical services due to the independency on critical infrastructures that were degraded.

Based on this example, it should come as no surprise that an adversary may try to capitalize on the strain a natural disaster has placed on emergency responders, security personnel, and the remaining critical infrastructure. This may lead to an increase in the threat of exploitation by adversaries intent on further degrading critical infrastructures and key assets, economic stability, and public morale.

2.10 COORDINATION OF CRITICAL INFRASTRUCTURE PROTECTION

The Department of Homeland Security coordinates with other appropriate federal departments and agencies to ensure the protection of critical infrastructure and key resources. The Department of Homeland Security developed a national indications and warnings architecture for critical infrastructure protection and capabilities that facilitates (1) an understanding of baseline infrastructure operations, (2) the identification of indicators and precursors to attacks, and (3) surge capacity for detecting and analyzing patterns of potential attacks.

Recognizing that each infrastructure sector possesses its own unique characteristics, the government has designated sector-specific federal departments and agencies that are responsible for coordinating the counterterrorism activities:

- Department of Agriculture: agriculture, food (meat, poultry, egg products).
- Department of Human Services: public healthcare and food (other than meat, poultry, egg products).
- Environmental Protection Agency: chemical industry, drinking water, and water treatment systems.
- Department of Energy: energy, including the production, refining, storage, and distribution of oil and gas, and electric power except for commercial nuclear power facilities.
- Department of the Treasury: banking and finance.
- Department of the Interior: national monuments and icons.
- Department of Defense: defense industrial base.

The Department of State and other appropriate agencies will work with foreign countries and international organizations to strengthen the protection of U.S. critical infrastructure and key assets.

Table 2.2 is a list of the federal agencies and the critical infrastructures for which they are tasked with coordinating protective measures.

TABLE 2.2. Critical Infrastructures and Key Assets Under HSPD 7

Lead Agency	Critical Infrastructure
Department of Homeland Security	Information technology; telecommunications; chemicals; transportation systems, including mass transit, aviation, maritime, ground/surface, and rail and pipeline systems; emergency services; postal and shipping services
Department of Agriculture	Agriculture, food (meat, poultry, egg products)
Department of Health and Human Services	Public health, healthcare, and food (other than meat, poultry, and egg products)
Environmental Protection Agency	Drinking water and wastewater treatment systems
Department of Energy	Energy, including the production, refining, storage, and distribution of oil and gas, electric power (except for nuclear power facilities)
Department of the Treasury	Banking and finance
Department of the Interior	National monuments and icons
Department of Defense	Defense industrial base

The Challenge of Protecting Critical Infrastructure

America is a large country that has porous borders. This provides some unique challenges in trying to secure the country to prevent the entry of adversaries or weapons of mass destruction. There are long stretches of both the northern and southern borders that are unpopulated, not secure, and not regularly patrolled by law enforcement personnel. The United States shares a 5525 mile border with Canada and a 1989 mile border with Mexico. Our maritime border includes over 96,000 miles of shoreline and navigable waterways as well as a 3.4 million square mile exclusive economic zone. There are 354 international airports and 146 seaports. All people and goods legally entering into the United States must be processed through an air, land, or sea port of entry. Each year, more than 500 million people legally enter the United States. Some 330 million are non-U.S. citizens; more than 85% enter via land borders, often as daily commuters. There are between 9 and 11 million illegal aliens living today in the continental Unites States. In 2002, 122 million cars, 11 million trucks, 2.4 million rail freight cars, and 56,596 vessels entered the United States at more than 3700 terminals and 301 ports of entry. There are 15 international mail facilities. An enormous volume of trade also crosses our borders every day—some $1.35 trillion in imports and $1 trillion in exports were processed in 2001.

Ninety percent of the world's general cargo moves inside seagoing shipping containers. Nearly 95% of all imported goods arrive in the United States via container ships. Each container can carry up to 65,000 pounds of cargo. Containers carry more than 20 billion tons of goods through U.S. ports and waterways each year. Nearly 9 million cargo containers are offloaded at U.S. seaports each year, and more than 200 million cargo containers move between the world's major ports each year, according to the U.S. Customs and Border Patrol.

The Vulnerabilities

Terrorism is a crime. Any crime, regardless how heinous, requires motive, means, and opportunity. In order to eliminate the means and opportunity, it is imperative that our critical infrastructures be identified, assessed, and have the appropriate countermeasures installed to reduce vulnerabilities. The reason for this is simple: it is quite likely that a terrorist may try to use our critical infrastructure against us by using it as a weapon of mass destruction. Here are two examples of how a terrorist could use our very own critical infrastructure as a weapon against us.

1. United States customs officials divide shipping containers into two categories: trusted and untrusted. A trusted container is one that has been shipped by an importer or consolidator (an intermediate that consolidates the contents or two or more containers into one) who is known to customs officials. A trusted importer is one who is familiar to customs officials and has no history of smuggling or attempting to violate U.S. laws. The containers shipped by a trusted importer are cleared by customs officers without any inspection or examination. Untrusted containers are those that come from the world's trouble spots or from new importers who are unfamiliar to customs officials. Untrusted containers are subject to inspection and examination. On average, overseas containers pass through 17 intermediate points before they arrive at their final destination in the United States. A possible scenario involving a shipping container being used as a weapon against us would start out with a radiological device being placed into a shipping container along with other commercial goods somewhere in the Middle East. This container moves along the global supply chain for several months, being transferred from ship to ship at the world's container ports. Ultimately, the container is carried to a U.S. port of entry by a trusted shipper. The container is offloaded from the ship and put on a truck. Since the container arrived in the U.S. from a trusted carrier, it is not inspected upon arrival. The container is transported to or near a critical infrastructure or key asset, and the radiological device is detonated.

2. According to the U.S. Environmental Protection Agency, there are 709 sites in the United States where the toll of death or injury from a catastrophic chemical release at a chemical plant could impact between 100,000 to more than 1 million people. A terrorist could cause a deliberate release of a chemical from a manufacturing or storage facility, causing mass casualties. For example, a terrorist could set off an explosive device on a railroad tanker containing 90 tons of liquid chlorine. When the liquid chlorine is released from its container, it immediately turns into a gas and is blown downwind, hugging the ground as it travels. Anyone in the path of the ensuing vapor cloud would be in grave danger of serious injury or death [13].

2.11 SELECTION OF CRITICAL INFRASTRUCTURE AND KEY ASSETS

It is important to select critical infrastructure, key resources, and key assets so that informed decisions can be made concerning proper resource allocation for their protection. Every jurisdiction, whether public sector or private sector, is obligated to identify its critical infrastructure, key assets, and key resources so they can be prioritized and have the proper security enhancements implemented to prevent exploitation.

The identification and importance of critical infrastructure, key resources, and key assets are certainly in the eye of the beholder. It is understood that what may be critical or key to a particular jurisdiction, whether owned by the public or private sector, may or may not be considered critical or key when compared to and prioritized against other assets on a regional or federal level. Each jurisdiction should identify and assess its own critical assets to prioritize their importance to the jurisdiction, identify the interdependencies between those assets and other systems, and prioritize which assets need to be protected first.

Critical infrastructure and key assets are prioritized based on which is the most essential in regard to the function it provides, or which poses the most significant danger to life and property if threatened or damaged. This information is necessary for developing an effective protection strategy.

The scope and complexity of critical infrastructure pose a significant challenge to identify which specific assets are in fact critical. The selection of critical infrastructure and key assets is at the discretion of the local jurisdiction or facility. Critical infrastructure and key assets are uniquely selected based on the particular circumstances concerning the entity involved. Critical infrastructures are not uniformly critical in nature, particularly in a national or regional context. For example, a small shopping center in a small town may be considered a critical infrastructure or key asset because it contributes significantly to the local economy in that town; however, in a large metropolitan city the same small shopping center may not be classified as a critical infrastructure or key asset because it contributes little to the economy of the city compared to other venues.

The criticality of individual assets is dynamic. Criticality varies as a function of time, risk, market conditions, population, and other critical infrastructure and key resources in the area. Therefore the critical infrastructure selection and prioritization process must be constantly reviewed and revised to reflect the most current and up to date situation.

As an example of a local jurisdiction's ability to select what are important critical infrastructure and key assets based on its particular circumstances, the state of New Jersey has created 23 critical infrastructure sectors (see Table 2.3).

There are tools available to help a jurisdiction select critical infrastructure and key assets based on local conditions. The "Critical Infrastructure/Key Asset Selection Matrix" identifies and quantifies four important criteria associated with critical infrastructure: occupancy, economic impact, business or service interruption, and interdependencies. This matrix allows for a jurisdiction to rate and prioritize each of its infrastructures and assets to determine which ones are more critical for the jurisdiction or facility to continue to operate or provide a service.

TABLE 2.3. New Jersey's Critical Infrastructure Sectors

911 Communications
Agriculture
Banking and insurance
Cable television
Chemical
Colleges and research
Commercial buildings
Construction
Dams
Electric
Food
Gas
Healthcare
Media
Nuclear
Petroleum
Pharmaceutical and biotechnology
Schools
Sports and entertainment
Telecommunications
Transportation
Wastewater
Water

2.12 IDENTIFICATION AND SELECTION OF SOFT TARGETS BY A JURISDICTION

Local jurisdictions must include a list of the potential soft targets along with their critical infrastructure, key resources, and key assets. Once all the soft targets have been inventoried, they must also be rated and categorized so a prioritization plan for their protection can be developed as well.

With limited resources in terms of security countermeasures and money, it is imperative that those soft targets that are the most attractive to an adversary for attack and that pose the greatest threat in terms of casualties, economic damage, or a negative impact on other interdependent critical infrastructure be protected. An attack on a soft target can and may impact other critical infrastructure, key resources, or key assets. An explosive device could be placed in a bus, and when the bus is adjacent to the local fire station the device could be detonated, impacting the ability of the fire department to provide emergency services.

The criteria for inventorying and prioritizing soft targets must be determined individually by each jurisdiction based on the specific local conditions. For example, a small popular chain restaurant in the center of a small community might be considered an attractive soft target and may receive a higher priority for protection than a small chemical processing facility on the outskirts of town where there are few homes, businesses, or groups of people that would be exposed in the event of a release of hazardous materials if the plant were attacked.

2.13 INVENTORYING AND PRIORITIZING CRITICAL INFRASTRUCTURE/KEY RESOURCES/KEY ASSETS/SOFT TARGETS

There are a number of tools that can be used to inventory and prioritize assets that are deemed critical and are potential targets for an adversary. There are slight differences in what qualifies an asset as critical for the public and private sectors. For example, the private sector may be more concerned about financial costs and downtime, while the public sector may be more concerned about damage to interdependent infrastructure and casualties.

The basic technique involves developing a matrix in which several critical parameters are identified by the jurisdiction, and a corresponding list of escalating consequences resulting from an attack is associated. For this preliminary assessment, the worst case scenario should be considered when evaluating that asset. Consideration should not be given to the likelihood of the attack, the difficulty of the attack, or the specific type of attack that is executed. A numerical value, which may or may not be weighted to reflect the importance of the particular loss, is assigned to each consequence. After each asset has been rated in this manner, the total score is calculated. The assets are then ranked based on the total score achieved in the evaluation process. The higher the score for an asset, the higher the priority is for protection.

The inventorying and evaluation of assets is best accomplished using a multidisciplinary team. For the evaluation of public sector assets, the team should include representatives from the following agencies:

- Law enforcement.
- Fire department.
- Emergency medical services.
- Health department.
- Engineering department.
- Finance department.
- Public works department.

In addition, a representative from the specific asset being evaluated should participate in the evaluation for that asset as the representative is more likely to know the specific adverse effects that will occur in the event the asset is attacked.

The key parameters considered will provide some indication of how attractive a target the asset is based on the adversary's goal of causing casualties, damage, and financial loss.

Critical Infrastructure/Key Resource/Key Asset/Soft Target Attractiveness Matrix: Public Sector

The following is an example of an inventory and prioritization methodology.

Occupants Exposed. How many people would be present at the asset at the time of maximum occupancy?

Score	Criteria
0	Asset is not normally occupied
1	Normal occupancy of 1–50 people
2	Normal occupancy of 51–250 people
3	Normal occupancy of 251–1000 people
4	Normal occupancy of 1001 and more people

Economic Impact. If the asset were attacked, what would the direct financial consequences be to repair or replace the physical asset and the associated equipment housed in the asset?

Score	Criteria
0	No significant economic effect is likely
1	Repair or replacement cost is less than $250,000
2	Repair or replacement cost is greater than $250,000 but less than $1,000,000
3	Repair or replacement cost is greater than $1,000,000 but less than $10,000,000
4	Repair or replacement cost is greater than $10,000,000

Business or Service Interruption. If the asset were successfully attacked, for what period of time would the asset be unable to provide its product or service?

Score	Criteria
0	Asset could start up or resume service with minimal procedural changes or repairs
1	Asset can provide partial services or product
2	Asset is shut down or unable to provide services for less than six months
3	Asset is shut down or unable to provide services more than six months
4	Asset is not expected to be rebuilt or services will not be provided in the future

Interdependencies. If the asset were successfully attacked, would there be an adverse effect on other assets that are interdependent?

Score	Criteria
0	No effect on the asset's normal operations or its ability to provide services
1	Asset is a standalone facility and is not interdependent with other assets; adverse effects would be limited to this asset only
2	Asset is a part of and interdependent with a larger system; however, adverse effects would not extend beyond this single asset
3	Asset is interdependent with or provides services to at least one other asset
4	Asset is interdependent with or provides services to the entire jurisdiction

Scoring. The matrix is completed for each individual asset. Once each element has been rated, the score is totaled. When all of the assets have been evaluated, they can be prioritized based on their total score. Maximum possible score is 16.

Score of	Importance	Meaning
10–16	High	Highly desirable target
5–9	Medium	Desirable target
1–4	Low	Not likely to be targeted

Exercise: Inventorying and Prioritizing Target Attractiveness—Public Sector Assets. Let's consider Anytown, USA. In this exercise, the critical infrastructure will be identified and prioritized. It is not important at this point to define what type of attack is perpetrated, how it might be executed, or whether or not it is likely to be successful. The purpose of completing the prioritization matrix is to determine the relative importance of the various potential targets in a jurisdiction. The matrix should be completed using the worst case scenario—that is, the maximum potential loss in the event of an attack.

Anytown, USA has a population of 25,000 people and is located in a suburban area of the state. A preliminary survey of Anytown reveals there are several pieces of critical infrastructure within the jurisdiction including:

- An elementary school with 1000 students plus a staff of 50, which accepts students from Anytown as well as the adjacent Mytown.
- A 35 member volunteer fire department, which provides fire protection for both Anytown and Mytown.
- A regional medical center with 250 beds and a staff of 200.
- A power generation plant with 50 employees that supplies electricity to all of Anytown.
- A Town Hall building, which employs 50 people and services approximately 10 citizens at any given time during the day.

For this exercise, the matrix would be completed as follows, using the worst case scenario.

- Assume the elementary school was attacked during a school day, and the building is a total loss after a terrorist attack. The total exposed population is 1050 people (1000 students, 50 staff) (4 points); replacement cost to rebuild the school would be $15,000,000 (4 points); the school would be closed and therefore unable to provide services for at least one year (3 points); and the school is a standalone facility not supporting any other critical infrastructure but provides services to the entire jurisdiction (4 points). The total score is therefore 15.
- Assume the volunteer fire station is not normally occupied, and the building, apparatus, and equipment housed therein are a total loss after a terrorist attack The total exposed population is zero since the building is normally empty (0 points); replacement cost for the fire station and equipment would cost $2,000,000 (3 points); services would be interrupted for less than one month until replacement apparatus and equipment were obtained (1 point); and the fire station provides services for two jurisdictions (4 points). The total score is therefore 8.
- Assume the medical center is being utilized at full capacity, being occupied by 250 patients and a staff of 80 on any given shift. The total exposed population is 280 (3 points); the large building is partially damaged and can be repaired for $5,000,000 (3 points); the ability to provide full services would be interrupted for three months until the damaged sections of the building were repaired (2 points); and the hospital provides medical services to the region (4 points). The total score is therefore 12 points.
- Assume the power generation plant operates with 15 employees per shift. The attack occurs at shift change, so a total of 30 employees are exposed (1 point). The plant is damaged in the attack, with repair costs estimated at $1,000,000 (2 points); and the plant provides electricity to all of Anytown (4 points). The total score is therefore 9 points.
- Assume the Town Hall building is attacked during business hours and is occupied by 50 employees and ten citizens. The total exposed population is 60 people (2 points). The building is partially damaged in the attack, with repair costs estimated at $200,000 (1 point); the ability to provide services would be interrupted for a short period of time to allow for debris cleanup and minor repairs (0 points); and the facility provides services to all of Anytown (4 points). The total score is therefore 7 points.

Based on the total scores for each individual facility, their importance to the jurisdiction can be prioritized in the following order.

1. Elementary school (15 points).
2. Medical center (12 points).

TABLE 2.4. Public Sector Critical Infrastructure Target Attractiveness Prioritization Matrix

Facility	Occupancy	Economic Impact	Business or Service Interruption	Interdependencies	Total
Elementary school	4	4	3	4	**15**
Fire station	0	3	1	4	**8**
Medical center	3	3	2	4	**12**
Power generation plant	1	2	2	4	**9**
Town Hall	2	1	0	4	**7**

3. Power generation plant (9 points).
4. Fire station (8 points).
5. Town Hall building (7 points).

These results provide the relative importance of each facility and would provide the order in which each facility was more fully analyzed to assess its security vulnerabilities and develop appropriate security enhancements to provide additional levels of protection.

Table 2.4 shows the completed target attractiveness prioritization matrix for this exercise.

Scenario: Attack on a Critical Infrastructure—Public Sector. A severe heat wave began in Europe in June 2003 and continued through mid-August. The month of August 2003 was a deadly month for the citizens of Europe, particularly France. There were record high temperatures across Europe, causing many heat-related deaths. Temperatures rose to a high of 104 °F across the continent. Power plants struggled to maintain sufficient levels of electricity.

In contrast to the United States, the overwhelming majority of homes and workplaces in Europe do not have any sort of air conditioning to counter the heat. Many people, particularly the elderly, were adversely affected by the heat. Over 35,000 heat-related fatalities were recorded in Europe, with almost 15,000 of those occurring in France. Physicians cited heat stroke and dehydration as the main causes of death.

Now, let's take that same scenario and manipulate the facts somewhat to turn the event into a terrorist attack. Assume it is August in the U.S. Gulf Coast region, where the temperatures in July and August approach 100 °F. The relative humidity is often very high, typically 70–80% in that time frame.

Let's assume that terrorists launch an attack against the electrical power sector. They launch simultaneous attacks against a number of key power plants, knocking them out of service for several months. They are also successful in destroying power distribution towers. The result is that electric power will be out for a period of six weeks. Although power can be rerouted to the affected area through the power grid, and portable generators brought in, electricity will be scarce and allocated only to the most critical infrastructures. Even with these temporary accommodations, frequent and long-lasting power outages will continue until the damaged equipment is brought on line.

The results of this attack from a casualty standpoint would be very similar to what occurred in Europe in 2003. With very high temperatures and very high humidity, the heat index would also be very high and, in fact, dangerous. Thousands of people, particularly the elderly, would succumb to heat-related illnesses.

As terrible as the human toll would be in this scenario, the damage does not stop there. Almost all other critical infrastructure sectors are interdependent on the electrical power sector. There would be a massive cascading effect as other infrastructure sectors were adversely impacted by the loss of electrical power. Many facilities would be shut down due to lack of power. Those essential critical infrastructures, such as hospitals, would have services severely curtailed due to the limited power supplied by alternate routes (such as generators) and routine, long-duration power outages. The financial loss would be staggering—not just the direct costs to repair the electric infrastructure damaged in the initial attack—but the indirect costs associated with the loss of lives and products and services degraded due to the loss of electric power.

Critical Infrastructure/Key Resource/Key Asset/Soft Target Attractiveness Matrix: Private Sector

The following is an example of an inventory and prioritization methodology.

Private sector critical infrastructures not only provide essential services and products but also contribute to the economy. Therefore an additional element has been added to the matrix. The "economic impact" element has been split into two categories—one to measure the repair or replacement costs of the asset if it were to be damaged or destroyed in an attack, and one to measure the effect the loss of the asset would have on the economy of both public and private jurisdictions.

The inventorying and evaluation of assets is best accomplished using a multidisciplinary team. For the evaluation of private sector assets, the team should include representatives from the local law enforcement and emergency response organizations, as well as experts from the various departments of the asset, such as operations, maintenance, and information technology.

Occupants Exposed. How many people would be present at the asset at the time of maximum occupancy?

Score	Criteria
0	Asset is not normally occupied
1	Normal occupancy of 1–50 people
2	Normal occupancy of 51–250 people
3	Normal occupancy of 251–1000 people
4	Normal occupancy of 1001 and more people

Economic Impact: Repair/Replacement. If the asset were attacked, what would the direct financial consequences be to repair or replace the physical asset and the associated equipment housed in the asset?

Score	Criteria
0	No significant economic effect is likely
1	Repair or replacement cost is less than $250,000
2	Repair or replacement cost is greater than $250,000 but less than $1,000,000
3	Repair or replacement cost is greater than $1,000,000 but less than $10,000,000
4	Repair or replacement cost is greater than $10,000,000

Economic Impact: Contribution to the Economy. If the asset were attacked, what effect would the attack have on the asset's contribution to the economy?

Score	Criteria
0	No significant economic effect likely
1	Impact on the individual asset's profitability of greater than 10%
2	Impact on the corporation's profitability greater than 10%
3	Impact on the state economy
4	Impact on the national economy

Business or Service Interruption. If the asset were successfully attacked, for what period of time would the asset be unable to provide its product or service?

Score	Criteria
0	Asset could start up or resume service with minimal procedural changes or repairs
1	Asset can provide partial services or product
2	Asset is shut down or unable to provide services for less than six months

Score	Criteria
3	Asset is shut down or unable to provide services more than six months
4	Asset is not expected to be rebuilt or services will not be provided in the future

Interdependencies. If the asset were successfully attacked, would there be an adverse effect on other self-contained assets or other assets that are interdependent?

Score	Criteria
0	No effect on the asset's normal operations or its ability to provide services
1	Asset is a standalone facility and is not interdependent with other assets; adverse effects would be limited to this asset only
2	Asset is a part of and interdependent with a larger system; however, adverse effects would not extend beyond this single asset
3	Asset is interdependent with or provides services to at least one other facility on site
4	Asset is interdependent with or provides services to external facilities

Scoring. The matrix is completed for each individual asset. Once each element has been rated, the score is totaled. When all of the assets have been evaluated, they can be prioritized based on their total score. Maximum possible score is 20.

Score of	Importance	Meaning
13–20	High	Highly desirable target
5–12	Medium	Desirable target
1–4	Low	Not likely to be targeted

Exercise: Inventorying and Prioritizing Target Attractiveness—Private Sector Assets. For this exercise, we will consider the Acme Manufacturing Company. In this exercise, the critical infrastructure and key assets will be identified and prioritized. It is not important at this point to define what type of attack is perpetrated, how it might be executed, or whether or not it is likely to be successful. The purpose of completing the prioritization matrix is to determine the relative importance of the various potential targets within a private sector jurisdiction. The matrix should be completed using the worst case scenario—that is, the maximum potential loss in the event of an attack.

This plant, located in Yourtown, USA, is the sole domestic manufacturer of widgets, which is a critical component in aircraft jet engines for both civilian and military aircraft. The Yourtown plant is one of three facilities owned by the Acme Manufacturing Company and accounts for 70% of the corporation's profits.

The Yourtown plant is considered a piece of critical infrastructure by the municipality. The manufacturing plant is a self-contained campus with several buildings located on 25 acres of land. The plant runs 24 hours per day, 7 days per week. The key assets at the Yourtown manufacturing plant include:

- A manufacturing building with 110 employees per shift.
- A quality control laboratory with eight employees per shift.
- A raw material warehouse with three employees per shift.
- A finished product warehouse with ten employees per shift.
- A boiler house with one employee per shift.
- An office building with 25 employees on day shift only.

For this exercise, the key assets that make up the critical manufacturing infrastructure are identified. The matrix would be completed as follows, using the worst case scenario.

- Assume the manufacturing building was attacked by terrorists and is a total loss. The total exposed population is 110 employees (2 points); the replacement cost of the building is $8 million (3 points); the loss of the building will impact the national economy as no jet engines can be repaired or manufactured without Acme's widget (4 points); services would be interrupted for at least one year (3 points); and the plant provides products supplied to other manufacturers (4 points). The total score is therefore 16.
- Assume the quality control laboratory is attacked by terrorists and the building is a total loss. The total exposed population is eight employees (1 point); the replacement cost of the lab building is $900,000 (2 points); there is no significant economic impact as a temporary lab can be set up relatively quickly (1 point); services would be interrupted for less than one month until replacement personnel and equipment are obtained (1 point); and the lab provides quality control services to the manufacturing building on site (3 points). The total score is therefore 8.
- Assume the raw material warehouse is attacked and destroyed. The total exposed population is eight employees (1 point); the loss of the building and inventory is valued at $20 million (4 points); the loss of the building and inventory will impact the plant's profitability 20% (2 points); replacement personnel could be hired quickly and a nearby offsite warehouse can be rented immediately to store raw materials (1 point); and the warehouse provides services to the manufacturing building (3 points). The total score is therefore 11.
- Assume the boiler house is attacked and damaged. The total exposed population is one employee (1 point); the repair costs will be $500,000 (2 points); there will be no significant economic impact to the company (0 points); the services can be provided after minor repairs (0 points); and the boiler house provides its products to other facilities onsite (3 points). The total score is therefore 6 points.

- Assume the finished product warehouse is attacked and destroyed. The total exposed population is ten employees (1 point); the replacement cost for the building and the inventory is $25 million (4 points); the loss of the building and the finished products it contained impacts the plant's profitability by 35% (2 points); a nearby offsite warehouse can be rented immediately to store finished product (1 point); and the warehouse provides services to the manufacturing building (3 points). The total score is therefore 11.
- Assume the office building is attacked and is slightly damaged at 2 am in the morning. The total exposed population is zero employees (0 points); the damage to the building can be repaired for less than $250,000 (1 point); the damage to the building will have no significant economic mpact (0 points); the attack has degraded the ability of the office to provide its services while undergoing repair (1 point) and the office provides services to the entire as (3 points). The total score is therefore 5.

Based on the total scores for each individual asset, their relative importance to the operation of the overall facility can be prioritized in the following order:

1. Manufacturing building (16 points).
2. Finished product warehouse (11 points).
3. Raw material warehouse (11 points).
4. Quality control laboratory (8 points).
5. Boiler house (6 points).
6. Office building (5 points).

These results provide the relative importance of each key asset that makes up the overall critical infrastructure and would provide the order in which each asset was more fully analyzed to assess its security vulnerabilities and develop appropriate security enhancements to provide additional levels of protection.

Table 2.5 shows the completed target attractiveness prioritization matrix for this exercise.

Case Study: Critical Infrastructure—Agriculture Sector. A Wisconsin man, Brian W. Lea, was convicted of product tampering in 2000. Mr. Lea was the owner of a rival milk ranch, dead livestock removal company, and animal food processing plant. The local police department received a tip that Lea twice contaminated liquid fat (tallow) intended as an ingredient in animal feed processed by National By-Products Incorporated, a major custom feed manufacturer, and a supplier to a Purina Mills animal feed plant. The tallow had been deliberately contaminated with the organochlorine pesticide Chlordane, which is used to kill termites, accumulates in fat, and is linked to cancer in humans. Based on the tip, Purina feed was tested and found to contain low levels of contamination; National By Products stopped a shipment of 300 tons of feed bound for four Midwest states. Within two days, all major customers were notified and the feed was replaced. Livestock at

TABLE 2.5. Private Sector Key Asset Prioritization Matrix

Facility	Critical Infrastructure/Key Asset/Soft Target	Occupancy	Economic Impact	Business or Service Interruption	Interdependencies	Total
Manufacturing building	Key asset	2	4	3	3	**12**
Finished product warehouse	Key asset	1	2	1	3	**7**
Raw material warehouse	Key asset	1	2	1	3	**7**
Quality control laboratory	Key asset	1	1	1	3	**6**
Office building	Key asset	0	1	1	3	**5**

the affected farms were tested, and luckily milk samples taken from some of the dairy herds that had eaten the affected feed were negative or contained levels well below those that pose a human health hazard. The contamination forced the company to recall product from 4000 dairy farms and to destroy 4000 tons of contaminated feed and 500,000 pounds of contaminated tallow, causing losses in excess of $4 million.

Exercise: Inventorying and Prioritizing Target Attractiveness—Soft Targets. Soft targets can be inventoried and prioritized for target attractiveness using either the public or private sector matrix.

For this exercise, we will visit Theirtown, USA. In this exercise, the soft targets will be identified and prioritized. It is not important at this point to define what type of attack is perpetrated, how it might be executed, or whether or not it is likely to be successful. The purpose of completing the prioritization matrix is to determine the relative importance of the various potential targets within a jurisdiction. The matrix should be completed using the worst case scenario—that is, the maximum potential loss in the event of an attack.

Theirtown, USA is a suburb of a major metropolis and has a population of 60,000 people. A preliminary survey of Theirtown reveals that there are several soft targets within the jurisdiction including:

- A large chain restaurant that has a typical occupancy of 100 customers and a staff of 15.
- A small shopping center with 75 employees that is visited by 500 people daily.
- A public library with an average occupancy of two staff and ten patrons.
- A regional bus service that maintains an average usage of 22 people and one driver per bus.

For this exercise, the matrix would be completed as follows, using the worst case scenario.

- Assume the restaurant was attacked by terrorists during a mealtime, and the building is a total loss. The total exposed population is 115 people (100 customers and 15 staff) (2 points); replacement cost to rebuild the restaurant would be $750,000 (2 points); the restaurant would be closed and therefore affect the facility's profitability (2 points); due to the stigma of the attack and the large number of casualties, the restaurant will not be rebuilt (4 points); and the restaurant is not interdependent with other critical infrastructure (1 point). The total score is therefore 11.
- Assume the shopping center is attacked on a busy Saturday night, with 500 patrons and 75 employees present at the time of the attack. Portions of the building and its contents are heavily damaged. The total exposed population is 575 people (3 points); the loss from the building damage and stock is $9,000,000 (3 points); profitability of the stores would be impacted more than 10%

(2 points); the shopping center would be closed for almost a year while undergoing repair (3 points); and the shopping center has embedded support systems and utilities that are shared by all of the individual stores in the mall (3 points). The total score is therefore 14.

- Assume the public library is attacked during exam week at the local high school. There are ten students and two staff in the library. The total exposed population is 12 (1 point); the cost to repair the minor damage to the building is $100,000 (1 point); there would be no significant economic effect based on the attack (0 points); the library could be reopened after some minor cleanup and repairs (0 points); and the library is not interdependent with any other assets (1 point). The total score is therefore 3.
- Assume a bus is attacked during the morning rush hour. A total of 23 people are exposed (1 point); the bus is destroyed in the attack at a loss of $200,000 (1 point); there would be no significant economic impact to the bus company from the loss of the single bus (0 points); it would take less than six months to rent or purchase a replacement bus (2 points); and the bus is not interdependent with any other assets (1 point). The total score is therefore 5.

Based on the total scores for each individual soft target, their relative attractiveness as a target can be prioritized in the following order:

1. Shopping center (14 points).
2. Restaurant (11 points).
3. Bus (5 points).
4. Public library (3 points).

These results provide a relative indicator as to how an adversary may perceive the attractiveness in attacking a particular soft target. This data provides the order in which each soft target should be more fully analyzed to assess its security vulnerabilities and develop appropriate security enhancements to provide additional levels of protection.

Table 2.6 shows the completed target attractiveness prioritization matrix for this exercise.

Case Study: Soft Target—Grocery Store. On December 31, 2002, a disgruntled supermarket employee in Byron Center, Michigan poisoned more than 100 people after mixing Black Leaf 40 (nicotine sulfate) insecticide into approximately 250 pounds of ground beef, then wrapping the meat for sale in packages of 1–3 pounds. Health officials stated that 111 people, including 40 children and a pregnant woman, were sickened after eating the tainted meat. No one died and none of the victims apparently suffered long-term health effects. The oil-like insecticide mixed into the meat uses high concentrations of the toxic substance. Tests indicated that a one-quarter pound burger made from the poisoned ground beef contained a potentially lethal amount of nicotine. The employee poisoned the beef

TABLE 2.6. Soft Target Prioritization Matrix

Facility	Critical Infrastructure/Key Asset/Soft Target	Occupancy	Replacement	Economic Impact	Business Interruption	Interdependencies	Total
Shopping center	Soft target	3	3	2	3	3	**14**
Restaurant	Soft target	2	2	2	4	1	**11**
Regional bus	Soft target	1	1	0	2	1	**5**
Public library	Soft target	1	1	0	0	1	**3**

because of a dispute with a former supervisor, and the employee said he did it in an effort to get his boss in trouble.

REFERENCES

1. U.S. Congressional Budget Office, *Public Works Infrastructure: Policy Considerations for the 1980s*, April 1983, page 1.
2. U.S. Congressional Budget Office, *New Directions for the Nation's Public Works*, September 1988, pages xi–xii.
3. Public Law 98-501 Section 203.
4. National Council on Public Works Improvement, *Fragile Foundations: A Report on America's Public Works*, Final Report to the President and Congress, February 1988, page 33.
5. Executive Order 13010, "Critical Infrastructure Protection," *Federal Register*, July 17, 1996, Volume 61, Number 138, page 37347.
6. *Defending America's Cyberspace: National Plan for Information System Protection*, Version 1.0, page 1.
7. *National Strategy for Homeland Security*, July 16, 2002.
8. HSPD 7, December 17, 2003, President George W. Bush, The White House, Washington, DC.
9. United States. Food and Drug Administration.
10. "Covert Biological Weapons Attack Against Agricultural Targets: Assessing the Impact Against U.S. Agriculture," Jason Pate and Gavin Cameron, August 2001, page 19.
11. www.csoonline.com/read/080105/range_bioterror_3765.html.
12. www.fb.org/news/fbn/html/agriculturalterrorism.html.
13. *Time Magazine*, "Why America is Still an Easy Target," Stephen Flynn, July 26, 2004.

APPENDIX 2.1 EXECUTIVE ORDER 13010 BY PRESIDENT WILLIAM J. CLINTON

Executive Order 13010 of July 15, 1996 Critical Infrastructure Protection

Certain national infrastructures are so vital that their incapacity or destruction would have a debilitating impact on the defense or economic security of the United States. These critical infrastructures include telecommunications, electrical power systems, gas and oil storage and transportation, banking and finance, transportation, water supply systems, emergency services (including medical, police, fire, and rescue), and continuity of government. Threats to these critical infrastructures fall into two categories: physical threats to tangible property ("physical threats"), and threats of electronic, radio-frequency, or computer-based attacks on the information or communications components that control critical infrastructures ("cyber threats"). Because many of these critical infrastructures are owned and operated by the private sector, it is essential that the government and private sector work together to develop a strategy for protecting them and assuring their continued operation.

By the authority vested in me as President by the Constitution and the laws of the United States of America, it is hereby ordered as follows:

Sec. 1. *Establishment.* There is hereby established the President's Commission on Critical Infrastructure Protection ("Commission").

(a) *Chair.* A qualified individual from outside the Federal Government shall be appointed by the President to serve as Chair of the Commission. The Commission Chair shall be employed on a full-time basis.

(b) *Members.* The head of each of the following executive branch departments and agencies shall nominate not more than two full-time members of the Commission:

(i) Department of the Treasury;
(ii) Department of Justice;
(iii) Department of Defense;
(iv) Department of Commerce;
(v) Department of Transportation;
(vi) Department of Energy;
(vii) Central Intelligence Agency;
(viii) Federal Emergency Management Agency;
(ix) Federal Bureau of Investigation;
(x) National Security Agency.

One of the nominees of each agency may be an individual from outside the Federal Government who shall be employed by the agency on a full-time basis. Each nominee must be approved by the Steering Committee.

Sec. 2. *The Principals Committee.* The Commission shall report to the President through a Principals Committee ("Principals Committee"), which shall review any reports or recommendations before submission to the President. The Principals Committee shall comprise the:

(i) Secretary of the Treasury;
(ii) Secretary of Defense;

(iii) Attorney General;
(iv) Secretary of Commerce;
(v) Secretary of Transportation;
(vi) Secretary of Energy;
(vii) Director of Central Intelligence;
(viii) Director of the Office of Management and Budget;
(ix) Director of the Federal Emergency Management Agency;
(x) Assistant to the President for National Security Affairs;
(xi) Assistant to the Vice President for National Security Affairs.

Sec. 3. *The Steering Committee of the President's Commission on Critical Infrastructure Protection.* A Steering Committee ("Steering Committee") shall oversee the work of the Commission on behalf of the Principals Committee. The Steering Committee shall comprise four members appointed by the President. One of the members shall be the Chair of the Commission and one shall be an employee of the Executive Office of the President. The Steering Committee will receive regular reports on the progress of the Commission's work and approve the submission of reports to the Principals Committee.

Sec. 4. *Mission.* The Commission shall:

(a) within 30 days of this order, produce a statement of its mission objectives, which will elaborate the general objectives set forth in this order, and a detailed schedule for addressing each mission objective, for approval by the Steering Committee;

(b) identify and consult with: (i) elements of the public and private sectors that conduct, support, or contribute to infrastructure assurance; (ii) owners and operators of the critical infrastructures; and (iii) other elements of the public and private sectors, including the Congress, that have an interest in critical infrastructure assurance issues and that may have differing perspectives on these issues;

(c) assess the scope and nature of the vulnerabilities of, and threats to, critical infrastructures;

(d) determine what legal and policy issues are raised by efforts to protect critical infrastructures and assess how these issues should be addressed;

(e) recommend a comprehensive national policy and implementation strategy for protecting critical infrastructures from physical and cyber threats and assuring their continued operation;

(f) propose any statutory or regulatory changes necessary to effect its recommendations; and

(g) produce reports and recommendations to the Steering Committee as they become available; it shall not limit itself to producing one final report.

Sec. 5. *Advisory Committee to the President's Commission on Critical Infrastructure Protection.*

(a) The Commission shall receive advice from an advisory committee ("Advisory Committee") composed of no more than ten individuals appointed by the President from the private sector who are knowledgeable about critical infrastructures. The Advisory Committee shall advise the Commission on the subjects of the

Commission's mission in whatever manner the Advisory Committee, the Commission Chair, and the Steering Committee deem appropriate.

(b) A Chair shall be designated by the President from among the members of the Advisory Committee.

(c) The Advisory Committee shall be established in compliance with the Federal Advisory Committee Act, as amended (5 U.S.C. App.). The Department of Defense shall perform the functions of the President under the Federal Advisory Committee Act for the Advisory Committee, except that of reporting to the Congress, in accordance with the guidelines and procedures established by the Administrator of General Services.

Sec. 6. *Administration.*

(a) All executive departments and agencies shall cooperate with the Commission and provide such assistance, information, and advice to the Commission as it may request, to the extent permitted by law.

(b) The Commission and the Advisory Committee may hold open and closed hearings, conduct inquiries, and establish subcommittees, as necessary.

(c) Members of the Advisory Committee shall serve without compensation for their work on the Advisory Committee. While engaged in the work of the Advisory Committee, members may be allowed travel expenses, including per diem in lieu of subsistence, as authorized by law for persons serving intermittently in the government service.

(d) To the extent permitted by law, and subject to the availability of appropriations, the Department of Defense shall provide the Commission and the Advisory Committee with administrative services, staff, other support services, and such funds as may be necessary for the performance of its functions and shall reimburse the executive branch components that provide representatives to the Commission for the compensation of those representatives.

(e) In order to augment the expertise of the Commission, the Department of Defense may, at the Commission's request, contract for the services of nongovernmental consultants who may prepare analyses, reports, background papers, and other materials for consideration by the Commission. In addition, at the Commission's request, executive departments and agencies shall request that existing Federal advisory committees consider and provide advice on issues of critical infrastructure protection, to the extent permitted by law.

(f) The Commission, the Principals Committee, the Steering Committee, and the Advisory Committee shall terminate 1 year from the date of this order, unless extended by the President prior to that date.

Sec. 7. *Interim Coordinating Mission.*

(a) While the Commission is conducting its analysis and until the President has an opportunity to consider and act on its recommendations, there is a need to increase coordination of existing infrastructure protection efforts in order to better address, and prevent, crises that would have a debilitating regional or national impact. There is hereby established an Infrastructure Protection Task Force ("IPTF") within the Department of Justice, chaired by the Federal Bureau of Investigation, to undertake this interim coordinating mission.

(b) The IPTF will not supplant any existing programs or organizations.

(c) The Steering Committee shall oversee the work of the IPTF.

(d) The IPTF shall include at least one full-time member each from the Federal Bureau of Investigation, the Department of Defense, and the National Security Agency. It shall also receive part-time assistance from other executive branch departments and agencies. Members shall be designated by their departments or agencies on the basis of their expertise in the protection of critical infrastructures. IPTF members' compensation shall be paid by their parent agency or department.

(e) The IPTF's function is to identify and coordinate existing expertise, inside and outside of the Federal Government, to:

 (i) provide, or facilitate and coordinate the provision of, expert guidance to critical infrastructures to detect, prevent, halt, or confine an attack and to recover and restore service;
 (ii) issue threat and warning notices in the event advance information is obtained about a threat;
 (iii) provide training and education on methods of reducing vulnerabilities and responding to attacks on critical infrastructures;
 (iv) conduct after-action analysis to determine possible future threats, targets, or methods of attack; and
 (v) coordinate with the pertinent law enforcement authorities during or after an attack to facilitate any resulting criminal investigation.

(f) All executive departments and agencies shall cooperate with the IPTF and provide such assistance, information, and advice as the IPTF may request, to the extent permitted by law.

(g) All executive departments and agencies shall share with the IPTF information about threats and warning of attacks, and about actual attacks on critical infrastructures, to the extent permitted by law.

(h) The IPTF shall terminate no later than 180 days after the termination of the Commission, unless extended by the President prior to that date. Sec. 8. General. (a) This order is not intended to change any existing statutes or Executive orders.

(i) This order is not intended to create any right, benefit, trust, or responsibility, substantive or procedural, enforceable at law or equity by a party against the United States, its agencies, its officers, or any person.

APPENDIX 2.2 PRESIDENTIAL DECISION DIRECTIVE 63 BY PRESIDENT WILLIAM J. CLINTON

PRESIDENTIAL DECISION DIRECTIVE/NSC-63

MEMORANDUM FOR THE VICE PRESIDENT
THE SECRETARY OF STATE
THE SECRETARY OF THE TREASURY
THE SECRETARY OF DEFENSE
THE ATTORNEY GENERAL
THE SECRETARY OF COMMERCE
THE SECRETARY OF HEALTH AND HUMAN SERVICES
THE SECRETARY OF TRANSPORTATION
THE SECRETARY OF ENERGY
THE SECRETARY OF VETERANS AFFAIRS
ADMINISTRATOR, ENVIRONMENTAL PROTECTION AGENCY
THE DIRECTOR, OFFICE OF MANAGEMENT AND BUDGET
THE DIRECTOR OF CENTRAL INTELLIGENCE
THE DIRECTOR, FEDERAL EMERGENCY MANAGEMENT AGENCY
THE ASSIST TO THE PRESIDENT FOR NATIONAL SECURITY AFFAIRS
THE ASSISTANT TO PRESIDENT FOR SCIENCE AND TECHNOLOGY
THE CHAIRMAN, JOINT CHIEFS OF STAFF
THE DIRECTOR, FEDERAL BUREAU OF INVESTIGATION
THE DIRECTOR, NATIONAL SECURITY AGENCY

SUBJECT: Critical Infrastructure Protection

I. *A Growing Potential Vulnerability*

The United States possesses both the world's strongest military and its largest national economy. Those two aspects of our power are mutually reinforcing and dependent. They are also increasingly reliant upon certain critical infrastructures and upon cyber-based information systems.

Critical infrastructures are those physical and cyber-based systems essential to the minimum operations of the economy and government. They include, but are not limited to, telecommunications, energy, banking and finance, transportation, water systems and emergency services, both governmental and private. Many of the nation's critical infrastructures have historically been physically and logically separate systems that had little interdependence. As a result of advances in information technology and the necessity of improved efficiency, however, these infrastructures have become increasingly automated and interlinked. These same advances have created new vulnerabilities to equipment failure, human error, weather and other natural causes, and physical and cyber attacks. Addressing these vulnerabilities will necessarily require flexible, evolutionary approaches that span both the public and private sectors, and protect both domestic and international security.

Because of our military strength, future enemies, whether nations, groups or individuals, may seek to harm us in non-traditional ways including attacks within the United States. Because our economy is increasingly reliant upon interdependent and cyber-supported infrastructures, non-traditional attacks on our infrastructure and information systems may be capable of significantly harming both our military power and our economy.

II. *President's Intent*

It has long been the policy of the United States to assure the continuity and viability of critical infrastructures. I intend that the United States will take all necessary measures to swiftly eliminate any significant vulnerability to both physical and cyber attacks on our critical infrastructures, including especially our cyber systems.

III. *A National Goal*

No later than the year 2000, the United States shall have achieved an initial operating capability and no later than five years from today the United States shall have achieved and shall maintain the ability to protect the nation's critical infrastructures from intentional acts that would significantly diminish the abilities of:

- the Federal Government to perform essential national security missions and to ensure the general public health and safety;
- state and local governments to maintain order and to deliver minimum essential public services.
- the private sector to ensure the orderly functioning of the economy and the delivery of essential telecommunications, energy, financial and transportation services.

Any interruptions or manipulations of these critical functions must be brief, infrequent, manageable, geographically isolated and minimally detrimental to the welfare of the United States.

IV. *A Public-Private Partnership to Reduce Vulnerability*

Since the targets of attacks on our critical infrastructure would likely include both facilities in the economy and those in the government, the elimination of our potential vulnerability requires a closely coordinated effort of both the government and the private sector. To succeed, this partnership must be genuine, mutual and cooperative. In seeking to meet our national goal to eliminate the vulnerabilities of our critical infrastructure, therefore, we should, to the extent feasible, seek to avoid outcomes that increase government regulation or expand unfunded government mandates to the private sector.

For each of the major sectors of our economy that are vulnerable to infrastructure attack, the Federal Government will appoint from a designated Lead Agency a senior officer of that agency as the Sector Liaison Official to work with the private sector. Sector Liaison Officials, after discussions and coordination with private sector entities of their infrastructure sector, will identify a private sector or counterpart (Sector Coordinator) to represent their sector.

Together these two individuals and the departments and corporations they represent shall contribute to a sectoral National Infrastructure Assurance Plan by:

- assessing the vulnerabilities of the sector to cyber or physical attacks;
- recommending a plan to eliminate significant vulnerabilities;
- proposing a system for identifying and preventing attempted major attacks;
- developing a plan for alerting, containing and rebuffing an attack in progress and then, in coordination with FEMA as appropriate, rapidly reconstituting minimum essential capabilities in the aftermath of an attack.

During the preparation of the sectoral plans, the National Coordinator (see section VI), in conjunction with the Lead Agency Sector Liaison Officials and a representative from the National Economic Council, shall ensure their overall coordination and the integration of the various sectoral plans, with a particular focus on interdependencies.

V. *Guidelines*

In addressing this potential vulnerability and the means of eliminating it, I want those involved to be mindful of the following general principles and concerns.

- We shall consult with, and seek input from, the Congress on approaches and programs to meet the objectives set forth in this directive.
- The protection of our critical infrastructures is necessarily a shared responsibility and partnership between owners, operators and the government. Furthermore, the Federal Government shall encourage international cooperation to help manage this increasingly global problem.
- Frequent assessments shall be made of our critical infrastructures' existing reliability, vulnerability and threat environment because, as technology and the nature of the threats to our critical infrastructures will continue to change rapidly, so must our protective measures and responses be robustly adaptive.
- The incentives that the market provides are the first choice for addressing the problem of critical infrastructure protection; regulation will be used only in the face of a material failure of the market to protect the health, safety or well-being of the American people. In such cases, agencies shall identify and assess available alternatives to direct regulation, including providing economic incentives to encourage the desired behavior, providing information upon which choices can be made by the private sector. These incentives, along with other action, shall be designed to help harness the latest technologies, bring about global solutions to international problems, and enable private sector owners and operators to achieve and maintain the maximum feasible security.
- The full authorities, capabilities and resources of the government, including law enforcement, regulation, foreign intelligence and defense preparedness shall be available, as appropriate, to ensure that critical infrastructure protection is achieved and maintained.
- Care must be taken to respect privacy rights. Consumers and operators must have confidence that information will be handled accurately, confidentially and reliably.
- The Federal Government shall, through its research, development and procurement, encourage the introduction of increasingly capable methods of infrastructure protection.

- The Federal Government shall serve as a model to the private sector on how infrastructure assurance is best achieved and shall, to the extent feasible, distribute the results of its endeavors.
- We must focus on preventive measure as well as threat and crisis management. To that end, private sector owners and operators should be encouraged to provide maximum feasible security for the infrastructures they control and to provide the government necessary information to assist them in that task. In order to engage the private sector fully, it is preferred that participation by owners and operators in a national infrastructure protection system be voluntary.
- Close cooperation and coordination with state and local governments and first responders is essential for a robust and flexible infrastructure protection program. All critical infrastructure protection plans and action shall take into consideration the needs, activities and responsibilities of state and local governments and first responders.

VI. *Structure and Organization*

The Federal Government will be organized for the purposes of this endeavor around four components (elaborated in Annex A).

1. *Lead Agencies for Sector Liaison*: For each infrastructure sector that could be a target for significant cyber or physical attack, there will be a single U.S. Government department which will serve as the lead agency for liaison. Secretary rank or higher to be the Sector Liaison Official for that area and to cooperate with the private sector representatives (Sector Coordinators) in addressing problems related to critical infrastructure protection and, in particular, in recommending components of the National Infrastructure Protection Plan. Together, the Lead Agency and the private sector counterparts will develop and implement a Vulnerability Awareness and Education Program for their sector.
2. *Lead Agencies for Special Functions*: There are, in addition, certain functions related to critical infrastructure protection that must be chiefly performed by the Federal Government (national defense, foreign affairs, intelligence, law enforcement). For each of those special functions, there shall be a Lead Agency which will be responsible for coordinating all of the activities of the United States Government in that area. Each lead agency will appoint a senior officer of Assistant Secretary rank or higher to serve as the Functional Coordinator for that function for the Federal Government.
3. *Interagency Coordination*: The Sector Liaison Officials and Functional Coordinators of the Lead Agencies, as well as representatives from other relevant departments and agencies, including the National Economic Council, will meet to coordinate the implementation of this directive under the auspices of a Critical Infrastructure Coordination Group (CICG), chaired by the National Coordinator for Security, Infrastructure Protection and Counter-Terrorism. The National Coordinator will be appointed by me and report to me through the Assistant to the President for National Security Affairs, who shall assure appropriate coordination with the Assistant to the President for Economic Affairs. Agency representatives to the CICG should be at a senior policy level (Assistant Secretary or higher). Where appropriate, the CICG will be assisted by extant policy structures, such as the Security Policy Board, Security Policy Forum and the National Security and Telecommunications and Information System Security Committee.

4. *National Infrastructure Assurance Council*: On the recommendation of the Lead Agencies, the National Economic Council and the National Coordinator, I will appoint a panel of major infrastructure providers and state and local government officials to serve as my National Infrastructure Assurance Council. I will appoint the Chairman. The National Coordinator will serve as the Council's Executive Director. The National Infrastructure Assurance Council will meet periodically to enhance the partnership of the public and private sectors in protecting our critical infrastructures and will provide reports to me as appropriate. Senior Federal Government officials will participate in the meetings of the National Infrastructure Assurance Council as appropriate.

VII. *Protecting Federal Government Critical Infrastructures*

Every department and agency of the Federal Government shall be responsible for protecting its own critical infrastructure, especially its cyber-based systems. Every department and agency Chief Information Officer (CIO) shall be responsible for information assurance. Every department and agency shall appoint a Chief Infrastructure Assurance Officer (CIAO) who shall be responsible for the protection of all of the other aspects of that department's critical infrastructure. The CIO may be double-hatted as the CIAO at the discretion of the individual department. These officials shall establish procedures for obtaining expedient and valid authorities to allow vulnerability assessments to be performed on government computer and physical systems. The Department of Justice shall establish legal guidelines for providing for such authorities.

No later than 180 days from the issuance of this directive, every department and agency shall develop a plan for protecting its own critical infrastructure, including but not limited to its cyber-based systems. The National Coordinator shall be responsible for coordinating analyses required by the departments and agencies of inter-governmental dependencies and the mitigation of those dependencies. The Critical infrastructure Coordination Group (CICG) shall sponsor an expert review process for those plans. No later than two years from today, those plans shall have been implemented and shall be updated every two years. In meeting this schedule, the Federal Government shall present a model to the private sector on how best to protect critical infrastructure.

VIII. *Tasks*

Within 180 days, the Principals Committee should submit to me a schedule for completion of a National Infrastructure Assurance Plan with milestones for accomplishing the following subordinate and related tasks.

1. *Vulnerability Analyses.* For each sector of the economy and each sector of the government that might be a target of infrastructure attack intended to significantly damage the United States, there shall be an initial vulnerability assessment, followed by periodic updates. As appropriate, these assessments shall also include the determination of the minimum essential infrastructure in each sector.
2. *Remedial Plan.* Based upon the vulnerability assessment, there shall be a recommended remedial plan. The plan shall identify timelines, for implementation, responsibilities and funding.

3. *Warning.* A national center to warn of significant infrastructure attacks will be established immediately (see Annex A). As soon thereafter as possible, we will put in place an enhanced system for detecting and analyzing such attacks, with maximum possible participation of the private sector.
4. *Response.* We shall develop a system for responding to a significant infrastructure attack while it is underway, with the goal of isolating and minimizing damage.
5. *Reconstitution.* For varying levels of successful infrastructure attacks, we shall have a system to reconstitute minimum required capabilities rapidly.
6. *Education and Awareness.* There shall be Vulnerability Awareness and Education Program within both the government and the private sector to sensitize people regarding the importance of security and to train them in security standards, particularly regarding cyber systems.
7. *Research and Development.* Federally-sponsored research and development in support of infrastructure protection shall be coordinated, be subject to multi-year planning, take into account private sector research, and be adequately funded to minimize our vulnerabilities on a rapid but achievable timetable.
8. *Intelligence.* The Intelligence Community shall develop and implement a plan for enhancing collection and analysis of the foreign threat to our national infrastructure, to include but not be limited to the foreign cyber/information warfare threat.
9. *International Cooperation.* There shall be a plan to expand cooperation on critical infrastructure protection with like-minded and friendly nations, international organizations and multinational corporations.
10. *Legislative and Budgetary Requirements.* There shall be an evaluation of the executive branch's legislative authorities and budgetary priorities regarding critical infrastructure, and ameliorative recommendations shall be made to me as necessary. The evaluations and recommendations, if any, shall be coordinated with the Director of OMB.

The CICG shall also review and schedule the taskings listed in Annex B.

IX. Implementation

In addition to the 180-day report, the National Coordinator, working with the National Economic Council, shall provide an annual report on the implementation of this directive to me and the heads of departments and agencies, through the Assistant to the President for National Security Affairs. The report should include an updated threat assessment, a status report on achieving the milestones identified for the National Plan and additional policy, legislative and budgetary recommendations. The evaluations and recommendations, if any, shall be coordinated with the Director of OMB. In addition, following the establishment of an initial operating capability in the year 2000, the National Coordinator shall conduct a zero-based review.

ANNEX A: STRUCTURE AND ORGANIZATION

Lead Agencies: Clear accountability within the U.S. Government must be designated for specific sectors and functions. The following assignments of responsibility will apply.

Lead Agencies for Sector Liaison:

Commerce	Information and communications
Treasury	Banking and finance
EPA	Water supply
Transportation	Aviation
	Highways (including trucking and intelligent transportation systems)
	Mass transit
	Pipelines
	Rail
	Waterborne commerce
Justice/FBI	Emergency law enforcement services
FEMA	Emergency fire service
	Continuity of government services
HHS	Public health services, including prevention, surveillance, laboratory services and personal health services
Energy	Electric power
	Oil and gas production and storage

Lead Agencies for Special Functions:

Justice/FBI	Law enforcement and internal security
CIA	Foreign intelligence
State	Foreign affairs
Defense	National defense

In addition, OSTP shall be responsible for coordinating research and development agendas and programs for the government through the National Science and Technology Council. Furthermore, while Commerce is the lead agency for information and communication, the Department of Defense will retain its Executive Agent responsibilities for the National Communications System and support of the President's National Security Telecommunications Advisory Committee.

National Coordinator: The National Coordinator for Security, Infrastructure Protection and Counter-Terrorism shall be responsible for coordinating the implementation of this directive. The National Coordinator will report to me through the Assistant to the President for National Security Affairs. The National Coordinator will also participate as a full member of Deputies or Principals Committee meetings when they meet to consider infrastructure issues. Although the National Coordinator will not direct Departments and Agencies, he or she will ensure interagency coordination for policy development and implementation, and will review crisis activities concerning infrastructure events with significant foreign involvement. The National Coordinator will provide advice, in the context of the established annual budget process, regarding agency budgets for critical infrastructure protection. The National Coordinator will chair the Critical Infrastructure Coordination Group (CICG), reporting to the Deputies Committee (or, at the call of its chair, the Principals Committee). The Sector Liaison officials and Special Function Coordinators shall attend the CIGC's meetings. Departments and agencies shall each appoint to the CIGC a senior official (Assistant Secretary level or higher) who will regularly attend its meetings. The National Security Advisor shall appoint a Senior Director for Infrastructure Protection on the NSC staff.

A National Plan Coordination (NPC) staff will be contributed on a non-reimbursable basis by the departments and agencies, consistent with law. The NPC staff will integrate the various sector plans into a National Infrastructure Assurance Plan and coordinate analyses of the U.S. Government's own dependencies on critical infrastructures. The NPC staff will also help coordinate a national education and awareness program, and legislative and public affairs.

The Defense Department shall continue to serve as Executive Agent for the Commission Transition Office, which will form the basis of the NPC, during the remainder of FY98. Beginning in FY99, the NPC shall be an office of the Commerce Department. The office of Personnel Management shall provide the necessary assistance in facilitating the NPC's operations. The NPC will terminate at the end of FY01, unless extended by Presidential directive.

Warning and Information Centers

As part of a national warning and information sharing system, I immediately authorize the FBI to expand its current organization to a full scale *National Infrastructure Protection Center* (NIPC). This organization shall serve as a national critical infrastructure threat assessment, warning, vulnerability, and law enforcement investigation and response entity. During the initial period of six to twelve months, I also direct the National Coordinator and the Sector Liaison Officials, working together with the Sector Coordinators, the Special Function Coordinators and representatives from the National Economic Council, as appropriate, to consult with owners and operators of the critical infrastructures to encourage the creation of a private sector sharing and analysis center, as described below.

National Infrastructure Protection Center (NIPC): The NIPC will include FBI, USSS, and other investigators experienced in computer crimes and infrastructure protection, as well as representatives detailed from the Department of Defense, the Intelligence Community and Lead Agencies. It will be linked electronically to the rest of the Federal Government, including other warning and operations centers, as well as any private sector sharing and analysis centers. Its mission will include providing timely warnings of international threats, comprehensive analyses and law enforcement investigation and response.

All executive departments and agencies shall cooperate with the NIPC and provide such assistance, information and advice that the NIPC may request, to the extent permitted by law. All executive departments shall also share with the NIPC information about threats and warning of attacks and about actual attacks on critical government and private sector infrastructures, to the extent permitted by law. The NIP will include elements responsible for warning, analysis, computer investigation, coordinating emergency response, training, outreach and development and application of technical tools. In addition, it will establish its own relations directly with others in the private sector and with any information sharing and analysis entity that the private sector may create, such as the Information Sharing and Analysis Center described below.

The NIPC, in conjunction with the information originating agency, will sanitize law enforcement and intelligence information for inclusion into analyses and reports that it will provide, in appropriate form, to relevant federal, state and local agencies; the relevant owners and operators of critical infrastructures; and to any private sector information sharing and analysis entity. Before disseminating national security or other information that originated from the intelligence community, the NIPC will coordinate fully with the intelligence community through existing procedures. Whether as sanitized or unsanitized reports, the NIPC will issue attack warnings or alerts to increases in threat condition to any private sector information sharing and analysis entity and to the owners and operators. These warnings may also include guidance regarding additional protection measures to be taken by owners and operators. Except in extreme emergencies, the NIPC shall coordinate with the National Coordinator before issuing public warnings of imminent attacks by international terrorists, foreign states or other malevolent foreign powers.

The NIPC will provide a national focal point for gathering information on threats to the infrastructures. Additionally, the NIPC will provide the principal means of facilitating and coordinating the Federal Government's response to an incident, mitigating attacks, investigating threats and monitoring reconstitution efforts. Depending on the nature and level of a foreign threat/attack, protocols established between special function agencies (DOJ/DOD/CIA), and the ultimate decision of the President, the NIPC may be placed in a direct support role to either DOD or the Intelligence Community.

Information Sharing and Analysis Center (ISAC): The National Coordinator, working with Sector Coordinators, Sector Liaison Officials and the National Economic Council, shall consult with owners and operators of the critical infrastructures to strongly encourage the creation of a private sector information sharing and analysis center. The actual design and functions of the center and its relation to the NIPC will be determined by the private sector, in consultation with and with assistance from the Federal Government. Within 180 days of this directive, the National Coordinator, with the assistance of the CICG including the National Economic Council, shall identify possible methods of providing federal assistance to facilitate the startup of an ISAC.

Such a center could serve as the mechanism for gathering, analyzing, appropriately sanitizing and disseminating private sector information to both industry and the NIPC. The center could also gather, analyze and disseminate information from the NIPC for further distribution to the private sector. While crucial to a successful government-industry partnership, this mechanism for sharing important information about vulnerabilities, threats, intrusions and anomalies is not to interfere with direct information exchanges between companies and the government.

As ultimately designed by private sector representatives, the ISAC may emulate particular aspects of such institutions as the Centers for Disease Control and Prevention that have proved highly effective, particularly it extensive interchanges with the private and non-federal sectors. Under such a model, the ISAC would possess a large degree of technical focus and expertise and non-regulatory and non-law enforcement missions. it would establish baseline statistics and patterns on the various infrastructures, become a clearinghouse for information within and among the various sectors, and provide a library for historical data to be used be the private sector and, as deemed appropriate by the ISAC, by the government. Critical to the success of such an institution would be its timeliness, accessibility, coordination, flexibility, utility and acceptability.

ANNEX B: ADDITIONAL TASKINGS

Studies

The National Coordinator shall commission studies on the following subjects:

- Liability issues arising from participation by private sector companies in the information sharing process.

- Existing legal impediments to information sharing, with an eye to proposals to remove these impediments, including through the drafting of model codes in cooperation with the American Legal Institute.
- The necessity of document and information classification and the impact of such classification on useful dissemination, as well as the methods and information systems by which threat and vulnerability information can be shared securely while avoiding disclosure or unacceptable risk of disclosure to those who will misuse it.
- The improved protection, including secure dissemination and information handling systems, of industry trade secrets and other confidential business data, law enforcement information and evidentiary material, classified national security information, unclassified material disclosing vulnerabilities of privately owned infrastructures and apparently innocuous information that, in the aggregate, it is unwise to disclose.
- The implications of sharing information with foreign entities where such sharing is deemed necessary to the security of United States infrastructures.
- The potential benefit to security standards of mandating, subsidizing, or otherwise assisting in the provision of insurance for selected critical infrastructure providers and requiring insurance tie-ins for foreign critical infrastructure providers hoping to do business with the United States.

Public Outreach

In order to foster a climate of enhanced public sensitivity to the problem of infrastructure protection, the following actions shall be taken:

- The White House, under the oversight of the National Coordinator, together with the relevant Cabinet agencies shall consider a series of conferences: (1) that will bring together national leaders in the public and private sectors to propose programs to increase the commitment to information security; (2) that convoke academic leaders from engineering, computer science, business and law schools to review the status of education in information security and will identify changes in the curricula and resources necessary to meet the national demand for professionals in this field; (3) on the issues around computer ethics as these relate to the K through 12 and general university populations.
- The National Academy of Science and the National Academy of Engineering shall consider a round table bringing together federal, state and local officials with industry and academic leaders to develop national strategies for enhancing infrastructure security.
- The intelligence community and law enforcement shall expand existing programs for briefing infrastructure owners and operators and senior government officials.
- The National Coordinator shall (1) establish a program for infrastructure assurance simulations involving senior public and private officials, the reports of which might be distributed as part of an awareness campaign; and (2) in coordination with the private sector, launch a continuing national awareness campaign, emphasizing improving infrastructure security.

Internal Federal Government Actions

In order for the Federal Government to improve its infrastructure security these immediate steps shall be taken:

- The Department of Commerce, the General Services Administration, and the Department of Defense shall assist federal agencies in the implementation of best practices for information assurance within their individual agencies.
- The National Coordinator shall coordinate a review of existing federal, state and local bodies charged with information assurance tasks, and provide recommendations on how these institutions can cooperate most effectively.
- All federal agencies shall make clear designations regarding who may authorize access to their computer systems.
- The Intelligence Community shall elevate and formalize the priority for enhanced collection and analysis of information on the foreign cyber/information warfare threat to our critical infrastructure.
- The Federal Bureau of Investigation, the Secret Service and other appropriate agencies shall: (1) vigorously recruit undergraduate and graduate students with the relevant computer-related technical skills full-time employment as well as for part-time work with regional computer crime squads; and (2) facilitate the hiring and retention of qualified personnel for technical analysis and investigation involving cyber attacks.
- The Department of Transportation, in consultation with the Department of Defense, shall undertake a thorough evaluation of the vulnerability of the national transportation infrastructure that relies on the Global Positioning System. This evaluation shall include sponsoring an independent, integrated assessment of risks to civilian users of GPS-based systems, with a view to basing decisions on the ultimate architecture of the modernized NAS on these evaluations.
- The Federal Aviation Administration shall develop and implement a comprehensive National Airspace System Security Program to protect the modernized NAS from information-based and other disruptions and attacks.
- GSA shall identify large procurements (such as the new Federal Telecommunications System ETS 2000) related to infrastructure assurance, study whether the procurement process reflects the importance of infrastructure protection and propose, if necessary, revisions to the overall procurement process to do so.
- OMB shall direct federal agencies to include assigned infrastructure assurance functions within their Government Performance and Review Act strategic planning and performance measurement framework.
- The NSA, in accordance with its National Manager responsibilities in NSD 42, shall provide assessments encompassing examinations of U.S. Government systems to interception and exploitation; disseminate threat and vulnerability information; establish standards; conduct research and development; and conduct issue security product evaluations.

Assisting the Private Sector

In order to assist the private sector in achieving and maintaining infrastructure security:

- The National Coordinator and the National Infrastructure Assurance Council shall propose and develop ways to encourage private industry to perform periodic risk assessments of critical processes, including information and telecommunications systems.

- The Department of Commerce and the Department of Defense shall work together, in coordination with the private sector, to offer their expertise to private owners and operators of critical infrastructure to develop security-related best practice standards.
- The Department of Justice and Department of the Treasury shall sponsor a comprehensive study compiling demographics of computer crime, comparing state approaches to computer crime and developing ways to deterring and responding to computer crime by juveniles.

APPENDIX 2.3 EXECUTIVE ORDER 13228 BY PRESIDENT GEORGE W. BUSH

EXECUTIVE ORDER 13228 OF OCTOBER 8, 2001

Establishing the Office of Homeland Security and the Homeland Security Council

By the authority vested in me as President by the Constitution and the laws of the United States of America, it is hereby ordered as follows:

Section 1. *Establishment.* I hereby establish within the Executive Office of the President an Office of Homeland Security (the "Office") to be headed by the Assistant to the President for Homeland Security.

Sec. 2. *Mission.* The mission of the Office shall be to develop and coordinate the implementation of a comprehensive national strategy to secure the United States from terrorist threats or attacks. The Office shall perform the functions necessary to carry out this mission, including the functions specified in section 3 of this order.

Sec. 3. *Functions.* The functions of the Office shall be to coordinate the executive branch's efforts to detect, prepare for, prevent, protect against, respond to, and recover from terrorist attacks within the United States.

(a) *National Strategy.* The Office shall work with executive departments and agencies, State and local governments, and private entities to ensure the adequacy of the national strategy for detecting, preparing for, preventing, protecting against, responding to, and recovering from terrorist threats or attacks within the United States and shall periodically review and coordinate revisions to that strategy as necessary.

(b) *Detection.* The Office shall identify priorities and coordinate efforts for collection and analysis of information within the United States regarding threats of terrorism against the United States and activities of terrorists or terrorist groups within the United States. The Office also shall identify, in coordination with the Assistant to the President for National Security Affairs, priorities for collection of intelligence outside the United States regarding threats of terrorism within the United States.

(i) In performing these functions, the Office shall work with Federal, State, and local agencies, as appropriate, to:

(A) facilitate collection from State and local governments and private entities of information pertaining to terrorist threats or activities within the United States;

(B) coordinate and prioritize the requirements for foreign intelligence relating to terrorism within the United States of executive departments and agencies responsible for homeland security and provide these requirements and priorities to the Director of Central Intelligence and other agencies responsible for collection of foreign intelligence;

(C) coordinate efforts to ensure that all executive departments and agencies that have intelligence collection responsibilities have sufficient technological capabilities and resources to collect intelligence and data relating to terrorist activities or possible terrorist acts within the United States, working with the Assistant to the President for National Security Affairs, as appropriate;

(D) coordinate development of monitoring protocols and equipment for use in detecting the release of biological, chemical, and radiological hazards; and

(E) ensure that, to the extent permitted by law, all appropriate and necessary intelligence and law enforcement information relating to homeland security is disseminated to and exchanged among appropriate executive departments and agencies responsible for homeland security and, where appropriate for reasons of homeland security, promote exchange of such information with and among State and local governments and private entities.

(ii) Executive departments and agencies shall, to the extent permitted by law, make available to the Office all information relating to terrorist threats and activities within the United States.

(c) *Preparedness.* The Office of Homeland Security shall coordinate national efforts to prepare for and mitigate the consequences of terrorist threats or attacks within the United States. In performing this function, the Office shall work with Federal, State, and local agencies, and private entities, as appropriate, to:

(i) review and assess the adequacy of the portions of all Federal emergency response plans that pertain to terrorist threats or attacks within the United States;

(ii) coordinate domestic exercises and simulations designed to assess and practice systems that would be called upon to respond to a terrorist threat or attack within the United States and coordinate programs and activities for training Federal, State, and local employees who would be called upon to respond to such a threat or attack;

(iii) coordinate national efforts to ensure public health preparedness for a terrorist attack, including reviewing vaccination policies and reviewing the adequacy of and, if necessary, increasing vaccine and pharmaceutical stockpiles and hospital capacity;

(iv) coordinate Federal assistance to State and local authorities and nongovernmental organizations to prepare for and respond to terrorist threats or attacks within the United States;

(v) ensure that national preparedness programs and activities for terrorist threats or attacks are developed and are regularly evaluated under appropriate standards and that resources are allocated to improving and sustaining preparedness based on such evaluations; and

(vi) ensure the readiness and coordinated deployment of Federal response teams to respond to terrorist threats or attacks, working with the Assistant to the President for National Security Affairs, when appropriate.

(d) *Prevention.* The Office shall coordinate efforts to prevent terrorist attacks within the United States. In performing this function, the Office shall work with Federal, State, and local agencies, and private entities, as appropriate to:

(i) facilitate the exchange of information among such agencies relating to immigration and visa matters and shipments of cargo; and, working with the Assistant to the President for National Security Affairs, ensure coordination among such agencies to prevent the entry of terrorists and terrorist materials and supplies into the United States and facilitate removal of such terrorists from the United States, when appropriate;

(ii) coordinate efforts to investigate terrorist threats and attacks within the United States; and

(iii) coordinate efforts to improve the security of United States borders, territorial waters, and airspace in order to prevent acts of terrorism within the United States, working with the Assistant to the President for National Security Affairs, when appropriate,

(e) *Protection.* The Office shall coordinate efforts to protect the United States and its critical infrastructure from the consequences of terrorist attacks. In performing this function, the Office shall work with Federal, State, and local agencies, and private entities, as appropriate, to:

(i) strengthen measures for protecting energy production, transmission, and distribution services and critical facilities; other utilities; telecommunications; facilities that produce, use, store, or dispose of nuclear material; and other critical infrastructure services and critical facilities within the United States from terrorist attack;

(ii) coordinate efforts to protect critical public and privately owned information systems within the United States from terrorist attack;

(iii) develop criteria for reviewing whether appropriate security measures are in place at major public and privately owned facilities within the United States;

(iv) coordinate domestic efforts to ensure that special events determined by appropriate senior officials to have national significance are protected from terrorist attack;

(v) coordinate efforts to protect transportation systems within the United States, including railways, highways, shipping, ports and waterways, and airports and civilian aircraft, from terrorist attack;

(vi) coordinate efforts to protect United States livestock, agriculture, and systems for the provision of water and food for human use and consumption from terrorist attack; and

(vii) coordinate efforts to prevent unauthorized access to, development of, and unlawful importation into the United States of, chemical, biological, radiological, nuclear, explosive, or other related materials that have the potential to be used in terrorist attacks.

(f) *Response and Recovery.* The Office shall coordinate efforts to respond to and promote recovery from terrorist threats or attacks within the United States. In performing this function, the Office shall work with Federal, State, and local agencies, and private entities, as appropriate, to:

(i) coordinate efforts to ensure rapid restoration of transportation systems, energy production, transmission, and distribution systems; telecommunications; other utilities; and other critical infrastructure facilities after disruption by a terrorist threat or attack;

(ii) coordinate efforts to ensure rapid restoration of public and private critical information systems after disruption by a terrorist threat or attack;

(iii) work with the National Economic Council to coordinate efforts to stabilize United States financial markets after a terrorist threat or attack and manage the immediate economic and financial consequences of the incident;

(iv) coordinate Federal plans and programs to provide medical, financial, and other assistance to victims of terrorist attacks and their families; and

(v) coordinate containment and removal of biological, chemical, radiological, explosive, or other hazardous materials in the event of a terrorist threat or attack involving such hazards and coordinate efforts to mitigate the effects of such an attack.

(g) *Incident Management.* The Assistant to the President for Homeland Security shall be the individual primarily responsible for coordinating the domestic response efforts of all departments and agencies in the event of an imminent terrorist threat and during and in the immediate aftermath of a terrorist attack within the United States and shall be the principal point of contact for and to the President with respect to coordination of such efforts. The Assistant to the President for Homeland Security shall coordinate with the Assistant to the President for National Security Affairs, as appropriate.

(h) *Continuity of Government.* The Assistant to the President for Homeland Security, in coordination with the Assistant to the President for National Security Affairs, shall review plans and preparations for ensuring the continuity of the Federal Government in the event of a terrorist attack that threatens the safety and security of the United States Government or its leadership.

(i) *Public Affairs.* The Office, subject to the direction of the White House Office of Communications, shall coordinate the strategy of the executive branch for communicating with the public in the event of a terrorist threat or attack within the United States. The Office also shall coordinate the development of programs for educating the public about the nature of terrorist threats and appropriate precautions and responses.

(j) *Cooperation with State and Local Governments and Private Entities.* The Office shall encourage and invite the participation of State and local governments and private entities, as appropriate, in carrying out the Office's functions.

(k) *Review of Legal Authorities and Development of Legislative Proposals.* The Office shall coordinate a periodic review and assessment of the legal authorities available to executive departments and agencies to permit them to perform the functions described in this order. When the Office determines that such legal authorities are inadequate, the Office shall develop, in consultation with executive departments and agencies, proposals for presidential action and legislative proposals for submission to the Office of Management and Budget to enhance the ability of executive departments and agencies to perform those functions. The Office shall work with State and local governments in assessing the adequacy of their legal authorities to permit them to detect, prepare for, prevent, protect against, and recover from terrorist threats and attacks.

(l) *Budget Review.* The Assistant to the President for Homeland Security, in. consultation with the Director of the Office of Management and Budget (the "Director") and the heads of executive departments and agencies, shall identify programs that contribute to the Administration's strategy for homeland security and, in the development of the President's annual budget submission, shall review and provide advice to the heads of departments and agencies for such programs. The Assistant to the President for Homeland Security shall provide advice to the Director on the level and use of funding in departments and agencies for homeland security-related activities and, prior to the Director's forwarding of the proposed annual budget submission to the President for transmittal to the Congress, shall certify to the Director the funding levels that the Assistant to the President for Homeland Security believes are necessary and appropriate for the homeland security-related activities of the executive branch.

Sec. 4. *Administration.*

(a) The Office of Homeland Security shall be directed by the Assistant to the President for Homeland Security.

(b) The Office of Administration within the Executive Office of the President shall provide the Office of Homeland Security with such personnel, funding, and administrative support, to the extent permitted by law and subject to the availability of appropriations, as directed by the Chief of Staff to carry out the provisions of this order.

(c) Heads of executive departments and agencies are authorized, to the extent permitted by law, to detail or assign personnel of such departments and agencies to the Office of Homeland Security upon request of the Assistant to the President for Homeland Security, subject to the approval of the Chief of Staff.

Sec. 5. *Establishment of Homeland Security Council.*

(a) I hereby establish a Homeland Security Council (the "Council"), which shall be responsible for advising and assisting the President with respect to all aspects of homeland security. The Council shall serve as the mechanism for ensuring coordination of homeland security-related activities of executive departments and agencies and effective development and implementation of homeland security policies.

(b) The Council shall have as its members the President, the Vice President, the Secretary of the Treasury, the Secretary of Defense, the Attorney General, the Secretary of Health and Human Services, the Secretary of Transportation, the Director of the Federal Emergency Management Agency, the Director of the Federal Bureau of Investigation, the Director of Central Intelligence, the Assistant to the President for Homeland Security, and such other officers of the executive branch as the President may from time to time designate. The Chief of Staff, the Chief of Staff to the Vice President, the Assistant to the President for National Security Affairs, the Counsel to the President, and the Director of the Office of Management and Budget also are invited to attend any Council meeting. The Secretary of State, the Secretary of Agriculture, the Secretary of the Interior, the Secretary of Energy, the Secretary of Labor, the Secretary of Commerce, the Secretary of Veterans Affairs, the Administrator of the Environmental Protection Agency, the Assistant to the President for Economic Policy, and the Assistant to the President for Domestic Policy shall be invited to attend meetings pertaining to their responsibilities. The heads of other executive departments and agencies and other senior officials shall be invited to attend Council meetings when appropriate.

(c) The Council shall meet at the President's direction. When the President is absent from a meeting of the Council, at the President's direction the Vice President may preside. The Assistant to the President for Homeland Security shall be responsible, at the President's direction, for determining the agenda, ensuring that necessary papers are prepared, and recording Council actions and Presidential decisions.

Sec. 6. *Original Classification Authority.* I hereby delegate the authority to classify information originally as Top Secret, in accordance with Executive Order 12958 or any successor Executive Order, to the Assistant to the President for Homeland Security.

Sec. 7. *Continuing Authorities.* This order does not alter the existing authorities of United States Government departments and agencies. All executive departments and agencies are directed to assist the Council and the Assistant to the President for Homeland Security in carrying out the purposes of this order.

Sec. 8. *General Provisions.*

(a) This order does not create any right or benefit, substantive or procedural, enforceable at law or equity by a party against the United States, its departments, agencies or instrumentalities, its officers or employees, or any other person.

(b) References in this order to State and local governments shall be construed to include tribal governments and United States territories and other possessions.

(c) References to the "United States" shall be construed to include United States territories and possessions.

Sec. 9. *Amendments to Executive Order 12656.* Executive Order 12656 of November 18, 1988, as amended, is hereby further amended as follows:

(a) Section 101(a) is amended by adding at the end of the fourth sentence: "except that the Homeland Security Council shall be responsible for administering such policy with respect to terrorist threats and attacks within the United States."

(b) Section 104(a) is amended by adding at the end: "except that the Homeland Security Council is the principal forum for consideration of policy relating to terrorist threats and attacks within the United States."

(c) Section 104(b) is amended by inserting the words "and the Homeland Security Council" after the words "National Security Council."

(d) The first sentence of section 104(c) is amended by inserting the words "and the Homeland Security Council" after the words "National Security Council."

(e) The second sentence of section 104(c) is replaced with the following two sentences: "Pursuant to such procedures for the organization and management of the National Security Council and Homeland Security Council processes as the President may establish, the Director of the Federal Emergency Management Agency also shall assist in the implementation of and management of those processes as the President may establish. The Director of the Federal Emergency Management Agency also shall assist in the implementation of national security emergency preparedness policy by coordinating with the other Federal departments and agencies and with State and local governments, and by providing periodic reports to the National Security Council and the Homeland Security Council on implementation of national security emergency preparedness policy."

(f) Section 201(7) is amended by inserting the words "and the Homeland Security Council" after the words "National Security Council."

(g) Section 206 is amended by inserting the words "and the Homeland Security Council" after the words "National Security Council."

(h) Section 208 is amended by inserting the words "or the Homeland Security Council" after the words "National Security Council."

APPENDIX 2.4 EXECUTIVE ORDER 13231 BY PRESIDENT GEORGE W. BUSH

EXECUTIVE ORDER 13231 OF OCTOBER 16, 2001

Critical Infrastructure Protection in the Information Age

By the authority vested in me as President by the Constitution and the laws of the United States of America, and in order to ensure protection of information systems for critical infrastructure, including emergency preparedness communications, and the physical assets that support such systems, in the information age, it is hereby ordered as follows:

Section 1. *Policy.*

(a) The information technology revolution has changed the way business is transacted, government operates, and national defense is conducted. Those three functions now depend on an interdependent network of critical information infrastructures. The protection program authorized by this order shall consist of continuous efforts to secure information systems for critical infrastructure, including emergency preparedness communications, and the physical assets that support such systems. Protection of these systems is essential to the telecommunications, energy, financial services, manufacturing, water, transportation, health care, and emergency services sectors.

(b) It is the policy of the United States to protect against disruption of the operation of information systems for critical infrastructure and thereby help to protect the people, economy, essential human and government services, and national security of the United States, and to ensure that any disruptions that occur are infrequent, of minimal duration, and manageable, and cause the least damage possible. The implementation of this policy shall include a voluntary public-private partnership, involving corporate and nongovernmental organizations.

Sec. 2. *Scope.* To achieve this policy, there shall be a senior executive branch board to coordinate and have cognizance of Federal efforts and programs that relate to protection of information systems and involve:

(a) cooperation with and protection of private sector critical infrastructure, State and local governments' critical infrastructure, and supporting programs in corporate and academic organizations;

(b) protection of Federal departments' and agencies' critical infrastructure; and

(c) related national security programs.

Sec. 3. *Establishment.* I hereby establish the "President's Critical Infrastructure Protection Board" (the "Board").

Sec. 4. *Continuing Authorities.* This order does not alter the existing authorities or roles of United States Government departments and agencies. Authorities set forth in 44 U.S.C. Chapter 35, and other applicable law, provide senior officials with responsibility for the security of Federal Government information systems.

(a) *Executive Branch Information Systems Security.* The Director of the Office of Management and Budget (OMB) has the responsibility to develop and oversee the implementation of government-wide policies, principles, standards, and guidelines for the security of information systems that support the executive branch departments and agencies, except those noted in section 4(b) of this order. The Director of OMB shall advise the President and the appropriate department or agency head when there is a critical deficiency in the security practices within the purview of this section in an executive branch department or agency. The Board shall assist and support the Director of OMB in this function and shall be reasonably cognizant of programs related to security of department and agency information systems.

(b) *National Security Information Systems.* The Secretary of Defense and the Director of Central Intelligence (DCI) shall have responsibility to oversee, develop, and ensure implementation of policies, principles, standards, and guidelines for the security of information systems that support the operations under their respective control. In consultation with the Assistant to the President for National Security Affairs and the affected departments and agencies, the Secretary of Defense and the DCI shall develop policies, principles, standards, and guidelines for the security of national security information systems that support the operations of other executive branch departments and agencies with national security information.

(i) Policies, principles, standards, and guidelines developed under this subsection may require more stringent protection than those developed in accordance with subsection 4(a) of this order.

(ii) The Assistant to the President for National Security Affairs shall advise the President and the appropriate department or agency head when there is a critical deficiency in the security practices of a department or agency within the purview of this section. The Board, or one of its standing or and hoc committees, shall be reasonably cognizant of programs to provide security and continuity to national security information systems.

(c) *Additional Responsibilities: The Heads of Executive Branch Departments and Agencies.* The heads of executive branch departments and agencies are responsible and accountable for providing and maintaining adequate levels of security for information systems, including emergency preparedness communications systems, for programs under their control. Heads of such departments and agencies shall ensure the development and, within available appropriations, funding of programs that adequately address these mission areas. Cost-effective security shall be built into and made an integral part of government information systems, especially those critical systems that support the national security and other essential government programs. Additionally, security should enable, and not unnecessarily impede, department and agency business operations.

Sec. 5. *Board Responsibilities.* Consistent with the responsibilities noted in section 4 of this order, the Board shall recommend policies and coordinate programs for protecting information systems for critical infrastructure, including emergency preparedness communications, and the physical assets that support such systems. Among its activities to implement these responsibilities, the Board shall:

(a) *Outreach to the Private Sector and State and Local Governments.* In consultation with affected executive branch departments and agencies, coordinate outreach to and consultation with the private sector, including corporations that own, operate, develop, and equip information, telecommunications, transportation, energy, water, health care, and financial services, on protection of information systems for critical infrastructure, including emergency preparedness communications, and the physical assets that support such systems; and coordinate outreach to State and local governments, as well as communities and representatives from academia and other relevant elements of society.

(i) When requested to do so, assist in the development of voluntary standards and best practices in a manner consistent with 15 U.S.C. Chapter 7;

(ii) Consult with potentially affected communities, including the legal, auditing, financial, and insurance communities, to the extent permitted by law, to determine areas of mutual concern; and

(iii) Coordinate the activities of senior liaison officers appointed by the Attorney General, the Secretaries of Energy, Commerce, Transportation, the Treasury, and Health and Human Services, and the Director of the Federal Emergency Management Agency for outreach on critical infrastructure protection issues with private sector organizations within the areas of concern to these departments and agencies. In these and other related functions, the Board shall work in coordination with the Critical Infrastructure Assurance Office (CIAO) and the National Institute of Standards and Technology of the Department of Commerce, the National Infrastructure Protection Center (NIPC), and the National Communications System (NCS).

(b) *Information Sharing.* Work with industry, State and local governments, and nongovernmental organizations to ensure that systems are created and well managed to share threat warning, analysis, and recovery information among government network operation centers, information sharing and analysis centers established on a voluntary basis by industry, and other related operations centers. In this and other related functions, the Board shall work in coordination with the NCS, the Federal Computer Incident Response Center, the NIPC, and other departments and agencies, as appropriate.

(c) *Incident Coordination and Crisis Response.* Coordinate programs and policies for responding to information systems security incidents that threaten information systems for critical infrastructure, including emergency preparedness communications, and the physical assets that support such systems. In this function, the Department of Justice, through the NIPC and the Manager of the NCS and other departments and agencies, as appropriate, shall work in coordination with the Board.

(d) *Recruitment, Retention, and Training Executive Branch Security Professionals.* In consultation with executive branch departments and agencies, coordinate programs to ensure that government employees with responsibilities for protecting information systems for critical infrastructure, including emergency preparedness communications, and the physical assets that support such systems, are adequately trained and evaluated. In this function, the Office of Personnel Management shall work in coordination with the Board, as appropriate.

(e) *Research and Development.* Coordinate with the Director of the Office of Science and Technology Policy (OSTP) on a program of Federal Government research and development for protection of information systems for critical infrastructure, including emergency preparedness communications, and the physical assets that support such systems, and ensure coordination of government activities in this field with corporations, universities, Federally funded research centers, and national laboratories. In this function, the Board shall work in coordination with the National Science Foundation, the Defense Advanced Research Projects Agency, and with other departments and agencies, as appropriate.

(f) *Law Enforcement Coordination with National Security Components.* Promote programs against cyber crime and assist Federal law enforcement agencies in gaining necessary cooperation from executive branch departments and agencies. Support Federal law enforcement agencies' investigation of illegal activities involving information systems for critical infrastructure, including emergency preparedness communications, and the physical assets that support such systems, and support coordination by these agencies with other departments and agencies with responsibilities to defend the Nation's security. In this function, the Board shall work in coordination with the Department of Justice, through the NIPC, and the Department of the Treasury, through the Secret Service, and with other departments and agencies, as appropriate.

(g) *International Information Infrastructure Protection.* Support the Department of State's coordination of United States Government programs for international cooperation covering international information infrastructure protection issues.

(h) *Legislation.* In accordance with OMB circular A–19, advise departments and agencies, the Director of OMB, and the Assistant to the President for Legislative Affairs on legislation relating to protection of information systems for critical infrastructure, including emergency preparedness communications, and the physical assets that support such systems.

(i) *Coordination with Office of Homeland Security.* Carry out those functions relating to protection of and recovery from attacks against information systems for critical infrastructure, including emergency preparedness communications, that were assigned to the Office of Homeland Security by Executive Order 13228 of October 8, 2001. The Assistant to the President for Homeland Security, in coordination with the Assistant to the President for National Security Affairs, shall be responsible for defining the responsibilities of the Board in coordinating efforts to protect physical assets that support information systems.

Sec. 6. *Membership.*

(a) Members of the Board shall be drawn from the executive branch departments, agencies, and offices listed below; in addition, concerned Federal departments and agencies may participate in the activities of appropriate committees of the Board. The Board shall be led by a Chair and Vice Chair, designated by the President. Its other members shall be the following senior officials or their designees:

(i) Secretary of State;
(ii) Secretary of the Treasury;
(iii) Secretary of Defense;
(iv) Attorney General;
(v) Secretary of Commerce;
(vi) Secretary of Health and Human Services;
(vii) Secretary of Transportation;

(viii) Secretary of Energy;
(ix) Director of Central Intelligence;
(x) Chairman of the Joint Chiefs of Staff;
(xi) Director of the Federal Emergency Management Agency;
(xii) Administrator of General Services;
(xiii) Director of the Office of Management and Budget;
(xiv) Director of the Office of Science and Technology Policy;
(xv) Chief of Staff to the Vice President;
(xvi) Director of the National Economic Council;
(xvii) Assistant to the President for National Security Affairs;
(xviii) Assistant to the President for Homeland Security;
(xix) Chief of Staff to the President; and
(xx) Such other executive branch officials as the President may designate.

Members of the Board and their designees shall be full-time or permanent part-time officers or employees of the Federal Government.

(b) In addition, the following officials shall serve as members of the Board and shall form the Board's Coordination Committee:
(i) Director, Critical Infrastructure Assurance Office, Department of Commerce;
(ii) Manager, National Communications System;
(iii) Vice Chair, Chief Information Officers' (CIO) Council;
(iv) Information Assurance Director, National Security Agency;
(v) Deputy Director of Central Intelligence for Community Management; and
(vi) Director, National Infrastructure Protection Center, Federal Bureau of Investigation, Department of Justice.

(c) The Chairman of the Federal Communications Commission may appoint a representative to the Board.

Sec. 7. *Chair.*

(a) The Chair also shall be the Special Advisor to the President for Cyberspace Security. Executive branch departments and agencies shall make all reasonable efforts to keep the Chair fully informed in a timely manner, and to the greatest extent permitted by law, of all programs and issues within the purview of the Board. The Chair, in consultation with the Board, shall call and preside at meetings of the Board and set the agenda for the Board. The Chair, in consultation with the Board, may propose policies and programs to appropriate officials to ensure the protection of the Nation's information systems for critical infrastructure, including emergency preparedness communications, and the physical assets that support such systems. To ensure full coordination between the responsibilities of the National Security Council (NSC) and the Office of Homeland Security, the Chair shall report to both the Assistant to the President for National Security Affairs and to the Assistant to the President for Homeland Security. The Chair shall coordinate with the Assistant to the President for Economic Policy on issues relating to private sector systems and economic effects and with the Director of OMB on issues relating to budgets and the security of computer networks addressed in subsection 4(a) of this order.

(b) The Chair shall be assisted by an appropriately sized staff within the White House Office. In addition, heads of executive branch departments and agencies are authorized, to the extent permitted by law, to detail or assign personnel of such departments and agencies to the Board's staff upon request of the Chair, subject to the approval of the Chief of Staff to the President. Members of the Board's staff with responsibilities relating to national security information systems, communications, and information warfare may, with respect to those responsibilities, also work at the direction of the Assistant to the President for National Security Affairs.

Sec. 8. *Standing Committees.*

(a) The Board may establish standing and ad hoc committees as appropriate. Representation on standing committees shall not be limited to those departments and agencies on the Board, but may include representatives of other concerned executive branch departments, and agencies.

(b) Chairs of standing and ad hoc committees shall report fully and regularly on the activities of the committees to the Board, which shall ensure that the committees are well coordinated with each other.

(c) There are established the following standing committees:

(i) *Private Sector and State and Local Government Outreach*, chaired by the designee of the Secretary of Commerce, to work in coordination with the designee of the Chairman of the National Economic Council.

(ii) *Executive Branch Information Systems Security*, chaired by the designee of the Director of OMB. The committee shall assist OMB in fulfilling its responsibilities under 44 U.S.C. Chapter 35 and other applicable law.

(iii) *National Security Systems.* The National Security Telecommunications and Information Systems Security Committee, as established by and consistent with NSD–42 and chaired by the Department of Defense, shall serve as a Board standing committee, and be redesignated the Committee on National Security Systems.

(iv) *Incident Response Coordination*, co-chaired by the designees of the Attorney General and the Secretary of Defense.

(v) *Research and Development*, chaired by a designee of the Director of OSTP.

(vi) *National Security and Emergency Preparedness Communications.* The NCS Committee of Principals is renamed the Board's Committee for National Security and Emergency Preparedness Communications. The reporting functions established above for standing committees are in addition to the functions set forth in Executive Order 12472 of April 3, 1984, and do not alter any function or role set forth therein.

(vii) *Physical Security*, co-chaired by the designees of the Secretary of Defense and the Attorney General, to coordinate programs to ensure the physical security of information systems for critical infrastructure, including emergency preparedness communications, and the physical assets that support such systems. The standing committee shall coordinate its work with the Office of Homeland Security and shall work closely with the Physical Security Working Group of the Records Access and Information Security Policy Coordinating Committee to ensure coordination of efforts.

(viii) *Infrastructure Interdependencies*, co-chaired by the designees of the Secretaries of Transportation and Energy, to coordinate programs to assess the unique risks, threats, and vulnerabilities associated with the interdependency of information systems for critical infrastructures, including the development of effective models, simulations, and other analytic tools and cost-effective technologies in this area.

(ix) *International Affairs*, chaired by a designee of the Secretary of State, to support Department of State coordination of United States Government programs for international cooperation covering international information infrastructure issues.

(x) *Financial and Banking Information Infrastructure*, chaired by a designee of the Secretary of the Treasury and including representatives of the banking and financial institution regulatory agencies.

(xi) *Other Committees*. Such other standing committees as may be established by the Board.

(d) *Subcommittees*. The chair of each standing committee may form necessary subcommittees with organizational representation as determined by the Chair.

(e) *Streamlining*. The Board shall develop procedures that specify the manner in which it or a subordinate committee will perform the responsibilities previously assigned to the Policy Coordinating Committee. The Board, in coordination with the Director of OSTP, shall review the functions of the joint Telecommunications Resources Board, established under Executive order 12472, and make recommendations about its future role.

See. 9. *Planning and Budget*.

(a) The Board, on a periodic basis, shall propose a National Plan or plans for subjects within its purview. The Board, in coordination with the Office of Homeland Security, also shall make recommendations to OMB on those portions of executive branch department and agency budgets that fall within the Board's purview, after review of relevant program requirements and resources.

(b) The Office of Administration within the Executive Office of the President shall provide the Board with such personnel, funding, and administrative support, to the extent permitted by law and subject to the availability of appropriations, as directed by the Chief of Staff to carry out the provisions of this order. Only those funds that are available for the Office of Homeland Security, established by Executive Order 13228, shall be available for such purposes. To the extent permitted by law and as appropriate, agencies represented on the Board also may provide administrative support for the Board. The National Security Agency shall ensure that the Board's information and communications systems are appropriately secured.

(c) The Board may annually request the National Science Foundation, Department of Energy, Department of Transportation, Environmental Protection Agency, Department of Commerce, Department of Defense, and the Intelligence Community, as that term is defined in Executive Order 12333 of December 4, 1981, to include in their budget requests to OMB funding for demonstration projects and research to support the Board's activities.

Sec. 10. *Presidential Advisory Panels*. The Chair shall work closely with panels of senior experts from outside of the government that advise the President, in particular:

the President's National Security Telecommunications Advisory Committee (NSTAC) created by Executive Order 12382 of September 13, 1982, as amended, and the National Infrastructure Advisory Council (NIAC or Council) created by this Executive Order. The Chair and Vice Chair of these two panels also may meet with the Board, as appropriate and to the extent permitted by law, to provide a private sector perspective.

(a) *NSTAC.* The NSTAC provides the President advice on the security and continuity of communications systems essential for national security and emergency preparedness.

(b) *NIAC.* There is hereby established the National Infrastructure Advisory Council, which shall provide the President advice on the security of information systems for critical infrastructure supporting other sectors of the economy: banking and finance, transportation, energy, manufacturing, and emergency government services. The NIAC shall be composed of not more than 30 members appointed by the President. The members of the NIAC shall be selected from the private sector, academia, and State and local government. Members of the NIAC shall have expertise relevant to the functions of the NIAC and generally shall be selected from industry Chief Executive Officers (and equivalently ranked leaders in other organizations) with responsibilities for the security of information infrastructure supporting the critical sectors of the economy, including banking and finance, transportation, energy, communications, and emergency government services. Members shall not be full-time officials or employees of the executive branch of the Federal Government.

   (i) The President shall designate a Chair and Vice Chair from among the members of the NIAC.

   (ii) The Chair of the Board established by this order will serve as the Executive Director of the NIAC.

(c) *NIAC Functions.* The NIAC will meet periodically to:

   (i) enhance the partnership of the public and private sectors in protecting information systems for critical infrastructures and provide reports on this issue to the President, as appropriate;

   (ii) propose and develop ways to encourage private industry to perform periodic risk assessments of critical information and telecommunications systems;

   (iii) monitor the development of private sector Information Sharing and Analysis Centers (ISACs) and provide recommendations to the Board on how these organizations can best foster improved cooperation among the ISACs, the NIPC, and other Federal Government entities;

   (iv) report to the President through the Board, which shall ensure appropriate coordination with the Assistant to the President for Economic Policy under the terms of this order; and

   (v) advise lead agencies with critical infrastructure responsibilities, sector coordinators, the NIPC, the ISACs, and the Board.

(d) *Administration of the NIAC.*

   (i) The NIAC may hold hearings, conduct inquiries, and establish subcommittees, as appropriate.

(ii) Upon the request of the Chair, and to the extent permitted by law, the heads of the executive branch departments and agencies shall provide the Council with information and advice relating to its functions.

(iii) Senior Federal Government officials may participate in the meetings of the NIAC, as appropriate.

(iv) Members shall serve without compensation for their work on the Council. However, members may be allowed travel expenses, including per diem in lieu of subsistence, as authorized by law for persons serving intermittently in Federal Government service (5 U.S.C. 5701–5707).

(v) To the extent permitted by law, and subject to the availability of appropriations, the Department of Commerce, through the CIAO, shall provide the NIAC with administrative services, staff; and other support services and such funds as may be necessary for the performance of the NIAC's functions.

(e) *General Provisions.*

(i) Insofar as the Federal Advisory Committee Act, as amended (5 U.S.C. App.), may apply to the NIAC, the functions of the President under that Act, except that of reporting to the Congress, shall be performed by the Department of Commerce in accordance with the guidelines and procedures established by the Administrator of General Services.

(ii) The Council shall terminate 2 years from the date of this order, unless extended by the President prior to that date.

(iii) Executive Order 13130 of July 14, 1999, is hereby revoked.

Sec. 11. *National Communications System.* Changes in technology are causing the convergence of much of telephony, data relay, and internet communications networks into an interconnected network of networks. The NCS and its National Coordinating Center shall support use of telephony, converged information, voice networks, and next generation networks for emergency preparedness and national security communications functions assigned to them in Executive Order 12472. All authorities and assignments of responsibilities to departments and agencies in that order, including the role of the Manager of NCS, remain unchanged except as explicitly modified by this order.

Sec. 12. *Counter-intelligence.* The Board shall coordinate its activities with those of the Office of the Counter-intelligence Executive to address the threat to programs within the Board's purview from hostile foreign intelligence services.

Sec. 13. *Classification Authority.* I hereby delegate to the Chair the authority to classify information originally as Top Secret, in accordance with Executive Order 12958 of April 17, 1995, as amended, or any successor Executive Order.

Sec. 14. *General Provisions.*

(a) Nothing in this order shall supersede any requirement made by or under law.

(b) This order does not create any right or benefit, substantive or procedural, enforceable at law or equity, against the United States, its departments, agencies or other entities, its officers or employees, or any other person.

APPENDIX 2.5 HOMELAND SECURITY PRESIDENTIAL DIRECTIVE 7 BY PRESIDENT GEORGE W. BUSH

Subject: Critical Infrastructure Identification, Prioritization, and Protection

Purpose

(1) This directive establishes a national policy for Federal departments and agencies to identify and prioritize United States critical infrastructure and key resources and to protect them from terrorist attacks.

Background

(2) Terrorists seek to destroy, incapacitate, or exploit critical infrastructure and key resources across the United States to threaten national security, cause mass casualties, weaken our economy, and damage public morale and confidence.

(3) America's open and technologically complex society includes a wide array of critical infrastructure and key resources that are potential terrorist targets. The majority of these are owned and operated by the private sector and State or local governments. These critical infrastructures and key resources are both physical and cyber-based and span all sectors of the economy.

(4) Critical infrastructure and key resources provide the essential services that underpin American society. The Nation possesses numerous key resources, whose exploitation or destruction by terrorists could cause catastrophic health effects or mass casualties comparable to those from the use of a weapon of mass destruction, or could profoundly affect our national prestige and morale. In addition, there is critical infrastructure so vital that its incapacitation, exploitation, or destruction, through terrorist attack, could have a debilitating effect on security and economic well-being.

(5) While it is not possible to protect or eliminate the vulnerability of all critical infrastructure and key resources throughout the country, strategic improvements in security can make it more difficult for attacks to succeed and can lessen the impact of attacks that may occur. In addition to strategic security enhancements, tactical security improvements can be rapidly implemented to deter, mitigate, or neutralize potential attacks.

Definitions

(6) In this directive:

(a) The term "critical infrastructure" has the meaning given to that term in section 1016(e) of the USA PATRIOT Act of 2001 (42 U.S.C. 5195c(e)).

(b) The term "key resources" has the meaning given that term in section 2(9) of the Homeland Security Act of 2002 (6 U.S.C. 101(9)).

(c) The term "the Department" means the Department of Homeland Security.

(d) The term "Federal departments and agencies" means those executive departments enumerated in 5 U.S.C. 101, and the Department of Homeland Security; independent establishments as defined by 5 U.S.C. 104(1); Government corporations as defined by 5 U.S.C. 103(1); and the United States Postal Service.

(e) The terms "State," and "local government," when used in a geographical sense, have the same meanings given to those terms in section 2 of the Homeland Security Act of 2002 (6 U.S.C. 101).

(f) The term "the Secretary" means the Secretary of Homeland Security.

(g) The term "Sector-Specific Agency" means a Federal department or agency responsible for infrastructure protection activities in a designated critical infrastructure sector or key resources category. Sector-Specific Agencies will conduct their activities under this directive in accordance with guidance provided by the Secretary.

(h) The terms "protect" and "secure" mean reducing the vulnerability of critical infrastructure or key resources in order to deter, mitigate, or neutralize terrorist attacks.

Policy

(7) It is the policy of the United States to enhance the protection of our Nation's critical infrastructure and key resources against terrorist acts that could:

(a) cause catastrophic health effects or mass casualties comparable to those from the use of a weapon of mass destruction;

(b) impair Federal departments and agencies' abilities to perform essential missions, or to ensure the public's health and safety;

(c) undermine State and local government capacities to maintain order and to deliver minimum essential public services;

(d) damage the private sector's capability to ensure the orderly functioning of the economy and delivery of essential services;

(e) have a negative effect on the economy through the cascading disruption of other critical infrastructure and key resources; or

(f) undermine the public's morale and confidence in our national economic and political institutions.

(8) Federal departments and agencies will identify, prioritize, and coordinate the protection of critical infrastructure and key resources in order to prevent, deter, and mitigate the effects of deliberate efforts to destroy, incapacitate, or exploit them. Federal departments and agencies will work with State and local governments and the private sector to accomplish this objective.

(9) Federal departments and agencies will ensure that homeland security programs do not diminish the overall economic security of the United States.

(10) Federal departments and agencies will appropriately protect information associated with carrying out this directive, including handling voluntarily provided information and information that would facilitate terrorist targeting of critical infrastructure and key resources consistent with the Homeland Security Act of 2002 and other applicable legal authorities.

(11) Federal departments and agencies shall implement this directive in a manner consistent with applicable provisions of law, including those protecting the rights of United States persons.

Roles and Responsibilities of the Secretary

(12) In carrying out the functions assigned in the Homeland Security Act of 2002, the Secretary shall be responsible for coordinating the overall national effort to enhance the protection of the critical infrastructure and key resources of the United States. The Secretary

shall serve as the principal Federal official to lead, integrate, and coordinate implementation of efforts among Federal departments and agencies, State and local governments, and the private sector to protect critical infrastructure and key resources.

(13) Consistent with this directive, the Secretary will identify, prioritize, and coordinate the protection of critical infrastructure and key resources with an emphasis on critical infrastructure and key resources that could be exploited to cause catastrophic health effects or mass casualties comparable to those from the use of a weapon of mass destruction.

(14) The Secretary will establish uniform policies, approaches, guidelines, and methodologies for integrating Federal infrastructure protection and risk management activities within and across sectors along with metrics and criteria for related programs and activities.

(15) The Secretary shall coordinate protection activities for each of the following critical infrastructure sectors: information technology; telecommunications; chemical; transportation systems, including mass transit, aviation, maritime, ground/surface, and rail and pipeline systems; emergency services; and postal and shipping. The Department shall coordinate with appropriate departments and agencies to ensure the protection of other key resources including dams, government facilities, and commercial facilities. In addition, in its role as overall cross-sector coordinator, the Department shall also evaluate the need for and coordinate the coverage of additional critical infrastructure and key resources categories over time, as appropriate.

(16) The Secretary will continue to maintain an organization to serve as a focal point for the security of cyberspace. The organization will facilitate interactions and collaborations between and among Federal departments and agencies, State and local governments, the private sector, academia and international organizations. To the extent permitted by law, Federal departments and agencies with cyber expertise, including but not limited to the Departments of Justice, Commerce, the Treasury, Defense, Energy, and State, and the Central Intelligence Agency, will collaborate with and support the organization in accomplishing its mission. The organization's mission includes analysis, warning, information sharing, vulnerability reduction, mitigation, and aiding national recovery efforts for critical infrastructure information systems. The organization will support the Department of Justice and other law enforcement agencies in their continuing missions to investigate and prosecute threats to and attacks against cyberspace, to the extent permitted by law.

(17) The Secretary will work closely with other Federal departments and agencies, State and local governments, and the private sector in accomplishing the objectives of this directive.

Roles and Responsibilities of Sector-Specific Federal Agencies

(18) Recognizing that each infrastructure sector possesses its own unique characteristics and operating models, there are designated Sector-Specific Agencies, including:

- (a) Department of Agriculture—agriculture, food (meat, poultry, egg products);
- (b) Health and Human Services—public health, healthcare, and food (other than meat, poultry, egg products);
- (c) Environmental Protection Agency—drinking water and water treatment systems;
- (d) Department of Energy—energy, including the production refining, storage, and distribution of oil and gas, and electric power except for commercial nuclear power facilities;
- (e) Department of the Treasury—banking and finance;
- (f) Department of the Interior—national monuments and icons; and
- (g) Department of Defense—defense industrial base.

(19) In accordance with guidance provided by the Secretary, Sector-Specific Agencies shall:

(a) collaborate with all relevant Federal departments and agencies, State and local governments, and the private sector, including with key persons and entities in their infrastructure sector,

(b) conduct or facilitate vulnerability assessments of the sector; and

(c) encourage risk management strategies to protect against and mitigate the effects of attacks against critical infrastructure and key resources.

(20) Nothing in this directive alters, or impedes the ability to carry out, the authorities of the Federal departments and agencies to perform their responsibilities under law and consistent with applicable legal authorities and presidential guidance.

(21) Federal departments and agencies shall cooperate with the Department in implementing this directive, consistent with the Homeland Security Act of 2002 and other applicable legal authorities.

Roles and Responsibilities of Other Departments, Agencies, and Offices

(22) In addition to the responsibilities given the Department and Sector-Specific Agencies, there are special functions of various Federal departments and agencies and components of the Executive Office of the President related to critical infrastructure and key resources protection.

(a) The Department of State, in conjunction with the Department, and the Departments of Justice, Commerce, Defense, the Treasury and other appropriate agencies, will work with foreign countries and international organizations to strengthen the protection of United States critical infrastructure and key resources.

(b) The Department of Justice, including the Federal Bureau of Investigation, will reduce domestic terrorist threats, and investigate and prosecute actual or attempted terrorist attacks on, sabotage of, or disruptions of critical infrastructure and key resources. The Attorney General and the Secretary shall use applicable statutory authority and attendant mechanisms for cooperation and coordination, including but not limited to those established by presidential directive.

(c) The Department of Commerce, in coordination with the Department, will work with private sector, research, academic, and government organizations to improve technology for cyber systems and promote other critical infrastructure efforts, including using its authority under the Defense Production Act to assure the timely availability of industrial products, materials, and services to meet homeland security, requirements.

(d) A Critical Infrastructure Protection Policy Coordinating Committee will advise the Homeland Security Council on interagency policy related to physical and cyber infrastructure protection. This PCC will be chaired by a Federal officer or employee designated by the Assistant to the President for Homeland Security.

(e) The Office of Science and Technology Policy, in coordination with the Department, will coordinate interagency research and development to enhance the protection of critical infrastructure and key resources.

(f) The Office of Management and Budget (OMB) shall oversee the implementation of government-wide policies, principles, standards, and guidelines for Federal government computer security programs. The Director of OMB will ensure the operation of a central Federal information security incident center consistent with the requirements of the Federal Information Security Management Act of 2002.

(g) Consistent with the E-Government Act of 2002, the Chief Information Officers Council shall be the principal interagency forum for improving agency practices related to the design, acquisition, development, modernization, use, operation, sharing, and performance of information resources of Federal departments and agencies.

(h) The Department of Transportation and the Department will collaborate on all matters relating to transportation security and transportation infrastructure protection. The Department of Transportation is responsible for operating the national air space system. The Department of Transportation and the Department will collaborate in regulating the transportation of hazardous materials by all modes (including pipelines).

(i) All Federal departments and agencies shall work with the sectors relevant to their responsibilities to reduce the consequences of catastrophic failures not caused by terrorism.

(23) The heads of all Federal departments and agencies will coordinate and cooperate with the Secretary as appropriate and consistent with their own responsibilities for protecting critical infrastructure and key resources.

(24) All Federal department and agency heads are responsible for the identification, prioritization, assessment, remediation, and protection of their respective internal critical infrastructure and key resources. Consistent with the Federal Information Security Management Act of 2002, agencies will identify and provide information security protections commensurate with the risk and magnitude of the harm resulting from the unauthorized access, use, disclosure, disruption, modification, or destruction of information.

Coordination with the Private Sector

(25) In accordance with applicable laws or regulations, the Department and the Sector-Specific Agencies will collaborate with appropriate private sector entities and continue to encourage the development of information sharing and analysis mechanisms. Additionally, the Department and Sector-Specific Agencies shall collaborate with the private sector and continue to support sector-coordinating mechanisms:

(a) to identify, prioritize, and coordinate the protection of critical infrastructure and key resources; and

(b) to facilitate sharing of information about physical and cyber threats, vulnerabilities, incidents, potential protective measures, and best practices.

National Special Security Events

(26) The Secretary, after consultation with the Homeland Security Council, shall be responsible for designating events as "National Special Security Events" (NSSEs). This directive supersedes language in previous presidential directives regarding the designation of NSSEs that is inconsistent herewith.

Implementation

(27) Consistent with the Homeland Security Act of 2002, the Secretary shall produce a comprehensive, integrated National Plan for Critical Infrastructure and Key Resources Protection to outline national goals, objectives, milestones, and key initiatives within 1 year from

the issuance of this directive. The Plan shall include, in addition to other Homeland Security-related elements as the Secretary deems appropriate, the following elements:

(a) a strategy to identify, prioritize, and coordinate the protection of critical infrastructure and key resources, including how the Department intends to work with Federal departments and agencies, State and local governments, the private sector, and foreign countries and international organizations;
(b) a summary of activities to be undertaken in order to: define and prioritize, reduce the vulnerability of, and coordinate the protection of critical infrastructure and key resources;
(c) a summary of initiatives for sharing critical infrastructure and key resources information and for providing critical infrastructure and key resources threat warning data to State and local governments and the private sector; and
(d) coordination and integration, as appropriate, with other Federal emergency management and preparedness activities including the National Response Plan and applicable national preparedness goals.

(28) The Secretary, consistent with the Homeland Security Act of 2002 and other applicable legal authorities and presidential guidance, shall establish appropriate systems, mechanisms, and procedures to share homeland security information relevant to threats and vulnerabilities in national critical infrastructure and key resources with other Federal departments and agencies, State and local governments, and the private sector in a timely manner.

(29) The Secretary will continue to work with the Nuclear Regulatory Commission and, as appropriate, the Department of Energy in order to ensure the necessary protection of:

(a) commercial nuclear reactors for generating electric power and non-power nuclear reactors used for research, testing, and training;
(b) nuclear materials in medical, industrial, and academic settings and facilities that fabricate nuclear fuel; and
(c) the transportation, storage, and disposal of nuclear materials and waste.

(30) In coordination with the Director of the Office of Science and Technology Policy, the Secretary shall prepare on an annual basis a Federal Research and Development Plan in support of this directive.

(31) The Secretary will collaborate with other appropriate Federal departments and agencies to develop a program, consistent with applicable law, to geospatially map, image, analyze, and sort critical infrastructure and key resources by utilizing commercial satellite and airborne systems, and existing capabilities within other agencies. National technical means should be considered as an option of last resort. The Secretary, with advice from the Director of Central Intelligence, the Secretaries of Defense and the Interior, and the heads of other appropriate Federal departments and agencies, shall develop mechanisms for accomplishing this initiative. The Attorney General shall provide legal advice as necessary.

(32) The Secretary will utilize existing, and develop new, capabilities as needed to model comprehensively the potential implications of terrorist exploitation of vulnerabilities in critical infrastructure and key resources, placing specific focus on densely populated areas. Agencies with relevant modeling capabilities shall cooperate with the Secretary to develop appropriate mechanisms for accomplishing this initiative.

(33) The Secretary will develop a national indications and warnings architecture for infrastructure protection and capabilities that will facilitate:

(a) an understanding of baseline infrastructure operations;

(b) the identification of indicators and precursors to an attack; and

(c) a surge capacity for detecting and analyzing patterns of potential attacks.

In developing a national indications and warnings architecture, the Department will work with Federal, State, local, and non-governmental entities to develop an integrated view of physical and cyber infrastructure and key resources.

(34) By July 2004, the heads of all Federal departments and agencies shall develop and submit to the Director of the OMB for approval plans for protecting the physical and cyber critical infrastructure and key resources that they own or operate. These plans shall address identification, prioritization, protection, and contingency planning, including the recovery and reconstitution of essential capabilities.

(35) On an annual basis, the Sector-Specific Agencies shall report to the Secretary on their efforts to identify, prioritize, and coordinate the protection of critical infrastructure and key resources in their respective sectors. The report shall be submitted within 1 year from the issuance of this directive and on an annual basis thereafter.

(36) The Assistant to the President for Homeland Security and the Assistant to the President for National Security Affairs will lead a national security and emergency preparedness communications policy review, with the heads of the appropriate Federal departments and agencies, related to convergence and next generation architecture. Within 6 months after the issuance of this directive, the Assistant to the President for Homeland Security and the Assistant to the President for National Security Affairs shall submit for my consideration any recommended changes to such policy.

(37) This directive supersedes Presidential Decision Directive/NSC-63 of. May 22,1998 ("Critical Infrastructure Protection"), and any Presidential directives issued prior to this directive to the extent of any inconsistency. Moreover, the Assistant to the President for Homeland Security and the Assistant to the President for National Security Affairs shall jointly submit for my consideration a Presidential directive to make changes in Presidential directives issued prior to this date that conform such directives to this directive.

(38) This directive is intended only to improve the internal management of the executive branch of the Federal Government, and it is not intended to, and does not, create any right or benefit, substantive or procedural, enforceable at law or in equity, against the United States, its departments, agencies, or other entities, its officers or employees, or any other person.

CHAPTER 3

Types of Terrorist Attacks

3.1 INTRODUCTION

Terrorism is a tactic in which an adversary uses random or premeditated violence to coerce and manipulate the target audience. In order to accomplish his/her goals, an adversary looks for low-risk, high-visibility, and high-impact targets against which to execute their attack. An adversary certainly does not want to expend any more resources than absolutely necessary to accomplish the mission. However, an adversary will risk whatever resources are necessary if the assumption is that the attack is not only likely to succeed, but that it will provide a sufficient amount of publicity and cause the maximum amount of casualties and/or damage to critical infrastructure of key asset.

An adversary has an almost unlimited selection of attacks to choose from, limited only by imagination and resources. The specific type of attack will be matched against an appropriate target to achieve specific goals. An adversary will not overexpend resources, meaning he/she will not dedicate more to an attack than is absolutely necessary to accomplish what needs to be done.

If an adversary crosses the line between an acceptable and unacceptable target, and an acceptable and unacceptable type of attack, he/she can very quickly lose support for the cause.

An adversary must be careful when selecting both the target and the type of attack that will be perpetrated in the furtherance of a cause. A terrorist wants to accomplish many things, including instilling fear within the population. However, if the wrong type of attack is executed at the wrong venue, a terrorist will likely instill rage in the population. Fear is instilled in the population because they have become sensitized to a certain amount of "acceptable" violence being perpetrated against certain targets. The population can become enraged when "unacceptable" violence is used to perpetrate attacks against "unacceptable" targets. For example, many Americans "accept" the risk of a terrorist bombing at tourist venues when traveling overseas, especially in the Middle East. While they have accepted both the method of attack and the target selected, there is an acceptable degree of fear that they could

Understanding, Assessing, and Responding to Terrorism: Protecting Critical Infrastructure and Personnel By Brian T. Bennett

become victims if they are traveling in these dangerous areas. As a contrast, the September 11 attack was deemed unacceptable by Americans. The attack used commercial aircraft, with innocent civilians aboard, as weapons against other innocent civilians, who did nothing wrong but go to work that fateful day. The targets, which were office buildings located in the homeland, were also seen as unacceptable. The end result of the attack was that individuals, organizations, and even governments that were supporters of the terrorists' cause have now abandoned them, and in some cases are working to eliminate them. Americans were outraged by both the method of attack and the targets selected, and this rage has been channeled into a relentless military campaign to extract revenge and eliminate the terrorist threat not only against the homeland, but against the world's citizens regardless of nationality or location.

3.2 TYPES OF DESTRUCTIVE EVENTS

A terrorist attack, by design, is intended to be destructive to people (in terms of casualties), to property (in terms of damage or degradation of services), and the economy (in terms of direct and indirect loss). However, terrorist attacks are not the only destructive events that can adversely impact us. There are three categories of destructive events:

- *Accidental Event.* An accidental event involves an unintentional act. An example of an accidental event would be an individual who unknowingly drops a lit cigarette onto a sofa cushion, which leads to a fire.
- *Natural Event.* A natural event is one that occurs naturally, without the direct involvement of humans. An example of a natural event is a hurricane.
- *Intentional Event.* An intentional event involves premeditation on the part of an individual or group to plan and execute the attack with the purpose of causing destruction. An example of an intentional event is a suicide bomber attacking a crowded restaurant.

3.3 WHO CAN EXECUTE AN ATTACK?

An attack against a target can be planned and executed by an individual working alone (such as the Unabomber) or by a group of people working toward a common goal. An attack can be perpetrated by any one or a combination of three adversary classifications:

1. *An Insider.* An attack may be perpetrated by a person inside the entity, organization, or jurisdiction. An insider may be an employee, a contractor, or other person who is authorized to be present in the area where the attack is executed. An insider can be motivated to attack for a number of reasons including

revenge, jealously, or financial gain. An insider may also be a terrorist, someone who has been in the area for some period of time, having integrated into the community and not raising any suspicions. This individual or group, known as a sleeper cell, has remained dormant in terms of the attack and has waited until the appropriate time and place to execute an attack.

2. *An Outsider.* An outsider is an adversary who is external to the entity, organization, or jurisdiction and is not normally authorized to be in the target area. Therefore the outsider usually initiates the attack from an area external to the target because there are effective countermeasures in place that do not allow access to the target area.
3. *In Collusion.* Collusion is when an outsider partners with an insider to perpetrate an attack. Effective adversaries are often on the lookout for vulnerable persons who may be exploited in some way to the adversary's advantage. For example, an adversary may become aware of an employee of a critical infrastructure who has been passed over for promotion and is disgruntled. The adversary may approach the disgruntled employee and offer to partner with him/her to exact revenge for the perceived wrong. An adversary may also be aware of an employee in a critical infrastructure who is in debt or has significant financial burdens. The adversary may approach this individual and offer to purchase information regarding the target or access to the target itself for a substantial fee. Once the adversary has secured the assistance of an insider, the two will work together in a cooperative manner to perpetrate the attack.

3.4 WAYS IN WHICH AN ASSET MAY BE ATTACKED

An asset may be attacked or exploited in one of four ways:

1. *The Asset May Be the Target.* The asset may be the actual target of the intended attack launched by an adversary. The asset is attacked because there is something present in the target location that the adversary wants to adversely impact: either people, information, or property. In the September 11 attack, the World Trade Center Towers 1 and 2 and the Pentagon were the targets.
2. *The Asset May Be Collateral Damage.* An asset may be adversely impacted because of its location. Collateral damage is unintended damage to personnel, information, or equipment from an attack on the primary target. The damage and subsequent destruction of the 47 story 7 World Trade Center building on September 11 is an example of collateral damage.
3. *The Asset May Be Used as a Diversion.* An asset may be attacked as a diversion from the primary attack. A diversionary attack is launched to draw resources away from the primary target, thus leaving it exposed and vulnerable to a subsequent attack. In April 1997, three members of the True

Knights of the Ku Klux Klan were arrested and have been found guilty for planning to place an improvised explosive device on a hydrogen sulfide storage tank at a refinery near Dallas, Texas as a diversionary attack prior to robbing an armored carrier.

4. *The Asset May Be Hijacked, Stolen, or Diverted.* There are assets that may be hijacked, stolen, or diverted and used at a later time against a more attractive target, which will cause more severe adverse effects. As an example, a gasoline tank truck, which contains approximately 8800 gallons of flammable gasoline, can be hijacked and stored in a warehouse. At some time in the future, it can be driven into the lobby of a multistory hotel and ignited, resulting in loss of life and destruction of the building.

3.5 TARGET SELECTION

Once an adversary has made the decision to attack, a sufficient amount of time and effort must be taken to select an appropriate target. There are a number of characteristics that lead to a target being selected for attack.

- *Association.* The target is selected for attack because of its affiliation or because it is part of an organization that is being targeted. For example, an El Al airliner may be attacked, not because the adversary wanted to attack an aircraft, but because the airline is associated with the Israeli government.
- *Importance.* The target is selected because it holds some importance to a jurisdiction, such as being a critical infrastructure, a key resource, or a key asset. The London bombings in July 2005 targeted transportation sector critical infrastructure—subways and buses.
- *Location.* The target is impacted only because of its location; this is commonly known as being in the wrong place at the wrong time. The target happened to be in the specific location at the specific time by chance when an attack was executed. The passengers on the airplanes during the September 11 terrorist attack in the United States were random victims of location.
- *Name.* The target is selected based on who or what it is. An adversary attacks a target by name to ensure a message is conveyed to the public. The assassination of U.S. President McKinley is an example of targeting by name.
- *Opportunity.* Targets of opportunity are very tempting to an adversary. The target is impacted because vulnerabilities that could easily be exploited by an adversary presented themselves. The chance for a successful attack was high, and the adversary took advantage of the opportunity presented and executed an attack. The attack on the USS Cole was a target of opportunity. The ship was vulnerable while tied up to the pier, the threat to the ship was misinterpreted as being low, people's guard was down, and there were few effective security countermeasures in place.

- *Recognition.* The target is selected because it is easily recognized by the adversary. The twin towers of the World Trade Center were targets of recognition because they were easily identifiable as the tallest buildings in New York City.
- *Symbol.* A symbolic target is one that is representative of a way of life, a person, or an organization. An adversary would attack a symbolic target as a means of affecting the greater entity. The Pentagon was a symbolic target on September 11. The building was symbolic of the U.S. military and its vast influence as a global superpower.

3.6 IDENTIFYING LUCRATIVE TARGETS

The U.S. Department of Defense has developed a system called DSHARPP to identify lucrative targets. The acronym DSHARPP is a useful tool in determining what may be considered a lucrative target for an adversary. Each letter in the acronym represents a vulnerability consideration:

Demography. Who is being targeted? Who are the occupants located at the potential target? Are the occupants at a target associated with a greater organization?

Symbolism. Does the target have some symbolic significance? Could it be perceived to represent a culture, corporation, or government?

History. Do adversaries have a history of attacking this type of target in the past? Does the target represent or commemorate an incident or target that was attacked in the past?

Accessibility. How easy is the target to approach? Does the security force appear vigilant? Is the target located near the perimeter? Can a person enter the target area unchallenged? Can the target be attacked with a low chance of compromise? Are effective security countermeasures in place?

Recognizability. Is the target easy to recognize? Can it be readily located and identified by an adversary?

Population. What is the population relative to other potential targets in the area? A basic assumption is that the higher the population, the more attractive it is as a terrorist target.

Proximity. Is the target located near other targets that might make it a less attractive target to an adversary? Unwanted collateral damage may be a deterrent to a terrorist attack.

Values from 1 to 5 are assigned to each factor based on the associated data for each target. Five represents the highest likelihood for attack, and one is the lowest. The higher the total overall score, the more lucrative the target is. The DSHARPP process is not a very scientific method, as it is very subjective. However, it does provide a system to ascertain the relative attractiveness of a key asset as a target.

Example: DSHARPP

For this example, we will evaluate some key assets located on a college campus:

- *Dormitory.* The dormitory is a six story masonry building housing 1000 male students.
- *Administrative Office.* The administration office is a three story masonry building housing the various administrative offices for the college.
- *Book Store.* The book store is a one story masonry building that sells student textbooks as well as miscellaneous items.
- *Classroom.* The classroom building is a three story masonry building located in the center of campus. It contains 20 classrooms plus various departmental offices.

Using the DSHARPP process, we find the following:

Building	D	S	H	A	R	P	P	Total
Dormitory	3	3	1	4	4	5	5	**25**
Office	5	5	3	4	4	3	4	**28**
Book store	1	1	1	5	3	2	2	**15**
Classroom	3	2	4	5	3	4	3	**24**

The result of the evaluation indicates that the office building is most at risk, followed by the dormitory, classroom, and bookstore.

3.7 DIFFERENCE BETWEEN TERRORISM AND INSURGENCY

There is a significant difference between terrorism and insurgency. A key difference is that an insurgency is a movement—a political effort with a specific aim. This sets it apart from both guerilla warfare and terrorism, as they are both methods available to pursue the goals of a political movement. Another difference is the intent of the component activities and operations of insurgencies versus terrorism. There is nothing inherent in either insurgency or guerilla warfare that requires the use of terror. While some of the more successful insurgencies and guerilla campaigns employed terrorism and terror tactics, and some developed into conflicts where terror tactics and terrorism became predominant, there have been others that effectively renounced terrorism. The ultimate goal of an insurgency is to challenge the existing government for control of all or a portion of its territory, or force concessions in sharing political power. Insurgencies require the active or tacit support of some portion of the population involved. External support, recognition, or approval from other countries or political entities can be useful to insurgents, but is not required. A terror group does not require and rarely has the active support or even the sympathy of a large fraction of the population. Terrorism does not attempt to challenge government forces directly, but acts to change perceptions as to the effectiveness or legitimacy of the government itself. This is done by ensuring the widest possible knowledge of the acts of terrorist violence among the target audience. Insurgency need not require the targeting of noncombatants. Terrorists do not discriminate between combatants and noncombatants. Ultimately, the difference between insurgency and terrorism comes down to the intent of the actor.

Insurgency movements and guerilla forces can adhere to international norms regarding the law of war in achieving their goals, but terrorists are by definition conducting crimes under both civil and military legal codes [1].

An insurgency differs from terrorism in that it is directed primarily against a military force. An insurgency is an organized rebellion that engages in deliberate actions to cause the downfall of a governmental authority through destruction and armed actions. Insurgents are those who carry out an insurgency. Insurgents engage in regular or guerilla combat against the armed forces of the established government, such as by sabotage or harassment. Insurgents are in opposition to a government primarily in order to overthrow or obtain a share in government, to further a separatist or revolutionary agenda, or improve their condition.

Insurgent tactics and strategies vary widely, as well as the type of targets that insurgents attack. Raids are among the most common actions taken by insurgents. Some elements of an insurgency may use bombs, kidnappings, hostage taking, hijackings, shootings, and other types of violence to target the establishments' power structure and other facilities with little regard for civilian casualties [2].

3.8 CHARACTERISTICS OF A TERRORIST ATTACK

- *Coercive*. A terrorist attack may be designed to maximize violence against people and maximize the destruction of property. These considerations are used in the commission of the attack to produce the desired effect. The threat or actual application of violence is used to coerce the target audience.
- *Deliberate*. The attack is premeditated and uses a specifically selected violent tactic against the target to achieve a particular goal. It is not a random act.
- *Dynamic*. Terrorist groups demand change, revolution, or political movement to further their cause. They utilize attacks to call attention to their cause and resort to drastic actions to destroy or alter the status quo and move people to support their cause.
- *Political*. A terrorist attack is usually designed to cause a political effect in support of a cause.
- *Psychological*. A terrorist attack is designed to instill terror and fear. A successful terrorist attack will affect the larger population—not just the actual victims who were the target of the attack.

3.9 RESULTS OF A TERRORIST ATTACK

Using an attack against a physical critical infrastructure target, an adversary will adversely impact one or some combination of:

- *People.* An adversary generally always targets people, with the goal of causing injuries or fatalities.
- *Products.* A critical infrastructure may provide an important product to the jurisdiction, such as electricity or a pharmaceutical drug.
- *Services.* A critical infrastructure may also provide an important service to the jurisdiction, such as water treatment or law enforcement.
- *Information.* An adversary may execute an attack to collect information that can used at a later time in a different attack, or to degrade or destroy information which will lead to an economic loss.

A successful attack will result in one of three outcomes that will have an impact on the targeted asset.

- *Degrade.* An asset is degraded when it is damaged to the point where it cannot provide its usual output of product or it cannot provide its full range of services. If a target is hardened to the point that an adversary is unlikely to destroy it, an option may be to degrade the target. For example, it may be very difficult to attack a power generation plant, but the electricity supply to the jurisdiction can be curtailed if an adversary were to attack the less protected, and hence more vulnerable, distribution system.
- *Destroy.* A physical asset may be damaged so severely that it cannot produce its product or services. In this case the asset has been damaged to the point where it will have to be rebuilt in order to provide its product or services. An asset may consist of people who provide a critical service. If an attack successfully incapacitates, injures, or kills people so that they cannot provide their services, such as physicians, it will have effectively destroyed that asset.
- *Exploit.* An adversary may also attempt to exploit a target during an attack. Exploitation means that vulnerabilities that exist are used by the adversary to the greatest possible advantage to ensure the success of the attack. A soft target can be exploited very easily since there are usually few, if any, security countermeasures in place.

An adversary may also exploit elements of a particular critical infrastructure to disrupt or destroy another target. For example, an electric power plant can be exploited to cause a release of a toxic chemical: by destroying a power plant in an attack, the loss of electricity could cause a release of hazardous materials from a neighboring chemical plant due to safety and control systems failure.

3.10 TERRORIST TACTICS

Terrorists learn about their target and adapt to the security countermeasures that have been implemented. They improve the likelihood that they will successfully execute an attack through research of the target and by practicing the attack.

There are a number of attacks an adversary can perpetrate against a target. Quite often, an attack will have multiple direct and indirect effects (e.g., an arson attack will also have economic effects). The types of attacks are described next.

Arson

Arson is the willful and malicious destruction or damaging of property through the use of fire. An adversary may execute an arson attack in a critical infrastructure, key resource, or key asset with the intent of damaging or destroying the asset, its product, or its ability to provide a service. An arson attack is less dramatic than other tactics, but it has the advantage of posing a low risk of the adversary being discovered or caught, and a successful attack requires only a low level of technical knowledge. The materials necessary to make an incendiary device are cheap, commonly available in commercial venues, and easy to hide. Thus an arson attack is easily perpetrated by an adversary that may not be as well organized, equipped, or trained as a major terrorist organization.

Example of an Arson Attack. On October 19, 1998, the Earth Liberation Front executed an arson attack at a ski resort that was undergoing an 880 acre expansion in Vail, Colorado. The fire caused $12 million in damages and destroyed a ski patrol headquarters building, a mountaintop restaurant, and several ski lifts. The attack was perpetrated to illustrate the group's displeasure with the construction occurring in a pristine environment.

Assassination

Assassination is the deliberate surprise killing of a strategically important individual for political or ideological reasons. The killing of prominent persons, symbolic enemies, as well as traitors who defect from the group often serves to instill a significant amount of fear in the target audience. Historically, terrorists have assassinated specific individuals for this very psychological effect.

Example of an Assassination Attack. In September 1981, Egyptian President Anwar Sadat began a crackdown on intellectuals and activists of all ideological causes. His extreme techniques included the arrest of over 1600 persons. On October 6, 1981, Sadat attended a military parade in Cairo celebrating the eighth anniversary of the 1973 Egypt–Israeli War. He was assassinated at the parade by army members who were part of the Egyptian Islamic Jihad, who were opposed to both his negotiations with Israel and his crackdown of the dissidents.

Interestingly, there are several ties to terrorists who many years later would become infamous in U.S. history. A fatwa approving the assassination had been obtained from Omar Abdul-Rahman, who was later convicted and imprisoned in the United States for his role in the first World Trade Center bombing in 1993. Over 300 Islamic radicals were indicted in the trial of the assassin, including Ayman al-Zawahiri. Zawahiri's fluency in English made him the spokesman for the defendants. He was released from prison in 1984, then traveled to Afghanistan and developed a close relationship with Osama bin Laden, later becoming the number two man in al Qaeda.

Cyber

Almost every facet of American life has become dependent on computers. The U.S. National Infrastructure Protection Center defines cyber terrorism as "a criminal act perpetrated by the use of computers and telecommunications capabilities, resulting in violence, destruction, and/or disruption of services." Cyber terrorism may involve the use of computer systems, computer programs, and data. Computer network tools can be used to shut down critical infrastructure such as energy or transportation.

A hacker is a computer programmer who creates and modifies computer hardware and software. A hacker employs a series of modifications to computer programs, administration, and security-related items to exploit a system or gain unauthorized access to a network. Once access to the system has been gained, a hacker can create a number of problems such as introducing computer viruses to incapacitate or destroy computer information systems.

Example of a Cyber Attack. On January 15, 1996, a 19 year old Swedish resident calling from London managed to hack into the network of Southern Bell. He was able to generate multiple, simultaneous telephone calls to eleven counties in west central Florida. He effectively jammed the 911 emergency phone system by tying up all telephone trunk lines, blocking any legitimate caller from placing an emergency call.

Damage/Destruction of Critical Infrastructure or Key Resources

Any asset could be considered an acceptable target to an adversary. The more valuable the asset is to a jurisdiction, the greater the attraction for an adversary to attack. Key resources such as significant landmarks and structures are also attractive potential targets. There are a number of ways a critical infrastructure or key resource can be damaged or destroyed.

Example a Destruction of a Key Resource. The Alfred Murrah Federal Building in Oklahoma City provided office space for various federal agencies. Timothy McVeigh, upset with the federal government's handling of the response to the Branch Davidian Complex in Waco, Texas, perpetrated the April 19, 1995 bombing which killed 168, wounded 642, and destroyed the building as well as several surrounding structures.

Economic

Terrorist groups realize that economic discomfort is extremely effective in persuading audiences. Bin Laden, in particular, has come to that conclusion and has issued fatwas calling for the destruction of the U.S. economy. A traditional terrorist attack can have immediate, varied, and far-ranging economic effects as we learned after the September 11 attack. Some of these adverse effects were the direct result of the attack, while still others were not but rather magnified the actions of the citizens as they changed their daily routines. The U.S. airline industry and high-profile vacation/entertainment venues suffered the worst of these indirect economic effects.

An economic attack is designed to cause financial loss to the intended target. In the case of a private sector asset, this loss may force the target to go out of business, spend money to repair or rebuild, or cause loss to the shareholders. An attack on a public sector asset would likely have an impact on a much broader population as the economic costs would be distributed across the jurisdiction's tax base or be passed on to customers through price increases for products or services. In any case, an economic attack is designed to cause an inconvenience to the general population by influencing how and when their money is spent.

Example of an Economic Attack. The Tylenol scare occurred in the fall of 1982. Someone apparently replaced Tylenol Extra Strength capsules with potassium cyanide laced capsules, resealed the packages, and deposited the adulterated product on the shelves of at least a half dozen pharmacies in the Chicago suburbs. It is believed the culprit entered various supermarkets and drug stores over a period of weeks, pilfered packages of Tylenol from the shelves, adulterated their contents with solid cyanide compound at another location, and then replaced the bottles. The contaminated product was ingested by unwitting victims, resulting in seven fatalities before action could be taken by the authorities.

The first victim was a 12 year old girl, who died on September 29, 1982 after waking her parents and telling them she did not feel well. Her parents gave her one Extra Strength Tylenol capsule. She was later found on the bathroom floor and taken to the hospital, where she was pronounced dead.

The second victim died on September 29, 1982. Paramedics were called to the home of a 27 year old male postal worker. He was found on the floor in respiratory distress. He was rushed to the local hospital where he died soon after arrival after resuscitation attempts failed.

The third and fourth victims died on the evening of the second victim's death. His grieving family gathered at his house to mourn his sudden passing and discuss funeral arrangements. His 25 year old brother and 19 year old sister-in-law were suffering from headaches attributed to the stress of losing a family member. They found the bottle of Extra Strength Tylenol capsules (the same bottle that killed victim #2) and took one capsule each. Shortly after taking the capsule, both victims collapsed to the floor. Paramedics transported both victims to the hospital; the brother died that day, and the sister-in-law died two days later.

By October 1, the poisoning had taken the lives of three other women. The fifth victim was a 27 year old female who was recovering from the birth of her fourth child. She died shortly after taking an Extra Strength Tylenol capsule. The sixth victim was a 35 year old flight attendant who was found dead in her apartment. The seventh and last victim was a 35 year old female also found dead in her home.

Investigators soon found the Tylenol link. Urgent warnings were broadcast, and police drove through Chicago neighborhoods broadcasting warnings over loudspeakers.

In addition to the five bottles that led to the victims deaths, three other tampered bottles were discovered.

Johnson & Johnson, the parent company of the manufacturer, McNeil Consumer Products, stopped product advertising and issued warnings to hospitals. Investigation of the manufacturing codes on the bottles revealed the tampered bottles came from different factories.

On October 5, a nationwide recall of Tylenol products was issued; an estimated 31 million bottles were in circulation with a retail value of over $100 million. The company also advertised in the national media for individuals not to consume any products that contained Tylenol.

Soon after the national news stories regarding the tragic deaths from the tainted Tylenol capsules, widespread fear swept the country, especially in Chicago and its suburbs. People across the country rushed home to dispose of their bottles of Tylenol. Hospitals and poison control centers were flooded with calls concerning Tylenol and fears of poisoning. Hospitals around the country admitted many patients under the suspicion of cyanide poisoning from Tylenol. Some state health departments banned all forms of Tylenol products. Many retailers completely removed Tylenol products from their shelves.

Before the crisis, Tylenol was the most successful over-the-counter product in the United States with over 100 million users. Tylenol was responsible for 19% of Johnson & Johnson's corporate profits during the first three quarters of 1982. Tylenol accounted for 13% of Johnson & Johnson's year-to-year sales growth and 33% of the company's year-to-year profit growth. Tylenol was the absolute leader in the painkiller field accounting for a 37% market share (out of a $1.2 billion pain relief market), outselling the next four leading painkillers combined. The market share of Tylenol collapsed from 37% to 8%. The company's market value fell by $1 billion as a result.

The capsules were found to contain 65 mg of cyanide each, more than 10,000 times the lethal dose to an adult. This is the first known deliberate tampering of a medication that led to death.

Environmental

Environmental attacks involve the deliberate introduction of a hazardous material into the environment, which will threaten or cause pollution.

Example of an Environmental Attack. There could be a number of reasons for the attack cited in this example: it could be an economic attack, whereby an oil tanker was damaged, the oil was burned, or the volatile petroleum market was shaken up; it could be an attack against the transportation infrastructure sector; or it could be an environmental attack, whereby the terrorists hoped to cause oil pollution on the water. It was certainly perpetrated to cause as much damage as possible through a number of adverse consequences. On October 6, 2002, a small boat laden with explosives was deliberately rammed into the 1000 foot French oil tanker Limburg as it approached an oil port in Yemen. The ship burned, oil was spilled into the gulf, and one crewman was killed in the attack.

Explosives

Conventional explosives or improvised explosive devices (IEDs) are used to damage or destroy a target. Modern explosive devices are smaller, harder to detect, and very destructive.

Example of an Explosive Attack. Sixty-three people were killed and 120 injured when a 400 pound suicide truck bomb was detonated at the U.S. Embassy in Beirut, Lebanon. The Islamic Jihad claimed responsibility.

Hijacking

Hijacking is the seizure by force of a vehicle. Hijacking is normally carried out to produce a spectacular hostage situation, murder, or ransom in the form of concessions or money. Although trains, buses, and ships have been hijacked, aircraft are the preferred target because of their greater mobility.

Example of a Hijacking Attack. TWA Flight 847, enroute from Athens to Rome, was hijacked on June 14, 1985 by Lebanese terrorists. The plane was forced to land in Lebanon, and U.S. Navy diver Robert Stetham, who was a passenger on the plane, was murdered and his body dumped on the tarmac. The remaining hostages were released in small groups over the next two weeks, with the final group released on July 1, 1985, after Israel agreed to release several hundred Palestinian detainees.

Hoaxes or Threats

A terrorist group may make a threat that it is capable of carrying out, while having no intention to do so. Any terrorist group that has established its credibility can employ a threat or hoax with considerable success. Threats and hoaxes require that resources (time, people, and money) are deployed by the jurisdiction to protect an asset that is not really being targeted. Also, false alarms dull the analytical and operational effectiveness of key personnel, thus degrading readiness. Hoaxes and threats at first heighten feelings of panic in the general public. However, once the threat or hoax has been discredited, the general population tends to become desensitized as to the real threat.

Hoaxes or threats can also be used to elicit a response by the jurisdiction, which can then be observed by the adversary to determine the response and countermeasures that would be implemented in response to a threat.

Example of a Hoax or Threat Attack. On January 24, 2001, executives of 300 of the largest water suppliers in the United States received the following fax from the Federal Bureau of Investigation: "Urgent: Last night, the FBI received a signed threat from a very credible, well funded North African based terrorist group indicating that they intend to disrupt water operations in twenty-eight U.S. cities. Because the threat comes from a credible, well known source, with an organizational structure capable of carrying out such a threat, the FBI has asked utilities, particularly large drinking water systems, to take precautions and to be on the lookout for anyone or anything out of the ordinary."

This threat turned out to be a hoax, but it was very disruptive to the water sector and very disturbing to the general public [3].

Hostage Taking

Hostage taking may involve the seizure of a facility or location or simply the taking of hostages to establish a bargaining position and to elicit publicity. This is usually an overt attempt to seize an individual or individuals with the intent of gaining publicity or other concessions in return for the release of the hostage. Unlike a kidnapping, hostage taking provokes a confrontation with authorities. It forces authorities either to make dramatic decisions or to comply with the terrorists' demands. The terrorists' intended target is the audience affected by the hostage's confinement, not the hostage.

Example of Hostage Taking. Approximately 500 Iranian student militants calling themselves the Muslim Students Following the Line of the Imam stormed the main U.S. Embassy building in Tehran, Iran on November 4, 1979. Of 90 occupants, 66 were taken hostage. Fourteen women, African Americans, and non-U.S. captives were released, leaving 52 Americans held hostage for 444 days, who were released on the day Ronald Reagan was inaugurated as president of the United States—January 20, 1981.

The students justified taking the hostages as retaliation for admission of the Shah of Iran into the United States.

Kidnapping

Kidnapping is similar to hostage taking, but it does have significant differences. Kidnapping is usually a covert seizure of an individual or individuals in order to extract specific demands. Kidnapping is one of the most difficult acts for an adversary to accomplish, but, if a kidnapping is successful, it can gain the adversary money, release of jailed comrades, and publicity for an extended period of time.

Example of Kidnapping. On December 17, 1981, U.S. Army Brigadier General James Dozier, the highest ranking NATO officer in Italy at the time, was kidnapped in Milan, Italy by leftist Red Brigade terrorists. Italian counterterrorist squads rescued him on January 28, 1982 after 42 days in captivity. Five Red Brigade members were captured. They had sought to highlight their cause by kidnapping and murdering prominent senior figures.

Murder

Civilian personnel are often targeted by terrorists, resulting in death or wounding of innocent men, women, and children in an effort to create terror. High-visibility, key officials may be specifically targeted for murder. Terrorist attacks occur at random and without warning, adding to the fear in the general population.

Example of Murder. The Islamic Jihad kidnapped, tortured, and murdered CIA Station Officer Lieutenant Colonel William Buckley, a top terrorism expert, on March 16, 1984 in Beirut, Lebanon. His remains were returned to the United States on December 28, 1991.

Raids/Attacks

A raid is a hostile or predatory incursion, usually a surprise attack by a relatively small force. Armed attacks on facilities are usually undertaken for one of three purposes:

- To gain access to media broadcast capabilities in order to make a statement.
- To demonstrate the government's inability to secure critical infrastructure, key resources, or soft targets.
- To acquire resources (e.g., robbery).

Example of a Raid. Shortly after noon on June 14, 1995, a group of some 195 Chechen fighters entered the town of Budennovsok, Russia in a convoy of trucks. The raiders held more than 1800 people hostage for six days; 47 people were killed, more than 400 people were injured, and over 160 buildings were damaged or destroyed. After the six day standoff with Russian authorities, an agreement was reached in which the hostages were released in exchange for safe passage back to Chechnya. The raid was conducted in an attempt to help begin the process of peacefully regulating the Chechen–Russian conflict.

Sabotage

Sabotage is the intentional destruction of property or the hindrance of production of a product or provision of a service. The primary objective is to demonstrate how vulnerable society is to terrorist actions.

Example of Sabotage. Ecoterrorists use sabotage to stop activities they consider contrary to their beliefs. The Earth Liberation Front has taken responsibility for several acts of sabotage. In July 2001, the group placed metal spikes in hundreds of trees at the Upper Greenhorn Timber Sale in the Cowlitz Valley Ranger District located in the Gifford Pinchot National Forest in Washington State. The group also took responsibility for the November 2001 spiking of trees throughout the Otter Wing Timber Sale in the Nez Perce National Forest, Idaho.

Seizure

Seizure is when something has been taken possession of illegally, usually by means of force. A seizure most commonly involves a building or other physical object that has some value.

Example of a Seizure. Within the Sunni Muslim tradition, Hanafi is one of four schools of law and is considered the oldest and most liberal school of law. On March 9, 1977, about one dozen Hanafi Muslim members armed with shotguns and machetes seized the City Hall Building, the B'nai B'rith Building, and the Islamic Center in Washington, DC. The group took 134 hostages and held them for more than 39 hours; they shot Washington, DC Councilman Marion Berry in the chest and shot and killed a radio reporter. The siege was conducted to seek revenge for the murders of Hamas leader Abdul Khaali's family in 1973 by the Black Muslims. The standoff ended and the hostages were freed after ambassadors from three Islamic nations joined the negotiations.

Weapons of Mass Destruction

Weapons of mass destruction are the ultimate weapon an adversary can employ. These weapons are usually military grade weapons and include the most destructive weapons ever developed. Terrorists have already used chemical and biological weapons, and there is the possibility that they may use nuclear/radiological weapons in the future.

Example of a Weapon of Mass Destruction Attack. The 2001 anthrax attacks started on September 18, 2001. Letters containing weaponized anthrax bacteria were mailed to several news media offices, and two U.S. senators. Five people were ultimately killed in the attack, and dozens of buildings were contaminated. One FBI document placed the cost of the cleanup at over $1 billion.

3.11 CASE STUDY OF A TERRORIST ATTACK

Chechen rebels executed an attack against Beslan Middle School #1, near the troubled Russian Republic of Chechnya, located in the North Ossetian town of Beslan. This three story school was for grades 1–11, with students aged 7–17.

The incident began after children at the school had been celebrating the start of the new school year. Twelve hundred students accompanied by their parents arrived at school with flowers for their new teachers. Shortly after 9 am, the attackers drove up in a covered truck similar to those used for military transport. This was the beginning of a three day hostage crisis. Most of the hostages were herded into the school gym, but others, primarily children, were ordered to stand at the windows. The terrorists were both men and women, with some women wearing bomb belts and some men carrying pistols and rifles. Terrorists threatened to kill five children for each terrorist that was killed, and to kill 20 children for each terrorist injured.

The devastation started when a vehicle from the emergency ministry was sent in to retrieve the bodies of those killed at the start of the siege. A series of explosive blasts rocked the gymnasium, bringing the roof down. Hostages started running. The attackers fired at them to try to block their escape, prompting the troops to shoot back. In the end, 27 hostage takers were killed, and three were arrested alive; 326 hostages were killed, and more than 725 were injured.

3.12 THE INTERRUPTED TERRORIST PLOTS

The potential threat from terrorists attacking targets in the United States remains very real. President George W. Bush underscored the current threat in a speech he presented on October 6, 2005 to the National Endowment for Democracy at the Ronald Reagan Building and International Trade Center in Washington, DC. In his speech, the president revealed that security countermeasures implemented after the September 11 attack had indeed thwarted attacks against the United States. "Overall, the United States and our partners have disrupted at least ten serious al Qaeda terrorist plots since September the 11th, including three al Qaeda plots to attack inside the United States. We've stopped at least five more al Qaeda efforts to case targets in the United States or infiltrate operatives into our country. Because of this steady progress, the enemy is wounded—but the enemy is still capable of global operations."

The ten terrorist plots are:

1. *The West Coast Airliner Plot.* In mid-2002, authorities disrupted a plot to attack targets on the West Coast of the United States using hijacked airplanes. The plotters included at least one major operational planner involved in planning the events of September 11.
2. *The East Coast Airliner Plot.* In mid-2003, U.S. authorities and a partner disrupted a plot to attack targets on the East Coast of the United States using hijacked commercial airplanes.
3. *The Jose Padilla Plot.* In May 2002, U.S. authorities disrupted a plot that involved blowing up apartment buildings in the United States. One of the plotters, Jose Padilla, also discussed the possibility of using a "dirty bomb" on U.S. targets.

4. *The 2004 UK Urban Targets Plot.* In mid-2004, U.S. authorities and partners disrupted a plot that involved using explosives against a variety of urban targets in the United Kingdom.
5. *The 2003 Karachi Plot.* In the spring of 2003, U.S. authorities and a partner disrupted a plot to attack Westerners at several targets in Karachi, Pakistan.
6. *The Heathrow Airport Plot.* In 2003, U.S. authorities and several partners disrupted a plot to attack Heathrow Airport using hijacked commercial airliners. The planning for this attack was undertaken by a major September 11 operational figure.
7. *The 2004 UK Plot.* In the spring of 2004, U.S. authorities and partners, using a combination of law enforcement and intelligence resources, disrupted a plot to conduct large-scale bombings in the UK.
8. *The 2002 Arabian Gulf Shipping Plot.* In late 2002 and early 2003, U.S. authorities and a partner nation disrupted a plot by al Qaeda operatives to attack ships in the Arabian Gulf.
9. *The 2002 Straits of Hormuz Plot.* In 2002, U.S. authorities and partners disrupted a plot to attack ships transiting the Straits of Hormuz.
10. *The 2003 Tourist Site Plot.* In 2003, U.S. authorities and a partner nation disrupted a plot to attack a tourist site outside the United States.

The five casings and infiltrations are:

1. *The U.S. Government and Tourist Sites Tasking.* In 2003 and 2004, an individual was tasked by al Qaeda to case important government and tourist targets within the United States.
2. *The Gas Station Tasking.* In approximately 2003, an individual was tasked to collect targeting information on U.S. gas stations and their support mechanisms on behalf of a senior al Qaeda planner.
3. *Iyman Faris and the Brooklyn Bridge.* In 2003, and in conjunction with a partner nation, the U.S. government arrested and prosecuted Iyman Faris, who was exploring the destruction of the Brooklyn Bridge in New York. Faris ultimately pleaded guilty to providing material support to al Qaeda and is now in a federal correctional facility.
4. *2001 Tasking.* In 2001, al Qaeda sent an individual to facilitate post-September 11 attacks in the United States. Federal law enforcement authorities arrested the individual.
5. *2003 Tasking.* In 2003, an individual was tasked by an al Qaeda leader to conduct reconnaissance on populated areas in the United States [4].

REFERENCES

1. www.terrorism-research.com/insurgency.
2. www.en.wikipedia.org/wiki/insurgency.
3. www.gale.com/pdf/samples/sp656113.pdf.
4. The White House, Office of the Press Secretary, October 6, 2005, *Fact Sheet: Plots, Casings, and Infiltrations Referenced in President Bush's Remarks on the War On Terror.*

CHAPTER 4

Weapons of Mass Destruction

4.1 INTRODUCTION

As we have seen in Chapter 3, there are a number of attacks an adversary can perpetrate to meet certain goals and objectives. This chapter focuses on the most heinous attacks and, arguably, the ones that if successful would cause the most damage.

Terrorists will not fight according to our notion of fairness. Terrorism is not just about causing casualties or damage against a specific target; it is about instilling fear in the general population. The disintegration of the Soviet Union left tens of thousands of nuclear weapons, vast quantities of chemical weapons and biological materials, and thousands of missiles scattered in what became 11 independent states. It should therefore not be unexpected that terrorists will attempt to obtain these or any other weapon that will cause the maximum amount of death and destruction. The ultimate weapon that achieves that goal is a weapon of mass destruction (WMD). Weapons of mass destruction differ from other weapons in that they involve the use of military grade chemical or biological warfare agents, radiological or nuclear materials, incendiary agents, and explosives. There are several acronyms that help to classify the five types of weapons of mass destruction, including BNICE (biological, nuclear, incendiary, chemical, and explosive) and CBRNE (chemical, biological, radiological, nuclear, and explosive). For the purpose of this text, WMD, CBRNE, and BNICE should all be considered synonymous.

An attack involving the use of a WMD will certainly result in a high-profile, high-impact event. Although the use of a WMD has the potential to cause great harm, its use as a terrorist tactic remains in its infancy as groups work toward obtaining the necessary knowledge and materials needed for a successful attack. The selection of an agent for use as a weapon is more complex than just considering its toxicity. Other factors, such as availability of precursors, availability of production knowledge and equipment, stability in storage, persistence, delivery to the target area, and dissemination techniques must also be considered and addressed in order to achieve success.

Understanding, Assessing, and Responding to Terrorism: Protecting Critical Infrastructure and Personnel By Brian T. Bennett

"I would say that from the perspective of terrorism, the overwhelming bulk of the evidence we have is that their efforts are focused on biological and chemical weapons," said U.S. Undersecretary of State for Arms Control and Disarmament, John Bolton. "Not to say there aren't any dealings with radiological materials, but the technology for biological and chemical is comparatively so much easier that that's where their efforts are concentrating. The thing to keep in mind is that while it is extremely difficult, we have highly motivated and intelligent people who would like to do it," said Daniel Benjamin, a senior fellow at the Center for Strategic and International Studies.

Terrorists would have to overcome significant technical and operational challenges to successfully manufacture and disseminate chemical or biological agents of sufficient quality and quantity to kill or injure large numbers of people. However, even an unsophisticated weapon will cause massive casualties. Whereas a military grade weapon would likely cause thousands or tens of thousands of casualties, a less sophisticated weapon may cause hundreds or thousands of casualties.

4.2 HISTORY OF WEAPONS OF MASS DESTRUCTION

The use of weapons of mass destruction to inflict mass casualties and cause panic within society is nothing new. These weapons have been used numerous times throughout history.

10,000 BC	The African San society used venom tipped arrows to kill their prey.
1000 BC	Chinese armies used arsenical smoke in battle.
600 BC	Assyrians contaminated enemy water supplies during the siege at Krissa.
429 BC	Spartans used noxious smoke against cities allied with Athens during the Peloponnesian War.
184 BC	Hannibal of Carthage had clay pots filled with poisonous snakes and instructed his soldiers to throw the pots onto the decks of Pergamene ships.
6 BC	Assyrians poisoned enemy wells with a fungus that would make the enemy delusional.
4 BC	Chinese troops pumped smoke from burning mustard and other toxic vegetables into tunnels being dug by enemy troops.
AD 1346	Tartars catapulted plague-infected corpses over the walls of the city of Kaffa. The plaque spread throughout the population and decimated the city.
1710	Russian forces attacked the Swedes by flinging plague-infected corpses over the city walls of Reval.
1763	During the French and Indian War in the United States, British soldiers gave Native American Indians a "gift" of smallpox-contaminated blankets. One-third of the Native American population died as a result.

1797	Napoleon attempted to infect Mantua with swamp fever.
1914–1918	Germans used chlorine gas against Allied troops in World War I.
1921–1927	The Spanish and French dropped mustard gas in Spanish-occupied Morocco to quell the Berber rebellion.
1931	Japanese attempted the assassination of the League of Nation Commission with cholera-laced fruit.
1935	Italians dropped mustard gas over a town during their invasion of Ethiopia.
1936	Japan invaded China, using mustard gas, phosgene, and hydrogen cyanide against troop concentrations.
1963–1967	Egypt used phosgene and mustard gases in support of South Yemen against the Yemeni royalist forces during the Yemeni civil war.
1980s	Iraq used mustard and nerve agents against the Iranians in the Iraq–Iran war, 5% of all Iranian casualties are directly attributable to the use of these agents.
1990s	Iraq uses nerve agent against its own people during the Kurdish uprising in northern Iraq.

4.3 WHY USE A WEAPON OF MASS DESTRUCTION?

The use of a WMD follows the escalatory pattern of violence. For more effective results, an adversary would need to be very creative in the design and use of a WMD, and new tactics to ensure the successful delivery of the weapon might have to be developed. An adversary may perceive several advantages from the use of a WMD:

- Small quantities of chemical or biological agents can readily be manufactured from commonly available commercial products, with just a basic knowledge of high school or college chemistry or biology. Recipes for chemical and biological weapons are readily available on the Internet or in publicly available books. Sophisticated processing equipment is not usually required for some basic weapons.
- Materials that could be used as a WMD are readily available. Commercial or industrial chemicals could be purchased, stolen, or diverted from industrial facilities, warehouses, or educational laboratories for use as a weapon. Radiological materials are readily available in many settings, including educational, construction, industrial, and health care. Biological material used to make a weapon can be found in hospital laboratories, university research facilities, garden centers, and even food stores.
- A WMD is cheap. One report quotes testimony before a United Nations panel that "for a large scale operation against a civilian population, manufacturing enough agent to cause causalities might cost about $600 per square kilometer with nerve gas and $1 per square kilometer with biological weapons" [1].
- Small quantities can have a tremendous effect. Weapons of mass destruction are highly toxic and can spread over large areas in dangerous concentrations very quickly.

- The use of a WMD would lead to a significant amount of worldwide media exposure. The use of a WMD would be the next step in the war and would undoubtedly lead to mass casualties, environmental damage, mass hysteria, and significant economic loss.
- Some weapons of mass destruction cannot be detected with existing methods used for explosives and firearms. Current protocol for searching for weapons includes the use of metal detectors and x-ray machines. A WMD can be transported in glass or plastic containers configured to look like everyday items such as hygiene or food products.
- Some agents can be used covertly, with little indication of agent deployment for hours or even days. The first indication of a chemical attack may be when people start to collapse. The first indication of a biological attack may be when people become symptomatic hours or even days after exposure to an infectious dose. There may not be an obvious indication of a radiological attack until many years later when those exposed start to develop diseases associated with radiation exposure.
- Favorable environmental conditions can rapidly spread dangerous concentrations over great distances very quickly. Biological agents can be spread unknowingly by human carriers as they travel across the country or even the world. With today's transportation systems, the globe can be circumnavigated in less than 24 hours.
- A good defense to protect the masses against the use of weapons of mass destruction is difficult. If the adversary successfully deploys a high-quality agent, many casualties will result.
- Use of a WMD will instill fear and confusion in the target population.

4.4 LIMITATIONS OF THE USE OF WEAPON OF MASS DESTRUCTION MATERIALS

Although Weapons of mass destruction are very effective if designed, manufactured, and disseminated properly, there are some limitations and negatives associated with their use:

- Chemical weapons must be used in large quantities, especially when disseminated outside buildings or in large areas.
- Delayed effects can detract from the desired impact. In order to make their political statement, adversaries must realize the results of their attack quickly. The possible uncertainty as to the cause of the attack, and the delay in seeing any measurable effect, will certainly detract from the potency of a political statement.
- The use of a WMD may be counterproductive to the adversary's cause. To a certain degree, there is a balance between the magnitude of the adversary's attack and the support or attention that it generates. Use of weapons abhorred

by the general public because they are considered morally reprehensible may therefore isolate an adversary's organization from its potential support base.

- The proper storage, packaging, and dissemination of a WMD are difficult to achieve. Some agents cannot be stored for long periods of time, because they begin to lose their effectiveness in a matter of hours or days. Getting the agent into the proper package for storage and delivery to the target location, without degradation of the agent, is difficult. Effective delivery of the agent against a target can also be problematic. A number of factors must be considered and addressed to ensure that the agent affects the maximum number of people.

4.5 INDICATORS OF A POSSIBLE WEAPON OF MASS DESTRUCTION ATTACK

Weapons of mass destruction possess some unique indicators that may help to reveal they have been deployed:

- *Unexplained Casualties.* These include multiple victims; definite casualty patterns; serious illnesses; and victims exhibiting nausea, disorientation, difficulty breathing, and convulsions.
- *Symptoms of Victims.* A WMD attack causes unique symptoms that differentiate an attack from other illnesses. Anytime a massive number of victims exhibit similar severe symptoms, a WMD attack should be suspected.
- *Unusual Number of Dead or Dying Animals, Lack of Insects.* Animals fall victim to the same effects of a WMD attack as humans, only more quickly. They are more likely to die of untreated injuries near the place where they were exposed.
- *Unusual Liquid, Spray, or Vapor.* This includes droplets, oily film, unexplained odor, or low hanging clouds unrelated to weather.
- *Suspicious Devices/Packages.* These include unusual metal debris, abandoned containers, or abandoned spray devices.

4.6 RESULTS OF A WEAPON OF MASS DESTRUCTION ATTACK

If a WMD were successfully deployed, there would be many significant adverse consequences:

- *Overwhelmed Emergency Responders.* A WMD attack will require immediate intervention to save lives. Intervention and mitigation by emergency responders may not be successful as they lack proper detection equipment, training, and personal protective equipment to operate in environments contaminated with supertoxic materials. A successful attack that caused hundreds or even thousands of casualties would quickly deplete the resources and ability of a typically staffed community to respond effectively.

- *Mass Casualties.* A WMD attack will result in mass casualties and psychological effects on both the injured and uninjured populations. Health care facilities may be quickly overwhelmed with victims and those who think they have been exposed. Hospital emergency room personnel unfamiliar with decontamination procedures and management of contaminated victims may become victims themselves from contacting residual agent on the clothing and skin of exposed victims.
- *Need for Mass Decontamination.* A WMD attack involving a chemical, biological, or radiological agent will require that all exposed victims be thoroughly decontaminated to limit the spread of the agent and to protect those who were not exposed in the initial attack. A successful attack may require the decontamination of thousands of people.
- *Chaos and Mass Hysteria.* People remote from the attack, and not directly impacted by the agent, will still want to be decontaminated and receive a medical evaluation. Others will change their daily routine as a result of the attack. Panic will likely ensue once the media reports the attack.
- *Lack of Scene Security and Safety.* It will be very difficult to maintain scene safety and security at a WMD incident. Emergency responders will likely be unable to immediately secure the area where an agent was deployed in order to limit the spread of contamination. Well-intentioned people will be rushing into the scene to provide assistance.

The success of a chemical or biological weapon attack is linked to five critical factors:

1. Quality of the agent.
2. Success of weaponization of the agent.
3. Delivery system.
4. Meteorological conditions at the target site.
5. Target conditions/terrain.

The quality of the agent depends of the knowledge of the person creating the agent, as well as the technical resources and equipment that were available to make the agent. The viability of the agent is crucial. As a general rule, as the particle size increases, the viability of cells in the aerosol increases. However, if the particle cell becomes too large it will not be inhaled and will not cause an infection. Weaponization involves modifying the agent to make it more deadly. The delivery system includes storing and transporting the agent, as well as disseminating it against the target. Although explosives are commonly linked to chemical and biological dissemination devices, the heat and shock wave from an explosive can kill a biological agent or incinerate a chemical agent. Spray equipment nozzles must be designed appropriately so the droplet or particle is of the proper size to remain suspended in the air. Meteorological conditions at the time of attack will determine the success of the attack. Meteorological conditions can adversely impact the effective dispersal of even a high-quality agent. Parameters such as temperature, cloud cover, wind speed and direction, humidity, air stability, and sunlight (e.g., ultraviolet radiation) must be considered before disseminating an agent. Finally, conditions at the target will also determine the effectiveness of the attack, such as the implementation defensive security countermeasures. If the targeted population has donned personal protective equipment, the agent would be ineffective. The terrain must also be considered. Vegetation may absorb the agent. The physical contours or topography may allow for the agent to collect in low areas, where the agent may not affect personnel.

4.7 HOW A CHEMICAL, BIOLOGICAL, OR RADIOLOGICAL AGENT CAN ENTER THE BODY

Weapons of mass destruction enter the body the same way as traditional hazardous materials:

1. *Inhalation.* This is the most common route of entry of a contaminant into the body; the agent is inhaled into the respiratory system.
2. *Ingestion.* A contaminant is admitted orally into the digestive system.
3. *Injection.* A piece of debris, such as glass or metal, that is contaminated punctures the skin and injects the contaminant into the circulatory system.
4. *Skin Absorbent.* The hazardous material actually soaks into body tissue through the skin.

There are two types of exposure: (1) *acute exposure*, in which a very high concentration of agent is introduced in a very short period of time; and (2) *chronic exposure*, in which a low concentration of agent is introduced over a long period of time.

Exposure to an agent will have one of two effects on the body: (1) *immediate effect*, in which symptoms manifest immediately after exposure, usually within seconds or minutes; and (2) *delayed effect*, in which symptoms manifest over long periods of time after exposure, usually days, weeks, months, or even years.

There are two types of effects on the body that can occur: (1) *local effect*, in which the adverse effect takes place at the point of exposure (e.g., blister agent will cause blisters to develop on exposed skin); and (2) *systemic effect*, in which the adverse effect is targeted to a particular organ or system, not necessarily the point at which the agent contacted the body (e.g., radiation may expose the skin, but the blood cells are adversely affected).

Definitions

There are some basic terms that must be defined to clarify our discussion.

Aerosol. A fine spray of a solid or liquid agent that is dispersed under pressure.

Gas. State of matter in which the matter occupies the volume of the container regardless of its quantity.

Persistency. A measure of the length of time that an agent remains effective after dissemination.

Specific Gravity. The ratio of the density of a particular substance to the density of water. If the specific gravity is less than 1, the substance will float on water; if it is greater than 1, it will sink.

Vapor. A liquid that has evaporated and is suspended in the air.

Vapor Density. The ratio of the density of a particular substance to the density of air. If the vapor density is less than 1, the substance will rise; if it is greater than 1, it will stay low to the ground, filling depressions.

Vapor Pressure. The pressure exerted by a vapor that is in equilibrium with its solid or liquid form.

Volatility. The tendency of a chemical to vaporize.

4.8 QUESTIONS ABOUT WEAPONS OF MASS DESTRUCTION

How Dangerous Are Weapons of Mass Destruction?

Weapons of mass destruction include the most deadly weapons ever developed by humankind. These weapons were designed for the single purpose of killing and have been engineered and manufactured to accomplish that objective very efficiently. The types of each weapon, rated in terms of their effectiveness to cause mass casualties, are:

1. *Biological agents* are the most effective at creating the most casualties.
2. A *nuclear weapon* would certainly be catastrophic, but it is widely believed to be beyond the capability of most terrorist groups.
3. *Chemical weapons* are the easiest and cheapest to produce, but massive quantities would be required to impact many people. Also, chemical agents generally produce instantaneous effects, as opposed to biological and nuclear/radiological weapons.
4. *Explosive devices* have been used widely across the globe to cause localized casualties. Explosives are effective against an individual target or small groups.
5. A *radiological dispersion device* would likely cause few casualties but would cause extensive psychological, economic, and environmental damage.

How Easy Is It to Obtain or Develop Weapons of Mass Destruction?

Unfortunately, it is very easy to obtain the relevant information, acquire the necessary materials, and prepare the agent for a WMD. Most formulations for chemical agents have been declassified by the military and are readily accessible in textbooks and on the Internet.

Does a WMD Need to Be a Military Grade Weapon?

A WMD does not have to be of military grade to be effective. An adversary does not need to use the ultrapure and ultraefficient weapons developed with the seemingly boundless resources of a state sponsor. Even weapons that are produced from readily available commercial or industrial origins can be very effective.

What Are the Obstacles for the Manufacture and Use of Weapons of Mass Destruction?

An adversary would face a number of obstacles that could prevent the effective and efficient deployment of a WMD and would need to overcome them in order to be successful. An adversary would have to:

1. *Possess the Requisite Technical Skills.* The manufacture of weapons of mass destruction and their dissemination systems requires a certain degree of technical expertise. Some agents are readily available and require little sophistication to obtain or use, but others are challenging to manufacture and deliver. The adversary must have access to these special skills in order to make an effective weapon.
2. *Have Adequate Financial Resources.* The costs associated with assembling a WMD can be substantial, depending on the type of weapon selected and the complexity of the dissemination system. The manufacture of nerve agents, for example, requires sophisticated laboratory equipment. Costs include not only the raw materials for the weapon itself, but the salaries for people who will develop the process and assemble the weapon, facilities and equipment to manufacture the weapon, storage and transportation of the device, and a dissemination system.
3. *Assume Personal Risk of Exposure to the Agent.* There may be some adverse health risk to the person or persons who are manufacturing, storing, transporting, and assembling the weapon. For some terrorists, this may not be an issue, but others may not be inclined to sacrifice their lives for the cause.
4. *Conduct Testing Procedures.* Tests may have to be run to ensure the weapon was assembled correctly and is effective, its storage container is properly designed, and the dissemination system works. Running a test, even in a remote unpopulated area, increases the probability of being reported to or discovered by law enforcement authorities.
5. *Avoid Detection.* In order for the mission to succeed, the attack must accomplish the adversary's goal of causing casualties, fear, or economic damage. Adversaries must go to great extremes to ensure they are not compromised before the attack is executed. There is a risk of detection during the manufacture of the agent, which might require large storage containers, or the manufacturing process itself may release irritating, toxic, or corrosive vapors and thus alert authorities.

6. *Recognize Environmental and Meteorological Conditions at the Time of Dissemination.* The most difficult step in the use of a WMD, especially for a chemical or biological agent, is the dissemination step. There are many factors that may influence the effectiveness of the dissemination system, including environmental and meteorological conditions at the time the agent is dispersed. Failure to consider the weather conditions in the dissemination plan can cause even a high-quality agent to be ineffective.

4.9 TYPES OF WEAPONS OF MASS DESTRUCTION

Biological

General. Biological agents can cause disease in people. The use of a biological weapon would certainly inflict a significant psychological impact on a population because it is silent, colorless, and odorless and does not present any warning that the agent had been dispersed and people were being exposed. Biological agents include toxins as well as bacteria, viruses, fungi, and other living microorganisms that can kill or incapacitate people. Toxins are poisons produced by insects, snakes, sea creatures, or plants. Some toxins can be synthesized through chemical processes. Biological warfare is the use of these pathogens or toxins as weapons. Pathogens as weapons could be used against targets such as food supplies or concentrations of people to create panic and cause casualties. Since they can reproduce, they have the unique potential to make the environment more dangerous over time. Some biological agents are also deadly to animals, although they are not usually the primary target. This characteristic may provide an early warning to emergency responders as animals and insects tend to be affected before humans. Toxins are considered to be less suitable for dispersion on a large scale and are more likely to be used to target a single person or small groups of people.

The primary route of exposure for biological agents is via inhalation or ingestion. Our skin provides a good barrier against biological agents. Unlike some chemical agents, biological agents cannot penetrate healthy, unbroken skin (an exception is T-2 mycotoxin).

Effectiveness of Biological Weapons. Biological agents are the most lethal of the weapons of mass destruction. By weight, biological agents are generally more toxic than chemical agents. For example, the toxin ricin is two to three times more toxic than the nerve agent VX, and the toxin botulinum is 5000–10,000 times more toxic than VX.

There are approximately 30 different pathogenic microbes that directly or indirectly affect humans and are considered biological weapons. Biological diseases are a very attractive weapon; in the U.S. Civil War, 65% of the Union soldiers' deaths were caused by infections. In World War I, 38% of American deaths were from infectious diseases [2].

For example, the bacteria anthrax is 100,000 times more deadly than the most toxic chemical warfare agent. A U.S. Congressional Office of Technology Assessment study concluded that 220 pounds of anthrax, thoroughly distributed in aerosol form over a large city, could kill as many as three million people.

According to another study of emergency responses to a hypothetical anthrax attack, completed in 2003 by operations researchers Lawrence Wein, David Craft, and Edward Kaplan, the release of just 2 pounds of weapons grade anthrax dispersed into the air from a tall building in an American city could result in more than 120,000 deaths [3].

Ideal Biological Weapon. The ideal biological WMD would have the following characteristics:

- Highly virulent so that people get sick very quickly.
- Highly contagious.
- No existing vaccine or prophylaxis.
- Very persistent.
- Cheap and easy to produce.

Categories of Biological Weapons. Biological weapons have been broken down into three categories by the U.S. Centers for Disease Control based on their ability to:

- Be easily disseminated or transmitted person to person.
- Cause a high mortality and present a major public health impact.
- Cause panic and social disruption.
- Require special action of public health preparedness.

Use of Biological Weapons. Biological agents are nonvolatile; they must be disseminated as a solid or liquid aerosol. Biological agents cannot be seen, tasted, or smelled. Environmental conditions such as temperature and humidity can adversely affect bacteria and viruses. Sunlight, in particular, ultraviolet light, will kill many of them.

Contagious Versus Noncontagious. A key question that must be answered very quickly if a biological attack occurs is whether the agent deployed is contagious or noncontagious. Contagious means an infectious disease can be spread between humans through direct or indirect contact or exposure. Noncontagious means the disease can only be spread through direct contact with the agent. An example of direct contact would be when an infected person sneezes, resulting in an aerosol being discharged into the area, which another person can inhale and hence catch the disease. An indirect exposure would be when a person handles contaminated clothing, resulting in the organism being suspended in the air and then inhaled.

Some bacteria and viruses can cause an epidemic, which is a widespread outbreak of disease, being spread from person to person.

Definitions. Infectivity of an agent reflects its capability to enter, survive, and multiply in a host. Virulence is the relative severity of the disease caused by a microorganism. The incubation period is the time elapsing between exposure to an infective agent and the first appearance of the signs of disease associated with the infection. Lethality reflects the ability of an agent to cause death in an infected population.

Ideal characteristics of biological weapons are high infectivity, high potency, no availability of vaccines, and delivery as an aerosol. Diseases are most likely to be considered for use as a biological weapon because of their lethality and robustness.

Types of Biological Agents. Biological agents have a variety of effects depending on the agent, the dose received, and the route of exposure, from skin irritation through death. There are three types of biological agents.

1. *Bacteria.* Bacteria can cause serious illness or death. Bacteria are single-cell living microorganisms that require nutrients to survive and reproduce by dividing. Bacteria reproduce asexually and quickly. Most bacteria can grow on nonliving surfaces. When infectious bacteria enter the body, they can make one sick. Bacteria make toxins that can damage specific cells that they have invaded. Some bacterial infections are contagious (such as strep throat and tuberculosis) and others (such as infections of the heart valves—endocarditis) are not. Bacteria can be controlled with antibiotics, which prevent cell growth. Bacteria can be inhaled or ingested or can cause skin illnesses. Examples of bacterial agents are anthrax and plague.

2. *Virus.* Viruses can also cause severe illness or death. Viruses are capsules of genetic material (DNA or RNA) and are infectious agents, much smaller than bacteria. A virus is not alive until it enters the cells of a living plant, human, or animal; so, unlike bacteria, viruses require a living host to multiply. When a virus enters the body, it invades some cells and takes over the cell machinery, redirecting host cells from their normal function to produce more of the virus. Viruses may eventually kill their host cells' or become part of these cells' genetic material. Some viruses are spread from person to person (such as influenza and the common cold), while other viruses (such as West Nile virus and yellow fever) are not. Viruses have an affinity for particular parts of the body. Viruses cannot survive or be grown on artificial media. Antiviral antibiotics are available for some types of viral infections, such as influenza and herpes. Viruses can be inhaled or ingested' or can cause skin illnesses. Examples of viral agents are smallpox (which attacks the skin), Ebola, and various viruses that cause hemorrhagic fevers.

3. *Toxin.* Biological toxins are poisonous substances that are of natural origin, produced by an animal, plant, or microbe. They are not living organisms, but rather chemical compounds. Toxins can be produced easily and cheaply without sophisticated laboratory equipment or training. Generally, toxins are nonvolatile. Toxins

can enter the body through inhalation, ingestion, or injection. Examples of toxins are rattlesnake venom, ricin, botulinum, and staphylococcal enterotoxin B (SEB).

There are two main types of toxins:

(a) *Neurotoxin.* This toxin attacks the nervous system. A neurotoxin is fairly quick acting and causes the opposite effect of nerve agents by preventing nerve to muscle stimulation. Symptoms such as mental confusion, loss of balance, vision problems, tremors, or seizures are common.

(b) *Cytotoxin.* This toxin attacks the cells. They are slower acting and can have a variety of symptoms including diarrhea, rashes, blisters, jaundice, bleeding, or general tissue deterioration.

Incubation Period. The incubation period is the time between the exposure to the biological agent and when symptoms begin to appear. During the incubation period, the agent is reproducing inside the body and defeating the body's natural defenses. The agent can also produce toxins that may poison the body. The incubation period can be as short as a few hours to as long as several weeks. Microbial pathogens require an incubation period of 25 hours to 6 weeks, while toxins are relatively fast acting. Some of the early symptoms of biological agent exposure are fever, vomiting, and diarrhea.

Aerosols. When biological agents are dispersed as an aerosol, the particles that have a size of 1–5 micrometers (μm) tend to behave like a gas and stay airborne. These particles are known as primary aerosols. The larger, heavier particles will fall to the ground and become secondary aerosols. Secondary aerosols are those particles that are heavier than air, settle to the ground, and need an applied force to suspend them in the air as an aerosol. Infections result when the smaller particle size primary aerosol is inhaled.

Case Study: Biological Attack. Bhagwan Shree Rajneesh founded the Rajneesh Foundation International. In 1981 the cult purchased a dilapidated ranch in Oregon, which became the site of Rajneeshpuram, a community of several thousand orange-robed disciples. The cult leaders planned to take over control of the Wasco County, Oregon Commission at the November election because of potential voter threat to their land due to zoning regulations. Their plan was to sicken so many people on election day that the group could get its own candidates elected. The cult purchased salmonella and other biological agents from a commercial supply house. The salmonella was mixed with water and placed into spray bottles. Followers sprayed the poison on salad bars at ten restaurants in Dalles, Oregon, resulting in 751 people being sickened with salmonella bacteria, 45 of whom were hospitalized.

Court testimony suggests that members of this cult considered various other, and more deadly, pathogens including *Salmonella typhi* (which causes typhoid) and the human immunodeficiency virus (HIV).

Nuclear/Radiological

General. Nuclear and radiological materials used as weapons of mass destruction involve the deliberate release of ionizing radiation. There are a number of ways in which nuclear/radiological material can be used as weapons of mass destruction. For terrorists, it's the fear of radiation that makes a nuclear/radiological weapon so attractive.

"I'm very surprised that a radiological device hasn't gone off," said Matthew Bunn, a nuclear expert at Harvard's Belfer Center for Science and International Affairs [4]. If you think about one of the primary goals of terrorism (fear among the population), the deliberate release of radiological material is the perfect weapon. Although that type of attack would unlikely cause many, if any, immediate fatalities or acute health effects, it is certainly a weapon that could be used to cause mass panic. If the attack were executed properly, the economic damage could be in the range of billions or even trillions of dollars. This is why this type of attack is often called a weapon of mass *disruption*.

Ionizing radiation can be defined simply as either electromagnetic or particulate emissions of energy from the disintegration of the nucleus of an atom. This energy, when impacting on or passing through material, including humans, can cause some form of adverse effect. When ionizing radiation is absorbed by our bodies, it can cause changes to our cells. Small amounts can be tolerated; larger amounts can be harmful. Radiation cannot be detected by our senses but can easily be detected and identified with instrumentation.

Radiological material is any material that gives off radiation.

There is a difference between the terms nuclear and radiological. *Nuclear* refers to the process of fission (splitting a nucleus) or fusion (combining nuclei). *Radiological* deals with radiation or material that emits radiation. *Radioactivity* is the process by which unstable atoms try to become stable by emitting ionizing energy.

Categories of Nuclear/Radiological Weapons. There are three ways in which a nuclear/radiological weapon can be employed:

- Detonation of a nuclear weapon.
- Intentional release of radiation.
- Use of conventional explosives to pulverize and spread radioactive material (e.g., a dirty bomb).

Two things are required to make a nuclear/radiological weapon: radioactive material and a dispersal mechanism. Since acquiring the nuclear/radioactive material is a prerequisite to the fabrication of a weapon, intensive efforts must be given to protect radioactive sources from being obtained for illicit purposes.

Ionizing Radiation. Radiation is a form of energy that is present all around us. Visible light, heat, radio waves, and microwaves are all types of radiation. Different types of radiation exist, some of which have more energy, and hence are more dangerous, than others. We can be harmed by each under certain circumstances. Ionizing radiation poses the most significant health effects as it can damage our cells. *Ionizing radiation* is the energy emitted through the process of removing electrons from atoms or molecules. Ionizing radiation cannot be seen, smelled, heard, or otherwise detected by our senses. Radiation originates inside atoms. The nucleus of an atom contains positively charged protons and neutrons, which have no charge. Electrons, with a negative charge, orbit the nucleus. In a stable atom, the forces among the protons and neutrons are balanced. An excess of either protons or neutrons unbalances the nucleus, leading to an excess of energy and an unstable atom. Unstable atoms shed particles or energy in an attempt to become stable. This shedding is known as radioactive decay.

The four basic types of ionizing radiation are described next.

- *Alpha Particles.* An alpha particle contains two protons and two neutrons and is emitted from the nucleus of an atom. Alpha particles have a positive charge, travel only a very short range (between 2 and 7 inches), and are easily shielded by a single piece of paper. Alpha particles cannot penetrate the outer layers of the skin and are not an external hazard. However, alpha particles are a significant internal hazard and can cause cancer and death if ingested, injected, or inhaled.
- *Beta Particles.* A beta particle occurs when a neutron breaks down into a proton and an electron, and the electron is ejected. Beta particles have a negative charge, can travel a longer range (up to 10 feet in air), and have more penetrating power than alpha particles. Aluminum foil or glass will stop beta particles. They can penetrate the outer layers of skin and are both an internal and external hazard. Beta particles can be inhaled, ingested, or injected into the body.
- *Gamma Rays.* Gamma rays are short-wavelength, high-frequency waves of pure electromagnetic energy. They travel at the speed of light through air, travel great distances (up to 1 mile), and have significant penetrating power. Only very dense materials such as steel, concrete, or lead can shield against gamma rays. Gamma rays can penetrate through the whole body and are an external and internal hazard. Intense gamma rays can cause tissue damage, radiation poisoning, or even death and may lead to cancer [5]. Just walking by a contaminated area can cause a radiation risk.
- *Neutron Radiation.* Neutron radiation comes from nuclear reactors or other industrial neutron sources. A nucleus with an excess of neutrons is radioactive; an extra neutron decays into a proton, an electron, and an antineutrino. This radiation can travel hundreds of feet through the air with high penetration ability, is very difficult to stop, and poses both an internal and external hazard. Plastic, water, and material containing hydrogen can shield against neutron radiation.

Health Effects of Radiation Exposure. The adverse health effects of ionizing radiation exposure may not become apparent for many years and can range from mild effects, such as skin reddening, to serious effects, such as cancer and death, depending on the amount of radiation absorbed by the body, the type of radiation, the route of exposure, and the length of time a person was exposed. Radiation exposure is cumulative.

Exposure to radiation will not make you contaminated and will not make you radioactive. Radioactive *contamination* occurs when materials containing radioactive atoms are deposited in an unwanted place. Radioactive contamination may readily be spread to other locations and other people or simply be suspended in the air. The material that contaminates you is emitting radiation, so you are exposed to radiation as well. Radioactive contamination may be in the form of a solid, liquid, or gas. Exposure to radiation does not indicate that radioactive contamination has necessarily occurred.

Radiation that gets inside our bodies causes *internal exposure*. Internal exposure occurs when unprotected people ingest, inhale, or are injected with radioactive material. Open wounds are a pathway for internal exposure. Individuals who have been exposed internally have also received an external exposure. *External exposure* is from radiation outside the body. Individuals who are externally contaminated are a source of exposure not only to themselves, but to everyone who is nearby. The effect of exposure to ionizing radiation depends on the dose, which is the total amount of ionizing radiation absorbed by the body.

An *acute dose* of radiation is a large amount of radiation received in a short period of time. A *chronic dose* of radiation is a small amount of radiation received over a long period of time.

Radiation sickness has a number of symptoms: burns, hair loss, weakness, fatigue, nausea, vomiting, sterility, low white blood cell count, abdominal discomfort and pain, diarrhea, and tachycardia. Cells that are rapidly dividing (e.g., blood, sperm, intestinal tract, hair follicles) are more sensitive to ionizing radiation. Children are more susceptible than adults. Exposure of an unborn child is of special concern, because the embryo or fetus is extremely sensitive to radiation.

Radiological material can pose both acute (immediate) and chronic (long-term) health effects. In all but the most extreme cases of a large exposure in a short period, it takes considerable time before an individual begins to show symptoms of radiation illness. The risk of adverse health effects from radiation is based on several factors:

- *Total Amount of Radiation Received (Dose).* The larger the dose received, the greater the health risk. A person's distance from the radioactive source will reduce the exposure.
- *Dose Rate.* How fast the dose is received is important: acute exposure poses a high health risk with symptoms occurring within hours or days; chronic exposure poses a smaller health risk delayed for years.

- *Specific Type of Radiation.* The type of radioactive source, its strength, and whether the exposure was an internal or external hazard are important factors.
- *Exposure.* Which body parts are exposed, the length of exposure, and the age/general health of the people exposed are important considerations.

Three concerns at a radiological incident in regard to health effects are the following:

- *Whole Body Exposure.* The more of the body exposed, the greater the danger. The torso and head are at the greatest risk due to the concentration of organs.
- *Ingestion/Inhalation of Radiation.* Internal contamination is much more dangerous than external contamination due to the proximity of internal organs.
- *Contamination.* Contamination will lead to continued exposure.

Very high levels of radiation result in cells' DNA and other components of the cells being damaged to such a degree that those cells are actually dying. Initial signs and symptoms of radiation exposure do not usually appear for 2–6 hours, even with high doses. Others may not become apparent for days, weeks, or months.

There are four effects that ionizing radiation can have on cells: (1) there is no damage; (2) the cells repair the damage and function normally; (3) the cells are damaged and function abnormally (e.g., cancer); and (4) the cells die as a result of the damage.

Radioactive material can enter the body through the same routes as any other hazardous material:

- *Inhalation.* Gaseous or contaminated dust particles can be inhaled into the lungs.
- *Ingestion.* Contamination may enter the body through the gastrointestinal tract by way of contaminated food and drink or swallowing contaminated mucus from the nose and mouth.
- *Absorption.* Radiation may be absorbed from the skin and mucous membranes.
- *Injection.* Radioactive material may enter through open wounds or be injected into the body by contaminated shrapnel such as glass or metal.

Availability of Nuclear/Radiological Materials. Until the demise of the Soviet Union, it was widely believed that there was no black market for fissionable materials. The International Atomic Energy Agency (IAEA) has documented over 400 cases of trafficking in nuclear or radiological materials since 1993. Many of these sources were obtained from poorly secured facilities around the world, particularly in the former Soviet Union. The concern is that terrorist organizations may obtain some of this readily available material and use it as a WMD. "Our database of smuggling . . . gives an indication that there is a market and there is an effort to obtain radioactive sources, and the obvious question is why" [6]. As an example of this black market activity, a deputy director of a company that operates and repairs Russia's nuclear powered ice breakers has been arrested for hoarding in his garage 2 kilograms of radioactive uranium 235. He was arrested as he tried to sell undercover investigators a suitcase containing the material. And it's not just radioactive material that is of concern. Thousands of nuclear weapons and missiles were left scattered after the former Soviet Union disintegrated into eleven successor states. It has been reported by Congressman Weldon that there are 85 missing tactical nuclear weapons from the former Soviet arsenal [7]. Also, in September 2003, Pyotr Simonenko, head of the Ukrainian parliament's Communist faction, told reporters in Kharkiv, Ukraine, that only 2200 of the 2400 nuclear warheads were transferred back to the Soviet Union at the time the Soviet Union disintegrated.

The problem is not one isolated to the eastern hemisphere. There are more than 17,000 radioactive material licenses in the United States [8]. "Stricter security measures are urgently needed to keep radioactive material out of the hands of terrorists, who could use it to spread havoc with dirty bombs" [7].

Possible WMD: Nuclear/Radiological Attacks. There are three types of possible attacks using nuclear/radiological materials.

Detonation of a Nuclear Weapon. The detonation of a nuclear weapon is an explosive release involving the fission or fusion of atoms to produce radioactive fallout. Nuclear weapons fall into three basic categories: the large megaton thermonuclear weapons, the smaller battlefield tactical nuclear weapons, and the even smaller "suitcase," "briefcase," or special atomic demolition munition (SADM or "backpack") weapons, which are small yield and easily transported. In 1998, former Russian General and National Security Advisor Ledbed said one of his assignments was to account for 132 suitcase size nuclear weapons that the Soviet Union had manufactured during the 1970s and 1980s, of which he can only find 48 (meaning 84 are missing). Although many U.S. authorities discount the likelihood of a nuclear detonation on American soil, Ayman al-Zawahiri, al Qaeda's number two leader, was quoted telling an Australian television station they have briefcase nuclear weapons [9].

The use of a nuclear weapon by a terrorist group would have devastating effects, including:

- Fires caused by the thermal (heat) pulse.
- Structural damage from the shock wave.
- Flash burns from the thermal (heat) pulse.
- Trauma from the shock wave.
- Radiation injuries from gamma and neutron radiation.
- Internal/external contamination from radioactive fallout.
- Electronic equipment failure because of the electromagnetic pulse.

A nuclear detonation would result in a bright flash and a vertical smoke column that is light brown or white in color. "Traditional" mushroom-shaped clouds result from higher yield weapons.

Intentional Release of Radiation. A terrorist group may intentionally release radiation, such as by attacking a nuclear power plant or a radioactive waste shipment or storage area. Due to the protective measures and security systems in place, this scenario is not believed to pose a likely threat. However, terrorists could obtain some readily available radioactive material and release radiation covertly or gradually, possibly employing one of the following methods:

- Aerosol or insecticide spraying devices or mechanical dispersion equipment.
- Dumping of radioactive material in the street.
- Contaminating food or water.
- Dispersing radiation in the thermal cloud of a fire.
- Dispersing radiation in a liquid, such as water.

In this case, people would be exposed to low levels of radiation, with few acute health effects. This type of attack would more likely produce mass hysteria among the population. The general public fears radiation and does not understand the actual levels of risk. It is likely that huge numbers of people will think they have been contaminated and are suffering ill effects. Large numbers of people will present themselves for radiation screening and medical evaluation. Decontamination of structures and land will be very costly and time consuming.

Radiological Dispersal Device (RDD)/The Dirty Bomb. The more likely nuclear/radiological attack would be the use of an RDD or dirty bomb. A dirty bomb is a conventional explosive such as dynamite that has been surrounded with radioactive material, which is pulverized and scattered when the explosive is detonated. A dirty bomb is not a nuclear weapon (dirty bombs do not use a nuclear reaction involving fission reactions). A dirty bomb primarily injures or kills through the explosive blast of the conventional explosive and, to a lesser degree, by the airborne dissemination of the radiological contaminant. British officials believe that the al Qaeda terrorist network successfully built a dirty bomb in Afghanistan [10].

It does not take a lot of expertise to make an effective dirty bomb; in fact, not much more than it takes to manufacture a conventional explosive device. The significant challenge is in obtaining the radioactive material, not in building the explosive device. The *Washington Post* reported in March 2002 that the Bush administration's opinion is that the al Qaeda terrorist network probably has obtained readily available radioactive material such as strontium 90 and cesium 137. "It is easy. It is going to happen some day" [11].

Terrorists might deploy an RDD not so much because of the potential heavy casualties, but rather for its ability to cause mass hysteria. It is not very likely that a dirty bomb would cause mass casualties. There will be some people in the immediate area of the blast who would be injured or killed by the detonation of the conventional explosive. However, depending on the size of the weapon, the type of radiological material used, the time of day, weather conditions, population density, and protective measures implemented, there could be mass panic over the radioactivity and emergency response operations that ensue. The area that is impacted by the radiological contamination would be off limits for months or years (again depending on the bomb's characteristics) during the cleanup effort. The potential economic damage and the public's fear would be far more catastrophic than the physical damage.

United States troops have also found detailed instructions on how to manufacture and use a dirty bomb in caves used by al Qaeda in Afghanistan [4].

What do we have to fear? The answer is fear itself. Dirty bombs can be as devastating as any conventional bomb. People will die in a dirty bomb attack. However, very few will become ill or die because of the radiation. The radiation will cause panic and psychological trauma stemming from our society's inherent fear of radiation. The weapons would not cause a lot of direct damage—they are more a weapon of disruption due to our fear of radiation. RDDs are generally not capable of producing acute health effects. Some people, fearing residual radiation, may never return to their homes or businesses located in the area where an RDD has been set off. The greatest impact of an RDD would likely be economic damage caused by the need to decontaminate the area.

The greatest risk of injury or death from a dirty bomb would result from the blast wave and shrapnel from the detonation of the conventional explosive. The radioactive material spread by the conventional explosive would coat everyone and everything within the dissemination plume. The worst case scenario would be radiation that is admitted directly into the body by shrapnel that pierces the skin.

A computer simulation by the Federation of American Scientists found that detonating a device containing 1.75 ounces of cesium in lower Manhattan would distribute radioactive fallout over 60 square blocks [12]. The explosion could damage buildings, expose people to radioactive material, and make buildings and land unusable for extended periods of time. Materials that might be used in a radiological attack can chemically bind to concrete and asphalt, while other materials would become physically lodged in crevices on the surfaces of buildings, sidewalks, and streets. Options for decontamination would range from sandblasting to demolition, with the latter likely being the only feasible option. Some radiological materials will become firmly attached to soil, with the only disposal method being large-scale removal of contaminated dirt. In short, there is a high risk that the area contaminated by a radiological attack would have to be deserted [13].

The destructive power would depend on the size of the conventional bomb, the volume and nature of the radioactive material, location of the release, weather conditions, and other factors.

There are two zones associated with the detonation of a dirty bomb:

- *Immediate Zone*. This is the area in which the conventional explosive was detonated. This area will include casualties from the explosion. There is a potential for large fragments of radioactive material to result in higher exposures. Victims with shrapnel wounds have the potential for greater radiation exposure.
- *Cloud Zone*. This is the area including the immediate zone extending downwind where radioactive materials are carried by the wind and dispersed. The concerns in the cloud zone are the health effects from the short-term initial exposure to radioactive particles and the long-term contamination of buildings and areas.

The real effects of an RDD would be psychological and economic shutdown due to the contamination.

Acquisition of Radiological Material. There are over two million licensed radioactive sources in the United States, and an average of 300 reports of lost, abandoned, or stolen radioactive sources each year, according to the Nuclear Regulatory Commission. Many types of radioactive materials are found in everyday military, industrial, household, educational, and medical applications. The military uses weapons grade uranium and plutonium. Industrial facilities use radiological materials for a number of reasons, most commonly gauging levels of liquids and density meters. Nuclear power plants handle spent nuclear fuel rods. The home contains radioactive sources in a number of appliances and devices, such as smoke detectors. Many colleges and universities have radioactive sources for experimentation and research. Radionuclear medicines used in cancer treatment and x-ray equipment contain radium and cesium isotopes. The effectiveness of the RDD depends on the physical form and intensity of the radioactive material. If just 3 curies (a fraction of a gram) of an appropriate isotope were spread over a square mile, the area would be uninhabitable according to the recommended exposure limits protecting the general population [14].

Radioactive Sources. Some readily available radioactive sources that would be of interest to one making an RDD are as follows:

Americium 241. Emits alpha particles and gamma rays, with a half-life of 432.7 years. Common applications: medical diagnostic devices, fluid density gauges, thickness gauges, aircraft fuel gauges, distance sensing devices, oil exploration, soil testing, moisture/density detection, and smoke detectors.

Californium 252. Emits alpha particles and neutrons, with a half-life of 2.7 years. Common applications: industrial radiography, moisture gauges, and well logging.

Cobalt 60. Emits beta particles and gamma rays, with a half-life of 5.27 years. Common applications: to preserve and irradiate food and kill bacteria, industrial radiography, level gauges, x-ray welds, to sterilize medical equipment, and cancer radiation therapy.

Cesium 137 (*cesium chloride*). Emits beta particles and gamma rays, with a half-life of 30.17 years. Common applications: measuring devices, irradiation of food, calibration of Geiger counters, medical radiation therapy devices, gauges to detect liquid flow through pipes, devices to measure thickness of materials, moisture gauges, level gauges, well-logging devices in the drilling industry to characterize rock strata, and sterilization.

Plutonium 239. Emits alpha particles, with a half-life of 24,400 years. Common applications: nuclear weapons development, space probes and satellites, nuclear powered generators, and nuclear power plants.

Strontium 90. Emits beta particles and gamma rays, with a half-life of 29.1 years. Common applications: thermoelectric generator (power source) for vehicles, remote weather stations, and navigational beacons; industrial gauges; medical applications (treat bone tumors); nuclear waste; radioactive tracer in medical and agricultural studies; electron tubes; thickness gauges; and treatment of eye diseases.

Uranium 235. Emits gamma rays, with a half-life of 700 million years. Common application: fuel for nuclear power plants and nuclear weapons.

Iodine 131. Emits beta particles and gamma rays, with a half-life of 8.06 days. Common applications: medical diagnoses, treatment of thyroid cancers, and industrial tracers.

Iridium 192. Emits beta particles and gamma rays, with a half-life of 74 days. Common applications: industrial radiography and medical applications.

Scenario: Radiological Dispersal Device. The Federation of American Scientists presented several dirty bomb scenarios before the Senate Committee on Foreign Relations on March 6, 2002. Below are summaries of the effects of two of these scenarios.

Scenario 1: Cobalt (Gamma Emitter). A single piece of radioactive cobalt (approximately 1 inch in diameter by 12 inches long) from a food irradiation plant was dispersed by an explosive at the lower tip of Manhattan. No immediate evacuation would be necessary, but an area of approximately 1000 square kilometers, extending over three states, would be contaminated. Over an area of 300 city blocks, there would be a 1 in 10 risk of death from cancer for residents living in the contaminated area for forty years. The entire borough of Manhattan would be so contaminated that anyone living there would have a 1 in 100 chance of dying from cancer caused by the residual radiation. It would be decades before the city was inhabitable again, and demolition might be necessary.

Scenario 2: Americium (Alpha Emitter). A typical americium source used in oil well surveying was blown up with 1 pound of TNT. People in a region roughly ten times the area of the initial bomb blast would require medical supervision and monitoring. An area 30 times the size of the first area (a swath 1 kilometer long covering 20 city blocks) would have to be evacuated within 30 minutes. An area 2 kilometers long covering 60 city blocks would be contaminated in excess of EPA safety guidelines. If the buildings in this area had to be demolished and rebuilt, the cost would exceed $50 billion.

Case Study: Radiological Dispersal Device. Although a terrorist group has never deployed an RDD as a weapon of mass destruction, we may be able to anticipate the consequences by analyzing an accidental release of a radiological material that occurred in 1987 in Goiania, Brazil. Junkyard workers pried open a metal canister from a cancer clinic. Inside was 3.5 ounces of glowing blue radioactive cesium 137 dust. By the next day, dozens of locals had been exposed. Several ingested it. Of the 20 seriously exposed victims, 4 died. But 112,000 plus people had to be medically evaluated. Most of these—47,000 people—had to take a shower and be monitored later on; 249 people had internal and/or external contamination. Some residences up to 100 miles away were contaminated. It was 11 days before radiation sickness was correctly diagnosed.

Incendiary

Incendiary agents are compounds that generate sufficient heat to cause destructive thermal degradation or destructive combustion. Arson is a favorite tactic of many domestic terrorist groups.

Case Study: Incendiary. ELF was deemed responsible for an arson fire on August 22, 2003 that destroyed 120 Hummer sport utility vehicles in West Covina, California.

Chemical

While the use of chemical weapons dates back many centuries, their effectiveness as a weapon in the terrorist arsenal is a recent phenomenon. Chemical agents use their toxic properties to incapacitate or kill victims. Access to readily available chemical precursors and chemists who can produce high-quality chemical weapons has escalated concern that such agents will be used in a terrorist attack. A few terrorist organizations have already managed to successfully deploy chemical agents relatively effectively. The ease with which ingredients can be inexpensively obtained from open commercial sources and synthesized without highly scientific knowledge makes chemicals an attractive weapon. Even an unsophisticated terrorist could create a chemical weapon that could cause localized casualties. However, to make a chemical weapon that would affect tens of thousands of people is a different story. The proper development and deployment of chemical weapons to affect very large numbers of people is a tricky task, with a high likelihood for failure for an unsophisticated adversary.

Even points of attack that have focused on fairly vulnerable critical infrastructure sectors, such as the food supply chain, have usually failed because of lack of research into the proper application of the chemical for use as a weapon. As an example, a group injected cyanide into grapes in 1978 in an attempt to poison consumers. However, this attack failed because the terrorists did not realize that the citric acid in the grapes broke down the cyanide. Even if an attack may appear successful initially, it may be quickly mitigated to reduce death and destruction. The Tylenol cyanide murders in 1982 caused seven fatalities, but the damage was mitigated through preventative actions taken by authorities and the manufacturer by quickly removing the product from store shelves.

An attacking involving a chemical WMD would be overt and, most likely, easily identifiable. Chemical incidents are characterized by the rapid onset of medical symptoms (typically minutes to hours) and easily observed signatures, such as colored clouds, mass casualties, dead insects and animals, damaged foliage, and strange odors.

Although the use of a chemical weapon would certainly cause a significant amount of psychological and shock value, chemicals, pound for pound, are a thousand times less toxic than biological agents. The chances for a successful outside attack are low. This means indoor targets are very appropriate for chemical agents.

Chemical agents can be broken down into two categories. (1) *chemical warfare agents* intended for use in military operations to kill, seriously injure, or incapacitate people; and (2) *toxic industrial chemicals* developed and manufactured for use in commercial or industrial operations (these chemicals are not primarily manufactured for the purpose of producing human casualties).

General Characteristics of Chemical Weapons. Chemical agents are generally liquid when containerized; some boil at low temperatures and become vapors. Chemical agents are usually best disseminated as an aerosol or vapor. The chemical cloud is influenced by weather conditions, such as direct sunlight, temperature, wind speed, humidity, and air stability. A chemical cloud will dissipate over time as air dilutes its concentration.

Persistence is an expression of the duration of effectiveness of a chemical agent. This is dependent on the physical and chemical properties of the agent, weather, methods of dissemination, and terrain. Nonpersistent agents, in general, lose their effectiveness as a weapon approximately 10–15 minutes after dissemination.

Desirable Properties of Chemical Agents

- Able to be produced in large quantities.
- Ability to deliver the agent as a gas, liquid, or aerosol.
- Capable of being dispersed.

- Availability of dispersal systems.
- Difficult to detect until onset of effects.
- High vapor pressure at ordinary temperature (meaning the liquids easily evaporate into a vapor).
- Lack of color and odor (thus no warning).
- Noncorrosive.
- Nonprotectable or limited protection available.
- Persistent.
- Resistant to environmental decomposition or hydrolysis.
- Small amounts are highly toxic via inhalation or absorption.
- Stable throughout in production, storage, and use.

Indicators of a Chemical Attack

- *Mass Casualties.* Unusual numbers of sick or dying people with common symptoms will be observed. Illness will develop suddenly and rapidly in those exposed to high levels of vapors.
- *Pattern of Casualties.* If the attack is outdoors, a downwind pattern of illness and death will be observed. The highest number of casualties and those with most severe symptoms will occur closest to the point of agent release. Casualties with milder symptoms will be observed further away and downwind. Very few, if any, casualties will be noted upwind from the agent release point. In confined areas or low-lying areas, casualties will probably be greater and grouped together due to the vapor concentration building up, confinement of the agent, lack of easy egress for the victims, and panic.
- *Unexplained Odors or Unusual Clouds, Fog, and Mists.* Unusual smells that are not normally present in an area should raise suspicion. There may be a colored cloud, a low-lying fog-type condition, pools of unusual liquid, and numerous surfaces coated with oily droplets or film.
- *Dead Insects, Birds, and Animals.* Numerous dead animals in the same general area will be noted. Normal insect activity (on the ground and in the air) is missing.
- *Defoliation.* Trees, lawns, shrubs, bushes, and crops will become discolored, wither, and die.
- *Debris, Containers, or Spraying Devices.* Presence of unexplained metal debris, abandoned storage containers such as cylinders or drums, and abandoned spraying equipment that may have been used to disseminate the agent may be observed.

Duration and Effectiveness of Chemical Agents. The duration and effectiveness of chemical agents can be determined by the method of dissemination, the agent's physical properties, weather conditions, and conditions of terrain or the target.

Classification of Chemical Weapons. Chemical weapons can be classified by their (1) physical state (solid, liquid, or gas), (2) physiological action (nerve, blister, blood, choking, incapacitating), and (3) use (kill or seriously injure, or temporarily incapacitate).

Classes of Chemical Weapons. Military grade chemical agents are supertoxic, designed and manufactured for the sole purpose of killing one's enemy. They are similar to commonly available industrial hazardous materials, but hundreds of times more toxic. There are five classes of chemical weapons.

1. *Nerve Agents.* Nerve agents are the most toxic, and hence the most feared, of the chemical agents. Nerve agents are essentially pesticides for humans. All are liquids at room temperature. The nerve agents enter the body through inhalation, ingestion, injection, or skin absorption. Once exposure has occurred, the nerve agent attacks and interferes with the normal chemistry at the nerve–muscle junction. To stimulate muscle contraction, the nerve endings activate a chemical called acetylcholine, which acts as an electrical conductor to bridge the gap between the nerve ending and the muscle. Following the contraction, the muscle secretes an enzyme called acetyl cholinesterase, which neutralizes the acetylcholine, breaking the electrical contact and allowing the muscle to relax. Nerve agents inhibit or capture the acetyl cholinesterase, thus preventing it from neutralizing the cholinesterase; thus the muscle is receiving a continuous stimulation. This constant stimulation results in muscle twitching. At the same time, fluids are building up in the tracheal area and there is bronchoconstriction, making it more difficult to breathe. Death usually results from cardiopulmonary failure. Table 4.1 lists the effects of a nerve agent liquid on the skin, and Table 4.2 lists the effects of a nerve agent vapor. Examples of nerve agents include VX, Tabun (GA), Soman (GD), and Sarin (GB).

Nerve agents are stable, easily dispersed, and highly toxic and cause rapid effects. Nerve agents are most effectively disseminated as a fine aerosol. Nerve agents are heavier than air and therefore tend to stay low to the ground. The "G" agents are fairly nonpersistent (meaning they will disperse quickly) while "V" agents are persistent (meaning they tend to linger). Nerve agents are 99%+ lethal. Six pounds of Sarin dispersed by a 3 pound burst charge at a height of 15 feet will deliver a median lethal dose to everyone within a 70,000 square feet area in one minute.

TABLE 4.1. Effect of Nerve Agent Liquid on the Skin

Very Small Dose
Sweating, twitching at the site of exposure (effect seen within 18 hours of exposure
Small Dose
Nausea, vomiting, diarrhea
Large Dose
Loss of consciousness, respiratory arrest, flaccid paralysis (effect seen within 30 minutes of exposure)

TABLE 4.2. Effect of Nerve Agent Vapor[a]

Small Amount
- Eyes: constricted pupils, red conjunctiva, dim/blurred vision, pain, nausea, vomiting
- Nose: runny nose
- Mouth: increased salivation
- Airways: tightness in chest, shortness of breath, cough

Large Amount
- Loss of consciousness
- Convulsions
- Flaccid paralysis
- Respiratory arrest
- Cardiac arrest

[a]Effects begin within seconds after exposure.

2. *Blister Agents.* Blister agents (also called vesicants) cause reddening of the skin and large blisters at the point of contact. Blister agents can enter the body through inhalation, ingestion, or skin absorption. The eyes and respiratory tract are particularly vulnerable to blister agents. If the contact is on the outside skin, large fluid-filled blisters develop. If the blister agent is inhaled or ingested, then the blisters form internally. Blisters that break within the respiratory system flood the lungs with fluid, and the victims die essentially by drowning. External blisters cause infection and hypergolic shock through massive fluid loss when they break. The early effects of blister agents are varied. There are no effects seen for hours with mustard gas; but Lewisite (phosgene oxime) will cause irritation and pain early on. Effects do not improve, even if victims are moved into fresh air, and even get worse with time.

These agents are normally disseminated as liquids; however, the vapors can cause blisters if in sufficient concentration. Under normal temperatures they have a low volatility (meaning they are unlikely to evaporate) and are persistent. Blister agents are about 40% lethal. Examples of blister agents include mustard gas (H agent), Lewisite (L agent), and phosgene oxime (CX agent).

3. *Blood Agents.* Blood agents interrupt the blood's ability to carry oxygen or block the normal transfer of oxygen from the blood to the individual cells. Blood agents are packaged as liquids but would rapidly vaporize once released into the atmosphere. The primary method of exposure is via inhalation, and the agent will immediately affect those exposed. Table 4.3 lists the effects of common blood agents, such as hydrogen cyanide (AC), which is lighter than air and thus will rise but is nonpersistent, and cyanogen chloride (CK).

4. *Choking Agents.* Choking agents (also called pulmonary agents) primarily attack the respiratory system, causing coughing, choking, burns, shortness of breath, respiratory arrest, and death. Exposure is primarily through inhalation. When the agent comes in contact with moisture on the skin or in the mucous membranes (eyes, nose, etc.), it hydrolyzes to an acid, which causes burns, which in turn

TABLE 4.3. Effects of Common Blood Agents[a]

Hydrogen Cyanide
Small amount: no effects
Medium amount: dizziness, nausea, feeling of weakness
Large amount: loss of consciousness, convulsions, respiratory arrest, death
Cyanogen Chloride
Small amount: irritation, giddiness, nausea, feeling of weakness
Large amount: loss of consciousness, convulsions

[a]Effects begin within seconds after exposure.

causes the membranes to secrete more fluid. Inhalation of choking agents causes extreme pulmonary edema (filling the lung sacs with fluid), which prevents oxygen from being absorbed by, and carbon dioxide being removed from, the blood. Death usually follows up to several hours later from chemical pneumonia or oxygen starvation (the victim is "choked"). Choking agents do not absorb through the skin; however, they will cause burns when they contact unprotected skin.

There are two military grade choking agents: phosgene (CG) and chlorine (Cl). Both are readily available as industrial chemicals. They have low boiling points, so once released they immediately become a gas. As a gas, both agents are non-persistent and both are heavier than air.

5. *Incapacitating Agents.* Incapacitating agents, or riot control agents, produce temporary physiological or mental effects, or both, which will render individuals incapable of concerted effort but ordinarily do not cause serious permanent harm. Incapacitating agents are therefore designed to incapacitate targets and render them unfit to fight, rather than kill them.

Case Study: Chemical Weapon. The Aum Shinrikyo religious group actually perpetrated two attacks in Japan involving the use of the nerve agent Sarin, which they had manufactured. The first attack was on a residential section in the city of Matsumoto on June 27, 1994, and affected over 600 residents. Seven people died, 500 were injured, and 58 were admitted to hospitals. A second attack occurred in a Tokyo subway station. Despite the poor quality of the Sarin used and its ineffective delivery system, 12 people were killed and over 5500 injured.

Matsumoto Attack. Aum Shinrikyo members sprayed Sarin gas from a truck moving through a residential neighborhood in the Kita-Fukashi district of Matsumoto. The Sarin seeped into the open windows of apartments and houses in the neighborhood. Climate conditions were hot and humid with a low wind speed of 0.5 meters per second from the southwest. These meteorological conditions would allow for maximum vaporization of Sarin in the vicinity of the release with a slow movement downwind. The first emergency call was from a man whose wife had fallen unconscious and his dog had suddenly died. The attack was reportedly aimed at disrupting ongoing litigation filed by local residents against the cult. The group was targeting the three judges presiding over the hearings. The Sarin was released within 30 feet of where the judges were staying. All three were affected by the Sarin gas and became ill.

The Sarin was sprayed out of a nozzle device attached to a truck specially outfitted for that purpose. Apparently an electric heater was used to heat the liquid into a gaseous state for dispersal by an electric fan. The release lasted approximately 10 minutes.

Subway Attack. On March 20, 1995, five Aum Shinrikyo members carried eleven packages onto five Tokyo subway trains running on three major lines. The subway has over 5 million riders daily. The selected trains were scheduled to arrive at the central Kasumigaseki station within four minutes of each other at the height of rush hour. The containers, which were thick nylon polyethylene bags wrapped in newspaper, were left on the floor or in baggage racks and punctured with sharpened umbrella tips, releasing the deadly Sarin liquid, which would vaporize. The choice of an underground, low-lying confined space in a crowded subway maximized the effect of Sarin's toxic properties. Sarin is much heavier than air and will collect in low-lying areas. The confined space of the subway restricted dispersion of the vapor and allowed concentrations to build up to high levels.

It was fortunate that a mistake was made by the terrorists in preparing the Sarin (it was only 30% pure) and an inferior dissemination method was used to deploy the agent; otherwise, there could have been tens of thousands of fatalities in the crowded subway system.

Industrial Chemicals

An adversary may not be able to obtain military grade chemical weapons due to security that is present around military weapons or due to the cost of obtaining them on the black market. However, there are alternatives that can be obtained either legally or illegally from industrial or commercial sources. Some chemicals that can be used as weapons can be obtained very easily, and in fact can be legally purchased at a relatively low cost. These chemicals are products that have everyday applications at home or in the workplace. Industrial chemical weapons are those made from materials that are readily and legally available in connection with industrial operations. There are abundant sources of industrial materials for use at little or no cost to an adversary. The most common types of industrial chemicals that can be used as weapons include irritants, choking agents, flammable liquids and gases, oxidizers, chemical asphyxiates, and organophosphate pesticides. The use of industrial chemical weapons provides an opportunity for terrorist to exploit and leverage potential vulnerabilities in critical infrastructure to further their cause. The adversary will not need a manufacturing capability in order for industrial chemicals to be used as weapons. Industrial chemicals used as weapons provide many of the same advantages that we have seen earlier: health hazards, physical damage,

TABLE 4.4. Industrial Chemicals that Could Be Used as Weapons

Irritants	Oxidizers
Acids	Oxygen
Ammonia	Peroxides
Acrylates	Chemical asphyxiants
Isocyanates	Argon
Choking agents	Carbon monoxide
Acid gases	Cyanides
Chlorine	Natural gas
Phosgene	Nitrogen
Flammables	Blister agents
Acetone	Dimethyl sulfate
Gasoline	Organophosphate pesticides
Hydrogen	Sevin
Propane	

contamination, and psychological effects resulting from their use. As an example, retreating Iraqi troops intentionally caused the release of crude petroleum from field protection facilities and ignited the oil to slow the advancing coalition forces, cause environmental and economic damage.

An adversary can resort to illegal activity to obtain chemicals that can be used as weapons, for example, by breaking into an industrial or commercial building to steal a chemical. The transportation system is also relatively insecure, and it would not be very hard for an adversary to steal chemicals while in transport via truck or railcar. There are many chemicals readily available; in the class of organophosphates alone, there are 50,000 known chemicals, all of which can be used to harm or kill. Table 4.4 lists some common industrial chemicals that can be used as weapons.

Case Study: Industrial Chemical. Abu Musab Zarqawi, leader of the Iraqi insurgency who was killed by U.S. forces in 2006, was determined to use extremely lethal tactics, especially chemical weapons. He was very interested in conducting a chemical attack against a Western interest and had proved he possessed the necessary technical knowledge to do so. Zarqawi was credited with the foiled April 2004 plot to use industrial chemical weapons in Amman, Jordan that could have killed in excess of 20,000 people if successful. The Jordanians stated they recovered more than 20 tons of chemicals. The plan was to disperse more than 71 chemicals, including blister agents, nerve agents, and choking agents with explosives. The targets were the U.S. Embassy, the Jordanian prime minister's office, and the headquarters of Jordanian intelligence.

Explosives

According to the FBI, over 70% of all terrorist attacks involve explosives. An explosion is an extremely rapid release of energy in the form of light, heat, sound, and a shock wave. The shock wave consists of highly compressed air traveling outward, in all directions, at supersonic speed. The use of explosives is extensively covered in the al Qaeda training manual. The manual states that "explosives are the safest weapon for the Mujahideen. Using explosives allows freedom fighters to get away from enemy personnel and to avoid being arrested." Terrorists favor explosives because they are easy to obtain and fabricate into an effective device. Also, the chemicals required for the manufacture of explosives are readily available as well. The technology for the manufacturing of most explosives is fairly simple, and recipes are readily available via the Internet. Plastics explosives are difficult to detect because a bomb maker can mold them into concealable or inconspicuous objects.

Definition of Explosive. An explosive is any substance, material, article, or device that rapidly converts a solid or liquid compound into gases having a much greater volume than the substances from which they are generated, accompanied by extremely high temperatures, shock waves, and loud noise.

Energetic Materials. Explosives are also known as energetic materials. An energetic material is a substance that can undergo an exothermic (e.g., releases heat) chemical reaction, rapidly releasing a large amount of energy. Energetic materials release energy in three forms: heat, light, and sound. The term explosive and energetic material can be used interchangeably.

Energetic materials can de divided into three categories, depending on their intended application:

1. *Pyrotechnics.* Pyrotechnics are designed to produce heat, smoke, light, and sound. Examples of pyrotechnics include fireworks and road flares.
2. *Propellants.* Propellants, which are considered low explosives, are designed to provide a controlled release of gas that can be used to perform useful work. Examples would be smokeless powder or a rocket motor.
3. *Explosives.* Explosives are designed to produce a near instantaneous release of energy. An example would be dynamite.

Explosives can also be divided into two categories based on the way they release energy: low-order explosives or high-order explosives. Low-order explosives deflagrate (burn) at a speed lower than 3300 feet per second. High-order explosives detonate (chemically decompose) at a speed greater than 3300 feet per second.

Attractiveness of Explosives

- Easy and inexpensive to produce.
- Various detonation techniques available, some of which may be low risk to the perpetrator.
- Attention-getting capability.
- Ability to control casualties through time of detonation and placement of the device.

Low-Order Explosives. There are two low-order explosives that can have terrorist applications.

- Black powder is typically composed of 75% potassium nitrate or sodium nitrate, 10% sulfur, and 15% charcoal. The mixture ranges in color from black to gray to brown. The grains may be in fine powder form or appear as large, dense pellets. Black powder is typically used as a propellant for ammunition, as the burning element in fuses, and in pyrotechnics. Black powder is very sensitive to friction, heat, impact, sparks, or flame, making it very dangerous to handle.
- Smokeless powders vary in form and color. Some are black to gray in color and are formed into rods, grains, or wafers. Others may be clear round or square flakes, orange to green in color, or may be a mixture. Smokeless powder is found in many of the world's weapons, such as small arms, cannons, and rockets. Smokeless powder is sensitive to friction, heat, impact, sparks, or flame.

High-Order Explosives. High-order explosives are designed to shatter and destroy. They do not need to be confined to cause damage. High-order explosives normally must be initiated by the shock of a detonator; they typically won't detonate by spark or flame.

High-order explosives fall into three categories based on their sensitivity:

- *Primary.* Primary high-order explosives are extremely sensitive to initiation by shock, friction, flame, or heat and hence are very dangerous to handle. Primary explosives are sufficiently powerful to cause complete, instantaneous detonation of other, less sensitive explosives. Common primary explosives include lead azide and mercury fulminate.
- *Secondary.* Secondary high-order explosives are relatively insensitive to shock, friction, flame, or heat and hence are less hazardous to handle. Secondary explosives must be initiated by both shock and heat. Common secondary explosives include dynamite, PETN, RDX, and C4.
- *Tertiary.* Tertiary high-order explosives are the most insensitive type of explosives. Tertiary explosives will only detonate when exposed to a large detonation of other explosive materials. A common tertiary explosive is an ammonium nitrate/fuel oil mixture (ANFO).

Initiation of Explosives. An external stimulus or initiator is required to cause the deflagration or detonation of explosives. There are six forms of stimuli that can be used to initiate an explosive device: (1) heat, (2) friction, (3) impact, (4) electrostatic discharge, (5) shock, and (6) radiofrequency energy.

For example, low-order explosives can be initiated by a flame, usually either a fuse or primer. High-order explosives are initiated by shock produced from a blasting cap or detonator.

Explosive Trains. A bomb may need a little bang to get a big boom. An explosive train is a series of explosions arranged to produce the most effective detonation or explosion of a particular explosive. The simplest explosive train requires only two steps, while more complex explosive trains of military explosives may require more than four separate steps to initiate a detonation. Explosive trains are classified as either low or high, depending on the classification of the final material in the train.

Example of a Low-Order Explosive Train (Pipe Bomb). A bomb maker inserts a length of black powder fuse into a pipe. When the fuse is lit with a match, the fuse transmits the flame into the low-order explosive in the pipe. When the low-order explosive is ignited, the confined gases produced by the ignition burst the pipe.

Example of a High-Order Explosive Train (ANFO Car Bomb). The bomb maker creates a three-step explosive train. A small amount of primary explosive is electrically detonated. The shock and heat from the electric detonator travels through a less sensitive secondary explosive, known as a booster charge. This leads to the detonation of the main charge of very insensitive tertiary explosive (ANFO).

Blast Injury. Explosives injure people in one of four ways.

- Primary injuries are caused by the blast front or shock wave of the blast itself. These blunt trauma injuries involve the tissue of the gastrointestinal tract, ear canals, and lung; all can be torn by the shock wave associated with these explosions.
- Secondary injuries are caused by fragmentation (when the explosive device itself comes apart) or shrapnel (components purposely added), creating penetrating trauma. In IEDs, materials such as nails, BB pellets, and screws have been used.
- Tertiary injuries occur when the patient is pushed to the ground by the blast wave. These injuries consist of neck and back injuries or other traumatic injuries incurred when hurled down or into something.
- Quaternary injuries are other medical and trauma complaints associated with the explosions. They can include asthma attacks from airborne particulates from the blast wave, a closed head injury, or other blunt trauma from structures collapsing onto the victims.

The blast from a relatively small bomb can cause serious injury or death at close range. Injuries are caused by the following explosion effects:

1. *Overpressure.* The explosion produces an overpressure. Injury is based on the dynamic impulse, which is the duration of the overpressure. This causes the most common and deadly of all explosives related injuries because it affects the internal organs of the body.
2. *Blast.* Victims are physically propelled due to the force of the explosion.

3. *Building Damage.* Victims can be hurt or killed by debris that falls from a structure or the collapse of a building or portion thereof.
4. *Fireball.* The explosion can produce a fireball that can cause thermal burns to anyone exposed.
5. *Fragmentation.* The shrapnel and fragmentation from the device, its container, or other things located at the blast site become projectiles. The blast wave from an explosion travels between 9000 and 22,500 feet per second, so fragmentation injuries are a major concern. Glass is one of the main causes of death and traumatic injury in an explosive attack.
6. *Noise.* Auditory damage can result from the concussion of the detonation.
7. *Thermal.* High heat, resulting from the explosion, causes burns.

Types of Blast Injury

- *Ear.* The ear is unable to respond to a pulse of less than 0.3 milliseconds. The attempt to do so causes a rupture of the eardrum.
- *Lungs.* The lungs are highly susceptible to serious damage. The primary blast injury to the lungs is hemorrhage.
- *Internal Organs.* The lungs can collapse and other internal organs can rupture from the blast overpressure.
- *Blunt Trauma.* Injury is caused by flying debris, the impact of being thrown against solid objects, and crushing from collapse.
- *Burns.* The heat generated by the explosion can cause thermal burns.

Table 4.5 lists the effects of overpressure on the human body and Table 4.6 lists the injuries that can be sustained when in proximity to a small bomb detonation.

TABLE 4.5. Direct Blast Effects of Explosions[a]: Fatalities and Injuries

Eardrum Rupture	
Threshold	5 psi
50% (20 or more years old)	15–20 psi
50% (less than 20 years old)	30–35 psi
Lung Damage	
Threshold	8–15 psi
Severe	20–37 psi
Lethality	
Threshold	30–50 psi
50% Lethality	50–75 psi
100% Lethality	75–115 psi

Source: *Effects of Nuclear Weapons*, Atomic Energy Commission, U.S. Department of Defense, Government Printing Office, Washington DC, 1977.
[a]Effective overpressure in psi (pounds per square inch). Overpressure duration is more than 100 milliseconds.

TABLE 4.6. Human Injury in Proximity to a Small Bomb Detonation[a]

Hearing	
Temporary loss	330.3 feet
Eardrum rupture threshold	31.1 feet
100% Eardrum rupture	12.5 feet
Lung Damage	
Collapse threshold	19.4 feet
100% Lethality	6.7 feet
Body	
Injury threshold	12.5 feet
Lethality threshold	10 feet
100% Lethality	6.1 feet

Source: Effects of Nuclear Weapons, Atomic Energy Commission, U.S. Department of Defense, Government Printing Office, Washington DC, 1977.

[a]Bomb size = 10 pounds (TNT equivalent); bomb's height = 0 feet, open air; individual's weight = 160 pounds.

Steps Leading to a Bombing Incident. In order for an explosive attack to be perpetrated, there are a number of steps that must be successfully achieved. It is quite likely that some of these steps will be occurring simultaneously and may overlap with others, thereby reducing the time necessary to plan, prepare, and execute an attack. The earlier an adversary is discovered, the more likely the attack can be prevented.

1. *Target Selection.* The adversary reviews the various critical infrastructure, key resources, key assets, and soft targets and selects potential targets.
2. *Reconnaissance.* The adversary will surveil and reconnoiter the potential targets to develop the maximum amount of information possible. Particular attention will be paid to determine if there are vulnerabilities present that can exploited, leading to a successful attack. The group will also look for security countermeasures that may be in place that would need to be overcome during the attack.
3. *Obtain Materials.* The adversary has decided to proceed with the attack and must now obtain the materials necessary to execute the attack, including the weapons, explosives, electronics (switch, timer, etc.), and delivery system or package (vehicle, vest, etc.).
4. *Construction of Device.* Once all of the materials have been obtained, the device must now be constructed and placed into its delivery package.
5. *Final Preparation.* In the final assembly of the device, an adversary will often spend many hours planning and reconnoitering a target before moving forward with an attack. At this step, great care is given to pertinent issues to ensure mission success.
6. *Deployment of Device.* Once all planning and operational issues have been addressed and the device built, it is deployed to the target area. Great care

is taken to avoid detection, and maximum effort is given to ensure the device is placed as close to the target as possible.

7. *Detonation of Device.* The device is in place and is detonated either by a suicide bomber or remotely.

Suicide Bombings. Suicide bombers are terrorists who attach explosives to themselves and die along with their victims in a bombing attack. Suicide bombers are also known as homicide bombers. Suicide bombers are common when one side in a violent conflict lacks means for effective, conventional attacks. Since a suicide bomber has already made the decision to die to ensure the success of his/her mission, more complex attacks can be considered than may otherwise be attempted since an escape plan from the area is unnecessary. Therefore suicide terrorism is a force multiplier and has advantages over other, more traditional, types of terrorist attacks. The use of a suicide bomber magnifies the psychological effect on the general population.

There is no real profile of the suicide bomber:

- Most bombers are male.
- Most bombers are single (87%).
- Most bombers are young (76% between the ages of 17 and 23).
- Most bombers are well educated (38% having university education and 47% a high school education).

However, suicide bombers can be either gender, can be older, and can be married. Behaviors are much more important than gender, age, or race/ethnicity. Adversaries will employ bombers and disguises that are most likely to deafeat security measures and profiling.

The first documented suicide attack occurred in Lebanon in 1983. A 2000 pound suicide truck bomb was detonated at the U.S. Embassy, killing 63 Americans and injuring hundreds more.

Handlers may accompany suicide bombers to attack and eliminate security personnel, distract security personnel, or assist the bomber to get into the proper position to ensure the maximum effect. Handlers may also detonate the suicide bomber's explosives if there is a malfunction in equipment, the bomber is incapacitated by security personnel, or even if the bomber loses the courage to initiate the explosives.

There are three ways a terrorist suicide bombing attack may be executed:

1. *Package Bomb.* The bomb is concealed in another package, such as a briefcase or box. The adversary attempts to match the package with the environment in which it will be delivered so as not to attract attention.
2. *Person-Borne Bomb.* Person-borne bombs involve the suicide bomber wearing the bomb on his/her body, usually as a vest or belt or sewn directly into garments. This method of deployment is useful because it allows the bomber to infiltrate the target area and get the bomb as close to the target

as possible. The explosives may be placed into metal or plastic pipe to increase the fragmentation effect.

3. *Vehicle Bomb.* Vehicle bombs allow the terrorist the use of the widest possible variety and quantity of explosives due to the large size of the container and the ability to carry and transport large weights. If there are no security checkpoints, a vehicle bomb may be positioned very close to the target, causing the maximum amount of damage.

Steps of a Suicide Attack

1. *Intent to Attack*
    - Evasive when questioned concerning past history and future plans, or such information is not realistic or verifiable.
    - Casing of properties or buildings in unusual ways.
    - Behavioral signs of intent to attack: (a) vague threats to manage emotions of anger, anxiety, or fear; (b) bragging to third parties of intent to attack; and (c) exaggerated, larger than life articulated fantasies of success or outcome of bombing (e.g., number of victims, joining other martyrs who have preceded them).
2. *Preparing to Attack*
    - No direct threats to the target, but continues to communicate with trusted third parties.
    - Boundary probing begins with physical approaches to measure access restriction, if any.
    - urveillance of target: begins to familiarize with area, makes decisions concerning dress and appearance and selection of time and day to maximize casualties; counter-surveillance of security personnel and barriers already in place.
    - Acquisition of materials for bomb begins, including the explosive, the detonation device, and the container.
    - May prepare a suicide note or video.
    - May give possessions away and get affairs in order.
    - Emotions are likely to be labile (quickly changing, irritable, sad, and easily upset).
    - May indulge in worldly sins that directly violate religious beliefs (visiting bars, strip clubs, gambling).
    - Will pay for items in cash.
    - Daily behaviors become more consistent with no future (forgetting to take change, purchasing one-way tickets).
    - Handler's involvement increases to help suicide bomber stay focused and manage anxiety.
    - May show arrogance and hatred through bragging, may express dislike of attitudes and decisions of the government, expresses superiority of religious beliefs, and has difficulty tolerating proximity to those he/she hates.
    - Will engage in private rituals within hours of the bombing that have religious and symbolic meaning, such as bathing, fasting, shaving of body hair, perfuming, and increased praying.

3. *Initiating the Attack*
   - Suspect may be carrying heavy luggage, bag, or wearing a backpack.
   - Suspect keeps his/her hands in pockets or repeatedly pats his/her upper body with hands.
   - Eyes appear to be focused and vigilant.
   - Does not respond to authoritative voice command or direct salutation from a distance.
   - Suspect is walking with deliberation but not running.
   - Just prior to detonation, suspect may hold his/her hands above the head or shout a phrase; or suspect will place hands and head close to the bomb to obliterate postmortem identification.
4. *Postoffense Behavior by the Attacker's Handlers or Associates*
   - Synchronized serial attacks implemented in stages, in close physical or temporal proximity to increase casualties of first responders.
   - Second attack is likely to occur within 20 minutes and be carried out along the evacuation route of casualties or near the first targeted area.
   - Surveillance of attack site to study first responders' behaviors and plan for future attacks.

Indicators of Suicide Bombers

- Unseasonable dress such as heavy clothing (sweatshirt, vest, or jacket) in hot weather; irregular dress such as loose fitting and/or bulky clothes, and long coats or skirts.
- Repeated and nervous patting or handling of self or parts of clothing.
- Profuse sweating, slow-paced walking.
- Evasive movements, attempts to avoid security personnel.
- Recently shaved face and short haircut.
- Appearance of being drugged.
- Irregular or inappropriate baggage or backpacks being carried such as a large briefcase into a club or a suitcase into a restaurant.
- Luggage, briefcase, gym bag, or backpack obviously weighed down more than normal.
- Hands in the pocket of trousers or outer clothing, apparently tightly gripping something; individual refuses to show hands when told to do so.
- Making threats directly to the target or indirectly to third parties.
- May appear nervous, unresponsive (blank stare), or preoccupied (tunnel vision).
- Stiff appearing torso/lack of lower mobility or flexibility; unusual or robotic-like gait.
- May smell of an unusual herbal/flower water as they may perfume themselves, their clothing, and their weapons to prepare themselves for paradise.
- Demonstrates forceful actions (e.g., pushing their way through a crowd or entering a restricted area).

- May be seen praying fervently to him/herself, giving the appearance of whispering to someone.
- Unusual or suspicious bulges around the midsection of the body.
- Support belts may visibly protrude from the bomber's clothing.
- Do not discount the prospect for male or female suicide bombers, or even male–female suicide teams.

The mnemonic ALERT is a summary of the above characteristics:

- **A**lone and nervous, sweating, walking slowly, or running suspiciously.
- **L**oose and/or bulky clothing that may not fit the weather conditions.
- **E**xposed wires, possibly through the sleeve of a jacket, shirt, backpack, handbag, or suitcase.
- **R**igid midsection (may indicate a concealed explosive vest or firearm).
- **T**ightened hands, which may be holding a detonation device.

Improvised Explosive Device (IED). An IED can be comprised of chemical constituents commonly found in the home or local community in various commercial operations. An IED is an explosive device that is disguised to appear as something harmless. The IED can be formed into an infinite number of shapes and sizes and encased in innocuous looking, commonly available things that do not appear out of place or will not attract attention; its design is limited only by the resources and imagination of the bomb maker.

To be most effective, IEDs are manufactured to fit in with the surroundings of the target area. For example, in April 2005, two suicide bombers drove a fire engine packed with explosives and dozens of propane tanks in a terrorist attack on a remote U.S. Marine outpost along the Syrian border in Iraq.

The effectiveness of an IED can be enhanced by packaging metal, such as nails, with the explosives. When the device explodes, the metal becomes shrapnel, increasing the number of casualties and the severity of injuries. IEDs can be placed at a target location, and the perpetrator can leave the area so as to avoid direct confrontation with the target or security personnel. Terrorists have learned to disguise IEDs to hinder detection and may booby trap the devices to detonate if disturbed.

Construction of an IED. The method used for constructing an IED is typically customized to produce the intended effect on the specific type of target. The major components of an IED are:

- *Power Supply.* The majority of IEDs contain an electric initiator and therefore require an electric power source. Batteries are a common power source. Mechanical detonators can also be used. A spring held compressed under pressure can store sufficient energy to cause the functioning of a nonelectric initiator.

- *Initiator.* Initiators are used to start the explosive train. Most initiators are shock sensitive. A blasting cap is an example of an initiator. The blasting cap starts the explosive train by providing a small explosion that sets off a larger one.
- *Explosives.* Explosives are the agent that causes the damage. Explosives can be military or commercial grade, depending on what is available to the bomber. Some explosives can be purchased legally, while others can be stolen from commercial or military stockpiles.
- *Switch.* A switch can be used to arm or trigger a device. Common switches used in IEDs include clockwork timers, pressure or pressure relief devices, pull or pull release devices, magnetic devices, vibration devices, alarm equipment, photocells, remote control devices, and mercury contact switches.

The IED must be contained and concealed in packaging to remain effective and facilitate delivery to its intended target. If the IED cannot be taken to the target, then the target must be brought to the IED. An example would be targeting a vehicle by placing the IED inside a garbage can or mailbox and detonating it as the vehicle passes in close proximity. IEDs can be delivered to the target in any number of ways, including a suicide bomber, through the postal system, or in a vehicle. IEDs can be concealed in almost any conceivable item.

Common IEDs include:

- *Letter/Package Bomb.* These IEDs do not normally contain a timing device. Rather, they are "victim activated," which means the triggering device is activated when the victim subjects the package to a certain action, such as opening it.
- *Vehicle Bomb.* A large U.S. made sedan can hold up to 1500 pounds of explosives; a midsized pickup truck could hold up to 3000 pounds of explosives; and a small box truck can hold up to 5000 pounds of explosives. These vehicles can cause catastrophic damage when detonated in proximity to people or buildings.

Potential Indicators that IEDs Are Being Built

- Chemical fires, toxic odors, brightly colored stains, or rusted metal fixtures in houses, apartments, motel rooms, or self-storage units.
- Containers of urine.
- Delivery of chemicals (that could be used in the manufacture of explosives) directly to a self-storage facility or to a residential address.
- Modification of a car, truck, or van with heavy duty suspension to handle heavier loads.
- Small test explosions in rural or wooded areas.
- Theft of explosives, blasting caps, or fusers or chemicals used to make explosives.
- Treatment of chemical burns, flash burns, or shrapnel injuries, or treatment for missing fingers/hands.

Potential Indicators of Mail or Package Bombs

- Distorted handwriting or labels made from cut-and-paste lettering.
- Excessive postage.
- Fictitious or nonexistent return address.
- Irregular shape, soft spots, or bulges.
- Marked with restricted endorsements, such a "Personal," "Private," or "Confidential."
- May feel lopsided, uneven, or rigid.
- Postmarked at a location different from the return address.
- Protruding wires or aluminum foil, oil stains, or a strange odor.
- Unprofessionally wrapped with several combinations of tape; may be endorsed with "Fragile," "Handle with Care," or "Rush Delivery."

Case Study: Explosives. Khobar Towers was part of a housing complex in the city of Khobar, Saudi Arabia. At the time of the attack, it was being used to house foreign military personnel, including Americans. On June 25, 1996, Hezbollah terrorists exploded a fuel truck containing 3000–5000 pounds of explosives adjacent to an eight story building that housed U.S. Air Force personnel. Nineteen U.S. servicepeople were killed and 372 were wounded. The force of the explosion was enormous. It heavily damaged or destroyed six high-rise apartment buildings in the complex. Windows were shattered in buildings up to one mile away from the epicenter. A crater, 85 feet wide and 35 feet deep, was left were the truck was parked. The attack was perpetrated in an attempt to persuade Americans to leave Saudi Arabia.

4.10 WEAPONIZATION OF CHEMICAL AND BIOLOGICAL AGENTS

General

Weaponization is the process to make a biological or chemical agent suitable for use as an effective WMD. A major technical obstacle to the effective use of weapons of mass destruction is not the production of the agents but rather the process of weaponization.

The weaponization process consists of four primary applications: (1) creating and modifying the agent; (2) packaging the agent so that the agent is kept alive or potent; (3) the delivering the agent such as in a bomb; and (4) developing an effective dissemination device.

Biological Agent Weaponization

For biological agents, selection of the virulent strain is the most important factor in agent weaponization. Biological agents must be small enough to get through the respiratory tract's natural filtering system and reach the small air sacs in the lungs. Processing biological agents into liquid or dry forms and into the right particle size is very difficult and requires expertise in a number of scientific disciplines. Although liquid agents are easier to produce, it is difficult to deliver them in the right particle size without reducing the strength of the mixture. Also, larger quantities of liquid agents are required as opposed to dry agents. Some biological agents can be stored indefinitely freeze dried or as a dry powder. Dry biological agents are easier to deliver, but more difficult to manufacture and less stable in storage.

For biological agents, the weaponization is the most challenging step. Biological agents in their raw form are very potent, but weaponization is necessary to make it effective over a wide area. Weaponization of a biological agent includes producing the agent in the correct formulation and in sufficient quantities to cause casualties, milling the agent to the proper aerodynamic diameter so that it is easily respired (1–5 μm in size) and penetrates into the alveoli deep within the lungs, stabilizing the agent, refining the powder to overcome natural adhesive forces, modifying the particle so that it has low gravitational settling velocities and is "ultralight" and stays airborne for extended periods of time, determining the proper liquid composition (for liquid agents), microencapsulating the agent in the correct storage and transport medium, adding powders to reduce electrostatic charges to prevent clumping, and determining the proper output rate.

Failure to manufacture the agent in the proper formulation will cause the agent to lose its toxicity in storage, will make it more difficult to effectively disperse, and will fail to have the desired effect on the human body. If the agent is not properly stabilized, the microorganisms will quickly deteriorate once they have been dispersed. The persistency of biological agents can be adversely affected by heat, oxidation, and desiccation. There are a number of techniques that can be used to increase the persistency of biological agents with the most common being freeze drying.

Biological agents can be genetically engineered to make the organism more lethal. Genes can be added for antibiotic resistance and extra toxin production, or the organism can be modified so that existing vaccines are not effective.

Chemical Agent Weaponization

The principal requirements of a chemical agent are that it be sufficiently toxic to produce large numbers of casualties, and thermally and mechanically stable enough so that it can survive dissemination. Industrial or commercial grade chemicals can be weaponized to make them more effective as weapons of mass destruction. Stability and volatilization are two major weaponization concerns with the use of chemical weapons:

1. Chemical additives may be added to an agent to allow for long-term storage or to enhance their effectiveness:
   - Stabilizers to extend the shelf life of the agent and prevent degradation of the agent.
   - An inhibitor to stop the agent from undergoing a chemical reaction and degrading.

- Thickeners to increase viscosity and persistence of the liquid agent.
- Carriers to improve dispersion characteristics and increase the airborne concentrations for agents that are not very volatile.
- A freeze point depressant to lower the freezing point of a liquid so that it can be used in winter conditions.
- Antiagglomerates to prevent the caking of powdered agents.

2. The agent must be inserted into the appropriate dissemination device. Chemical dissemination devices are designed to convert bulk liquid or powdered agent into an aerosol or microscopic droplets (1–7 μm in diameter), which remain airborne for hours and are readily inhaled into the deep passages of the lungs, or into particles that can readily be absorbed by the lungs, or into a spray of relatively large droplets (greater than 70 μm in diameter) that can be absorbed by the skin.

Chemical agents can be deployed as a unitary or binary agent. Unitary agents come in one container that holds the active ready-to-use agent. The use of binary agents as a chemical weapon is very desirable, because it is safer for the people handling and working with the agent since they are not exposed to the final product until dissemination, and it ensures maximum potency of the agent when the two components are mixed since the agent will not need to be stabilized to prevent degradation. In binary devices, the two chemical components are stored in separate containers until the time of use, when they are mixed and allowed to react and form the harmful agent. Because of their high level of toxicity, nerve agents are often stored and transported as binary agents.

Dissemination

Dissemination is the process of releasing the agent from its container into the environment. The purpose of dissemination is to place the agent at the intended target. Chemical agents can be disseminated in any physical form:

Vapor or Gas. Gases are materials in the gaseous state and remain that way when compressed at ordinary temperatures. Vapors are produced by evaporating liquids or sublimating solids. They resume their liquid or solid state under high pressure at ordinary temperatures.

Aerosols and Sprays. Aerosols and sprays are liquid droplets or dry particles suspended in air. Aerosols have droplets or particles that are small enough to remain suspended in air and inhaled. Sprays have bigger droplets or particles that fall to the ground more quickly and are more likely to be absorbed through the skin or ingested.

Liquids. Many agents are liquids at normal pressures and temperatures. Agents can be dissolved to improve flow characteristics and make them easier to disseminate. Liquid agents can be disseminated as liquids or aerosols.

Solids. Solids may take the form of particulates (powder), which can be inhaled or absorbed. They can also be dissolved to form liquid agents.

Carriers are materials added to facilitate the transport of the chemical agent. Once released outside, an aerosol cloud gradually dilutes and dissipates over time as a result of meteorological conditions. There are several meteorological factors that may degrade the agent and impact the effectiveness of the agent dissemination including:

Time of Day. Sunlight (ultraviolet rays).

Air Quality. Pollution, oxygen content.

Atmospheric Turbulence. Eddy currents can dilute or move the cloud to an unfavorable location.

Temperature. High air temperatures may cause evaporation of aerosol particles, decreasing their size and improving their inhalability. High or low ground temperatures can either increase or decrease evaporation rates and persistence.

Humidity. Mist, fog. High relative humidity may enlarge aerosol particles, lessening their inhalability. High humidity plus high temperature can cause people to sweat more, and moisture intensifies the effects of certain chemical agents.

Precipitation. Rain, snow. Light rain disperses and spreads agents and also causes faster evaporation. Heavy rain dilutes and disperses agents. Snow slows evaporation and increases persistence.

Wind. Speed, swirling, direction. Wind speed determines how fast a cloud will move. Wind direction dictates which areas will be impacted by the cloud. High winds can rapidly disperse and dilute a cloud.

Inversion. An attack could be potentially devastating if an inversion condition existed. An inversion occurs when a layer of colder air acts as a cap, holding down a layer of warmer air at ground level, thus preventing the vertical dissipation of the agent.

An interior release of an agent would be subject to many of the same issues. One of the more significant concerns with an indoor dissemination would be the effect the heating, ventilating, and air condition (HVAC) system has on the dispersion pattern of the agent. It is possible that the HVAC system could quickly eliminate the agent from the building based on the air exchange rate of the system.

Terrain and buildings can also affect the effectiveness of an agent. Ground type affects evaporation, absorption, persistence, and rate of vapor movement across the surface. Forestation and hills can interfere with vapor movement and increase exposure by trapping an agent in a relatively confined area.

Although liquid agents are relatively easy to make, they are very difficult to disseminate as a small size particle aerosol.

Physical Properties of Chemical and Biological Agents that Affect Dissemination Methods. Physical properties of an agent will affect its effectiveness as a weapon, the ways it can best be disseminated, and the severity of effects it produces in victims.

- *Concentration.* Concentration is the relative content of the agent in the mixture, or its strength. A higher concentration may mean less volume is needed.
- *Contamination Density.* Contamination density is the amount of agent applied to a given area, measured in mass of agent per unit area.
- *Corrosiveness.* Some agents are very corrosive. For those agents, great care must be taken in selecting the appropriate compatible processing, storage, transport, and dissemination equipment.
- *Flow Characteristics.* Dissolving solid and viscous liquids gives them better flow characteristics. The flow characteristics of an agent affect the ease with which it can be dispersed through an aerosol nozzle and whether it forms a fine mist.
- *Lethality.* Lethality is the ease with which an agent causes death.
- *Persistence.* Persistence is the length of time an agent remains effective after dissemination. Persistence depends on meteorological conditions, the type of agent used, and the amount of agent used. Nonpersistent agents last minutes to hours; semipersistent agents last less than 12 hours; and persistent agents last more than 12 hours.
- *Rate of Action.* Rate of action refers to how quickly symptoms appear after exposure. The rate of action depends on several factors, including the specific agent used, the concentration of the agent, whether a victim was protected, and the individual victim's medical history and condition. A precipitous agent will have an effect within minutes; a rapid agent will have an effect within a few minutes to ten minutes; and a delayed agent will have an effect within 10 minutes to several hours.
- *Stability.* Refers to the ability of the aerosolized agent to survive the influence of environmental factors such as sunlight, air pollution, surface forces, and drying, while remaining effective.
- *Toxicity.* Toxicity is the relative severity of the illness or incapacitation caused by the agent.
- *Volatility.* Volatility is the ease with which an agent evaporates. If an agent is not volatile, it is not a good candidate to be used in an inhalation exposure scenario. Likewise, if an agent is very volatile, it would not be a good choice as a skin absorption weapon. Volatility is related to several other factors such as temperature, vapor pressure, and persistence.

Dissemination Devices. Regardless of the type of WMD that is used, a dissemination device is required. The dissemination device is what is used to carry the weapon to its point of use and release it to the atmosphere. For biological weapons, the agent must be dispersed in a particulate form and sized to effectively travel through the air, lodge in human lungs, and cause an infection. Biological agents are best disseminated as low latitude aerosol clouds. Chemical agents are also most effectively deployed in an aerosol form, ensuring inhalation or absorption. For a radiological weapon, the particles must also be pulverized small enough to be inhaled and deposited deep in the respiratory tract or ingested into the body. There are eight major categories of dissemination devices that can be used to deploy weapons of mass destruction:

1. *Direct Deposit*. Direct deposit devices are mechanical devices employed to execute an attack on a specific target with minimal collateral damage. These devices are normally constructed to inject the agent directly into the target. There is no danger of downwind hazards from a direct deposit device, and the effects of these devices are the most easily controlled. An example of a direct deposit device is a syringe.

Example: On December 12, 1994, Aum Shinrikyo members attacked Tadahiro Hamaguchi by spraying him with the nerve agent VX dispensed from a syringe while he was walking on the street in Osaka. He died on December 22, 1994.

2. *Breaking Devices*. Breaking devices are mechanical devices that encapsulate the agent and release it once the container is broken. They are optimally constructed from common items such as light bulbs, balloons, or thermos bottles. The agent is inserted in the device then sealed. The devices are employed by simply throwing them at the intended victims. Breaking devices cause point dissemination and create some degree of downwind hazard. A related device may contain a binary agent, which requires the mixing of two components to make the desired agent.

Example: The Aum Shinrikyo group once again used a very basic system that was simple in concept and execution. Their target was the Tokyo subway system. This attack was staged during a national holiday when the system was loaded with people leaving the city for vacation. Cult members placed plastic bags containing sulfuric acid and sodium cyanide in a men's toilet in an underground subway concourse at Shinjuku Station on May 5, 1995. They had intended for the two substances to mix, generating poisonous hydrogen cyanide gas. The bags were placed near a vent where the gas would be dispersed through the subway ventilation system. The unattended bags were reported to station attendants by observant passengers and safely removed. Experts have estimated that the amount of gas that would have been released would have been sufficient to kill between 10,000 and 20,000 people [15]. However, the attack was unsuccessful because the heat of the chemical reaction set the paper bag on fire. The fire was extinguished before the chemical reaction could fully take place.

3. *Bursting/Exploding Devices*. Bursting/exploding devices are mechanical devices that employ an explosive to break the agent container and disseminate the agent. Bursting devices have an agent reservoir and a chamber for the explosive and usually employ a timer or a command detonation switch. These devices pose a wider area hazard than either the direct deposit or breaking devices and may produce a larger downwind hazard area due to the increased amount of agent involved and the explosive nature of the dissemination. Exploding devices may

not be an effective dissemination means for chemical or biological agents as the agent may be destroyed by the heat or pressure from the detonation.

Example: In World War I, artillery shells were filled with chlorine and shot at enemy troops. When they exploded, the chlorine was released, forming a toxic cloud.

4. *Spraying Devices*. Spraying devices vaporize, aerosolize, or spray the agent. Mechanical spraying devices contain an agent reservoir along with a pressure storage container. The pressure may be supplied independently or applied directly into the agent reservoir. The pressure is released and disseminates the agent. Spraying devices can include small hand-held aerosol cans (such as for deodorant or spray paint), pump type sprayers (such as garden or paint sprayers), aerosol generators (such as a small truck-mounted unit used to spray crops), or crop dusting aircraft. Spraying devices can be employed as a point source device (such as an aerosol directed at the intended victim) or as a line source device (such as when a container is opened as a vehicle travels along its path). This method is the least controllable and can impact the largest area. Line source dissemination is accomplished by discharging the agent perpendicular to the wind, with the wind carrying the agent many miles downwind across the target area. This is by far the most effective way to disseminate a biological or chemical weapon in an outdoor environment. Line source dissemination is very susceptible to meteorological conditions such as changing wind direction. Care must be taken to ensure that too much heat is not used in the spraying process, which can kill a biological agent or destroy a chemical agent.

Example: A large-scale biological aerosol test was conducted to demonstrate the vulnerability of a large seaport. The test was conducted off the San Francisco coast on September 20–26, 1950. Two species of bacteria that are easily detected and act as biological agent simulants, bacillus globigii (BG) and serratia marcescens, were used. A small U.S. Navy ship equipped with spraying devices discharged a line of agents (line source dissemination) 2 miles long 2 miles offshore just after sundown. The agents were disseminated as a liquid; there was a strong inversion, and a gentle 10 mph wind. The cloud spread more than 30 miles, with the result being 117 square miles were contaminated. This concentration would have led to more than 60% of the population being infected.

5. *Vectors*. Vectors usually disseminate only living organisms. A vector is a carrier and may be an insect or a contaminated item such as clothing, food, or water. Vectors are the least controllable and predictable of the dissemination methods.

Example: Female mosquitoes ingest the malaria parasite by feeding on human carriers. The infected mosquito can carry and transmit malaria to humans, other mammals, birds, and reptiles.

6. *Contamination*. Contamination is the intentional introduction of an agent into something else that will have contact with the intended victims. Food and water are potentially vulnerable to contamination.

Example: In March 1989, it was reported that grapes imported from South America had been injected with cyanide. However, this attempt to poison people through contamination of the food supply would very likely be unsuccessful. The cyanide ion that would be present in the grape juice is converted to ammonia upon a spontaneous saponification reaction of the cyanohydrins rapidly formed from the reaction of cyanide with sugars.

7. *Sabotage or Attack on a Facility*. Potential weapons of mass destruction have many dual uses, meaning they can not only be used as a weapon but have peaceful applications in the manufacture of products, production of energy, construction, and medical procedures. A terrorist group may attempt to attack a fixed or mobile facility with the intent of causing a deliberate release of a hazardous material.

Example: On December 2–3, 1984, the Union Carbide Chemical Plant in Bhopal, India began leaking 27 tons of the toxic gas methyl isocyanate. Approximately 500,00 people were exposed, resulting in 20,000 fatalities to date. The cause of the release was water that had flowed into the storage tank, causing a reaction that led to the release of the gas. Although this incident appears to be accidental in nature, it serves to illustrate the potential that could result from sabotage or a successful attack on a fixed facility by an adversary.

8. *Human Carrier*. Human carriers could potentially spread a communicable biological agent. This means of dissemination has several advantages: the biological agent need not be highly weaponized as the terrorist would only have to directly infect one person; and the need for other complex and potentially expensive dissemination devices would be eliminated. If a highly contagious agent were chosen, the infected person could unobtrusively infect a significant number of people without attracting attention.

Example: Viral hepatitis is one of the most common infectious diseases, causing an estimated 1.5 million deaths worldwide per year. A large number of people worldwide are carriers, meaning their immune systems tolerate the virus. Carriers thus do not have any symptoms and can knowingly or unknowingly infect other people. For an adversary whose mission is to spread a virus, it is not imperative that the carrier be immune to the virus.

Case Study: Dissemination Devices. There are three case studies that illustrate the importance of designing a proper dissemination device. Even if the agent is of high quality, if it is not disseminated properly, it is ineffective as a weapon.

The Aum Shinrikyo group had decided to destroy Japanese society in order to accelerate the coming apocalypse. They had become convinced that by eliminating the Japanese Diet (the equivalent of the U.S. Congress), the destruction of society would follow.

Botulin toxin is a poison made by the bacterium *Clostridium botulinum*. It is one of the most poisonous substances known to humans. The fatal dose of botulin toxin by injection or inhalation is about 1 nanogram (1 billionth of a gram) per kilogram of weight. The toxin is relatively fast acting, producing death between 1 and 3 days in 80% of the victims.

The first plan was for cult members to drive in circles around the Diet building in a modified truck, spraying the toxin into the air. Fortunately, the attack failed. The spraying device designed to disseminate the toxin had actually destroyed the biological agent.

The second attack involved attacking world dignitaries attending the royal wedding of Prince Naruhito. Modifications were made to the spraying device after the failed attack against the Japanese Diet. The cult planned to again disseminate botulin toxin while driving in downtown Tokyo as close to the royal wedding as possible while spraying the toxin into the air. The delivery system failed again. As the toxin passed through a number of steps to vaporize it into a fine mist, it had again been exposed to environmental stressors that exceeded tolerable parameters.

For the third biological attack, the cult decided to employ anthrax. Not only did they change the agent, but they changed their dissemination technique. Instead of a mobile delivery system, they decided to spray anthrax spores from a stationary location. The plan was to pour the anthrax spores into a modified steam generator located in a downtown Tokyo building owned by the cult. The anthrax saturated steam was discharged through the stack and blown across the city for four consecutive days. Once again, the attack failed.

It is not fully known why the anthrax spores failed to kill. The most likely scenario is the scientists misjudged the incubation period of the biological agent. Another possibility is the spores were killed by the elevated temperature of the steam.

REFERENCES

1. *NJ CBRNE Awareness Course*, 4th edition, NJ State Police, page 13.
2. www.lsic.ucla.edu/classes/mimg/robinson/micro12/m12webnotes/biowarfare/warfare.html.
3. *Time Magazine*, July 26, 2004, page 41.
4. *The Star Ledger*, Newark, NJ May 9, 2004.
5. *Nuclear Waste News*, October 2, 2003.
6. Mohammed El Baradei, Chief of the International Atomic Energy Agency, www.washingtonpost.com March 11, 2003.
7. www.firehouse.com/tech/news/2001/1211.
8. *The Synergist*, December 2003.
9. www.aolsvc.news March 21, 2004.
10. *USA Today*, January 30, 2003.
11. USAF Colonel Randy Larsen, Director of ANSER Institute for Homeland Security, www.cnn.com June 11, 2002.
12. *LA Times*, May 9, 2004.
13. Testimony of Dr. Henry Kelly, President of the Federation of American Scientists, before the Senate Committee on Foreign Relations, March 6, 2002.
14. Statement of Dr. Steven E. Koonin on radiological terrorism before the Senate Foreign Relations Committee, March 6, 2002.
15. www.ict.org.il/inter/attackdet/cfm?Incident = 1738.

CHAPTER 5

The Terrorist's Preparation for an Attack

5.1 GENERAL

Terrorists are relentless, patient, opportunistic, and flexible. Terrorists have learned from their experience and have modified their operational tactics and targeting of assets to take security countermeasures into consideration when planning an attack. Terrorists now seem to favor quick strike, small-scale attacks instead of the more elaborate September 11 style attacks.

Once a terrorist group has made the fundamental decision to perpetrate an attack, the preparation phase must begin.

A potential indicator that an attack may be forthcoming involves the amount of communications between cell members and the number of threats received. Once the chatter has diminished and threats decreased, that may be a sign that the adversary has moved into the operational mode and an attack may therefore be imminent.

The complexity of an adversary's attack depends on the technology available to the group and the points of weakness of the target.

5.2 TARGET CONSIDERATIONS

Before an adversary will attempt to plan an attack against a target, there are several considerations that must be evaluated to determine if the target warrants the expenditure of resources in an attack.

- *Target Attractiveness.* An estimate of the real or perceived value of a target is made. Will an attack accomplish the goals of the adversary?
- *Threat.* Potential acts that can result in service disruption, property damage, injury, or death are considered. Can the adversary initiate an attack that will accomplish a favorable result?

Understanding, Assessing, and Responding to Terrorism: Protecting Critical Infrastructure and Personnel By Brian T. Bennett

- *Vulnerability.* Conditions that allow or promote a threat to be carried out are discovered. Are there inadequate security measures that will allow the adversary with a weapon close access to the target?

5.3 THE TERRORIST'S INVESTMENT

An adversary must make an investment in order to plan and execute an attack.

1. *People.* Some attacks require many people to conduct planning, surveillance, rehearsal, and execution. Still others may require only one person to complete all of the necessary activities. An adversary must devote an appropriate amount of time to recruit and select the proper person(s) necessary to fit into the organization. This person certainly must share ideologies and must be willing to commit to the cause. The person recruited must also be capable of being trained to accomplish the tasks that will be assigned.

2. *Money.* The financial resources necessary to plan and execute an attack can, in some cases, be substantial. This is especially true if several operatives were to be recruited and then deployed as a sleeper cell, awaiting orders for months or even years to execute their attack. Costs include the travel expenses to move operatives into the target area; housing and living expenses, such as rent, food, and utilities; and the equipment needed to plan and execute the attack, such as cameras, vehicles, and weapons. An adversary most likely has somewhat limited resources and therefore is very judicious with those resources when planning an attack. The adversary wants to receive the maximum benefit for the expenditure of scarce resources. An adversary also wants to reap the positive benefits of a successful attack, among them being additional support for the cause through extensive press coverage, which will lead to monetary donations, and additional volunteers and supporters of the effort. Therefore an adversary is very unlikely to execute an attack against a target that appears to be secure and defended. Adversaries are not likely to get the chance to execute a second attack against the same target in the event the first one fails. As an example, of the financial resources necessary to plan and execute an attack the September 11 Commission estimated the terrorists' attacks perpetrated against the United States cost approximately $500,000.

The main funding for terrorist activities comes from:

- *Charities.* Donations were at one time the largest source of terrorist funding, coming primarily from various charities and wealthy individuals.
- *Illegal Activities.* The largest source of terrorist funding is now illegal activity, primarily the illegal drug trade, although other illegal commerce provides funds as well. It was widely reported that the Madrid train bombers sold counterfeit CDs and illegal drugs to finance their operation.
- *Front Companies.* Many terrorist organizations operate legitimate businesses to generate funds or to launder money. In 2001, the *New York Times* reported

Osama bin Laden owned and operated a string of retail honey shops throughout the Middle East and Pakistan. In addition to generating revenue, the honey was used to conceal shipments of money and weapons [1].

3. *Materials*. There are many resources that will be necessary to execute an attack. First, there is the weapon itself that will be used to perpetrate the attack. This may include the raw materials to manufacture the weapon, or it may be the weapon itself. There will be the materials necessary to support the attack, such as surveillance equipment and cameras. Vehicles will also be needed to transport the adversaries and weapons to the target area.

4. *Time*. The last investment an adversary will make in planning and executing an attack is time. Some attacks, such as a suicide bombing, may only require one or two persons devoting a few hours to planning. However, more complex attacks may take a cadre of individuals months or even years to develop.

5.4 EXAMPLE OF TERRORIST FINANCING

There are few reliable data on the cost of attempting terrorist attacks. One account from terrorists themselves is the Jordanian Islamic Action Front (IAF) statement that Hamas' July 31, 2002 bombing of Hebrew University cost $50,000. An attempt to estimate the cost of major terrorist attacks was made in an August 2004 United Nations Monitoring Team report on al Qaeda and the Taliban. Consider its estimate for the costs of various terrorist attacks:

- Madrid train bombing, March 11, 2004: $10,000.
- Istanbul truck bomb attacks, November 15 and 20, 2003: $40,000.
- Jakarta JW Marriot Hotel Bombing, August 5, 2003: $30,000.
- Bali bombings, October 12, 2002: $50,000.
- USS *Cole* attack, October 12, 2002: $10,000.
- East African embassy bombings, August 7, 1998: $50,000.

These UN estimates might be too low. Consider the East African embassy bombings, about which much evidence emerged in the trials of the perpetrators and in subsequent reports by the U.S. and British governments. The evidence suggests the bombings incurred a wide array of costs well in excess of $50,000 [2]:

- Setting up and maintaining al Qaeda run businesses.
- Travel for senior al Qaeda members to Nairobi.
- Training East African al Qaeda operatives in various skills, such as bomb making, hijacking, kidnapping, assassination, and intelligence gathering, in al Qaeda training camps, including sending operatives to Lebanon to train at Hezbollah terrorist camps.

- Renting an upscale residential estate in Nairobi and turning it into a virtual bomb factory.
- Renting another estate in the Illah district of Dar es Salaam.
- Maintaining a communications network between Osama bin Laden and East African terror cells, including using satellite phones costing $80,000 each.
- Bribing local border officials.
- Purchasing electronic equipment including state-of-the-art video cameras from China and Germany for surveillance.
- Purchasing the Nissan and Toyota trucks used to bomb both embassies.
- Purchasing the TNT bombs used at both buildings.

5.5 EIGHT INDICATORS OF TERRORISM

There are no physical characteristics common to all terrorists that would assist in their identification and apprehension. However, there are activities that could be observed and, if promptly reported to law enforcement authorities, could provide information to prevent future terrorist attacks. Some terrorist indicators, such as attempts to obtain information regarding potential targets, may be observed as trespasser incidents, prowlers, or other suspicious circumstances. Any of these events may appear, by itself, unrelated to terrorist activity. However, when the individual events are viewed together, patterns could begin to emerge that could assist in the identification of the terrorist activity. Since it is very difficult for a layperson to ascertain whether or not an observation is terrorist related, it is best to report any suspicious observation to law enforcement personnel immediately.

It is important to remember that preincident indicators may be observed months or even years before an attack. Therefore it is extremely important to document every fragment of information, no matter how insignificant it may appear at the time, and forward the information to the local law enforcement authority. Each indicator can result from legitimate recreational or commercial activities or criminal activity not related to terrorism; however, multiple indicators combined with other information can suggest a threat exists and should be reported to law enforcement personnel for investigation.

U.S. Air Force intelligence units have observed signs that have led up to terrorist attacks, such as those against the Khobar Towers in Saudi Arabia. The Michigan State Police have refined these items and created an awareness video to assist in identifying potential terrorist activities. We now discuss our eight indicators or signs.

Sign #1: Preoperational Surveillance

Surveillance is conducted on a critical infrastructure, key resource, or key asset to determine target suitability, security measures in place, and noticeable patterns in a target's movements, physical security, and the surrounding environment. In cases where law enforcement officials are unable to detect a terrorist plot, recognizing terrorist surveillance may be the only other effective means of preempting an attack.

Usually the first indication that a terrorist attack may be in the planning stage is the surveillance of the potential target. Surveillance is most effective if it is conducted during all hours—day and night, weekday and weekend—to determine all patterns and ascertain if any changes in the level of security occur. An adversary surveilling a target may use equipment to assist with the task, such as cameras with zoom lenses, video recording devices, telescopes, or night vision equipment. Adversaries have been known to use advanced technology such as modern optoelectronics, communications equipment, video cameras, commercial and military night vision devices, global positioning systems, and cellular phones. It should be assumed that many adversaries have access to expensive technological equipment.

The surveillance may be conducted from a public area, such as a street, from an adjacent building, or from inside a vehicle. Surveillance may also be conducted from mass transit vehicles as they pass by a target, from the water in a boat, or from the air in a private plane or helicopter. Tourist vehicles such as tour buses are particularly effective since they would not raise suspicions if they slowed down and scrutinized a target. The surveillance would be attributed to normal tourist activity and would not necessarily be considered suspicious. As the tourist vehicle passes by potential targets, people (both tourists and adversaries) would be observing characteristics of the target, taking photographs, and asking questions.

The adversary will need to plan the various access routes to and from the target, including alternatives in case of heightened security, traffic, or construction activities. It is possible that an adversary may be observed annotating access routes on a map, paying particular attention to mass transit facilities (e.g., schedules, bus stops, subway stations, taxi cab stands, number of riders), or identifying alternate access routes to the target via side streets, common basements, or interconnected buildings.

An adversary may be observed in the area monitoring activities. The adversary will observe the target, attempting to collect as much information about the target as possible. As the adversary observes the target, it is quite likely that the information obtained will be recorded in the form of pictures, video, audio recording, sketches, or written notes. The purpose of the adversary's surveillance is to determine the asset's attractiveness as a target, physical strengths and weaknesses, security measures in place, opportunities for exploitation, vulnerabilities, and emergency response capability. Particular attention would be given to the number of security officers available to respond to an incident, and what capabilities were available to them to repel an attack. (For example, are security officers armed or unarmed?). The adversary may have previously collected information such as blueprints, floor plans, photographs, or other specific information that will need to be verified as still correct.

Surveillance and probing of potential targets is consistent with known practices of al Qaeda and other terrorist organizations that seek to maximize the likelihood of operation success through careful planning.

Surveillance may be conducted individually or in teams. With teams, each individual is assigned to collect specific information about a particular area of the target. They will later reconvene and merge and share the information collected. Team members may also be used to cause a diversion to draw attention away from a fellow adversary who will then have unimpeded access to surveil a particular aspect of the target.

The adversary will likely make attempts to fit into the surrounding area so as not to draw attention or be confronted by law enforcement or security personnel. The adversary will dress appropriately and make attempts to stay concealed in crowds.

The adversary will look to exploit any opportunities that may exist to ensure the success of an attack. Weather conditions, time of day, movement of the target, deliveries, and shift change are all potential opportunities that may provide a distraction or cover for an adversary to get into position to execute the attack.

An adversary may try to get into a target to facilitate surveillance: for example, legally, by getting hired as an employee or contractor, by making a delivery to the target, or by posing as a visitor; and illegally, by breaking in.

An adversary may gain some advantage by observing the actions of the security personnel or occupants of the target. For example, an adversary could phone in a bomb threat to a target and observe the response of the security personnel and emergency responders, and how the target occupants react, such as whether or not they evacuate the area, and to where they evacuate.

An adversary's surveillance operation can fixed, mobile, or progressive.

Fixed surveillance is conducted from a static position, such as from an adjacent building, business, or other facility. In fixed surveillance scenarios, an adversary may establish him/herself in a public location over a period of time, such as by sitting on a public bench each day at the same time. This method would make the adversary familiar to other people in the area and so it would not be considered an unusual occurrence to see that person there each day. Another method of fixed surveillance involves the adversary donning a disguise (such as a homeless person) or occupation (such as street vendor, tourist, repair or deliveryperson, photographer, or even demonstrator). It is critical that the adversary select a disguise or occupation that would fit in with the target area and not arouse suspicion.

Mobile surveillance usually entails observing and following persons or individual human targets. This type of surveillance is conducted when an adversary is targeting a specific individual. The adversary will attempt to ascertain patterns in the target's movements and schedules and determine if there are any security measures in place such as body guards. Mobile surveillance can also be conducted against nonmobile facilities. This type of surveillance of fixed targets is conducted from vehicles as they move past the target area. An example of this type of surveillance would be collecting information while driving by a building in a car. To enhance mobile surveillance, many adversaries have become more adept at progressive surveillance.

Progressive surveillance is a technique whereby the adversary will follow a target for a short period of time from point A to point B, withdraw for a time, possibly days or even weeks, and then resume surveillance from point B to point C. This will continue until the adversary identifies noticeable patterns in the target's movements. Another option would be for several adversaries to conduct the surveillance of the target, switching adversaries at predetermined locations. Progressive surveillance makes it much more difficult to detect adversaries or predict their activities.

There are a number of ways an adversary can collect information.

Human intelligence (HUMINT). HUMINT is intelligence derived from information collected and provided by human sources in an overt, covert, or clandestine manner. HUMINT does not necessarily refer to people involved in covert activities. The persons providing the information could be hostile, friendly, or neutral. Of particular concern are persons who may be familiar with a target and inadvertently reveal sensitive information to an adversary in the course of a discussion.

Open source intelligence (OSINT) is intelligence that is retrieved and analyzed from sources that are unclassified, open to the public, and readily accessible through books, technical manuals, and asset websites. An example of the proliferation of open source intelligence is the Internet; it is loaded with a myriad of information, provided by both official and unofficial sources, which would prove valuable to an adversary. The biggest challenge in dealing with OSINT is in identifying reliable sources from the vast amount of information available.

Imagery intelligence (IMINT) is intelligence that is obtained from satellites or aerial photography. Aerial photography can be used to provide high-resolution images of the target that could not be obtained from restricted or inaccessible areas on the ground. For example, an adversary could rent a small aircraft or helicopter and take photographs of a restricted area from a distance using high-resolution camera equipment.

Signal intelligence (SIGINT) is the collection of intelligence through the interception of signals. In today's world, a tremendous amount of data is transmitted via wireless telecommunications, such as cellular phone, fax, and radio. An adversary can obtain information pertaining to a target, or the emergency response of the target, via a radio scanner, which could intercept cellular phone or radio transmissions.

There are several key activities that may suggest a possible adversary is conducting surveillance of a target:

- An increase in anonymous threats followed by individuals noticeably observing security reaction drills or procedures. Questioning of security or facility personnel by an individual who appears benign.
- Foot surveillance involving two or three individuals working together.
- Mobile surveillance using bicycles, scooters, motorcycles, sport utility vehicles, cars, trucks, boats, or small aircraft.
- Persons or vehicles being seen in the same location on multiple occasions; people sitting in parked cars for an extended period of time.
- Persons not fitting into the surrounding environment, such as wearing inappropriate clothing for the location, or persons drawing pictures or taking notes in an area not normally of interest to a tourist.

- Persons using possible ruses to cover their activities, such as taking on the disguise of a beggar, demonstrator, shoe shiner, and fruit or food vendor not previously recognized in the area.
- Persons videotaping or photographing security cameras or other security countermeasures, guard locations or showing unusual or prolonged interest in security measures or personnel, entry points and access controls, or perimeter barriers such as fences or walls.

It is critical that personnel be trained to collect the proper information when suspicious activity is observed. Personnel must also be trained on what to do with the information they collect (e.g., who should it be reported to). Effective information collection enables a faster and more effective follow-up by law enforcement personnel. The following types of information will greatly facilitate their investigative process:

- Date and time of incident.
- Specific location of the incident.
- Description of the incident (e.g., what made the circumstances suspicious).
- Description/identification of the facility or person being targeted.
- From where was the target being surveiled?
- How many adversaries where conducting the surveillance?
- Have these individuals been observed in the area previously?
- Have the individuals conducting the surveillance left the area? If so, in which direction did they travel and by what means?
- For suspicious people, a name, physical description, description of clothing, or description of items being carried.
- For suspicious vehicles, the make, model, color, and year; license plate number and state; markings, signs, or labels; damage; or embellishments (e.g., aluminum wheel covers).
- For suspicious aircraft, the type (e.g., fixed wing, helicopter, ultralight, hang glider), color, or markings.
- For suspicious watercraft, the type (e.g., motorboat, row boat, jet ski), color, registration number, or name.
- For surveillance equipment, the equipment being used (e.g., video camera, still camera, binoculars) and what was being photographed or observed.
- Contact information for the person making the report to the law enforcement agency.

The mnemonic CYMBAL can be helpful for remembering the relevant information about suspicious activities that should be reported to law enforcement:

C: color of vehicle, or person's hairs, eyes, clothing, and so on.

Y: year of vehicle or person's age.

M: make and model of vehicle or a person's race or ethnicity.

B: vehicle body type or a person's build (height and weight).

A: additional specific descriptive features such as a markings on a vehicle or person's clothes.

L: vehicle license plate number or a person's distinguishing looks (e.g., tattoos, scars, facial hair).

Example of Surveillance. In June of 2004, two Iranian security guards employed at the Iranian Mission to the United Nations in New York City were expelled from the United States for conducting surveillance of landmarks and transportation assets in the city in a manner "inconsistent with their stated duties." A U.S. counterterrorism official at the time stated: "We cannot think of any reason for this activity other than this was reconnaissance for some kind of potential targeting for terrorists" [3].

Sign #2: Seeking Information/Elicitation

An adversary may attempt to gather information concerning a target by elicitation. Elicitation, or asking questions, involves anyone who is attempting to obtain specific information about a target or its security systems; this can be accomplished via telephone, fax, e-mail, or in person. A seemingly harmless inquiry can lead to a critical piece of information being disclosed to an adversary that will aid in the planning or execution of an attack. Personnel should be instructed not to disclose any sensitive information about the target, people who are or may be present security procedures or countermeasures installed, or operations without proper authorization based on a need to know.

An adversary may not be able to overcome the security measures in place to prevent the disclosure of sensitive information. In that case, an adversary may make attempts to establish a relationship with an insider familiar with the target and obtain information from that person either by striking up a conversation or by offering to purchase information or sensitive documents. Employees of potential targets may be approached while in the community, such as in a grocery store, by a seemingly friendly person attempting to initiate a conversation, and be asked questions about the target, its operations, or security procedures. An adversary may also attempt to gain access to restricted areas within the target through the newly befriended person.

Adversaries could also use electronic means to obtain sensitive information, such as wiretapping, interception of wireless communication, or hacking into computer systems.

There have been occasions where potentially sensitive information about a target and its operations has readily been available in the public domain at little or no cost. Potential targets should carefully review their advertising materials, websites, or publicly distributed materials to ensure all sensitive information that could possibly be exploited to assist an adversary in planning an attack has been removed. Public tours (such as an open house) of potential targets may have to be significantly modified or suspended so as not to provide sensitive information to an adversary.

The following are examples of typical indicators of elicitation:

- Inquiries about size of security force.
- Inquiries concerning access to sensitive areas.
- Inquiries involving heating, ventilation, and air conditioning systems by persons not associated with service agencies or providers.
- Inquiries into the purchase of an ambulance, school bus, limousine, or any other vehicle that would generally be regarded as innocuous.
- Inquiries regarding the licensing/certification for hazardous materials transportation.
- Inquiries regarding local chemical, biological, or radiological materials sales, storage, or disposal sites.

There are many pieces of information about a critical infrastructure, key asset, or key resource that may be useful to an adversary planning an attack. Some of the more common pieces of information include:

- The target's method of construction, building materials, and construction features.
- Type of occupancy and use of the target, such as manufacturing, office, or tourist attraction.
- Number of employees, contractors, and visitors present at various times of the day and/or night.
- Building floor plans, layout, location of key areas such as ventilation system intakes and controls, offices of key personnel, exits.
- Arrival and departure schedules for key personnel, shift changes, arrival times of large groups of people.
- Schedules of deliveries and shipments that pose a target of opportunity, such as a material that could be used as a WMD.
- Key target operational aspects: length of shifts, duration frequency, and route of security patrols, routine of personnel on site, security guards' routines including patrol routes.
- Policies and procedures such as security measures, background check procedure, search procedure.
- Security features such as number and competency of security guards, checkpoints, access control equipment, locks.

The captured al Qaeda manual titled *Military Studies in the Jihad Against the Tyrants* states that public information can provide 80% of the information needed about a potential target, demonstrating that there must be a careful review of what is available on the Internet and other public domains.

Example of Elicitation. A group is planning an attack on a high-profile executive. Although the group has a sophisticated surveillance system, it has been unable to penetrate the security measures in place to ascertain the security systems that have been implemented to protect the executive and determine his travel schedule. Through a surveillance operation, the group has learned that an aide, who is likely to be familiar with the necessary information, frequents a neighborhood bar after work. The group details a female adversary to go to the bar and start a conversation with the aide. After a few weeks, the two develop a close friendship. The female adversary feigns she is interested in the aide's work. The female adversary is soon able to extract the necessary information required to plan and execute an attack against the executive, through the seemingly harmless collection of critical information obtained through the casual conversation between two friends.

Sign #3: Probing/Tests of Security

Probing or tests of security are techniques an adversary may use in an attempt to gather data by examining and studying existing security protocols at a specific target. Probing is usually accomplished by penetrating guarded or sensitive areas to elicit a response in an effort to observe the reactions by security or law enforcement, to ascertain the ease of approaching and withdrawing from a target, and to test the reaction of the civilian population to a potential attack situation. These tests of security are likely to confirm what has already been observed during the surveillance phase of the operation. It is critical to the success of the attack that an adversary be aware of how the target will react to different threat scenarios so appropriate tactics can be developed to ensure mission success. Sometimes, what appear to be comprehensive security policies and procedures at a target are not fully understood and implemented properly by employees and the security force. What appear to be robust physical countermeasures may actually be ineffective because employees and the security force do not properly employ the countermeasures, or equipment is not in proper operating condition due to poor maintenance. Finally, complacency may have set in and employees and the security force do not fully appreciate the risk to the target and therefore do not ensure the proper implementation of the protective systems in place. Probing by an adversary will quickly reveal whether these deficiencies exist, and whether or not the target has vulnerabilities that can easily be exploited by an adversary to ensure the success of an attack.

An adversary may employ many different tactics in an attempt to determine the effectiveness of security measures installed at a target. Among the techniques that could be used by an adversary to probe a target are:

- A pattern or series of false alarms requiring law enforcement or emergency services response.
- Attempts to penetrate physical security barriers.
- Attempts to gain access to sensitive areas of the target.
- Attempts to test physical security/response procedures at key facilities.

An adversary can attempt to bypass or circumvent existing security measures by probing in an attempt to gauge their effectiveness. The purpose of these probes is to determine how stringent the polices and procedures are enforced by employees and security personnel, what route the law enforcement and emergency services take to the target, what type of response is provided by local law enforcement and emergency services (e.g., how many responders show up), what equipment is provided by local law enforcement and emergency services (e.g., SWAT team, hazardous materials team), or how robust the physical countermeasures are and how difficult it will be to penetrate them. Such probes may include:

- Attempting to bypass a physical security barrier such as a fence by climbing over or under it, cutting through it, or cutting a gate lock.
- Attempting to get through locked doors by following an authorized person through; having an accomplice prop open a normally locked door; using illicit means to obtain a key or pass code for a door lock; or trying to pick a lock.
- Attempting to get weapons or other restricted materials through a security checkpoint, such as a metal detector or bag search point.
- Attempting to circumvent background check procedures by not providing all information or erroneous information.
- Attempting to penetrate off-limit areas once inside the target area as an authorized visitor.

An adversary may also attempt to test security at a target by initiating a false alarm (such as a bomb threat). The adversary then observes how the target is secured and how the security force responds, how emergency services respond, ascertains the strengths and weaknesses of procedures and physical countermeasures, and notes how employees and other personnel at the target area behave. In these tests of security, individuals would noticeably be observing the response of personnel and the implementation of security procedures. It is possible that an adversary may even casually question security or facility personnel about the procedures and response that were implemented in an attempt to extract additional information. Examples of how an adversary may test procedures and responses include:

- Phone in a bomb threat to the target and observe what actions are taken such as evacuation, searching for the device, or emergency response from the municipal emergency services.
- Have an accomplice penetrate a secure area and observe how long it takes to be discovered and what the response is by employees and the security force once an intruder has been discovered.
- Park a vehicle in an area where parking is prohibited and determine how long it stays there before it is observed and reported to the security force, and what actions the security force takes once the presence of the vehicle has been reported.

Example of Probing. Journalist Annie Jacobsen, a passenger on The June 29, 2004 Northwest Airlines flight #327 from Detroit, Michigan to Los Angeles, California, described a frightening series of events that occurred on board the aircraft. The story, reported in an article entitled "Terror in the Skies Again" on Women's Wall Street.com, recounts the events. "After seeing 14 Middle Eastern men board the aircraft (six together, eight individually) and then act as a group, watching their unusual glances, observing their bizarre bathroom activities, watching them congregate in small groups, knowing that the flight attendants and the pilots were seriously concerned, and now knowing that federal air marshals were on board, I was terrified."

Shortly after takeoff, the unusual activity began. One of the men got up and entered the restroom at the front of the coach section, taking with him a large McDonald's bag. Leaving the restroom, he passed the bag to another man and gave him a thumbs up sign. For the next hour, the men used the restroom consecutively. They congregated in groups at the rear of the plane. One of them stood in first class a foot from the cockpit door. Two were standing midcabin, and two more were standing in the galley, keeping an eye on the flight attendant. Others spent the flight patrolling the aisles, scrutinizing increasingly nervous passengers. As the plane prepared to land, seven of the men suddenly stood up in unison and walked to the front and back lavatories of the coach cabin. One by one, they entered the lavatories, each spending about four minutes inside. Two men stood against the emergency exit door; another stood blocking the aisle. At the back of the plane, two more men stood next to the bathroom, blocking the aisle. They ignored repeated orders from the flight attendant to sit down. The last man came out of the bathroom, and as he passed one of his colleagues, ran his forefinger across his neck and mouthed the work "no." As the Syrians deplaned, they were detained and later released by law enforcement personnel [4].

According to Peter Leitner, cofounder of the Higgins Counterterrorism Research Center in Arlington, Virginia, this event was "undoubtedly a probing attack" [5].

Sign #4: Intrusion

Intrusion is different from probing, in that an adversary has actually gained access to a restricted area. Intrusion occurs when unauthorized personnel enter a restricted area for the purpose of collecting information or stealing something associated with the target (which may be of value in executing an attack later on, such as floor plans). An intruder may also enter a restricted area with malicious intent, damaging or manipulating some system of the target which will either facilitate the execution of an attack or increase the severity of the outcome of an attack. Once inside the restricted area of the target, an intruder may execute an attack.

An adversary can also intrude into a computer network. Once an adversary hacks into the computer network, the network can be used to provide information regarding the target, can assist in the execution of an attack, or can be used to attack the target.

Example of Intrusion. An adversary is able to obtain access into an office building's restricted area and obtains the operating instructions for the building's heating, ventilating, and air conditioning system. This information will prove useful to the adversary in the future when an attack, which will involve the release of a chemical agent into the ventilation system, will be perpetrated.

Sign #5: Acquiring Supplies

The adversary will need to obtain the materials necessary for an attack. These items may be purchased legally through commercially available sources (e.g., purchasing a cell phone at a local shopping center). Other items may need to be stolen because they cannot be obtained legally (e.g., explosives stolen from a construction site). Materials that could be used as a weapon may be diverted or hijacked from a commercial, industrial, educational, or medical facility. For example, a shipment of toxic chemicals can be hijacked while in transport and be used by an adversary to create a chemical WMD.

The items that are necessary for the execution of an attack include:

- *Weapons.* This would include the actual device used to perpetrate the attack, such as an explosive, as well as the individual weapons necessary for the adversaries themselves, such as side arms and automatic weapons.
- *Uniforms.* It may be helpful for an adversary to assume the identity of an individual who would not arouse suspicion in the target area. Uniforms can be made; stolen from a legitimate person's home, car, or workplace; or stolen from a commercial establishment such as a uniform shop or dry cleaners. There are vendors who legally sell authentic official apparel (such as purchasing military uniforms from an Army Navy store). For example, if an adversary were to obtain an airline pilot's uniform, it may be possible to bypass certain security measures simply because they are in uniform. His/her presence in a secure area may not arouse the suspicions of others in the area or trigger a security alert based on the fact that the adversary is in the proper uniform for the area or location.
- *Identification.* An adversary may be able to steal or create fraudulent documentation and identification cards, and when used with the appropriate uniform, this would allow the adversary to bypass security checkpoints and access sensitive areas. Because a person has the proper documentation, access cards, or identification, his/her presence in the target area may not be questioned.
- *Vehicles.* Vehicles can include almost any type of transportation device, such as bicycles, motorcycles, cars, trucks, boats, and planes. Vehicles may be purchased legally, stolen, or hijacked. Vehicles are necessary for two purposes: (1) to transport the adversaries from their safe house to the target area and possibly back to a safe area; and (2) for use as a component of the weapon system itself, such as a car bomb.

Adversaries may also attempt to acquire information that will be useful in planning or executing the attack. Such information may include aircraft flight manuals; heating, ventilating, and air conditioning (HVAC) systems operating manuals; or chemical or biological agent technical manuals. Once again, this information may be obtained legally through various commercial enterprises, through the Internet, or at the local library. It can also be stolen from secure areas within the target.

Adversaries may also use false or stolen identification documents such as passports, driver's licenses, or official credentials. This identification can be used to access confidential information or to gain entrance to a secure or prohibited area at a target. For this reason, great care must be given by security personnel and employees to ensure that anyone wearing a uniform also has the appropriate identification with them.

Once the adversary has obtained the supplies necessary for an attack, they must be stored and assembled in a secure location. The adversary must assemble the various component materials necessary to complete the weapon without being detected. Therefore it is likely that the various components will be stored at separate locations to help avoid detection and suspicion if the adversary is caught. The various components will likely be brought to a central location only at the time the weapon is ready to be assembled. Experience has shown that the various components are brought together and the weapon assembled immediately before deployment. Likewise, the various other materials necessary for the attack will be stored in secure locations until such time as they are ready to be used.

It is quite likely that only one or two members of the terrorist cell will have advance knowledge of all the details of the entire operation, of the components that have been obtained, and the location of the various storage areas to avoid compromise of the operation if a cell member is captured by law enforcement.

Following are some indicators that an adversary is beginning to acquire the supplies necessary to perpetrate an attack:

- Suspicious or improper attempts to acquire official vehicles, uniforms, badges, access cards, or identification for key facilities.
- Theft of two-way radios or scanners.
- Theft or purchase of respirators or chemical mixing devices.
- Theft or purchase of specialized fuels, agricultural or industrial chemicals, explosives, blasting caps or fuses for explosives, weapons, ammunition, dangerous chemicals, flight manuals, or other materials that could be used in a terrorist attack.
- Theft or purchase of paint or logos similar to those found on security or emergency vehicles.
- Attempts to gain sensitive information regarding key facilities or personnel through personal contact or by telephone, mail, or e-mail.
- Stockpiling of suspicious materials or obtaining potential containers for explosives (e.g., vehicles, suitcases).

Example of Acquiring Supplies. An adversary is interested in planting an explosive device on an airplane. The adversary's surveillance has indicated that security in place at the airports will make it impossible to smuggle an explosive device through the security checkpoint. Therefore a change in plan is made so it is more likely that the attack will succeed. Once again, surveillance has indicated that aircraft pilots in uniform go through a special security checkpoint, which is not as thorough as the one for the general public. The adversaries steal a pilot's car, which contains several uniforms and identification cards. The adversaries use the stolen identification cards as a template to create their own using commercially available software. The explosive device is modified to be sewn into the uniform jacket, and the adversary impersonating the pilot proceeds through the crew-only security checkpoint during a busy time at the airport.

Sign #6: Suspicious People Who Do Not Belong

Another preincident indicator is observing suspicious people who don't belong. This can include people who have entered the country illegally through border crossings, stowaways aboard a ship or airplane, or a person who jumps ship while in a port.

People are suspicious not necessarily because of their race, religion, or sex, but rather because of their behaviors or actions.

Suspicious people can be observed almost anywhere—in a workplace, a tourist venue, a building, or a neighborhood or business establishment. Suspicious people do not fit in because of their demeanor the unusual questions they ask the statements they make or their very presence in a restricted area. Suspicious people may be conducting surveillance, probing a potential target, practicing an attack, or getting ready to execute an attack.

It is likely that several adversaries may meet periodically at a safe house to develop the attack plan and the weapon to be used in the attack. Signs of planning activities may include people coming and going at odd hours, both day and night; shades and blinds drawn closed; and the residents of the safe house staying to themselves and not socializing or mingling with neighbors.

Personnel who observe suspicious people should be trained to document their description and suspicious activity and notify law enforcement personnel immediately. The following should arouse suspicion:

- Persons or vehicles observed in the same location on multiple occasions and/or those who engage in unusual behavior.
- Persons observed near a potential target using or carrying video, still camera, or visual enhancement devices (telescopes, binoculars, night vision goggles).
- Persons showing an interest in or photographing the security measures at a target.
- Persons drawing pictures or taking notes in a nontourist area not normally known to have such activity.
- Persons observed with facility maps, photographs, diagrams, or notes regarding infrastructure or listing of certain key personnel.
- Unusual or prolonged interest in security measures or personnel, entry points, and access controls or perimeter barriers such as fences or walls.
- Unusual behavior such as staring or quickly looking away from personnel or vehicles entering or leaving designated facilities or parking areas.

- Observation of security reaction drills or procedures.
- Foot surveillance involving two or three individuals working together.
- Mobile surveillance using bicycles, scooters, motorcycles, cars, trucks, sport utility vehicles, limousines, boats, or small aircraft.
- Prolonged static surveillance using operatives disguised as panhandlers, shoe shiners, food or flower vendors, news agents, or street sweepers not previously seen in the area.
- Use of multiple sets of clothing and identification.
- Presence of individuals who do not appear to belong in the workplace, business establishment, or near a key facility.
- Behavior that appears to denote planning for terrorist activity, such as mapping out routes, playing out scenarios, monitoring key facilities, and timing traffic flow or signals.

Example of Suspicious People Who Do Not Belong. A suspicious man is observed in a restaurant located across the street from a government building. He insisted on being seated at a table along the windows that faced the government building. He has ordered only a coffee and appears to be taking notes as vehicles enter and exit the underground parking garage under the government building. He has questioned the waitress about various activities that occur at the building. He was observed making a cell phone call, and several minutes later the government building was evacuated for a bomb threat. At that point, the man departs the restaurant and mingles with the evacuated employees from the building. He is taking some photographs and asks the employees questions related to their bomb threat procedure and evacuation plans.

Sign #7: Dry Run/Trial Run

A dry run may be at the heart of the planning phase of a terrorist act. Before the execution of the final plan or operation, a practice session will be held to work out the flaws and unanticipated problems. Dry runs expose strengths and weaknesses in an attack plan. Multiple dry runs are normally conducted at or near the target area. The dry run would be conducted as close to the actual date of the attack as possible to ensure the most likely conditions present on the day of the attack are encountered which will allow the adversary to adopt their plans to the current conditions. What seems to be a good plan on paper may not be able to be executed practically. Each step of the operation should be rehearsed to ensure it is achievable. If, for example, the crux of the operational plan is to be able to get weapons through a security checkpoint, then it should be practiced at the location and at the same time of the real attack. It would be a good idea to have someone other than the person who will conduct the actual attack perform the dry run. Ideally, this person should not be familiar with the attack planning. This will protect the viability of the attack plan if the operative is caught and questioned by law enforcement. It will also serve to protect the operative who will conduct the attack as he/she will not be recognized by security force personnel. Performing a dry run of this type will allow for a simulation of the exact conditions that will be encountered at the time of the actual attack. Security force personnel can be evaluated to see how thoroughly they perform their jobs, how quickly they act based on the volume of people going through security at the time, and how they react and what the procedure is if they find contraband material. Another type of dry run may involve establishing time frames to execute an attack. This is especially important if the attack will be coordinated with other attacks or must be performed in a particular sequence. A mobile target may only be exposed for a short period of time, so the timing of the attack must be exact. Dry runs to establish the timing of events will involve moving from the safe area to the target area at the precise time of the actual attack using the same mode of transportation. This will allow for traffic conditions to be evaluated and the proper mode of transportation selected. Also, alternate routes, and the timing associated with travel of those routes, should be selected in case of unexpected conditions at the time of attack (emergency construction, accident, etc.). Weather conditions should also be considered in the timing, as rainy, foggy, or snowy conditions tend to slow traffic down. The dry run will involve studying not only the route to the target but also the exit route, if applicable. Some attacks may involve several teams working together, and each team may depart from a different safe area and take a different route to and from the target area. The dry run may reveal problems associated with accessing the target. It may be discovered that recently implemented security procedures or physical hardening prevent direct access to the target. By conducting the dry run, it may be possible to discover these issues and modify the attack plan to circumvent the countermeasures. Each team's route must be carefully rehearsed. Quite often multiple dry runs will be conducted at or near the target to gain additional planning intelligence.

Both the September 11 airliner attacks and the July 2005 London train and bus bombings were prefaced by dry runs.

Potential indicators of a dry run are:

- Suspicious persons sitting in a parked car for an extended period of time for no apparent reason.
- Persons observed monitoring a police radiofrequency and recording emergency response times.
- Persons observed mapping out routes and determining the timing of traffic lights and traffic flow.
- Persons questioning key asset personnel or security guards.

Example of a Dry Run. An adversary wants to smuggle a weapon onto an aircraft. As part of the overall plan, a dry run is conducted. An operative, who is not part of the team that will execute the attack, is selected to attempt to breach security with the weapon. The operative will attempt to smuggle a small knife past security; a second adversary will position himself in such a way as to observe the security process. The operative has been given instructions on how to behave and what to say if the knife is found.

Sign #8: Deploying Assets/Getting into Position

The final sign that a terrorist attack is imminent is the deployment of assets or getting people and weapons into position for the attack. This is the last chance one would have to detect the presence of the adversary and alert law enforcement authorities before the actual attack occurs.

The members of the group may meet in a single location immediately before deploying assets to begin the process of finalizing the attack plans. The adversaries may be observed discussing plans and assembling the weapon or loading weapons and other supplies into vehicles before beginning the trip to the target area.

Once arriving at the target area, the adversary will need to get the weapon as close to the target as possible. Once close to the target, the adversary will complete the final preparations and deploy personnel and weapons for the attack. Personnel should be on the alert for anyone who is observed acting suspiciously.

Example of Deploying Assets. The adversaries have spent the last six months planning an attack and conducting surveillance of the target. The group has finalized all of the preparatory work and is now ready to execute the attack. The group members will meet at the safe house and bring the various components of the weapon with them. Once everyone has arrived at the safe house, the group will review the final details of the plan, assemble the weapon, and load it into the van for transport to the target area.

Once the van arrives at the target area, the adversaries will place the vehicle as close to the target building as possible and then exit to a safe area. At the appropriate time, the adversaries will remotely detonate the bomb and make their escape in a second vehicle that was staged nearby.

5.6 RAISING SUSPICION

Following are some suspicious behaviors and circumstances that may be indicators of terrorist activity. Some of these indicators could very well be innocent activities being conducted by innocent people. Therefore it is best that laypeople do not intervene, but rather simply notify law enforcement personnel of the suspicious activity so that it can be investigated further.

- *Unexplainable Behaviors*

  Individuals possessing large sums of currency.

  Individuals buying or renting goods, services, vehicles, and accommodations with cash or by fraudulent means, such as stolen credit cards or checks, or otherwise operating through false identities or indirect ownership.

  Individuals traveling by plane, train, bus, or other means and staying at hotels or other public accommodations, without reservations or accurate information.

  Individuals in vehicles arriving at or departing from locations at odd times of the day or night.

Individuals living under unusual circumstances (e.g., several persons renting a house with little or no furnishings or other items commonly found in residences).

Individuals in possession of firearms or other dangerous items.

Suspicious purchases of odd items or items in odd quantities (e.g., an apartment dweller purchasing large quantities of lawn fertilizer).

Individuals observed sketching, photographing, or loitering near critical infrastructures.

Persons exhibiting excessive nervousness.

Persons trying to conceal their faces or activities.

Persons wearing clothing that is inconsistent with the area/weather or wearing uniforms inconsistent with activity.

Persons using binoculars, cameras, and/or night vision goggles or making notes or sketches of a nontourist facility.

Persons sitting in a parked vehicle for no apparent reason.

- *Strange Objects*

Bottle or pipe with attached wire or battery.

Briefcase, package, or bag in a questionable location.

Parcels, or luggage left unattended.

Common objects of value left unattended.

Vehicles left unattended or abandoned or that appear to be out of place.

- *Unusual Circumstances*

Two or more people experiencing unidentifiable odor, coughing, nausea, or blurred vision.

Agitated person entering a sensitive area, looking around, and quickly departing.

Nontraditional use of specialty vehicles such as an emergency vehicle or delivery truck.

Specialty vehicles parked in uncharacteristic places (such as a gas truck at a school).

Unidentified vehicles parked in sensitive areas.

5.7 SUMMARY OF ATTACK PROCESS

The attack process includes the following steps:

Step 1. Initiation

Selecting a target

Gathering intelligence

Operational planning

Selection and training perpetrators

Obtaining materials and supplies necessary for the attack

Step 2. Escalation

Assembling the weapon

Transporting the adversaries and weapon to the target

Executing the attack

Step 3. Deescalation

Withdrawing from the target area (if applicable)

Withdrawing from the safe house

Step 4. Termination

Wrapping up loose ends associated with the attack and moving on to the next mission

REFERENCES

1. Council on Foreign Relations, *Tracking Down Terrorist Financing*, April 4, 2006.
2. The Washington Institute for Near East Policy, *Policy Watch #1041*, November 1, 2005.
3. Testimony of Matthew A. Levitt, Joint Hearing of the Committee of International Relations, United States House of Representatives, February 16, 2005.
4. www.nationalreview.com/comment/morse200510260833.asp.
5. www.newsmax.com/archives/articles/2004/8/9/115651.shtml.

CHAPTER 6

Risk and Threat Assessment

6.1 INTRODUCTION

As adversaries continue to threaten attacks against our critical infrastructure, key resources, key assets, and soft targets, it is imperative that we develop the necessary systems to obtain and analyze intelligence concerning their plans. The basic premise is that the terrorist threat is credible and the terrorists are highly motivated and capable of causing us great harm. We must identify and analyze the vulnerabilities of our assets and implement the appropriate security countermeasures to reduce the risk of an attack. As part of this process, a threat identification, threat credibility, and risk assessment process must be developed. Figure 6.1 illustrates the complete cycle of identifying and protecting critical infrastructure.

6.2 DEFINITIONS

Attack. An attack is a threatening, aggressive offensive assault against an enemy. An attack is a potential source of harm to an asset.

Consequence. A consequence is the type and magnitude of adverse impact resulting from an attack.

Harm. Harm is a measure of the physical or psychological injury to the health of people, or damage to property, the economy, or the environment.

Hazard. A hazard is an act or condition posing a source of potential danger or adverse condition.

Impact. Impact is the adverse effect of a potential attack on a target. Impact is a measure of the seriousness of a threat.

Probability. Probability is the chance, likelihood, or mathematical certainty that a given event, condition, or situation will occur.

Risk. Risk is a quantified measure of the possibility that a key asset will suffer some degree of harm or loss; more specifically, that a defined threat will

Understanding, Assessing, and Responding to Terrorism: Protecting Critical Infrastructure and Personnel By Brian T. Bennett

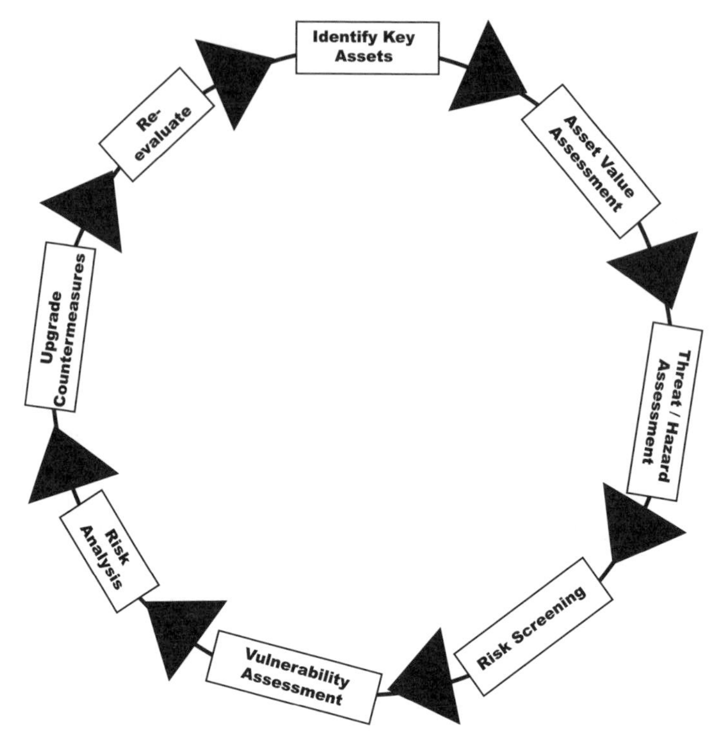

FIGURE 6.1. The cycle of identification and protection of critical infrastructure.

target and successfully exploit a specific vulnerability of a key asset and cause a given set of adverse consequences generally resulting in a loss of some kind.

Risk Avoidance. Risk avoidance is an informed decision not to become involved in a risk situation. This is accomplished by identifying the risks and neutralizing or eliminating the hazards that create the risk.

Security Incident. A security-related occurrence or action that can result in an undesirable event, such as casualties, damage to or destruction of an asset, degradation of services, or financial loss.

Severity. Severity is the level of harm (negative consequences) resulting from a successful attack against a target.

Threat. A threat is a declaration that something unpleasant is about to happen. A threat that is successfully executed can adversely impact an asset. A threat is a capability coupled with an intent.

Threat Analysis. Potential threats are identified and analyzed based on current events, intelligence, and historical data.

Vulnerability. Vulnerability is the state of being assailable or exposed to a threat; a measure of the probability that a weakness will be exploited due to a flaw in the security protection process.

Vulnerability Analysis. Potential vulnerabilities are quantified on the basis of asset and threat analysis, and existing security countermeasures are tested for effectiveness.

6.3 THE RISK OF ATTACK

The adversary needs to have various capabilities in order to perpetrate an attack. The key asset must present features that make it an attractive target for an adversary to attack. The following criteria can be used to determine whether the adversary has obtained the necessary capabilities in order to pose a potential threat and whether the key asset is an attractive target.

- *Access to a Weapon.* Can the adversary acquire the materials necessary to build a weapon and execute an attack?
- *Knowledge and Expertise.* Does the adversary have the skills and resources necessary to create or obtain a weapon and execute an attack?
- *History of Threat.* Has the key asset or a similar key asset or critical infrastructure been targeted before? Has intelligence indicated that the key asset or a similar key asset or critical infrastructure is attractive as a target?
- *Key Asset Visibility.* Does the key asset provide some economic, cultural, financial, symbolic or other importance to society that would make it an attractive target to the adversary?
- *Key Asset Accessibility.* Can the adversary get into a favorable position from which to launch an attack against the intended target?
- *Key Asset Population.* Are the demographics such that the key asset would be an attractive target?
- *Key Asset Value.* Would degradation or destruction of the key asset cause a huge impact on society?
- *Security Systems in Place.* Do the security counter measures currently installed provide a level of defense against each of the potential threats?

6.4 DETERMINING KEY ASSET AND ITS VALUE

The first step of the risk assessment process is to determine all key assets and their values to help prioritize the evaluation process.

A key asset is any resource of value that requires protection; it can be tangible (such as a building) or intangible (such as a corporation's reputation). Determination of key assets can be accomplished by assembling a multidisciplinary team of the jurisdiction's stakeholders. Input from the stakeholders will be helpful in identifying the most valuable key assets. Identifying a jurisdiction's key assets is a two-step process:

1. Define and fully understand the key asset's core functions in terms of products or services provided to the jurisdiction.
   (a) What are the primary products or services provided?
   (b) What critical activities take place at the key asset?
   (c) Is the key asset interconnected with other critical infrastructures or key assets such that an attack at another location could have an adverse impact here or vice versa?
2. Identify the jurisdiction's individual critical components and their value.
   (a) How many people work in or visit the key asset and could become casualties in the event of an attack?
   (b) What are the specific physical locations of all critical key assets?
   (c) Can the key asset continue to operate somewhat effectively, providing its product or service, if it is damaged (degraded) in an attack?
   (d) What is the effect on the jurisdiction if the key asset is destroyed?
   (e) Are backups or replacements for the key asset readily available?
   (f) What are the availability and readiness of emergency response assets that would mitigate the effects of a successful attack?

Asset Criticality

Once all of the key assets have been inventoried, they should be prioritized to reflect their importance to the specific jurisdiction. Typically, people are a jurisdiction's most critical asset and therefore are most at risk and require protection. Asset criticality is defined as a critical infrastructure, key asset, or key resource's perceived value or the significance of its system in the event of a loss. The criticality of an asset is determined by evaluating the consequences if the integrity and/or availability of the asset or the asset function is compromised. Key assets are rated in terms of their importance; this rating is used to determine which key assets get priority in terms of resources for the implementation of security countermeasures. In order to prioritize them, they should be assigned an importance value. There are a number of asset value scales available, but the principle is the same: higher asset values reflect a more significant loss.

Consequence of Loss	Asset Value
Very high	10
High	8–9
Medium high	7
Medium	5–6
Medium low	4
Low	2–3
Very low	1

Very high indicates loss or damage of the key asset would have exceptionally grave consequences. *High* means loss or damage of the key asset would have grave consequences. *Medium high* indicates loss or damage of the key asset would have serious consequences, while *medium* means loss or damage of the asset would have moderate to serious consequences. *Medium low* indicates loss or damage of the key asset would have moderate consequences, while *low* means loss or damage of the key asset would have minor consequences or impact. *Very low* indicates loss or damage of the key asset would have negligible consequences or impact.

Asset Value Example

The jurisdiction to be assessed in this example is a three story elementary school. The school has 1000 students and 50 staff. The scenario involves an adversary who hijacks a gasoline tank truck loaded with 8800 gallons of gasoline. The truck is driven into the main lobby of the school and the gasoline is ignited. An assessment team is assembled to develop a list of key assets, assign an asset value, and prioritize the assets for protection. The key assets present include:

- The students and staff.
- The school building itself.
- The boiler room, which provides heat to the school.
- The library, which houses the books and computer systems used by the students and staff.
- The garage, where the school buses are repaired and stored.

An asset value is then assigned to each key asset-to reflect the consequences of there loss

Key Asset	Asset Value
Students and staff	Very high (10)
School building	Very high (10)
Boiler room	Medium (5)
Library/information systems	Low (3)
Garage	Low (3)

The result of this assessment and key asset valuation indicates that maximum effort must be given to protect the people and the building.

6.5 THREATS

Threat Identification

Since September 11, 2001, we have lived under the increased threat that terrorists may attempt additional attacks against our country. A threat is simply the potential for an attack. Threats come in different forms and from different sources. It is important to understand who the people are who intend to cause harm. It is also essential to understand the weapons and tactics that could be used to cause harm. Threats from outside the facility could affect people and the facility itself and may involve trespassing, unauthorized entry, theft, burglary, or vandalism. Threats from inside the facility may arise from inadequate designs, management systems, staffing or training, or other internal problems. These may include theft, substance abuse, sabotage, disgruntled employee or contractor actions, or workplace violence, among others. Threats are not restricted to people and property and could also involve sensitive facility information. Both facility outsiders or employees or contractors could pose threats to data storage and data transmissions of, for example, proprietary information, privacy data, and contract information. They could also pose a threat to computer-controlled equipment. These threats may include breaches in data access and storage, uncontrolled dissemination of information, or destruction of information or automated information systems[1].

Terrorism has become a significant threat to our way of life here in the United States. There is a generalized concern at all levels that the terrorism threat is real, but the concern is not universally accepted. There is a trend toward more aggressive and frequent foreign and domestic terrorism. The terrorist threat is dynamic and has evolved in response to social, political, and technological changes. Terrorist attacks will continue to evolve with even more efficient ways discovered to cause death and destruction. The tactics and weapons that can be used are limited only by the adversary's creativity. Threat analysis includes not only the likelihood of becoming a target, but also whether or not the security countermeasures that are implemented are sufficient to discourage an attack.

Personnel must be trained to identify the potential and real sources of threat to a key asset. This will include identifying all pertinent deliberate threats from internal and external sources, as well as all accidental threats from human and natural sources. A threat is a combination of the *motivation* to do harm, the *capability* to do harm, the *opportunity* to do harm, and the potential *impact* of the harm. Threats against a target can be natural (a flood or hurricane), accidental (a fire or damaged equipment), or intentional (a terrorist attack), and cause an undesirable impact. To assist in the risk analysis process, a listing of each potential threat should be compiled. This list would capture the various specific types of threats from each of the three categories that may occur and adversely affect a key asset. The threat must be described in specific terms to determine a key asset's vulnerability and to establish protective security countermeasures. This description should include the tactics that adversaries will use to attack the key asset. These types of threat descriptions can be used to design detailed protective security systems to mitigate the threat.

Threat can be defined as

$$\text{Threat} = \text{Motivation} + \text{Capability} + \text{Opportunity} + \text{Impact}$$

Motivation. An adversary must have the proper motivation in order to plan and execute an attack against a key asset. In the case of terrorism, most motivations are driven by political or religious factors.

Capability. An adversary must have the technical and financial capability to plan and execute an attack. Designing, building, storing, transporting, and disseminating a weapon of mass destruction (WMD) not only requires adequate financial resources but also sound technical knowledge.

Opportunity. In order for a threat to translate into an actual attack, an opportunity to attack must exist. Opportunities are usually security vulnerabilities that are exploited by an adversary to advantage.

Impact. The impact is the adverse effect that is achieved when an adversary successfully executes an attack against a key asset. Impact can range from no noticeable effect to degradation and/or destruction of the key asset.

Threat Assessment

The first most important step in the risk assessment and management process is a threat assessment. A threat assessment is a statement of threats that are related to vulnerabilities of a key asset. A threat assessment considers all potential adversary threats, as well as their capabilities, against a specific key asset. Threat and risk assessments are widely recognized as effective decision support tools for prioritizing security countermeasure investments. The threat assessment should examine supporting information to evaluate the likelihood of occurrence for each specific threat.

There are two general categories of threat assessments:

1. *General Threat Assessment*. A general description of the threat is required to estimate the likelihood that adversaries might attempt an attack against a key asset. This description includes the type of adversary and the tactics and capabilities (e.g., the number of members in a group, weapons, equipment, and mode of transportation) associated with each potential threat.
2. *Site-Specific Threat Assessment*. The threat must also be specifically defined for each individual key asset. This includes the number of adversaries involved in the attack, their likely modus operandi for an attack against the specific key asset, the types of tools and weapons they would use, and the specific types of event or act they are willing to commit.

The four major functions of a threat assessment are the following:

1. *Identification of Assets at Risk*. How attractive is the key asset? Estimate the real or perceived value of the key asset in the eyes of the adversary.
2. *Identification of Potential Adversaries*. Stakeholders of critical infrastructure, key assets and key resources must work cooperatively with law enforcement to identify potential adversaries. Once credible intelligence has been obtained, it must be conveyed to the affected individuals and organizations so that appropriate security countermeasures can be implemented. Potential adversaries include insiders (employees or other persons who have authorized

access to the target), outsiders (persons external to the key asset being targeted), and conspirators (an insider working cooperatively with an outsider).

3. *Assessment of the Risks Posed by the Potential Adversary.* Information must be gathered on the potential adversary as well as the potential target. Multiple sources of information should be consulted to ensure high reliability. This information will lead to an assessment of the capabilities of the potential adversary, which can be compared to the security countermeasures in place at the potential target to reduce risk.
4. *Management of Target Risks.* Evaluate existing and planned security countermeasures to prevent an attack, or at least minimize the risks posed by a successful attack to an acceptable level. The more effective the countermeasures, the less likely the adversary will succeed.

Threat is expressed as a function of the likelihood that an adversary will successfully exploit a vulnerability present at a key asset. This vulnerability can be triggered accidentally or intentionally. Without a vulnerability that can be exploited, the threat does not pose a risk to the target.

Homeland Security Presidential Directive 3 (HSPD 3; See Appendix 6.1) and the FBI's National Threat Warning System (NTWS) provide appropriate factors for the assignment of threat conditions. The NTWS ensures that vital information regarding terrorism reaches the U.S. counterterrorism and law enforcement communities. The guidelines governing the NTWS also provide specific policy regarding public notification procedures.

HSPD 3 and NTWS provide certain criteria that should be considered when conducting a threat analysis. These criteria include a variety of considerations before reaching a decision on the threat condition. Higher threat conditions indicate a greater risk of a terrorist act, with the risk including severity and probability. The most important factor in determining the threat risk is the quality of the information. The evaluation of threat information usually includes:

- *The Credibility of the Threat.* Was the information obtained through a reliable source?
- *The Level of Corroboration Regarding the Threat.* Was the information confirmed by other, independent sources?
- *The Degree to Which the Threat is Imminent.* Is the threat likely to occur in the near term?
- *Threat Specificity.* Was a specific target identified?
- *The Gravity of the Consequences if the Threat is Acted Upon.* What will be the adverse impacts if the attack is successful?
- *The Assessed Vulnerability of the Target.* Is the target one that has been analyzed and is hardened with physical and administrative countermeasures or is the target a relatively unprotected soft target?

Factors that determine the credibility of a threat include:

The Source of the Threat. From where was the information obtained?

Source Dependency and Reliability. Is there a high level of confidence in the information obtained from this source based on the accuracy of previous information obtained from this source?

Credibility of the Source's Access to Certain Information. Is it likely that the source would have access to the adversary, or the adversary's key personnel, in order to obtain the information reported?

Purpose and Objective of the Terrorist Group Involved in the Threat. Are the goals and objectives of the attack consistent with the terrorist adversary's goals and objectives? Have they perpetrated this type of attack before?

Capability and Resources of the Terrorist Group Involved in the Threat. Does the adversary group have the financial, technical, and operational capabilities to plan and execute this type of attack?

Specificity of the Source's Information. When, where, and from whom was the source's information obtained?

To corroborate a threat, the following information should be ascertained:

Does the threat serve the stated or philosophical purpose of the group?

Has intelligence indicated that planning or operational activities consistent with the threat have been underway?

Do other intelligence sources confirm activities consistent with the threat are underway?

If a specific threat exists against a specific target, it is necessary to determine what the adverse impacts would be if the target were to be successfully attacked:

What will the effect on a critical infrastructure, key resource, or key asset such that a successful attack will result in the disruption of essential services, cause significant adverse financial impact, or lead to casualties?

What would be the psychological adverse effect on the public sector, private sector, or general public of the loss or degradation of the target?

If the threat is imminent, is there sufficient time between the threat determination and the attack to implement security countermeasures to foil the attack?

Can the target be made less attractive by implementing security countermeasures?

Can the threat be interrupted if law enforcement personnel catch the adversary and prevent the attack from being perpetrated?

Is there sufficient time to warn the target of the impending attack so that security countermeasures can be implemented or personnel can be evacuated from the target area?

Threat Analysis

A common method to evaluate an adversary's threat is to analyze five factors: existence, capability, history, intention, and targeting.

Existence addresses the questions:

Who is hostile to the key asset or jurisdiction?

Are they present or thought to be present?

Are they able to enter the country and are they readily identifiable in a local community upon arrival?

Capability addresses the questions:

What weapons have been used in carrying out past attacks?

Do the adversaries need to bring weapons into the area or are they available locally?

History addresses the questions:

What attacks has the potential adversary committed in the past and how many times?

When was the most recent incident and where and against what target?

What tactics did the adversary use?

Is the adversary supported by another group or individuals?

How did the adversary acquire the demonstrated capability?

Intention addresses the questions:

What does the potential adversary hope to achieve?

How do we know this?

Targeting addresses the questions [2]:

Do we know if an adversary is performing surveillance on the key asset or on a similar key asset?

Is this information current and credible and indicative of preparations for terrorist operations?

Threats are examined based on the basis of their likelihood of occurring. The Commonwealth of Kentucky Office of Homeland Security has taken the five factors commonly used to evaluate terrorist threats and layered them into the Homeland Security Advisory System levels.

	Threat Analysis Factors				
Threat Level	Existence	Capability	History	Intention	Targeting
Severe (Red)	X	X	X	X	X
High (Orange)	X	X	X	X	O
Elevated (Yellow)	X	X	X	O	
Guarded (Blue)	X	X	O		
Low (Green)	X	O			

X = Factor must be present O = Factor may or may not be present

Please note that the Federal Department of Homeland Security does not use these threat analysis factors to determine threat level.

Threat Likelihood

After the threats and their potential impacts have been identified, an analysis of the probability of these threats being carried out must be completed to properly evaluate the risk. Each threat is assigned a value, either quantitative or qualitative.

Prioritizing the Response to Threat

After the severity of each undesired event and the likelihood of attack for each adversary group have been determined, these values are ranked in a matrix. Priority cases would be those with a matrix value closer to 1.

Once the threats and corresponding risks have been identified, a key asset must take steps to reduce its vulnerability by (1) eliminating or reducing risks as far as possible by inherently safe design and construction, (2) enacting protective security measures, and (3) informing users of residual risk.

6.6 PROBABILITY OF ATTACK OCCURRENCE

There are a number of descriptors that can be used to ascertain the probability of an attack, given that the adversary has met all of the other prerequisites needed to execute the attack (e.g., technical, financial, and operational).

The following parameters can be used to indicate the likelihood or probability of an attack occurring:

0 Impossible—the probability of occurrence is zero
1 Remote—the attack is not likely to occur but is possible
2 Possible—the attack might occur
3 Probable—the attack is likely to occur
4 Certain—the attack has occurred or will occur

6.7 CONSEQUENCES OF A SUCCESSFUL ATTACK

The consequences of a successful attack, also known as the severity, are a qualitative comparison between the adverse effects (impact) and the security countermeasures in place (mitigation). Therefore

$$\text{Severity} = \text{Impact} - \text{Mitigation}$$

The more security countermeasures in place, the less severe the consequences of a successful attack are likely to be.

There are a number of scales that can be used to categorize the consequences or severity of a successful attack.

Severity of Loss	Value
Catastrophic (death of personnel, destruction of key asset)	4
Critical (severe injuries, degradation of key asset's ability to provide product or service)	3
Marginal (minor injuries, minor damage to key asset)	2
Negligible (no significant injuries or damage to key asset)	1

The chart below helps define the areas of concern by comparing the severity of the consequences resulting from a successful attack against the probability of an attack being perpetrated. It is helpful to complete this chart by plotting the threat when making recommendations for the implementation of security countermeasures, in order to ensure that resources are being allocated to the appropriate threat. High probability and high severity threats should receive priority for the implementation of countermeasures.

Low Probability High Severity	High Probability High Severity
Low Probability Low Severity	High Probability Low Severity

6.8 RISK

Components of Risk

Risk has three components: (1) there must be a *threat* to a key asset; (2) the key asset must be *vulnerable* to a threat; and (3) there is an adverse *consequence* or adverse impact if an attack against a key asset is successful. Therefore

$$\text{Risk} = (\text{Threat}) \times (\text{Vulnerability}) \times (\text{Consequence})$$

Understanding Risk

Understanding the risk that a key asset faces from a successful attack requires answering the following questions:

How important is the key asset to the jurisdiction?

What vulnerabilities exist that can be exploited by an adversary in the furtherance of an attack?

Is an adversary targeting a particular key asset?

How likely is it that the attack will occur?

What are the adverse consequences resulting from a successful attack?

Principle of Risk Minimization

Managing a security risk posed by an adversary, in its most simple form, means defining what the risk to the asset is, determining the likelihood of an attack, assessing the relative magnitude (or severity) of the risk, identifying the vulnerabilities, and installing security countermeasures.

It should be noted that there is no way to protect against every threat that an adversary can make against an asset. There is no such thing as absolute security, regardless of the time, effort, and material invested, which assures 100% protection against all possible threats, at all times; to do so would involve exorbitant costs and would impede the free and easy access that critical infrastructures and soft targets often need in order to make their product or provide their service. Therefore the goal of the risk management process is to manage the risk posed by an adversary to an acceptable level, at an acceptable cost, within tolerable limits. This technique is known as *risk minimization*.

Risk Estimation

To estimate risk, a number of factors must be considered. The first is to determine the *value* of the key asset, in terms of the products or services it provides to the jurisdiction. The *vulnerabilities* that exist at the key asset and could be exploited by an adversary are quantified. Next, identify and rate the *threats* that could cause harm to the key asset. The *likelihood* of an attack is predicted, and the adverse *consequences* of a successful attack are determined. Therefore the risk from an attack on a key asset can be defined mathematically as

$$\text{Risk} = (\text{Value}) \times (\text{Vulnerabilities}) \times (\text{Threats}) \times (\text{Likelihood}) \times (\text{Consequences})$$

Acceptable Risk

Acceptable risk is a measure of the amount of risk that will be tolerated by an individual, group, or society in exchange for the benefits of having access to or use of something. Whether a risk is acceptable or not will depend on the advantage that the person or group perceives to be obtainable in return for taking the risk.

Unacceptable Risk

There are times when a threat poses a risk to people, information, or property, which is so severe that it cannot be considered acceptable. This is known as an unacceptable risk. When unacceptable risk is present, more work must be done to mitigate the adverse effects posed by the threat by implementing additional risk reduction measures until the level of risk becomes acceptable.

Risk Analysis

As part of the critical infrastructure, key resource, and key asset protection process, risk analysis occurs when a jurisdiction determines that one or more threatened key assets are vulnerable to deliberate attacks, natural disasters, or accidents. Risk analysis begins with an examination of the negative effects of the degradation or loss of a key asset. The likelihood of the occurrence is determined, and appropriate security countermeasures are developed. Following this action is an evaluation of the cost of the security countermeasures in terms of available resources (e.g., time, money, personnel, and materials). The probable negative effects caused by doing nothing to prevent the degradation or loss of a critical infrastructure are then weighed against the cost of doing something with protective measures. Decision makers should conclude that a risk is unacceptable if the impact of the degradation or loss of the key asset will be catastrophic to the jurisdiction.

Risk analysis is a detailed identification, examination, and assessment performed to understand the nature of unwanted, negative consequences resulting from undesired events. The level of risk is based on (1) the value of the key assets, (2) threats to the key assets, and (3) their vulnerabilities and likelihood of exploitation.

The goals of risk analysis are the identification of all key assets, threats, and vulnerabilities of key assets along with the estimation of the impact of a successful attack.

Based on the evaluations and assessments performed previously, the key assets that are susceptible to compromise by the various threats through the exploitation of system vulnerabilities will be identified. A combination of the impact of loss rating and the vulnerability rating can be used to evaluate the potential risk to the key asset from a given threat.

Risk analysis can be quantitative or qualitative, but in most cases it is partly both. There are many variants of risk analysis that are known by many different names—hazard analysis, consequence analysis, worst case analysis, fault tree analysis, failure modes and effects analysis—and there are numerous models and tools that can be used in a systematic assessment. Whether qualitative or quantitative, simple or complex, some type of systematic analysis of the risks needs to be done in all cases to serve as the basis for developing an effective risk management strategy.

Quantitative Risk Analysis

Quantitative relates to, concerns, or is based on the amount or number of something; so risk is capable of being measured or expressed in numerical terms. Quantitative risk analysis is a formalized and specialized method of estimating the magnitude of risk by calculating a numerical value for both consequences and likelihood. It provides a degree of objectivity for ranking risks and establishing priorities for protective security countermeasures. The approach employs two fundamental elements: the probability of an event occurring and the likely loss should it occur.

The advantage of a quantitative analysis is that it provides a measurement of the magnitude that can be used in the cost–benefit analysis of the recommended security countermeasures. The disadvantage is that, depending on the units in which the measurement is expressed, the meaning of a quantitative analysis may be unclear, requiring the result to be interpreted in a qualitative manner.

An example of the quantitative analysis of hazards involves assigning a numeric value to criteria such as:

The probability of exposure to an attack.

The frequency with which an attack may occur.

The number of persons at risk.

A descriptive phrase should be assigned to the numerical values, such as:

0—No damage to the structure.

1—Attack likely to occur within the next 6 months.

2—Casualties would be in the range of 50–100 people.

The numerical values may be weighted to reflect their perceived importance. For example, the loss of a life is more significant than destruction of a structure, so the loss of life can be weighted by a factor of 5 to reflect its significance.

After the screening has identified the specific threats against the specific key assets, the next step is to develop a risk matrix. The vertical column of the risk matrix can be arranged by key asset or specific threat. An example of a risk matrix arranged by key asset for a manufacturing complex would include:

- Administrative office.
- Manufacturing area.
- Quality control lab.
- Information technology.

- Maintenance.
- Warehousing/shipping.

An example of a risk matrix arranged by threat against the manufacturing complex would include:

- Vehicle-borne improvised explosive device.
- Chemical agent attack.
- Biological agent attack.
- Cyber attack.

The horizontal axis of the risk matrix would include the consequences of the specific threat against the key asset or execution of the threat. An example of the consequences in a risk matrix would include:

- Casualties.
- Damage/destruction of physical assets.
- Economic damage.
- Environmental damage.

The matrix table is completed by measuring the consequence of an attack against a key asset or execution of a specific threat. For example,

0 = No injuries
1 = Minor injuries
2 = Major injuries
3 = Fatalities (less than 10)
4 = Mass fatalities (more than 10)

Another type of quantitative risk analysis is available for very specific threats against very specific targets. The basic process for this technique is as follows.

Step 1. Determine the key asset value and the consequence of loss. Key assets that are vulnerable and require security countermeasures are identified and ranked according to the consequence of their loss (most important ranked first).

Step 2. Identify the specific threats that could adversely impact the key asset.

Step 3. Identify key asset vulnerabilities. Which key asset can be exploited by the specific threats raised in Step 2? Determine the nature and source of these attacks.

Step 4. Determine the specific risk scenarios of how undesirable events may occur and determine the effect on each key asset. Each valid threat should be addressed in at least one scenario. Assign high medium low risk rating for each scenario based on the severity of the consequences and the likelihood of the scenario occurring. Identify the frequency of a potential attack (e.g., frequent = 1–2 times per year).

Step 5. Identify security countermeasures that can either eliminate or reduce the effects of one or more vulnerabilities. Security countermeasures are selected for implementation based on factors such as whether they reduce the probability of an undesired event from occurring, their implementation cost, and risk–benefit analysis.

Step 6. Reevaluate the risk. Implemented security countermeasures are inserted into the scenario, and the risk rating is recalculated by starting the quantitative analysis process over again.

Some of the disadvantages of using a quantitative risk assessment methodology include:

- Undesirable effects can vary from person to person conducting the assessment depending on their perceived values and preferences.
- Organizational failures are not taken into account.
- If there is no weighing of individual factors, equal weight can be attributed to a low-probability, high-risk event and a high-probability, high-risk event.

Example: Quantitative Risk Analysis. The Acme Company employees 25 employees to process orders that are placed via the Internet by its customers. The total compensation for each employee is \$50 per hour (salary, benefits, and taxes). Acme's customers place an average of \$50,000 worth of orders each hour via the Internet.

An adversary can launch a cyber attack against the Acme Company by placing a virus in the computer system, which causes the system, to go down for 4 hours. The probability that a virus could be placed into the computer system and cause the system to go down is estimated to be 80% in this example. It is estimated that without appropriate security countermeasures in place, an adversary could perpetrate at least one attack per month.

The quantitative risk analysis of the potential financial loss in this example is:

$$\begin{aligned}
&4 \text{ hours} \times 25 \text{ employees} \times \$50/\text{hour} = \$5000\\
&\text{Business loss per occurrence}\\
&\quad = \$50{,}000(\$5000 + \$50{,}000) \times 80\% \text{ probability of success}\\
&\quad = \$44{,}000 \text{ loss per occurrence}
\end{aligned}$$

So the cost of the risk per occurrence is \$44,000. If this type of attack is successfully perpetrated monthly, the annual cost now becomes

$$\$44{,}000 \text{ per occurrence} \times 12 \text{ occurrences/year} = \$528{,}000$$

The computer system has a life expectancy of three years. Therefore the total potential loss is

$$3 \text{ years} \times \$528{,}000 \text{ per year} = \$1{,}584{,}000$$

The cost of the risk can now be compared to the cost of the security countermeasure(s) to protect the computer system from a cyber attack. An antivirus software program and license costs $128,000 to protect Acme's computer system from this type of attack. The cost to train the employees to operate within the new software system is $6000. Therefore the one-time cost of the security countermeasure is $134,000. Thus the analysis indicates that a one-time $134,000 investment in security countermeasures will prevent a potential total loss of $1,584,000!

Someone at the facility must be empowered to:

- Determine if the appropriate security countermeasure(s) should be implemented.
- Determine if and when the risks have been minimized to an acceptable level by the installation of the security countermeasure(s).
- Determine if the cost–benefit analysis justifies the expenditure to implement the proposed security countermeasures to prevent the attack.

Qualitative Risk Analysis

Qualitative analysis involves distinctions based on qualities. Qualitative risk assessment usually uses a matrix. This methodology uses a qualitative, event descriptive, scalable table for hazard likelihood and consequences by reviewing considerations such as people, assets, environmental damage, financial aspects, business or service interruption, and corporate reputation.

Qualitative risk analysis is by far the most widely used risk analysis methodology. The advantage of a qualitative risk analysis is that it provides a relative prioritization of the specific risks that an attack may pose and identifies immediate areas for improvement to reduce the risks posed by the vulnerabilities present at the key asset. The disadvantage of qualitative risk analysis is that it does not provide specific quantifiable measurements of the magnitudes of the impact, thereby making the cost–benefit analysis difficult.

Example: Qualitative Risk Analysis. The soft target to be evaluated in this example is a local shopping center. The shopping center contains 100 stores, with 800 generally unskilled, part-time employees working at any given time. The stores include retailers, service providers, and a food court. Competition between the stores is fierce. The shopping center's hours of operation are 9:00 am until 10:00 pm, 7 days per week. There is an average of 3000 shoppers in the shopping center at any given time, serving primarily middle income clientele. The shopping center generates approximately $1,000,000 in gross sales daily and pays $1,250,000 in property taxes to the municipality annually. The shopping center pays $21.9 million in sales tax to the state annually. The shopping center has an insured replacement cost of $150,000,000 and the inventory of the various stores is insured for $75,000,000. Deliveries to the stores in the shopping center occur between 8:00 am and noon, Monday through Friday. There are a total of eight security guards on site during normal business hours. The security guards are hired from a private company, are unarmed, and have only basic security training. There are no security guards present during nonbusiness hours. Each store has a metal, roll-down security door that is closed and locked when the store is closed. All entrances to the shopping center, as well as the individual stores, are equipped with a burglar alarm system. Typical response time of the local police department to the shopping center is 5 minutes.

Using the basic processes described previously, the qualitative risk analysis for the shopping center would be completed as follows.

Step 1. Identification of the Assessment Team. For a relatively simple risk analysis, one or two employees can perform the assessment. If the use of a team is desired, it should be comprised of multidisciplinary personnel. For this example, the assessment team for the risk analysis would likely consist of the following personnel: local law enforcement, local fire department, local emergency medical service, shopping center loss prevention specialist, and shopping center safety and health staff.

Step 2. Purpose of the Assessment. The purpose of the risk analysis is to evaluate several possible attack scenarios against the shopping center, prioritize which specific key assets within the shopping center pose the greatest risk to the shopping center and personnel, and develop recommendations concerning enhanced security countermeasures.

Step 3. Scope of the Assessment.

The soft target to be evaluated is described: the shopping center, the shopping center parking lot, its employees, and its customers and visitors.

The mission of the soft target is evaluated: the mission of the shopping center is to provide a safe and secure venue for people to shop and dine, and to provide gainful employment for its employees, suppliers, and contractors.

The soft target systems are identified: each of the 100 stores, the common shopping center areas, the shopping center parking lot, and the employees, customers, and visitors.

Soft target boundaries and the interconnectivity with other critical infrastructure or key assets are enumerated. The soft target boundaries will be the shopping center property, including the shopping center building and the parking lot. For the purpose of this risk analysis, interconnectivity will not be considered.

Step 4. Identification of the Soft Targets to Be Protected and Valuation of Assets.

People include employees, contractors, visitors, vendors, and truck drivers.

There are many stores within the shopping center that provide functional services to customers. The shopping center itself, as well as the individual stores, provides functional services to employees, suppliers, and contractors.

The shopping center owns several electrical transformers and substations on their property, which receive electricity from the local power utility. These facilities step down the electricity to the proper voltage and distribute it to the various occupancies on the property. Water, natural gas (for heating and cooking), and telecommunications are provided by the respective utility companies to the individual stores as needed.

Physical property includes the structure itself, the inventory in each store, and the cash in each store. Some stores that provide services also have intangible assets such as intellectual property.

Core business includes the products and services sold by the various tenants of the shopping center, as well as the shopping center's reputation as a safe and secure venue in which to shop.

Many stores have computer systems including hardware and software associated with data, telecommunications, and computer processing for the conduct of their business.

The valuations of the physical assets pertaining to the shopping center are as follows:

- The replacement cost of the shopping center is $150,000,000.
- The value of the individual stores' inventory and equipment is $75,000,000.
- The shopping center gross sales are $1,000,000 daily.
- The shopping center pays $1,250,000 in local property taxes annually.

Step 5. Specific Loss Risk Events Likely to Occur.

Shoplifting and theft from the stores are a moderate concern based on the three year statistics provided by the local police department as well as incident reports provided by the individual stores.

Car theft from the parking lot is a moderate problem based on statistics provided by the local police department.

Assault and other violent crimes are a minor problem based on complaints filed with the local police department by employees and shoppers.

Intelligence from federal, state, and local law enforcement agencies has indicated that shopping centers are a soft target, and terrorist organizations have indicated that a concerted effort to attack a shopping center in this area is underway.

Based on intelligence provided by the law enforcement agencies, the following types of WMD attack against the shopping center are possible:

- A chemical weapon involving a choking agent deployed inside the shopping center.
- A biological weapon mixed into the food sold at the food court.
- An explosive weapon, most likely a vehicle-borne improvised explosive device, detonated in a densely occupied area.

Step 6. Probability of Loss Risk and Frequency of Events. The probability of loss risk is based on the following.

History of prior incidents indicates inadequate security to deal with this type of threat, with few physical or administrative security countermeasures in place or planned.

There have been no terrorist attacks against this type of soft target in the homeland. Thus there are no trends to analyze or frequency data available for review.

There are active intelligence warnings issued to the shopping center from law enforcement agencies based on terrorist threats.

Step 7. Impact of Events. If a terrorist were to successfully execute a WMD attack in the shopping center, the adverse impacts include the following.

Casualties would be significant, with fatalities ranging up to several hundred and injuries approaching one thousand.

Equipment damage would depend on the type of weapon deployed. The shopping center may have to be decontaminated (in the event of a biological or chemical attack) or repaired or rebuilt (in the event of an explosive attack).

The shopping center would likely be closed for an extended period of time due to the investigation, cleanup, and repair after the attack. Services provided by the shopping center may be unavailable for several months.

There would be a significant amount of psychological damage to the general populace in the event of a WMD attack on a soft target such as a shopping center. Many people would likely be scared to return to this type of venue until they were assured the appropriate security countermeasures to prevent another attack had been implemented.

The financial costs attributable to a successful attack could run into tens or even hundreds of millions of dollars. There would be costs associated with the cleanup, repair, and replacement of the tangible assets such as structures and inventory. However, the costs associated with the intangible assets, such as loss of business due to fear from another attack and the impending lawsuits from the occupants of the shopping center at the time of the attack, would be very significant.

Step 8. Existing Security Countermeasures. There is not much security currently present at the shopping center to deal with this type of threat. Most security that is present is focused on traditional loss prevention (i.e., theft from the stores). There are a small number of inadequately trained, unarmed security guards on site during business hours. There are no security guards present when the shopping center is closed. The security guards and store employees have not received any training concerning suspicious persons, activities, or packages.

Step 9. Options to Mitigate and Manage the Risk. There are several options available to prevent, mitigate, and respond to the risks identified in the threat intelligence:

Restrict all vehicle parking within 300 feet of the building.

Install security stations at each entry portal and search all packages carried by visitors and employees as they enter the mall.

Search all delivery trucks at a remote location before they approach the loading docks.

Train all security guards and store employees about suspicious persons, activities, and packages.

Arm the security guards.

Develop and implement an emergency response plan to respond to a WMD attack.

Coordinate the shopping center emergency response plan with local authorities.

Conduct frequent drills and exercises with employees and the local emergency responders to test the emergency response plan.

Step 10. Feasibility of Implementation of Security Countermeasures.

Restrict all vehicle parking within 300 feet of the building. This option is not feasible under normal circumstances as it would result in the loss of approximately 15% of available parking spaces.

Search all packages carried by visitors and employees as they enter the shopping center. This option is not feasible as it would present an undue inconvenience to customers and would likely result in a loss of business to other shopping centers where searches were not conducted.

Search all delivery trucks at a remote location before they approach the loading docks. This option is practical and can be implemented with limited disruption to normal operations and at minimal cost.

Train all security guards and store employees about suspicious persons, activities, and packages. This option is practical and can be implemented with little to no disruption of daily operations.

Arm all security guards. This option is feasible.

Develop and implement an emergency response plan to respond to a WMD attack. This option will be implemented.

Coordinate the shopping center emergency response plan with local authorities. This option will be implemented.

Conduct frequent drills and exercises with employees and the local emergency responders to test the emergency response plan. This option will be implemented.

Step 11. Cost–Benefit Analysis.

- Restrict all vehicle parking within 300 feet of the building.

  The direct cost to implement this option would include the purchase and installation of 400 concrete barriers to restrict vehicle parking from the restricted areas, new signage, and restriping of new parking spots. Total direct cost would be $125,000.

  The annually recurring costs include maintenance of the barrier system.

  The indirect cost would include possible loss of business due to public perception that the shopping center may be threatened by an imminent terrorist attack.

The benefit of installing this countermeasure would be prevention or minimization of structural damage to the building and elimination of casualties to visitors and employees.

- Search all packages carried by visitors and employees as they enter the shopping center.

  The direct costs to implement this option would include new modifications to the existing entrances to accommodate the security force and facilitate the search process; fencing to direct patrons to the search area; and new signage, inspection equipment, and 20 additional security guards to staff two guards at each of the ten entrances to the shopping center. Total direct costs for implementation would be $1,000,000.

  Annually recurring costs are the salaries for the 20 newly hired security guards, plus maintenance of the security areas, security equipment, and fencing system.

  The indirect costs would be public perception that the shopping center may be threatened by an imminent attack and the intrusion into patrons' privacy by inspecting their parcels.

  The benefit of installing this countermeasure would be to prevent casualties to visitors and employees by reducing the likelihood that a chemical or biological agent may be brought into the shopping center.

- Search all delivery trucks at a remote location before they approach the loading docks.

  The direct costs to implement this option would include the purchase and installation of several concrete barriers to redirect delivery trucks to the remote inspection area; a new security inspection area/building; new signage; inspection equipment; and the hiring of two additional security guards to staff the inspection area. Total direct costs would be $160,000.

  The annually recurring costs include maintenance of the security station/building, barrier system, and inspection equipment plus the salary of the two security guards.

  The indirect costs would be public perception that the shopping center may be threatened by an imminent attack.

  The benefit of installing this countermeasure would be prevention or minimization of structural damage to the building and elimination of casualties to visitors and employees.

- Train all security guards and store employees about suspicious persons, activities, and packages.

  The direct cost to implement this option would include the hiring of an expert consultant to conduct the training, and the time cost for employees and security guards to attend the training. Total direct cost would be $6000.

  There are no annually recurring costs.

  There is no indirect cost.

The benefit of installing this countermeasure would be prevention or minimization of structural damage to the building and elimination of casualties to visitors and employees by discovering an adversary before an attack is executed.

- Arm the security guards.

  The direct cost to implement this suggestion would include the training and certification of the security guards to carry weapons plus the weapons themselves. The total direct cost for this option would be $12,000.

  The annual recurring costs include retraining and recertification of the security guards. Total annual costs would be $6000.

  An indirect benefit of implementing this option may be that the shopping center patrons feel more secure knowing the security guards are armed.

- Develop and implement an emergency response plan to respond to a WMD attack.

  The direct cost to implement this option would include assigning responsibility to an employee or consultant to write the plan. Total direct cost would be $2500.

  The annually recurring costs include the updating of the response plan to reflect current conditions.

  The indirect cost includes the training of employees on the contents of the plan and their responsibilities.

  The benefit of installing this countermeasure would be to have a plan to effectively respond in the event of an attack.

- Coordinate the shopping center emergency response plan with local authorities.

  The direct cost to implement this option would include assigning responsibility to an employee or consultant to coordinate the plan with the local authorities. Total direct cost would be $1000.

  The annually recurring costs include the updating of the response plan to reflect current conditions.

  There is no indirect cost.

- Conduct frequent drills and exercises with employees and the local emergency responders to test the emergency response plan.

  The direct cost to implement this enhancement would be approximately $2000 for supplies necessary to conduct the drills and exercise.

  The annually recurring costs would also be $2000 for supplies.

  The indirect benefit of implementing this option would be patrons of the shopping center feeling more secure knowing a fully implemented and tested emergency response plan is in place at the shopping center.

Risk Management

Risk is present in everything we do. However, risk can be controlled. It is up to us to control and minimize the unnecessary risks faced each day. Risk management involves using all of the information gathered during the risk analysis and assessment processes to evaluate security policy options. Risk management is the process involved in the identification, selection, and adoption of security measures justified by the identified risks to a key asset, and the reduction of these risks to acceptable levels. The goal of risk management is to enable individuals and organizations to isolate separate risks and to identify potential mitigation options. The challenge of risk management is to find the balance between protecting key assets, not interfering with the primary mission of the key asset, and avoiding fiscal collapse in the process of implementing security countermeasures.

The management of risk involves:

- Understanding the risk.
- Defining the risk objectives and guidelines.
- Determining what appropriate security countermeasures can be implemented to minimize the risks identified in the risk analysis and assessment process.
- Determining the associated trade-offs of implementing the identified risk management options.
- Identifying future impacts of implementing management options made at the present time.
- Instituting and monitoring the appropriate risk controls.

Effective risk management consists of a comprehensive analysis of the risks, costs, benefits, and technical feasibility of protecting a key asset.

Definitions of Risk

Residual risk is the risk remaining after protective measures have been developed and implemented to protect a key asset. *Tolerable risk* is the risk that is accepted in a given context based on the current values of society and on the cost to reduce or eliminate the remaining risk.

Residual Risk

Few, if any, key assets will ever be completely risk-free. Every key asset will always have some residual risk. Residual risk is the amount of risk remaining after security countermeasures have been implemented. Each jurisdiction must take the responsibility to determine the amount and type of risk it is willing to accept. The decision about accepting residual risk is based on the risk assessment process and cost–benefit analysis to implement the appropriate security countermeasures.

Risk Management Principle: ALARP

When attempting to implement the appropriate security countermeasures, it is sometimes helpful to remember the acronym ALARP, which stands for *a*s *l*ow *a*s *r*easonably *p*racticable. It means that a residual risk is low enough that attempting to make it lower would actually be more costly than any cost likely to come from the risk itself. The ALARP principle arises from the fact that it would be possible to spend *infinite* time, effort, and money attempting to reduce all risks to zero.

Four Key Risk Management Principles

There are four risk management principles that will help to reduce risk and therefore should be incorporated into a comprehensive risk management program:

1. *Accept No Unnecessary Risks.* If all the hazards that could have been detected have not been detected, then unnecessary risks are being accepted by the key asset. This reemphasizes the need for a strong intelligence gathering and evaluation process involving not only law enforcement but key asset personnel. Once the intelligence information has been gathered and analyzed, it must be communicated to the appropriate levels of personnel within the organization to ensure the appropriate security countermeasures can be implemented.
2. *Make Risk Decisions at the Appropriate Level.* Risk decisions should be made at the lowest possible level in the organization. This will allow for the timeliest decision to be made and allow for the quickest response time to implement appropriate security countermeasures. Appropriate personnel should be empowered and assigned the resources to make and implement these risk management decisions.
3. *Accept Risks When the Benefits Outweigh the Costs.* The fundamental objective of risk management is to minimize and ultimately eliminate risk. Someone will need to make the decision not to implement a particular security countermeasure to address a specific threat. This decision must be made after a careful evaluation of the threat, the risk, the security countermeasures, and the cost–benefit ratio. Everything can be protected; it's just a matter of time, money, and resources. Sometimes it is more practical to accept the risk based on the analysis that an attack is unlikely to occur or will be unsuccessful.
4. *Integrate Risk Management into Operations and Planning at All Levels.* Risk management must be incorporated at all levels of an organization in everyday planning and security operations. Risk management must be conducted at the source in order for the timeliest decisions to be made.

Elements of an Effective Risk Management Program

An effective risk management process has a number of common baseline programs:

- *Management Commitment.* Senior management must demonstrate commitment to ongoing improvements through security policies, procedures, communications, and resources.
- *Employee Participation.* Employees are front-line players in identifying and managing risks. They have the greatest possibility of observing surveillance

operations or suspicious activity. Employees must have a direct conduit to management to communicate suggestions for improvement and report suspicious occurrences.

- *Training.* Employees and contractors must have a thorough understanding of the security risks, threats to the facility, and risk management plan. They should be trained to recognize suspicious activities, how to report these concerns, what actions to take, and emergency procedures. Periodic emergency response drills and exercises involving all personnel should be conducted, and at least one drill or exercise per year should involve outside emergency response and law enforcement agencies.
- *Standard Operating Procedures.* Key assets should develop and implement comprehensive standard operating procedures that provide clear instructions to all employees and contractors as regards security and risk management procedures. Applicable employees should be trained on their responsibilities in the risk management plan and emergency response plan.
- *Incident Reporting.* All potential security-related incidents should immediately be reported to management and investigated by law enforcement authorities if appropriate. Corrective actions to improve security and reduce risk should be developed and implemented in response to each security incident reported.
- *Emergency Preparedness and Response.* If all else fails, key assets should have a comprehensive and specific emergency preparedness and response plan in the event security is breached and an attack is launched against the key asset. As a minimum, each employee should know his/her responsibilities in the emergency response plan and the emergency evacuation procedure.

Risk Treatments

Once the threats and risks have been identified and assessed, the risks must be treated through the implementation of security countermeasures. The major option categories for managing risk include the following

- *Accept the Risk.* Accept the potential adverse consequences by doing nothing to mitigate the effects of the risk. An example of accepting the risk is smoking cigarettes while understanding they cause cancer.
- *Avoid the Risk.* Avoid the risk by not performing the activity that could carry a risk. An example would be not flying on an airplane to avoid the risk that it could crash.
- *Modify the Risk.* Modify the risk by simply changing an activity or process to make it less risky. Wearing a helmet while riding a bicycle is an example of risk modification.
- *Reduce the Risk.* Reduce the risk, which in turn will reduce the severity of the loss, by implementing security measures or designing and building the asset to be inherently safe. Burglar alarms reduce the risk of robbery.

- *Retain the Risk.* Retain the risk and accept the loss when it occurs. Usually, when retaining the risk, nothing is done to reduce the risk because the costs to protect against the risk are greater than the loss itself. This category includes risks that are so severe they will result in large or catastrophic losses that cannot be protected against due to unfeasible costs. An example of risk retention would be someone who builds a home on the shoreline of a barrier island, increasing the risk it will be destroyed in a storm.
- *Share the Risk.* Share the risk with another organization or jurisdiction. An example would be multiple partners who invest in a business and will share the profits or losses from the venture.
- *Transfer the Risk.* Transfer the risk to someone else. An insurance policy is an example of transferring risk from one person to another.

Implementation of Security Countermeasures

Based on the results of the risk analysis, the next step in the process is to identify security countermeasures that will lower the risk posed to the key asset to an acceptable level. There are usually numerous risk reduction opportunities for which various kinds of interventions could reduce the risk. Based on the risk analysis results, the most important risks associated with current operations should be prioritized for immediate remediation. Options include new security countermeasures, modification of existing security countermeasures, and the removal of security countermeasures considered unnecessary or obsolete. As it is impossible to completely eliminate all risk, residual risks should be identified and quantified so that they can be evaluated and an informed determination can be made as to whether or not they are acceptable.

Dissemination of Information

The applicable threat, vulnerability, risk, and security countermeasure information must be shared with all applicable parties. This information must be communicated to ensure that all affected parties fully understand the process of and information generated by the risk analysis, and their responsibilities in ensuring the integrity of the security countermeasures and reducing the risk to the key asset.

Reevaluation of Risks

The risk management process is a never ending process. Risk management demands continuous improvement. Even though the threats and vulnerabilities have been assessed, and security countermeasures installed, the process is not complete. The final step in the risk analysis process is to reevaluate the vulnerabilities and the impact of a loss, taking into consideration the newly implemented security countermeasures as well as changes in the socio-political landscape. A reevaluation of the vulnerabilities and risks must be completed after security countermeasures have been implemented to see if anything was missed on the original analysis, or if the security countermeasures have created new vulnerabilities and risk.

Example: Risk Analysis. In this example, we review the threats posed to Hometown, USA. Hometown has a population of 15,000 residents. A multidisciplinary team was assembled to review the threats and develop a security countermeasures program. The team identified the jurisdiction as everything contained within the borders of Hometown. To keep this example simple, we select only four key assets, we assume the attack occurs at a time when there are no people present at the key asset, the attack is a truck bomb, and the key asset is destroyed. However, when conducting an actual assessment, these limitations would not be applied and all potential circumstances would be evaluated.

Among the key assets within the jurisdiction are (1) the town hall, (2) the fire house, (3) the water distribution plant, and (4) the power plant.

The key assets losses are then valued:

Key Asset	Loss Value
Town hall	Medium low (4)
Fire house	Medium high (7)
Water distribution plant	Medium (6)
Power plant	High (8)

Each of the threats posed against the key assets are then identified in terms of

- *Who*—international terrorist
- *Weapon*—improvised explosive device
- *Tactic*—truck bomb

The probability of the attack is then determined: the probability of an adversary using a truck bomb to attack a key asset is possible (2).

The severity of loss of each of the key assets is then determined.

Key Asset	Severity of Loss
Town Hall	Critical (3)—can work out of temporary facilities
Fire house	Critical (3)—can use a neighboring town to handle fire calls
Water distribution plant	Critical (3)—can use bottled water and bring in water tankers
Power plant	Catastrophic (4)—no long-term dependable source of electricity until plant is rebuilt

Using a severity–probability table, the power plant would receive priority for security countermeasures since it is a high-probability–high-severity occurrence.

Finally, the risk factors need to be addressed for the power plant:

- The destruction of the power plant is an unacceptable risk.
- The recommended risk treatment is to reduce the risk.

- Security countermeasures are recommended: (1) install barriers so a truck cannot get close to the power plant; (2) install new blast-resistant windows to reduce the risk of flying glass in a detonation; (3) train employees to recognize suspicious circumstances/characters; and (4) implement a vehicle search program.
- Review the residual risk if the recommended countermeasures are implemented: (1) the power plant can still be damaged (acceptable risk); (2) employees can be injured (acceptable risk); and (3) deliveries to the power plant will be delayed because of increased security (acceptable risk).

At some point after the recommended security countermeasures are installed, the key assets should be reevaluated for threats and risk.

6.9 THE CARVER ASSESSMENT TOOL

The CARVER matrix was developed by the U.S. Special Forces during the Viet Nam War and is a decision tool used by the Special Forces for rating the relative desirability of potential targets and for properly allocating attack resources. CARVER is used in the analysis and examination of the interrelationships between assets, threats, vulnerabilities, and countermeasures that protect a facility.

The CARVER selection factors assist in selecting which targets would be most open to attack. The selection factors range from 1 to 10 and are not weighted; all key assets are alike and use the same model. As the factors are analyzed and values assigned, a decision matrix is formed, indicating the target most likely to be attacked. The CARVER tool has been modified so that it can be used in the vulnerability and risk assessment process.

C—Criticality. Identify critical assets, single points of failure, or choke points. Criticality is the target value: the importance of a system, subsystem, complex, or component. A target is critical when its destruction or damage has a significant impact on the output of the target system, subsystem, or complex. A successful attack will significantly impair or damage political, economic, and government operations, or civil society.

Criticality depends on several factors:

Time. How rapidly will the impact of target destruction affect operations?

Quantity. What percentage of output is curtailed by target destruction?

Backup. Do substitutes for the output product or service exist?

Number of Targets and Their Positions in the System or Complex Flow Diagram.

A—Accessibility. Determine ease of access to critical assets. Accessibility is the ease with which a target can be reached, either physically or with a standoff weapon. A target is accessible when an adversary element can physically infiltrate the target, or if the target can be attacked by direct or indirect methods. Accessibility varies with the infiltration/exfiltration, survival, and escape potential from the target area, the security situation enroute to and at the target, and the need for barrier penetration at the target. The use of standoff weapons such as vehicle bombs should always be considered when evaluating accessibility. Survivability of the adversary is not always correlated to a target's accessibility.

R—Recuperability. Determine how long it would take to repair, replace, bypass, or restore a key asset from the destruction or damage inflicted in the attack. If a target is cheap, modular, and easy to fix, it may be a poor target for terrorism (but a great target for vandalism). Recuperability deals with things, not people. Recuperability varies with the sources and ages of targeted components and with spare parts or redundant capabilities inherent in the key asset.

V—Vulnerability. A target is vulnerable if an adversary has the capability and intent to attack it and achieve a significant level of damage using available resources. An evaluation of the effectiveness of security countermeasures against the adversary's capabilities should be conducted at this stage. Vulnerability depends on (1) the nature and construction of the target; (2) the amount of damage required/desired; (3) the resources available to the adversary; and (4) the adversary's personnel, expertise, and mindset.

E—Effect. Consider the scope and magnitude of adverse consequences that would result from a successful attack.

R—Recognizability. Recognizability is the degree to which a target can be recognized without confusion with other targets or components. Factors that influence recognizability include the size and complexity of the target, the existence of distinctive target signatures, and the technical sophistication and training of the attackers. An evaluation of the likelihood that potential adversaries would recognize that an asset was critical should also be made.

Why Use CARVER?

Target analysis is the procedure by which an attacking force chooses the proper venue and/or person for attack. In general, target analysis provides attackers with the identification of the most effective attack loci coupled with a determination of the least effort needed to achieve the goal and/or the lowest personnel losses (capture/death). Defending forces, of course, apply target analysis to identify their weaknesses and/or most probable areas for attack. By using target analysis in this manner, it is possible to reverse engineer an attack scenario to provide the most effective defense.

Variants of CARVER

There are a number of CARVER variants in use:

- CARVER2 is used by the U.S. Department of Homeland Security for developing buffer zone protection plans.
- CARVER + Shock is used by the U.S. Food and Drug Administration (USFDA) for food security assessments.
- DSHARPP is used by the U.S. Department of Defense.
- MSHARPP is used by the U.S. Department of Defense and state and local governments.

Example: CARVER + Shock. The USFDA uses the CARVER + Shock methodology to assess vulnerabilities and establish protective measures to prepare for, guard against, and respond to potential attacks on the food infrastructure. The CARVER + Shock process uses the same CARVER factors described earlier but an additional factor is added for the "Shock." The shock dimension involves evaluating the psychological effect a successful attack on the target will have.

Scales Used by USFDA and USDA

We now define the attribute used by the USFDA and USDA to conduct their vulnerability assessments and provide the scales used by the agencies for scoring each attribute. These scales were developed with the mindset that mass mortality is a goal of terrorist organizations. It is important to remember, however, that any intentional food contamination could also have major psychological and economic impacts on the affected industry.

Criticality. A target is critical when introduction of threat agents into food at this location would have significant health or economic impact. Example metrics are:

Criticality Criteria	Scale
Loss of over 10,000 lives OR loss of more than $100 billion	9–10
Loss of life between 1000 and 10,000 OR loss between $10 and $100 billion	7–8
Loss of life between 100 and 1000 OR loss between $1 and $10 billion	5–6
Loss of life less than 100 OR loss less than $1 billion	3–4
No loss of life OR loss less than $100 million	1–2

Accessibility. A target is accessible when an attacker can reach the target to conduct the attack and egress the target undetected. Accessibility is the openness of the target to the threat. This measure is independent of the probability of successful introduction of threat agents. Example metrics are:

Accessibility Criteria	Scale
Easily accessible (e.g., target is outside building and no perimeter fence). Limited physical or human barriers or observation. Attacker has relatively unlimited access to the target. Attack can be carried out using medium or large volumes of contaminant without undue concern of detection. Multiple sources of information concerning the facility and the target are easily available.	9–10

Accessibility Criteria	Scale
Accessible (e.g., target is inside building but in unsecured part of facility). Limited human observation and physical barriers. Attacker has access to the target for an hour or less. Attack can be carried out with moderate to large volumes of contaminant, but requires the use of stealth. Only limited specific information is available on the facility and the target.	7–8
Partially accessible (e.g., inside building but in a relatively unsecured, but busy, part of facility). Under constant possible human observation. Some physical barriers may be present. Contaminant must be disguised, and time limitations are significant. Only general, nonspecific information is available on the facility and the target.	5–6
Hardly accessible (e.g., inside building in a secured part of facility). Human observation and physical barriers with an established means of detection. Access generally restricted to operators or authorized persons. Contaminant must be disguised and time limitations are extreme. Limited general information available on the facility and the target.	3–4
Not accessible. Physical barriers, alarms, and human observation. Defined means of intervention in place. Attacker can access target for less than 5 minutes with all equipment carried in pockets. No useful publicly available information concerning the target.	1–2

Recuperability. A target's recuperability is measured in the time it will take for the specific facility to recover productivity. The effect of a possible decrease in demand is not considered under this criterion. Example metrics are:

Recuperability Criteria	Scale
More than 1 year	9–10
6 months to 1 year	7–8
3–6 months	5–6
1–3 months	3–4
Less than 1 month	1–2

Vulnerability. This is a measure of the ease with which threat agents can be introduced in quantities sufficient to achieve the attacker's purpose once the target has been reached. Vulnerability is determined by both the characteristics of the target (e.g., ease of introducing agents, ability to uniformly mix agents into target) and the characteristics of the surrounding environment (ability to work unobserved, time available for introduction of agents). It is also important to consider what interventions are already in place that might thwart an attack. Example metrics are:

Vulnerability Criteria	Scale
Target characteristics allow for easy introduction of sufficient agents to achieve aim	9–10
Target characteristics almost always allow for introduction of sufficient agents to achieve aim	7–8
Target characteristics allow 30–60% probability that sufficient agents can be added to achieve aim	5–6
Target characteristics allow moderate probability (10–30%) that sufficient agents can be added to achieve aim	3–4
Target characteristics allow low probability (less than 10%) that sufficient agents can be added to achieve aim	1–2

Effect. Effect is a measure of the percentage of system productivity damaged by an attack at a single facility. Thus effect is inversely related to the total number of facilities producing the same product. Example metrics are:

Effect Criteria	Scale
Greater than 50% of the system's production impacted	9–10
25–50% of the system's production impacted	7–8
10–25% of the system's production impacted	5–6
1–10% of the system's production impacted	3–4
Less than 1% of the system's production impacted	1–2

Recognizability. A target's recognizability is the degree to which it can be identified by an attacker without confusion with other targets or components. Example metrics are:

Recognizability Criteria	Scale
Target is clearly recognizable and requires little or no training for recognition	9–10
Target is easily recognizable and requires only a small amount of training for recognition	7–8
Target is difficult to recognize or might be confused with other targets or target components and requires some training for recognition	5–6
Target is difficult to recognize, is easily confused with other targets or components, and requires extensive training for recognition	3–4
Target cannot be recognized, under any conditions, except by experts	2–1

Shock. Shock is the final attribute considered in the methodology. Shock is the combined measure of health, psychological, and collateral national economic impacts of a successful attack on the target system. Shock is considered on a national level. The psychological impact will be increased if there are a large number of deaths or the target has historical, cultural, religious, or other symbolic significance. Mass casualties are not required to achieve widespread economic loss or psychological damage. Collateral economic damage includes such items as decreased national economic activity and increased unemployment in collateral industries. Psychological impact will be increased if victims are members of sensitive subpopulations such as children or the elderly. Example metrics are:

Shock	Scale
Target has major historical, cultural, religious, or other symbolic importance. Loss of over 10,000 lives. Major impact on sensitive subpopulations (e.g., children or elderly) is experienced. National economic impact more than $100 billion.	9–10
Target has high historical, cultural, religious, or other symbolic importance. Loss of between 1000 and 10,000 lives. Significant impact on sensitive subpopulations such as children or the elderly. National economic impact between $10 and $100 billion.	7–8
Target has moderate historical, cultural, religious, or other symbolic importance. Loss of between 100 and 1000 lives. Moderate impact on sensitive subpopulations such as children or the elderly. National economic impact between $1 and $10 billion.	5–6
Target has little historical, cultural, religious, or other symbolic importance. Loss of less than 100 lives. Small impact on sensitive subpopulations such as children or the elderly. National economic impact between $100 million and $1 billion.	3–4
Target has no historical, cultural, religious, or other symbolic importance. Loss of less than 100 lives. No impact on sensitive subpopulations such as children or the elderly. National economic impact less than $100 million.	1–2

By definition, terrorists attempt to achieve strong emotional responses from their target audience. Aspects of targets that terrorists view as increasing a target's shock value are symbolism (e.g., the Pentagon), large number of casualties, sensitive nature of facilities (e.g., nuclear facilities), and the ability to strike at core values and primal emotions (e.g., targeting children).

Calculation of Final Values and Interpretation. Once the ranking on each of the attribute scales has been calculated for a given node within the food supply system, the ranking on all of the scales can then be totaled to give an overall value for that node. This should be repeated for each node within a food supply system. The overall values for all the nodes can then be compared to rank the vulnerability of the different nodes relative to each other. The nodes with the highest total rating have the highest potential vulnerability and should be the focus of countermeasure efforts.

REFERENCES

1. *Chemical Accident Prevention: Site Security*, United States Environmental Protection Association, February 2000.
2. *FEMA 426 Risk Management Series*, December 2003.

APPENDIX 6.1 HOMELAND SECURITY PRESIDENTIAL DIRECTIVE 3 BY PRESIDENT GEORGE BUSH

Purpose

The Nation requires a Homeland Security Advisory System to provide a comprehensive and effective means to disseminate information regarding the risk of terrorist acts to Federal, State, and local authorities and to the American people. Such a system would provide warnings in the form of a set of graduated "Threat Conditions" that would increase as the risk of the threat increases. At each Threat Condition, Federal departments and agencies would implement a corresponding set of "Protective Measures" to further reduce vulnerability or increase response capability during a period of heightened alert.

This system is intended to create a common vocabulary, context, and structure for an ongoing national discussion about the nature of the threats that confront the homeland and the appropriate measures that should be taken in response. It seeks to inform and facilitate decisions appropriate to different levels of government and to private citizens at home and at work.

Homeland Security Advisory System

The Homeland Security Advisory System shall be binding on the executive branch and suggested, although voluntary, to other levels of government and the private sector. There are five Threat Conditions, each identified by a description and corresponding color. From lowest to highest, the levels and colors are:

Low = Green;
Guarded = Blue;
Elevated = Yellow;
High = Orange;
Severe = Red.

The higher the Threat Condition, the greater the risk of a terrorist attack. Risk includes both the probability of an attack occurring and its potential gravity. Threat Conditions shall be assigned by the Attorney General in consultation with the Assistant to the President for Homeland Security. Except in exigent circumstances, the Attorney General shall seek the views of the appropriate Homeland Security Principals or their subordinates, and other parties as appropriate, on the Threat Condition to be assigned. Threat Conditions may be assigned for the entire Nation, or they may be set for a particular geographic area or industrial sector. Assigned Threat Conditions shall be reviewed at regular intervals to determine whether adjustments are warranted.

For facilities, personnel, and operations inside the territorial United States, all Federal departments, agencies, and offices other than military facilities shall conform their existing threat advisory systems to this system and henceforth administer their systems consistent with the determination of the Attorney General with regard to the Threat Condition in effect.

The assignment of a Threat Condition shall prompt the implementation of an appropriate set of Protective Measures. Protective Measures are the specific steps an organization shall take to reduce its vulnerability or increase its ability to respond during a period of heightened alert. The authority to craft and implement Protective Measures rests with the Federal departments and agencies. It is recognized that departments and agencies may have several preplanned sets of responses to a particular Threat Condition to facilitate a rapid, appropriate, and tailored response. Department and agency heads are responsible for developing their own Protective Measures and other antiterrorism or self-protection and continuity plans, and resourcing, rehearsing, documenting, and maintaining these plans. Likewise, they retain the authority to respond, as necessary, to risks, threats, incidents, or events at facilities within the specific jurisdiction of their department or agency, and, as authorized by law, to direct agencies and industries to implement their own Protective Measures. They shall continue to be responsible for taking all appropriate proactive steps to reduce the vulnerability of their personnel and facilities to terrorist attack. Federal department and agency heads shall submit an annual written report to the President, through the Assistant to the President for Homeland Security, describing the steps they have taken to develop and implement appropriate Protective Measures for each Threat Condition. Governors, mayors, and the leaders of other organizations are encouraged to conduct a similar review of their organizations = Protective Measures.

The decision whether to publicly announce Threat Conditions shall be made on a case-by-case basis by the Attorney General in consultation with the Assistant to the President for Homeland Security. Every effort shall be made to share as much information regarding the threat as possible, consistent with the safety of the Nation. The Attorney General shall ensure, consistent with the safety of the Nation, that State and local government officials and law enforcement authorities are provided the most relevant and timely information. The Attorney General shall be responsible for identifying any other information developed in the threat assessment process that would be useful to State and local officials and others and conveying it to them as permitted consistent with the constraints of classification. The Attorney General shall establish a process and a system for conveying relevant information to Federal, State, and local government officials, law enforcement authorities, and the private sector expeditiously.

The Director of Central Intelligence and the Attorney General shall ensure that a continuous and timely flow of integrated threat assessments and reports is provided to the President, the Vice President, Assistant to the President and Chief of Staff, the Assistant to the President for Homeland Security, and the Assistant to the President for National Security Affairs. Whenever possible and practicable, these integrated threat assessments and reports shall be reviewed and commented upon by the wider interagency community.

A decision on which Threat Condition to assign shall integrate a variety of considerations. This integration will rely on qualitative assessment, not quantitative calculation. Higher Threat Conditions indicate greater risk of a terrorist act, with risk including both probability and gravity. Despite best efforts, there can be no guarantee that, at any given Threat Condition, a terrorist attack will not occur. An initial and important factor is the quality of the threat information itself. The evaluation of this threat information shall include, but not be limited to, the following factors:

1. To what degree is the threat information credible?
2. To what degree is the threat information corroborated?
3. To what degree is the threat specific and/or imminent?
4. How grave are the potential consequences of the threat?

Threat Conditions and Associated Protective Measures

The world has changed since September, 11, 2001. We remain a Nation at risk to terrorist attacks and will remain at risk for the foreseeable future. At all Threat Conditions, we must remain vigilant, prepared, and ready to deter terrorist attacks. The following Threat Conditions each represent an increasing risk of terrorist attacks. Beneath each Threat Condition are some suggested Protective Measures, recognizing that the heads of Federal departments and agencies are responsible for developing and implementing appropriate agency-specific Protective Measures:

1. *Low Condition (Green).* This condition is declared when there is a low risk of terrorist attacks. Federal departments and agencies should consider the following general measures in addition to the agency-specific Protective Measures they develop and implement:
   1. Refining and exercising as appropriate preplanned Protective Measures;
   2. Ensuring personnel receive proper training on the Homeland Security Advisory System and specific preplanned department or agency Protective Measures; and
   3. Institutionalizing a process to assure that all facilities and regulated sectors are regularly assessed for vulnerabilities to terrorist attacks, and all reasonable measures are taken to mitigate these vulnerabilities.
2. *Guarded Condition (Blue).* This condition is declared when there is a general risk of terrorist attacks. In addition to the Protective Measures taken in the previous Threat Condition, Federal departments and agencies should consider the following general measures in addition to the agency-specific Protective Measures that they will develop and implement:
   1. Checking communications with designated emergency response or command locations;
   2. Reviewing and updating emergency response procedures; and
   3. Providing the public with any information that would strengthen its ability to act appropriately.
3. *Elevated Condition (Yellow).* An Elevated Condition is declared when there is a significant risk of terrorist attacks. In addition to the Protective Measures taken in the previous Threat Conditions, Federal departments and agencies should consider the following general measures in addition to the Protective Measures that they will develop and implement:
   1. Increasing surveillance of critical locations;
   2. Coordinating emergency plans as appropriate with nearby jurisdictions;
   3. Assessing whether the precise characteristics of the threat require the further refinement of preplanned Protective Measures; and
   4. Implementing, as appropriate, contingency and emergency response plans.
4. *High Condition (Orange).* A High Condition is declared when there is a high risk of terrorist attacks. In addition to the Protective Measures taken in the previous Threat Conditions, Federal departments and agencies should consider the following general measures in addition to the agency-specific Protective Measures that they will develop and implement:
   1. Coordinating necessary security efforts with Federal, State, and local law enforcement agencies or any National Guard or other appropriate armed forces organizations;
   2. Taking additional precautions at public events and possibly considering alternative venues or even cancellation;
   3. Preparing to execute contingency procedures, such as moving to an alternate site or dispersing their workforce; and
   4. Restricting threatened facility access to essential personnel only.

5. *Severe Condition (Red).* A Severe Condition reflects a severe risk of terrorist attacks. Under most circumstances, the Protective Measures for a Severe Condition are not intended to be sustained for substantial periods of time. In addition to the Protective Measures in the previous Threat Conditions, Federal departments and agencies also should consider the following general measures in addition to the agency-specific Protective Measures that they will develop and implement:
   1. Increasing or redirecting personnel to address critical emergency needs;
   2. Assigning emergency response personnel and pre-positioning and mobilizing specially trained teams or resources;
   3. Monitoring, redirecting, or constraining transportation systems; and
   4. Closing public and government facilities.

Comment and Review Periods

The Attorney General, in consultation and coordination with the Assistant to the President for Homeland Security, shall, for 45 days from the date of this directive, seek the views of government officials at all levels and of public interest groups and the private sector on the proposed Homeland Security Advisory System.

One hundred thirty-five days from the date of this directive the Attorney General, after consultation and coordination with the Assistant to the President for Homeland Security, and having considered the views received during the comment period, shall recommend to the President in writing proposed refinements to the Homeland Security Advisory System.

CHAPTER 7

Protecting Critical Infrastructure, Key Resources, and Key Assets

7.1 INTRODUCTION

A terrorist attack on a critical infrastructure, key resource, or key asset could significantly disrupt the ability of the public and the private sector to provide the services or products depended on by the citizens. A successful terrorist attack could also produce cascading effects far beyond the targeted sector and physical location of the incident. The protection of the nation's key assets is one of six critical mission areas assigned to the Department of Homeland Security in the Homeland Security Act of 2002.

When it comes to protecting our key assets, the mantra is *if it's predictable, it's preventable*. In this chapter, we discuss how to determine if an attack is predictable based on vulnerabilities that exist in the security systems at a critical infrastructure, key asset, or key resource. Once these vulnerabilities have been identified and evaluated, security countermeasures can be installed and implemented to reduce the risk of a successful attack.

We need to minimize the opportunities our adversaries have to beat us. Be proactive and look at key assets from the outside in.

7.2 PURPOSE OF SECURITY VULNERABILITY ANALYSIS (SVA)

The security vulnerability assessment is the last in the series of analytical processes used to identify and categorize our critical infrastructure, key resources, and key assets, and screen them for risks posed by an adversary who is intent on causing them harm. The security vulnerability assessment focuses on the security system vulnerabilities that exist and can be exploited by an adversary to enhance an attack.

Once all of the credible threats have been identified from the assessment process covered in Chapter 6, a security vulnerability analysis might be the next logical step

Understanding, Assessing, and Responding to Terrorism: Protecting Critical Infrastructure and Personnel By Brian T. Bennett

in the overall protection process. The vulnerability analysis considers the potential adverse impacts from a successful attack by an adversary, by examining the vulnerability of the key asset to an attack. A security vulnerability analysis is a qualitative analysis of the interrelationships between key assets, threats, vulnerabilities, and security countermeasures. The security vulnerability analysis is a systematic, risk-based approach in which risk is a function of severity of consequences of an undesired event, the likelihood of an adversary attack, and the likelihood of adversary success in causing the undesired event to occur. Security vulnerability analysis identifies the probable security risks that could adversely impact a key asset, prioritizes the threats, and provides the information that will be used to implement appropriate cost-effective security countermeasures. If the security risks are deemed unacceptable, recommendations can be developed for security countermeasures to eliminate the risks or at least reduce the risks to an acceptable level. The completion of a security vulnerability analysis allows a jurisdiction to identify and evaluate existing security vulnerabilities in order to plan enhancements to the security systems, which will reduce the overall threat to the key asset.

Key assets have different values based on the audience; for example, a key asset may have an economic value or a symbolic value, or it may be a critical infrastructure. Therefore an examination is required to prioritize the importance, the vulnerabilities, and the investment required to install or implement the proper security countermeasures. Whereas some key assets are not critical, and therefore would not justify large expenditures for security countermeasures, others are so important that they must be protected regardless of the cost to install effective security countermeasures.

Vulnerability assessments that were conducted prior to September 11, 2001 were primarily focused on accidental or natural threats. Now, with the advent of terrorism in the homeland, these assessments must now begin to consider the intentional act as well. Protective measures that were installed based on these early risk analyses were not designed to protect key assets from intentional acts, nor from the severity of a WMD attack. In many cases, security systems must be significantly enhanced to deal with intentional threats.

The basic questions to be addressed when conducting a security vulnerability analysis include, but are not limited to, the following [1]:

What specific security threats exist that could adversely impact the critical infrastructure, key resource, or key asset?

What characteristics are present that might lead an adversary to find a particular target more attractive than another?

What security vulnerabilities exist that could be exploited to aid in the furtherance of an attack?

How significant could the adverse effects of an attack be?

Are the security countermeasures sufficient to reduce the threat to the target?

What enhanced security countermeasures are justified to further reduce the risks and consequences of an attack?

The completion of a security vulnerability analysis may assist a jurisdiction to (1) identify and prioritize critical infrastructure, key resources, and key assets for protection; (2) prioritize risks posed to a potential target; and (3) prioritize the implementation of security countermeasures to protect assets.

Following are general considerations that may be taken into account when conducting a security vulnerability analysis:

- Develop a screening process to identify the critical infrastructure, key resources, and key assets within a jurisdiction.
- Coordinate security response requirements with the appropriate law enforcement officials at the federal, regional, and local levels to assure good communication and coordination in protecting the asset.
- Develop an emergency management response process to reduce or mitigate impacts of a loss of service or deliverability of product.
- Prepare a formal mutual assistance agreement at the appropriate local, state, or regional level to support response, repair, and restoration activities for the disrupted critical infrastructure, key resource, or key asset.

There are two primary time frames in which to conduct a security vulnerability analysis: proactive or reactive.

A *proactive analysis* is conducted before a threat has reached the point to be of significant concern to the key asset. Proactive reasons to select a key asset for a security vulnerability analysis include:

- The key asset is critical; that is, loss of the key asset would have significant adverse national or regional economic impact, disrupt essential services, and/or affect public health.
- Preplanning identifies vulnerabilities at a critical infrastructure, key resource, or key asset and allows formulation of effective and appropriate security countermeasures and emergency response plans.
- Development of a coordinated plan to enhance security countermeasures will reduce the risk at a key asset.
- The key asset is of such complexity or unique design that it would be beneficial to conduct a security vulnerability analysis.

A *reactive analysis* is conducted once there is a specific, credible threat directed toward a critical infrastructure or key asset or an attack has already occurred. Reasons to conduct a reactive security vulnerability analysis include:

- The specific key asset (or the entire critical infrastructure sector) is under threat of attack from an adversary.
- The key asset supports or is in close proximity to a national special security event.

- The key asset, or a similar asset, has already been attacked.
- A key asset in the vicinity has been attacked.

There are six primary reasons to conduct a security vulnerability assessment:

1. *Initial Review.* If a key asset has never been evaluated using a security vulnerability analysis, one should be done immediately to ascertain the threats and vulnerabilities and enhance the security countermeasures.

2. *Threat Changes.* Law enforcement may share information with a key asset indicating that an adversary's tactics may have changed or a new, previously unconsidered, threat has emerged. Essentially, if the original threat assumptions change, then the security vulnerability analysis must be redone to take the new threat into consideration.

3. *Function of the Key Asset Changes.* It is possible that an asset was not considered a key asset when the original assessment of the jurisdiction was completed based on its activity. However, over time, the function may have changed so the asset may now be considered a key asset (e.g., during the initial assessment the facility was manufacturing a consumer product; it has changed its operation and is now manufacturing a critical component for the military's cruise missile). Or perhaps, a key asset has changed its operation (e.g., an asset has changed its process so that large quantities of a highly toxic material are now being used).

4. *After a Significant Security Incident at the Key Asset.* If a significant incident resulting in the violation of a security policy or procedure or a security breach at the key asset occurs, a security vulnerability analysis should be conducted to reevaluate the threats and vulnerabilities that exist. The security incident that triggers this requirement does not necessarily have to be perpetrated by an adversary intent on causing intentional harm. It can be an "accidental" or seemingly harmless security breach, but nonetheless there was a system failure and it needs to be re-evaluated so more effective security countermeasures can be implemented to prevent recurrence.

5. *After an Attack at a Similar Key Asset or an Attack in the Jurisdiction or Nearby Jurisdiction.* If an adversary attacks a similar key asset anywhere or attacks any key asset in the area, a new security vulnerability assessment should be completed to take into account the lessons learned.

6. *Periodic Revisions.* In keeping with the spirit of continuous improvement, it is recommended that the security vulnerability assessment be redone every three to five years. The reason for this is to consider any subtle changes in the operation, threat, vulnerabilities, or effectiveness of the security countermeasures that are in place and revalidate the findings of the original analysis. When assembling the revalidation team, it is also recommended that the majority of the analysis team be members different from those members on the previous analysis. By incorporating new members, there will be people looking at different things from different perspectives. Some individuals from the previous analysis team should participate to provide a sense of consistency between the analyses.

The security vulnerability analysis is really a risk assessment and management technique. The purpose of a security vulnerability analysis is to investigate the threats and vulnerabilities to include the events caused by accidental, natural, and intentional threats that may have an adverse effect on a key asset.

The security vulnerability analysis is a detailed study of the key asset and the threats and risks posed against it. A comprehensive security vulnerability analysis can take days, weeks, or even months to complete, depending on the key assets studied and the level of their complexity. Whereas some of the basic screenings that were conducted previously may have been completed by one or two persons, the security vulnerability analysis is much more comprehensive and detailed and necessitates the use of a multidisciplinary team that may consist of several dozen persons, again depending on the size and complexity of the asset being analyzed.

The end product of a security vulnerability analysis is a series of recommendations identifying specifically what should be done to reduce or eliminate the risk of attack against the key asset.

7.3 PREPARING TO CONDUCT A SECURITY VULNERABILITY ANALYSIS

In the asset analysis phase, the analysis team identifies critical infrastructure, key resources, and key assets to determine the adverse impact to the jurisdiction if the assets were damaged or destroyed. Also included in this analysis is the identification of undesirable events that could adversely affect the value of these assets. Using this information allows the assets to be prioritized based on the potential adverse consequences of their loss.

In the threat analysis phase, the analysis team determines which adversaries are most likely to cause harm to the key assets. To determine the threat level, the analysis team will review and access information related to current events, attractiveness as a target, historical information, and intelligence about the capabilities and intent of potential adversaries. Completion of the asset and threat analysis provides the data for an effective security vulnerability analysis.

This phase requires the analysis team to analyze an asset through the eyes and mind of a potential adversary. The team must answer questions such as:

If I were a terrorist or criminal, how would I attempt to destroy this asset?

What is the probable adverse impact if the asset is damaged or lost to an adversary's attack?

How likely is it that an adversary will attempt to attack the identified assets?

What are the most likely security vulnerabilities that the adversary will target and attempt to exploit?

During the security vulnerability analysis phase, a matrix is developed to show the relationship between the asset, the threat, and the consequence of the loss. The matrix shows which assets face the highest probability of attack and which threats pose the greatest risk to the jurisdiction so that security vulnerabilities can be rated as to their overall risk.

7.4 THE SECURITY VULNERABILITY ANALYSIS PROCESS

Before the security vulnerability analysis is started, the jurisdiction must determine what their approach will be. There must be complete support for this endeavor from the chief executive of the jurisdiction, thus ensuring the proper resources, in terms of time, people, and money, are committed to the process. The chief executive must establish the management system that will guide the vulnerability analysis through completion, ensuring the right people are participating in the analysis, the analysis is meeting the stated goals and objectives, the quality of work is appropriate, and the analysis is proceeding on schedule. Finally, the chief executive will ultimately be the individual who will make the final decision on whether or not to implement the recommended security countermeasures and provide the funding to do so.

The jurisdiction's chief executive should assign one person to coordinate and oversee the security vulnerability analysis to ensure the project progresses on schedule and drives the process to completion. This individual should provide periodic status reports to the chief executive.

The security vulnerability analysis process is founded on a risk-based approach to controlling hazards. There is a formal process used to conduct the security vulnerability analysis process, which will be reviewed next. Once the potential targets and threats have been identified, each threat that is applicable to the key asset is analyzed to determine what security vulnerabilities are present with the existing security countermeasures implemented.

The security vulnerability analysis process includes seven steps.

Step 1: Planning

Security vulnerability assessments are best conducted by a multidisciplinary team. If the right members are not selected for the team, it is likely the analysis will be incomplete and ineffective, and the overall goal, which is to reduce the risk of loss, will not be achieved. The team members should include representatives of all stakeholders and should be considered experts in their field. Typical membership of a security vulnerability analysis team includes representatives from the various departments of the key asset, such as safety, security, operations, maintenance, and information technology; representatives from the applicable local, state, or federal law enforcement agencies; and representatives from the local emergency response agencies, such as the fire department and emergency medical services. It is recommended that the team be comprised of both management workers as well as line workers. This is important as each group of workers has different perspectives of what is important and what might be exploited.

The inclusion of line workers is considered critical to the analysis as they are on the "front lines" and typically have intimate knowledge in the day to day operations of the key asset and are likely to know where the vulnerabilities are and how they could be exploited to cause adverse effects.

The analysis team should be educated on the following:

- The scope of the security vulnerability analysis, including specifically what is to be analyzed and against which threats. Typically, the analysis team arrives at a scenario beyond which it will not proceed. For example, many facilities have decided they will not analyze scenarios that involve armed attack by a group of adversaries because it is beyond their ability to provide effective protection.
- The specific security vulnerability analysis methodology used and the general process and techniques that will be used to analyze the key asset.
- The goals and objectives of the security vulnerability assessment: what is hoped to be achieved with this endeavor.
- The timing of the security vulnerability assessment, including the start date, key milestones, and the completion date.
- A review of the team members roles and responsibilities, specifically who will be responsible for completing specific assignments. The team members should be introduced to each other, and they should provide a synopsis of their particular area of expertise.
- The timing and format of the completed security vulnerability analysis report, including who will receive a copy and who will be responsible for following up on the recommended security countermeasures.

The analysis team should refer to the screening that was completed previously to help ascertain which key assets are considered to be at risk by the various threats posed by an adversary. The team should also identify and request access to any supporting documentation that may be necessary to help facilitate the completion of the security vulnerability analysis, such as floor plans, construction details, or technical manuals.

The identification of threats and risks to the key asset, as well as developing security countermeasures, must be conducted as a partnership between the key asset and local law enforcement personnel and emergency responders. This is important as law enforcement personnel are a resource in terms of sharing threat information obtained from various intelligence sources that can be used to identify potential adversary actions. Also, law enforcement will likely be called upon to supplement or even take primary responsibility for protecting the key asset in times of heightened concern. In order for law enforcement personnel to properly secure a key asset, they must be fully aware of the vulnerabilities that exist, know how the vulnerabilities can be exploited, and be familiar with the adverse impacts if an attack is successful. Similarly, firefighters and emergency medical services personnel must also be involved in the analysis process, as they will have primary responsibility for protecting the community by mitigating the consequences of a successful attack and treating victims. These emergency responders must be aware of the adverse impacts resulting from a successful attack so they can develop effective response procedures, purchase the appropriate personal protective equipment and mitigation supplies, and receive the training necessary to operate safely and effectively.

The analysis team should also become familiar with the key asset itself, reviewing such things as:

- The security systems that are in place, such as policies, procedures, and physical hardening techniques.
- The basic operational aspects of the key asset, such as number of employees, hours of operation, products and or services provided.
- The likely scenarios that would harm employees or the community if a successful attack were to be perpetrated.

Step 2: Asset and Risk Characterization and Screening

Although the characterization of key assets was covered previously, we will provide a quick refresher of the process.

Information on the jurisdiction's critical assets is taken directly from a detailed examination of the jurisdiction's operation, physical plant, and criticality within the related infrastructure. The team should next characterize the facility, to identify the specific assets present within the jurisdiction that may be targeted by an adversary. The analysis team should develop a list of the individual specific components that make up the key asset that could be the target of an attack, including people, information, and property (product/service).

The characterization includes identification of the potential key assets, of the threats, of the adverse consequences resulting from a successful attack on an asset and its surroundings, and of existing security countermeasures that have been implemented at the key asset and determination of the key asset's attractiveness as a target. The characterization should list others who may be adversely impacted by a successful attack, such as employees at the key asset; visitors, contractors, and delivery persons at the key asset; neighbors of the key asset; other critical infrastructure, key resources, or key assets; the key asset's finances; the local, state, national, or worldwide economy; and the key asset's reputation.

The characterization of an asset includes a description of building structures, traffic areas, infrastructure, terrain, weather conditions, and operational conditions. To know how operations at the key asset can be interrupted, it is necessary to know what is required for the key asset to operate effectively. Information that will be helpful in identifying potential security vulnerabilities and was requested from the key asset during the planning stage should be reviewed in detail by the analysis team. The types of documentation include the following policy and procedure documents: unusual occurrence reports, existing threat assessment information, results from past security surveys and audits, building blueprints and plans for future structures, site plans, existing security systems and countermeasures in place, and operational procedures.

After the documentation has been reviewed by the analysis team, the following information should be extracted to characterize the facility

- *Site Plans.* These will help identify property borders and entrance/exit routes to and from the key asset. The site plans would assist in identifying other areas of concern, such as specific vulnerable areas in and around the key asset (e.g., adjacent buildings that a sniper could use to target the key asset); adjacent parking lots and related security countermeasures; neighboring building locations and characteristics (purpose of the building, who is allowed access, and operational conditions); a description of adjacent residential or commercial areas; and existing physical protection features.
- *Access to Control Systems.*
- *Operational Conditions.* The conditions are described by length and number of day and night shifts; activities typical to each shift and the associated security implications; the number of employees, contractors, and visitors in the area during each shift and the level of access to the facility during weekdays, weekends, and holidays; the availability of security and safety personnel, including law enforcement; and weather conditions for the region and time of the year.
- *Procedural Information.* This includes entry control procedures to the facility for visitors, delivery persons, contractors, and vendors; evacuation procedures; emergency operations procedures in case of evacuation; security procedures; policies related to alarm assessment and communication with responding security personnel or local law enforcement; and safety procedures and features.

The characterization is facilitated if the analysis team conducts a walk through and around the key asset to be analyzed. The walk through should be conducted both inside and outside the key asset's perimeter and afford an opportunity for the analysis team to become familiar with the key asset and its surroundings. The walk through should be conducted from the perspective of the adversary, looking for potential vulnerabilities that can be exploited to facilitate an attack. Particular attention should be given to observing for weaknesses that exist from the outside perimeter of the key asset, since it is from this location that the key asset would most likely be attacked. The analysis team should review the key asset's existing *rings of protection* (see Section 8.10) and existing *layers of protection*.

Risk Characterization. Risk characterization asks two basic questions:

What do we have that can be used as a weapon of mass destruction?

Could we be the target of a weapon of mass destruction? An affirmative answer to either of these questions would bring us to the next step.

Risk Screening. It is recommended that the formal assessment process start with a screening process to prioritize the various critical components that constitute the key asset; that is, things like utilities, critical equipment, manufacturing buildings, storage tanks, maintenance areas, warehouses, computer systems, and large groups of people. Each key asset would be evaluated to determine the consequences of a successful attack against five criteria:

1. Casualties.
2. Environmental impact.
3. Economic impact.
4. Business impact.
5. Impact on the facility's infrastructure.

Sample Key Asset Screening Assessment Methodology

Score	Casualties
0	None expected
1	Non-life-threatening injuries likely both on and off the key asset property
2	Life-threatening injuries likely both on and off the key asset property
3	On-site fatalities likely
4	Off-site fatalities likely

Score	Environmental Impact
0	Not applicable/biodegradable
1	Will not leave the key asset's property
2	Likely to leave the key asset's property; however, nonpersistent and no decontamination and/or remediation required
3	Likely to leave the key asset's property; however, nonpersistent and decontamination and/or remediation required
4	Likely to leave the key asset's property; persistent and long-term remediation required

Score	Economic Impact
0	No significant effect likely
1	Impact on division or business unit profitability $>10\%$
2	Impact on corporate profitability $>10\%$
3	Impact on U.S. economy
4	Impact on world economy

Score	Business Impact
0	Startup facility with minor changes
1	Facility shut down and unable to provide products or services for less than 1 month
2	Facility shut down and unable to provide products or services for less than 6 months
3	Facility shut down and unable to provide products or services for less than 1 year
4	Facility destroyed and not expected to be rebuilt

Score	Infrastructure Impact
0	No effect on operations
1	Damage limited to the specific building/area only
2	Damage to support systems and/or utilities
3	Damage to other production or service facilities
4	Damage to the entire site

Impact	Weighting Factors
Casualties	Rating × 5
Environmental	Rating × 4
Economic	Rating × 3
Business interruption	Rating × 2
Infrastructure	Rating × 1

After each critical asset and scenario have been screened, the scores would be used to prioritize the sequence of conducting a complete vulnerability assessment.

Some questions to ask during the screening phase include:

- Do we have large groups of people?
- Do we have explosive, nuclear, biological, or chemical materials that could be used as a weapon of mass destruction?
- Do we make or provide controversial products or services?
- Do we provide essential services (e.g., water treatment facility)?
- Do we share an occupancy with a possible targeted group (e.g., governmental agency)?
- Are we in or near a high-profile structure that as historic, religious, or national importance?
- Are we in a heavily populated area?
- Are we in a gridlocked area with limited access/egress?

Step 3: Threat Identification

The next step involves identifying and evaluating the various possible threats that could endanger the key asset, and the likelihood of its occurrence. The threat assessment process was covered in Chapter 6.

Adversaries are those who could harm the key asset. An adversary does not necessarily have to be a terrorist executing an attack involving a weapon of mass destruction; adversaries can include other attacks that cause a loss to the key asset, such as vandalism, theft, or product adulteration. Potential adversaries include:

- *Insiders*. This includes disgruntled employees, employees on strike, and criminals.
- *Outsiders*. This includes vandals, extremists, community activists, burglars, terrorists, organized crime, corrupt politicians, and contractors.
- *Outsiders in collusion with Insiders*.

The threat review should include the identification and prioritization of adverse consequences (impacts) posed by internal threats, external threats, and collusion threats. The process of identifying and evaluating threats should include a review of local, regional, or national intelligence information that may provide information concerning adversaries who may be planning to attack the key asset. As part of the threat review, the type of potential adversaries should also be considered:

The casual criminal who perpetrates a crime of opportunity.

The adversary who works alone to perpetrate an attack.

A small group of adversaries, working together using small unit military tactics.

A large group of international adversaries, highly trained and well financed.

The capabilities of the adversaries should also be considered:

Capable of obtaining and deploying small explosives and using automatic weapons.

Capable of developing and deploying large improvised explosive devices.

Capable of obtaining and deploying shoulder-fired rockets and other military grade weapons.

Capable of developing and deploying chemical, biological, or radiological weapons.

Step 4: Vulnerability Analysis

The security vulnerability analysis is the culmination of the risk evaluation process. The security vulnerability analysis is a very detailed examination of the threats and vulnerabilities that may put a key asset at risk.

The security vulnerability analysis involves evaluating each specific key asset against each of the potential relevant threats posed by an adversary. As part of the vulnerability analysis, existing security countermeasures that have been implemented to reduce the vulnerabilities and risks to the key asset should be identified and their level of effectiveness should be evaluated and considered in the overall risk management strategy. The information gathered from the vulnerability analysis will result in a prioritized plan for risk and threat reduction to the key asset.

Each key asset should be compared to each threat individually, fully analyzing the adverse impact consequences of each specific threat.

There are two basic methodologies for assessing the risk posed to a key asset: scenario-based approach and asset-based approach.

The *scenario-based approach* is the more detailed analysis. A scenario-based analysis involves identifying each of the potential adversaries who might plan to attack the key asset. After each adversary has been identified, the analysis team should determine and analyze each of the various ways in which the potential adversaries might attempt to harm or attack a key asset, such as by disseminating a chemical agent into a building's heating, ventilation, and air conditioning system or by detonating an improvised explosive device concealed in a truck.

The scenario-based approach requires that an adversary as well as an attack tactic be selected; then one determines the likelihood of success based on the security countermeasures that are currently in place. It is important to ensure that the attack scenario is realistic for this analysis to be worthwhile. Once again, the best way to develop realistic and credible attack scenarios would be for members of the analysis team to put themselves in the role of the adversary and ask themselves: "How would I accomplish this?" The analysis team will then need to compare the realistic attack scenario against the effectiveness of the security countermeasures in place to determine the likelihood of success.

An *asset-based analysis* involves evaluating each individual component that constitutes the key asset and making a determination as to its attractiveness as a target, the potential threats, the adverse impacts that might arise as a result of a successful attack, the vulnerabilities that may be exploited by an adversary, the existing security countermeasures that have been implemented to protect against an attack, and recommendations for enhancements to the security countermeasures. For the asset-based analysis, the method of the attack is immaterial. There is no consideration given as to how an adversary would perpetrate an attack; it is just assumed that the key asset is attacked by an adversary and destroyed.

The asset-based approach is less detail oriented than the scenario-based approach and therefore can be completed in less time. If there are limited resources or many key assets to be analyzed, this approach may be the better option.

The final step in the vulnerability assessment phase is to prioritize the scenarios based on the likelihood of occurrence and adverse impact if they were to occur so that the appropriate security countermeasures can be developed to provide adequate protection against attack.

Step 5: Security Countermeasures Assessment

The next step in the security vulnerability analysis process is to review the effectiveness of the existing security countermeasures and recommend additional security countermeasures that can be implemented or upgrades to enhance security and reduce the risk posed by an adversary. The analysis team will have to ascertain whether the existing countermeasures are adequate to prevent a successful attack, which was developed during the vulnerability phase, from being executed. If this analysis finds the existing security countermeasures are insufficient, then it would be appropriate for the analysis team to make recommendations for upgrades to the security systems.

The security countermeasure recommendations should be based on the adverse consequences resulting from a successful attack and likelihood that the layered rings of protection are breached. Recommendations for upgraded security countermeasures should measurably reduce risks by reducing security vulnerabilities and/or adverse consequences. The assets whose destruction would have the greatest adverse impact should receive priority for the implementation of new security countermeasures.

Step 6: Drill and Exercise

All security countermeasures, policies, plans, and procedures should be periodically evaluated for effectiveness by drilling and exercising with an involved personnel and agencies.

Step 7: Re-evaluation

All security countermeasures, policies, plans, and procedures should periodically be re-evaluated to ensure they are complete and effective.

7.5 ADMINISTRATIVE FUNCTIONS IN SECURITY VULNERABILITY ANALYSIS PROCESS

Report

Once the security vulnerability analysis team has completed their work, a written report should be prepared that summarizes the analysis and provides recommendations for enhanced security of the key asset. Since the report will contain confidential information that would prove very useful to an adversary, its control is very important. There should be strict controls on who can view or receive copies of the report. The report should be stored in a secure area with limited access. Only those personnel with a legitimate need to know should be provided access to the report.

TABLE 7.1. Example of an Asset Based Analysis

Problem	Risk	Existing Countermeasures	Recommendations	Priority	Assigned to Completion Date	Status
Church is open and unlocked 24 hours per day	Theft/Vandalism		Lock doors between 9 pm and 6 am	3	J. Doe	Completed
List of members is on a computer network that can be remotely accessed; no firewalls installed	Cyber		Install firewall	3	J. Jones 7-15-2007	Open
Protestors due to church's controversial stance on various social issues	Disruption of activities		Develop a procedure with the Police Department to minimize disruption	2	J. Smith 4-15-2007	In progress
International terrorist attack	Chemical, biological, radiological or explosive attack		Coordinate intelligence with Police Department	2	J. Harris 4-15-2007	In progress
Domestic terrorist attack	Incendiary or explosive attack		Coordinate intelligence with Police Department	2	J. Harris 4-15-2007	In progress
Collateral Damage (from government office building next door)	Explosive attack		Train staff to recognize suspicious activity and behaviors	2	J. Johnson 6-15-06	Open
			Develop an emergency response plan		J. Jackson 6-15-06	In progress
Assault	Injury		Train staff on preventative measures	1	J. Bond	Completed

TABLE 7.2. Example of a Scenario Based Analysis

Type of Attack	Consequences	Existing Countermeasures	Recommendations	Assigned to Completion Date	Status
Truck bomb detonates in front of church	Death Injury Property damage	None	Install barricades to prevent trucks from parking within 300 feet of the church	G. Washington 9-1-2007	Open
Intruder opens fire with a rifle during church services	Death Injury	None	Install metal detectors at entrances	R. Reagan 8-1-2007	Open

Example: Security Vulnerability Analysis

A municipality has decided to conduct a security vulnerability analysis of the critical infrastructure and key assets located in their jurisdiction. The have decided to use the seven step process.

Step 1. Planning. The jurisdiction will use a multi-discipline team. Both public and private sector assets will be analyzed, so the team will include stakeholders from both sectors. The multi-discipline team would include:

- Municipal Fire Department representative
- Municipal Police Department representative
- Municipal Emergency Medical Service representative
- Municipal Health Department representative
- Municipal Engineering/Building Department representative
- Asset Safety, Health, and Environmental representative
- Asset Security Department representative
- Asset Operations Department representative
- Asset Engineering Department representative
- Asset front line worker

Once the team members have been assembled, they are briefed on the scope, goals, and objectives of the vulnerability analysis. They also review the applicable supporting documentation, such as the threat and risk assessment, operational aspects, floor plans, construction plans, technical manuals, current threat intelligence information, current security countermeasures in place, etc.

Step 2. Asset and Risk Characterization Screening. The team would review the previously completed asset characterization to become familiar with the asset and the risks associated with an attack.

Step 3. Threat Identification. The team would review the previously completed threat assessment to become familiar with the potential threats posed by insiders, outsiders, and collusion against the asset.

Step 4. Vulnerability Analysis. The team would next begin the detailed analysis of potential security vulnerabilities present at the asset. The team would evaluate all critical infrastructure and key assets using both the scenario based and asset based approach.

For the asset based analysis, the analysis team would identify each critical infrastructure and key asset present in the jurisdiction. For the purpose of this example, only one asset will be considered: a nationally recognized house of worship.

In the asset based analysis, the team will consider all of the various types of events that could cause a loss at the asset, not just terrorist events. Examples of the various items to be considered include:

- Activist protests, such as animal rights and right to life
- Assassination of key personnel

- Assault, kidnapping, rape, murder
- Car jacking, truck jacking, diversion of raw materials or products
- Chemical, biological, radiological, incendiary, or explosive attack by terrorists
- Civil unrest, including riots
- Collateral damage from an attack on a neighboring asset
- Crime, such as theft, trespassing, and vandalism
- Cyber attacks
- Financial, such as fraud and corruption
- Gang and hate group activity
- Hoaxes
- Hostage taking of personnel or the asset itself
- Labor issues, such as strikes and sabotage
- Loss due to interdependcies (e.g., an attack on the power plant)
- Protection of sensitive information
- Suspicious letters, packages, or deliveries

Each loss event would be evaluated, with the resulting loss stated if the event were to occur (see Table 7.1).

In the scenario based analysis, the team will consider the potential adversaries and the specific type of attack they may execute. The analysis team considers all of the various specific scenarios and determines the consequences that will occur if the attack is successful. The existing security countermeasures are evaluated for their effectiveness in preventing or mitigating the effects of an attack, and recommendations for improvement are made. Finally, the recommendations are assigned to a responsible person for action and a targeted completion date is assigned (see Table 7.2).

Step 5. Security Countermeasures Assessment. The analysis team will review each of the existing security countermeasures that are installed and evaluate their effectiveness in preventing or mitigating the attack that was generated in the analysis. If the existing countermeasures are inadequate, recommendations for additional security countermeasures to further reduce risk will be made by the analysis team to cover gaps that are discovered in the existing protective systems. Each recommendation is prioritized for implementation, and is assigned to a responsible person for completion in the desired timeframe.

Step 6. Drill and Exercise. The analysis team should create an action item in their report requiring the testing of security policies, plans and procedures on at least an annual basis.

Step 7. Re-evaluation. The analysis team should include in their report an action item the re-evaluation of the key asset at a specific interval.

Security Countermeasure Recommendations

As part of its work, the analysis team will develop recommendations for improvement in the key asset's security system. These recommendations should be reviewed on a timely basis, and a decision should be made on whether to accept or reject the recommendations.

For recommendations that are rejected, there should be some documentation as to who made the decision to reject the recommendation as well as the justification for rejection. This documentation should be considered confidential and stored with the security vulnerability analysis report.

For recommendations that are accepted, an action plan should be developed. There may be cases where recommendations are modified, then accepted. In these cases, documentation should be created which indicates who authorized the modification and the justification for the modification. The action plan should assign someone the responsibility of completing the recommendation. A deadline should be assigned to complete the implementation of the recommendation. A person should be designated the responsibility to periodically follow-up on the progress of all accepted recommendations to ensure corrective actions are completed on schedule. This documentation should also be considered confidential and stored with the security vulnerability analysis report.

Revalidation of the Security Vulnerability Assessment

The security vulnerability analysis should be revalidated on a periodic basis, as it is likely that key assets will be added and deleted, and threats and vulnerabilities will change. The chief executive of the jurisdiction should designate a person to be responsible for ensuring the revalidation is completed on schedule.

7.6 RISK ASSESSMENT

Definition

A risk assessment is nothing more than a careful examination to ascertain how high the probability is of an attack occurring and causing harm to critical infrastructure, key resources, or key assets, so that an assessment can be made as to whether enough security precautions have been taken to prevent adverse impacts. The risk assessment involves a comprehensive review of the vulnerabilities that exist, and how they can be exploited to cause harm.

The important output from a risk assessment is to determine if a hazard is significant and whether sufficient security countermeasures have been taken so that the risk to the asset is small.

Principles of Risk Assessment

Risk assessment is a process for individuals and organizations to use to determine the level of acceptable risk. Risk assessment is not an exact science, but rather a process that uses scientific methods and analysis techniques to form an educated opinion on where a particular key asset may be at risk, what the adverse effect of that risk will be, and what security countermeasures are in place already or can be implemented to reduce that risk. The goal of this process is the determination of levels of risk, whether additional security countermeasures should be implemented to further reduce risk, the appropriate level of residual risk, and whether the risk is at an acceptable level.

A risk assessment is a process that can be completed relatively quickly by an individual working alone. It should not be confused with the much more comprehensive security vulnerability analysis, which is best completed by a multidisciplinary team working together.

The techniques discussed next are for illustrative purposes only; specific jurisdictions should customize the information presented so that it better illustrates the specific issues present in their particular situation.

The basic questions involved with the risk assessment process are:

What are we trying to protect?
What are the threats?
What are the vulnerabilities?
What are the risks associated with those threats?
How significant is the risk?
Who or what can be harmed?
What are the implications if the asset is damaged or lost?
What security countermeasures are in place?
What security countermeasures are needed?
Is the key asset easily replaced?

7.7 PREPARING TO CONDUCT A THREAT AND RISK ANALYSIS

There is a difference between threat and risk. The threat posed against a key asset by an adversary is defined in the detailed threat analysis, which is conducted by the law enforcement and intelligence community. Risk is the correlation of how, or if, that threat can adversely impact a key asset. Before a threat and risk analysis can be started, a planning stage is required. The planning stage will provide the foundation on which all subsequent work will be built, so it must be completed thoroughly and accurately. Items that should be covered in the planning stage include the following.

- *Identification of the Analysis Team.* The analysis team can be a multidisciplinary team that captures representatives from each interested group that has a stake in the asset. However, since a risk analysis is usually a relatively quick evaluation of the threats that could adversely affect an asset, the analysis is usually completed by an individual working alone.

- *Purpose of the Analysis*. The general purpose of the analysis is to identify the various threats posed by an adversary that could adversely impact an asset. As part of the risk analysis, the process must also identify the consequences of an attack, and what security measures are in place and as well as what additional countermeasures can be installed to reduce the unfavorable outcomes of an attack.
- *Scope of the Risk Analysis*. This would include a description of the asset to be evaluated; the mission of the asset to be evaluated (e.g., what services or products are provided or produced); identification and nature of the asset systems (e.g., the key assets that comprise the asset); and the asset boundaries and its interconnectivity with other assets (e.g., what assets are considered to compose the target and any interdependencies with other critical infrastructure).
- *Identification and Valuation of Specific Key Assets*. The infrastructure of a facility, a company, or a critical infrastructure sector consists of an array of assets that are necessary for the production and/or delivery of goods or services. Similarly, the critical infrastructure of a city, state, or nation consists of an array of assets necessary for the economic and social activity of the city and region, and the public health and welfare of its citizens.

  Key assets are broadly defined as people, information, products/services, and property.

  People, including employees, contractors, visitors, guests, passengers, vendors, truck drivers, and anyone else directly or indirectly connected with the organization.

  Information, which includes any general or proprietary information that relates to the organization's products or services, such as formulations, customer lists, trade secrets, and price schedules.

  Functional services are those activities provided to both internal and external customers.

  Utilities are those assets that support the primary endeavor, such as electricity, water, and telecommunications.

  Property includes all tangible assets such as real estate, structures, equipment, and cash, and intangible assets such as intellectual property.

  Core business is the primary business, including products and services. Also included in this category is the organization's reputation and good will.

  Computer networks include all systems, hardware, and software associated with data, telecommunications, and computer processing.

Each key asset must be identified and have its value quantified in terms of dollars. Determine what warrants protection—inventory key assets and determine their worth. The value should be based on the criticality of the key asset.

Determine how each key asset can be harmed. Walk around the key asset, both inside and outside the perimeter, and look at what could reasonably be expected to cause harm. Since we can't prevent every possible threat scenario locally (e.g., crashing a plane into a building), ignore those extreme hazards and concentrate on the hazards that could result in serious harm to the key asset.

The analysis team must fully understand the various operational aspects of the key asset to be evaluated, as well as the risks posed against the key asset. For example, consider the hours of operation of the facility, staffing levels, types of products produced or services rendered, special issues such as environmental concerns, and type of labor force (e.g., unskilled, white collar, collective bargaining agent).

- *Determination of Key Asset Criticality.* Not every key asset is as important as another. In order to focus assessment resources, the analysis should focus on those key assets judged to be most critical. Criticality is defined and quantified in terms of impact of loss. Loss is defined as the destruction of the key asset or degradation, which leads to the inability to function properly.

The impact of loss is measured in terms of four specific quantifiable areas: (1) its initial costs, (2) temporary replacement costs, (3) permanent replacement costs, and (4) the remaining related costs that would result from loss or damage to the key asset. The resultant loss is usually expressed in dollars. Each key asset that needs to be safeguarded is evaluated in terms of this impact of loss.

The more the loss of a key asset threatens the survival or viability of a society, the more critical it becomes. Criticality depends on several factors, including the perception of the individual conducting the analysis. Three factors that determine the degree of criticality are (1) *scope*—the extent of the population and geographic area covered; *magnitude*—the potential effect of the impact; and *time effect*—additional damage caused by extended duration of serious impact.

While the immediate impact is certainly important, so too is the amount of time and resources required to replace the lost capability of the key asset once it is attacked. If losing a key asset results in a large immediate disruption, but the key asset can be replaced quickly and cheaply or there are cost-effective substitutes, the total adverse consequences of the attack may not be so great. Alternatively, if losing a key asset results in a small immediate disruption but that disruption continues for a long period of time because of the difficulty in reconstituting the lost capability, the total adverse consequences of the attack may be very great.

Another issue concerns whether the loss of a particular key asset could lead to cascading effects, not only within the facility or company but affecting other critical infrastructures within a jurisdiction.

Adverse consequences can be categorized in a number of ways: casulties, economic, financial, environmental, health and safety, technological, operational, and time-related.

Once the criticality of the key asset has been determined, a numeric rating should be assigned to signify its significance. For example, this numeric value can vary from 1 (catastrophic) to 4 (not serious).

- *Identification of Specific Threats.* All threats posed against the key asset must be identified. A threat can be any indication, circumstance, or event that has the potential to cause damage to or loss of the key asset's ability to provide its products or services. The likelihood of incidents occurring is based on intelligence, the history of such events, or the circumstances in the local jurisdiction. Every threat associated with a key asset, if it occurs, does not necessarily result in a loss event. When a loss event does occur, it always results in quantifiable, physical damage, destruction, or degradation of the key asset. The three types of potential loss events should be analyzed (1) *natural hazard* (hurricane, flood, etc.), *accidental hazard* (power loss, fire, etc.), and *intentional hazard* (sabotage, terrorist attack, etc.).

  The information sources that may be consulted to determine the likelihood of these potential loss events include:

  Geological surveys (Is the facility sited on an earthquake fault line?).

  Weather statistics (snow, flooding, tornado, hurricane, etc).

  Local police reports and crime statistics.

  The organization's or jurisdiction's loss reports, incident reports, and crime statistics.

  Demographic/social data.

  Prior complaints from employees, contractors, visitors, and truck drivers regarding potential losses.

  Intelligence from federal, state, or local law enforcement agencies.

  The types of threat to be considered in the analysis are usually selected by the key asset stakeholders in conjunction with the analysis team.

- *Probability of a Loss Risk and Frequency of Events.* The likelihood of an attack is based on two things: whether or not the key asset represents a tempting target based on the goals and motivation of the adversary; and whether the adversary has the capability to attack the key asset. The probability of loss risk is not based on mathematical certainty, but rather is qualitative and based on the history of prior incidents, trends, warnings, or threats to the organization or jurisdiction in the past. The frequency of events relates to the regularity of the loss event occurring. The probability of a risk event occurring is usually based on the intrinsic values of the key asset. The potential loss risk events can be determined through a security vulnerability analysis.
- *Determination of the Adverse Impact of Events.* There can be many direct and indirect adverse effects that may result from a terrorist attack, including casualties, equipment damage, service degradation, loss of business, negative media coverage, and psychological and financial aspects associated with the loss of tangible or intangible key assets of an organization or jurisdiction. Impacts are evaluated based on the basis of their scope.
- *Likeliness of Harm to the Key Asset.* Evaluate the existing security countermeasures that are already in place, which could be used to counteract the

effect of an attack. Countermeasures are those actions taken to eliminate, reduce, or control vulnerabilities to specific threats. This evaluation should consider all existing administrative and physical security countermeasures that are already in place and should include a measurement of their effectiveness. Existing countermeasures must be identified and assessed to determine the extent to which they are providing the intended vulnerability reduction.

- *Development of New Options to Mitigate and Manage Risk.* Determine all appropriate risk reduction countermeasures, and their associated costs, necessary to reduce the identified risk to a key asset to an acceptable level. Consider available options to prevent, mitigate, and respond to losses through physical or administrative security processes. This is a brainstorming exercise; therefore all options should be presented. Identify all cost-effective countermeasure approaches.
- *Feasibility of Implementation of Security Countermeasure Options.* Before implementing these countermeasures, a study addressing the cost, availability, feasibility, and practicality of the various options should be conducted to ensure they would not substantially interfere with the normal operation of the key asset. The goal is to make all risks to the key asset as small as possible.
- *Cost–Benefit Analysis.* A systematic evaluation should be performed to measure and analyze the value of all benefits afforded by the proposed security countermeasure versus the specific direct and indirect expenditures to implement and maintain the countermeasure. The four steps usually involved in this process include: (1) identification of all direct and indirect consequences of implementing the security countermeasure; (2) assignment of a monetary value to all costs resulting from installation of the security countermeasure; (3) determination of the value of what will be protected by the implementation of the security countermeasure; and (4) weighing of the implementation costs against the impact of the loss in terms of both direct and indirect costs.

Sample Risk Analysis

Following is a basic outline that illustrates the content of a risk analysis.

Introduction. The introduction contains a brief description of the analysis team and the process used to conduct the analysis.

Purpose. The purpose of the risk analysis is to identify the key asset, the vulnerabilities that exist and can be exploited by an adversary, the type of threat posed by the adversary, the impact if the attack is successfully perpetrated, the likelihood of the attack occurring, and the security countermeasures that can be implemented to mitigate or reduce the risk to the key asset.

Scope. The scope includes the specific assets that will be analyzed. The scope should provide a detailed description of the asset, including system components, construction, cyber systems, and any other information that may be useful in conducting the analysis. Blueprints, floor plans, and process flow diagrams should be provided to assist those who will be conducting the analysis to understand the scope of the project.

Risk Assessment Approach. A risk assessment can be conducted in one of two ways: after an attack has taken place or considering the likelihood of an attack taking place in the future. The approach taken should be documented in this section.

Asset Characterization. This section provides the information where components and information that constitute the asset and its boundaries are identified in order to provide the foundation for the remaining steps in the risk assessment process. The characterization statement provides a detailed view of the key asset and its components.

Threat Statement. This section identifies and explains the existing threats to the key asset and lists them specifically in terms of the potential adverse effects they can cause.

Findings. The findings form the basis for the recommended security countermeasures to be evaluated for implementation. Each finding must include:

- A discussion of the threat and existing vulnerability that can be exploited by an adversary.
- Identification of all existing security countermeasures that have been implemented.
- A discussion of the adverse impact that would be achieved with a successful attack.
- A qualitative or quantitative rating of the risk posed.
- Recommended security countermeasures to mitigate the risk to the key asset.

Evaluating Risk

Once the risk has been assessed, it must now be evaluated and prioritized for the implementation of appropriate security countermeasures. Risk is evaluated on the basis of vulnerability. The risk assessment process is the systematic evaluation resulting from the analyses of the potential losses and impacts associated with a key asset due to the risk posed by an adversary exploiting vulnerabilities, so that a jurisdiction can gauge the risk presented and implement the appropriate security countermeasures to ensure sufficient protection. The severity of the consequences for each specific attack must be determined.

A risk evaluation is a useful tool to identify the security-related risks from internal and external threats to key assets and their vulnerabilities. A risk evaluation provides the information necessary to make an informed decision on how to manage risk, including priority setting for the implementation of security countermeasures. Risk evaluation is the first phase in analyzing a system and determining what can go wrong, with what likelihood, and whether the level of risk is sufficiently serious to warrant the installation of security countermeasures. If the risk evaluation indicates that a potential threat is not of concern, then a more comprehensive analysis may not be necessary. However, if the evaluation indicates that a potential threat is of concern, then a more comprehensive review to estimate the risk and develop security countermeasures is necessary.

Risk evaluations provide a method of prioritizing the criticality of assets (or the impact of the loss of a key asset), threats posed against the key asset, and recommended security countermeasure strategies. A structured risk evaluation process allows for the documentation of the risk by a team of subject matter experts based on their judgments and assumptions. The final product is a broad set of priorities that contribute to the protection of the key asset.

The risk evaluation stage attempts to answer three main questions:

1. What are the risks and what are the scenarios that jeopardize the asset?
2. What is the likelihood of the risk occurring and what is the probability the risk will happen?
3. What are the adverse consequences resulting from the risk and the adverse effects to the target and its surroundings?

Risk evaluations assess the sensitivity and criticality of the critical infrastructure, key asset, or key resource to the vulnerabilities, threats, impacts, and security countermeasures that may exist. Existing security programs, including administrative security, personnel security, and physical security, must be reviewed and assessed for adequacy. The identification of vulnerabilities that can be exploited by an adversary to cause harm and a final assessment gauging the risk for each key asset lead to the recommendation for the implementation of security countermeasures.

Three factors are considered when considering risk evaluation:

1. What will be adversely affected if the attack should occur (potential impacts)? Key assets will generally have multiple risks. Different assets will have different risks associated with them. Some risk will impact all key assets of a facility while in other cases the risk may have a limited impact against specific components of a facility. All exploitable weaknesses resulting from inadequate or deficient security countermeasures should be identified. For example, a large truck bomb may destroy an entire facility. A computer virus may only have an adverse localized affect on the computer system.

2. What is the probability of the attack occurring? After the threats and their potential adverse impacts have been identified, an assessment of the probability of these threats occurring (e.g., the likelihood of occurrence) must be completed to properly evaluate the risk. For terrorist threats, the attractiveness of the target is a primary consideration. The probability of a risk occurring is a combination of vulnerability and threat. Factors that contribute to the probability include the intent, motivation and capabilities of the adversary; the type and severity of the

vulnerability; and the effectiveness of the installed security countermeasures. The method of attack that is most likely to succeed is the one most likely to be chosen by an adversary. If the existing security countermeasures indicate that a successful attack is unlikely, the adversary will likely move to an alternate target. While there are any number of potential threats that could be made against a key asset, not all threats are probable. For example, it is highly probable that a hurricane could strike a key asset in Florida, but not highly probable that a hurricane will strike a key asset in Kansas. Historical data may provide an indication of how probable some risks are of occurring based on previous events, such as natural events like flooding, accidental events such as fire, and intentional acts such as theft.

3. What will be the cost of an attack, if it should occur? The cost of an attack is simply all direct and indirect monetary losses associated with the attack should it occur. This dollar loss can then be compared to the replacement cost of the asset, and the cost of the security countermeasures necessary to protect the asset. This leads to a cost–benefit analysis to determine if the loss due to a risk is worth protecting against.

Remember to consider interdependencies among critical infrastructures when evaluating the adverse consequences of an attack. An incident in one critical infrastructure can cascade to other infrastructure sectors, causing additional adverse effects.

Reducing the Risk

Once the risks have been fully evaluated and prioritized, a plan should be established to start eliminating (or minimizing) the vulnerabilities and reducing both the risk of a successful attack and the unfavorable outcomes of a successful attack. One of the best ways to reduce risk is to incorporate inherent safety in all operations. The hierarchy of inherent safety includes (1) reducing or eliminating the *possibility* of an attack by choosing inherently safe materials and technologies; (2) reducing the *probability* of negative impacts through secondary prevention measures; and (3) reducing the *potential severity* of the impacts through coordination with local authorities and developing plans for appropriate mitigation measures.

During the implementation of security countermeasures to reduce risk, an assessment must be made to determine whether current security measures effectively address these new and unforeseen threats.

Reevaluating the Risk

Provision must be included in the overall assessment process that mandates a periodic reevaluation of the security programs. The reevaluation can serve as a validation that the changes made have been effective and can also serve to identify previously undiscovered vulnerabilities. It is beneficial to have the reevaluation conducted by person(s) other than those who did the original assessment in order to have an unbiased and "fresh set of eyes" look at the asset. A security specialist from a reputable firm should participate in the validation of the overall security program. Having a local law enforcement official participate in the validation fosters community involvement and also helps to ensure the assets written plans are coordinated with the municipality's plans.

7.8 THE BUFFER ZONE PROTECTION PLAN (BZPP)

The BZPP was created by the Department of Homeland Security to reestablish buffer zones of critical infrastructure facilities due to the increasing expansion of urban areas. Buffer zones provide separation for a facility from surrounding areas and sensitive populations. This makes it harder to locate and attack a facility and also provides some protection to the community in the event of an incident at the key asset.

The BZPP is unlike the security vulnerability analysis in that it is designed for the assessors to look at the critical infrastructure, key resource, and key asset from the outside in. This technique allows the assessors to observe the asset, and its vulnerabilities, from the same perspective as an adversary. The concept behind this technique is that an adversary can legally be present in the public areas that may surround the asset. While in this public area, the adversary can conduct surveillance operations, observe the implementation of security countermeasures, and conduct practice sessions. The end product of conducting the buffer zone review is to make it more difficult for adversaries to conduct planning activities or successfully launch attacks from the immediate vicinity of a critical infrastructure, key resource, or key asset target. The BZPP is designed to increase the general protective capacity and preparedness surrounding the key assets by establishing protected buffer zones around individual assets.

Specifically, BZPPs will:

- Define the buffer zone outside the security perimeter of a potential critical infrastructure, key resource, or key asset target.
- Identify the specific threats and vulnerabilities associated with the buffer zone.
- Analyze and categorize the level of risk associated with each vulnerability.
- Recommend corrective measures within a buffer zone that will reduce the risk of a successful adversary attack by (1) devaluing a target by making it less attractive or too costly for an adversary to attack; (2) deterring an attack from occurring (e.g., through warning signs, physical barriers, cameras, and security guards); (3) detecting an adversary who is planning or committing an attack or the presence of a hazardous device or weapon; and (4) defending against attack by delaying or preventing an adversary's movement toward the asset or use of weapons and explosives.
- Define the command and control structure for terrorism prevention specific to an individual critical infrastructure target.
- Review established security measures to ensure they are consistent with the Homeland Security Advisory System (HSAS) and disseminate the information to appropriate authorities and emergency responders.

The BZPP is a strategic document that (1) applies to a critical infrastructure, key resource, or key asset site; (2) provides planning guidance and suggested actions to be taken during each HSAS level; and (3) illustrates ways in which federal, state, and local agencies can most effectively synchronize their preventive actions.

The BZPP should not supersede existing asset response plans that were developed for response to terrorist threats or attacks. Rather, it is intended to foster a cooperative environment in which federal, state, and local authorities, along with the private sector, can carry out their respective protection responsibilities more efficiently and effectively.

BZPP development steps include the following:

1. *Determine the Jurisdiction's Critical Assets.* Identify the specific individual key assets that are present at the jurisdiction.
2. *Identify Threats.* Identify the specific threats that present a risk to the key asset.
3. *Identify Vulnerabilities.* Identify each of the specific vulnerabilities that can be exploited by an adversary to perpetrate an attack or increase the effectiveness of an attack.
4. *Develop Protective Plan.* Begin the development of a specific protection plan to reduce the vulnerabilities that could be exploited from the buffer zone surrounding the key asset.
   a. *Definition of Specific Protective Team Tasks.* Each team member should use his/her expertise in a particular field to identify and then counter any threats that pose a risk to the key asset.
   b. *Resource Identification and Acquisition.* The team should identify the resources necessary to assist the local law enforcement and emergency response agencies in preventing and responding to an attack on the key asset. The team should assist the jurisdiction in preparing the necessary justification for obtaining the necessary resources through governmental homeland security grants.
5. *Department of Homeland Security Follow-up with State and Local Jurisdictions.* The Department of Homeland Security shall coordinate with the state and local jurisdictions responsible for implementing the BZPP program to ensure activities are progressing on schedule.

The BZPP assumes that the local law enforcement agencies and the key asset's management actively participate in a life cycle of domestic incident management activities, including:

Awareness. Participate in security awareness practices and adhere to HSAS levels as appropriate.

Prevention. Practice prevention to avoid incidents, intervene as necessary in order to stop incidents from occurring, and attempt to mitigate a given incident's effects.

Preparedness. Be involved in activities to identify risks or threats and requirements or shortfalls and have plans to remedy shortfalls over time.

Response and Recovery. Cooperate actively with federal, state, and local entities in emergency response and recovery activities as needed.

The buffer zone assessment team usually consists of six to twelve people from federal, state, and local governments. Included in the team are experts in the area of explosives and military small unit tactics.

7.9 THE CARVER TARGET ANALYSIS TOOL

The BZPP program also uses the CARVER target analysis tool to conduct the assessment.

1. *Criticality*. Criticality refers to the key asset's value as a target. Criticality would be a primary consideration in the eyes of an adversary planning an attack, since a successful attack on a critical target would have a significant adverse impact.

Criticality depends on several factors:

Time. How rapidly will the impact of the target attack affect operations?

Quality. What percentage of output, production, or service will be curtailed by target damage?

Surrogates. What will the effect be on the output, production, and service?

Relativity. How many targets are there? What are their positions? How is their relative value determined? What will be affected in the system?

The criticality values are:

Criteria	Scale
Immediate halt in output, production, or service; target cannot function without it	9–10
Halt within 1 day, or 66% curtailment in output, production, or service	7–8
Halt within 1 week, or 33% curtailment in output, production, or service	5–6
Halt within 10 days, or 10% curtailment in output, production, or service	3–4
No significant effect on output, production, or service	1–2

2. *Accessibility*. A target is accessible when an adversary can reach the key asset with sufficient personnel and equipment to execute an attack. The four basic steps in identifying accessibility are:

Infiltration to the key asset

Movement from the point of entry to the target

Movement to the target's critical element

Escape

The accessibility values are:

Criteria	Scale
Easily accessible; standoff weapons can be employed	9–10
Inside a perimeter fence but outdoors	7–8
Inside a building but on a ground floor	5–6
Inside a building but on second floor or in basement—climbing or lowering required	3–4
Not accessible without extreme difficulty	1–2

3. *Recuperability*. Recuperability refers to how long it will take to replace, repair, or bypass the damage or destruction caused at a key asset by a successful attack. Factors that should be considered when assessing recuperability include the availability of:

On-hand equipment (or equipment that can be cannabilized) such as railroad cranes and dry docks.

Restoration and substitution through redundancies.

On-hand spares.

Equivalent equipment sets that back up critical equipment or components.

The effects of economic embargoes and labor unrest.

The recuperability values are:

Criteria	Scale
Replacement, repair, or substitution requires 1 month or more	9–10
Replacement, repair, or substitution requires 1 week to 1 month	7–8
Replacement, repair, or substitution requires 72 hours to 1 week	5–6
Replacement, repair, or substitution requires 24–72 hours	3–4
Same day replacement, repair, or substitution	1–2

4. *Vulnerability*. A key asset is vulnerable if an adversary has the means and expertise to successfully attack it. Specifically, vulnerability depends on:

The nature and construction of the target.

The amount of damage required.

The resources available to the adversary.

The vulnerability values are:

Criteria	Scale
Vulnerable to small arms fire or explosive charges of 5 pounds or less	9–10
Vulnerable to light anti-armor weapons fire or explosive charges of 5–10 pounds	7–8
Vulnerable to medium anti-armor weapons fire, bulk explosive charges of 10–30 pounds, or very careful placement of smaller charges	5–6
Vulnerable to heavy anti-armor fire, bulk explosive charges of 30–50 pounds, or specialized weapons	3–4
Invulnerable to all but the most extreme targeting measures	1–2

5. *Effect.* The effect of an attack on a key asset is a measure of the possible military, political, economic, psychological, and sociological impacts at the target and beyond. Effects can also include:

The triggering of security countermeasures by law enforcement

Support or negation of the individual's or group's goals or intentions.

Unemployment in the industry.

Panic in the population.

Collateral damage to other components in the industry.

The effect values are:

Criteria	Scale
Overwhelmingly positive effects; no significant negative effects	9–10
Moderately positive effects; few significant negative effects	7–8
No significant effects; neutral	5–6
Moderately negative effects; few significant positive effects	3–4
Overwhelmingly negative effects; no significant positive effects	1–2

6. *Recognizability.* A key asset's recognizability is the degree to which it can be recognized by an adversary under varying conditions. Factors that influence recognizability include:

Weather

Distance

Light

Season

Landscaping

Size and complexity of the key asset

Distinctive features

Presence of masking or camouflage

The recognizability values are:

Criteria	Scale
Target is clearly recognizable under all conditions and from a distance; it requires little or no training for recognition	9–10
Target is easily recognizable at small arms range and requires a small amount of training for recognition	7–8
Target is difficult to recognize at night in bad weather or might be confused with other targets or target components; it requires some training for recognition	5–6
Target is difficult to recognize at night or in bad weather, even within small arms range; it is easily confused with other targets or components and it requires extensive training for recognition	3–4
Target cannot be recognized under any conditions, except by experts	1–2

REFERENCE

1. *Analyzing and Managing the Security Vulnerabilities of Fixed Chemical Sites*, CCPS, 2003.

CHAPTER 8

Principles of Protective Security

8.1 INTRODUCTION

Once all of the threats, vulnerabilities, and risks have been identified and analyzed, the next step is to develop security countermeasures that can be implemented to reduce the occurrence and severity of adverse consequences resulting from an attack.

Now that we have a basic understanding of what the weapons of mass destruction (WMD) threat is and the types of weapons that may be used against us, we need to start the protection process. Predicting the location of the next terrorist target and the type of attack is obviously very difficult. Therefore it is incumbent upon everyone to be prepared. Since the WMD scenarios originate with deliberate acts instead of equipment or human failures, the safeguards that were installed against accidental threat scenarios may not be adequate to protect against terrorist threats. As part of an overall comprehensive security/loss prevention program, we should protect not only against terrorism, but theft, industrial espionage, sabotage of equipment, or adulteration of product.

Protecting our critical infrastructure, key resources, and key assets not only makes the nation more secure from terrorism, but it also helps to reduce the vulnerability to those threats that are more likely to occur, such as natural disasters, accidents, and organized crime.

However, adversaries continue to adapt to our protective measures and develop new attack tactics, techniques, and procedures. Therefore we must continually reevaluate the threat and develop new and creative security countermeasures.

8.2 PREVENTION

The old adage expresses a basic truth: the easiest battle to win is the one that is never fought. We can apply this principle to our efforts to secure our assets from attack by an adversary. The best way to respond to a terrorist attack is to prevent it from ever

Understanding, Assessing, and Responding to Terrorism: Protecting Critical Infrastructure and Personnel By Brian T. Bennett

happening. Some security countermeasures are very inexpensive—in terms of personnel, money, and physical resources—to implement and can be very effective in dissuading an adversary from attacking a target. As was previously discussed, adversaries have limited resources and are unlikely to waste them on targets where the chance of a successful mission is questionable. Perhaps one of the easiest ways to prevent an attack is to raise the level of awareness of all personnel present at a potential target to the threat an adversary may pose. This responsibility does not apply to just law enforcement or security personnel. If all personnel present at the potential target site are trained and aware of the adversary's threat, the security force has been significantly increased in size. Terrorists and criminals cannot easily accomplish their mission when competent, trained personnel are on the alert at potential target locations. In order to be effective, everyone must be aware of their surroundings, be on the alert for suspicious activity, and know how to process that information appropriately so the proper response can be initiated. Experience has shown that criminals and terrorists conduct surveillance and planning activities in the target area well before the attack itself. If their surveillance reveals a highly trained and aware group of people are present at the potential target, the adversary is likely to move on to an alternate, less protected asset.

8.3 INFORMATION COLLECTION

Information collection is a key element in preventing a terrorist attack. It is imperative that all information is properly collected, analyzed, and shared in order to prevent an attack from occurring. All citizens must be part of the intelligence gathering network. Any observation of suspicious activity should be reported to law enforcement immediately for an appropriate investigation. Some of the information may be criminal in nature, and some may be noncriminal in nature. The data in and of itself does not provide the basis for a reasonable suspicion that a terrorist plot is in the making.

8.4 INFORMATION SHARING

Once information has been analyzed, it should be disseminated to all applicable law enforcement agencies for appropriate action. This information may include data that is not indicative of immediate criminal or terrorist intent or action but is suspicious and may be an indicator or more devious activities in the future. Information should also be shared with the private and public sector critical infrastructure, key resources, key assets, or soft targets that may be impacted by terrorist activity so they are aware of the threat and appropriate countermeasures can be implemented.

8.5 RISK MITIGATION

In order to mitigate risk, the security vulnerabilities must first be identified. Once these vulnerabilities have been identified, it must be determined if they can be exploited by an adversary to cause harm. If they can be exploited, an adversary will determine if the existing vulnerabilities make the attack attractive. In determining whether or not to attack, the adversary will consider the cost versus gain. If this evaluation indicates that the gain from perpetrating the attack exceeds the adversary's cost to execute the attack, then it is likely the attack will be executed.

Risk mitigation involves the implementation or installation of security countermeasures intended to sufficiently reduce the identified risks to the key asset based on the results of the risk assessment process. The goal in selecting security countermeasures is to reduce the level of risk to an acceptable level, without adversely affecting the other asset capabilities. Remember, the elimination of all risk is usually impractical and probably impossible. Therefore the goal is to protect the key asset with cost-effective and practical security countermeasures that are applicable to the key asset being protected.

To mitigate risk, there are three approaches that are usually taken:

1. *Prevent.* Prevention involves eliminating the threat by removing the existing shortcomings in the security countermeasures, which have been identified in the security vulnerability assessment process.
2. *Limit.* Limiting involves implementing security countermeasures that constrain the adverse impact of a threat.
3. *Detect and Respond.* Detect and respond involves the implementation of security countermeasures to detect security vulnerabilities and take the appropriate steps to mitigate the adverse outcomes.

If the determination is made that unacceptable risks are present at the key asset due to an adversary's threat, corrective action is warranted. Some basic tenets to consider when implementing corrective measures include:

- If a security vulnerability exists, countermeasures to reduce the likelihood of the vulnerability being exploited should be implemented.
- Security countermeasures should be implemented to provide a layered protection, regardless of whether administrative or physical countermeasures are employed.
- If the adversary's cost to execute the attack is less than the gain, apply additional security countermeasures to increase the adversary's cost to perpetrate the attack.
- If the risk of the loss is significant, apply security countermeasures that will limit the magnitude of the attack, thereby reducing the loss.

8.6 COST–BENEFIT ANALYSIS

For many reasons, primarily financial, it is not possible to implement all of the recommended security countermeasures that may be proposed as part of the risk management process. In order to properly select those countermeasures that are appropriate and will be implemented, a cost–benefit analysis for each proposed countermeasure should be conducted. Cost–benefit analysis can be qualitative or quantitative. The purpose of the cost–benefit analysis is to demonstrate that funds spent on implementing the countermeasure can be justified with a corresponding reduction in risk to the key asset.

The first step in conducting a cost–benefit analysis is to identify all of the benefits that will be realized if the specific security countermeasure is implemented relative to the cost of implementation, control, and maintenance of the countermeasure. The level of risk reduction in terms of likelihood and adverse impact in the event of a successful attack can then be measured.

8.7 SITUATIONAL AWARENESS

Situational awareness is the knowledge of where you are, where other friendly elements are, and the status, state, and location of the enemy. Situational awareness is therefore being aware of everything that is happening around oneself and the relative importance of everything observed. Situational awareness is the degree of accuracy by which one's perception of the current environment mirrors reality.

Situational awareness is important for effective decision making and performance in any complex and dynamic environment. An individual's understanding and classification of a situation forms the basis for all subsequent decision making and performance.

There are three levels of situational awareness:

Level 1 situational awareness involves perceiving the critical factors in the environment.

Level 2 situational awareness is understanding what those factors mean, particularly when integrated together in relation to the decision maker's goals.

Level 3 situational awareness is the highest level, which is an understanding of what will happen with the system in the near future.

The loss of situational awareness usually occurs over a period of time and will leave a trail of clues. The following clues warn of lost or diminished situational awareness:

- *Confusion or a Gut Feeling.* Disorder within the team exists or a gut feeling that things "are not right." This clue is one of the most reliable because our bodies are able to detect a stimulus long before we have consciously put it all together.
- *No One Watching or Looking for Hazards.* The proper assignment and performance of tasks, particularly supervisory ones, is essential to situational awareness.
- *Use of Improper Procedures.* This puts the individual or team in a gray area where no one may be able to predict outcomes with any certainty.

- *Departure from Regulations.* In addition to violating procedures, operations are now being conducted in an unknown area where the consequences of our actions cannot be predicted with any degree of certainty.
- *Failure to Meet Planned Goals.* During each operation, certain goals or targets are set to be met. When they are not met, we must question why and systematically begin to evaluate the situation.
- *Unresolved Discrepancies.* When two or more pieces of information do not agree, we must continue to search for more information until the discrepancy is resolved.
- *Ambiguity.* When needed information is confusing or unclear, we must clarify or fill in the missing pieces before proceeding.
- *Fixation or Preoccupation.* When an individual fixates on one task or becomes preoccupied with work or personal matters, he/she loses the ability to detect other important information.

Practicing Situational Awareness

"Know the routines. Be alert as you go about your daily business. This will help you learn the normal routines of your neighborhood, community, and workplace. Understanding these routines will help you spot anything out of place.

Be aware. Get to know your neighbors at home and while traveling. Be on the lookout for suspicious activities such as unusual conduct in your neighborhood, in your workplace, or while traveling. Learn to spot suspicious packages, luggage, or mail abandoned in a crowded place like an office building, an airport, a school, or a shopping center.

Take what you hear seriously. If you hear or know of someone who has bragged or talked about plans to harm citizens in violent attacks or who claims membership in a terrorist organization, take it seriously and report it to law enforcement immediately" [1].

Why Is Situational Awareness Important?

Experience has shown that when situational awareness is lost, especially in cases involving an adversary who is trying to cause harm, people get hurt or killed. It is critical that all personnel present at a potential target, or those who will be responding to mitigate an attack at a key asset, be trained to ensure they maintain a high level of situational awareness at all times.

Barriers to Situational Awareness

The following barriers reduce the ability to understand a situation. Recognizing these barriers and taking the appropriate corrective action is the responsibility of all team members.

- *Perception Based on Faulty Information Processing*. Perception is our mental picture of reality. The amount and quality of information available limit all pictures of our current operational state. Insufficient information makes it difficult to ensure that our mental picture is always aligned with reality. Our mental picture is affected by:

  Past Experiences. We act on information based on our knowledge. When something looks similar to what we are familiar with, we may react as if it were the same.

  Expectations. We interpret information in such as way that it affirms the planned action.

  Filters. We are provided with information, but we don't use it. We don't pay attention to information that doesn't match our mental picture.

- *Excessive Motivation*. This behavior imposes expectations and filters our ability to fully access the situation and any safety risks. It includes an overriding sense of mission importance. Using an effective decision making strategy and seeking feedback on judgments can reduce the potential for unsafe acts.
- *Complacency*. Assuming everything is under control affects vigilance. When things are slow and tasks are routine, complacency can occur. Challenging yourself and/or the team to be prepared for contingencies (e.g., planning and training) can deter complacency.
- *Overload*. Overload causes distraction, fixation, increased errors, and high stress. Prioritizing and delegating tasks and minimizing job distractions can improve safety in conditions of overload.
- *Fatigue*. Fatigue affects vigilance. Adjusting work routine and imposing sleep discipline to prevent wake cycles longer than 18 hours and permit at least 5, and preferably 8, hours per day of sound sleep can minimize sleep deprivation.
- *Poor Communications*. The level of situational awareness achieved is related to the level and quality of communications.

Case Study: Situational Awareness

The Madrid train bombers used backpacks to carry the explosives aboard several trains. The first of ten bombs placed aboard four trains detonated at 7:39 am. Once the bombs were detonated, the police responded and began their investigation. At some point during the investigation, the police decided to move the victim's personal belongings such as pocketbooks and briefcases to a police station for safe keeping.

A backpack was moved from the train station at El Pozo to the Vallecas Police Station. It was later discovered that this backpack contained an explosive device. After the backpack was removed from the police station and rendered safe, it was found that the device did not detonate because the terrorists had misprogrammed a cellular phone that was used to initiate the detonation by setting it 12 hours late.

This case study illustrates the importance of situational awareness. Even though there were multiple explosions on trains involving explosive devices carried onto the trains in personal belongings, at least some police officers lost situational awareness. Although they thought they were doing the right thing—moving the victim's personal belongings to a secure area—they inadvertently moved an explosive device into a police station. Had the device detonated in the police station, it certainly would have caused a significant amount of damage and multiple casualties.

8.8 SECURITY

Perception of Security

As with many things in the adversaries' world, perception is reality. It is not very difficult to portray the perception that a target has a very sophisticated and robust security program, when in reality it may not.

Adversaries will form their opinion on the attractiveness of a target based what they see, or more correctly, their perception of what they see. Adversaries may conduct their surveillance operations against a potential target and observe that all visitors gaining access to a particular target are required to walk through a metal detector and their parcels are searched by what appears to be highly trained, competent, and efficient security guards. This example could be considered reality, if in fact the conclusions drawn from the surveillance are accurate. However, the conclusions drawn from the surveillance may not be very accurate. True, the visitors were required to walk through a metal detector when entering the target area. But how did the security force react if the detector sounded an alarm? Was the person simply allowed to talk his/her way out of further scrutiny by the security guards by claiming the alarm was due to coins, keys, or steel toe work boots, or was a more detailed search conducted and the person required to go through the metal detector a second time? Parcels were also searched, but how alert were the security guards and how thorough were the searches? Were the searches conducted halfheartedly by the security guards while they carried on conversations, or were the contents removed from each parcel and thoroughly scrutinized?

What Are We Trying to Protect?

Protecting key assets is a complicated task. There are several issues that must be considered in preparation for implementing security countermeasures:

- What are the critical infrastructure, key resources, and key assets that should be protected?
- Against what threats do they need protection?
- What are the threats, vulnerabilities, and risks?
- How can the most cost-effective risk mitigation measures be selected?
- How are money and resources best allocated?

Standoff Distance

Distance is the most effective and desirable countermeasure because other measures may vary in effectiveness, are more costly, and often have unintended consequences.

The distance between a key asset and a threat is referred to as the *standoff distance*. There is no ideal standoff distance; it is determined by the type of threat, the layout and construction of the key asset, and the desired level of protection.

Maximizing the standoff distance may be the most cost-effective solution to ensuring adequate protection of a key asset. Maximum standoff distance also ensures that there is an opportunity in the future to upgrade key assets to meet increased threats or to accommodate additional security countermeasures.

Standoff distance must be coupled with appropriate hardening of the key asset to provide the necessary protection.

Operational Security (OPSEC)

OPSEC is a five step analytic risk management process used by military and security personnel to protect sensitive information that adversaries could collect and use to their advantage. OPSEC does not replace other security measures; it supplements them. OPSEC is a fluid process that can be constantly updated and reviewed based on current threats and missions.

According to an al Qaeda training manual for jihad that was recovered in Afghanistan, "using public sources openly and without resorting to illegal means, it is possible to gather at least 80% of the information about the enemy."

The basic concept of OPSEC is that the accumulation of one or more elements of seemingly harmless information could damage security when combined together. Any organization that develops proprietary information needs to protect that information. The goal of OPSEC, therefore, is to deny an adversary these pieces of the intelligence puzzle.

The information that is often used against us is not classified information; it is information that is openly available to anyone who knows where to look and what to ask.

There is nothing new about the principles underlying OPSEC. In fact, we can trace OPSEC practices back to the colonial days and the Revolutionary War. George Washington was a known OPSEC practitioner. General Washington was

1. Identify critical information
2. Conduct a threat analysis
3. Perform a vulnerability analysis
4. Assess risks
5. Implement countermeasures

FIGURE 8.1. Steps to ensure operational security.

quoted as saying: "Even minutiae should have a place in our collection, for things of a seemingly trifling nature, when enjoined with others of a more serious cast, may lead to a valuable conclusion."

The basic premises of OPSEC are the following:

- Any organization that develops proprietary information needs to protect that information.
- OPSEC is a discipline that works with other traditional security programs.
- OPSEC is the study of indicators to detect potential vulnerabilities.
- The whole point of OPSEC is to have a set of operational (daily, habit ingrained) practices that make it harder for another group to compile critical information.

OPSEC is a necessary discipline to protect sensitive information and activities which are susceptible to adversary surveillance and information collection behaviors.

- Prohibit the presence of cell phones and related communication tools in sensitive areas.
- Remove sensitive information from websites and all other sharing venues.
- Refuse discussion of sensitive matters on unsecured communications devices.
- Shred all confidential documents no longer needed regardless of perceived sensitivity.
- Stop leaving sensitive documents in unattended vehicles.
- Ensure access to networks and databases is limited to only those with the need to know.
- Avoid the discussion of sensitive matters in unsecured areas.
- Screen all information that is released to the public through any medium.

The whole point of OPSEC is to have a set of operational practices that make it harder for an adversary to compile critical information about a target.

The Five Step OPSEC Process

1. *Identification of Critical Information.* The purpose of this step is to determine what needs to be protected. This may not be traditional "classified" information, but rather a piece of the puzzle or "indicator" that can reveal a jurisdiction's plans. Critical information can include intentions, capabilities, strengths, limitations, weaknesses, technology, and tactics.

- Basic to the OPSEC process is determining what information, if available to one or more adversaries, would harm a jurisdiction's ability to effectively carry out the operation or activity. As part of the process, the length of time the information needs to be protected should be ascertained.

- What is the value of this information? Is it important to you? Would it be important to someone else? If someone else had access to this information, could it be a threat to you?
- What are some tricks or methods an adversary could use to get this information or resource or perhaps modify it? What are the capabilities of a potential adversary? Could an adversary possibly access and utilize the information?
- How likely is it that someone can get at this information?

2. *Analysis of Threats.* Knowing who the adversaries are, what their capabilities are, and whether they have the intent and capability to harm us is crucial. What information do they require to meet their objectives? This analysis is essential in determining what information is truly critical to a jurisdiction's mission effectiveness. The purpose of this step is to identify all vulnerabilities and/or indicators. An indicator is information obtained from publicly available open sources or from observations of actions that an adversary can exploit to draw conclusions concerning intention, capability, or activity. There are three types of indicators:

- *Profile.* Activity patterns indicate how activities are normally conducted. For example, an adversary observes that the security force always starts its perimeter patrol on the hour, the same route is taken, and the patrol is completed in 15 minutes.
- *Deviation.* Profile changes help an adversary learn about intentions and preparations. For example, security personnel are observed moving metal detectors into place at an entrance portal, leading an adversary to determine that increased security checks will soon be implemented.
- *Tip Off.* Certain actions can warn or show an adversary of impending security. For example, before a show of force detail, security force members are observed taking out their weapons and inspecting them; or security force members may perform radio communication checks and begin to don protective equipment in advance of a drill.

3. *Analysis of Vulnerabilities.* Determining a jurisdiction's vulnerabilities involves systems analysis of how operations or activities are actually conducted by the jurisdiction. The jurisdiction and its activities must be viewed as the adversaries will view it. Perform a vulnerability analysis to determine how an individual or group might disrupt operations or security by using the information. The purpose of this step is to identify possible OPSEC measures for each vulnerability and indicator. Vulnerabilities are opportunities for adversaries to exploit critical information, such as publishing sensitive information on public websites or talking about sensitive matters on cell phones that are easily monitored. Vulnerabilities can be reduced by taking action to maintain protection of essential information by the implementation of appropriate countermeasures. Determine how an adversary might cause an adverse impact by using the information.

4. *Assessment of Risks.* Vulnerabilities and the specific threat must be matched. Assess risks and determine the probability that an adversary will obtain critical information and how that could impact operations. The purpose of this step is to select OPSEC countermeasures for implementation based on the perceived risk. Care must be taken to balance the need for operational success versus implementing the appropriate countermeasures.

5. *Application of Countermeasures.* Countermeasures need to be developed that eliminate the vulnerabilities, threats, or utility of the information to the adversaries. Implement countermeasures to minimize an attacker's ability to discover your weaknesses and strike at your vulnerabilities. The purpose of this step is to implement the selected controls to eliminate indicators or countermeasures to enhance security. Countermeasures should be monitored for effectiveness before, during, and after execution. There should be a mechanism to improve the effectiveness or implement enhanced countermeasures when new vulnerabilities are identified [2].

Practicing OPSEC

- Prohibit the use of cellular phones (which may contain a camera) in the key asset's restricted areas.
- Remove sensitive information such as home addresses and home telephone numbers of key personnel from websites.
- Reconsider providing open houses for the general public at key assets.
- Do not leave sensitive documents unattended on desks or in vehicles.

Example of OPSEC. When you are getting ready to go on a trip, have you ever:

Stopped delivery of newspapers so they would not pile up outside and send a signal that you are not home?

Asked your neighbor to pick up your mail so the mailbox would not fill up, also indicating that you were away?

Connected your porch lights and inside lights to a timer so they would go on at preset times to make it look like someone was home?

Left a vehicle parked in the driveway?

Connected a radio to a timer so that it comes on at various times to make it sound like someone is inside?

If you have done any of these things, you have practiced OPSEC [3].

8.9 SUSPICIOUS ACTIVITY

It is very important that everyone understand they have a part in preventing an adversary attack from occurring. As adversaries begin to plan an operation, suspicious activities may start to increase. One way everyone can participate in everyday counterterrorism efforts is to be aware of these suspicious activities. The general public should refrain from confronting suspicious people or investigating suspicious activity due to the potential risk to themselves. Suspicious activities or circumstances may be an indicator that something is not right and should be reported to local law enforcement authorities immediately for further investigation. The information provided to law enforcement should provide as much detail as possible to facilitate appropriate investigation and follow-up. Nothing is too insignificant.

There are five key things to remember when reporting suspicious activity:

1. What is happening?
2. Who is doing it?
3. Where is it taking place?
4. When did you observe it?
5. Why are you suspicious?

Suspicious people may be observed in vehicles at odd times, exiting secure locations, loitering at nonpublic areas near critical infrastructure/key resources/key assets, wearing odd clothing, or exhibiting odd behavior.

Suspicious vehicles may be abandoned vehicles, possible mobile surveillance units, those with unusual decals or signage or vehicle frame modifications.

Suspicious actions/objects include suspicious packages or luggage left unattended, chemical fires and/or toxic odors, unusual test explosions, illicit access to blueprints or requests to see files and plans, heavy mailed packages with excessive postage, unusual activity, an increase in anonymous telephone or e-mail threats to facilities in conjunction with suspected surveillance activities, and the questioning of personnel at a key asset.

8.10 WHAT CAN BE DONE TO PROTECT PEOPLE AND FACILITIES

An adversary has literally tens of thousands of potential targets spread across the various critical infrastructure sectors, key resources, and key assets from which to choose. In order to protect our people and facilities, we need to convince adversaries that they do not want to risk expending their resources on an attack that is not likely to succeed. Jurisdictions need to implement rings of protection for our critical assets, whether they are people, infrastructure, equipment, products, or intellectual capability.

The basic formula for vulnerability to attack is

$$\text{Intent} \times \text{Motivation} \times \text{Capability} \times \text{Ease}$$

Intent includes the adversary's intentions, such as causing casualties or destroying key assets. *Motivation* is the strategic logic behind an adversary's action, which is typically religious or politically induced. *Capability* is the technical and financial wherewithal necessary for an adversary to plan a mission as well as acquire, assemble, and deploy a weapon against a target. *Ease* is the opportunity afforded an adversary to exploit an existing vulnerability and execute an attack against a key asset.

If any one element is removed, the chain is broken and vulnerability approaches zero. Clearly, the only element over which a single, local jurisdiction will have direct control is ease of attack. Therefore once the threat and vulnerabilities have been assessed, specific security countermeasures must be installed and implemented. It is imperative that a jurisdiction carefully consider each recommendation for reducing vulnerabilities and implement the countermeasures that will yield the biggest bang for the dollar spent.

Remember, adversaries need the attack to be successful in order to justify the expenditure of their scarce resources, so they will not go against strength, or even perceived strength. The countermeasures that are implemented to secure a key asset must convey the perception to the adversary that stringent security policies and procedures are in place, and the target has been sufficiently hardened so that an attack would be unwise. If we are successful in this endeavor, the adversary will be convinced that an attack against this key asset would not succeed and therefore would be a poor investment of resources.

Rings of Protection

Properly selected, developed, and implemented security countermeasures will increase the difficulty of attacking a critical infrastructure, key resource, or key asset and decrease the probability of a successful attack. A well structured protection plan for a key asset will have eight layered, overlapping, and intermixed rings of protection. The greatest advantage occurs when countermeasures have benefits in more than one area.

Rings of protection that are properly deployed will not only provide real security but will also provide a perception of security that goes beyond the actual improvements installed. The chances for success of dissuading an attack increase greatly and become value added when the rings of protection overlap and one enhancement provides value in multiple areas (e.g., a properly trained and equipped security guard can deter, detect, delay, defend, and respond).

The eight rings of protection provide both proactive and reactive countermeasures to secure a key asset from attack by an adversary. The rings of protection that include devalue and deter are *proactive* countermeasures, meaning they are deployed before the adversary arrives at the key asset and generally tend to prevent an aggressive, offensive posture by the adversary. Proactive countermeasures are the preferred method of addressing the adversary threat since they are preventative in nature. The rings of protection that include detect, delay, deny, defend, respond, and recover are *reactive* countermeasures. Reactive countermeasures are those that are designed to identify or stop an adversary once they have arrived at the key asset and have begun to initiate operations against the key asset. Reactive countermeasures generally come into play after the proactive countermeasures have failed or have been breached by the adversary. The reactive countermeasures must be very effective in their design and implementation to ensure that the adversary is caught as early into the operation as possible.

The eight rings of protection are described next.

Devalue. The first ring of protection involves devaluing the target. An adversary will attack a target because it presents one or more attractive characteristics, such as the ability to cause casualties. If a jurisdiction can eliminate the attractiveness possessed by a key asset as a target, the adversary will likely choose not to attack that asset. Therefore the jurisdiction must ascertain what makes a target attractive from an adversary's point of view, and then eliminate (or at least minimize) that characteristic to avoid an attack. Devaluing tactics include things such as reducing inventories of hazardous substances or substituting a less hazardous substance for the more dangerous one, spreading out groups of people or hazardous materials into smaller quantities over large areas, and moving high-level officials from a building.

Example of Devaluing a Target. An adversary has ascertained through surveillance that a municipal water treatment facility stores two railcars on its property, each containing 90 tons of liquid chlorine. The adversary has used commercially available software to model the effects of a release of the chlorine. The software reveals that if the railcar is breached, the liquid will rapidly vaporize and be carried downwind into the nearby town, where 80,000 people could be adversely affected by the chlorine gas. The adversary moves into the next phase of the attack plan by formulating a plan involving the breaching of the chlorine-containing railcars using an explosive device.

The water treatment facility has an assessment team conduct a security vulnerability assessment and the team has determined that the chlorine-containing railcars make an attractive target for an adversary. The team follows the rings of protection theory when developing recommendations for security countermeasures. The team arrives at the conclusion that if the chlorine is removed from the water treatment plant area, the facility is no longer a very attractive target. The team begins to evaluate the need for the chlorine and discovers that the usage rate of chlorine is such that the inventory can be reduced from 180 tons of liquid chlorine stored in two railcars to 6 tons of gaseous chlorine stored in cylinders. Thus, by changing the physical characteristics of the chlorine from the much more dangerous liquid state to the gaseous state, and reducing the inventory down to 6 tons, the team has devalued the attractiveness of the facility as a target. Once the adversary becomes aware of the change in inventory, he/she is likely to abandon this facility as a potential target as the casualties resulting from a breach of the smaller gaseous chlorine containers are significantly less than what the adversary wants to achieve with this type of attack.

Deter. The second ring of protection, and the first in terms of hardening a potential target, is to deter adversaries before they can plan or execute an attack against a key asset. Remember, perception is reality to adversaries. Every critical infrastructure, key resource, and key asset is a potential target, so there are plenty of choices to select from and plenty of opportunity to attempt an attack. The best indicator that an asset may be targeted is direct observation or evidence that an asset is or has been under surveillance by an adversary. Therefore the goal at this outermost ring of protection is to scare the adversary away before start of the surveillance operation. The countermeasures installed need to be highly visible so as to convince the adversary that the chance of successfully surveilling or executing an attack against this asset is low, and not worth expending resources there. In order to ensure an adversary can observe the countermeasures, there should be some obvious systems installed at the perimeter of the key asset, which can be viewed from the public domain. Experience has shown that adversaries will reconnoiter a target before executing an attack, so if we can scare them away before they even start the operation, we can interrupt the planning process and avoid being targeted. Examples of deter include highly visible and professional appearing security forces that make frequent, random patrols as well as fixed and manned security points; appropriate levels of fencing, lighting, access control, and intrusion detection; and provisions for personnel and vehicle inspections, as well as identification and background checks of individuals as one gets closer to the critical asset.

Example of Deter. As part of its security vulnerability assessment, the municipal water treatment plant's assessment determines that the chlorine containing railcars are the primary key asset that would be targeted by an adversary. Therefore the assessment team develops the appropriate deterrent countermeasures that would be recommended for implementation to scare adversaries away before they could cause harm to the key asset:

- Install 8 foot high chain link fencing with screening so adversaries cannot easily observe the railcars from the public way surrounding the water treatment plant. Landscaping may also be used to screen the key asset so adversaries do not have a clear line of sight to the potential target. Something as simple as planting some hedges to obstruct the view of the target might be enough to deter adversaries. If adversaries cannot observe the target area and collect intelligence about it, they certainly cannot plan an operation.
- Install an intrusion detection system tied into a closed circuit camera system that would sound an alarm in the security office if an intruder was in the area of the railcars.
- Hire professional security guards to secure the facility. The guards would make frequent, random patrols of the perimeter of the facility to observe for suspicious activity.
- Purchase night vision equipment for the security guards to use as they make their patrols at night.
- Install lighting to assist the security guards in their observation of the perimeter.
- Develop and implement a stringent access control procedure that would deter unauthorized personnel from attempting to gain access to the facility.

Detect. The third ring of protection is detecting the adversary. The earlier the planning, reconnaissance of the key asset, or attack itself is discovered and interrupted, the less likely it is to succeed. Optimally, the threat should be detected during the planning or reconnaissance stage by having systems in place to reveal the presence of the adversary trying to collect intelligence about the key asset. Training employees about specific activities that should be considered suspicious and how to report this to the appropriate authority would be the outermost level of detection. Background checks and searches are valuable in screening potential employees, contractors, truck drivers, and visitors before they enter the facility. Detection can also occur during the intelligence stage conducted by law enforcement agencies. It is very helpful to have a system in place to share information between law enforcement agencies and critical infrastructure, key resources, and key assets. This shared information can be used to monitor and identify the threat before it penetrates the key asset's perimeter. Intrusion detection systems, surveillance cameras, alarms, and frequent, random inspection rounds by security guards make up the innermost level of the detect ring.

Example of Detect. The water treatment plant's assessment team has developed a number of security countermeasures that will help to detect the presence of an adversary. As the assessment team has deduced that the adversary will likely be reconnoitering the chlorine-containing railcars in order to gather the intelligence necessary to plan and execute an attack, the primary resources will be allocated to detecting an adversary in this area of the key asset. As mentioned previously, security countermeasures are particularly efficient and cost effective if they provide beneficial enhancements in more than one ring of protection. For this example, many of the security countermeasures that would be implemented in the deter ring of protection could also be applied in this ring as well. Among the possible enhancements to help detect an adversary are the following:

- Install an intrusion detection system. As the railcars are close to the property line of the water treatment facility, it will be possible for an adversary to view the railcars and activities occurring within the facility by staying in the public way. By installing an intrusion detection system, the facility security guards would be made aware if someone were to approach the fence line. The effectiveness of the intrusion detection system can be enhanced by tying it into a closed circuit camera system. If the intrusion detection system were to sound an alarm, the security guard could observe the area remotely using a security camera to ascertain the conditions in the area (e.g., alarm set off by an intruder or by an animal).
- Develop and implement a robust background check procedure. If the adversary cannot get close enough or observe the target area to gather intelligence from the public way, he/she may try to gain access to it from the inside. A possible way an adversary can gain access to the inside of the perimeter would be to attempt to gain entry as an employee, contractor, visitor, or delivery person.

Therefore the key asset should develop a comprehensive background check for all persons attempting to gain access to the facility.

- A specific training program should be developed and presented to all personnel who normally work at the key asset. This training program should include a review of what the threats are against the facility, which key assets an adversary might attempt to exploit or attack, what activities are considered suspicious, and what an employee should do if suspicious circumstances are observed. As part of the training program, there should be a reporting system established, which will ensure all pertinent information regarding suspicious activity is collected and reported to the proper authority immediately.
- A search procedure for all persons, packages, and vehicles entering (and leaving if something can be removed from the facility and used as a WMD elsewhere) the facility should be implemented. It is possible that an adversary might try to smuggle a weapon into the facility to initiate an attack by posing as a visitor or delivery person. Therefore the search procedure should call for the inspection of all parcels and vehicles at a location remote from the key asset.

Deny. The fourth ring of protect is to deny the adversary the ability to cause casualties or damage to key assets by designing or using infrastructure or equipment that can withstand the effects of a weapon of mass destruction.

Example of Deny. The water treatment facility's assessment team has recommended the implementation of a number of security countermeasures that, if installed, will result in less damage to the facility and less casualties on site. These recommendations include:

- The glass windows in the office building should be replaced with a blast resistant design that will not shatter in the event of a detonation. If the possibility of flying glass from windows shattered by a detonation can be reduced, casualties will be reduced.
- Heating, ventilating, and air conditioning system filters in the office building should be replaced with filters that can eliminate the entry of a chemical, biological, or radiological agent into the building.
- Decorative concrete planters should be positioned around the key assets at the facility to prevent explosive-laden vehicles from getting close enough to the key assets to cause significant damage.
- Key structures on site should be reinforced to withstand the effects of a vehicle bomb.
- Remote access to the facility's computer network should be physically disconnected when not in use to prevent an adversary from hacking into it.

Delay. The fifth ring of protection is to delay the adversary. If we are unable to deter or detect the adversary, and the adversary is able to gain access to the key asset, there must be sufficient physical and administrative barriers in place to make it difficult to gain clear, unimpeded, easy, and direct access to the targeted key asset. Typical delaying tactics include remote check-in points before entering a key asset; verification of identity and purpose of visit; searching of people, parcels, and vehicles; multiple layers of fencing or other physical blocking devices such as tire shredders and "jersey barriers"; and locked doors with access control systems.

Example of Delay. The water treatment facility's assessment team has realized that if an adversary has penetrated the third ring of protection, that adversary is now very close to successfully executing an attack. Therefore the assessment team has developed a number of delaying countermeasures that can be implemented to stop the adversary from having direct access to the chlorine containing railcars.

The assessment team has recognized that the adversary's weapon of choice in executing this attack will be an explosive device. The explosive device can be delivered in one of two ways: carried by a vehicle or carried by a person.

The delaying tactics that could be recommended in the case of a vehicle-borne device are the following:

- Install concrete "jersey" barriers both on the access road to the chlorine-containing railcars and surrounding the railcars. Placement of the barriers in the roadway will necessitate that the vehicle drive slowly, making it likely it could be stopped by the other countermeasures in place. By surrounding the railcars with concrete barriers, a standoff distance has been created. The vehicle is unlikely to be able to penetrate through the barriers; therefore it will not be close enough, even if the device is detonated, to allow for significant damage to the railcars, which could lead to a release of the liquid chlorine.
- Tire shredders can be installed along the road that leads to the railroad cars. These devices will shred the tires of a vehicle and are effective at stopping vehicles. By placing the shredders at several locations enroute to the railcars, there is a good chance the vehicle will be stopped before it reaches the target.
- A soil berm several feet high could be installed around the railcars. The berm would have a steep angle, making it unlikely that a vehicle could negotiate its way over it and access the railcars.

The delaying tactics that could be recommended in the case of a backpack device carried by a person are the following:

- Eight foot high fencing topped with three strands of barbed wire surrounding the railcars would be effective in stopping an intruder short of the intended target.
- An aggressive search procedure that includes all packages and parcels carried by individuals and vehicles into the facility would likely discover a person trying to smuggle an explosive device into the facility. The checkpoint should be located far enough away from key assets at the facility so that if

the device were detonated at the checkpoint it would not adversely impact key assets at the facility.

Defend. There are times when a key asset may have to be defended as a last ditch effort to protect the asset from harm. Not all key assets warrant a defense; only those assets that are of extremely high value or that, if successfully attacked, would lead to a catastrophic impact would typically be defended. Defending tactics include the use of weapons such as armed security, law enforcement, or military personnel; military weapons such as armored vehicles or helicopters; or other defensive systems that would present the application of deadly force against a potential adversary. As an example, U.S. airlines frequently have armed air marshals aboard should an adversary try to commandeer an aircraft. As a last ditch defensive measure, some pilots are now armed with handguns in the cockpit in case all other countermeasures fail and the adversary is able to breach the cockpit door.

Example of Defend. The assessment team has come to the conclusion that if an adversary successfully accesses the chlorine-containing railcars, the casualties in the community that will result from the escaping chlorine gas will be extremely high. Because of that conclusion, the team has made a recommendation to implement defensive countermeasures if the specific intelligence available indicates the threat to the facility is high and an attack is likely. The defensive countermeasures recommended will also provide some degree of deterrence if the adversary becomes aware of the increased hardening of the facility. Among the recommended defensive countermeasures that could be considered are the following:

- Uniformed and highly visible national guard troops will conduct continuous patrols of the perimeter in armored vehicles equipped with automatic weapons 24 hours per day.
- Armed local law enforcement personnel will supplement the security guards and assume responsibility for searching employees, contractors, visitors, and truck drivers, their parcels, and vehicles. Marked police cars will be parked at the various entrances to the facility as a form of deterrence.
- There will be armed guards stationed around the chlorine-containing railcars to provide last ditch defense in the event an adversary penetrates all of the other countermeasures. These guards will have the authorization to use deadly force in order to stop an adversary.

Respond. If all else fails, the jurisdiction must have the appropriate capability to respond to the likely consequences of a successful attack by an adversary. Emergency preplanning activities in preparation for an emergency must change focus from the traditional "accidental" damage scenario, which usually results in minor damage and few casualties, to the current "on purpose" scenario whereby an adversary is intentionally trying to cause the greatest amount of damage and casualties. In the past, fire and emergency medical responders typically participated in the development of pre-emergency plans. Local law enforcement agencies must now also participate in the pre-emergency planning process to address security issues. Careful review and coordination of both the municipal and private industry joint response capabilities and equipment must be completed, with clearly delineated areas of responsibility. Interoperability of all responding jurisdictions should become a priority. Interoperability means all of the responding jurisdictions share common communications frequencies, equipment, and operating procedures to facilitate an effective response. There must also be redundant capabilities for communications and mitigation plans and equipment. Joint pre-emergency planning and periodic emergency exercises between the key asset and fire, emergency medical services, and law enforcement increase the chances of good response in the event of a successful attack. A strong emergency response capability can also serve as a deterrent to an attack if the adversaries believe the consequences will be quickly and successfully mitigated.

Example of Respond. The water treatment facility's assessment team has developed several recommendations to deal with the unlikely scenario of an adversary circumventing all of the other rings of protection and executing a successful attack against the railcars. If the adversary is successful and breaches the railcars, resulting in a release of chlorine, a timely and effective response is necessary to minimize the number of casualties. The assessment team has recognized that if the key asset and local emergency responders work together to mitigate the incident, the likelihood of success is great. Therefore the team's recommendations include a number of items relating to shared responsibility for emergency response and interoperability.

- The emergency response plan should be modified to call for shared responsibility for emergency response. Clear lines of responsibility should be developed for both the water treatment facility as well as the local emergency responders.
- Personal protective equipment and mitigation equipment that is purchased to support emergency response operations at the key asset should be compatible between the key asset and the local emergency responders.
- Emergency response personal protective equipment and mitigation equipment should be dispersed at several locations within the key asset to local emergency responders to avoid having the equipment inaccessible or destroyed in a successful attack.
- Communications systems should be synchronized so that the key asset can communicate directly with the emergency responders in the event of an attack. Backup, redundant communication systems should also be developed.
- Emergency response operating procedures should be standardized between the key asset and local emergency responders. This will greatly facilitate operations in the event of an attack.
- Emergency response drills and exercises should be conducted frequently and should involve both the key asset and local emergency responders. A thorough postexercise analysis should be conducted to identify weaknesses in the plans or procedures and the appropriate corrective actions should be taken.

Recover. If all else fails and the attack is successful, the emergency response activities will commence. Once the emergency has been stabilized, the recovery ring is activated. Recovery involves all the activities necessary to repair the degraded or destroyed products or services of the key asset. Recovery operations actually begin well before the attack occurs. The key asset should have developed a business continuity plan, which will detail how the key asset will get back into operation. Typically, the recovery plan will address things such as how to replace personnel injured or killed in the attack; how damaged equipment can be expeditiously repaired or replaced; and alternate means to provide the product or service, such as using an alternate supplier.

Example of Recovery. The assessment team for the water treatment facility has identified the facility as a piece of critical infrastructure. As such, it is important that a recovery plan (or business continuity plan) be established in the event the facility is degraded or destroyed in an attack. Among the recommendations from the assessment team are the following:

- A plan to replace injured or killed workers should be developed. The water treatment facility has a sister operation in another nearby town. The employees located at the sister facility are familiar with the general operation of this facility. It is recommended that once per year employees from the sister facility visit this facility to refresh themselves on the specific operations and equipment located here. These individuals will be available to fill positions if necessary.
- An up-to-date phone list should be created listing all personnel at both this facility as well as the sister facility. This list should be readily available in the event an attack occurs and employees need to be replaced to repair or operate the facility.
- An inventory of all critical equipment should be created. This list should include the part numbers, suppliers, cost, and availability for delivery. In the event the facility is attacked and the equipment is damaged or destroyed, it is critical to make repairs and start up the operation as soon as possible. By creating this list in advance of the attack, valuable time can be saved.
- A contingency plan should be developed in case the facility is destroyed or degraded to the point where it cannot provide its services.

  Is there an alternate facility that can provide the lost services?

  Is there a supplier who can provide chlorine if the railcars are destroyed?

  Is there a supplier who can replace damaged or destroyed equipment quickly?

8.11 CONCLUSION

Every asset is a potential target, and every asset can be protected. The adversary needs an attack to be successful and therefore will not go against a perceived strength. Our job is to establish overlapping and intermixed rings that will provide perceived and actual protection against an adversary's attack. The only real defense we have in preventing an attack against our asset is to eliminate the adversary's perception that an attack can easily be executed. We must revisit our hazard assessments and emergency preplans with an eye toward the intentional act and the more severe consequences this type of a successful attack will bring. We must work closely not only with the fire and emergency medical services, but with law enforcement as well in the planning and execution of emergency plans, procedures, and exercises. We must partner with the local municipal emergency responders to pool our personnel and equipment to ensure the quickest, most efficient, and safest response in the event of an attack.

REFERENCES

1. *United for a Stronger America: Citizens Preparedness Guide*, US Freedom Corps, 2002, page 2.
2. U.S. Coast Guard, 7th Coast Guard District.
3. www.defendamerica.mil/articles/a021202b.html.

CHAPTER 9

Effective Security Countermeasures

9.1 INTRODUCTION

"The fact that we are arguably the world's most powerful nation does not bestow invulnerability; in fact, it may make us a larger target for those who don't share our interests, values, or beliefs.... We must take care to be on guard watching our every step and looking far ahead" [1].

Once all of the characterizations, screenings, and analysis of the key assets have been completed, it is time to implement the appropriate security countermeasures (also known as protective measures) to minimize the threat of attack and thereby reduce risk. In Chapter 7, the mantra of "If it's predictable, it's preventable" was introduced. Remember that protective measures cannot be implemented if what needs protection is unknown. We have already discussed how an attack may be predictable by observing and reporting suspicious activities. In this chapter, we present concepts that will prevent an adversary attack against a critical infrastructure, key asset, or key resource. If the security countermeasures are not able to prevent a successful attack, they should be able to mitigate the effects of the deliberate efforts to destroy, incapacitate, or exploit the key asset without disruption or incapacitation.

It is a well established fact that key assets cannot prevent or protect against all known or suspected adversary threats. However, there are reasonable measures and approaches that can be taken for certain threats that pose an unreasonable risk to the key assets. When expending scarce resources to enhance security countermeasures, priority should be given to those threats that are more likely to occur and pose an unacceptable risk.

The key to justification of committing resources to improve security at a key asset is a risk assessment. As part of the risk assessment, security countermeasures should be developed to reduce the adverse impact on the key asset based on the threat and should be installed with the intent of reducing the risk posed by the threat to an acceptable level.

When developing security countermeasures that deal with people, we should not profile individuals; rather, we should profile behaviors that put key assets at risk.

Understanding, Assessing, and Responding to Terrorism: Protecting Critical Infrastructure and Personnel By Brian T. Bennett

Potential adversaries come in all shapes and sizes, both genders, and all races and ethnicities. The implementation of security countermeasures should not infringe on people's rights guaranteed in the U.S. Constitution.

9.2 COUNTERTERRORISM POLICY: NATIONAL SECURITY STRATEGY

Current U.S. policy in countering terrorism was first stated by the Reagan administration and has been reaffirmed by every president since:

1. The United States will make no concessions to terrorists.
2. The United States will treat terrorists as criminals and apply the rule of law.
3. The United States will apply maximum pressure on state sponsors of terrorism.

The Clinton administration added a corollary to these rules:

4. The United States will help other governments improve their capabilities to combat terrorism.

9.3 HARDENING

Hardening is simply the process of making a key asset more robust so that it can resist an attack with a minimum of casualties and damage. Since hardening is concerned with minimizing damage to a key asset, hardening techniques can run the gamut from something as simple as a sandbag to as complex as adding structural members to provide additional support. Strengthening can be defined as the measures taken to increase the overall strength and stability of a structure. Strengthening and hardening are often used together to protect key assets.

Examples of hardening a building include:

- *Windows.* Block up all unnecessary windows, reduce the size of windows by partially boarding them up, and/or remove glass from windows (glass is a major cause of injury in explosions).
- *Doors.* Block up unnecessary doors, keep doors closed when not in use, use horizontal beams to hold door closed, clad wooden doors with metal plates, and rehang doors to open out instead of in.
- *Walls.* Mound up earth outside the building to create a berm.

9.4 WHAT ARE SECURITY COUNTERMEASURES?

Security countermeasures usually include personnel, equipment, and procedures intended to safeguard a critical infrastructure, key resource, or key asset against threats or to mitigate the effects of a successful attack. Selected countermeasures can be implemented on a permanent basis to serve as routine protection for a key asset, while others are implemented only during periods of increased threats or heightened alert.

Security countermeasures should be applied to all critical infrastructures, key resources, or key assets that are vulnerable to natural, accidental, or intentional hazards and are at serious risk of degradation or loss in the event the hazard is applied. There are many different security countermeasures that can be implemented. Some are simple and cost very little, some are complex and expensive, and others are the result of creativity and ingenuity. Many are applicable to a wide range of threats, while others are designed to meet the unique needs of a specific threat. Some security countermeasures may be tactical, but others may address long-term strategic requirements. However, the overall intent in implementing security countermeasures is to make the adversary's effort to execute a successful attack too great.

Resources to implement security countermeasures should be allocated in proportion to the risk from an attack.

Security countermeasures should be coordinated with the rings of protection, which were covered in Chapter 8. Protective actions installed at a key asset should include:

- Countermeasures that devalue: systems that minimize the adverse impacts of a successful attack.
- Countermeasures that deter: systems that reduce the adversaries' interest in the target.
- Countermeasures that detect: systems that indicate a potential threat.
- Countermeasures that delay: systems that make access to the target difficult.
- Countermeasures that defend: systems that provide self-defense.
- Countermeasures that respond: systems that mitigate the adverse impact of a threat.
- Countermeasures that recover: systems that help repair and restore the key asset to a functional level.

Each ring of security countermeasures can be thought of as a sieve, reducing the size of the threat that may gain access to the key asset. The rings of protection should overlap and provide layered protection. Layers of protection are simply several protective systems that work together to reduce the likelihood of an undesirable event.

An adversary could respond to security countermeasures by targeting a different key asset that is less protected. The risk of an attack could be shifted from a normally high profile, attractive target to another key asset that is normally considered safe and would not otherwise be considered a primary target.

The threat of terrorism is dynamic in that it adapts to current conditions. The same tactics used at one target could be very effective, while being ineffective at another target. For example, an adversary could choose to use a car bomb to execute an attack. The soft target could be a hotel, and the attack could cause a large number of casualties and a considerable amount of damage. The adversary could use the same tactic and attack a hardened target, such as a federal building. The chances are the number of casualties and the amount of physical damage will be much less due to the fact the building was hardened.

As a reminder, the installation of effective security countermeasures should not be seen as a panacea for all potential adversary threats. Risk reduction does not necessarily equal risk elimination.

Types of Security Countermeasures

Security countermeasures can differ in terms of feasibility, expense, and effectiveness. They can be simple or complex actions limited only by one's imagination and creativity.

There are two basic types of security countermeasures (also called protective measures) that can be implemented to enhance the security systems that have been designed to protect a key asset: (1) physical systems (both passive and active) and (2) administrative systems (procedural). Together, these elements provide a systems approach to protecting critical assets.

Physical Systems. Physical systems are those security countermeasures that tend to harden a key asset from an attack by an adversary. Physical systems are tangible and include equipment such as fences, cameras, and intrusion detection systems. Passive measures function simply because they exist such as doors, windows, and fences. Active measures involve actions, such as installing barriers, locks, alarms, and intrusion detection systems.

Physical security countermeasures mitigate the threat from inside and outside the key asset. A physical security program may include deterrence and prevention strategies. A systems approach is advisable, where detection, assessment, communication, and response are planned and supported by adequate policies, procedures, and resources.

Administrative Systems. Administrative systems are policies and procedures that are developed and implemented to enhance the security of a key asset. Administrative systems are designed to install procedural barriers that are implemented to protect the key asset: for example background checks, access control procedures, and personnel and vehicle search procedures.

There are a number of administrative enhancements that can be made to strengthen the security at critical infrastructure, key resources, and key assets. When developing these administrative procedures, they should be customized to fit the specific circumstances that exist at the key asset. Care must be taken when developing these policies and procedures to ensure they are applicable and can be fully implemented; avoid writing rules that will not be fully implemented and enforced. Also, this is an opportunity to protect the key asset not only from an adversary but also from general loss. With this in mind, the policies and procedures should be expanded to enhance good security practices.

The policies and procedures should be safeguarded from general distribution so as to protect the integrity of the security program. The contents of the policies and procedures should be communicated only on a need to know basis.

When prohibitive costs or other factors delay the installation of active physical security countermeasures, there is a greater consideration and dependence on administrative countermeasures. The implementation of administrative countermeasures serves as an acceptable alternative means to avoid unacceptable risk and to provide a proactive response in protecting key assets.

Pros and Cons of the Two Types of Security Countermeasures

Security countermeasures must also be designed to prevent and mitigate attacks from both inside and outside the key asset. For example, cyber security countermeasures mitigate the threat posed to the key asset from outside the organization. Employee background checks mitigate the threat from inside the organization.

Remember that there are key assets other than people and physical assets that need to be protected with appropriate security countermeasures. Protecting potentially sensitive information reduces the likelihood that information could be exploited by those intending to utilize it to perpetrate an attack, which could damage key assets, disrupt operations, or harm individuals.

Although it may appear on the surface that the installation of physical systems always provides the best opportunity to enhance security, that is not always the case. Although physical systems can certainly improve security at a key asset, they are often expensive to install and have annually recurring costs. For example, a recommendation may be made to hire armed security guards to protect a key asset. There is a significant amount of cost associated with this option, such as:

Installation of a guard shack or other workstation.

Supervision and/or management of the security guards.

Uniforms.

Weapons and ammunition.

Salary and benefits.

Training.

Some of these costs, such as training, are annually recurring costs that typically increase each year.

Although it may not appear as obvious, administrative systems are often more cost effective and, in most cases, more efficient in assuring that a key asset can be properly secured. Well written, comprehensive administrative systems often provide the foundation for effective security systems as they provide the policies and procedures that set the operational aspects of the key asset in terms of security. Administrative systems are relatively easy and inexpensive to develop. Once they have been implemented, there are little annually recurring costs to maintain these systems.

Implementation of Security Countermeasures

Security countermeasures should be installed commensurate with the risks that exist at a key asset. The installation of appropriate security countermeasures can consume a considerable amount of resources in terms of time, effort, and material. Oftentimes, these otherwise effective countermeasures are compromised because of inadequate forethought being devoted to ensure an adversary could not figure out a way to circumvent them. One of the easiest ways for an adversary to develop a plan to bypass installed security countermeasures is through the surveillance phase of the operation. To maintain their effectiveness, the security countermeasures that are implemented should not be repetitious or predictable. For example, a key asset may employ armed and very highly trained security guards who make periodic rounds to inspect the perimeter of the key asset. However, if the rounds are made at the same time and follow the same route every time, an adversary can figure out a way to bypass that particular security countermeasure and exploit that observation to advantage. Therefore, whenever possible, security countermeasures should be changed in a random, unpredictable manner to maximize their effectiveness. Here's an example.

Day	Security Countermeasure Week 1	Security Countermeasure Week 2
Monday	Random vehicle inspection	Everyone goes through a metal detector
Tuesday	Extra random security patrols	Double the security force
Wednesday	Use alternate entrance	All packages searched
Thursday	All vehicles are inspected	Everyone entering gets patted down
Friday	Show of force demonstration	Municipal police supplement guard force
Saturday	Change layout to entrance	Bomb dog checks all vehicles
Sunday	Security guards are armed	Helicopter used for surveillance

Security countermeasures that are implemented should be *redundant*—if a component of a countermeasure fails, other countermeasures can take over for the failed component until the component is repaired; and *resilient*—if part of a countermeasure fails, the overall system is able to maintain at least partial functionality.

Security countermeasures should provide (1) protection for vulnerabilities that pose an unacceptable risk, (2) balanced protection commensurate with the risks, (3) appropriate protection that reduces the risks to an acceptable level, and (4) layered protection in depth, which means that an adversary would be required to avoid or defeat several protective devices in sequence to achieve a successful attack.

No security countermeasure will reduce the likelihood of attack to zero. Adversaries who are determined to cause malicious events will be difficult to completely stop. Security countermeasures recommended in the security vulnerability analysis should be feasible and should make it more difficult for adversaries to reach the targets of concern. For example, security countermeasures designed to repel a determined, armed attack on a target by multiple paramilitary adversaries are not appropriate for most key assets. However, countermeasures to detect the presence of such an attack force and to quickly sound an alarm or call for help are appropriate.

9.5 MANAGEMENT OF CHANGE

Key assets should consider implementing a management of change procedure to ensure that any and all physical, procedural, or operational changes that may impact security be analyzed before they are implemented. Changes should be evaluated to determine (1) if the introduction of the change makes the key asset more vulnerable; (2) if there are risks associated with the changes; (3) if the new risks are acceptable or unacceptable; (4) if the benefits offered by the change are greater than the risks they represent; and (5) if new or enhanced security countermeasures are warranted.

For example, based on the flow of visitors, a key asset determines that additional parking space must be provided to accommodate the influx of vehicles. Currently, visitors park their vehicles in a parking garage one block away from the key asset. However, that garage has reached capacity. The key asset formulates a plan to purchase a vacant lot immediately adjacent to its property and build a parking lot.

The management of change procedure should be implemented to analyze the effects of the change: (1) the change will make the key asset more vulnerable as vehicles (possibly packed with explosives) will be parked close to the key asset; (2) the risks associated with this change include the possibility of physical damage and casualties if a vehicle bomb is detonated; (3) the risks are unacceptable and must be reduced; (4) the benefits of the change are greater assuming the risks can be reduced; and (5) new security countermeasures, both physical and administrative, will be required to manage the risks associated with the change.

If the risks are extensive, a full security vulnerability analysis may need to be conducted to ensure completeness in the evaluation of the treats, hazards, and risks.

9.6 RISK MANAGEMENT

Risk management is part of the common sense employed on a daily basis. Individuals and organizations balance the cost of a protective measure against risk that is mitigated.

Minimizing risk is the fundamental reason why individuals and organizations carry out security measures. All security-related activities are part of risk management. Risk management decisions are involved in the entire life cycle of the key asset.

9.7 CRITICAL INFRASTRUCTURE RESILIENCY

There has been a recent development in the area of critical infrastructure protection called resiliency. Resiliency has been touted as a cost-effective alternative to key asset protection. Resiliency refers to the ability of a jurisdiction to expeditiously recover and reconstitute, with minimum disruption, a key asset's ability to produce a product or provide service after a successful attack. Resiliency may have some benefit, especially when critical infrastructures, key resources, or key assets cannot be adequately protected from all threats because of insufficient resources. Resiliency embraces the concept of acceptable losses.

The Infrastructure Security Partnership (www.tisp.org) has made a subtle but important change in its focus from critical infrastructure protection to critical infrastructure resilience. This paradigm shift has been initiated because of the recognition that it is nearly impossible to protect key assets against all major threats and disasters, and therefore resiliency should be the goal. A resilient key asset is "one that has the capability to withstand significant incidents or attacks with some damage and then recover to provide critical services with minimum downtime or damage to public safety and health, the economy, and security."

The Multidisciplinary Center for Earthquake Engineering Research (Buffalo, New York) created a framework for measuring resiliency: *robustness* (strength to withstand the hit), *redundancy* (containing elements that are substitutable to continue the function), *resourcefulness* (capacity to identify problems and mobilize resources), and *rapidity* (speed of recovery).

Continuity of Operations

Not only must critical infrastructure, key resources, and key assets be protected from physical damage, they must also be protected so as to provide the continuation of their crucial functions during any emergency that may degrade or incapacitate normal operations. The *continuity of operations planning* (COOP) process specifically addresses the people, materials, and systems necessary for recovery of mission tasks. The COOP process enhances the survivability of the key asset and its vital products and services.

Every key asset should have a plan that specifies step-by-step recovery procedures to follow during and after a natural or intentional disaster. The COOP process identifies the critical and time sensitive applications, vital records, processes, and functions that must be maintained, as well as the personnel and procedures necessary to do so.

A summary of the COOP process is the following:

- Involve all stakeholders in the planning process.
- Acquire the total commitment of all stakeholders to successfully finalize a COOP process.
- Write up the COOP process and safeguard the document.
- Include preplanning strategies as well as recovery activities.

- Pinpoint what would cause mission failure and how to mitigate those causes.
- Identify the key assets and essential tasks for appropriate protective measures.
- Define who will be responsible to complete each crucial response and recovery task.
- Prepare succession lists for the jurisdiction's senior leadership as well as all other essential tasks.
- Select and equip an alternate site from which to sustain operations when necessary.
- Establish redundant voice and data communications and cyber systems.
- Determine actions when logistics (e.g., fuel, supply, and repair) are disrupted.
- Protect vital records and operations plans from damage or loss.
- Ascertain what automatic and mutual aid can be expected under all conditions.
- Annually train, test, evaluate, and revise the COOP process.

A COOP process reduces the likelihood of prolonged interruptions and enhances prompt resumption of key services and product manufacture.

Continuity of Government

Just as it is important to maintain continuity of operations to ensure key products and services are provided, it is also important to ensure *continuity of government* (COG).

Continuity of government refers to the continued functioning of constitutional government under all circumstances including terrorist attacks or natural disasters. Arrangements for the continued operation of the federal government are specified in numerous documents, some of which are classified and thus not available to the general public.

Continuity of government assures provisions are in place to (1) quickly fill vacancies in elected positions, (2) ensure succession of key leadership positions, and (3) achieve quorums for legislative sessions, especially involving cases where legislators are temporarily incapacitated.

Actions that have recently been implemented to ensure continuity of the federal government include the following:

- President George W. Bush has signed several Executive Orders prescribing the line of succession within the departments in the event that a cabinet secretary is killed or incapacitated.
- Federal departments and agencies have been assigned emergency preparedness responsibilities, including planning for the continuity of government.
- Evacuation plans have been developed for the president and other principal executive officials to locales outside the seat of government.
- Relocation has been determined for key officials to secondary or satellite management centers where they can continue to perform their administrative responsibilities.

Local jurisdictions, both public and private sectors, should follow the lead of the federal government to ensure emergency planning, including the lines of succession for key officials, is completed in a timely manner to ensure continued efficient operations and management.

9.8 CRITICAL INFRASTRUCTURE PROTECTION

Critical infrastructure protection (CIP) is the proactive system of activities used to protect the indispensable people, physical assets, and cyber systems that we depend on. More formally, it is the analytical process to guide the systematic protection of critical infrastructures by the application of a reliable decision sequence to determine exactly what needs protection and when security measures must occur [2]. The objective of critical infrastructure protection is to deter or mitigate attacks on critical infrastructure. The process ensures the protection of only those infrastructures on which survivability and mission success actually depend. Critical infrastructure protection involves the application of a systemic analytical process fully integrated into all plans and operations.

The basic tenets of homeland security are fundamentally different from the historically defined tenets of national security. Traditionally, national security has been recognized largely as the responsibility of the federal government. National security is underpinned by the collective efforts of the military, foreign policy establishment, and intelligence community in the defense of our airspace and national borders, as well as operations overseas to protect our national interests. Homeland security, particularly in the context of critical infrastructure and key asset protection, is a shared responsibility that cannot be accomplished by the federal government alone. It requires coordinated action on the part of federal, state, and local governments; the private sector; and concerned citizens across the country [3].

Critical Infrastructure Protection Process Question Navigator [4]

- Is the person, thing, or system part of the organization's infrastructure?
- Is this infrastructure essential for survivability and mission success?
- Is there potential for deliberate, natural, or accidental attack (threats) against this critical infrastructure?
- Is the threat of an attack against this critical infrastructure a truly credible one?
- Is there a security vulnerability (or weakness) in the threatened critical infrastructure?
- Does this vulnerability (or weakness) render the critical infrastructure susceptible to disruption or loss?
- Is it acceptable to assume risk and delay the allocation of resources and the application of security countermeasures?
- Apply security countermeasures to protect this critical infrastructure as soon as available resources permit.

The CIP process is an all hazards discipline that guides the jurisdiction to consider threats (i.e., plausible sources of an attack) from all hazards. There is the possibility of multiple threats against critical infrastructure; only threats that will potentially degrade survivability, continuity of operations, and mission accomplishment are pertinent in this process. This determination enables leaders to focus on the guiding principle for threat analysis: apply precious resources to protect only those critical infrastructures against which a credible threat exists.

Critical infrastructure protection can reduce the chances of some future attacks, make it more difficult for the attacks to succeed or degrade critical infrastructure, and mitigate the adverse effects when attacks are successful. Critical infrastructure protection may also be a means to change the behavior of adversaries. The proper protection of critical infrastructure has the potential to develop a new mindset among terrorists that their actions will be futile and not yield the results they seek.

From a municipal perspective, the CIP philosophy is to first protect those critical infrastructures absolutely required for citizen survivability and continuity of crucial community operations.

Follow-up

Once all of the recommendations for security system enhancements have been reviewed and the appropriate ones selected for implementation, a person should be assigned responsibility to ensure the security countermeasures are installed as per the plan and on schedule. Periodic updates should be provided to the jurisdiction's chief executive so he/she is apprised of the current work status.

Coordination with Local Agencies

A well developed and thoroughly integrated communications program between the key asset and the local law enforcement and emergency response agencies ensures the effectiveness of threat response, emergency management, and business continuity plans. If a strong communications plan has not already been developed, consideration should be given to establishing relationships with federal, state, county, and local law enforcement and emergency response agencies.

Public–Private Sector Partnerships

There must be a closely coordinated public–private sector partnership to reduce security vulnerabilities. Each sector has resources that can be effective in helping to prevent an attack by an adversary at a key asset. In order to be effective, there must be a strong, well ingrained communications process in place. The sectors should regularly share intelligence information that may be of value.

The cross-sector partnership can also help alleviate issues of insufficient resources. Oftentimes, the private sector has resources (such as trained emergency responders and emergency response equipment) that can complement and supplement the public sector's resources, and vice versa. Once again, there must be careful planning and coordination to fully develop this relationship. The partnership can be formalized through the execution of a mutual assistance agreement between the two sectors.

To ensure that the partnership is particularly effective, the two sectors must work together to coordinate emergency response plans, operational guidelines, and training. It is also important that communications systems, such as two-way radios, allow for communication between the sectors. The culmination of these efforts should be a joint emergency exercise, where all of the various systems are tested and evaluated, with opportunities for improvement identified.

Equipment purchases should be coordinated so that tools and personal protective equipment are interchangeable and there are no incompatibilities between the two sectors. For example, if the private sector is purchasing fire hose, it should ensure that the hose threads are compatible with those of the municipal fire department.

This cooperative partnership of mutual assistance will result in a synergistic effect, whereby the sum of the two sectors working together is greater than the sum of their individual capabilities had they worked in isolation. The partnership will also result in a greater likelihood of organizational survivability and business continuity and will enhance the overall emergency response capabilities in the event of a successful attack.

9.9 ALL HAZARDS PROTECTION

Homeland Security Presidential Directive 8 (HSPD 8), entitled *National Preparedness* and issued on December 17, 2003 by President George W. Bush, outlines the nation's plans for responding to all hazards. All hazards protection refers to preparedness for domestic terrorist attacks, major accidental emergencies, and natural disasters. Preparedness is simply the existence of plans, procedures, policies, training, and equipment necessary to maximize the ability to prevent, respond to, and recover from major incidents. Appendix 9.1 is a copy of HSPD 8.

The concept for all hazards protection is that when implementing enhancements to critical infrastructure, key resources, and key assets, they should be designed to address any type of emergency, regardless of its source. This concept will provide the maximum amount of protection and help to justify costs.

9.10 COST–BENEFIT ANALYSIS

There will probably never be enough resources (i.e., dollars, personnel, time, and materials) to achieve total preparedness and reduce the risk of adverse impacts against a key asset. Therefore the management team at a key asset must make tough decisions about what specific assets really need protection by the application of scarce resources. There should be no tolerance for waste and misguided spending in the business of critical infrastructure, key resource, or key asset protection.

Cost–benefit analysis is a process in planning, related to the decision to commit funds or assets. This is a systematic attempt to measure or analyze the value of all the benefits that would be achieved from a particular expenditure. Usually, the process involves three steps:

1. Identification of all direct and indirect consequences of the expenditure.
2. Assignment of a monetary value to all costs and benefits resulting from the expenditure.
3. Discounting expected future costs and revenues accruing from the expenditure to express those costs and revenues in current monetary values.

Once all of the costs associated with the implementation of a security countermeasure are known, than an evaluation can be made as to whether the expense for implementation is justified in terms of benefits gained by the implementation of the countermeasure.

9.11 INFORMATION SHARING AND ANALYSIS CENTERS

One of the significant lessons learned from the September 11, 2001 attack was the need to share intelligence information concerning adversary threats, not only between the various public sector and law enforcement agencies, but between the public and private sectors. Homeland Security Presidential Directive 7 (HSPD 7) specifically mandates that the public and private sectors share information about physical and cyber threats and vulnerabilities to help protect critical infrastructure.

The Information Sharing and Analysis Centers (ISACs) were created to facilitate the sharing of information about threats, vulnerabilities, incidents, potential protective measures, and best practices between the public and private sectors. Each critical infrastructure sector maintains an ISAC for their specific information.

The ISACs provide timely notification specifically designed to help protect critical infrastructure from threats posed by an adversary. The information is obtained from ISAC members, commercial security firms, federal, state, and local governments, law enforcement agencies, and other trusted sources.

9.12 PRIVATE SECTOR'S RESPONSIBILITY

As mentioned previously, 85% of the critical infrastructure in the United States is owned by the private sector. The private sector cannot defer all of the responsibility to protect these assets to the public sector; it must take responsibility for its own protection. The private sector must become more self-reliant to prepare for and prevent terrorist attacks. Preparedness includes greater awareness, cooperation between different sectors and disciplines, and sharing of information.

9.13 PROTECTING CRITICAL INFRASTRUCTURE, KEY RESOURCES, AND KEY ASSETS

The Department of Homeland Security's *National Strategy for the Physical Protection of Critical Infrastructures and Key Assets* notes the complexity of the nation's critical infrastructure and key resources and emphasizes that protecting critical infrastructures and key resource sites is a shared responsibility requiring cooperation among all levels of government—federal, state, and local—and the involvement of the private sector.

The President's National Strategy of the Physical Protection of Critical Infrastructure and Key Assets of February 2003 directed the development of a comprehensive national approach to physical protection. This strategy identified the specific initiatives to drive near term national protection priorities, and updated the resource allocation process.

Homeland Security Presidential Directive 7

Homeland Security Presidential Directive 7 (HSPD 7, see Appendix 2.5) discusses the need to protect critical infrastructure, key resources, and key assets from attack. Specifically, per HSPD 7: "It is the policy of the United States to enhance the protection of our Nation's critical infrastructure and key resources against terrorist attacks that could:

(a) cause catastrophic health effects or mass casualties comparable to those from the use of a weapon of mass destruction;
(b) impair Federal departments and agencies' abilities to perform essential missions, or to ensure the public's health and safety;
(c) undermine State and local government capacities to maintain order and to deliver minimum essential public services;
(d) damage the private sector's capability to ensure the orderly functioning of the economy and delivery of essential services;
(e) have a negative effect on the economy through the cascading disruption of other critical infrastructure and key resources; or
(f) undermine the public's morale and confidence in our national economic and political institutions."

The Homeland Security Advisory System

The federal government has developed a standardized threat warning system to publicize the current terrorist threat level. This system, called the Homeland Security Advisory System (HSAS), is an effort to improve coordination and cooperation among all levels of government and the general public in the fight against terrorism. The system was intended to create a common vocabulary and a common understanding of the meaning behind the changes in threat conditions. The purpose of the system is to provide a comprehensive and effective means to disseminate information regarding the risk of terrorist acts to federal, state, and local authorities and to the American people. Risk includes both the probability of an attack and its potential gravity. The threat conditions can be assigned nationally, regionally, by infrastructure sector, or to a potential target. Factors that will be considered when assigning the threat level include:

To what degree is the threat information credible?
To what degree is the threat information corroborated?
To what degree is the threat specific and/or imminent?
How grave are the potential consequences of the threat?

The Homeland Security Advisory System uses a five tier, color-coded system to indicate the current threat level. The higher the threat condition, the greater the risks of a terrorist attack. Facilities should implement a corresponding set of protective measures to further reduce vulnerability or increase response capability during a period of heightened alert.

Low Condition (Green): Low Risk of Terrorist Attack.
Refining and exercising protective measures.
Train personnel on specific measures.
Regular assessment of facilities for vulnerabilities and taking corrective action.
Guarded Condition (Blue): General Risk of Terrorist Attack.
Checking communication systems.
Reviewing/updating emergency response procedures.
Providing the public with necessary information.
Elevated Condition (Yellow): Significant Risk of Terrorist Attack.
Increased surveillance of critical locations.
Coordination of emergency plans with local jurisdiction.
Assessing further refinement of protective measures.
Implementing emergency and contingency plans.
High Condition (Orange): High Risk of Terrorist Attack.
Coordinating security efforts with armed forces or law enforcement.
Taking additional precautions at public events.
Preparing to work at an alternate site with a dispersed workforce.
Access restricted to essential personnel only.
Severe Condition (Red): Severe Risk of Terrorist Attack.
Assign emergency response personnel and preposition equipment.
Monitor, redirect, or constrain transportation systems.
Close public and government facilities.
Increase or redirect personnel to address critical emergency needs.

Incremental Threat Response

If the HSAS or intelligence reveals that a key asset is under increased risk of attack, security efforts should be enhanced to deal with the threat. The incremental threat response plan is develop to address this period of heightened concern. The incremental threat response plan will list the specific security system enhancements that will be made in response to a threat.

For example, credible intelligence has indicated that an adversary may attempt to mail an explosive device into a key asset. The Department of Homeland Security has disseminated this information to all critical infrastructure sectors and has raised the HSAS to level "orange" in response. As part of its incremental threat response plan, a key asset has implemented enhanced security countermeasures as follows:

- At HSAS "yellow" level the mail entering a key asset may be inspected by the security guard at the main entrance to the key asset. Once all of the mail has been inspected and no suspicious packages have been found, the mail can be released for distribution.
- At HSAS "orange" level the mail will be inspected at the postal facility by the security guard. Once all of the mail has been inspected and no suspicious packages have been found, the security guard will bring the mail to the key asset and release it for distribution.

This example serves to illustrate how a key asset has implemented its incremental threat response system in response to a threat by adding specific enhancements to its security systems to counter the threat.

Each critical infrastructure, key resource, and key asset should develop a comprehensive incremental threat response plan to indicate specifically how security measures will be enhanced for each change in the HSAS level.

Dealing with the Community

As mentioned previously, there is a need to establish a clear communications and information link with the local authorities. It is recommended that any information concerning security-related issues are cleared with law enforcement officials before it is released to the general public or media. Certainly, security assessment vulnerabilities should not be released to the general public or media. Security discussions with the community should be limited to generalities. Brochures and websites should be sanitized to remove any information that can be used to facilitate an attack. The following are some considerations for dealing with the community:

- Any information concerning security-related issues must be cleared with local law enforcement authorities before being released to the media or general public.
- Limit security-related discussions with the public to generalities.
- Restrict participation in security assessments to company and/or law enforcement authorities only.

- DO NOT share the findings of any site security assessments with the media or general public.
- Reconsider providing tours or "open houses" of your facility.
- Sanitize websites or brochures that highlight information that could be used against a facility.
- Redirect requests for right to know information or material safety data sheets from unknown people to the local law enforcement authorities.

Recovery

If all of the protective countermeasures fail, the attack will be executed and damage, to some degree, will occur to the key asset. Once the attack is completed and the emergency situation mitigated, the recovery operations must begin.

The first step in the recovery process is damage assessment. Damage assessment includes the procedures and technologies that assist in initial assessment of structural and other types of damage to the key asset to determine the effect of the attack on functionality and what must be repaired. Next, the key asset should implement its functional continuity plan. This plan includes the contingency plans for reestablishing key asset functionality, including the use of available alternatives and emergency repairs. The final step in the recovery process is reconstitution, which is the permanent restoration of the key asset's ability to provide its full capacity of products or services.

Potential Security Enhancements

Some best practices include the following.

1. *Communication with Authorities.* The first and most important step in the risk reduction phase is coordination with local, state, and federal law enforcement and emergency response agencies. All of a key asset's risk reduction plans must be incorporated into the local emergency response plan. Law enforcement and emergency response agencies can be very helpful in providing risk reduction techniques. Additionally, these agencies must be fully informed so they can provide appropriate emergency response, in coordination with the key asset's emergency response resources, in the event of an attack.

2. *Physical Security/Perimeter Protection/Access Control.* Consideration should be given to providing increased hardening to make access to a key asset more difficult. Increased physical security and perimeter protection includes fencing, concrete barriers, surveillance cameras, increased security guard patrols, defoliation of fence lines to increase observation, and intrusion detection systems. All entrances to the key asset should be locked and, preferably, guarded. Employees should have to use some sort of access control system (swipe card or password protected electronic locks) to enter. Adequate lighting should be provided to facilitate perimeter surveillance. Projectile shields can be used to protect vulnerable targets.

Landscaping should be installed to block clear lines of sight of key infrastructures from the public way.

3. *Backup System for Utilities.* Any critical infrastructure that could lead to an emergency, or increase the severity of an emergency, should have a backup in place in case the attack affects one of the critical suppliers. In the event backup utilities are not possible, efforts should be made to reduce the negative effect their loss will have on the key asset.

4. *Training, Plans, Policies, and Procedures.* Written plans must be developed to address the various specific responses to the identified vulnerabilities. For example, many key assets have developed and implemented a program for designated employees to screen the incoming mail for suspicious packages. Employees were provided with awareness training on how to identify the package, and what to do with the package once it has been identified. Other written policies and procedures, along with the associated awareness training, which should be implemented as necessary include:

- Access control.
- Background checks for employees, contractors, and truck drivers.
- Dealing with civil disturbances.
- Employee misconduct policy.
- General weapons policy.
- Identification, handling, and reporting of suspicious people, activity, inquiries, or calls.
- Mail and package screening procedure.
- Personnel and vehicle search procedure.
- Protection of electronic and proprietary information procedure.
- Workplace violence policy.

5. *Conduct Background Checks for New Employees and Contractors.* Background checks help to ensure potential employee or contractor personnel do not have a history that is of concern. There are a number of background checks that are available and the most useful include:

- Criminal background check: a national felony conviction check; a felony conviction check for each county resided and employed in; and a check of the FBI's terrorist "be on the lookout" list.
- Credit check: to establish the history of residency, employment, and sources of income.
- Citizenship/immigration check: to determine if the individual is a United States citizen, is in the United States legally, and is authorized to hold a job.

If a company does not want to take responsibility for conducting background checks on contractors, the company should require that contractor management certify, in writing, that the background checks were completed by management as specified and were found to be acceptable.

6. *Conduct Background Checks for Truck Drivers.* Background checks should be completed for drivers transporting dangerous or sensitive materials into or out of the key asset. This background check should include the same elements as those for employees and contractors.

7. *Reporting of Security Incidents.* A procedure should be established which outlines how employees can report security-related incidents to management. All security incidents should be investigated thoroughly so corrective actions to prevent recurrence can be implemented.

8. *Protection of a Facility's Heating, Ventilating, and Air Conditioning (HVAC) System.* Key assets that have large populations in a single building are attractive targets due to the high concentration of people in a relatively small area. HVAC system air intakes are a potential introduction source for chemical, biological, or radiological weapons into the building. Therefore a thorough assessment must be conducted concerning the design and operation of the HVAC system. Air intakes, because they are usually easily assessible, must be protected:

- Access to the intake must be restricted by providing locked fencing.
- Access to rooftop units must be restricted by locked doors or access ladders.
- Intakes should be ducted as high as possible to restrict direct access.
- Intakes should be grated and sloped to make throwing something into the intakes more difficult.
- Intrusion alarms, cameras, and frequent patrols should provide monitoring for the HVAC intakes.

9. *Emergency Response.* Key assets must develop comprehensive written emergency response plans and ensure they are coordinated with the local responders. These written plans should be tested, by conducting drills periodically, and updated as necessary after a drill critique has been conducted. Key asset evacuation and personnel accountability procedures are especially critical in an emergency, and these procedures should be practiced regularly with all employees.

Based on the overall assessment process, if a key asset determines it may be a potential target or may be impacted by a nearby potential target, it may need to develop some level of emergency response capability to protect its facility and people, such as the training and equipment necessary to provide at least a basic capability for facility personnel to don appropriate personal protective equipment, rescue and treat victims, conduct air monitoring for chemical and radiological agents, and decontaminate personnel and victims.

9.14 ADMINISTRATIVE SECURITY ENHANCEMENTS

Examples of administrative policies and procedures that should be considered for implementation are discussed in this section.

Security Policy

A security policy should be developed that places the necessary importance on the security program. The policy should be signed by the chief executive of the jurisdiction and should be posted in prominent locations for all personnel to view.

The policy should include:

- The importance of security as a core value of the jurisdiction.
- The need for all personnel to be familiar with and carry out their responsibilities in the security plan.
- The need for all personnel to report any security concerns or incidents to the proper authority immediately so they can be investigated in a timely manner.
- The involvement of law enforcement agencies to investigate security incidents.
- The requirement for periodic audits of the security systems and procedures.

Security Organization

The security organization policy should establish which individuals have responsibility for key elements within the security program. Among the key positions are (1) the person with overall responsibility for security risk management and (2) the security coordinator, who has primary responsibility for security at the key asset. The security coordinator is also often the counterterrorism coordinator.

The organization policy should also designate departmental responsibilities for security items:

- *Security Department.*

  Prioritize and conduct periodic security vulnerability assessments.

  Develop, administer, and implement the key asset security policies and procedures.

  Develop and implement the key asset's counterterrorism procedures.

  Develop and implement security measures commensurate with risks.

  Audit the various security programs.

  Train employees and outside agencies on security topics.

  Train and equip the emergency response team to deal with credible terrorism incidents.

  Administer the security incident reporting system.

  Evaluate, respond to, and investigate all security incidents.

  Coordinate with federal, state, local, and corporate security agencies.

  Update and amend the security manual as needed.

  Implement security measures as appropriate.

  Maintain documentation of security management programs, processes, and procedures.

Evaluate, respond to, report, and communicate security threats.

Maintain a communications dialog and information exchange on appropriate security issues with stakeholders.

Supervise the security guard force.

- *Human Resources Department.*

  Conduct preemployment background checks for employee candidates.

  Collect information concerning employee-initiated restraining orders that include company premises.

  Administer the substance abuse program.

  Manage all incidents that involve or potentially involve employee disciplinary action.

- *Logistics Department.*

  Administer the contractor screening program.

  Administer the truck driver screening program.

- *Security Guard Force.*

  Administer the access control procedure.

  Administer the personal and vehicle search procedure.

  Conduct periodic perimeter and internal security inspections.

Security Training

It is essential that all employees receive basic security training so that they understand the threat against the key asset, what constitutes suspicious behavior, and how to respond if they observe something suspicious. If the jurisdiction maintains an emergency response team, the team members should receive training commensurate with their responsibilities. Annual refresher training should be completed for all personnel. All training activities should be appropriately documented.

- *Initial Training*. All new hires shall receive the following training (as applicable to their job function) provided by the Security Department as part of the new employee orientation.

  (i) *Terrorism and Security Awareness Training*. All employees shall be trained on basic terrorism awareness; recognition of suspicious persons, inquiries, activities, and purchases; and the generic security policies and procedures that have been developed to protect the site and personnel.

  (ii) *Specific Security Procedure Training*. Employees shall be trained on the specific security policies and procedures that affect them directly. Employees shall also receive training on the specific security policies and procedures that affect the conduct of their normal responsibilities.

- *Emergency Responder Training.*
  - (i) *Weapons of Mass Destruction—Awareness Training.* All members of the Emergency Response Team (ERT) shall receive Weapons of Mass Destruction—Awareness level training. This training provides a basic overview of the basic types of potential terrorism attacks, how to recognize the presence of this type of attack, how to respond safely to protect themselves and others, how to preserve evidence, and how to minimize the impact of such an attack.
  - (ii) *Weapons of Mass Destruction—Operational Training.* All members of the ERT shall receive Weapons of Mass Destruction—Operational level training. This training provides the basic information necessary to conduct defensive operations in response to a terrorist attack.
- *Refresher Training.* All employees shall receive annual refresher training for the above topics provided by the Security Department, as applicable to their job function.
- *Training Records.* Security training shall be documented on a training sign-in sheet, entered into the training database, and filed.

Access Control Procedure

The jurisdiction should establish a procedure that establishes how access is controlled into key assets, such as buildings for all employees, visitors, contractors, and truck drivers.

The purpose of the access control procedure is to (1) limit access to the site to authorized personnel only; (2) provide an accurate headcount of all employees, contractors, visitors, and truck drivers on site for use during an emergency; (3) identify/screen/search individuals entering the site; and (4) ensure employee, contractor, and visitor vehicles are parked in appropriate areas.

Employee Access Procedure

1. Each employee shall enter and exit the site through the main entrance, using the electronic access card issued by the jurisdiction.
2. An employee who does not use the electronic access card issued by the jurisdiction must sign in and out with the security guard at the main entrance for each and every entrance and exit.
3. The security guard shall confirm the identity of each employee by comparison with the jurisdiction's photo database.

Visitor Access Procedure

1. All visitors shall sign in and out with the security guard at the main entrance for each and every entrance and exit.
2. The security guard shall confirm with an employee that the visitor is expected.

3. The visitor must provide one form of positive identification (i.e., picture ID) to the security guard.
4. An employee must escort the visitor to and from the guard station. No visitor shall enter the key asset unescorted. Visitors must be accompanied by an employee throughout the visitor's time at the key asset.
5. If a visitor does not produce a positive form of identification and an employee cannot confirm the visitor's identity, the visitor shall not be allowed entry into the key asset.

Contractor Access Procedure

1. All contractors and contractor employees shall sign in and out with the security guard at the main entrance for each and every entrance and exit.
2. The security guard shall confirm with the contractor's liaison that the contractor employee is expected.
3. The security guard shall confirm that the contractor company and the specific contractor employee are on the approved contractor list.
4. The security guard shall confirm the identity of the contractor by checking the photo database. If the contractor is not in the photo database, the contractor must provide one form of positive identification to the security guard. Once the identity of the contractor has been confirmed, the security guard shall take his/her picture and insert it into the photo database.
5. Contractor work vehicles may enter the key asset only with the express permission of the Security Department.
6. Contractor work vehicles shall be inspected upon entering and exiting the key asset.
7. If a contractor employee does not produce a positive form of identification and an employee or contractor management representative cannot confirm the individual's identity, such individual shall not be allowed entry into the key asset.

Truck Driver Access Procedures

1. Pickup/delivery trucks shall sign in and out at the delivery.
2. The security guard shall confirm with the Logistics Department that a pickup/delivery has been scheduled and the truck is expected at this time.
3. The truck shall not be allowed into the key asset if the driver does not have:
   (a) A valid commercial driver's license and hazardous materials endorsement (for chemicals only).
   (b) A valid company identification card.
   (c) His/her presence confirmed by the carrier.
   (d) A matching photo in the truck driver photo database.
   (e) A valid shipping/receiving order prepared by the Logistics Department.

4. If the truck driver is not in the photo database, the truck driver must provide a form of positive identification to the security guard. Once the identity of the truck driver has been confirmed, the security guard shall take his/her picture and insert it into the photo database.
5. If a truck driver does not produce a positive form of identification and is not in the truck driver photo database, the truck driver shall not be allowed entry into the key asset.
6. If a truck driver does not allow the security guard to search the vehicle, the truck driver and the vehicle shall not be allowed entry into the key asset.

Identification of Personnel

1. Positive identification shall be confirmed via:
   (a) Comparison of the person with the photo stored in the database.
   (b) Government credentials/badge (with photo).
   (c) Driver's license (with or without photo).
   (d) Company-issued identification card (with photo).
   (e) Verification of identity by an authorized employee.
2. In cases when increased scrutiny is required, the Security Department shall verify identity by calling the home office/headquarters of the person involved to confirm the individual's job position and to confirm the individual's assignment and reason to be at the key asset. The verification from the person's home office/headquarters shall be made to a direct, main telephone phone number obtained from a commercial source (telephone book, telephone operator, etc.) and not a number provided by the involved individual.

Contractor Screening

The jurisdiction should require that contractor companies and contractor employees be screened before being allowed to work at a key asset. Background checks shall be performed before issuing a purchase order for a job. A third party shall be utilized to conduct the background checks.

The jurisdiction should require that each contractor company screen its employees in accordance with the jurisdiction's specifications and certify in writing that any and all employees sent to work at the key asset have passed the required background checks.

Contractor Employee Background Screening Procedure

1. All contractor employees who will work at the key asset shall undergo the following screens:
   (a) Identification.
   (b) Criminal record check for all towns and states in which such contractor resides or has resided.
   (c) Motor vehicle record.

   (d) Credit history.
   (e) INS Form 9.
2. Any misrepresentation or failure to disclose material information shall disqualify the contractor employee from working at the key asset.
3. Any felony conviction, whether disclosed by the contractor employee or discovered in a background check, may result in the immediate disqualification of the contractor employee to enter the key asset. In making a disqualification determination, the company may consider the effect and bearing that the crime or offense may have on the performance of the work or the presence of the individual on company premises. Such crimes or offenses which may cause a disqualification determination include, but are not limited to, the following:
   (a) Arson.
   (b) Theft (e.g., robbery, burglary, hot checks).
   (c) Fraud or embezzlement.
   (d) Industrial espionage or trade secret theft.
   (e) Physical violence (e.g., assault, battery, or homicide).
   (f) Sexual crimes.
   (g) Sale, distribution, or possession of illegal substances.
   (h) Weapons or contraband related offenses.
   (i) Driving while intoxicated, driving under the influence, public intoxication, or other alcohol or drug offenses.
4. In addition, the jurisdiction may consider mitigating factors such as commission of the felony or misdemeanor when an underage minor and where a significant period of time has elapsed since the conviction, in making a decision whether to disqualify the individual. The jurisdiction may consider such cases in making the disqualification determination provided that the contractor company provides the pertinent mitigating information.
5. If a contractor company fails to complete the stipulated background checks, that company shall not work at the key asset without the express authorization of the Security Department.

Contractor Company Background Screening Procedure. The Logistics Department shall conduct a background check of all contractor companies awarded work at the key asset using a third party agency to ensure they are legitimate business entities. The background checks to be completed include a Dunn and Bradstreet financial history.

A contractor company shall be disqualified from working at the site in the following circumstances:

1. History of poor performance on past jobs.
2. Poor feedback from references.
3. Poor Dunn and Bradstreet financial rating [6–9].

If the Logistics Department has not conducted the stipulated background checks on a contractor company, the contractor company shall be precluded from working at the key asset without the express authorization of the Security Department.

Handling of Suspicious Persons and Intruders

Identification of Suspicious People. Suspicious people are those who may be trying to collect information concerning the key asset that can be used for illicit purposes. There are many different indicators that may be of concern:

1. May be observed hanging around the key asset.
2. May make an effort to strike up a conversation with an employee concerning the key asset or its operations.
3. May attempt to contact vendors or delivery people to ascertain information concerning the key asset or its operations.
4. May attempt to contact suppliers or customers for information about the key asset or its operations.
5. May be observed taking photographs of the key asset.

How to Handle Suspicious People or Vehicles. All personnel should remain alert and diligent in order to identify potential risks to the key asset. If an individual is observed who may be acting suspiciously, the following actions should be taken:

1. Immediately notify security.
2. Remember the physical description of the suspicious individual(s), including hair color, eye color, distinguishing marks, clothing, height, weight, and any packages that may be carried.
3. Remember the description of the individual's vehicle, including make, model, color, license plate, markings, and damage. Also make note of the direction of travel if the individual leaves the area.
4. Remember exactly what made the individual(s)/vehicle(s) suspicious, such as questions asked, photos being taken, or circling the key asset.
5. Do not confront or detain the individual(s) if you do not feel comfortable with the situation.

Identification of Intruders. Intruders are those people who gain access to the key asset without authorization. Intruders may be trying to collect information concerning the key asset which can be used for illicit purposes, or may be trying to cause damage or steal material. Intruders may (1) try to bluff their way into the key asset, or (2) try to force their way into the key asset through doors or windows, or (3) try to gain access by breaching or climbing the fence.

How to Handle Intruders. All personnel should remain alert and diligent in order to identify potential risks to the key asset. If an intruder is observed within the key asset, the following actions should be taken:

1. Immediately notify security.
2. Remember the description of the suspicious individual, including hair color, eye color, distinguishing marks, clothing, height, weight, and any packages that may be carried.
3. Remember exactly what the individual was doing, location, how he/she entered the key asset, direction of travel, packages/items being carried.
4. Do not confront or detain the individual.
5. Try to follow the individual and observe from a safe distance while maintaining contact with the Security Department. Report where the intruder is going, what he/she is carrying, and what he/she is doing.

Mail, Package, and Delivery Screening

To ensure the safety and health of employees, the Security Department shall screen all mail and packages (U.S. Postal Service, federal express, courier deliveries, etc.) delivered each day to the key asset. Once the mail and packages have been screened for any suspicious indicators, they shall be released for distribution to the recipients. The screener shall not open mail and packages, but rather shall perform an external inspection. Therefore even though the Security Department screened the mail and packages, employees must be cautious, as the screener did not open the packages and they may contain a hazard inside.

Mail and Package Screening Procedure

1. The mail and packages shall be screened by the Security Department in a location remote from the key asset and away from other personnel.
2. The screener shall wear the following personal protective equipment when inspecting mail and packages: (a) safety glasses with side shields and (b) latex gloves.
3. Each individual piece of mail and each package shall be externally inspected by the Security Department for the following suspicious indicators:
   (a) Excessive postage and/or weight.
   (b) Handwritten or poorly typed addresses.
   (c) Incorrect titles or title with no name.
   (d) Misspellings of common words.
   (e) Oily stains, discoloration, or odor.
   (f) No return address.
   (g) Lopsided or uneven envelope.
   (h) Protruding wires, plastic wrap, or aluminum foil.

(i) Excessive security material, such as masking tape and string.
(j) Visual distractions.
(k) Ticking sound.
(l) Marked with restrictive endorsements, such as "Personal" or "Confidential."
(m) Shows a city or state in the postmark that does not match the return address.

4. Suspicious mail or packages shall be placed in a plastic bag to prevent leakage of the contents.
5. The screener shall remove his/her gloves after completing the screening and dispose of them in the receptacle provided.

Handling Suspicious Mail and Packages

1. Mail and packages that have been determined to be suspicious, and any other mail or packages they contacted, shall remain isolated (i.e., not distributed until further investigation by the Security Department).
2. Do not shake, bump, or empty the contents of any suspicious package.
3. Do not open, smell, touch, or taste the contents of any suspicious package.
4. Do not put in water or a confined space.
5. If you haven't opened the package, do not.
6. Leave the package where it is.
7. Stay with the mail/package. Do not leave the area until authorized to do so to minimize the spread of contamination.
8. Do not allow other personnel into the area.
9. There is no need to sound the emergency alarm or evacuate the area!

Handling Mail or a Package Containing Powder

1. Do not clean up the powder. Cover the spilled contents immediately.
2. Notify the appropriate emergency responders immediately!
3. Prevent others from entering the area.
4. Do not leave the area until authorized, to minimize the spread of contamination.

Handling Personnel Contaminated with Powder

1. The emergency responders shall make the appropriate decision regarding the need for decontamination and/or medical evaluation for personnel contaminated with a suspicious material.
2. The general practice is to prevent contact with your face until the hands have been washed with soap and water.

Procedure for Deliveries (Such as United Parcel Service, Trucks)

1. Upon arrival of a delivery, the security guard shall confirm the shipment against a purchase order issued by the Logistics Department. The delivery shall not be unloaded until the confirmation has been made. If no purchase order has been issued, the delivery shall be refused. The transporter shall be directed to remove the delivery from the key asset immediately.
2. The delivery shall be inspected at a remote location from the key asset and away from personnel. The screener shall not open boxes.
3. Each individual package shall be externally inspected by the Security Department for the following suspicious indicators:
   (a) Excessive postage and/or weight.
   (b) Handwritten or poorly typed addresses.
   (c) Incorrect titles or title with no name.
   (d) Misspellings of common words.
   (e) Oily stains, discoloration, or odor.
   (f) No return address.
   (g) Lopsided or uneven envelope.
   (h) Protruding wires, plastic wrap, or aluminum foil.
   (i) Excessive security material, such as masking tape and string.
   (j) Visual distractions.
   (k) Ticking sound.
   (l) Marked with restrictive endorsements, such as "Personal" or "Confidential."
   (m) Shows a city or state in the postmark that does not match the return address.
4. Suspicious deliveries shall be segregated and emergency responders notified ASAP.
5. The Security Department shall release deliveries for distribution after screening.

Handling Suspicious Deliveries

1. Deliveries that have been determined to be suspicious, and any other package they contacted, shall remain isolated (i.e., not distributed) in the remote location until further investigated by the emergency responders.
2. Do not shake or empty the contents of any suspicious package.
3. If you haven't opened the package, do not.
4. Leave the package where it is.
5. Do not allow other personnel into the area.
6. There is no need to sound the emergency alarm or evacuate the area!
7. Wash your hands with soap and water. Prevent contact with your face until hands are washed.

Personnel and Vehicle Search Procedure

Search of Personnel

1. Patting down or otherwise searching personnel shall not ordinarily be done.
2. Patting down or searching personnel shall only be done if the presence of weapons, drugs, or alcohol is reasonably suspected.
3. If the security guard identifies an individual, who the Security Guard reasonably suspects is carrying weapons, drugs or alcohol, the Police Department shall be notified immediately.
4. If an individual must be searched or patted down, the Police Department shall be notified and will conduct the pat down or search of the individual, if any.

Search of Personal Belongings

1. The security guard shall request to search every parcel (e.g., briefcase, purse, lunch box) brought into or out of the key asset by contractors, visitors, or truck drivers.
2. The security guard shall request to search parcels brought into or out of the key asset by employees. Such searches may occur on a random basis as determined by management.
3. Consent shall be obtained before searching any personal belongings being brought into the key asset. If consent is not given, then:
   (a) Notify the Police Department immediately.
   (b) The individual shall be requested to place the parcel in his/her vehicle.
   (c) The vehicle shall be moved away from the key asset.
   (d) If the individual does not meet (b) and (c) above, the individual shall be requested to leave the premises.
4. If consent is obtained, the owner shall be requested to:
   (a) Open the parcel.
   (b) Remove or adjust the contents so everything can be observed by the security guard.
   (c) Replace the contents back into the parcel when the search is complete.
5. If consent to search is not obtained upon the visitor exiting the key asset, the security guard shall:
   (a) Not confront the individual.
   (b) Notify the Police Department ASAP.
6. The security guard shall:
   (a) Respect the privacy of the owner at all times.
   (b) Conduct the search in plain site in an open area (desktop, countertop).
   (c) Conduct the search in the presence of the owner.
   (d) Not touch or remove the contents of the parcel.

7. If suspicious or contraband material is discovered during the search, the security guard shall:
   (a) Not confront the individual.
   (b) Instruct the individual to repack the parcel.
   (c) Notify the Police Department ASAP.
8. The security guard shall not:
   (a) Become argumentative with personnel.
   (b) Search when consent has not been received.
   (c) Detain anyone from leaving the property.
9. As a general rule, known emergency responders will not be searched when responding to emergencies, unless suspicious behavior or material is observed.

Search of Vehicles Entering/Exiting the Key Asset

1. The security guard shall request to search every vehicle entering or exiting the key asset.
2. Consent shall be obtained before searching a vehicle. If consent is not obtained, then notify the Police Department immediately.
   (a) If the vehicle is trying to enter the key asset, deny entry to the site. The vehicle shall be moved away from the key asset.
   (b) If the vehicle is trying to exit the key asset, do not confront the individual and notify the Police Department ASAP.
3. If consent is obtained, the vehicle driver shall be requested to:
   (a) Open the passenger compartment.
   (b) Open the trunk.
   (c) Open tool boxes or compartments.
   (d) Remove or adjust the contents so everything can be observed by the security guard.
   (e) Replace the contents into the vehicle when the search is complete.
4. The security guard shall:
   (a) Respect the privacy of the driver at all times.
   (b) Conduct the search in plain site in an open area.
   (c) Conduct the search in the presence of the driver.
   (d) Not touch or remove the contents of the vehicle.
5. If suspicious or contraband material is discovered during the search, the security guard shall:
   (a) Not confront the individual.
   (b) Notify the Police Department ASAP.
6. The security guard shall not:
   (a) Become argumentative with personnel.

   (b) Search when consent has not been received.
   (c) Detain anyone from leaving the property.
7. The security guard shall pay particular attention for the following for vehicles entering the key asset:
   (a) Illegal or contraband material.
   (b) Unusual containers or packages, such as drums, cylinders, or flasks.
   (c) Packages labeled explosive, radioactive, or poison.
   (d) Leaking packages, containers, drums, cylinders, or flasks.

Pre-employment Screening

The key asset requires pre-employment screening, as specified below, as a means of verifying applicant data prior to hire. This policy applies to all employment, including rehires where the separation period is more than 30 days.

Background checks shall be made after extension of a contingent offer but prior to the start of employment.

Screening shall be conducted by a third party agency secured by the key asset. Copies of all investigative reports shall be retained by the key asset's Human Resources Department.

Employee Background Screening Procedure. All candidates for employment by the key asset shall undergo the following screens:

1. Positive verification of identity.
2. Employment history.
3. Education.
4. Criminal record check for all towns and states in which the applicant resides and has resided.
5. Motor vehicle record.
6. Credit history.
7. Military record.
8. Professional certifications/licenses.
9. INS Form 9.
10. Preplacement medical examination and/or drug screening (postemployment offer).

Any misrepresentation or failure to disclose material information on the employment application/resume shall be reviewed by the Human Resources Department and may result in the immediate revocation of the employment offer, or termination of employment if the candidate has been employed.

Any felony conviction, whether disclosed by the employee or discovered in a background check, may result in the immediate revocation of the employment offer, or termination of employment if the individual is employed. In making a decision to rescind an offer of employment or to terminate employment, the key asset may consider the effect and bearing that the crime or offense may have on the performance of the work or the presence of the individual on key asset premises. Such crimes or offenses that may cause a disqualification determination include, but are not limited to, the following:

- Theft (e.g., robbery, burglary, hot checks).
- Fraud or embezzlement.
- Industrial espionage or trade secret theft.
- Physical violence (e.g., assault, battery, homicide).
- Sexual crimes.
- Sale, distribution, or possession of illegal substances.
- Weapons or contraband related offenses.
- DWI, DUI, public intoxication, or other alcohol or drug offenses.

In addition, the key asset may consider mitigating factors such as commission of the felony when an underage minor and where a significant period of time has elapsed since the conviction, in making a decision to rescind an offer of employment or to terminate employment. The key asset may consider such cases, provided that the individual provides the pertinent mitigating information.

In all cases, the key asset shall comply with the requirements set forth in the Fair Credit Reporting Act and any state or local law or regulation governing employment investigations.

Protection of Information Procedure

The key asset maintains a significant amount of information, such as business plans, financial reports, and technical information, which are vital to success and must be protected as a precious resource. Any nonpublic information relating to the key asset which, if disclosed in an untimely or unauthorized manner, would be detrimental to the best interests of the key asset or would give an unfair business or personal advantage is proprietary and confidential. Therefore the key asset should implement an appropriate level of protection to ensure this information is not corrupted, shared with unauthorized personnel, or lost.

Information Technology Disaster Contingency Plan. The key asset should maintain an Information Technology Disaster Contingency Plan. The purpose of this plan is to develop, demonstrate, and sustain the capability to restore the network computing environment to the key asset before the unavailability of these systems causes the site to experience unacceptable financial losses, disruption to the organization, or inability to meet customer obligations.

Information Technology Manual. The key asset should maintain an information technology (IT) manual that further stipulates security measures for both hardware and software. The contents of the IT manual include computer usage, user account manager, passwords, physical security, data security, data encryption, protection against viruses, Intranet and Internet security, remote access security, and external networks security.

Personal Computers. The key asset should issue a personal computer security guide. The purpose of this document is to inform the users of the vulnerability of data and information as unauthorized modification, disclosure, and destruction, whether deliberate or accidental. This guide alerts employees to some of the undesirable things that can happen to data, provides practical solutions to reduce risks of these threats, and provides rules that must be adhered to when using any personal computer issued by the jurisdiction.

Personal computers shall not be "on" while unattended. Screen savers that are password protected shall be enabled. Employees shall log off the network or shut down their computers at the end of the day or if away from their workstation for any period of time.

Internal Network Security. Employees frequently access the key asset's Intranet to conduct their routine daily business. The key asset's information technology coordinator should control access to the key asset Intranet. Each employee should be issued a login name and personal password that will provide access to the authorized files. Employees must not divulge their passwords to others and must not write down or keep their passwords in a location that may be accessed by others. Employees are granted access to certain files and programs based on their job responsibilities. Employees are instructed not to try to access programs or documents for which authorization has not been granted.

External Network Security. The key asset's corporate policy should not allow simultaneous connections between the jurisdiction's network and other networks that are not approved by the key asset. If an employee must connect to another network, they must physically disconnect from the key asset's network before making the connection. This includes connecting to customer networks or connecting for Internet access while being connected to the key asset's network. Internet access is only available to specifically designated employees.

Telephone Communications. Telephone conversations may be overheard or intercepted by unauthorized personnel. Cellular telephones are particularly susceptible to being monitored. Therefore employees are cautioned to ensure that privacy has not been compromised when discussing confidential or proprietary information on hard line telephones. Employees are advised not to discuss confidential or proprietary matters while on cellular telephones.

Fax Communications. The key asset should place language on the cover sheets of facsimile transmissions stating that the fax should not be read, copied, or distributed (and should be returned to the sender immediately) if it is received by someone other than the intended recipient. Employees are cautioned to ensure the fax number is correct, and the recipient is aware the fax is being sent, when confidential or proprietary information is being transmitted.

E-Mail Communications. The key asset should direct employees to insert language on e-mail transmissions stating that the e-mail should not be read, copied, or distributed (and should be returned to the sender immediately) if it is received by someone other than the intended recipient. Employees should be cautioned to ensure the e-mail address is correct when company confidential or proprietary information is being transmitted.

Document Control. The key asset generates a significant amount of hard copy documentation pertinent to its employees and business. Many confidential documents, such as operating procedures, are typically placed in an electronic document control system and should not be printed. Many memos and technical reports are also prepared and distributed via electronic systems. Employees should be cautioned about printing documents unless absolutely necessary. The control, retention, and appropriate disposal of all documents are further detailed in the key asset's document control policy.

Employees shall take all appropriate efforts to safeguard sensitive paperwork, including but not limited to storing sensitive papers out of sight and in secure locations, and locking doors and/or files when unattended.

Release of Documents to Persons Outside the Jurisdiction. The key asset should consider all key asset documents to be confidential and proprietary. Therefore management approval must be obtained before releasing documents to persons external to the key asset. Additionally, management may require the marking of documents as "confidential," "proprietary," or "secret."

Suspicious Persons Procedure

Objective. In an effort to thwart terrorism, employees should be directed to report any suspicious persons who may be attempting to collect information about the key asset or potentially cause damage to the key asset.

Who Is a Suspicious Person? This procedure shall cover potential suspicious activities conducted by persons who may be attempting to enter and/or conduct surveillance of the key asset. The intent of this procedure is to identify those who attempt to obtain information in the furtherance of criminal or terrorist activity.

What Should You Do If You Encounter a Suspicious Person? If you feel you have encountered a suspicious person, you should immediately notify the Security Department.

Guidelines. The following guidelines are provided to assist employees to more readily identify suspicious persons who may be attempting to collect information that could be used in an act of terrorism or for the production of weapons of mass destruction or for purely criminal activity.

Potential Identifiers

- Unusual or prolonged interest in security measures or personnel, entry points and access controls, or perimeter barriers such as fences.
- Unusual behavior such as quickly looking away from personnel or vehicles entering or leaving the site or parking facilities.
- Observation of emergency response or security drills.
- Foot surveillance involving two or three individuals working together.
- Mobile surveillance using bicycles, scooters, motorcycles, trucks, SUVs, taxicabs, boats, or small aircraft.
- Prolonged static surveillance using operatives disguised as panhandlers, demonstrators, food/flower vendors, or street sweepers, not previously seen in the area.
- Discreet use of still cameras, video recorders, or note taking.
- Use of multiple sets of clothing and/or identifications, or the use of sketching materials (paper, pencils, etc.).
- Questioning of security or facility personnel.
- Unusual activities or behavior, including surveillance, during the loading or unloading of trucks.
- Probing of boundaries with physical approaches to measure access restrictions.
- Arrogance and hatred toward Americans (bragging, expressed dislike of attitudes and decisions of the U.S. government, superiority of religious beliefs, and difficulty tolerating proximity to those hated).
- Clothing out of sync with the weather or social position (well groomed but wearing sloppy clothing) or location (wearing a coat inside a building).
- Loose clothing.
- Carrying heavy baggage, bags, or wearing a backpack.
- Keeps hands in pockets.
- Repeatedly pats upper body with hands.
- Pale face from recently shaved beard.
- No obvious emotion seen on face.
- Eyes appear to be focused and vigilant.
- Does not respond to authoritative voice commands or direct salutation from a distance.

Security Drill and Exercise Procedure

All Employees

1. All employees shall participate in at least one security drill annually.
2. The purpose of the security drill shall be to:
    (a) Test employees' knowledge of their security responsibilities.

(b) Test employees' response to a security breach.
(c) Test employees' knowledge of emergency procedures.

Security Guards

1. All security guards shall participate in at least one security drill quarterly.
2. The purpose of the security drill shall be to:
   (a) Test the guards' knowledge of their security responsibilities.
   (b) Test the guards' response to a security breach.
   (c) Test the guards' proficiency to properly utilize their equipment.
   (d) Test the guards' knowledge of emergency procedures.

Emergency Response Team (ERT)

1. All ERT members shall participate in at least one security drill annually.
2. The purpose of the security drill shall be to:
   (a) Test the ERT members' proficiency to properly utilize their equipment.
   (b) Test the ERT members' knowledge of emergency procedures.

Incident Command Staff

1. All ICS staff members shall participate in at least one security drill annually.
2. The purpose of the security drill shall be to test the ICS staff members' knowledge of emergency procedures.

Police Department

1. The Security Department shall provide site specific security/counterterrorism training to the Police Department annually.
2. The site shall conduct one security/counterterrorism drill or exercise involving outside agencies annually.

Security Incident Reporting Procedure

Definition. A security incident is defined as any violation of an established security procedure, any breach of the security system, or any suspicious activity resulting in (or which could result in) damage to equipment, injury to personnel, and/or loss of raw material or product.

Procedure

1. Whenever an employee observes or is involved in a security incident, no matter how minor, he/she shall report the incident to the Security Department immediately.
2. The security manager, in consultation with the Law Department, shall determine whether federal, state, and/or local law enforcement or other agencies should be notified. If a notification is required, the security manager shall make such notification.

3. When outside law enforcement or other agencies are involved, the Security Department, with the advice of the Law Department, shall coordinate the investigation and the results with such agencies, as may be necessary.
4. The Security Department shall begin an investigation along with the affected employee(s) or contractors and any witness(es) immediately after the security incident has been resolved. It is highly recommended that the investigation commence immediately while the facts of the incident are fresh in everyone's mind. The investigation shall include a physical inspection of the area where the incident occurred.
5. For any significant security incident (breach of physical security, property damage, or personal injury), the security manager shall be notified immediately, and he/she shall participate in the investigation.
6. At the request of and under the direction of the Law Department, a Security Incident Investigation Report shall be generated by the persons stated above using a Security Incident Form.
7. The completed Security Incident Investigation form shall be reviewed for completeness by the security manager. Prior to issuing any investigation report, the security manager will review the report with in-house counsel.
8. The security manager, at the direction of the Law Department, shall distribute the final Security Incident Investigation Report to all personnel who have a need to know, within seven days of the incident.
9. Each department manager shall ensure all applicable employees have reviewed the Security Incident Investigation Report as soon as practical.
10. Any corrective measures taken to prevent reoccurrence shall have a responsible manager and completion date assigned.
11. Action items shall be tracked to completion.
12. The security manager shall maintain all Security Incident Investigation materials for a minimum of five years (or such longer period as the Law Department shall dictate) in a secure file. No person shall have access to such file without the prior approval of the Law Department.

9.15 RECOMMENDATIONS FOR ENHANCED SECURITY THROUGH VARIOUS ISACs

General Protective Measures for Controlled and Uncontrolled Access

- Encourage personnel to take notice of and report unattended packages, devices, briefcases, or other unusual materials immediately; inform them not to handle or attempt to move any such object, especially near air intakes.
- Encourage personnel to know emergency exits and stairwells and the locations of rally points to ensure the safe egress of people present.
- Increase the number of visible security personnel wherever possible.

- Institute/increase vehicle, foot, and roving security patrols varying in size, timing, and routes.
- Enclosed spaces, such as restrooms, should be regularly inspected.
- Deliveries to concessions in stadiums, arenas, and conference centers should be inspected prior to scheduled events.
- Implement random security guard shift changes.
- Limit the number of access points and strictly enforce access control procedures.
- Deploy visible security cameras and motion sensors.
- Arrange for law enforcement vehicles to be parked randomly near entrances and exits.
- Review current contingency plans and, if not already in place, develop and implement procedures for receiving and acting on threat information, alert notification procedures, terrorist incident response procedures, evacuation procedures, bomb threat procedures, hostage and barricade procedures, chemical, biological, radioactive, and nuclear (CBRN) procedures, consequence and crisis management procedures, accountability procedures, and media procedures.
- Conduct internal training exercises and invite local emergency responders (fire, rescue, medical, bomb squads) to participate in joint exercises.
- Inspect vendor items being brought into area.
- Inspect all items being carried in by patrons.
- Ensure proper badging and identification of all working staff.
- Conduct a security sweep prior to an event.

Vehicle-Borne Improvised Explosive Device Protective Measures

- Approach all illegally parked vehicles in and around facilities, question drivers, and direct them to move immediately. If an owner cannot be identified, have the vehicle towed.
- Conduct vulnerability studies focusing on physical security, structural engineering, infrastructure engineering, power, water, and air infiltration, if feasible.
- Deploy explosive detection devices and explosive detection canine teams.
- Encourage personnel to be alert and to immediately report any situation that appears to constitute a threat or suspicious activity.
- Implement a robust vehicle inspection program, including but not limited to checking the undercarriage of vehicles, under the hood, and in the trunk. Provide vehicle inspection training to security personnel.
- Implement random security guard shift changes.
- Increase perimeter lighting.
- Institute/increase visible vehicle, foot, and roving security patrols that vary in size, timing, and route.

- Rearrange vehicle barriers, traffic cones, and roadblocks to alter traffic patterns near facilities.
- Remove vegetation in and around perimeters and maintain regularly.
- Review security camera footage daily to detect possible indicators of preoperational surveillance.

Suicide Bomber Countermeasures

- Proactively pursue through investigation and questioning any individual reported to be a threat to bomb or carry out a terrorist act and arousing suspicion in others.
- Interview collaterals (family, friends, employers, neighbors, and co-religionists) who observe changes in the individual's behavior, such as withdrawal from previous social contacts, radicalization of beliefs, increased travel to countries known to be supportive of terrorist activities, associations with other suspected terrorists, new and unidentified sources of income, or an increase in religiosity.
- Conduct surveys of retail outlets for bomb making materials to identify the suspect's acquisition behavior and gather evidence.
- Conduct countersurveillance of the identified targets.
- Harden the identified target to reduce or impede access by a suicide bomber or other terrorists.
- Monitor e-mail or cell phone usage of the suspect bomber.
- Continue surveillance of the suspect's behavior.
- Call or shout a voice command from a distance to break suspect's concentration.
- Make physical contact with the suspect to distract his/her attention and physically impede his/her forward movement.
- Ensure physical control before questioning, especially the hands and arms.
- Ensure the safety of civilian targets in the immediate area.
- Make countersurveillance team a part of the first response.
- Include bomb disposal experts in the first response to search for additional explosives.
- Alter primary entrances and exits, if possible.
- Implement stringent identification procedures, to include conducting 100% hands-on checks of security badges for all personnel.
- Remind personnel to properly display badges and enforce visibility.
- Require two forms of photo identification for all visitors.
- Escort all visitors.
- X-ray packages and inspect handbags and briefcases at entry points.
- Validate vendor lists for all routine deliveries and repair services.

Protection of Information

The following information should be shredded or otherwise destroyed upon disposal:

- Proprietary information, including diagrams, first generation drawings, program summaries, and meeting notes.
- Incident records, standard operating procedures, directives, administrative regulations, publications, and directories.
- Personal rosters and phone lists indicating leadership positions and where personnel fit into the organization.
- Memoranda and discarded electronic correspondence and paper notes that might include passwords, specific activities, personal information, and account names.
- Discarded computer equipment packaging that alerts information thieves to the purchase of new equipment and provides brand names that could help them hack into a system based on known vulnerabilities associated with certain equipment models.
- Credit card statements, offers, receipts, bank statements, insurance forms, inventory lists, social security numbers, dates of birth, addresses, and personal telephone numbers.
- CDs and tapes unless properly erased or written over, and CDs that have failed to copy correctly when burned but still could contain information.

Emergency Plans and Supplies

- Have an emergency plan that is developed and approved by local emergency responders.
- Keep the plan uncomplicated, practical, and absolutely realistic.
- Annually review and improve the plan.
- Incorporate all new personnel, equipment, and systems into the plan.
- Ensure complete comprehension and compliance with the plan.
- Periodically exercise and train with the approved plan.
- Guarantee potential incident commanders are capable of implementing the plan.
- Implement the plan when any disaster or emergency occurs.
- Review and improve the plan again after each implementation.
- Back up power.
- Store alternative dependable sources of vehicle and generator fuel.
- Store alternative, dependable sources of water, nonperishable food supplies, and additional expendable or consumable equipment, materials, and supplies.
- Have a supply of satellite radios/phones.

Elimination of Insider Threat

- Enforce identification checks of all personnel entering any facilities.
- Safeguard facilities particularly from imposters seeking entry.
- Guard against anyone using social engineering as a ruse to gain access.
- Prohibit entry of all unauthorized personnel to data and information processing sites.
- Secure contracts only with vendors who conduct thorough pre-employment screening.
- Inspect parcels, packages, tool kits, and baggage of anyone permitted access.

Key Activities Suggesting Possible Terrorist Surveillance Is in Progress

- Foot surveillance involving two or three individuals working together.
- Mobile surveillance using bicycles, scooters, motorcycles, sport utility vehicles, cars, trucks, boats, or small aircraft.
- Persons or vehicles seen in the same location on multiple occasions; persons sitting in a parked car for an extended period of time.
- Persons not fitting into the surrounding environment, such as wearing improper attire for the location, or persons drawing pictures or taking notes in an area not normally of interest to a tourist.
- Persons using possible ruses to cover their activities, such as taking on a disguise as a beggar, demonstrator, shoe shiner, fruit/food vendor, street sweeper, or a newspaper or flower vendor not previously recognized in the area.
- Persons videotaping or photographing security cameras or guard locations. Unusual or prolonged interest in security measures or personnel, entry points and access controls, or perimeter barriers such as fences or walls.
- An increase in anonymous threats followed by individuals noticeably observing security reaction drills or procedures. Questioning of security or facility personnel by an individual who appears benign.

Business and Small Government Protective Actions

- Maintain situational awareness of world events and ongoing threats.
- Ensure all levels of personnel are notified via briefings, e-mail, voice mail, and signage of any changes in threat conditions and protective measures.
- Encourage personnel to be alert and immediately report any situation that appears to constitute a threat or suspicious activity.
- Encourage personnel to take notice and report suspicious packages, devices, unattended briefcases, or other unusual materials immediately; inform them not to handle or attempt to move any such object.
- Encourage personnel to keep their family members and supervisors apprised of their whereabouts.

- Encourage personnel to know the locations of emergency exits and stairwells and rally points to ensure the safe egress of all employees.
- Increase the number of visible security personnel.
- Rearrange exterior vehicle barriers, traffic cones, and road blocks to alter traffic patterns near facilities and patrols by alert security forces.
- Institute/increase vehicle, foot, and roving security patrols varying in size, timing, and routes.
- Implement random security guard shift changes.
- Arrange for law enforcement vehicles to be parked randomly near entrances and exits.
- Review current contingency plans and, if not already in place, develop and implement procedures for receiving and acting on threat information, alert notification procedures, terrorist incident response procedures, evacuation procedures, bomb threat procedures, hostage and barricade procedures, CBRN (chemical, biological, radiological, and nuclear) procedures, consequence and crisis management procedures, accountability procedures, and media procedures.
- When the aforementioned plans and procedures have been implemented, conduct internal training exercises and invite local emergency responders (police, fire, rescue, medical and bomb squads) to participate in joint exercises.
- Coordinate and establish partnerships with local authorities to develop intelligence and information sharing relationships.
- Place personnel on standby for contingency planning.
- Limit the number of access points and strictly enforce access control procedures.
- Approach all illegally parked vehicles in and around facilities. Question drivers and direct them to move immediately; if owner cannot be identified, have vehicle towed by law enforcement.
- Consider installing telephone caller ID; record phone call if necessary.
- Increase perimeter lighting.
- Deploy visible security cameras and motion sensors.
- Remove vegetation in and around perimeters; maintain regularly.
- Institute a robust vehicle inspection program to include checking the undercarriage of vehicles, under the hood, and in the trunk. Provide vehicle inspections training to security personnel.
- Deploy explosive detection devices and explosive detection canine teams.
- Conduct vulnerability studies focusing on physical security, structural engineering, infrastructure engineering, power, water, and air infiltration, if feasible.
- Initiate a system to enhance mail and package screening procedures (both announced and unannounced).
- Install special locking devices on access hole covers in and around facilities.

Indicators of the Use of Dangerous Materials that May Be Discovered by Emergency Responders

- Report sudden, unexplained illness of livestock herds or human population in local area, particularly that involving viruses or unusual disease(s) not normally associated with the area (e.g., malaria in dry or nontropical climate).
- Report detection or treatment of unexplained chemical burns or chemical exposure injuries, particularly if associated with vague, irrational, or deceptive explanations.
- Note unusual burns or illness in animals, which may be indicative of unauthorized materials or biological testing.
- Report use of facilities (e.g., warehouses, self-storage rentals) to store unusual or unexplained quantities of chemicals, Hazmat, or biological material.
- Report unusual, unexplained, or unauthorized use or rental of chemical sprayers, spraying vehicles, or aircraft.
- Note evidence of unusual or unauthorized attempts to obtain a license to handle pesticides.
- Report suspicious purchase or rental of motorized personal aerial vehicles (e.g., ultralights) not requiring pilot license to operate.
- Repot suspicious deliveries to new or nontraditional customers of chemical, radiological, or geological material directly from the manufacturer to a self-storage facility, urban residence, or rural area.
- Report unusual chemical containers (type/quantity) discarded in storage unit dumpsters.
- Report complaints of unusual fumes, liquids, or odors from storage unit customers or neighbors.
- Report frequent off-hours visits to storage units, remote storage sites, or abandoned barns, fields, vacant warehouses, or other secluded areas.
- Report rescues made from burning buildings or vehicles where the victims seem reluctant to describe details or give inconsistent or conflicting versions of what happened.
- Note attempts to avoid reporting of fires or minor explosions in residences or storage facilities.
- Note occupant attempts to restrict access of first responders to areas of a residence or facility, or attempts to flee before or after the first responders arrive.
- Report evidence of chemical fires, toxic odors, brightly colored stains, or rusted metal fixtures in apartments, hotel/motel rooms, commercial offices, self-storage units, or garages.
- Report possession or acquisition of the following materials by persons with no apparent knowledge or skills related to their use: (i) portable safety enclosures with chemical fume hood; (ii) chemical protective garments and/or masks; (iii) 30–50 liter glass stills; (iv) quantities of Teflon or other glass storage containers (particularly 3–15 liter sizes); (v) established commercial, chemical, or

biological testing business or laboratory; (vi) chemical sprayers, spraying vehicles, or aircraft; (vii) various standard laboratory glassware; (viii) portable neutron generators of any type; and (ix) nuclear material transporting containers.

Attempt to Acquire Specialized Training or Expertise

- Report unauthorized or unusual attempts to obtain or conduct organized training in security concepts, conventional military weapons and tactics, and CBRNE (chemical, biological, radiological, nuclear, and explosive) weapons.
- Report unauthorized or unusual attempts to obtain specialized training concerning explosives, firearms, survival, flying, or defensive driving.
- Report semi-truck or large vehicle driver training conducted by uncertified individuals—particularly in remote areas such as fields or vacant parking lots at night.
- Report lack of interest by commercial driver's license students in finding follow-on employment.
- Report unusual interest in training in surveillance, weapons, intelligence gathering, or countersurveillance or counterintelligence techniques.
- Report attempts to threaten, coerce, or bribe trainers for certifications or licenses.

Use of Materials or Financing to Support Terrorist Activity

- Report unusual purchases of tools or equipment (e.g., lamination machines, specialized software, blank forms, documents) associated with document forgery.
- Report evidence of funding transfers between federally listed terrorist organizations and known suppliers of CBRNE weapons, devices, or materials.
- Report multiple suspicious financial transactions initiating from or terminating at the same location.
- Report cache(s) of funds, some of which may be held by unwitting associates.
- Report establishment or management of financial accounts or channels used by known or suspected terrorists or affiliated organizations. Note bank accounts that show indications of structuring.
- Report transactions involving a high volume of incoming or outgoing wire transfers, with no logical or apparent purpose, that come in from, go to, or transit through locations of concern (e.g., sanctioned countries, noncooperative nations, or sympathizer nations).
- Report unexplainable clearing or negotiation of third party checks and their deposits in foreign bank accounts.
- Report corporate layering, that is, transfers between bank accounts of related entities or charities for no apparent reason.

- Report wire transfers by charitable organizations to companies located in countries known to be bank or tax havens.
- Report lack of apparent fund-raising activity (e.g., lack of small checks or typical donations) associated with charitable bank deposits.
- Report use of multiple accounts to collect funds that are then transferred to the same foreign beneficiaries.
- Report transactions with no logical economic purpose (e.g., no link between the activity of the organization and other parties involved in the transaction).
- Report use of a business account to collect and then funnel funds to a small number of foreign beneficiaries, both individual and business.
- Report use of a business account that would not normally generate the volume of wire transfer activity, into and out of the account, as reported.
- Report use of multiple individuals to structure transactions under the reporting threshold to circumvent reporting requirements and then funnel funds to a foreign beneficiary.
- Report structuring of money order purchases at multiple locations to circumvent federal Currency Transaction Report requirements and Bank Secrecy Act recordkeeping.
- Report apparent intent to circumvent remittance company's internal requirements of presentation of identification through purchase of money orders in small amounts.
- Report import/export businesses acting as an unlicensed remitter to conduct wire transfers.
- Report business account activity conducted by nationals of countries associated with terrorist activity with no obvious connection to the business.
- Report use of alternate money remittance systems and/or informal banking methods, or commodities to transfer (e.g., drugs, weapons, cigarettes, diamonds, and gold).

Physical Security Planning

- Acquire the assistance of a physical security specialist (usually from a law enforcement agency) to conduct annual physical security vulnerability assessments to determine where improvements are needed.
- Randomly inspect the security and condition of all facilities, storage areas, and HVAC systems.
- Increase observation and scrutiny of all facilities, storage, and surrounding areas.
- Keep all doors (including apparatus bay doors) and windows closed and locked unless these access points are continuously monitored so intruders can be immediately intercepted.
- Use appropriate locking systems for all access points (e.g., single cylinder locks for solid core doors and double cylinder locks for doors with glass).

- Obtain a monitored security alert system for buildings and storage areas that are not always occupied and in regular use.
- Guarantee that all apparatus, vehicles, and equipment maintained in exterior parking or storage areas are always locked when unattended.
- Periodically test security systems, back-up power sources, and emergency communications.
- Initiate and enforce a reliable identification system for department personnel and property.
- Screen all visitors (including vendors) and deny entry to anyone who refuses inspection.
- Develop inspection practices for incoming deliveries including postal packages and mail.
- Implement a dependable visitor/vendor identification and accountability system that includes escorting nondepartment personnel as much as practicable.
- Restrict access to communication centers and equipment including computer systems and networks to the few essential department personnel and authorized technicians.
- Prepare an SOP containing the organization's physical security policy and practices.
- Train department personnel regarding the application and enforcement of all physical security measures.

Considerations Before Catastrophe Strikes

- Issue and mandate the wearing of picture identification while on duty.
- Require 100% identification check at suspicious incidents.
- Maintain 100% personnel accountability at all incidents.
- Be observant and preserve situational awareness during the performance of duties.
- Attempt to know as many of your employees as possible.
- Recognize the employees of neighboring businesses.
- Establish aggressive controls over vehicle access to the key asset.
- Completely destroy unserviceable clothing, equipment, and accessories before discarding.

Protective Measures for Public Gatherings

- Develop provisions to validate the identity of official personnel, guests, and vehicles that may be seen at or near planned gatherings.
- Become familiar with local first responder uniforms and vehicles, including those from mutual aid partners and other adjacent municipalities.

- Establish strict internal accountability for uniforms, accouterments, vehicles, operating devices, codes, and anything else that can be used by adversaries to "legitimize" their presence or to facilitate illicit acts.
- Reliably ascertain if there is any group (violent or nonviolent) that plans to appear at local celebrations with or without a formally approved permit.
- Rehearse plans to professionally intercept and remove individuals or groups that unlawfully disrupt proceedings.
- Confirm the readiness of local stakeholders and mutual aid partners to execute emergency response plans if an attack or violence occurs.
- Reinforce the National Incident Management System and the Incident Command System.

Indicators of Surveillance, Probing, and Reconnaissance of Key Assets

- Report attempts to test or conduct reconnaissance of security operations at key asset facilities, high resource facilities, high profile venues, or sector specific events.
- Report any persons showing uncommon interest in security measures or personnel, entry points or access controls, or perimeter barriers such as fences or walls.
- Report any persons showing uncommon interest in key asset facilities, networks, or systems (e.g., photographing or videotaping assets).
- Report all suspicious attempts to recruit employees or persons knowledgeable about key personnel or key asset facilities, networks, or systems.
- Report any persons loitering for no apparent purpose near key asset facilities who do not fit the surrounding environment, such as individuals wearing improper attire for conditions not normally present in the area.
    - (i) Note any responses from such individuals to questions posed by security personnel which appear practiced.
    - (ii) Note possession by such individuals of uniforms (military, clerical, medical, civil service, law enforcement), which do not match their stated profession.
- Report pedestrian surveillance near key asset facilities involving any surveillance activity of sensitive operations, including photography, videotaping, or extensive note taking/use of audio recorder (regardless of number of individuals involved), or mobile surveillance by cars, trucks, motorcycles, boats, or small aircraft.
    - (i) Note suspicious behavior, such as staring or quickly looking away from personnel, unexplained vehicle movement, or sudden movement by personnel or vehicles when approached or observed by security personnel.
    - (ii) Note apparent foot surveillance involving two or more individuals working together, and prolonged static surveillance by personnel performing apparent work functions for unusually long durations.

(iii) Note mobile surveillance using bicycles, scooters, cars, aircraft, watercraft, or other vehicles. Where possible, attempt to identify make, model, and license number.

(iv) Note secretive or nonsecretive use of still cameras, video recorders, sketching, or note taking around key asset facilities not normally associated with normal tourist interest or behavior.

If you encounter a person making suspicious inquiries, request their identification and make a photocopy, contact local law enforcement agency before the visitors leave the premises, obtain an accurate vehicle description and license plate number, and preserve any surveillance videotape that may exist.

Cyber Countermeasures

- Close holes by obtaining and applying software security patches as soon as they become available.
- Block intruders with a quality firewall.
- Stop infections caused by hostile software that can still infiltrate the computer (e.g., others connected to a local area network).
- Prevent subversion by adding one or more firewalls that prevent spyware or other malware from being installed.
- Lock down the machine by using hard to crack passwords and/or encrypting and by password protecting files, folders, or even entire drives.

Miscellaneous

- Maintain situational awareness of world events and ongoing threats.
- Ensure all levels of personnel are notified via briefings, e-mail, voice mail, and signage of any changes in threat conditions and protective measures.
- Encourage personnel to be alert and immediately report any situation that may constitute a threat or suspicious activity.
- Encourage personnel to avoid routines, to vary times and routes, to preplan, and to keep a low profile, especially during periods of high threats.
- Encourage personnel to take notice and report suspicious packages, devices, unattended briefcases, or other unusual materials immediately; inform them not to handle or attempt to move any such object.
- Encourage personnel to keep their family members and supervisors appraised of their whereabouts.
- Encourage personnel to know emergency exits and stairwells.
- Increase the number of visible security personnel wherever possible.
- Rearrange exterior vehicle barriers, traffic cones, and roadblocks to alter traffic patterns near facilities and cover by alert security forces.

- Institute/increase vehicle, foot, and roving security patrols varying in size, timing, and routes.
- Implement random security guard shift changes.
- Arrange for law enforcement vehicles to be parked randomly near entrances and exits.
- Review current contingency plans and, if not already in place, develop and implement procedures for receiving and acting on threat information, alert notification procedures, terrorist incident response procedures, evacuation procedures, bomb threat procedures, hostage and barricade procedures, CBRN procedures, consequence and crisis management procedures, accountability procedures, and media procedures.
- When aforementioned plans and procedures have been implemented, conduct internal training exercises and invite local emergency responders to participate in joint exercises.
- Coordinate and establish partnerships with local authorities to develop intelligence and information sharing relationships.
- Place personnel on standby for contingency planning.
- Limit the number of access points and strictly enforce access control procedures.
- Consider installing telephone caller ID; record phone calls if necessary.
- Deploy visible security cameras and motion sensors.
- Initiate a system to enhance mail and package screening procedures (both announced and unannounced).
- Install special locking devices on access hole covers in and around facilities.
- Implement a countersurveillance detection program.

REFERENCES

1. George Tenet, CIA Director, March 21, 2000 statement before the U.S. Foreign Relations Committee.
2. *U.S. Fire Administration Fact Sheet*, December 2004.
3. *The National Strategy for the Physical Protection of Critical Infrastructure and Key Assets*, The White House, 2003.
4. U.S. Fire Administration, *The CIP Process Job Aid*, May 2002.

APPENDIX 9.1 HOMELAND SECURITY PRESIDENTIAL DIRECTIVE 8 BY PRESIDENT GEORGE W. BUSH

SUBJECT: NATIONAL PREPAREDNESS

Purpose

(1) This directive establishes policies to strengthen the preparedness of the United States to prevent and respond to threatened or actual domestic terrorist attacks, major disasters, and other emergencies by requiring a national domestic all-hazards preparedness goal, establishing mechanisms for improved delivery of Federal preparedness assistance to State and local governments, and outlining actions to strengthen preparedness capabilities of Federal, State, and local entities.

Definitions

(2) For the purposes of this directive:

(a) The term "all-hazards preparedness" refers to preparedness for domestic terrorist attacks, major disasters, and other emergencies.

(b) The term "Federal departments and agencies" means those executive departments enumerated in 5 U.S.C. 101, and the Department of Homeland Security; independent establishments as defined by 5 U.S.C. 104(1); Government corporations as defined by 5 U.S.C. 103(1); and the United States Postal Service.

(c) The term "Federal preparedness assistance" means Federal department and agency grants, cooperative agreements, loans, loan guarantees, training, and/or technical assistance provided to State and local governments and the private sector to prevent, prepare for, respond to, and recover from terrorist attacks, major disasters, and other emergencies. Unless noted otherwise, the term "assistance" will refer to Federal assistance programs.

(d) The term "first responder" refers to those individuals who in the early stages of an incident are responsible for the protection and preservation of life, property, evidence, and the environment, including emergency response providers as defined in section 2 of the Homeland Security Act of 2002 (6 U.S.C. 101), as well as emergency management, public health, clinical care, public works, and other skilled support personnel (such as equipment operators) that provide immediate support services during prevention, response, and recovery operations.

(e) The terms "major disaster" and "emergency" have the meanings given in section 102 of the Robert T. Stafford Disaster Relief and Emergency Assistance Act (42 U.S.C. 5122).

(f) The term "major events" refers to domestic terrorist attacks, major disasters, and other emergencies.

(g) The term "national homeland security preparedness-related exercises" refers to homeland security-related exercises that train and test national decision makers and utilize resources of multiple Federal departments and agencies. Such exercises may involve State and local first responders when appropriate. Such exercises do not include those exercises conducted solely within a single Federal department or agency.

(h) The term "preparedness" refers to the existence of plans, procedures, policies, training, and equipment necessary at the Federal, State, and local level to maximize the ability to prevent, respond to, and recover from major events. The term "readiness" is used interchangeably with preparedness.

(i) The term "prevention" refers to activities undertaken by the first responder community during the early stages of an incident to reduce the likelihood or consequences of threatened or actual terrorist attacks. More general and broader efforts to deter, disrupt, or thwart terrorism are not addressed in this directive.

(j) The term "Secretary" means the Secretary of Homeland Security.

(k) The terms "State," and "local government," when used in a geographical sense, have the same meanings given to those terms in section 2 of the Homeland Security Act of 2002 (6 U.S.C. 101).

Relationship to HSPD-5

(3) This directive is a companion to HSPD-5, which identifies steps for improved coordination in response to incidents. This directive describes the way Federal departments and agencies will prepare for such a response, including prevention activities during the early stages of a terrorism incident.

Development of a National Preparedness Goal

(4) The Secretary is the principal Federal official for coordinating the implementation of all-hazards preparedness in the United States. In cooperation with other Federal departments and agencies, the Secretary coordinates the preparedness of Federal response assets, and the support for, and assessment of, the preparedness of State and local first responders.

(5) To help ensure the preparedness of the Nation to prevent, respond to, and recover from threatened and actual domestic terrorist attacks, major disasters, and other emergencies, the Secretary, in coordination with the heads of other appropriate Federal departments and agencies and in consultation with State and local governments, shall develop a national domestic all-hazards preparedness goal. Federal departments and agencies will work to achieve this goal by:

(a) providing for effective, efficient, and timely delivery of Federal preparedness assistance to State and local governments; and

(b) supporting efforts to ensure first responders are prepared to respond to major events, especially prevention of and response to threatened terrorist attacks.

(6) The national preparedness goal will establish measurable readiness priorities and targets that appropriately balance the potential threat and magnitude of terrorist attacks, major disasters, and other emergencies with the resources required to prevent, respond to, and recover from them. It will also include readiness metrics and elements that support the national preparedness goal including standards for preparedness assessments and strategies, and a system for assessing the Nation's overall preparedness to respond to major events, especially those involving acts of terrorism.

(7) The Secretary will submit the national preparedness goal to me through the Homeland Security Council (HSC) for review and approval prior to, or concurrently with, the Department of Homeland Security's Fiscal Year 2006 budget submission to the Office of Management and Budget.

Federal Preparedness Assistance

(8) The Secretary, in coordination with the Attorney General, the Secretary of Health and Human Services (HHS), and the heads of other Federal departments and agencies that provide assistance for first responder preparedness, will establish a single point of access to Federal preparedness assistance program information within 60 days of the issuance of this directive. The Secretary will submit to me through the HSC recommendations of specific Federal department and agency programs to be part of the coordinated approach. All Federal departments and agencies will cooperate with this effort. Agencies will continue to issue financial assistance awards consistent with applicable laws and regulations and will ensure that program announcements, solicitations, application instructions, and other guidance documents are consistent with other Federal preparedness programs to the extent possible. Full implementation of a closely coordinated interagency grant process will be completed by September 30, 2005.

(9) To the extent permitted by law, the primary mechanism for delivery of Federal preparedness assistance will be awards to the States. Awards will be delivered in a form that allows the recipients to apply the assistance to the highest priority preparedness requirements at the appropriate level of government. To the extent permitted by law, Federal preparedness assistance will be predicated on adoption of Statewide comprehensive all-hazards preparedness strategies. The strategies should be consistent with the national preparedness goal, should assess the most effective ways to enhance preparedness, should address areas facing higher risk, especially to terrorism, and should also address local government concerns and Citizen Corps efforts. The Secretary, in coordination with the heads of other appropriate Federal departments and agencies, will review and approve strategies submitted by the States. To the extent permitted by law, adoption of approved Statewide strategies will be a requirement for receiving Federal preparedness assistance at all levels of government by September 30, 2005.

(10) In making allocations of Federal preparedness assistance to the States, the Secretary, the Attorney General, the Secretary of HHS, the Secretary of Transportation, the Secretary of Energy, the Secretary of Veterans Affairs, the Administrator of the Environmental Protection Agency, and the heads of other Federal departments and agencies that provide assistance for first responder preparedness will base those allocations on assessments of population concentrations, critical infrastructures, and other significant risk factors, particularly terrorism threats, to the extent permitted by law.

(11) Federal preparedness assistance will support State and local entities' efforts including planning, training, exercises, interoperability, and equipment acquisition for major events as well as capacity building for prevention activities such as information gathering, detection, deterrence, and collaboration related to terrorist attacks. Such assistance is not primarily intended to support existing capacity to address normal local first responder operations, but to build capacity to address major events, especially terrorism.

(12) The Attorney General, the Secretary of HHS, the Secretary of Transportation, the Secretary of Energy, the Secretary of Veterans Affairs, the Administrator of the Environmental Protection Agency, and the heads of other Federal departments and agencies that provide assistance for first responder preparedness shall coordinate with the Secretary to ensure that such assistance supports and is consistent with the national preparedness goal.

(13) Federal departments and agencies will develop appropriate mechanisms to ensure rapid obligation and disbursement of funds from their programs to the States, from States to the local community level, and from local entities to the end users to derive maximum

benefit from the assistance provided. Federal departments and agencies will report annually to the Secretary on the obligation, expenditure status, and the use of funds associated with Federal preparedness assistance programs.

Equipment

(14) The Secretary, in coordination with State and local officials, first responder organizations, the private sector and other Federal civilian departments and agencies, shall establish and implement streamlined procedures for the ongoing development and adoption of appropriate first responder equipment standards that support nationwide interoperability and other capabilities consistent with the national preparedness goal, including the safety and health of first responders.

(15) To the extent permitted by law, equipment purchased through Federal preparedness assistance for first responders shall conform to equipment standards in place at time of purchase. Other Federal departments and agencies that support the purchase of first responder equipment will coordinate their programs with the Department of Homeland Security and conform to the same standards.

(16) The Secretary, in coordination with other appropriate Federal departments and agencies and in consultation with State and local governments, will develop plans to identify and address national first responder equipment research and development needs based upon assessments of current and future threats. Other Federal departments and agencies that support preparedness research and development activities shall coordinate their efforts with the Department of Homeland Security and ensure they support the national preparedness goal.

Training and Exercises

(17) The Secretary, in coordination with the Secretary of HHS, the Attorney General, and other appropriate Federal departments and agencies and in consultation with State and local governments, shall establish and maintain a comprehensive training program to meet the national preparedness goal. The program will identify standards and maximize the effectiveness of existing Federal programs and financial assistance and include training for the Nation's first responders, officials, and others with major event preparedness, prevention, response, and recovery roles. Federal departments and agencies shall include private organizations in the accreditation and delivery of preparedness training as appropriate and to the extent permitted by law.

(18) The Secretary, in coordination with other appropriate Federal departments and agencies, shall establish a national program and a multi-year planning system to conduct homeland security preparedness-related exercises that reinforces identified training standards, provides for evaluation of readiness, and supports the national preparedness goal. The establishment and maintenance of the program will be conducted in maximum collaboration with State and local governments and appropriate private sector entities. All Federal departments and agencies that conduct national homeland security preparedness-related exercises shall participate in a collaborative, interagency process to designate such exercises on a consensus basis and create a master exercise calendar. The Secretary will ensure that exercises included in the calendar support the national preparedness goal. At the time of designation, Federal departments and agencies will identify their level of participation in national homeland security preparedness-related exercises. The Secretary will develop a multi-year national homeland security preparedness-related exercise plan and submit the plan to me through the HSC for review and approval.

(19) The Secretary shall develop and maintain a system to collect, analyze, and disseminate lessons learned, best practices, and information from exercises, training events, research, and other sources, including actual incidents, and establish procedures to improve national preparedness to prevent, respond to, and recover from major events. The Secretary, in coordination with other Federal departments and agencies and State and local governments, will identify relevant classes of homeland-security related information and appropriate means of transmission for the information to be included in the system. Federal departments and agencies are directed, and State and local governments are requested, to provide this information to the Secretary to the extent permitted by law.

Federal Department and Agency Preparedness

(20) The head of each Federal department or agency shall undertake actions to support the national preparedness goal, including adoption of quantifiable performance measurements in the areas of training, planning, equipment, and exercises for Federal incident management and asset preparedness, to the extent permitted by law. Specialized Federal assets such as teams, stockpiles, and caches shall be maintained at levels consistent with the national preparedness goal and be available for response activities as set forth in the National Response Plan, other appropriate operational documents, and applicable authorities or guidance. Relevant Federal regulatory requirements should be consistent with the national preparedness goal. Nothing in this directive shall limit the authority of the Secretary of Defense with regard to the command and control, training, planning, equipment, exercises, or employment of Department of Defense forces, or the allocation of Department of Defense resources.

(21) The Secretary, in coordination with other appropriate Federal civilian departments and agencies, shall develop and maintain a Federal response capability inventory that includes the performance parameters of the capability, the timeframe within which the capability can be brought to bear on an incident, and the readiness of such capability to respond to domestic incidents. The Department of Defense will provide to the Secretary information describing the organizations and functions within the Department of Defense that may be utilized to provide support to civil authorities during a domestic crisis.

Citizen Participation

(22) The Secretary shall work with other appropriate Federal departments and agencies as well as State and local governments and the private sector to encourage active citizen participation and involvement in preparedness efforts. The Secretary shall periodically review and identify the best community practices for integrating private citizen capabilities into local preparedness efforts.

Public Communication

(23) The Secretary, in consultation with other Federal departments and agencies, State and local governments, and non-governmental organizations, shall develop a comprehensive plan to provide accurate and timely preparedness information to public citizens, first responders, units of government, the private sector, and other interested parties and mechanisms for coordination at all levels of government.

Assessment and Evaluation

(24) The Secretary shall provide to me through the Assistant to the President for Homeland Security an annual status report of the Nation's level of preparedness, including State capabilities, the readiness of Federal civil response assets, the utilization of mutual aid, and an assessment of how the Federal first responder preparedness assistance programs support the national preparedness goal. The first report will be provided within 1 year of establishment of the national preparedness goal.

(25) Nothing in this directive alters, or impedes the ability to carry out, the authorities of the Federal departments and agencies to perform their responsibilities under law and consistent with applicable legal authorities and presidential guidance.

(26) Actions pertaining to the funding and administration of financial assistance and all other activities, efforts, and policies in this directive shall be executed in accordance with law. To the extent permitted by law, these policies will be established and carried out in consultation with State and local governments.

(27) This directive is intended only to improve the internal management of the executive branch of the Federal Government, and it is not intended to, and does not, create any right or benefit, substantive or procedural, enforceable at law or in equity, against the United States, its departments, agencies, or other entities, its officers or employees, or any other person.

CHAPTER 10

General Emergency Response Considerations

10.1 INTRODUCTION

Emergencies come in many sizes, from a relatively simple event such as a minor laceration or rupture of a 55 gallon drum of hazardous materials, to complex situations such as a major fire in a high rise office building or a large chemical explosion or toxic release. Now, emergency responders face an even greater challenge—the use of weapons of mass destruction by an adversary.

Emergency situations also seem to occur at the most inopportune times—bad weather, few personnel available. Some emergencies can become significant in that they can impact wide areas of land, water, or air. Emergency incidents have no regard for jurisdictional boundaries and often spread through jurisdictions, impacting many people.

10.2 DEFINITION OF FIRST RESPONDER

The definitions of "first responder" in Homeland Security Presidential Directive 8 (HSPD 8) and the Homeland Security Act are much broader than the traditional fire, emergency medical, law enforcement, and emergency management. The term "first responder" refers to those individuals who in the early stages of an incident are responsible for the protection and preservation of life, property, evidence, and the environment, including emergency response providers as defined in Section 2 of the Homeland Security Act of 2002 (6 U.S.C. 101), as well as emergency management, public health, clinical care, public workers, and other skilled support personnel who provide immediate support services during prevention, response, and recovery operations (from HSPD 8).

The term "emergency response providers" includes federal, state, and local emergency public safety, law enforcement, emergency response, emergency medical

Understanding, Assessing, and Responding to Terrorism: Protecting Critical Infrastructure and Personnel By Brian T. Bennett

(including hospital emergency facilities), and related personnel, agencies, and authorities (from Homeland Security Act).

10.3 EMERGENCY RESPONSE PLANS

Written emergency response plans are what employees and emergency responders will follow in the event of an emergency. Emergency response plans should be developed to cover all potential emergencies that may arise within the jurisdiction. Written emergency response plans should contain the following basic elements as a minimum.

- *Shelter in Place.* This section should review the decision making process as to whether personnel should be protected in place rather than be removed from the area in the event of an emergency. Sheltering in place is a viable protective option, especially when large numbers of people might have to be protected. It is sometimes safer to leave people where they are than move them into or through a dangerous area as part of the evacuation process.
- *Evacuation.* Evacuation is the physical displacement and relocation of personnel from a dangerous area to a safer area. Because of the logistics involved in moving large numbers of people, evacuation should be considered as a last resort. Evacuation is appropriate whenever people are in more danger remaining in their present locations than if they were moved.
- *Medical Emergencies.* Medical emergencies can arise at any time, and not necessarily related to an attack by an adversary. Emergency response plans should address the actions to be taken if someone were to need medical care. The plan should cover who to notify (the appropriate organization for help) and how to notify them, such as emergency phone numbers.
- *Fire.* All personnel should be knowledgeable about how to summon help in the event of a fire. The local emergency number should be included in the plan.
- *Incident Command System.* The jurisdiction-specific incident command system (ICS) should be delineated, so each person knows his/her role and how he/she fits into the overall incident management plan. There should be a minimum of one backup person for each ICS function in case the primary person is unavailable to fulfill the role.
- *Responsibilities.* Emergency response plans should spell out each individual's role. If the jurisdiction maintains an emergency response and mitigation capability, there should be a mission statement that outlines the functions and responsibilities of the emergency responders.
- *Emergency Communications.* The plan should include emergency telephone numbers for the municipal police, fire, and emergency medical services. If the jurisdiction maintains its own emergency responders, the in-house emergency telephone number should also be listed. If two-way radios are used,

the appropriate frequencies and specific procedures should be listed. Finally, emergency numbers for key personnel should be provided, including off-hours telephone numbers.

- *Account for People.* There should be a system to account for all personnel present within the area if an emergency occurs and results in sheltering in place or an evacuation. Specific individuals should be assigned to account for personnel and report to the command post. A system should also be developed to locate people who were unaccounted for.
- *Communicate with Personnel.* There are times when emergency information, such as evacuation orders, must be communicated to personnel present within a jurisdiction. This may be people who are located in a large office building, or the citizens of a town or section thereof. There must be plans in place that outline how the information will be communicated and by whom.

Emergency response plans should be developed in cooperation with the local emergency responders. This coordination will ensure that each agency is fully aware of its responsibilities under the plan and that each agency has the capabilities necessary to fulfill that responsibility.

Once an emergency response plan has been written and coordinated with the applicable agencies, the plan should be tested to ensure it will function as designed. The way to test an emergency response plan is through exercises. Each specific element in the emergency response plan should be tested.

Once an emergency response exercise has been completed, a postincident analysis should be conducted. This analysis is essentially a critique of the exercise, with the goal of finding deficiencies in the plan and correcting them. Once the analysis has been completed, the emergency response plan should be updated to reflect the recommended changes. Then the process starts again with another exercise and critique, with the goal being continuous improvement.

An emergency response plan is only effective if the information it contains is current. Therefore periodic reviews of the written plan must be conducted to ensure all of the information and procedures are complete and reflect the current situation.

10.4 PRE-EMERGENCY PLANS

Pre-emergency plans are an integral part of a comprehensive emergency preparedness and response program. Pre-emergency plans are essentially scripts that will be used to guide the response to certain emergency situations. They are prepared in advance of the emergency, usually by a committee, and put into written form. The preplans are then built into the training program for emergency responders so that they can be practiced. Once they have been practiced, they should be evaluated for completeness and updated as necessary.

In the event of a real emergency, emergency responders will have a documented plan they can use as a template to mitigate the emergency. The advantage of the pre-emergency plan, other than having the plan for responding to the incident, is that the operational risk management plan has already been completed for the likely emergency scenarios.

As with all other emergency response documents, the pre-emergency plans should be developed, practiced, evaluated, and updated with both in-house and outside agency emergency responders.

Pre-emergency plans should be developed for likely accidental, natural, or intentional hazard scenarios, such as storms, hurricanes, floods, tornadoes, earthquakes, fires, and hazardous materials releases. These same plans can be used to respond to incidents caused by an expanding "spectrum of threats" including terrorism or other human-caused disasters.

Effective pre-emergency plans typically include the following information:

- A broad description of the incident command system and emergency management organization.
- A general description of the emergency response priorities.
- Pre-evaluation of potential hazards.
- Proper personal protective equipment required for a safe response.
- Tools and equipment necessary for mitigation.
- Specific mitigation procedures.
- Air monitoring equipment and techniques.
- Decontamination solutions and protocols.
- First aid procedures.
- Communication systems, including radio frequencies, and phone numbers.
- Location of critical equipment and utility shutoffs.
- Contingency plans that are appropriate and flexible.
- A formal and defined emergency management process to mitigate incidents and restore services quickly.
- Formal mutual assistance agreements.

10.5 DRILLS AND EXERCISES

There are two categories of exercises. The type of exercise that best meets a jurisdiction's requirements is identified through an analysis of the stated exercise purpose, proposed objectives, experience, operations, historical precedence, and recommended level of performance.

The first type of exercise is the discussion-based exercise. This type of exercise is normally used as a starting point in the exercise process, to highlight existing plans, policies, mutual aid agreements, and procedures. They are excellent tools for familiarizing agencies and personnel with current or expected capabilities. Discussion-based exercises typically focus on strategic, policy-oriented issues.

Facilitators keep participants focused and on track while meeting the objectives of the exercise.

Discussion-based exercises include seminars, workshops, tabletop exercises, and games.

Seminars. Seminars are employed to orient participants to authorities, strategies, plans, policies, procedures, protocols, response resources, concepts, and ideas. Seminars offer the following attributes: low-stress environment, informal discussions, lack of time constraints, and effectiveness with both large and small groups.

Workshops. Workshops offer increased participant interaction and are focused on achieving or building a product, such as a plan or policy. Workshops are an ideal forum for collecting or sharing information; obtaining new or different perspectives; testing new ideas, policies, procedures, or processes; training groups in coordinated activities; problem solving complex issues; obtaining consensus; and team building.

Tabletop Exercises. Tabletop exercises involve senior staff, elected or appointed officials, or other key personnel in an informal setting, discussing simulated situations. This type of exercise is designed to stimulate discussion of various issues regarding a hypothetical situation. It can be used to access plans, policies, and procedures or to assess the types of systems needed to guide the prevention of, response to, and recovery from a defined event. Tabletop exercise attributes include practicing group problem solving, familiarizing senior officials with a situation, conducting a specific case study, examining personnel contingencies, testing group message interpretation, participating in sharing information, assessing interagency coordination, and achieving limited or specified objectives.

Games. A game is a simulation of operations that often involves two or more teams, usually in a competitive environment, using rules, data, and procedures designed to depict an actual or assumed real-life situation. It does not involve the use of actual resources, and the sequence of events affects, and in turn is affected by, the decisions made by the players.

The second type of exercise is the operations-based exercise. This type of exercise is used to validate the plans, policies, agreements, and procedures solidified in discussion-based exercises. Operations-based exercises are characterized by actual response, mobilization of apparatus and resources, and commitment of personnel, usually over an extended period of time.

Operations-based exercises include drills, functional exercises, and full-scale exercises.

Drills. A drill is a coordinated, supervised activity usually employed to test a single specific operation or function in a single agency. Drills are commonly used to provide training on new equipment, develop or test new policies or procedures, or practice or maintain current skills. Typical attributes of drills include a narrow focus, measured against established standards; instant feedback; realistic environment; and performance in isolation.

Functional Exercises. A functional exercise (also known as a command post exercise) is designed to test and evaluate individual capabilities, multiple functions or activities within a function, or interdependent groups of functions. Functional exercises are generally focused on exercising the plans, policies, procedures, and staffs of the direction and control nodes of Incident Command and Unified Command. The objective of a functional exercise is to execute specific plans and procedures and apply established policies, plans, and procedures under crisis conditions. Attributes of functional exercises include evaluating functions; evaluating Emergency Operations Centers, headquarters, and staff; reinforcing established policies and procedures; measuring resource adequacy; and examining interjurisdictional relationships.

Full-Scale Exercises. Full-scale exercises are multiagency, multijurisdictional exercises that test many facets of emergency response and recovery. A full-scale exercise focuses on implementing and analyzing the plans, policies, and procedures developed in discussion-based exercises and practiced in previous, smaller, operations-based exercises. The events are projected through a scripted exercise scenario with built-in flexibility to allow updates to drive activities. It is conducted in a real-time, stressful environment that closely mirrors a real event. First responders and resources are mobilized and deployed to the scene, where they conduct their actions as if a real incident had occurred. Typical attributes include assessing organizational and individual performance; demonstrating interagency cooperation; allocating resources and personnel; assessing equipment capabilities; activating personnel and equipment; assessing interjurisdictional cooperation; exercising public information systems; testing communications systems and procedures; and analyzing memorandums of understanding (MOUs), standard operating procedures, plans, policies, and procedures [1].

A debriefing and detailed analysis are essential to ensure the lessons learned from the exercise are applied for continuous improvement.

10.6 EMERGENCY RESPONSE PRIORITIES

Emergency incidents have the potential of causing an extensive amount of damage, including injuries and death to exposed personnel. While emergency responders have the training and equipment to mitigate emergencies, they are often injured or killed because they fail to prioritize their emergency activities.

Emergency response priorities have been established to help guide responders to achieve a safe response. These priorities are one of the few things at an emergency incident that must never change. The emergency response priorities are:

1. Life safety.
2. Incident stabilization/protection of the environment.
3. Property conservation.

What these priorities tell us is that life is the most important issue when responding to an incident. That means that the emergency responder must ensure that he/she is protected first, and only after that, start other emergency activities. There are several critical activities that must occur to ensure an emergency responder's life safety is protected during an emergency response:

The materials involved in the incident must be identified.

The appropriate level of personal protective equipment must be available and worn correctly.

A sufficient number of responders must be assembled before starting operations (each responder should at least have a "buddy").

There must be an action plan.

The necessary equipment to conduct the task must be available.

Emergency responders must have the training necessary to implement the action plan.

Once the life safety of the responder is addressed, then rescue of victims can be started. There are too many case studies of well-intentioned, yet unprotected, untrained, or ill-equipped emergency responders becoming fatalities. The primary responsibility of every emergency responder is to safeguard his/her own safety first, then their safety of their "buddy," and then the safety of the victims. If all safety considerations have been met, and viable victims are present, then all necessary resources should be dedicated to victim rescue. However, there are times when these safety considerations cannot be met and therefore operations should not be started.

Once all of the life safety issues confronting the emergency responders and victims have been addressed, the next response priority is that of stabilizing the incident. The responders should take whatever mitigation actions are appropriate to minimize the adverse effects of the emergency.

The last response priority is that of property conservation. Only after all other issues have been addressed should responders be committed to saving equipment or property.

Depending on the number of responders available and the type of emergency at hand, it may be possible to conduct two or three of these tasks at the same time.

10.7 OPERATIONAL RISK MANAGEMENT

Operational risk management is very similar to the risk management process covered earlier. However, instead of evaluating and managing the risk to a key asset, operational risk management evaluates the risk to the emergency responder based on the operations that will be performed.

Any emergency response operation is inherently dangerous, and the risk can almost never be reduced to zero. However, when responding to a weapon of mass destruction (WMD) attack, the hazards and risks to emergency responders will increase exponentially. Therefore an effective operational risk management process is even more important than in a "normal" emergency response. Emergency responders must be highly trained and rein in the urge to rush in before conducting an assessment. Operating procedures and drills must enforce the principle of operational risk management assessment before conducting any task. Unlike the risk management process discussed earlier to assess assets, a trained individual emergency responder can very quickly perform a risk assessment. Obviously, the assessments performed by individual emergency responders before they start a task will be completed mentally and not necessarily written down.

Operational risk management is the process of identifying, assessing, and controlling the risks that are inherent in the daily operations of an organization—in this case an emergency response organization—and making decisions that balance risk costs with the benefits of an aggressive response. Emergency response leaders must understand the importance of the process in achieving the response goals and conserving resources. Operational risk management is an ongoing process that continues response to response. It must be integral to each decision that is made.

The basic tenets of operational risk management are:

- *Risk a Lot to Save a Lot.* Emergency responders will risk their safety to achieve a significant goal, such as saving a life.
- *Risk a Little to Save a Little.* Emergency responders will accept a little risk to save valuable assets.
- *Risk Nothing to Save What is Already Lost.* Emergency responders will not endanger their safety to save something that has no value.

Operational Risk Management Principles

The basic tenets are supported by four basic operational risk management principles:

1. *Accept no Unnecessary Risk—Understand Those Risks that are Accepted.* There must be some value in performing an operation that poses a risk to an emergency responder. Responders are willing to accept a significant amount of risk in order to save something of great value. However, since not all of the risk has been mitigated, the responders should have a full understanding of the residual risk that they are accepting by performing the operation.

2. *Accept Risk When Benefits Outweigh the Costs.* There are situations when the risk analysis process indicates that much can be saved with little cost in terms of risk to the emergency responder. In these situations, the operation should proceed.

3. *Anticipate Risk by Integrating Operational Risk Management into Operations and Planning at all Levels.* Emergency response organizations must fully understand that there is risk in all emergency response activities. In order to protect the organization's assets (in this case, the emergency responders themselves), the concept of organizational risk management must be built into all aspects of the planning and operational phases of the emergency response operation.

4. *Make Risk Decisions at the Correct Level.* The operational risk management process dictates that the risk assessment is conducted at all levels. Each individual emergency responder should conduct a risk assessment for his/her own tasks. Supervisors should be assessing the risk for the tasks assigned to their subordinates. And finally, the Incident Commander should be conducting a risk assessment for the overall incident.

The factors listed below become the basis of a decision making system to guide supervisors in conducting the operational risk management analysis:

Who has operational control and responsibility?

Who is the senior person at the scene?

Who possesses best insight into the full benefits and costs of risk?

Who has the resources to mitigate the risk?

What level makes the most operational sense?

There are seven developmental steps in the overall operational risk management process.

1. *Mission and Task Identification.* Clearly state the objective of the emergency response. Define what tasks are required to accomplish the objectives. Define the conditions under which to accomplish the task.

2. *Hazard and Risk Identification.* This is done by traditional methods including site surveys and review of material safety data sheets, operational equipment in use, and resources being used. Risk identification includes items such as any real or potential condition that can cause mission degradation, injury, illness, or death to emergency responders, and damage to or loss of equipment or property. Hazard identification answers the following questions: What can go wrong? (Focus on the critical components of your mission: equipment, personnel/experience, environment, timeline.) What safeguards exist and how effective are they?

3. *Hazard and Risk Assessment and Evaluation.* This is the step that associates the hazards with the risks. Determine the associated risk in terms of severity and probability and determine suitable controls for those hazards. The hazard is a condition that can impair the accomplishment of the emergency response objectives. When reviewing hazards associated with a task, their significance in terms of accomplishing the

emergency response objectives should not be considered so as not to skew the assessment.

Risk is a hazard for which we have estimated the severity, probability, and exposure to determine the scope with which it can impact our mission. Severity is the potential consequences measured in terms of degree of impact on the mission, the emergency responders, and equipment. Probability is the likelihood that potential adverse consequences will occur (e.g., very likely). Exposure is the duration, repetition (frequency), and number of people and/or equipment involved in the event (e.g., great, moderate). Frequency is based on reviewing data of similar activities and tasks and the frequency of the various associated incidents.

By ranking hazards, they can be remediated on a worst first basis. This is vital because risk control resources are always limited and should be directed at the big problems first to assure maximum bang for the buck.

4. *Risk Versus Gain Evaluation.* The person conducting the operational risk management assessment should evaluate what will be gained in performing the specific task in relation to the risks assumed by the emergency responders performing the task. Gain should balance or outweigh the risk. The goal should always be to get to the point where all tasks are low risk, high gain. However, realistically, this does not happen all that frequently with emergency response operations.

5. *Risk Decisions/Priorities.* This responsibility must ultimately be assigned to the Incident Commander given the current primary goal of the operation (e.g., rescue or recovery) and the operational effect of the recommended controls. Are risks acceptable or unacceptable? Can the emergency response objectives be modified to reduce risk? Are any safeguards missing? What new options should be considered?

When identifying options and establishing priorities, attack the worst problems first.

6. *Risk Control.* Execute the decision and implement risk and hazard control options. Ensure that control decisions are communicated to all personnel on scene, implemented properly, and complied with by all emergency responders.

7. *Monitor Activities.* Follow up to evaluate that controls are working and recommend appropriate modifications. Ensure risk control options are effective. Identify changes requiring further risk assessment and management. Capture and apply the lessons learned.

10.8 SITUATIONAL AWARENESS

Situational awareness is genuinely heightened awareness or cognizance of what is currently developing or occurring around you. Situational awareness failures can jeopardize personnel and physical assets. Hence situational awareness is essential for effective decision making and performance in complex and dynamic operational environments (such as an emergency response) often confronting first responders and their leadership.

Acquiring situational awareness is a daunting challenge for emergency services personnel. Duty, performance, unfamiliar settings, varied resources, confusing circumstances, time pressures, multiple incidents, and the risks of injury or death are all barriers to quality situational awareness.

Factors that reduce situational awareness for emergency responders include:

- *Insufficient Communication.* Progress reports from those "on the front lines" back to the supervisors are sometimes inadequate. Likewise, risk and hazard information reports from leadership to the front lines are often insufficient.
- *Fatigue and Stress.* Emergency response activities, especially when using encapsulating personal protective equipment that would be necessary in a WMD attack, cause a considerable amount of physiological and psychological stress on the body. Fatigue and stress often result, which can cause skewed reasoning and decision making.
- *Task Overload and Underload.* When emergency responders are overwhelmed with tasks, their focus is on completing the tasks and attention to other issues is compromised. Similarly, when emergency responders are underutilized, they tend to lose focus on the situation.
- *Group Mindset.* When there is a group of emergency responders, tasks tend to get put off because everyone thinks someone else will do it. In reality, no one does it.
- *"Press on Regardless" Philosophy.* Emergency responders often compromise their own safety in order to help others. Emergency responders are known to find innovative ways to accomplish very tough missions. Too often, the mentality is to press on regardless of the hazards and risks.
- *Degraded Operating Conditions.* Once emergency scene conditions deteriorate, things get disorganized very quickly. Usually when emergency scene operations degrade, that means bad things are starting to happen. Oftentimes, in an attempt to regain control of the incident, things that should get done do not.

10.9 HOMELAND SECURITY PRESIDENTIAL DIRECTIVE 5 (HSPD 5)

On February 28, 2003, President George W. Bush issued Homeland Security Presidential Directive 5 (HSPD 5) entitled. *Management of Domestic Incidents.*

The purpose of HSPD 5 is to enhance the ability of the United States to manage domestic incidents by establishing a single, comprehensive national incident management system to deal with both natural and human-caused disasters.

HSPD 5 directs the Secretary of Homeland Security to coordinate utilization of the federal government's resources in major disasters if any of the following four conditions apply:

1. A federal department or agency acting under its own authority has requested the assistance of the Department of Homeland Security.
2. The resources of state and local authorities are overwhelmed and federal assistance has been requested by the appropriate state and local authorities.

3. More than one federal department or agency has become substantially involved in responding to the incident.
4. The Secretary of Homeland Security has been directed to assume responsibility for managing the domestic incident by the president.

HSPD 5 also directs the Secretary of Homeland Security to develop, submit for review to the Homeland Security Council, and administer a National Response Plan.

Appendix 10.1 is a copy of HSPD 5.

National Incident Management System

HSPD 5 directs the Secretary of Homeland Security to develop and administer a National Incident Management System (NIMS). NIMS provides a consistent nationwide template to enable all public sector, private sector, and nongovernmental organizations to work effectively and efficiently together to prepare for, prevent, respond to, and recover from domestic incidents, regardless of size or complexity and whether they be caused by natural, accidental, or intentional circumstances.

The NIMS enhances the management of domestic incidents by establishing a single, comprehensive system for incident management and will help achieve greater cooperation among departments and agencies at all levels of government. To provide for interoperability and compatibility among federal, state, and local capabilities, the NIMS will include a core set of concepts, principles, terminology, and technologies covering the incident command system; multiagency coordination systems; unified command; training; identification and management of resources (including systems for classifying types of resources); qualifications and certification; and the collection, tracking, and reporting of incident information and incident resources.

NIMS is a comprehensive, national approach to incident management that is applicable at all jurisdictional levels and across functional disciplines. The intent of NIMS is to (1) be applicable across a full spectrum of potential incidents and hazard scenarios, regardless of size or complexity; and (2) improve coordination and cooperation between the public and private sectors while managing domestic incidents.

NIMS Concepts and Components

NIMS provides a flexible framework that facilitates public and private entities at all levels working together to manage domestic incidents. NIMS also provides a set of standardized organizational structures, as well as requirements for processes, procedures, and systems designed to improve interoperability.

Interoperability. Interoperability is the ability of tools, systems, and management processes to work together to accomplish a common task. Interoperability includes some degree of standardization.

For emergency responders, interoperability means jurisdictions that work together have standardized such things as:

- *Communications Systems.* Emergency responders from various jurisdictions, both public and private sectors, have common communications frequencies so that they can communicate with each other directly during an emergency incident. For example, jurisdictions can share a common radiofrequency.
- *Equipment.* Jurisdictions have purchased and trained on similar equipment, so that emergency responders from various jurisdictions are familiar with and can use the equipment. Additionally, this standardization allows for sharing resources and facilitates repairs. For example, jurisdictions can share fire hoses if all hoses have common threads.
- *Personal Protective Equipment.* Jurisdictions can maximize their inventories of protective equipment available if the equipment can be shared between jurisdictions. For example, one jurisdiction can purchase and inventory less self-contained breathing apparatus bottles if the other jurisdictions in the area maintain the same brand of bottles.
- *Operating Procedures.* Emergency response operations are facilitated, and in fact safer, if all responding emergency response jurisdictions use the same operating procedures. For example, all responding jurisdictions use the same operating procedure to combat the release of a biological agent into a building's HVAC system.

NIMS Components. NIMS is comprised of six components that work together as a system to provide a national framework to prepare for, prevent, respond to, and recover from domestic incidents.

1. *Command and Management.* NIMS standard incident management structures are based on three key organizational systems:

The Incident Command System (ICS), which defines the operating characteristics, management components, and structure of incident management organization in an incident.

Multiagency coordination systems, which define the operating characteristics, management components, and organizational structure of supporting entities.

Public information systems, which include the processes, procedures, and systems for communicating timely and accurate information to the public during emergency incidents.

2. *Preparedness.* Effective incident management begins with a host of preparedness activities. These activities are prepared well in advance of a potential incident. Preparedness involves a combination of planning, training, and exercises; personnel

qualifications and training standards; equipment acquisition and certification standards; publication management processes and activities; and mutual aid agreements and Emergency Management Assistance Compacts.

3. *Resource Management.* NIMS defines standardized mechanisms and establishes requirements for describing, inventorying, mobilizing, dispatching, tracking, and recovering resources during an emergency incident.

4. *Communications and Information Management.* NIMS identifies the requirements for a standardized framework for communications, information management, and information sharing support at all levels of incident management. Incident management organizations must ensure that effective, interoperable communications processes, procedures, and systems exist across all agencies and jurisdictions. Information management systems help ensure that information flows efficiently through a commonly accepted architecture. Effective information management enhances incident management and response by helping to ensure that decision making is better informed.

5. *Supporting Technologies.* Technology and technological systems provide supporting capabilities essential to implementing and refining NIMS. Examples include voice and data communication systems; information management systems, such as recordkeeping and resource tracking; and data display systems. Supporting technologies also include specialized technologies that facilitate ongoing operations and incident management activities in situations that call for unique technology-based capabilities.

6. *Ongoing Management and Maintenance.* The Department of Homeland Security established the NIMS Integration Center to provide strategic direction and oversight in support of routine review and continual refinement of both the system and its components.

Area Command

An Area Command is an organization established to oversee the management of multiple incidents that are each being managed by an ICS organization and large incidents that cross jurisdictional boundaries. Area Commands are particularly relevant to public health emergencies because these incidents are typically not site specific, not immediately identifiable, and geographically dispersed and evolving over time. These types of incidents call for a coordinated response, with large-scale coordination typically found at a higher jurisdictional level.

What Does Area Command Do? The Area Command has the responsibility for:

- Setting overall strategy and priorities.
- Allocating critical resources according to the incident priorities.
- Ensuring that incidents are properly managed.

- Ensuring that objectives are met.
- Ensuring that strategies are followed.

An Area Command may become a Unified Area Command when incidents are multijurisdictional.

How Is an Area Command Organized? An Area Command is organized similar to an ICS structure but, because operations are conducted on scene, there is no Operations Section in an Area Command. Other sections and functions are represented in an Area Command structure.

Multiagency Coordination System

On large or wide scale emergencies that require higher level resource management or information management, a Multiagency Coordination System may be needed.

What Are Multiagency Coordination Systems? Multiagency Coordination Systems are a combination of resources that are integrated into a common framework for coordinating and supporting domestic incident management activities. These resources may include facilities, equipment, personnel, procedures, and communications.

What Do Multiagency Coordination Systems Do? The primary functions of Multiagency Coordination Systems are to:

- Support incident management policies and priorities.
- Facilitate logistics support and resource tracking.
- Make resource allocation decisions based on incident management priorities.
- Coordinate incident-related information.
- Coordinate interagency and intergovernmental issues regarding incident management policies, priorities, and strategies.

Direct tactical and operational responsibility for the conduct of incident management activities rests with the On Scene Incident Commander.

Multiagency Coordination System Elements Multiagency Coordination Systems include Emergency Operations Centers (EOCs) and in certain multijurisdictional or complex incidents, Multiagency Coordination Entities.

EOCs are the locations from which the coordination of information and resources to support incident activities takes place. EOCs are typically established by the emergency management agency at the local level. Multiagency Coordination Entities typically consist of principals from organizations with direct incident management responsibilities or with significant incident management support or resource responsibilities. These entities may be used to facilitate incident management and policy coordination.

Emergency Operations Centers. EOC organization and staffing are flexible but should include coordination, communications, resource dispatching and tracking, and information collection, analysis, and dissemination. EOCs may also support multiagency coordination and joint information activities.

EOCs may be staffed by personnel representing multiple jurisdictions and functional disciplines. The size, staffing, and equipment at an EOC will depend on the size of the jurisdiction, the resources available, and the anticipated incident needs.

Multiagency Coordination Entity Incident Responsibilities. Regardless of their form or structure, Multiagency Coordination Entities are typically responsible for:

- Ensuring that each involved agency is providing situation and resource status information.
- Establishing priorities between incidents and/or Area Commands in concert with the Incident Commander.
- Acquiring and allocating resources required by incident management personnel.
- Coordinating and identifying future resource requirements.
- Coordinating and resolving policy issues.
- Providing strategic coordination.

Multiagency Coordination Entity Postincident Responsibilities. Following incidents, Multiagency Coordination Entities are typically responsible for ensuring that revisions are acted upon. Revisions may be made to plans, procedures, communications, staffing, and other capabilities necessary for improved incident management. These revisions are based on lessons learned from the incident. They should be coordinated with the emergency planning team in the jurisdiction and with mutual aid partners.

National Response Plan

HSPD 5 directs the Secretary of Homeland Security to develop a National Response Plan (NRP). The NRP will establish a single, comprehensive approach to domestic incident management to prevent, prepare for, respond to, and recover from terrorist attacks, major disasters, and other emergencies. The NRP will be an all-hazards plan built on the template of the NIMS.

The NRP will integrate the federal government's domestic prevention, preparedness, response, and recovery plans into one all-discipline, all-hazards plan. The NRP, using NIMS, with regard to response to domestic incidents, will provide the structure and mechanisms for national level policy and operational direction for federal support to state and local incident managers and for exercising direct federal authorities and responsibilities, as appropriate.

The NRP will include protocols for (1) operating under different threats or threat levels; (2) incorporation of existing federal emergency and incident management plans (with appropriate modifications and revisions) as either integrated components of the NRP or as supporting operational plans; and (3) additional operational plans or annexes, as appropriate, including public affairs and intergovernmental communications.

The NRP will provide a consistent approach for reporting incidents, providing assessments, and making recommendations to the president, the Secretary of Homeland Security, and the Homeland Security Council.

The NRP will include rigorous requirements for continuous improvements for testing, exercising, experience with incidents, and new information and technologies.

The heads of federal departments and agencies are to adopt the NIMS within their departments and agencies and provide support and assistance to the Secretary of Homeland Security in the development and maintenance of NIMS. All federal departments and agencies will use the NIMS in their domestic incident management and emergency prevention, preparedness, response, recovery, and mitigation activities, as well as those actions taken in support of state or local entities. The heads of federal departments and agencies are to participate in the NRP, to assist and support the development and maintenance of the NRP, and to participate in and use domestic incident reporting systems and protocols.

The NRP applies to all incidents requiring a coordinated federal response as part of an appropriate combination of federal, state, local, tribal, private sector, and nongovernmental entities.

Incident of National Significance. An Incident of National Significance (INS) is an actual or potential high-impact event that requires robust coordination of the federal response in order to save lives and minimize damage, and provides the basis for long-term community and economic recovery.

The Secretary of Homeland Security, in consultation with other departments and agencies, and the White House, as appropriate, declares Incidents of National Significance.

Role of the Private Sector in the NRP. The NRP recognizes the private sector as a key partner in domestic incident management, particularly in the area of critical infrastructure protection and restoration. Private sector entities are also called upon to contribute necessary items and services to the impacted area.

The Department of Homeland Security and other federal departments and agencies coordinate with the private sector to effectively share information, formulate courses of action, and incorporate available resources to prevent, prepare for, respond to, and recover from incidents of various types.

10.10 HOMELAND SECURITY PRESIDENTIAL DIRECTIVE 8—NATIONAL PREPAREDNESS

On December 17, 2003, President George W. Bush issued Homeland Security Presidential Directive 8 (HSPD 8), entitled *National Preparedness*. This directive is a companion to HSPD 5. This directive describes the way federal departments and agencies will prepare and respond to major emergencies, including prevention activities during the early stages of a terrorist incident.

This directive establishes policies to strengthen the preparedness of the United States to respond to threatened or actual domestic terrorist attacks, major disasters, and other emergencies requiring a national domestic all-hazards preparedness goal, establishing mechanisms for immediate delivery of federal preparedness assistance to state and local governments, and outlining and strengthening preparedness capabilities for federal, state, and local entities.

The term all-hazard preparedness refers to preparedness for domestic terrorist attacks, major disasters, and other emergencies. The term federal preparedness assistance means federal department and agency grants, cooperative agreements, loans, loan guarantees, training, and/or technical assistance provided to state and local governments and the private sector to prevent, prepare for, respond to, and recover from terrorist attacks, major disasters, and other emergencies.

The term preparedness refers to the existence of plans, procedures, policies, training, and equipment necessary at the federal, state, and local level to maximize the ability to prevent, respond to, and recover from major events. The term readiness is used interchangeably with preparedness.

10.11 THE INCIDENT COMMAND SYSTEM

A tool available for emergency responders is the Incident Command System (ICS). The purpose of the ICS, which is a modular and flexible system for managing a safe and effective response, is to prepare personnel to manage the emergency situation, be it large or small. The emergency situation may involve multiple agencies and/or jurisdictions, depending on the magnitude of the situation. Records show that an incident can be successfully mitigated if a viable ICS is in place.

Managing an emergency situation requires a calm, cool hand at the helm in order to achieve the established goals. Managing an emergency situation is very stressful, and careful consideration must be given to the selection of Incident Commanders. Subordinate staff functions are also very important, as they feed the necessary information to the Incident Commander. From this information, the Incident Commander will develop the strategy and tactics that will drive the mitigation efforts.

The complexity of incident management, along with the likelihood of multiagency and multijurisdictional involvement on incidents, requires the need for a single, standard incident management system.

ICS training will not provide a responder with solutions on how to mitigate specific incidents; however, it will provide the template and tools needed to successfully manage emergency incidents. ICS is just another tool for emergency response mitigation.

A jurisdiction's response to an emergency is one of its most visible activities. Only through adequate pre-emergency planning and rehearsal through drills and exercises can excellence be achieved. A jurisdiction-specific ICS must be rehearsed and integrated into the jurisdiction's plan for it to be truly effective.

Incident Commander

Responders at the Incident Commander (IC) level are those persons who are responsible for decisions relating to the management of an incident. The IC will use his/her expertise in formulating response objectives, action options, and the plan of action.

Even though an IC is responsible for directing and coordinating a response, some management functions may have to be delegated to others. The IC will establish the necessary branch(es) based on the magnitude and complexity of the incident.

The characteristics of an effective IC are very direct and simple to understand. The effective IC must be proactive, decisive, objective, calm, patient, a good listener, firm, and a quick thinker. To handle all necessary responsibilities, the IC must also be adaptable, flexible, and realistic about personnel and equipment limitations.

Response Safety

Safety must be considered in every action taken at an emergency incident scene because risks will always be present. By demonstrating the knowledge and skills included in these competencies, an IC should be able to reduce the risk inherent in an emergency incident.

All emergency response incidents are inherently dangerous by nature, and it is very unlikely that all hazards and risk will be completely eliminated before a responder is expected to act. One of the biggest responsibilities held by responders in a leadership position is analyzing this risk and determining when and how to intervene in an emergency.

There are two basic requirements to help ensure responder safety:

1. *Buddy System.* Each responder must operate with a buddy when in a hazardous area. The buddy must be wearing the same level (or a higher level) of protective equipment and is responsible for the safety of his/her partner.
2. *Backup Teams.* A minimum of two responders, dressed in an identical or higher level of personal protective equipment as the entrants, shall be on standby to provide immediate assistance to responders who may be in distress and need help.

Background of the Incident Command System

In the early 1970s, a series of major wild land fires in southern California prompted municipal, county, state, and federal fire authorities to form a cooperative effort to develop a system to manage multiagency emergency response incidents. Issues addressed included ineffective communications, accountability of emergency responders, and use of a well-defined command structure. Their efforts resulted in the development of the original Incident Command System (ICS). The ICS assists in the command, control, coordination, and communication aspects of emergency management. Although initially designed for fire emergencies, it evolved into an "all-risk" system for all types of emergency response incidents.

The ICS incorporates the management principles of unity of command and span of control. It provides a structure where numerous individuals and agencies can work together under one Incident Commander (IC) to implement common action plans and achieve strategic goals. The ICS is activated from the top down by the IC in a modular fashion, commensurate with the complexity of the incident.

The primary objective of the ICS is to give the IC the ability to effectively utilize resources (both personnel and equipment) for maximum efficiency, productivity, and safety at emergency response incidents. The ICS also ensures that there are no "freelance" operations, and that all responders operate under the same incident strategy. Each responder is accountable to one person only.

Laws and Standards Requiring the Use of an ICS

Emergency responders must have a management system to address all types of emergency response incidents. Additionally, the following laws and standards require the use of an ICS to manage emergency response activities:

- SARA requires organizations handling hazardous materials incidents to operate within an ICS.
- OSHA requires employers responding to hazardous materials incidents to operate under an ICS and interface their ICS with that of other responding agencies (29 CFR 1910.120).
- NFPA standards 1500 and 1561 require the use of ICS and set the framework that should be included when developing an ICS.
- HSPD 5 requires the use of a standardized incident management system.

Common Characteristics of Emergency Incidents

Each emergency is unique and dynamic. However, all emergencies share some common characteristics:

They usually occur with no advance notice.
They develop rapidly.
They may grow in size and complexity.
Danger to responders and public may be high.
There are often several agencies with some on-scene responsibility.
They can very easily become multijurisdictional.
They often have high public and media visibility.
Risk of property loss can be high.
Cost of response needs to be considered.

Because of these many characteristics, Incident Commanders (ICS) must ensure all relevant information used in the decision making process has been double verified.

Factors that Affect Emergency Management

Although many similarities exist between business and emergency management, several factors make emergency management more difficult. Emergency management is carried out in a constantly changing environment. Although the situation may get better or worse, it seldom stays the same. The dynamics of a constantly changing environment present additional challenges to the IC. The dynamics of the incident may create difficulty in gathering accurate and current information, especially due to the limited time available at an emergency scene. Additionally, personnel reporting to the IC may not be able to judge the total picture. An emergency incident, being dynamic, may require frequent shifts from offensive to defensive modes.

Control the Situation, or It Will Control You!

The intricacy of an incident complicates emergency management. Command activities include strategic goal setting, developing and implementing action plans, controlling and coordinating incident operations, using all available resources, considering safety in decision making, providing logistical support, and evaluating the action plan.

In addition to stabilizing the emergency incident, the IC is also responsible for managing or delegating the safety of all personnel, coordinating with other agencies, responding to media requests for information, and documenting all incident activities. Complicating matters further is the fact that interagency cooperation is required from municipal responders, mutual aid teams, local utility companies, public works departments, board of health, and state and federal agencies.

Time constraints cause confusion. Where business managers may have weeks or months to develop a strategy, an IC may have only seconds. Feedback methods may not be established to utilize the existing communication network. Possible breakdown of feedback at an emergency incident scene may occur as a result of inadequate procedures, improperly functioning equipment, or lack of interagency training.

Collecting and Interpreting Hazard and Response Information

The IC must be able to collect and interpret hazard and response information from a variety of sources, including reference manuals, hazardous materials databases, technical information centers, technical information specialists, and monitoring equipment.

The IC is expected to understand the types of resources that are available and the types of information each can provide. The IC is not expected to be able to personally operate the various resource materials, but should understand the advantages and disadvantages of each, and how to interpret and utilize the information obtained from each.

Terms Used in Hazardous Materials Incidents

In order to determine the potential outcomes of hazardous materials incidents, some basic health terms must be understood to clearly recognize the potential hazards of the products that may be involved.

Parts per Billion (ppb) and Parts per Million (ppm). The values used to establish exposure limits are quantified in parts per million or parts per billion. A good reference to remember is that 1% equals 10,000 ppm, or 1% equals 1000 ppb. So if you obtain a reading from a sampling instrument of 0.5%, that is equivalent to 500 ppm, or 50 ppb. If you then determine the threshold limit value (TLV) is 7500 ppm, you can relate the reading from the instrument to determine the degree of hazard.

Lethal Concentration (LC_{50}). The median lethal concentration of a hazardous material. It is defined as the concentration of a material in air that, on the basis of laboratory tests (inhalation route), is expected to kill 50% of a group of test animals when administered in a specific time period.

Lethal Dose (LD_{50}). The LD_{50} of a substance is a single dose that will cause the death of 50% of a group of test animals exposed to it by any route other than inhalation.

Permissible Exposure Limit (PEL). The maximum concentration, averaged over 8 hours, to which 95% of healthy adults can be repeatedly exposed for 8 hours per day, 40 hours per week without suffering adverse health effects.

Threshold Limit Value Ceiling (TLV-C). The maximum concentration to which a healthy adult can be exposed without risk of injury. It is comparable to the IDLH (see below), and exposures to higher concentrations should not occur.

Threshold Limit Value Short-Term Exposure Limit (TLV-STEL). The maximum average concentration, averaged over a 15 minute period, to which a healthy adult can safely be exposed for up to 15 minutes continuously. Exposure should not occur more than four times a day with at least 1 hour between exposures.

Threshold Limit Value Time-Weighted Average (TLV-TWA). The maximum concentration, averaged over 8 hours, to which a healthy adult can repeatedly be exposed for 8 hours per day, 40 hours per week without suffering adverse health effects.

Immediately Dangerous to Life and Health Value (IDLH). The maximum level to which a healthy worker can be exposed for 30 minutes and escape without suffering irreversible health effects or impairment. If at all possible, exposure to this level should be avoided.

Radiation is present in most residential, commercial, and industrial occupancies. It is therefore necessary that a responder have a basic knowledge of radiation.

There are four kinds of radiation:

Alpha. Alpha radiation involves the alpha particle, a positively charged particle emitted by some radioactive materials. It is less penetrating than beta and gamma radiation and is not considered dangerous unless ingested. If ingested, alpha radiation will attack internal organs.

Beta. Beta radiation involves the beta particle, which is much smaller but more penetrating than the alpha particle. Beta particles can damage skin tissue and internal organs if they enter the body. Full protective clothing, including positive pressure self-contained breathing apparatus, will protect against most beta radiation.

Gamma. Gamma radiation is especially harmful since it has great penetrating power. Gamma rays are a form of ionizing radiation with high energy that travels at the speed of light. It can cause skin burns and can severely injure internal organs. Protective clothing is inadequate in preventing gamma radiation from harming the body.

Neutrons. Neutron radiation consists of particles that are ejected from an atom's nucleus. Neutron radiation can travel great distances and is highly penetrating. It is best shielded with high hydrogen content material (e.g., water, plastic).

The radiation absorbed dose (rad) and the roentgen equivalent man (rem) are used to measure the amount and effect of ionizing radiation absorbed by humans. The average radiation dose received by a person in the United States is about 180 millrems per year.

There are two basic ways to protect yourself from the effects of radiation:

Half-Life. A measure of the rate of decay of a radioactive material. It indicates the time needed for one-half of a given amount of radioactive material to change to another nuclear form or element. This technique is not usually effective for emergency responders.

Time, Distance, Shielding. The shorter the time of exposure, the lower the dosage. The farther the distance from the exposure, the lower the amount of radiation one is exposed to (this is known as the inverse square law). Shielding refers to blocking radiation by using varying thicknesses of different materials. This is the typical method responders use to protect themselves.

To determine the risk to both the responder and the general public, the IC must understand some basic toxicological principles:

Acute and Chronic Toxicity. Acute toxicity refers to the sudden, severe onset of symptoms due to a short-duration, high-concentration exposure (e.g., to ammonia). Chronic toxicity refers to the delayed effects that may not develop for hours, months, or years (e.g., mesothelioma due to asbestos exposure).

Routes of Exposure to Toxic Materials. Hazardous materials can enter the human body through four routes of exposure:

1. *Contact.* Physical contact is made between the hazardous material and the body, causing localized damage.
2. *Absorption.* Hazardous material soaks through the skin and causes localized damage, or it is picked up by the blood and carried through the body.
3. *Inhalation.* Hazardous vapor, gas, or dust is drawn into the body through normal respiration.
4. *Ingestion.* Contaminated food, fingers, cigarettes, and so on are admitted into the body orally due to inadequate isolation or decontamination.

Local and Systemic Effects. Local effects are those in which the result of the exposure occurs at the point of contact (e.g., acid burns). Systemic effects are those that occur at a specific organ or system of the body (e.g., carbon tetrachloride in the liver).

Dose Response. The chemical, biological, or radiological dose relationship refers to the response produced in a human body. It is a cause–effect relationship. The magnitude of the body's response will depend on the concentration of the exposure at the site, the material itself, and the dose administered.

Synergistic Effects. Toxicity, exposure, and dose must all be analyzed to understand the risk that more than one product will have on the victim (e.g., asbestos and cigarette smoking).

Use of properly selected and worn personal protective equipment (PPE) will reduce the chance of a contaminant getting into your body.

Identifying Response Objectives

Response objectives are determined based on the emergency response priorities and the potential outcomes. The following steps should be taken when determining response objectives:

1. Estimate the number of exposed individuals who can be saved. The level of response and the acceptable risk associated with a response is based on the number of exposed persons who can be saved. The number of exposed persons who can be saved is based on the estimated outcomes minus the number of exposed persons already lost.
2. Determine the response objectives. The response objectives, based on the stage of the incident, are the tactical goals for stopping the event now occurring or keeping future events from occurring. Decisions should focus on changing the actions of the stressors, the containment system, and the hazardous material.

10.12 DETERMINING POTENTIAL OUTCOMES

One of the first tasks undertaken by the IC at an incident is to "size up" or establish what the current circumstances are. Once the facts of the incident are known, the potential outcomes must be determined. Potential outcomes are simply what may or may not happen as a result of the incident. All potential outcomes, both good and bad, must be considered. Once the potential outcomes are known, then a plan of action may be established.

Strategy and Tactics

Once the incident priorities have been established, the IC should decide upon a strategy. The strategy should be communicated to others in the organization so the appropriate tactics can be developed.

Strategy is the overall outcome that is desired from the management of an emergency incident. Generally, strategy will not change unless a major event has occurred (such as a sudden escalation). Tactics are the specific means that will be used to achieve the strategic goal. Tactics change quite frequently as various means and techniques are used to achieve the overall goal. It is not uncommon to have to execute several tactical options before success is achieved. For example, the strategy is to stop the chlorine from leaking from a 1 ton cylinder. The tactics will include using a chlorine "B" patch kit.

Identifying the Potential Action Options

There are three types of action options available to emergency responders based on the strategy and tactics chosen:

Offensive. These actions require specialized training, equipment, and personal protective equipment. Aggressive action is taken to mitigate the emergency.

Defensive. These actions can be taken from a distance. No specialized tools, training, or equipment are required for these tasks.

Nonintervention. This is basically a nonaction. There are insufficient levels of training, knowledge, experience, or number of responders, or inadequate or insufficient equipment available to start a response, or the gain does not outweigh the risks.

It is common to start with nonintervention until the situation is assessed, then switch to a defensive mode as more information is obtained, and finally to an offensive mode once the proper resources to mitigate the emergency have been collected.

10.13 APPROVING THE LEVEL OF PERSONAL PROTECTIVE EQUIPMENT

Levels of Protection

Personnel in the ICS are expected to "approve" the personal protective equipment (PPE) used by the emergency responders. Chemical protective clothing (CPC) provides a barrier between the skin and skin-absorbable or skin-destructive hazardous materials. Respiratory protection protects the lungs and respiratory tract.

Personal protective equipment for hazardous materials incidents have been divided into four levels depending on the degree of protection afforded to protect the body against contact with known or suspected hazardous materials.

Level A should be worn when the greatest level of respiratory, skin, and eye protection is required.

Level B should be worn when the greatest level of respiratory protection is needed, but a lesser level of skin protection is needed.

Level C should be worn when all hazardous materials have been identified and quantified and found to be within acceptable limits without chance of increasing.

Level D should be worn only as a work uniform, and not when any skin, eye, or respiratory hazard is present.

Please note that structural turnout gear offers NO chemical protection and therefore is considered level D.

How CPC Can be Compromised

Besides physical destruction by tearing or ripping, any one or more of the following may compromise CPC:

Degradation is the total loss of the physical capabilities of the fabric.

Penetration occurs when a hazardous material works its way through flaws in the CPC (e.g., seams, stitch holes, zippers).

Permeation occurs when a hazardous material works its way through and then flow in between the molecules that make up the fabric.

The responder should be able to recognize when one of these situations has occurred. Once CPC has been compromised, the responder should leave the area, go through decontamination, and don a new suit.

Safety Considerations When Wearing CPC

Working efficiently in CPC takes practice. Because personnel wearing CPC may experience a loss of dexterity, vision, and communications capability, it is important for responders to be closely monitored. Backup personnel must be available to assist the entry team in an emergency. Hand signals should be established to aid in communications. All responders must also have their vital signs monitored and be observed for the effects of heat-related injuries. A proper on-scene rehabilitation program should be in place to replenish fluids and allow for rest and recovery of all individuals responding to an incident.

Physical and Psychological Stresses Affecting Users of CPC

CPC, particularly fully encapsulating garments, increases the stress a responder may feel when working at a hazardous materials incident. Responders wearing CPC usually experience a loss of mobility and restricted visibility and communications. The higher the level of CPC, the greater these hindrances will be. Wearing CPC also increases the likelihood of heat stress and heat exhaustion. While fit individuals may be able to work under conditions of extreme heat and physical exertion for longer periods of time without adverse medical problems, there is still a limit to any person's endurance. Medical monitoring for all personnel wearing CPC at the scene is required.

10.14 DEVELOPING A PLAN OF ACTION

A plan of action will describe the response objectives and any options toward achieving the objectives. The basis of the plan will be the site's emergency response plan. Safety and health considerations, necessary personnel, and the control equipment necessary should be listed in the plan.

The following components must be considered when developing an action plan:

- *Site Restrictions.* Any areas/activities that are off limits to the responders.
- *Entry Objectives.* What is hoped to be achieved when entering into the hot zone.
- *On-Scene Organization and Control.* An organization chart listing all positions of the ICS that are filled, and by whom.
- *PPE.* The protective equipment that is needed for the various tasks to be performed.
- *Hazard Evaluation.* A thorough review of the various hazards present at the incident.
- *Communications Procedures.* Radiofrequencies, hand signals, and so on to be used.
- *Emergency Procedures.* Areas of refuge, what to do in the event of an emergency, what to do if CPC/SCBA fails, what to do if injured in the hot zone.
- *Personal Accountability.* How all responders will be accounted for to ensure no one is lost.
- *Emergency Medical Care.* How, where, and by whom injuries will be treated.
- *Rehabilitation Plan.* Location of the rehab area, who will provide assistance in the rehab area, and what services will be provided.
- *Decontamination Procedures.* The location and type of decontamination to be performed.
- *Debriefing.* Where and when the debriefing will occur.

Protecting the Public

This evaluation is designed to reduce or prevent contamination of the public directly exposed to the hazardous material. If members of the public are safe in their present location, and the structure where they are located can be protected from contamination (by closing windows and doors, shutting off HVAC systems, etc.), it is better to leave those people in place until the incident is controlled. Evacuation, which is the physical removal of people from the area, should be done only as a last resort due the logistical issues involved with this option.

Arrival Reports

The first arriving emergency responder should make an arrival report. It should paint a picture of what is actually being seen by those on the scene, allowing other emergency responders enroute to the scene to begin to "see" the incident. Such reports should be brief but concise, including all pertinent information. Mitigation efforts consistent with company policy should be initiated and command assumed. The arrival report should provide a description, including size, of the incident (spill, fire, collapse), any vehicles involved, any hazardous material involved or suspected, exposure, injuries, how enroute responders should approach the scene, what actions they should perform, and what actions the initial responders are taking.

If the person providing the arrival report assumes command, he/she must also indicate the location of the Command Post and issue instructions to other responders. If the person who provides the arrival report decides to pass command (because a higher ranking official is enroute and will arrive shortly), the report must describe the strategic goal (e.g., entering the area to rescue victims) and describe the tactical objectives (e.g., using a fire hose to suppress vapors).

Site Safety Plan

The Incident Commander must ensure that emergency responder safety remains a prime concern. A site safety plan including initial recommendations should be assembled. Whether it is written or not will be dependent on the size and complexity of the incident.

Coordination with the Municipality

The private sector's emergency response plan must be coordinated with the municipality's plan. Each agency must take responsibility for the various activities it will perform during the emergency, such as medical assistance, fire suppression, or offensive Hazmat operations. Emergency drills and exercises are critical to ensure success during an emergency. Tabletop, functional, and full-scale exercises should be completed annually.

Emergency preplans are developed to address possible emergency scenarios that may develop on-site. These plans should identify the proper response efforts that should be employed to mitigate the emergency. These plans should be tested and refined through the use of drills and exercises.

Safe Operating Practices

The following practices should be employed to ensure safe operations at a hazardous materials incident:

- All responders are trained and certified to their respective training level.
- Activities that present a significant risk to the safety of responders are limited to situations where there is a potential to save endangered lives.
- No risk to the safety of responders is acceptable when there is no possibility to save lives, protect the environment, or save property.
- All responders working in the hot and warm zone are under direct supervision.
- Personnel accountability procedures are utilized.
- A rest and rehabilitation area is set up and manned.
- An Incident Safety Officer has been designated and is operating.
- Radio communication and hand signals are established and in use.
- Properly selected and donned CPC is in use to protect responders from potential hazards and exposure.
- All operations are done using the buddy system. A backup team is in place.
- Responders have their vital signs monitored before and after donning CPC.
- A safety briefing is completed before entry.

Safety Briefing

An important component of the action plan is the safety briefing. The Incident Safety Officer presents the safety briefing to all responders before mitigation efforts start. Topics covered in the safety briefing include hazard communications material, emergency procedures, proper levels of CPC, location of decontamination corridor, communications plan, and task assignments.

It is also a good practice to have the responders check in with the Incident Safety Officer before they leave the cold zone. The Incident Safety Officer should inspect the responders to ensure the proper level of CPC is donned correctly, should perform a radio check, should review the hazard communications material and task assignment information, and should log the responders out for accountability purposes.

10.15 REQUIREMENTS FOR THE INCIDENT COMMAND SYSTEM

To be effective, an Incident Command System must be suitable for use regardless of the type of jurisdiction or agency involved. An Incident Command System (ICS) is based on the following basic tenets:

1. The ICS must provide for the following kinds of operations: single jurisdiction/single agency involvement, single jurisdiction/multiagency involvement, and multijurisdiction/multiagency involvement.

2. The ICS organizational structure must be able to adapt to any emergency or incident.
3. The ICS must be applicable and acceptable to users throughout the emergency response network.
4. The ICS must be able to expand in a logical and organized manner from the initial response into a major incident.
5. The ICS must have common elements in organization, terminology, and procedures.
6. Implementation of the ICS must have the least possible disruption to existing systems.

Components of the Incident Command System

The Incident Command System has ten major components:

1. *Common Terminology.* It is essential for any management system, especially one that will be utilized by multiagency and multijurisdictional organizations, to communicate effectively. The ICS uses common terminology that addresses organizational functions (major functions and functional units as well as organizational structure), resource elements (equipment and personnel used in tactical operations), and facilities (command posts and staging areas).

2. *Modular Organization.* The ICS organization develops in a modular fashion from the top down based on the magnitude and complexity of the emergency incident. If one individual (the Incident Commander) can effectively manage all functional areas, no further organization is required. If one or more of the areas requires independent management, an individual is appointed to manage that section subordinate to the Incident Commander.

3. There are four organizational terms relevant to the ICS:

Section. Sections are the specific functions that make up the general staff.

Branch. A branch is a major operational area at an incident. Its function usually requires several components to work together to complete an assignment. Each branch is supervised by an officer (e.g., a hazardous materials spill branch at a large hazardous materials incident may have several operational groups such as leak control, confinement, and decontamination).

Division. Areas created by dividing a large incident by geographic boundaries to better coordinate functions.

Group. A group is an individual or team with specific responsibilities to be accomplished.

4. *Integrated Communications.* For any emergency response effort to succeed, an efficient communications system must be in place and used. For this communications system to be truly effective and useful to all agencies involved, communications must be made in "plain English." No codes should be used, and all

messages should be limited to those essential to the operation. Redundant communications systems are a must for large incidents (hard wire telephone, radio, cellular phone, fax, messenger, public address systems, etc.).

The Incident Commander (IC), or designee, must ensure appropriate notifications are made to other jurisdictions that may be adversely impacted, as appropriate.

5. *Unified Command Structure*. Command may be passed "up the chain of command" as more senior personnel arrive at the emergency scene. For example, a shift supervisor may be the initial IC. Command will be transferred to the department head upon his/her arrival at the emergency scene. Assuming command of an emergency incident requires that the incoming IC receive a complete and up-to-date incident briefing from the immediate predecessor. The IC will assume command of an incident after the overall situation has been reviewed, and a smooth transition of command can occur. The new IC must make it known to the subordinate staff that command has been transferred. The outgoing IC should be kept on as a Deputy IC for assistance if needed.

6. *Command Mode*. Based on the specific geographic location of an emergency incident, one of two types of command may be implemented: single command or unified command.

A *single command* is used when one organization is responding to an incident, and one individual has been designated by the proper authority to assume command. A *unified command* is used when either several organizations are responding to an incident, or an incident extends into more than one jurisdiction. For example, the local fire chief, emergency management coordinator, state health department representative, and industrial facility IC may establish a unified command, where all involved agency ICs work together to reach mutual decisions. State law, municipal ordinance, or prearranged agreement (home rule) usually establishes the overall IC.

7. *Consolidated Action Plan*. Once the strategic goals for the incident have been established, the next step is to consolidate those goals into an action plan. The IC, in concert with the general staff, will develop objectives and strategy for the emergency incident. Each functional section should then develops its specific, tactical action plans after receiving instructions from the IC.

For small, minor incidents of short impact, magnitude, and/or duration, the action plan generally is not extensive or written. Examples of "minor" incidents, where action plans are generally simple and not written, include a single minor injury; a minor fire, such as one involving ordinary combustibles in a dumpster with no exposures; a minor automobile accident with no significant injuries; or a spill of a small amount of hazardous materials with no environmental or life safety exposures.

However, for significant, major incidents with major impact to people and/or the environment, large magnitude, or long duration, action plans need to be written. Examples of "major" incidents, where action plans generally are complex and written, include numerous injuries and fatalities at a local shopping mall as a result of an explosion; a structure fire at an occupied grammar school, with numerous students missing or injured; an accident involving a tour bus, with numerous entrapments, serious injuries, and fatalities; or a release of 45 tons of chlorine in the middle of a suburban town.

Generally, action plans should be written in the following situations:

When resources from multiple agencies are being used.

When more than one jurisdiction is involved.

When the incident involves staging of equipment or relief personnel.

When municipal and industrial teams are working together.

8. *Manageable Span of Control.* Span of control refers to the number of people reporting directly to an individual. Safety considerations as well as sound management techniques influence span of control considerations. The type, hazards, and magnitude of the emergency incident will influence span of control considerations. An important consideration in span of control is to anticipate change and prepare for it. This is especially true during rapid buildup of the ICS in the initial stages of an incident. For emergency response activities, the span of control for any one individual should range from three to seven, with five considered optimum. Of course, there will always be exceptions taking into account local specific situations.

9. *Predesignated Incident Facilities.* There are two basic types of facilities that may be established in and around an emergency incident area. The need for and location of these facilities will be determined by the IC based on the type and magnitude of the emergency situation.

- *Command Post.* The Command Post (CP) is the location from which all incident operations are directed. The CP should be stationary and located in an appropriate location either at the scene or removed from it. Personnel who should be in the CP include the command and general staff, plus representatives from each of the other responding agencies.

  There should be only one CP for the incident. In a unified command structure, the individuals designated by their respective agencies would be located in the single CP. Although a CP may vary in size and type depending on the emergency incident, a good CP would have the following characteristics:

  Far enough away from the incident so as not to be affected by the incident (water runoff, plumes, etc.).

  Large enough in area to comfortably accommodate all command and general staff indoors.

  Suitable redundant communication capabilities.

  View of the incident, if practical.

  Easily secured to keep unauthorized personnel out.

  The necessary equipment (status boards, communications, etc.).

- *Staging Area.* Staging areas are established for temporary location of available equipment and personnel. Resources in the staging area must be able to respond to the emergency incident within 3 minutes of notification. A good staging area would have the following characteristics:

Large enough to accommodate a large amount of equipment and personnel.

Temporary sanitation and fueling services.

Rest areas and food/drink for personnel.

10. *Comprehensive Resource Management.* Resources are classified into one of three categories:

- *Single Resource.* A single resource is assigned a primary tactical responsibility, or task, to be accomplished. A single resource consists of the equipment plus the individuals required to properly utilize it (e.g., an ambulance plus 3 EMTs).
- *Teams.* Teams are a set number of resources of the same type and kind that have an established minimum number of personnel. Teams have leaders and will have common communications (e.g., a fire hose crew).
- *Task Force.* A task force is any combination of resources that can be assembled for a specific mission. All resource elements within a task force must have common communications and a leader (e.g., using an industrial ERT and a municipal fire department to conduct a search and rescue operation).

In order to maintain an up-to-date status of resources, it is necessary that all resources be assigned a current status. The three status conditions established for tactical operations are:

Assigned. Performing an active assignment.

Available. In staging and ready for assignment within 3 minutes of notification.

Out of Service. Not ready for assignment due to mechanical problems, insufficient personnel, and so on.

ICS Organization and Overview

An Incident Command System is customized to meet the needs of the agencies involved in the emergency response. Positions are filled as necessary based on incident magnitude and complexity. The ICS will expand and contract as the incident dictates. As the emergency is mitigated, and resources can be released, the ICS will begin to be terminated. The ICS should shrink as rapidly as it was built up, keeping only the necessary organization. The last position to be terminated will be the Incident Commander. Once the organization is terminated, the incident debriefing, investigation, and postincident analysis activities will begin.

The Command Staff consists of the Incident Commander, Incident Safety Officer, Liaison Officer, Information Officer, and Documentation Officer. The General Staff encompasses responsibility for finance/administration, logistics, operations and planning.

Command and General Staff Functions

Command Staff

Incident Commander (IC). The IC has the responsibility for the overall management of all incident activities including the development and implementation of strategy and for ordering and releasing resources. The IC also has the responsibility for developing the ICS specific for the incident at hand and must fill the applicable subordinate staff and support functions. The IC will assume positions not filled by subordinates.

In multijurisdictional incidents, the duties of the IC may be carried out by a unified command.

Basic responsibilities of the IC include:

- Assess incident situation.
- Develop tactical and strategic goals.
- Conduct initial and periodic briefings.
- Activate elements of the Incident Command System (ICS).
- Brief staff and section officers.
- Develop appropriate organizational structure.
- Coordinate staff activities.
- Manage incident operations.
- Manage resources.
- Approve requests for additional resources and requests for release of resources.
- Authorize release of information to the news media.
- Assign prior IC to a position within the ICS.
- Make appropriate notifications to other jurisdictions potentially adversely impacted.
- Ensure necessary reports are filled with applicable regulatory agencies.

Incident Safety Officer. The Incident Safety Officer is responsible for the overall safety and health of all personnel involved in the emergency incident. The Incident Safety Officer will assess all plans prior to implementation and assure safety and health considerations have been addressed. The Incident Safety Officer has the authority to stop any activity that poses an imminent danger to responders or the general population. The Incident Safety Officer will then consult with the IC to resolve the areas of concern.

Liaison Officer. The Liaison Officer is the prime point of contact for the representatives from other agencies. The Liaison Officer is responsible for briefing and coordinating the activities of the various agencies involved in the mitigation efforts. Reports from the various agencies are channeled through the Liaison Officer to the IC.

Public Information Officer. The Public Information Officer is responsible for preparing accurate and complete press releases regarding incident particulars and disseminating information to the news media at periodic intervals after receiving permission from the IC. The Public Information Officer will also lead tours of the emergency scene when the incident is under control.

Documentation Officer. The Documentation Officer is responsible for documenting the activities that occur in the Command Post, as well as collecting and collating the logs from the various sections involved in the mitigation effort. Once all logs are assembled, collated, transcribed, and reviewed, detailed after action reports and a critique can be developed. All documentation, logs notes, and so on pertaining to the incident must be preserved for use in civil or criminal actions that may arise as a result of the emergency situation.

General Staff

Operations Officer. The Operations Officer has the responsibility to organize and operate the Operations Section and has the responsibility for the management of all tactical operations directly applicable to the emergency incident mitigation plan.

The Operations Officer runs or supervises operations and staging in accordance with the action plan. The Operations Officer directs the formulation and execution of branch plans and requests and releases resources.

Basic responsibilities of the Operations Officer include:

- Obtain briefing from the IC.
- Develop tactical operations plan.
- Brief and assign operation personnel.
- Establish staging areas.
- Determine need for and request additional resources.
- Implement the action plan.
- Report to the IC.
- Evaluate the operations plan.
- Maintain personnel accountability.

The Operations Section typically has the following branch organization:

Safety Branch
Sampling Branch
Staging Branch

Hazardous Materials Branch
Fire Branch
Decontamination Branch
Emergency Medical Service Branch
Search and Rescue Branch
Supply Branch

The *Safety Branch* has the following responsibilities specific to Operations Section personnel:

- Obtain briefing from the Operations Officer.
- Evaluate all plans and actions to assure the safety and health of section personnel.
- Advise the Operations Officer as necessary.
- Coordinate activities with the Incident Safety Officer.
- Ensure all personnel are wearing proper level of PPE.
- Ensure proper decontamination of personnel and equipment.
- Monitor breathing air consumption of personnel.
- Maintain accountability of all section personnel.
- Maintain branch logs.
- Ensure personnel are working in teams.

The *Sampling Branch* has the following responsibilities:

- Obtain briefing from the Operations Officer.
- Perform air sampling to determine appropriate work zones and levels of PPE.
- Perform sampling of water runoff.
- Delineate extent of surface water contamination.
- Use appropriate sampling techniques to delineate soil contamination.

The *Staging Branch* has the following responsibilities:

- Obtain briefing from the Operations Officer.
- Establish staging area layout.
- Determine support needs (food, security, sanitation, etc.).
- Establish check-in procedure.
- Respond to request for resources.
- Ensure resources are deployable within 3 minutes.
- Report resource status to Operations Officer at 1 hour intervals.
- Maintain branch log.

The *Hazardous Materials Branch* has the following responsibilities:

- Obtain briefing from Operations Officer.
- Perform initial reconnaissance of involved materials to obtain placard and label information, container shape, magnitude of the spill, and so on.
- Initiate offensive action to mitigate the spill.
- Provide emergency backup for offensive teams.
- Initiate defensive action to minimize impact of the spill.

The *Fire Branch* has the following responsibilities:

- Obtain briefing from the Operations Officer.
- Supply fire suppression equipment and personnel as necessary.
- Supply vapor suppression or firefighting foam, equipment, and personnel as needed.

The *Decontamination Branch* has the following responsibilities:

- Obtain briefing from Operations Officer.
- Set up an appropriate decontamination facility before the entry team enters the hot zone.
- Provide decontamination services for victims, equipment, and emergency response personnel.

The *Emergency Medical Services Branch* has the following responsibilities:

- Obtain briefing from Operations Officer.
- Monitor and document vital signs of Hazmat personnel before and after entry into the work zones.
- Set up and manage the rehabilitation area.
- Provide basic life support equipment and personnel at the onset of the emergency response.
- Provide advanced life support equipment and personnel as necessary.

The *Search and Rescue Branch* has the following responsibilities:

- Obtain briefing from the Operations Officer.
- Provide search and rescue teams to locate and remove any victims.
- Provide initial first aid to victims.
- Bring victims to decontamination area.

The *Supply Branch* has the following responsibilities:

- Obtain briefing from the Operations Officer.
- Ensure supplies necessary for incident mitigation are available and in proper repair.
- Bring full SCBA bottles to the decontamination area.
- Fill empty SCBA bottles.
- Assist in the set-up of equipment as necessary.

Planning Officer. The Planning Officer has the responsibility to organize and operate the Planning Section and is responsible for the collection, evaluation, dissemination, and use of information pertinent to the emergency situation. The Planning Officer should ensure adequate documentation, information, and specialists are available for consultation in the mitigation efforts.

The Planning Officer will also coordinate with the Operations Officer to ensure information is available for preparation of an action plan that will ensure a safe and efficient mitigation of the emergency incident. The Planning Officer will fill subordinate positions as necessary, depending on the size and complexity of the emergency incident.

Basic responsibilities of the Planning Officer include:

- Obtain instructions from the IC.
- Develop action plan for Planning Section functions.
- Brief staff, make assignments, and evaluate performance.
- Brief the IC concerning Planning Section activities as necessary.
- Maintain contact with responding agencies, technical specialists, utility liaisons, and contractors regarding planning matters.
- Obtain technical information (MSDS, water supply diagrams, etc.) relative to the emergency incident.
- Schedule and run periodic Planning Section briefings.
- Identify need for use of specialized resources.
- Assemble information on alternative strategies.
- Provide periodic predictions on incident potential.
- Maintain status log of injured personnel and coordinate with next of kin.
- Advise IC of environmental concerns relevant to the emergency incident.
- Complete necessary forms and reports for submittal to the IC prior to demobilization.
- Maintain Planning Section log.

The Planning Section typically has the following branch organization:

Technical Branch
Environmental Branch
Personnel Branch

The *Technical Branch* is responsible for assembling, evaluating, and disseminating all pertinent information and technical specialists relative to the emergency incident. Information that the Technical Branch will assemble includes:

- Material safety data sheets.
- Names of technical specialists.
- Reference material.
- Drawings and maps.
- Printed equipment specification manuals.
- Utility drawings (water, electric, etc.).
- Piping and instrumentation diagrams.
- Process flow diagrams.

The *Environmental Branch* is responsible for determining the need for, and making, any notifications relating to the incident to federal, state, or local authorities, evaluating the air and water sampling data reported by the Operations Section, and developing action plans for: evacuation of exposed personnel; minimizing environmental exposure/damage; neutralization, dispersion, and containment of hazardous materials or runoff; and ultimate cleanup and recovery of the impacted area. Information that the Environmental Branch will assemble includes:

- List of equipment and contractors necessary to contain, clean up, and recover affected site.
- Toxicological data necessary to make isolation and evacuation recommendations.
- Recommended procedures to contain, clean up, and recover affected area.
- Meteorological data.
- Documentation of reports made to applicable federal, state, and local agencies.

The *Personnel Branch* is responsible for tracking injuries or fatalities, keeping the status log of all hospitalized personnel, notifying the next of kin of injured/dead personnel, and arranging for food, clothing, and shelter for emergency responders as necessary. Information that the Personnel Branch will assemble includes:

- Personnel data for all emergency responders, including next of kin and medical history.
- A list of vendors and contractors needed to provide food, clothing, or shelter.
- Location of the local hospital and medical examiner.

Finance Officer. The Finance Officer has the responsibility to organize and operate the Finance Section and will oversee all financial and cost analysis aspects of the incident. For agencies assisting at an incident in your jurisdiction, remuneration may be required for expendables, personnel, and damaged/lost equipment. The

Finance Officer should ensure adequate documentation, inventories, and time sheets are maintained for tracking purposes. Coordination with the Operations Section is helpful to track the use of consumables and equipment.

The Finance Officer is usually involved with any compensation claims that may arise as a result of the emergency operation. The Finance Officer will also work in conjunction with the Logistics Officer to ensure purchase orders and billing procedures are prepared for contractors or equipment necessary for the mitigation efforts. The Finance Officer will fill subordinate positions as necessary, depending on the size and complexity of the emergency incident.

Basic responsibilities of the Finance Officer include:

- Obtain instructions from the IC.
- Develop action plan for Finance Section functions.
- Brief staff, make assignments, and evaluate performance.
- Brief the IC concerning Finance Section activities as necessary.
- Maintain contact with responding agencies, industrial contacts, vendors, and contractors regarding financial matters.
- Maintain personnel, expendables, and equipment inventories, logs, and cost records.
- Schedule and run periodic Finance Section briefings.
- Complete necessary forms and reports for submittal to the IC prior to demobilization.
- Maintain Finance Section log.

The Finance Section typically has the following branch organization:

Time Unit Branch
Cost Unit Branch
Compensation/Claims Branch
Procurement Branch
Documentation Branch

The *Time Unit Branch* is responsible for maintaining personnel time logs for manpower used in the mitigation efforts. Its major functions include:

- Obtain instructions from the Finance Officer.
- Establish contact with appropriate agency representatives.
- Ensure personnel time recording documentation is in place and approved by appropriate personnel.
- Post personnel travel and work hours, and specific pay provisions, for payment.
- Prepare necessary forms and reports for submittal to the Finance Officer prior to demobilization.
- Brief Finance Officer as necessary regarding pertinent branch activities.

The *Cost Unit Branch* is responsible for collecting all cost data, preparing cost data summaries, providing cost estimates, and providing cost reduction recommendations specific to the emergency incident. Its major functions include:

- Obtain instructions from the Finance Officer.
- Ensure all contractors, vendors, and agencies requiring payment have been identified.
- Obtain and record all cost data.
- Prepare cost data summaries.
- Prepare cost estimates for planning purposes.
- Make recommendations for cost reductions to Finance Officer.
- Ensure that all cost documentation is properly prepared, approved, and signed.
- Prepare necessary forms and reports for submittal to the Finance Officer prior to demobilization.
- Brief Finance Officer as necessary regarding pertinent branch activities.

The *Compensation/Claims Branch* is responsible for the collection and management of all compensatory claims filed as a result of the emergency incident, either from emergency responders or the general population. Its major functions include:

- Obtain instructions from the Finance Officer.
- Establish contact with applicable agency representatives.
- Obtain documentation of medical treatment and maintain injury log.
- Obtain documentation of damages or destroyed property or equipment.
- Obtain witness statements from involved personnel.
- Designate a local medical provider to examine injured personnel.
- Designate claims adjusters to evaluate extent of property loss.
- Coordinate with Operations Officer to document extent and intensity of any exposures for personnel and property.
- Ensure timely payment of treatment and claims bills.
- Prepare necessary forms and reports for submittal to the Finance Officer prior to demobilization.
- Brief Finance Officer as necessary regarding pertinent branch activities.

The *Procurement Branch* is responsible for the administration of all financial matters pertaining to vendors and contractors. Its major functions include:

- Obtain instructions from the Finance Officer.
- Coordinate activities with the Logistics Section.
- Establish, prepare, and sign purchase orders and contracts as necessary.
- Draft memorandums of understanding.
- Complete processing and approve payment orders.

- Prepare necessary forms and reports for submittal to the Finance Officer prior to demobilization.
- Brief Finance Officer as necessary regarding pertinent branch activities.

The *Documentation Branch* is responsible for maintaining the appropriate logs of section and branch activities for use in the investigation, debriefing, and critique of the emergency incident. Logs should be submitted to the Finance Officer prior to demobilization.

The Documentation Officer has the following responsibilities:

- Obtain briefing from the Operations Officer.
- Document all Command Post activities.
- Coordinate with the various Operations Branches to collate on Operations Section activity log.

Logistics Officer. The Logistics Officer has the responsibility to organize and operate the logistics section, and is responsible for providing all materials, services, and facilities in support of the incident. The Logistics Officer should coordinate with the Operations Section to become aware of the action plan and develop a supply plan for consumables, contractors, and equipment.

The Logistics Officer will also work in conjunction with the Finance Officer to ensure purchase orders and billing procedures are prepared for contractors or equipment for the mitigation efforts. The Logistics Officer will fill subordinate positions as necessary, depending on the size and complexity of the emergency incident.

Basic responsibilities of the Logistics Officer include:

- Obtain instructions from the IC.
- Develop action plan for Logistics Section functions.
- Brief staff, make assignments, and evaluate performance.
- Brief the IC concerning Logistics Section activities as necessary.
- Maintain contact with industrial contacts, vendors, and contractors regarding availability of materials and personnel.
- Identify service and support requirements for planned and expected operations.
- Coordinate and process requests for additional resources.
- Schedule and run periodic Logistics Section briefings.
- Complete necessary forms and reports for submittal to the IC prior to demobilization.
- Maintain Logistics Section log.

The Logistics Section typically has the following branch organization:

Services Branch
Support Branch
Facilities Branch

The *Services Branch* is responsible for ensuring all personnel requests necessary for the mitigation efforts are available. Its major functions include:

- Obtain instructions from the Logistics Officer.
- Establish contact with appropriate contractors, mutual aid organizations, and so on.
- Post personnel travel and work hours as necessary.

The *Support Branch* is responsible for ensuring all support requests necessary for the mitigation efforts are available. Its major functions include:

- Obtain instructions from the Logistics Officer.
- Coordinate with the IC for a list of supplies that will be needed.
- Coordinate with the Finance Section to develop a payment plan for necessary supplies.
- Arrange for fueling, maintenance, and repairing of equipment.
- Arrange for transportation of personnel and equipment, if necessary.

The *Facilities Branch* is responsible for providing security for the immediate incident area and providing for the needs of the ICS personnel. Its major functions include:

- Ensure adequate security personnel are available to guard the immediate incident scene, command posts, and rehabilitation area.
- Ensure an adequate supply of potable water, food, clothes, shelter, port-o-potty, and so on are available.

Media Relations

Emergency incidents, by their very nature, are newsworthy. Both the print and electronic news media will most likely cover incidents of even minor consequence. While satisfying the news media may be considered a "nuisance" chore, this is not the attitude from which it should be approached. In fact, it should be looked upon as an "opportunity"—to inform a large number of people about the true situation at the emergency scene.

Just as emergency responders regard themselves as having some particular knowledge and skill to mitigate emergencies, so too the representatives of the media look upon themselves as fulfilling their job in a first class manner. Their superiors have given them an assignment and they will carry it out to the best of their ability. Thus they will get their story with or without the cooperation of those in charge of the incident.

While the media are often criticized (some of it is justified), many times misinformation and poor facts appearing in the media can be traced to a situation where little or no cooperation was received from the Incident Commander, and reporters had to gather information from other unofficial sources. For these reasons, it is in the best interest of the Incident Commander to answer legitimate questions from the media. If this attitude is adopted and carried out, experience has shown the media are cooperative.

A Public Information Officer (PIO) must be designated as soon into the emergency incident as possible. The PIO's name should be conveyed to the press as soon as possible. The PIO should designate a location and schedule for press briefings on a periodic basis. Additionally, a phone number for a PIO should be designated to allow for clarification of issues or questions in the future.

A good PIO should be articulate, able to withstand pressure, well presented and appropriately dressed, credible, and knowledgeable and have a positive, friendly demeanor.

The following guidelines are useful when dealing with the press:

- Designate a PIO and advise all Command Staff, public officials, and news media of the name and location of this individual. Before issuing a statement, the PIO will have a meeting with the Incident Commander (IC) staff to ensure facts are correct. If possible, have IC staff attend the briefing to answer specific detailed questions.
- Be courteous and cooperative. Reporters get the news regardless, but if the IC treats them with respect and cooperation, and the media have confidence in the spokesperson, they will be respectful and courteous in return. All questions deserve an answer. If you don't know the answer, tell the press you will get it and follow up promptly.
- Maintain control. Keep your cool and do not be defensive. Start any briefing with a statement of the current situation. Be prepared to answer questions. Make sure statements and answers are consistent. Answer only one question at a time. Keep control of the meeting and do not become overwhelmed. If "facts" presented by the questioner are incorrect, state the correct facts before answering the question. Be wary of questions that start with "Are you telling me . . ." or "Is it true that . . . ." Make sure the statements reflect what was said, and if not, state the situation correctly.
- Ignore attempts to interrupt. Do not attempt to out talk the questioner, wait until he/she is finished and then commence by saying "as I was saying."
- Do not be verbose, but do not be curt; there is a happy medium.
- Maintain control of the situation.
- Don't speculate. At the outset, don't attempt to speculate on fault or cause. It takes time to gather and assess the relevant facts.
- Avoid professional jargon. Try to put explanations in comprehensible terms. The purpose of the media is to explain a situation to the average person, not to write a technical paper on a subject. Remember that it is the speaker's responsibility to be understood.
- Present facts. Give the facts as they are known. Do not volunteer opinions.

- Know the situation before starting the briefing. If utilizing personnel not immediately familiar with the emergency incident, provide them with a briefing before meeting the media.
- Anticipate questions and have the answers ready. Members of the staff can role play reporters. "What if" questions should be responded to with facts, not speculation.

Initial Press Release

When starting the initial press briefing, the PIO should introduce himself/herself and any other personnel who may be involved in the briefing. Phone numbers or another method of contact for the PIO should be provided at this time. It is an excellent idea to have representatives from all participating jurisdictions (mayor, fire chief, private sector representative, etc.) involved with the PIO during the briefing as this conveys the perception of cooperation, openness, and teamwork.

Press briefings should be prepared in advance and rehearsed if possible. Never proceed into a briefing blind. The PIO may want to state "I have a prepared statement to read, after which I will answer questions for 5 minutes." The next briefing and location should be announced at the conclusion of the initial briefing.

The location where the press briefing is conducted is also very important. The press, if they had their druthers, would prefer interviews to be conducted with the smoldering ruins of the facility or giant fireball in the background. From a perception standpoint, this venue is not good. Therefore a facility away from the emergency incident, such as a hotel meeting room, would be more suitable. For long-duration events, the media could use this room to prepare their stories. More importantly, it gives the media a place to assemble and stay. This is good because it keeps them from roaming and possibly finding unknowledgeable or unauthorized "witnesses." Generally, having refreshments and making equipment available (tables, phones, etc.) ensures the press will not leave.

If the press wants photo or video opportunities, a "pool" camera may be the best way to go. A pool camera would entail selecting a limited number of cameras into the affected area, and that tape or photo is shared with all reporters. A pool is a good idea when the scene is not yet fully secured; it is also easier to control a few camera people than many.

The following items *should be* included in the initial press release:

- *Nature of the Emergency.* A general description of what happened, so far as is known, and any possible consequences.
- *Incident Facts.* Time, place of incident, and number of personnel injured, killed, and missing to the extent known. Use numbers only, but split into employees, civilians, and so on. *Do not* provide any names.
- *Description of Damage.* Provide a description of damage, effect on operations, on going activities, who is involved in these activities, and what is upcoming.

- *Material Involved.* Type of product involved and amount, if clearly established. Give general terms such as toxic, flammable, corrosive, and hazardous.
- *Impact.* Describe the effect on the community, such as need to evacuate.
- *Future.* Duration of remediation, if known.
- *Contact People.* Identify the Incident Commander and PIO. Request that queries for information be processed through the designated person. Assure the media of continued cooperation, and that information will be provided at periodic intervals. Controlled access to the emergency site will be allowed when cleared from a safety standpoint.
- *Credibility.* It is imperative that the flow of information at the start of an emergency incident be as frequent as possible since the situation will be changing. Do not say information will be available at a certain time and then not meet the commitment. By having a frequent flow of information, the media tend to stay in one place rather than walk around talking to personnel. Remember though that camera crews will always walk around or find other ways to get their photo opportunities.

The following information *should not* be included in the initial releases. The professional public affairs personnel should address these questions.

- *Cause.* The cause of the incident should be released as the situation unfolds and statements can be made with a high degree of certainty.
- *Loss.* Monetary estimates of losses should not be released until they can be ascertained with some assurance of accuracy.
- *Negligence.* Any statement at any time implying negligence should be avoided.
- *Names.* Identification of killed, injured, or missing personnel must not be released until it has been confirmed and the next of kin have been notified.

Other important tips to remember: always have a positive response to a negative question; never lie or bluff; and *never* say "no comment."

It bears repeating that dealing with media should be looked upon as an integral part of the mitigation effort, and the same care should be made in handling this aspect as with any other part of the emergency incident.

10.16 EVALUATING PROGRESS OF THE PLAN OF ACTION

The emergency response leadership must continually evaluate the progress of the action plan to ensure the mitigation efforts are accomplishing the response objectives. This evaluation must be a continual process. As one action plan is implemented, work should be ongoing to develop alternate plans.

To determine whether the actions being taken at an incident are effective and the response objectives are being met, responders must determine whether the incident is stabilizing or increasing in intensity. Feedback from the responders in the field will allow modification of either the strategic goals or the tactics being employed. The feedback from the field should include information on the effectiveness of personnel, on the responders' PPE, on control zones, decontamination procedures, specific mitigation techniques being employed, and other pertinent information.

The IC should determine whether events at an incident are occurring as predicted, occurring out of predicted sequence, or are different than expected. The IC should also determine if events that were predicted to occur as part of the mitigation, response, or overall plan are occurring as anticipated. This evaluation should continue until the incident has been terminated so that there are no "surprises" during the postemergency response operations.

10.17 TERMINATING THE INCIDENT

As with many jobs, using specific procedures will ensure that no unfinished items are left behind. Following these procedures will ensure that you gain the most from the lessons you learn from each incident.

Transferring Command

Transferring authority at an incident generally means transferring command, or the role of IC, from one person to another. Authority may be transferred from one person to another with higher rank or authority. The three main reasons for transferring command include arrival of a higher ranking person, extended operations, and the incident becomes multijurisdictional. Authority may also be transferred when the emergency phase has ended and the postemergency response phase begins.

Conducting a Debriefing

The first step in termination is debriefing. This should occur immediately after the incident and should cover the main details of the incident. The debriefing is not a comprehensive analysis; it is the gathering of information intended to provide an overall summary of the activities of each branch, section, or division during the incident. The objectives of a debriefing are to identify who responded, what they did, when they did it, and how effective their operations were. The debriefing should also document any injuries suffered, note the type of treatment given, and indicate whether any follow-up medical treatment is needed. Responders should understand what if any hazardous materials were involved and how they were identified. The strategy employed should be explained as well as the details of the site safety plan. Initial decisions as well as additional considerations should also be explained. Special concerns of personnel must be addressed. This is the same debriefing used when dealing with critical incident stress.

The levels of exposure should be identified and documented at this point. Responders must be notified of the symptoms of overexposure and actions to be taken by responders for medical surveillance. There should be a contact person to notify if symptoms develop and all responders should know how to reach that person. Exposure reports must be filed for all responders exposed.

Incident Investigation

The next step in the termination process is incident investigation, which involves review and analysis of the incident, debriefing, and interviews with those involved. The investigation should be started as soon as the emergency is under control. For major incidents, investigations may take several weeks or even months. This step is used to identify the causes of the emergency, as well as areas where action is needed and strengths to build upon. Investigations are usually done by a committee, involving representatives of the jurisdictions involved, such as emergency response organizations and corporate staff personnel, personnel directly involved in the incident, and a neutral third party. Some incidents may be significant enough as to involve federal, state, or local authorities as mandated by law.

Conducting a Multiagency Postincident Analysis

The last step is the postincident analysis, or operational evaluation. The postincident analysis is usually done after the incident investigation, so all relevant facts are available for discussion. The postincident analysis is used to identify and document accomplishments, problems, and shortcomings. It should be held in a positive manner. If problems are identified, focus on the issues and problems, not the people involved.

Postincident analyses should follow this general plan:

- *Operations.* Did tactical operations meet strategic goals?
- *Command.* Did it function through all transfers of command?
- *Resources.* Were resources requested, staged, delivered, and used appropriately?
- *SOPs.* Were existing SOPs appropriate for this incident or are new ones needed? Can existing ones be modified?

The postincident analysis must be conducted in a professional, not personal, manner. It must be constructive and must not assign blame. A critique is like any other incident investigation: it is designed to gather information to ensure a better outcome next time. Participants should be open and honest. Don't forget to focus on the positive as well as negative aspects. A written record of the critique should be made.

Reporting and Documenting the Incident

The IC must be aware of the reporting requirements necessary to deal with the incident. Personnel should be familiar with all of their local, state, and federal reporting requirements. Questions about an incident may not arise until someone files a claim sometime after the incident is over. If information documenting the incident is not available, it could have serious ramifications for all personnel involved. Thus both documenting information about personnel training and exposure and keeping incident and critique reports on file are critical to ensuring questions that might arise about the handling of the incident can be effectively, accurately, and appropriately answered.

No job is ever complete until the paperwork is done! After action reports, consisting of the written findings and other incident documents such as MSDS, unit logs are the next step in the process. Confidential personnel and medical files might need to be updated, injury reports must be written, and decontamination procedures must be documented. If contaminated equipment was disposed of, appropriate records must be maintained.

After action follow-up assures implementation of any recommendations made as a result of the incident. All recommendations should have a time frame and responsible individuals assigned. The first priority should be given to safety and health issues.

Victim Family Notification Guidelines

One of the most traumatic and emotional events that can occur to employees in the workplace is having a fellow employee injured or killed. Just as we take care in how we treat our employees' emotional well-being, we must take even greater care when notifying family members that an injury or fatality has occurred. Generally, this very difficult task falls on the Incident Commander, or his/her designee, usually a senior manager. It is always a good idea to send at least two people, including at least one person who is available to answer any questions the family may have, providing assistance to the family, and helping make any arrangements that may be necessary as a result of the workplace incident.

Reactions to bad news can be many, but the three usual major reactions include violence, shock, and unphased. The person making the notification should be prepared to deal with any or all of these emotions.

The first issue that needs to be addressed is providing all pertinent information to the family regarding the incident. The same principles apply when speaking with the family as talking with the media. Generally, the following items are important to discuss: (1) facts relative to the incident, as known up to this point; and (2) immediate condition of employee—medical diagnosis, current medical status, extent of injuries, and location of employee. It is not a good idea to speculate on prognosis—leave that to the doctors.

Assistance and arrangements for the family can include:

Arranging for transportation to the hospital as necessary. This may include lodging and meals depending on the situation.

Reassurance of the jurisdiction's responsibility for all associated medical costs, and insistence of appropriate medical care as indicated.

Arranging for babysitting services for children, if necessary.

Review of the jurisdiction's life insurance and funeral allowance policies.

Arranging any counseling that may be required by family members.

Assistance with the filing of necessary paperwork for benefits.

For cases where employees will be away from work, periodic updates and contact with the employee and family during convalescence are helpful.

For noncritical injuries, the IC can notify the family via telephone and meet the family at the hospital. If the family members do not have transportation to the hospital, the company will arrange this. It is very important that company personnel are available to meet with and support the family for the extent of the treatment and convalescence of the victim.

For a fatality, the IC (or designee) and additional personnel should go to the family's home and make notification personally, if possible. A clear understanding between the jurisdiction and local authorities as to who will notify the family must be obtained. Usually, local authorities will accompany jurisdiction personnel when notification is made. Other support personnel, if available, such as the family's personal clergy (if known) and counselor should be involved. It is not a good idea to leave the family alone once they have been notified.

Only after the family has been notified should the name of the injured or deceased be released to the media.

Employees will also need crisis intervention counseling for cases of serious injury or fatality.

10.18 CRITICAL INCIDENT STRESS

Emergency responders, by definition, frequently are exposed to traumatic events. During emergency incidents, they are thrust into dangerous and ambiguous situations. Their actions or inactions may result in serious consequences for the victims of the incident, other responders, or the community at large. Additionally, because of what responders see and are asked to do—sometimes involving seriously or fatally injured personnel (who may be friends or relatives)—they are under a lot of stress.

Stress has been defined as the body's nonspecific response to demands placed upon it. It is typically seen while responding to emergencies. Medical monitoring has shown increased pulse and respiration, elevated blood pressure and blood sugar levels, as well as rapid increases in adrenaline level.

Incident Commanders must anticipate stress, be familiar with its causes, and be ready to respond to the needs of their personnel. While stress injuries are not as apparent as broken limbs, they are just as real and require treatment.

Common symptoms of stress-induced problems include headaches, fatigue, insomnia, loss of appetite, poor concentration, low productivity, isolation, negative attitude, and tension. In extreme cases, responders might suffer from, post-traumatic stress disorder (PTSD). These people might have difficulty sleeping or be seriously bothered by nightmares containing flashbacks to a particularly difficult emergency situation. Without intervention, these symptoms can get worse, often leading to substance abuse.

Incident Commanders and other leaders can help reduce the effects of stress at an incident by developing a positive work environment. Use of an appropriate ICS will control accountability and ensure responder protection and decontamination. Stress caused by a particularly gruesome incident will be defused by debriefing responders.

An effective stress debriefing consists of several steps, the first of which is on-scene debriefing. It should be conducted one-on-one by someone not involved in the incident (e.g., a different supervisor or counselor). The facilitator allows the responders to vent their feelings, allows them to talk about their feelings, and evaluates their well-being. This phase should be mandatory for all responders at an incident involving serious injury or fatality.

The next step, critical incident stress debriefing, is initiated within 24–48 hours of the incident. It involves all responders and is conducted by a trained individual or team. Typically, this involves a six step process:

1. *Introduction*. Rules for debriefing are laid out and confidentiality is emphasized. Nobody will be criticized for how they feel.
2. *Facts*. The history of the event is recounted.
3. *Feelings*. People express their feelings, which may include fear, anxiety, concern, guilt, or anger.
4. *Symptoms*. Usually things people have experienced during or after an incident.
5. *Teaching*. Allows the facilitator to instruct the group on stress response methods, emphasizing that these symptoms are normal and can be managed.
6. *Reentry*. Deals with lingering concerns, summarizes comments, and provides additional referrals.

The last step of a full debriefing process will take place several weeks or months later. The follow-up debriefing must be performed by a trained individual and will concentrate on those who seem to have problems dealing with the incident.

10.19 FAMILY PREPAREDNESS

Everyone should have a role in preparing for an unexpected emergency. Individuals or families can prepare by:

- *Identifying Meeting Locations in Case of an Emergency*. Most families are not together 24 hours per day; thus planning ahead is important. Location points should be accessible locations; schools, public places, or friends' homes may be ideal places to meet.
- *Developing a Family Emergency Contact List*. The emergency contact list should include an out-of-town family contact, work phone numbers, neighbors' phone numbers, school phone numbers, and local emergency management phone numbers.

- *Developing an Emergency Plan.* This includes two or more ways to stay in contact (e-mail and phone), escape routes from work or home and a selected meeting location, name and phone number of an out-of-state emergency family contact, a description of health needs that will need attention, and a plan for what to do with pets.
- *Assembling a Disaster Supply Kit.* This should include food and water, first aid supplies, prescription/nonprescription medication, blankets and pillows, clothing, toiletries, tools, flashlight and batteries, battery-operated radio, and cash and identification.

REFERENCE

1. U.S. Department of Homeland Security, Homeland Security Exercise and Evaluation Program, May 2004.

APPENDIX 10.1 HOMELAND SECURITY PRESIDENTIAL DIRECTIVE 5 BY PRESIDENT GEORGE W. BUSH

SUBJECT: MANAGEMENT OF DOMESTIC INCIDENTS

Purpose

(1) To enhance the ability of the United States to manage domestic incidents by establishing a single, comprehensive national incident management system.

Definitions

(2) In this directive:

(a) the term "Secretary" means the Secretary of Homeland Security.

(b) the term "Federal departments and agencies" means those executive departments enumerated in 5 U.S.C. 101, together with the Department of Homeland Security; independent establishments as defined by 5 U.S.C. 104(1); government corporations as defined by 5 U.S.C. 103(1); and the United States Postal Service.

(c) the terms "State," "local," and the "United States" when it is used in a geographical sense, have the same meanings as used in the Homeland Security Act of 2002, Public Law 107-296.

Policy

(3) To prevent, prepare for, respond to, and recover from terrorist attacks, major disasters, and other emergencies, the United States Government shall establish a single, comprehensive approach to domestic incident management. The objective of the United States Government is to ensure that all levels of government across the Nation have the capability to work efficiently and effectively together, using a national approach to domestic incident management. In these efforts, with regard to domestic incidents, the United States Government treats crisis management and consequence management as a single, integrated function, rather than as two separate functions.

(4) The Secretary of Homeland Security is the principal Federal official for domestic incident management. Pursuant to the Homeland Security Act of 2002, the Secretary is responsible for coordinating Federal operations within the United States to prepare for, respond to, and recover from terrorist attacks, major disasters, and other emergencies. The Secretary shall coordinate the Federal Government's resources utilized in response to or recovery from terrorist attacks, major disasters, or other emergencies if and when any one of the following four conditions applies: (1) a Federal department or agency acting under its own authority has requested the assistance of the Secretary; (2) the resources of State and local authorities are overwhelmed and Federal assistance has been requested by the appropriate State and local authorities; (3) more than one Federal department or agency has become substantially involved in responding to the incident; or (4) the Secretary has been directed to assume responsibility for managing the domestic incident by the President.

(5) Nothing in this directive alters, or impedes the ability to carry out, the authorities of Federal departments and agencies to perform their responsibilities under law. All Federal departments and agencies shall cooperate with the Secretary in the Secretary's domestic incident management role.

(6) The Federal Government recognizes the roles and responsibilities of State and local authorities in domestic incident management. Initial responsibility for managing domestic incidents generally falls on State and local authorities. The Federal Government will assist State and local authorities when their resources are overwhelmed, or when Federal interests are involved. The Secretary will coordinate with State and local governments to ensure adequate planning, equipment, training, and exercise activities. The Secretary will also provide assistance to State and local governments to develop all-hazards plans and capabilities, including those of greatest importance to the security of the United States, and will ensure that State, local, and Federal plans are compatible.

(7) The Federal Government recognizes the role that the private and nongovernmental sectors play in preventing, preparing for, responding to, and recovering from terrorist attacks, major disasters, and other emergencies. The Secretary will coordinate with the private and nongovernmental sectors to ensure adequate planning, equipment, training, and exercise activities and to promote partnerships to address incident management capabilities.

(8) The Attorney General has lead responsibility for criminal investigations of terrorist acts or terrorist threats by individuals or groups inside the United States, or directed at United States citizens or institutions abroad, where such acts are within the Federal criminal jurisdiction of the United States, as well as for related intelligence collection activities within the United States, subject to the National Security Act of 1947 and other applicable law, Executive Order 12333, and Attorney General-approved procedures pursuant to that Executive Order. Generally acting through the Federal Bureau of Investigation, the Attorney General, in cooperation with other Federal departments and agencies engaged in activities to protect our national security, shall also coordinate the activities of the other members of the law enforcement community to detect, prevent, preempt, and disrupt terrorist attacks against the United States. Following a terrorist threat or an actual incident that falls within the criminal jurisdiction of the United States, the full capabilities of the United States shall be dedicated, consistent with United States law and with activities of other Federal departments and agencies to protect our national security, to assisting the Attorney General to identify the perpetrators and bring them to justice. The Attorney General and the Secretary shall establish appropriate relationships and mechanisms for cooperation and coordination between their two departments.

(9) Nothing in this directive impairs or otherwise affects the authority of the Secretary of Defense over the Department of Defense, including the chain of command for military forces from the President as Commander in Chief, to the Secretary of Defense, to the commander of military forces, or military command and control procedures. The Secretary of Defense shall provide military support to civil authorities for domestic incidents as directed by the President or when consistent with military readiness and appropriate under the circumstances and the law. The Secretary of Defense shall retain command of military forces providing civil support. The Secretary of Defense and the Secretary shall establish appropriate relationships and mechanisms for cooperation and coordination between their two departments.

(10) The Secretary of State has the responsibility, consistent with other United States Government activities to protect our national security, to coordinate international activities related to the prevention, preparation, response, and recovery from a domestic incident, and for the protection of United States citizens and United States interests overseas. The Secretary of State and the Secretary shall establish appropriate relationships and mechanisms for cooperation and coordination between their two departments.

(11) The Assistant to the President for Homeland Security and the Assistant to the President for National Security Affairs shall be responsible for interagency policy

coordination on domestic and international incident management, respectively, as directed by the President. The Assistant to the President for Homeland Security and the Assistant to the President for National Security Affairs shall work together to ensure that the United States domestic and international incident management efforts are seamlessly united.

(12) The Secretary shall ensure that, as appropriate, information related to domestic incidents is gathered and provided to the public, the private sector, State and local authorities, Federal departments and agencies, and, generally through the Assistant to the President for Homeland Security, to the President. The Secretary shall provide standardized, quantitative reports to the Assistant to the President for Homeland Security on the readiness and preparedness of the Nation—at all levels of government—to prevent, prepare for, respond to, and recover from domestic incidents.

(13) Nothing in this directive shall be construed to grant to any Assistant to the President any authority to issue orders to Federal departments and agencies, their officers, or their employees.

Tasking

(14) The heads of all Federal departments and agencies are directed to provide their full and prompt cooperation, resources, and support, as appropriate and consistent with their own responsibilities for protecting our national security, to the Secretary, the Attorney General, the Secretary of Defense, and the Secretary of State in the exercise of the individual leadership responsibilities and missions assigned in paragraphs (4), (8), (9), and (10), respectively, above.

(15) The Secretary shall develop, submit for review to the Homeland Security Council, and administer a National Incident Management System (NIMS). This system will provide a consistent nationwide approach for Federal, State, and local governments to work effectively and efficiently together to prepare for, respond to, and recover from domestic incidents, regardless of cause, size, or complexity. To provide for interoperability and compatibility among Federal, State, and local capabilities, the NIMS will include a core set of concepts, principles, terminology, and technologies covering the incident command system; multi-agency coordination systems; unified command; training; identification and management of resources (including systems for classifying types of resources); qualifications and certification; and the collection, tracking, and reporting of incident information and incident resources.

(16) The Secretary shall develop, submit for review to the Homeland Security Council, and administer a National Response Plan (NRP). The Secretary shall consult with appropriate Assistants to the President (including the Assistant to the President for Economic Policy) and the Director of the Office of Science and Technology Policy, and other such Federal officials as may be appropriate, in developing and implementing the NRP. This plan shall integrate Federal Government domestic prevention, preparedness, response, and recovery plans into one all-discipline, all-hazards plan. The NRP shall be unclassified. If certain operational aspects require classification, they shall be included in classified annexes to the NRP.

(a) The NRP, using the NIMS, shall, with regard to response to domestic incidents, provide the structure and mechanisms for national level policy and operational direction for Federal support to State and local incident managers and for exercising direct Federal authorities and responsibilities, as appropriate.

(b) The NRP will include protocols for operating under different threats or threat levels; incorporation of existing Federal emergency and incident management plans (with appropriate modifications and revisions) as either integrated components of the

NRP or as supporting operational plans; and additional operational plans or annexes, as appropriate, including public affairs and intergovernmental communications.

(c) The NRP will include a consistent approach to reporting incidents, providing assessments, and making recommendations to the President, the Secretary, and the Homeland Security Council.

(d) The NRP will include rigorous requirements for continuous improvements from testing, exercising, experience with incidents, and new information and technologies.

(17) The Secretary shall:

(a) By April 1, 2003, (1) develop and publish an initial version of the NRP, in consultation with other Federal departments and agencies; and (2) provide the Assistant to the President for Homeland Security with a plan for full development and implementation of the NRP.

(b) By June 1, 2003, (1) in consultation with Federal departments and agencies and with State and local governments, develop a national system of standards, guidelines, and protocols to implement the NIMS; and (2) establish a mechanism for ensuring ongoing management and maintenance of the NIMS, including regular consultation with other Federal departments and agencies and with State and local governments.

(c) By September 1, 2003, in consultation with Federal departments and agencies and the Assistant to the President for Homeland Security, review existing authorities and regulations and prepare recommendations for the President on revisions necessary to implement fully the NRP.

(18) The heads of Federal departments and agencies shall adopt the NIMS within their departments and agencies and shall provide support and assistance to the Secretary in the development and maintenance of the NIMS. All Federal departments and agencies will use the NIMS in their domestic incident management and emergency prevention, preparedness, response, recovery, and mitigation activities, as well as those actions taken in support of State or local entities. The heads of Federal departments and agencies shall participate in the NRP, shall assist and support the Secretary in the development and maintenance of the NRP, and shall participate in and use domestic incident reporting systems and protocols established by the Secretary.

(19) The head of each Federal department and agency shall:

(a) By June 1, 2003, make initial revisions to existing plans in accordance with the initial version of the NRP.

(b) By August 1, 2003, submit a plan to adopt and implement the NIMS to the Secretary and the Assistant to the President for Homeland Security. The Assistant to the President for Homeland Security shall advise the President on whether such plans effectively implement the NIMS.

(20) Beginning in Fiscal Year 2005, Federal departments and agencies shall make adoption of the NIMS a requirement, to the extent permitted by law, for providing Federal preparedness assistance through grants, contracts, or other activities. The Secretary shall develop standards and guidelines for determining whether a State or local entity has adopted the NIMS.

Technical and Conforming Amendments to National Security Presidential Directive-1 (NSPD-1)

(21) NSPD-1 ("Organization of the National Security Council System") is amended by replacing the fifth sentence of the third paragraph on the first page with the following: "The Attorney General, the Secretary of Homeland Security, and the Director of the Office of Management and Budget shall be invited to attend meetings pertaining to their responsibilities."

Technical and Conforming Amendments to National Security Presidential Directive-8 (NSPD-8)

(22) NSPD-8 ("National Director and Deputy National Security Advisor for Combating Terrorism") is amended by striking "and the Office of Homeland Security," on page 4, and inserting "the Department of Homeland Security, and the Homeland Security Council" in lieu thereof.

Technical and Conforming Amendments to Homeland Security Presidential Directive-2 (HSPD-2)

(23) HSPD-2 ("Combating Terrorism Through Immigration Policies") is amended as follows:

(a) striking "the Commissioner of the Immigration and Naturalization Service (INS)" in the second sentence of the second paragraph in section 1, and inserting "the Secretary of Homeland Security" in lieu thereof;

(b) striking "the INS," in the third paragraph in section 1, and inserting "the Department of Homeland Security" in lieu thereof;

(c) inserting "the Secretary of Homeland Security," after "The Attorney General" in the fourth paragraph in section 1;

(d) inserting "the Secretary of Homeland Security," after "the Attorney General" in the fifth paragraph in section 1;

(e) striking "the INS and the Customs Service" in the first sentence of the first paragraph of section 2, and inserting "the Department of Homeland Security" in lieu thereof;

(f) striking "Customs and INS" in the first sentence of the second paragraph of section 2, and inserting "the Department of Homeland Security" in lieu thereof;

(g) striking "the two agencies" in the second sentence of the second paragraph of section 2, and inserting "the Department of Homeland Security" in lieu thereof;

(h) striking "the Secretary of the Treasury" wherever it appears in section 2, and inserting "the Secretary of Homeland Security" in lieu thereof;

(i) inserting "the Secretary of Homeland Security," after "The Secretary of State" wherever the latter appears in section 3;

(j) inserting "the Department of Homeland Security," after "the Department of State," in the second sentence in the third paragraph in section 3;

(k) inserting "the Secretary of Homeland Security," after "the Secretary of State," in the first sentence of the fifth paragraph of section 3;

(l) striking "INS" in the first sentence of the sixth paragraph of section 3, and inserting "Department of Homeland Security" in lieu thereof;
(m) striking "the Treasury" wherever it appears in section 4 and inserting "Homeland Security" in lieu thereof;
(n) inserting "the Secretary of Homeland Security," after "the Attorney General" in the first sentence in section 5; and
(o) inserting "Homeland Security" after "State" in the first sentence of section 6.

Technical and Conforming Amendments to Homeland Security Presidential Directive-3 (HSPD-3)

(24) The Homeland Security Act of 2002 assigned the responsibility for administering the Homeland Security Advisory System to the Secretary of Homeland Security. Accordingly, HSPD-3 of March 11, 2002 ("Homeland Security Advisory System") is amended as follows:

(a) replacing the third sentence of the second paragraph entitled "Homeland Security Advisory System" with "Except in exigent circumstances, the Secretary of Homeland Security shall seek the views of the Attorney General, and any other federal agency heads the Secretary deems appropriate, including other members of the Homeland Security Council, on the Threat Condition to be assigned."
(b) inserting "At the request of the Secretary of Homeland Security, the Department of Justice shall permit and facilitate the use of delivery systems administered or managed by the Department of Justice for the purposes of delivering threat information pursuant to the Homeland Security Advisory System" as a new paragraph after the fifth paragraph of the section entitled "Homeland Security Advisory System."
(c) inserting "the Secretary of Homeland Security" after "The Director of Central Intelligence" in the first sentence of the seventh paragraph of the section entitled "Homeland Security Advisory System."
(d) striking "Attorney General" wherever it appears (except in the sentences referred to in subsections (a) and (c) above), and inserting "the Secretary of Homeland Security" in lieu thereof; and
(e) striking the section entitled "Comment and Review Periods."

CHAPTER 11

Emergency Response to a Weapon of Mass Destruction Attack

11.1 INTRODUCTION

Routine responses to accidental emergency incidents pose a number of risks to even the most highly trained and experienced responder. Emergency response to an intentional incident, caused by an adversary bent on causing the greatest possible amount of damage and casualties, is much more dangerous. If the intentional act involves the use of a weapon of mass destruction (WMD), the hazards are extreme because the weapon was designed, manufactured, and employed for the sole purpose of killing people. Effective response to WMD incidents requires comprehensive standard operating procedures, highly effective personal protective equipment, and hundreds of hours of specialized training.

Some adversaries have decided to attack the emergency responders who are attempting to help those in need. This intentional targeting of emergency responders is done for several reasons:

- To demotivate the emergency responders by injuring or killing their fellow emergency responders.
- To demotivate the citizens by proving that emergency responders will not be able to provide aid, and that the government cannot ensure their safety and security.
- To impede the provision of emergency services. If a secondary device is suspected or discovered, emergency responders will most likely withdraw from the area until the device can be rendered safe or neutralized. Of course while that process is occurring, casualties will be left untreated, and other results of the attack, such as fires, will not be mitigated.
- To add to the casualty count. The detonation of a secondary device will certainly add to the number of casualties, both civilians and emergency responders.

Understanding, Assessing, and Responding to Terrorism: Protecting Critical Infrastructure and Personnel By Brian T. Bennett

11.2 USE OF A WEAPON OF MASS DESTRUCTION

Chemical, biological, or radiological agents can be dispersed in the air we breathe, the water we drink, or the food we eat. Dispersion of the weapons can be as simple as opening a container and allowing the agent to spread out over a wide area. The potential for these weapons to cause massive harm makes them very attractive to an adversary.

When responding to a WMD attack, there is no such thing as a routine response.

11.3 THE EMERGENCY SCENE AS A CRIME SCENE

A terrorist attack is a crime; therefore if a terrorist were to deploy a WMD, the area would become a crime scene. Although the first priority of emergency responders would be to save lives and minimize property damage, an effort must be made to preserve the scene and its evidence as much as possible to assist law enforcement agencies in their investigation. A crime scene resulting from a terrorist's use of a WMD will be much different from any other crime scene. The area will be very dangerous because of the weapon deployed, and there will be mass casualties who need rescue and treatment. The crime scene will likely be spread out over a very large area. For example, the bombing of Pan Am Flight 103 over Lockerbie, Scotland resulted in a crime scene that encompassed over 65 square miles. Evidence that is present in the crime scene will need to be protected as best as possible.

Sample Procedure: Preservation of Evidence

1. If possible, photograph or videotape the scene as soon as possible.
2. Establish a record of all personnel entering into the crime scene area. Record name of entrant, time entering/exiting, area entered, and purpose of entry.
3. Identify and document all emergency vehicles that enter or leave the crime scene. Vehicle tires and clothing can pick up or damage key evidence. Record identity of vehicle entering/exiting the scene, where it was within the scene, the purpose of entering/exiting the scene, driver/occupants of the vehicle, and destination of vehicles exiting the scene.
4. Do not allow any preliminary examination of crime scene debris (either formally or informally) unless it is conducted by a recognized law enforcement evidence collection unit.
5. Segregate any witness(es) in a safe area pending interview by law enforcement personnel.
6. Responders should ensure that the general conditions found at the incident scene are not disturbed. Potential evidence should be moved only for life safety or incident stabilization.

7. Responders should ensure that debris or other materials found at the incident scene are not disturbed or moved, unless necessary to mitigate the incident or treat a victim.
8. If a responder must disturb evidence, an effort should be made to document its location with the Incident Commander. The material should be moved only as far from its original location as absolutely necessary.
9. Do not replace any evidence that was moved back into its original position.
10. Law enforcement should be notified as soon as practical and requested to collect evidence.
11. Potential evidence includes (a) victim's clothing, (b) deceased victims, (c) dissemination devices, (d) sampling media, (e) shrapnel, (f) dead animals and birds, (g) samples of agent, (h) containers, (i) unexploded devices, and (j) components of devices.

11.4 SIZE UP

Size up is the process of ascertaining the extent of the emergency situation and determining a course of action to follow to mitigate the problem. When dealing with terrorism incidents, the threat must be determined and included in the size up process. Threat assessments should be made in a unified manner in consultation with all of the stakeholders involved. Threat assessment involves analyzing the circumstances surrounding the incident, the target, and any specific threats or warnings concerning the attack. The threat determination also includes the intended target of the weapon (inside or outside area) and where the weapon was found within the target (in a mailroom, by computer servers). Any suspicious packages should be considered a high threat, and the appropriate response agencies notified.

Determination of the level of threat should impact all facets of the emergency response. As threat credibility increases, the response should be increased.

Handling Hoaxes

In the event that the threat assessment determines there is no credibility, the threat component of the size up does not exist. The Incident Commander will need to determine if a public safety emergency exists, or if the emergency response operation can be terminated.

If the threat has been deemed to be a hoax, the scene should be turned over to law enforcement personnel for investigation and collection of any evidence, if appropriate.

11.5 THE SECONDARY DEVICE

Secondary devices are explosive weapons that are placed at the scene of an ongoing emergency response which are intended to specifically target and cause casualties among emergency responders. Typically, the secondary device is concealed or camouflaged so as to be unseen by the emergency responders when they arrive on scene. The concept of the secondary device is to allow emergency responders to assemble on scene and begin their mitigation activities. Shortly after the emergency responders arrive, the secondary explosives are detonated after the primary attack. Secondary devices are intended to inflict additional casualties, primarily among the emergency responders, cause further damage, and instill fear in the emergency responders and the general public.

The threat of a secondary device presents unique tactical considerations. In a terrorism incident, emergency responders should always assume that a secondary device is present.

Protecting Against the Secondary Device

There are some measures emergency responders can take to protect themselves against the adversary's use of a secondary device:

1. *Recognition of Secondary Devices.* Emergency responders should be trained to recognize:

- When a secondary device might be utilized by an adversary: an adversary can deploy a secondary device any time, any place. It would most likely be used at the scene of a mass casualty incident, probably that has already involved the use of an explosive device in the primary attack, when there are numerous emergency responders present.
- What a secondary device could look like: a secondary device is an improvised explosive device; therefore it can be disguised to look like almost anything, limited only by the builder's imagination.
- Where it is likely to be planted: the secondary device must be hidden from view of the emergency responders. It can be placed almost anywhere, such as in dumpsters, mailboxes, vehicles, or even strapped on a person.
- What to do if one is suspected: emergency responders should be trained on how to respond to the discovery of a secondary device. First, the device should not be touched or moved; second, all emergency responders should immediately evacuate the area; and third, bomb squad personnel should be notified.

2. *Variation of Routine.* Experience has shown that an adversary will observe the operations of emergency responders prior to utilizing a secondary device. The adversary will attempt to collect information that can be used to ensure maximum effectiveness of the weapon. The adversary would be interested in things like:

- Do the emergency responders always respond to a key asset using the same route? If so, a device could be placed along the response route, such as inside a parked vehicle.
- Do the emergency responders always park their apparatus in the same general area? If so, an adversary might be able to plant a secondary device in a nearby parked vehicle or other object, such as a mailbox or dumpster.

- Do the emergency responders tend to cluster together? This may pose an attractive target for a secondary device.
- Do the emergency responders tend to use the same access and egress routes into and out of the key asset? If so, a secondary device could be planted along that route.
- Does the Command Post tend to be located in the same location each time, for example, in the security guard station in the lobby of an office building? If so, a secondary device could be used to eliminate the emergency management leadership.

3. *Evacuation Locations.* Emergency responders should have a minimum of two access and egress routes preplanned for each key asset. These routes should include the roads taken to respond to the key asset, as well as routes into and out of the key asset once they arrive on scene. As an example, if the incident is in a building, emergency responders should have planned evacuation routes using a minimum of two different doors so they are not always using the same path.

4. *Becoming More Aware of Unusual Activity or Situational Awareness.* Maintaining situational awareness is a simple concept that can help save lives. Emergency responders must always remember where they are and what is occurring around them. If they have responded to a terrorist incident, they must be aware it is very likely that a secondary device may be present. Emergency responders must also be on the lookout for suspicious activity, which may be an indicator that the adversary is observing their actions, deploying weapons, or preparing to execute another attack.

Case Study: Secondary Device

There have been two highly publicized events involving secondary devices that have targeted emergency responders in the United States. On January 27, 1997, a bomb was detonated at the Northside Planning Service, a women's health facility, in Atlanta, Georgia, causing significant damage to the clinic. Within an hour, a second explosive device detonated, wounding several law enforcement and emergency responders. On February 21, 1997, a secondary device was detonated at an alternate lifestyle nightclub, The Otherside Lounge, also in Atlanta, Georgia. The explosive injured five people. An additional secondary device was discovered by law enforcement personnel and was successfully disarmed.

11.6 EVACUATION OF PERSONNEL IN A WEAPON OF MASS DESTRUCTION ATTACK

The first instinct when a threat has been received or an attack executed against a target is to evacuate personnel from the "danger area" to a perceived "safe area." However, there are times when evacuation is not the best option to protect people. Problems associated with evacuation include:

- The need to move large numbers of people very quickly. An attractive target would have many people who need to be moved from the key asset to a safe area.

- Where to put the people. Once all of the people were evacuated from the key asset, where would they assemble and how would they get there?
- How to account for everyone. Once everyone is assembled in the safe area, how would they be accounted for?
- People with special needs. How would people with special needs be safely evacuated from the key asset and moved to the safe area?
- Moving people from a safe area through a dangerous area. Would the people being evacuated have to move through a dangerous area (such as a chemical, biological, or radiological cloud) between the key asset and the safe area? Can they be protected during their trek?
- Moving people from a safe area to a dangerous area. Is it possible the people would actually be moved from a relatively safe area to a more dangerous area?

An evacuation can provide an enticing target for an adversary. Typically, an evacuation results in a large number of people grouped together. An adversary may use the tactic of calling in a bomb threat or activating the fire alarm system to cause an evacuation. The adversary may use this tactic in a hardened facility, when access to people would normally not be present in the key asset. The adversary could deploy a chemical, biological, radiological, or explosive weapon once personnel are outside the protected area of the key asset and are grouped together.

Sheltering in place may, at times, provide a better solution to the problem.

Sheltering in Place

Sheltering in place, also known as protecting in place, means personnel are told to stay where they are when an emergency occurs. Sheltering in place sometimes provides a better option to protect personnel rather than evacuation. This is especially true if there are large numbers of people, people with special needs, or if the evacuees would need to travel through a dangerous area.

Techniques for sheltering in place include:

- Move to the center of the building, away from windows and external doors that might allow a chemical, biological, or radiological agent to enter. Windows can also pose a hazard in the event an explosive device is detonated and the window glass is shattered.
- Shut down the building's HVAC system to reduce the chance of a chemical, biological, or radiological agent from entering the building.
- Stay out of rooms with an exhaust fan as contaminants can enter into the building through this route.

Who Makes the Decision to Evacuate or Not?

Each local emergency response jurisdiction will have its own policy for dealing with this issue. However, in most cases, the decision on whether to evacuate or not is given to the key asset's chief executive. For example, if a bomb threat is received at the local high school, the principal usually has the ultimate responsibility to make the decision.

However, this decision should not be taken lightly. The decision maker must resist the inclination to avoid disrupting the normal routine. It is recommended that the key asset's chief executive and the local emergency response and law enforcement officials meet to review the threat, risk, and intelligence data. Once all of the pertinent information is reviewed and analyzed, an informed decision can be made. If there is any uncertainty, it is always better to err on the side of caution and protect personnel.

Communications also plays a part in the evacuation process. There must be some thought put into how all of the personnel affected will be notified of the evacuation in a timely manner, without causing undo panic.

Evacuation of Personnel

When a bomb threat is received, a decision must be made concerning what to do with the personnel who are in the potentially affected area. There are three choices available:

1. *Do Nothing*. The do nothing option is typically utilized when there is a high probability that the threat is a hoax. When the threat appears to be a hoax, oftentimes the best option is to do nothing rather than disrupt the normal operations at the key asset, especially when there are large numbers of people or people with special needs involved. An evacuation that is conducted unnecessarily will likely cause some degree of panic and can put people at risk.

2. *Partial Evacuation*. Partial evacuation can be used if there is some credibility to the threat. A partial evacuation is used to move people from a potentially affected area of the key asset but leaves the remainder of the personnel in place. Partial evacuation may also be used if there are sensitive populations, such as small children, who will require additional time to evacuate the area. A plan must be in place to inform the balance of the population who remain in place why they are not being evacuated.

3. *Full Evacuation*. Full evacuation of a key asset is a major undertaking and should only be done when the credibility of a threat is high. There should be a plan in place to evacuate personnel in a prearranged, staged, and orderly manner so that the evacuation can be accomplished efficiently and safely. The plan must also address the issue of where the evacuated personnel will go, who will perform a headcount to make sure everyone has evacuated, and how to handle personnel who are reported missing.

11.7 PROTECTING BUILDING ENVIRONMENTS FROM AIRBORNE AGENTS

There are actions that can be taken to minimize the adverse effects to the occupants of buildings if an adversary deploys an airborne biological, chemical, or radiological agent. The most significant portal for these agents to enter into a building is via the heating, ventilation, and air conditioning (HVAC) system. Therefore most efforts should be devoted to enhancing the protection of this system.

Some of the techniques that can be used to minimize the adverse effects of an attack should be addressed in advance of an attack, such as:

- Securing mechanical rooms that house the HVAC controls.
- Securing HVAC intakes and exhausts.
- Controlling the distribution of a building's floor plans and engineering drawings.
- Isolating HVAC systems in the lobby, mailroom, loading docks, and storage areas (high-risk areas where materials can enter the building through packages).
- Evaluating HVAC control options.
- Assessing HVAC filtration systems.
- Sealing gaps in buildings to prevent infiltration.

11.8 EMERGENCY RESPONSE ACTIONS AT THE SCENE OF A WEAPON OF MASS DESTRUCTION INCIDENT

The following tasks should be conducted upon initial arrival of the emergency responders at a WMD attack:

1. Conduct an incident size up.
2. Establish scene control, including the establishment of a perimeter.
3. Identify the agent involved.
4. Conduct a hazard and risk assessment.
5. Establish incident goals and objectives.
6. Select appropriate personal protective equipment.
7. Establish an emergency decontamination area.
8. Execute incident action plan.
9. Order additional resources as needed.

Emergency Response Procedures: Biological Agents

Personal Protective Equipment. Level C personal protective equipment (PPE), using a full face air purifying respirator, is effective for most biological agents. This level of PPE will present less stress to the emergency responders and allow them to work longer and more efficiently.

Decontamination. Most biological agents can be destroyed by decontaminating with sodium hypochlorite (common household bleach). Other antiseptics and disinfectants may also be effective. Household bleach can be diluted with water (1 part bleach to 9 parts of water) and left on the biological agent for 15 minutes. After 15 minutes, the bleach can be washed away with water to dilute the corrosive effects of the bleach.

If decontaminating solid agents are dispersed as a powder, they should be wet carefully to prevent suspending the powder in the air.

What to Do If You Receive a Letter/Package Containing Powder

1. Notify local law enforcement and emergency response agencies.
2. Do not (a) move the letter/package, (b) shake or empty the contents of the letter/package, (c) attempt to clean up the powder.
3. Isolate the letter/package. Place the letter/package in a plastic bag or cover it with a towel (or something similar) to prevent the spread of the powder.
4. Remove everyone from the area, except those exposed, to a safe area.
5. Those who were exposed should be segregated.
6. Close the door to the room containing the letter/package, and do not allow anyone in (except emergency responders).
7. Ensure everyone who came in contact with the letter washes their hands with soap and water. Shower with soap and water as soon as possible.

Sample Procedure: Biological Agent

General

1. Protect yourself by using personal protective equipment.
2. Practice body fluid isolation.
3. The situation should be thoroughly assessed before committing emergency responders to an operation.
4. Do not touch any suspicious substance and/or dissemination device.
5. Avoid contamination.
6. Isolate and contain the agent if possible.
7. Keep exposed personnel together in a secure location awaiting decontamination and treatment.
8. Beware of a secondary device.
9. Decontamination should be set up before the emergency responders enter the hot zone.
10. When confronted with an unknown WMD agent, the sampling protocol is (a) flammability, radiation; (b) M8/M9 paper; (c) M256 kit; and (d) colorimetric tubes.

Detection of Bacterial Agents. No reliable field test is currently available. New detection devices are currently under development.

PPE for Bacterial Agents

1. Polycoated Tyvek suit.

2. Air purifying respirator with HEPA filters.
3. Latex or PVC gloves.

Decontamination for Bacterial Agents

1. Remove clothing.
2. Decontaminate with a bleach solution.
3. Potentially contaminated personal belongings and clothing should be bagged and segregated.

Treatment of Bacterial Agent Injuries

1. Decontaminate victim.
2. Maintain an open airway.
3. Administer oxygen if necessary.
4. Transport to a designated medical facility.

Detection of Viral Agents. No reliable field test is available at this time.

PPE for Viral Agents

1. Polycoated Tyvek suit.
2. Air purifying respirator with HEPA filters.
3. Latex or PVC gloves.

Decontamination for Viral Agents

1. Remove clothing.
2. Use a mild bleach solution.
3. Potentially contaminated personal belongings and clothing should be bagged and segregated.

Treatment of Viral Agent Injuries

1. Decontaminate victim.
2. Maintain an open airway.
3. Administer oxygen if necessary.
4. Transport to a designated medical facility.

Biological Toxins

1. Abrin
   (a) Appearance: yellowish-white powder.
   (b) Routes of exposure: all.

   (c) Acute effects: severe vomiting and diarrhea (resulting in severe dehydration); multisystem organ failure (GI tract, kidney, liver, pancreas).

2. Ricin
   (a) Appearance: white powder.
   (b) Routes of exposure: all.
   (c) Acute effects: severe vomiting and diarrhea (resulting in severe dehydration); multisystem organ failure (GI tract, kidney, liver, pancreas). Potentially fatal due to severe allergic reaction.

Signs and Symptoms of Biological Toxins

1. Abrin
   (a) Skin: potential for allergic skin reaction—redness, blister, pain.
   (b) Eyes: tearing, swelling of eyelids, pain, redness, corneal injury.
   (c) Ingestion: very low blood pressure; fast and/or irregular heart beat; drowsiness, disorientation, hallucinations, seizures, coma; burning pain in mouth, abdominal pain, nausea, vomiting, diarrhea, blood in urine; muscle weakness, tremors, spasm; dilated pupils and bleeding in back of eyes; cyanosis and flushing of skin.
2. Ricin
   (a) Skin: potential for allergic skin reaction—redness, blister, pain.
   (b) Eyes: tearing, swelling of eyelids, pain, redness, corneal injury.
   (c) Ingestion: fever, thirst, sore throat, headache; abdominal pain, cramping, nausea, vomiting, diarrhea, blood in urine; dilated pupils; vascular collapse and shock.

Detection of Biological Toxins. No reliable field test is available at this time.

PPE for Biological Toxins

1. Entry
   (a) SCBA.
   (b) Responder or Tychem BR suit.
2. Decontamination
   (a) Polycoated Tyvek suit.
   (b) Full face air purifying respirator with HEPA filters.
   (c) Latex or PVC gloves.

Decontamination for Biological Toxins

1. Wash with soap and water, then decontaminate with an alkaline solution.
2. Avoid using hot water.
3. Avoid vigorous scrubbing.

4. Use large amounts of water.
5. Potentially contaminated personal belongings and clothing should be bagged and segregated.

Treatment for Biological Toxins

1. Decontaminate victim.
2. Maintain an open airway.
3. Administer high flow oxygen.
4. Notify advanced life support personnel.
5. Transport to a designated medical facility.

Emergency Response Procedures: Nuclear/Radiological Agents

Defining the hot zone is the most important task in a radiological emergency. The PPE could include turnout gear and air purifying respirators with HEPA filters. Decontamination is done with soap and water.

A radiological incident should be handled like any mass casualty incident involving a hazardous material. Terrorists are counting on the fear of radiation by emergency responders to slow down the response to the attack. Defining the hot zone is the most important task in a radiological emergency in order to limit the spread of contamination.

Responders should approach from an uphill and upwind position. Look for fires, wires, and sharp or falling objects. Wear an SCBA or air purifying respirator with HEPA filters to reduce the risk of breathing radioactive dust. Remember, radioactive dust can collect on clothes, so decontamination will be critical. The basic protective measures for response to a radiological incident is time, distance, and shielding. Responders should minimize their time in the presence of a radioactive source. The longer you stay near a radiological source, the more of a dose you receive. Responders should stay as far away from a radiological source as possible. The strength of a source decreases as the distance between a responder and the source increases. The intensity of the radiation field decreases drastically as the distance from the source increases. This is known as the inverse square rule. For example, if the exposure rate is 1000 millirem per hour at a distance of 1 foot from the source, the exposure at 2 feet will be only one-quarter as much, or 250 millirem per hour. Therefore the more distance there is between an individual and a radiation source, the less exposure the individual receives. And finally, responders should attempt to put shielding between their bodies and the radioactive source. This shielding may be a building, turnout gear, or a fire truck. The more massive the shielding, the greater the protection from the sources. The more shielding between an individual and a radioactive source, the less exposure received. If a radiological agent is thought to be present, avoid inhalation and ingestion of radioactive particles. This can be achieved by moving to unaffected areas inside a building, shutting down a building's HVAC system, donning SCBA or an air purifying respirator, and not eating, drinking, or smoking in the hot or warm zones. A radiation survey meter should be used as you move in toward the incident scene. Departments must establish standard operating guidelines for response to radiological incidents. Standard operating procedures should include action levels for responders and public protection. For example, if the projected dose is 1–5 rem, you should consider evacuation; if the dose exceeds 5 rem, evacuation should be mandatory.

All persons within the hot zone must be surveyed before they are allowed to leave the area. Survey areas should be established in several locations, preferably located away from the decontamination and treatment areas. Victims can only be declared "clean" after being surveyed. Standard advice to citizens awaiting assistance from emergency responders should be for them to go inside a building, turn off the HVAC system, and await further instructions from authorities.

Radiological Decontamination. Radiological contamination occurs when radioactive material exists in an unwanted place, particularly where its presence may be harmful. Decontamination is the process of removing, destroying, or covering a contaminant to an acceptable level that facilitates normal operations. However, unlike chemicals, radiation is not diluted, destroyed, or neutralized during the decontamination process. Therefore any materials (rags, water, etc.) used during the decontamination process need to be contained and disposed of properly. For this reason, the use of copious amounts of water during the radiological decontamination process is discouraged. Eighty to ninety percent of radioactive surface contamination can be eliminated by simply removing your clothes. Washing the hair, hands, and feet will eliminate most of the remaining radioactive material.

It is recommended that there are separate decontamination lines for the emergency responders and victims. The preferred location for the decontamination station is indoors, away from contaminated dust particles that may be in the air. A major concern in decontamination operations is the resuspension of radioactive contamination into the air. Efforts must be taken to minimize this hazard as a victim's clothing is removed. Decontamination crews must wear respiratory protection to prevent inhalation of radioactive particles.

The decontamination process for radiological incidents consists of ten stations.

Station #1: Initial Radiological Survey. Decontamination should be performed based on the results of a body survey done with a radiation survey instrument. Whole-body decontamination may not be necessary; areas of radiation can be pinpointed with the survey instrument, spot decontamination performed, and the area resurveyed. A survey must be conducted after each decontamination attempted to ensure the contamination has been successfully removed. Typically, a person is considered decontaminated when the radiation levels are no more than twice the normal background level.

Station #2: Dry Decontamination. Once "hot" areas have been identified, decontamination can be accomplished by removing clothing and any foreign material (e.g., dust) that may be present on the skin. Particular attention must be paid to shoes. Dry decontamination excludes the use of water and hence the need to contain runoff. Dry decontamination relies on the physical removal of radioactive contamination by removing clothing, brushing, or removing the contamination with tape. The dry decontamination process will ordinarily remove a minimum of 90% of the contamination.

Station #3: Radiological Survey. The "hot" area should be resurveyed after the decontamination process to ensure radioactive particles have been removed. If the area is still hot, move to the partial dry decontamination station.

Station #4: Partial Dry Decontamination. "Hot" areas are wiped with a soapy wet cloth or a gentle spray of soapy water, and then wiped with a cloth. A minimum amount of water should be used at this station.

Station #5: Radiological Survey. The "hot" area should be resurveyed after the decontamination process to ensure radioactive particles have been removed. If the area is still hot, move to the wet decontamination station.

Station #6: Wet Decontamination. The wet decontamination method should only be used when a victim is still "hot" after both the dry and partial dry decontamination steps. Wet decontamination consists of the traditional flushing with copious amounts of water followed by a soap scrub. Large amounts of water runoff will need to be contained at this station.

Station #7: Radiological Survey. The "hot" area should be resurveyed after the decontamination process to ensure radioactive particles have been removed. If the area is still hot, move to the second wet decontamination station.

Station #8: Second Wet Decontamination. The second wet decontamination station is identical to the first wet decontamination station.

Station #9: Radiological Survey. The "hot" area should be resurveyed after the decontamination process to ensure radioactive particles have been removed. If the area is still hot, move to the partial dry decontamination station.

Station #10: Special Evaluation. If a victim is still "hot" after the second wet decontamination, the victim must be isolated and evaluated by a radiation specialist—it is possible they have internal contamination.

Treatment of Contaminated Victims. Occasionally, people will experience nausea and vomiting after a presumed exposure, for example, after hearing that a radiological device been set off, even though there was no actual exposure. If radiation is released, many people will transport themselves to local medical facilities for treatment. Others will remain in the immediate area and await the arrival of emergency responders. In either case, we cannot prevent contaminated victims from reaching the hospital.

Victims may be contaminated with radiation after the deployment of a radiological weapon. Separate contaminated victims from noncontaminated victims, and then further separate victims into ambulatory and nonambulatory. Noncontaminated, uninjured victims can be sent home after the survey with the advice of taking a shower. Noncontaminated injured victims should be treated immediately per existing mass casualty protocols. Decontamination of injured victims may be necessary based on the results of the radiation survey. The walking wounded should be surveyed and decontaminated if the survey instrument indicates the presence of radiation. As casualties are removed from the decontamination line, they should be sent to a dedicated location known as the casualty collection point (CCP) for further medical evaluation and treatment. Optimally, the CCP should be located between the decontamination location and the hospital.

The basic rules for handling severely injured contaminated victims are: (1) treat life-threatening injuries without regard to contamination; (2) isolate patients and restrict access to the treatment/evaluation area; and (3) maintain contamination control.

The big difference between a radiological incident and a typical Hazmat incident involves the decontamination of injured victims. Decontamination should not initially be performed on an unstable, injured victim. Immediate life-saving medical procedures and transportation to a medical facility must always be the first priority over decontamination. The rationale for this is if the victim is still alive, whatever radiation exposure the responders receive from the contaminated victim will not be life-threatening. Also, internal contamination poses a minimal risk to emergency responders. Seriously injured contaminated victims will die from medical instability, not contamination.

Care must be taken when decontaminating in or around open wounds. Open wounds and abrasions, as well as other body openings (e.g., mouth, nose, and ears) must be protected so the radioactive contamination is not flushed directly into the body.

Radiological Incident Phases. The U.S. Environmental Protection Agency has developed the following chart, which indicates the appropriate protective actions that should be implemented for the various nuclear/radiological incident phases.

Incident Phase	Exposure Pathway	Protective Action
Early	External radiation from a facility	Shelter in place Evacuation Control access
Early	External radiation from a plume	Shelter in place Evacuation Control access
Early/ intermediate	Inhalation of radiation from plume	Shelter in place Administration of stable iodine Evacuation Control access

Incident Phase	Exposure Pathway	Protective Action
Intermediate	Contamination of skin and clothes	Shelter in place Evacuation Personnel decontamination
Intermediate	External radiation from ground deposition of radioactivity	Evacuation Relocation Decontamination of land and property
Intermediate/late	Ingestion of contaminated food and water	Food and water controls
Late	Inhalation of resuspended radioactive particles	Relocation

Sample Procedure: Nuclear/Radiological Agent

General

1. Protect yourself by using personal protective equipment.
2. Avoid contamination.
3. Do not touch any suspicious substance and/or dissemination device.
4. Isolate and contain the device if possible.
5. Exposure to radiological material should be limited by practicing the time, distance, and shielding principle.
6. The situation should be thoroughly assessed before committing emergency responders to an operation.
7. Stay upwind and an appropriate distance away from the fallout.
8. Keep exposed personnel together in a secure location awaiting decontamination and treatment.
9. Beware of a secondary device.
10. Practice universal precautions to minimize spread of radiological material.
11. Decontamination should be set up before emergency responders enter the hot zone.
12. The emergency responders' time in the hot zone should be guided by the attached "stay time chart."
13. When confronted with an unknown WMD agent, the sampling protocol is (a) flammability, radiation; (b) M8/M9 paper; (c) M256 kit; and (d) colorimetric tubes.

Detection of Radiological Material

1. The radiation detection meter can be used to detect radiological material that emits alpha, beta, or gamma radiation.

2. The emergency responders should determine the background radiation level immediately before entering the hot zone.
3. The hot zone should encompass the area that is 2 millirem over background.
4. The warm zone should encompass the area from background to 2 millirem over background.

PPE for Radiological Materials

1. Respiratory protection (SCBA, air line respirator, or full face respirator with HEPA filters).
2. Protective clothing (Tyvek suit or turnout gear).
3. Foot covering (bunker boots or disposable latex Hazmat boot).
4. Gloves (latex).

Decontamination for Radiological Materials—General

1. A modified standard decontamination station should be used for radiological incidents.
2. Two adjacent decontamination lines should be established—one for ambulatory victims and one for nonambulatory victims.
3. Victims should be triaged at the equipment drop station. Victims classified as "immediate" should be sent for medical treatment without being decontaminated.
4. Victims/responders should be checked with a radiation survey meter at the equipment drop station before starting the decontamination process.
5. Ambulatory victims who are not contaminated should be released from the scene without going through the decontamination line.
6. Nonambulatory victims who are not contaminated should be released for medical treatment without going through the decontamination line.
7. Particular attention should be given to the feet during the survey and decontamination.

Decontamination for Radiological Materials—Ambulatory Victims

1. If the initial radiation survey indicates ambulatory victims are contaminated, they should be directed to remove and bag their clothing and report to the ambulatory victim decontamination line.
2. Flush eyes with water or saline solution, if needed.
3. After clothing has been removed, another radiation survey should be performed. Particular attention should be given to identifying localized contamination.
4. The hands and feet should be given particular attention during the decontamination process.
5. Dry decontamination is the preferred method.

6. After dry decontamination, victims should be checked with a survey meter for contamination.
7. If dry decontamination was effective, victims should be advised to shower as soon as possible.
8. If "hot" spots exist on the body, decontaminate by wiping with a soapy wet cloth.
9. Perform a radiation survey to determine decontamination effectiveness.
10. If necessary, decontaminate the skin again with a minimal amount of tepid water and a mild soap.
11. Recheck for contamination by conducting another radiation survey.
12. If there are still hot spots, victims should shower.
13. After showering, victims should be surveyed for residual radiation. If there is still contamination, transport the victims to a medical facility for evaluation of possible internal radiation contamination.

Decontamination for Radiological Materials—Nonambulatory Victims

1. If the radiation survey indicates nonambulatory victims are contaminated, the decontamination team should remove and bag their clothing and the victims should be taken to the nonambulatory victim decontamination line.
2. Flush eyes with water or saline solution, if needed.
3. After clothing has been removed, another radiation survey should be performed. Particular attention should be given to identifying localized contamination.
4. The hands and feet should be given particular attention during the decontamination process.
5. Dry decontamination is the preferred method.
6. After dry decontamination, victims should be checked with a survey meter for contamination.
7. If dry decontamination was effective, victims should be given a shower as soon as possible.
8. If "hot" spots exist on the body, decontaminate by wiping with a soapy wet cloth.
9. Perform a radiation survey to determine decontamination effectiveness. If necessary, decontaminate the skin again with a minimal amount of tepid water and a mild soap.
10. Recheck for contamination by conducting another radiation survey.
11. If there are still hot spots, victims should be given a shower.
12. After showering, victims should be surveyed for residual radiation. If there is still contamination, transport victims to a medical facility for evaluation of possible internal radiation contamination.

Treatment of Radiological Injuries

1. The general symptom of radiation exposure is burns without pain. Skin may turn red and look puffy. Burns may not appear for several hours.
2. Move the victim away from radiological material.
3. Flush eyes with water or saline solution.
4. Decontaminate the skin with tepid water and a mild soap.
5. Maintain an open airway.
6. Administer high flow oxygen.
7. Treat thermal burns.
8. Control bleeding (usually nose, gums).

Emergency Response Procedures: Chemical Agents

An incident involving a chemical WMD should be treated just as any other hazardous materials incident. The most significant difference is the fact that a chemical WMD is supertoxic when compared to ordinary hazardous materials. The same personal protective equipment, mitigation tools, air monitoring devices, and decontamination equipment and procedures are generally equally effective.

General Response Guidelines to a Chemical Agent Attack. First responders should take specific protective measures in case of a suspected chemical attack, including:

- Park vehicles and position responders upwind and at a safe distance.
- Don chemical protective clothing and use respiratory protection.
- Immediately notify your agency dispatcher that you are involved in a possible chemical incident and provide your dispatcher with as much detailed information as possible.
- Establish an isolation distance (hot zone) and prohibit traffic from passing through the incident.
- Evacuate people downwind.
- If incident is outdoors, seal doors and windows and turn off HVAC systems.
- Be alert for signs of escaping materials or agents: note sounds of escaping gas or odd smells.
- Follow decontamination procedures when clear of the contaminated area.

Personal Protective Equipment. Once the size up has been completed and the threat and hazards assessed, the proper emergency responder personal protective equipment must be selected. Standard compatibility charts are available from suit and glove manufacturers, which will help in the selection of the proper protective equipment for specific agents. The general rule of thumb is to use Level A chemical protective clothing for chemical agents, with Level B being an acceptable alternative in most cases. Decontamination crews should done either Level B or Level C protection, depending on the concentrations of agent present.

Monitoring for Chemical Agents. As with an accidental hazardous materials release, it is important that air monitoring be conducted immediately upon the emergency responders' arrival on scene. Air monitoring devices should be used to identify the agent involved, as well as the concentrations present. The results of monitoring will provide the information necessary to:

- Establish the hot, warm, and cold zones.
- Conduct a complete hazard and risk assessment.
- Establish the goals and objectives of the response.
- Determine the need for sheltering in place or evacuation.
- Select proper levels of personal protective equipment.
- Select the proper level of decontamination and decontamination solution.
- Establish the proper level of medical care necessary.

Some typical inexpensive monitoring equipment used for chemical agent detection includes:

- M8/M9 paper—used to detect nerve, blood, and blister agents. Liquid is placed on the paper, and a color change occurs indicating the agent.
- M256 kit—used to detect nerve, blood, and blister agents. A qualitative test is run in a contaminated atmosphere, resulting in a color change, which indicates the agent present.
- Chemical-specific meters—electronic meters used to detect specific airborne chemicals, such as chlorine.
- Colorimetric tubes—used to detect airborne contaminants. An air sample is drawn into a tube that contains a reagent medium; a color change indicates the identity of the agent and relative concentration present.

Additional, more expensive chemical warfare agent detectors are also available.

Sample Procedure Chemical Agent

General

1. Protect yourself by using personal protective equipment.
2. The situation should be thoroughly assessed before committing emergency responders to an operation.
3. Do not touch any suspicious substance and/or dissemination device.
4. Avoid becoming contaminated or spreading contamination.
5. Isolate and contain the agent if possible.

6. Stay upwind and an appropriate distance away from the cloud/agent.
7. Keep exposed personnel together in a secure location awaiting decontamination and treatment.
8. Beware of a secondary device.
9. Decontamination should be set up before emergency responders enter the hot zone.
10. When confronted with an unknown WMD agent, the sampling protocol is (a) flammability, radiation; (b) M8/M9 paper; (c) M256 kit; and (d) colorimetric tubes.

Identification of Nerve Agents

1. Sarin (North American Emergency Response Guidebook Guide #153)
   - Colorless liquid; odorless in pure form.
   - Heavier than air.
2. VX (North American Emergency Response Guidebook Guide #153)
   - Colorless to straw colored liquid; odorless; similar in appearance to motor oil.
   - Heavier than air.

Detection of Nerve Agents

1. The following Drager colorimetric tubes can be used to detect nerve agents:

Agent	Drager Tube	Detection Range
Tabun (GA)	Phosphoric acid esters	0.05 ppm
Sarin (GB)	Phosphoric acid esters	0.05 ppm
Soman (GD)	Phosphoric acid esters	0.05 ppm
Chloropicrin	Carbon tetrachloride	1–15 ppm

2. M8 paper can be used to detect G and V nerve agents.
3. The M256 kit can be used to detect G and V nerve agents.

PPE for Nerve Agents

1. Tabun (GA)
   (a) Entry: Tychem Level A.
   (b) Decon: Saranex Level B.
   (c) Gloves: Butyl.
2. Sarin (GB)
   (a) Entry: Responder or Tychem Level A.
   (b) Decon: Saranex Level B.
   (c) Gloves: Butyl.

3. Soman (GD)
   (a) Entry: Tychem Level A.
   (b) Decon: Saranex Level B.
   (c) Gloves: Butyl.
4. Chloropicrin
   (a) Entry: Responder Level A.
   (b) Decon: Saranex Level B.
   (c) Gloves: Butyl.
5. VX
   (a) Entry: Responder Level A.
   (b) Decon: Saranex Level B.
   (c) Gloves: Butyl.

Decontamination for Nerve Agents

1. Remove clothing and remove agent by absorption.
2. Warm or hot water works well unless thickening agents have been added to the agent.
3. Soap increases efficiency of decontamination.
4. Flush eyes with water or saline solution.
5. A bleach solution works best (5% for equipment, 0.5% for people).
6. Special decontamination solutions include (a) baking soda solution for "G" agents, (b) borax powder for thickened agents, and (c) chloramine for mustard and "V" agents.

Treatment of Nerve Agent Injuries

1. Decontaminate victim.
2. Maintain an open airway.
3. Administer high flow oxygen.
4. Monitor and suction victim.
5. Notify advanced life support personnel.

Identification of Blood Agents

1. Hydrogen cyanide
   - Colorless gas or liquid with characteristic odor.
   - The gas mixes well with air, and explosive mixtures are easily formed.
   - Gas is lighter than air.
2. Cyanogen Chloride
   - Colorless compressed liquefied gas with a pungent odor.
   - Gas is heavier than air.

3. Potassium Cyanide
   - White granular powder or hygroscopic crystals or solid with characteristic odor.
   - Contact with metals may produce hydrogen gas.
4. Sodium Cyanide
   - White hygroscopic crystalline powder with characteristic odor; odorless when dry.

Detection of Blood Agents

1. The following Drager colorimetric tubes can be used to detect blood agents:

Agent	Drager Tube	Detection Range
Hydrogen cyanide (AC)	Hydrocyanic acid	2–30 ppm
Cyanogen chloride (CK)	Cyanogen chloride	0.25–5 ppm

2. The M256 kit can be used to detect hydrogen cyanide (AC) and cyanogen chloride (CK).

PPE for Blood Agents

1. Hydrogen Cyanide (North American Emergency Response Guidebook Guide #117)
   (a) Entry: Responder or Tychem Level A.
   (b) Decon: Saranex Level B.
   (c) Gloves: Butyl.
2. Cyanogen Chloride (North American Emergency Response Guidebook Guide #125)
   (a) Entry: Responder or Tychem Level A.
   (b) Decon: Saranex Level B.
   (c) Gloves: Butyl.
3. Potassium Cyanide (North American Emergency Response Guidebook Guide #157)
   (a) Entry: Responder or Tychem Level A.
   (b) Decon: Saranex Level B.
   (c) Gloves: Butyl.
4. Sodium Cyanide
   (a) Entry: Responder or Tychem Level A.
   (b) Decon: Saranex Level B.
   (c) Gloves: Butyl.

Decontamination for Blood Agents

1. Remove clothing.

2. Flush eyes with water or saline solution.
3. Use a soap and water solution for skin.

Treatment of Blood Agent Injuries

1. Decontaminate victim.
2. Maintain open airway.
3. Administer high flow oxygen.
4. Notify advanced life support personnel.

Detection of Choking Agents

1. The following Drager colorimetric tubes can be used to detect choking agents:

Agent	Drager Tube	Detection Range
Chlorine (CL)	Chlorine	2–30 ppm
Phosgene (CG)	Phosgene	0.02–1 ppm

PPE for Choking Agents

1. Chlorine
   (a) Entry: Responder Level A.
   (b) Decon: Saranex Level B.
   (c) Gloves: Nitrile.
2. Phosgene
   (a) Entry: Responder Level A.
   (b) Decon: Saranex Level B.
   (c) Gloves: Nitrile.
3. Ammonia
   (a) Entry: Responder Level A.
   (b) Decon: Saranex Level B.
   (c) Gloves: Nitrile.

Decontamination for Choking Agents

1. Decontamination with a solution is not normally required unless there was a direct skin contact (then use soap and water).
2. Flush eyes with water or saline solution.
3. Clothing should be removed to prevent off gassing.

Treatment of Choking Agent Injuries

1. Maintain an open airway.
2. Position victim in semi-upright position.

3. Administer high flow oxygen.
4. Notify advanced life support personnel.

Identification of Blister Agents

1. Mustard (H, HD, HS) (North American Emergency Response Guidebook Guide #153)
   - Pure liquid is colorless and odorless; forms yellow prisms on cooling. Agent grade material is yellow to dark brown or black.
   - Heavier than air.
2. Nitrogen Mustard (HN1, HN2, HN3) (North American Emergency Response Guidebook Guide #153)
   - HN1: Colorless to yellow oily liquid with faint, fishy or musty odor.
   - HN2: Clear liquid with fishy odor; turns yellow to amber on storage.
   - HN3: Colorless to pale yellow liquid with faint odor resembling fish and soap.

Detection of Blister Agents

1. The following Drager colorimetric tubes can be used to detect blister agents:

Agent	Drager Tube	Detection Range
Mustard (HD)	Thioether	1 mg/m^3
Nitrogen mustard (HN)	Nitrogen compounds	1 mg/m^3
Lewisite (L)	Arsine	0.05–3 ppm
Phosgene oxime (CX)	Phosgene	0.02–1 ppm

2. The M256 kit can be used to detect mustard (H and HD), phosgene oxime (CX), and Lewisite (L).

PPE for Blister Agents

1. Mustard (H, HD, HS) (North American Emergency Response Guidebook Guide #153)
   (a) Entry: Responder Level A.
   (b) Decon: Saranex Level B.
   (c) Gloves: Butyl, neoprene, nitrile, or PVC.
2. Nitrogen Mustard (HN)
   (a) Entry: Responder Level A.
   (b) Decon: Saranex Level B.
   (c) Gloves: Butyl, neoprene, nitrile, or PVC.
3. Lewisite (L)
   (a) Entry: Responder Level A.

   (b) Decon: Saranex Level B.
   (c) Gloves: Nitrile.
4. Phosgene Oxime (CX)
   (a) Entry: Responder Level A.
   (b) Decon: Saranex Level B.
   (c) Gloves: Nitrile.

Decontamination for Blister Agents

1. Decontamination must be immediate.
2. Remove clothing.
3. Flush eyes with water or saline solution.
4. Blot agent off skin (do not wipe).
5. Decontaminate with soap and water, followed by a bleach solution, followed by soap and water.

Treatment of Blister Agent Injuries

1. Maintain an open airway.
2. Administer high flow oxygen if necessary.
3. Transport to hospital.

Detection of Riot Control Agents

1. The following Drager colorimetric tubes can be used to detect riot control agents:

Agent	Drager Tube	Detection Range
Pepper spray	Olefins	1–55 mg/L
Mace	Chloroformates	2–10 ppm

PPE for Riot Control Agents

1. Pepper Spray
   (a) Entry: Saranex Level B.
   (b) Decon: Level D.
   (c) Gloves: Latex.
2. Mace
   (a) Entry: Saranex Level B.
   (b) Decon: Level D.
   (c) Gloves: Latex.

Decontamination for Riot Control Agents

1. Remove clothing if off gassing.

2. Flush eyes with water.
3. Decontaminate skin with soap and water.

Treatment of Riot Control Agent Injuries

1. Maintain an open airway.
2. Administer oxygen if necessary.
3. Detoxification takes approximately 30 minutes.

Chemical Weapon Indicators

Agent	Odor	Symptoms
Tabun, VX, Sarin, Soman	Fruity	Excessive twitching, runny nose, sweating, drooling, pinpoint pupils, urinating, defecating, vomiting, convulsions.
Mustard agent	Garlic	No immediate symptoms, severe shortness of breath, eye irritation, fluid-filled blisters.
Lewisite	Geraniums	Immediate pain, eye and lung burning, bee sting type blisters.
Phosgene	New mown hay	Coughing, choking, pneumonia.
Chlorine	Bleach	Coughing, choking.
Cyanide	Bitter almonds	Bright red lips and skin, headache, gasping, nausea.

Emergency Response Procedures: Explosives

Bomb incidents can fit into three categories: (1) bomb threat, (2) suspicious package, and (3) actual explosive device.

The bomb threat is the most difficult of the three categories to deal with. The bomb threat is usually communicated via telephone, but it can be received in many different ways, including written, via e-mail, or posted on an Internet site. The threat may or may not provide details concerning the type of device, its location, and time it will detonate. The first issue that must be addressed when a bomb threat is received is whether or not to evacuate the area. Overreacting can be expensive and disruptive and cause panic. Underreacting can lead to injuries and deaths. Statistically, most bomb threats turn out to be pranks. However, threats should not be taken lightly. They should be evaluated based on the information provided in the threat, and the appropriate actions taken.

The suspicious package should illicit more of a concern than a threat. Once a suspicious package has been identified, whether it be a pocketbook, briefcase, backpack, or box, it should be considered to be an explosive device and treated accordingly. Suspicious packages should not be touched by anyone other than trained explosive ordinance disposal technicians (e.g., the bomb squad). Some devices can be detonated with the slightest movement, or worse yet, can be detonated remotely by the perpetrator once people approach it.

The third category, the presence of an actual explosive device, is obviously the most dangerous situation of the three categories. Once a device has been identified, the area must be promptly evacuated and the decision made by the bomb squad technicians on how to ultimately dispose of the device. An actual explosion of a device would also fall into the third category. Once a device has detonated, the emergency response operations begin.

Types of Explosive Incident Response. There are two types of explosive incident response. A *preblast response* to an incident occurs when the explosive device has not yet detonated. Activities prior to a bomb detonating include building searches, evacuation, and render safe procedures. A *postblast response* occurs after an explosive device has detonated. Activities after a bomb has detonated include responding to casualties, fire, and structural instability.

Risks Associated with Explosive Incidents

1. *Weakened Structural Elements/Damaged Utilities.* Just a few tenths of a pound per square inch of overpressure resulting from an explosion can damage and weaken structures. Emergency responders must be alert for damaged structures, partial structural collapses, and exposed utilities such as live electrical wires or leaking natural gas pipes when responding to an explosion.
2. *Secondary Explosive Devices/Booby Trapped Environments.* As mentioned previously, secondary explosive devices are always a threat to emergency responders. Responders should maintain situational awareness and be alert for indications of a secondary device when responding to an explosion.
3. *Chemical/Biological/Radiological Exposures.* An adversary may use an explosive device to disperse a biological, chemical, or radiological agent. It is prudent for emergency responders to monitor for these agents when responding to an explosive incident.

Dealing with the Bomb Threat. A caller may report a bomb threat for one of two reasons: (1) the caller has knowledge that an explosive device will be or has been placed and wants to minimize damage and casualties; or (2) the caller wants to create panic in the population and disrupt the normal operations of the key asset.

Once a bomb threat has been received, the fundamental decision to be made is whether to evacuate the area or ignore the threat and do nothing.

A threat and risk assessment must be conducted in order to make an informed decision. Among items to consider when evaluating the threat against the key asset are:

- Has the key asset received bomb threats in the past?
- Is there intelligence indicating that an attack may be imminent?
- How secure is the key asset? Would it be possible for an adversary to breach the

physical and administrative security countermeasures and place the device in the target area?

- What is the current situation at the key asset? Could a disgruntled insider call in a threat? Could an unhappy outsider call in a threat? Are any of the following conditions existent at the key asset: contract negotiations, strike, layoffs/downsizing, facility closing, exam week at a school, early Friday afternoon of a three-day weekend at an office building, visiting dignitary, or involvement in producing a controversial product (e.g., weapons facility) or providing controversial services (e.g., abortion clinic)?
- What was the exact wording of the threat? Was the threat very specific with respect to:

  The reason the device was planted ("I was just layed off after thirty years of faithful service").

  The design and construction of the device ("I placed 5 pounds of black powder and a pound of sheetrock screws in a cast iron pipe").

  The location of the device ("I placed the bomb in the cabinet at the back of Mrs. Jones's classroom where the microscopes are stored").

  The time the device will detonate ("I set it to go off at noon because I know that is when there are hundreds of people in the cafeteria").

The risk assessment will be similar to what was done previously:

Are people at risk?
Is property at risk?
Are products/services at risk?
Is information at risk?
Will the adversary receive favorable press coverage?
Will the attack accomplish the stated goals of the adversary?

Telephone Threats. When a bomb threat is phoned in, the person receiving the call should:

1. Complete the bomb threat checklist (see Figure 11.1).
2. More than one person should listen to the call if possible.
3. Keep the caller on the phone as long as possible. Collect as much information as possible.
4. Have the caller repeat the message so it can be confirmed.
5. If the caller has not already provided the location of the bomb and time of detonation, ask for that information.
6. Listen carefully for background noises that may help to identify the location of the caller.

BOMB THREAT CHECKLIST

1. When is the bomb going to explode?
2. Where is the bomb right now?
3. What does the bomb look like?
4. What kind of bomb is it?
5. What will cause the bomb to explode?
6. Did you place the bomb?
7. Why?
8. What is the address?
9. What is your name?

EXACT WORDING OF BOMB THREAT:

____

____

____

____

____

Sex of Caller: _______ Race: _______

Age: _______ Length of Call: _______

Telephone number at which call is received: ____________________________

Time Call Received: ______________

Date Call Received: ____ / ____ / ____

Caller's Voice:

☐ Calm	☐ Soft	☐ Stutter	☐ Excited
☐ Laughter	☐ Rasp	☐ Rapid	☐ Nasal
☐ Angry	☐ Loud	☐ Lisp	☐ Slow
☐ Crying	☐ Deep	☐ Normal	☐ Slurred
☐ Ragged	☐ Deep breathing	☐ Disguised	☐ Distinct
☐ Whispered	☐ Clearing throat	☐ Cracking voice	☐ Accent

☐ Familiar (*If voice is familiar, who did it sound like?*) ______________________

FIGURE 11.1. Sample bomb threat checklist. (*Source*: Bureau of Alcohol, Tobacco, and Firearms).

BACKGROUND SOUNDS:

☐ Street noises	☐ Voices	☐ Animal noises	☐ PA system
☐ Music	☐ Long distance	☐ Motor	☐ Booth
☐ Factory machinery	☐ Crockery	☐ Clear	☐ Static
☐ House noises	☐ Local	☐ Office machinery	

☐ Other (*Please Specify*) ______________________________

BOMB THREAT LANGUAGE:

☐ Well spoken (educated)	☐ Foul	☐ Incoherent
☐ Message read by threat maker	☐ Taped	☐ Irrational

REMARKS:

____

____

Your Name: ______________________________

Your Position: ______________________________

Your Telephone Number: ______________________

Date Checklist Completed: ____ / ____ / ____

FIGURE 11.1. *Continued.*

7. Listen to the caller's voice (male or female), voice quality (calm or excited), accents or speech impediments.
8. Report the call to the appropriate law enforcement agencies immediately.

A sample bomb threat checklist is provided in Figure 11.1.

Searching Buildings for a Bomb. The decision to search a key asset for a bomb is once again a joint decision between the key asset's chief executive and the local authorities. If a decision to search the key asset is made, the next step is to decide who will conduct the search. Oftentimes, personnel from the key asset are asked to participate in the search with the local authorities. The reason for this is the personnel from the key asset are familiar with the area and would know if something did not belong and may be a suspicious package. Personnel should be asked to search through their immediate work areas. Volunteers can be solicited to search the common areas and exterior of the building. Searchers should work in teams of at least two people.

Key assets should have a written bomb threat procedure as part of their pre-emergency plans, and personnel should receive periodic training on its contents as well as on search techniques.

The search for a bomb must be conducted in a planned, methodical manner. The first rule in searching for a bomb is that if a suspicious package or device is found, *it must not be touched.* Once it has been discovered, its location and a description of it should be provided to the bomb technicians and all personnel removed from the area. Another rule of thumb when searching for a bomb is that transmitting devices, such as two-way radios or cellular phones, should not be used as they are a potential source of ignition. The third basic rule when searching for a bomb is never let an explosive device get between the searchers and the exit. Therefore searches should start on the ground floor and work up. If the building has a basement, the first floor should be searched, then the basement, then work upwards.

The guidelines for conducting a bomb search include:

1. All searches should begin from the outside of a structure and gradually work in toward the interior.
2. When searching the exterior of a building, search closest to the building first, working out a minimum of 25 feet. Pay particular attention to places where an explosive devices can be hidden, such as waste receptacles, vehicles, HVAC ductwork, landscaping (shrubs, etc.), loading docks, and entranceways.
3. Searches of the building interior should be divided into two areas:
   (a) Areas to which the general public has access—these are the most likely areas where a device may be located, so these areas should be searched first.
   (b) Areas that have restricted access are less vulnerable than public access areas but may still contain a device. An adversary can gain access to restricted areas by posing as an authorized contractor, vendor, or visitor; breaching security; or working in collusion with an insider.
4. Areas to check inside a building include offices, lobbies, closets, storage areas, stairwells, elevator shafts, mechanical equipment rooms, and rest rooms.
5. Areas should be searched using a grid method to make sure the entire area is completely searched.
6. Searchers should divide rooms into four zones to facilitate the search: (a) floor to waist level (area where most devices will be found), (b) waist to head level, (c) head to ceiling level, and (d) hidden and enclosed areas. If the room has removable ceiling tiles, then the area above the tiles will need to be searched.

The searchers should inspect the area from outside in, and from the bottom up. Using this method, the entire area can be checked in a consistent and complete manner. Ideally, two teams of two persons will search each room, to ensure all areas are overlapped and thoroughly searched.

Searchers must also be alert to the presence of trip wires and other booby traps, which may have been placed by the adversary to hinder search efforts. Runners, or messengers, should be used to communicate the search progress back to the Command Post.

Searching Vehicles for a Bomb. Many keys assets routinely search vehicles for explosive devices. Many of the principles used in the search of a building will be used to search vehicles.

The easiest way to prevent a vehicle bomb from adversely impacting a key asset is to restrict access so the vehicle cannot get close enough to the key asset to cause damage. If vehicle access is necessary, then the following techniques can be used to search for an explosive device:

1. The inspection area should be far enough from the key asset so that if the vehicle detonates at the search area, it will not adversely impact the key asset. The inspection area should also contain the fewest number of people necessary for the same reason.
2. An external search of the vehicle should be conducted first. Any signs of modifications to the vehicle should be considered suspicious. As part of the external search, the undercarriage should also be checked.
3. The interior of the vehicle should be searched last. All compartments, such as the glove box, trunk, and tool boxes, should be opened and inspected. Particular attention should be paid to the battery and electrical system, as this may be the source of the power to detonate the device. For this reason, the engine compartment should be inspected first.

Safe Operations at Explosive Incidents

- Do not use two-way radios (or any transmitting device) within 300 feet.
- Notify proper authorities (e.g., bomb disposal unit).
- Stage emergency medical service, fire, and police units at a safe location until the area has been cleared by explosive disposal personnel.
- Do not approach a suspected device as it may contain an acoustic or motion triggering device.
- Blast pressures decay rapidly with distance. Standoff distance is the best defense to blast effects.

Sample Procedure Explosive Weapon

Receipt of a Bomb Threat

1. If a bomb threat is received, the Incident Command staff should immediately convene.
2. The Police Department should be notified.
3. The Unified Incident Commander should review the threat and situation, and determine if the threat is considered credible.
4. If the threat is considered noncredible, no further action is required.

Dealing with a Credible Bomb Threat. The Unified Command should determine whether to evacuate on-site and/or off-site personnel.

Searching for a Suspected Device

1. The Unified Incident Commander determines if a search for the suspected device should be initiated. This determination is made after a thorough risk analysis and risk–benefit analysis have been completed.
2. Two-way radios and cellular phones are not to be used when searching for an explosive device.
3. Hard line telephones and runners are the communication methods to be used when searching for an explosive device.
4. Turnout gear and SCBA are the PPE to be used when searching for an explosive device.
5. The Incident Commander should (a) obtain all available information concerning the bomb threat; (b) ensure the doors and windows to all buildings are opened; (c) thoroughly assess the situation before committing responders; and (d) consider the possibility of the presence of a secondary device; and (e) consider the possibility the explosive device may be used to disseminate a chemical, biological, or radiological device.
6. If key asset personnel will be used to search for a bomb:
   (a) Key asset personnel should be teamed up with a law enforcement officer.
   (b) The most important areas should be searched first.
   (c) Search the areas most related to the threat if possible.
   (d) DO NOT touch a strange or suspicious object.
   (e) If a suspicious object is found, personnel should withdraw to a safe area.
   (f) Law enforcement personnel should be responsible for securing the suspicious object.
7. The following search techniques should be used:
   (a) Start with the exterior areas of the facility most accessible to the public.
   (b) Move to the interior areas.
   (c) Each of the two searchers begin at the same point in the area.
   (d) Each person works in opposite directions and back toward the starting point.
   (e) The search patterns should overlap somewhat.
   (f) First area search covers the floor to hip area.
   (g) Second area search covers the hip to head area.
   (h) Third area search covers the head to ceiling area.
   (i) Fourth area search covers hidden and enclosed areas.
   (j) Listen for clockwork device.

8. If a suspicious object or device is located:
   (a) DO NOT touch the suspected device.
   (b) DO NOT put device in water or in a confined space (e.g., desk drawer, cabinet).
   (c) Report location and description of device.
   (d) Evacuate all personnel to the evacuation distances given below.
   (e) Position personnel so they are not in direct line of sight of the device, are away from glass and parked cars, can utilize structural and/or natural barriers to assist with protection, and are away from secondary hazards (storage tanks, electrical lines, etc.).
   (f) Do not permit reentry into the area until the bomb squad has declared the area safe.
   (g) Treat the area as a crime scene and preserve evidence.
   (h) Continue searching the rest of the facility.

Evacuation Distances. If a suspicious package is found, the following minimum evacuation distances apply:

Container	Distance
Small box (<28 pounds)	985 feet
Briefcase	1123 feet
Compact sedan	1500 feet
Full size sedan	1750 feet
Passenger or cargo van	2750 feet
Small box van (14 foot box)	3750 feet
Box van/fuel truck	6500 feet
Semi-trailer	7000 feet

Dealing with an Unattended Article

1. Interview person(s) who found the article and anyone who may have been in the area.
2. Attempt to determine the owner/custodian of the article.
3. DO NOT physically examine or disturb the article.
4. Notify the Police Department if the article is not claimed.

Treatment of Bomb Injuries

1. Basic treatment for crush injuries is primarily supportive.
2. Administer high flow oxygen.
3. Position victim for shock.
4. Notify advanced life support personnel.

If There Is an Explosion

1. DO NOT approach the point of explosion. There may be undetonated or partially detonated explosives present.
2. Establish the crime scene perimeter. Look for the furthest debris or damage from the blast center, and then double that distance as a minimum crime scene perimeter (the distance may be increased if it seems too small).
3. If you are in a building when a detonation occurs, stay low to the floor and exit the building as soon as possible.
4. If you are trapped in debris, do not light a match, do not move about or kick up dust, and rhythmically tap on a pipe or wall so rescuers can hear you.
5. When confronted with an unknown WMD agent, the sampling protocol is (a) LEL, radiation, pH paper; (b) M8/M9 paper; (c) M256 kit; and (d) colorimetric tubes.

INDEX

Understanding, Assessing, and Responding to Terrorism: Protecting Critical Infrastructure and Personnel By Brian T. Bennett